Income Distribution in Macroeconomic Models

Income Distribution in Macroeconomic Models

Giuseppe Bertola
Reto Foellmi
Josef Zweimüller

PRINCETON UNIVERSITY PRESS
PRINCETON AND OXFORD

Published by Princeton University Press, 41 William Street, Princeton, New Jersey 08540

In the United Kingdom: Princeton University Press, 3 Market Place, Woodstock, Oxfordshire OX20 1SY

Library of Congress Cataloging-in-Publication Data
Bertola, Giuseppe.
   Income distribution in macroeconomic models / Giuseppe Bertola, Reto Foellmi, and Josef Zweimüller.
      p. cm.
   Includes bibliographical references and index.
   ISBN: 0-691-12171-0 (alk. paper)
   1. Income distribution—Econometric models. 2. Economic development—Econometric models. 3. Wealth—Econometric models. 4. Equality—Econometric models. I. Foellmi, Reto. II. Zweimüller, Josef. III. Title.

HB523.B47 2006+

339.2'01'51—dc22   2005048825

British Library Cataloging-in-Publication Data is available

This book has been composed in Sabon

Printed on acid-free paper. ∞

pup.princeton.edu

Printed in the United States of America

10 9 8 7 6 5 4 3 2 1

Contents

Introduction

THIS BOOK FOCUSES ON two main sets of issues. The first relates to the dynamics of aggregate variables when the population is heterogeneous. Under which conditions are the dynamics of capital accumulation affected by the distribution of income and wealth? When is a more equal distribution of income and wealth beneficial or harmful for accumulation and growth? The second set of issues refers to the dynamics of the distribution of income and/or wealth. How does the distribution of income and wealth evolve in a market economy? When does the gap between rich and poor people in market economy increase over time? Conversely, under which conditions will this gap tend to disappear eventually?

ISSUES

Interest in the distribution of income used to be central in economics. Classical economists were concerned with the issue of how an economy's output is divided among the various classes in society, which, for David Ricardo, was even "the principal problem of Political Economy." While classical economists were primarily interested in the *functional* distribution of income among factors of production (wages, profits, and land rents), in modern societies distributional concerns focus at least as much on the *personal* (or *size*) distribution of income. In contrast to its paramount importance in nineteenth-century classical economics, however, income distribution became a topic of minor interest in recent decades. Atkinson and Bourguignon (2001, 7265) note that "in the second half of the century, there were indeed times when interest in the distribution of income was at a low ebb, economists appearing to believe that differences in distributive outcomes were of second order importance compared with changes in overall economic performance."

This is especially true regarding macroeconomics and growth theories. While early growth models in the post-Keynesian tradition were still strongly concerned with distributional issues (see, in particular, Kalecki 1954 and Kaldor 1955, 1956), subsequent "new classical" theoretical developments removed distribution from the set of macroeconomic issues of interest. Crucial progress in microfounding behavioral relationships in terms of optimal choices and expectations accompanied heavy reliance on "representative agent" modeling strategies. The distribution of income and wealth across consumers was viewed as a passive outcome of aggregate dynamics and market interactions, and little attention was paid to feedback effects from distribution into growth and other macroeconomic phenomena.

The prominence of economic inequality as a macroeconomic issue is much larger at the beginning of the twenty-first century. Renewed interest in issues of whether and how income and wealth inequality interact with production and growth is the result of dramatic changes in the distribution of incomes that have been taking place all over the world in the late portion of the twentieth century. Rising wealthiness coexists with persistent poverty in rich and in poor countries alike. China and India, comprising almost 40 percent of the world's population, have experienced extraordinarily high growth rates, leading to a strong reduction in (global) poverty (see, e.g., Bourguignon and Morrison 2002; Sala-i-Martin 2002; or Deaton 2004, among others). At the same time, inequality within these countries has been increasing. In other parts of the world, in particular in most countries of sub-Saharan Africa, no such growth has been taking place, and dramatic levels of poverty and excessive inequalities persist. Similarly, growth in many countries of Latin America was sluggish in the past decades, and inequality persisted at high levels.

Furthermore, empirical evidence suggests there are interesting links between distribution and long-run growth. For instance, countries in East and Southeast Asia had low inequality levels in the first place and managed to catch up quite considerably in terms of per capita incomes. More generally, there is a negative correlation between inequality and long-run growth rates across countries. For instance, in fast-growing countries such as the East Asian Tigers, India, and China, inequality had been much lower than in slow-growing countries of Latin America and sub-Saharan Africa. This suggests that excessive inequalities may be an obstacle for growth, whereas low inequality may be growth enhancing. Conversely, it is likely that the process of growth and development brings about systematic changes in the distribution of incomes and wealth. Kuznets (1955) was among the first who speculated about a systematic relationship between inequality and the process of development. According to Kuznets, inequality increases in early stages of development (as workers move from the traditional to the modern sector) and decreases again (when the modern sector takes over the entire economy), resulting in the famous "Kuznets curve," an inverse-U relationship between inequality and per capita incomes. However, it is not clear whether this is an appropriate description of the actual inequality experiences across countries. For instance, high-growth countries such as India and China experienced an increase in inequality during the past decades. Similarly, such increases in inequality have taken place also in industrialized countries, in particular in the United States and the United Kingdom. This suggests that the relationship between economic growth and income inequality might be much more complex than suggested by Kuznets (1955).

While no consensus on the empirical issues has yet been reached, it is obvious that, by the beginning of the twenty-first century, issues of income distribution are back on the agenda. Changes in inequality and its relationship to growth, global trade opportunities, and new technologies have drawn attention to issues relating to income distribution in the 1990s.

METHODS

While these issues may motivate many of our readers, not only empirical trends but also methodological advances underlie recent interest in the interaction of macroeconomic and distributional phenomena.

Modern optimization-based macroeconomic models typically rely on the representative agent paradigm. Recent research, however, has relaxed many aspects of the representative agent framework of analysis. We do not provide an exhaustive survey of all relevant empirical and theoretical aspects.[1] Rather, we take stock of results and methods discovered (or rediscovered) in the context of the 1990s revival of growth theory, which reconciled rigorous optimization-based technical tools with realistic market imperfections and politico-economic interactions. Without aiming at covering cutting-edge research in a fast-evolving literature, we focus on technical insights that have proved useful in this and other contexts where a compromise needs to be struck between formulation of concise relationships between aggregate variables, and appropriate attention to the distributional issues disregarded when modeling aggregate phenomena in terms of a single representative agent's microeconomic behavior.

A representative agent perspective on macroeconomic phenomena, of course, recommends itself on grounds of tractability rather than realism. The objectives and economic circumstances of real-life individuals are certainly highly heterogeneous, but it would be impossible to obtain results of any generality from models featuring millions of intrinsically different individuals. With a representative agent framework, we implicitly assume that cross-sectional differences can be smoothed and aggregated so as to ensure that the economy's behavior is well described by that of an average individual whose decisions represent all the real agents regarding variables relevant for macroeconomic analysis. When economists are interested in distribution, however, they can now exploit a vast tool kit of modeling

---

[1] The strand of literature ranging from classical to postwar contributions is surveyed by Hahn and Matthews (1964). Recent developments are surveyed by Bénabou (1996c), papers in the January 1997 special issue of the *Journal of Economic Dynamics and Control*, the *Handbook of Income Distribution* (Amsterdam: North-Holland, 1999, especially chap. 8, 9, and 10), and Aghion, Caroli, and Garcia-Penalosa (1999).

strategies and methodological insights. This book offers a hands-on approach to macroeconomic treatment of inequality and distribution. Using the standard tools of microfounded macroeconomic analysis, we outline and analyze modeling assumptions that support representative agent analysis, and discuss how suitable modifications of those assumptions may introduce realistic interactions between macroeconomic phenomena and distributional issues. This sequencing of the argument makes it clear that, while the issues disregarded by a representative agent perspective are important in principle, they may be neglected in practice if the assumptions supporting that perspective are deemed realistic for some specific purpose. And it also makes it clear that any insightful macroeconomic model of distribution does need to restrict appropriately the extent and character of cross-sectional heterogeneity, trading some loss of microeconomic detail for macroeconomic tractability and insights.

Achieving a satisfactory balance of tractability and realism is key to macroeconomic analysis and, indeed, to all applied economics. Hence our treatment may be of interest independently of the inequality issues we focus on. As is also typical of much economic analysis, it is not possible to reach definitive conclusions regarding, for example, the dynamics of inequality. But it is possible, and useful, to highlight channels through which inequality may increase or decrease, depending on the structure of an economy's technology, markets, and institutions. We necessarily focus on a limited set of methodological issues that are key to the application of modern optimization-based techniques to realistic economies where agents are heterogeneous and, because of market imperfections, their behavior fails to aggregate to that of a hypothetical social planner. Making extensive use of simple formal examples and exercises, the exposition aims at familiarizing readers with basic insights in practice as well as in theory.

In this spirit, we illustrate how modern analytical tools may highlight important interactions between the distribution of income and wealth on the one side and macroeconomic outcomes on the other side. The contrast between representative agent and distributional perspectives is clearly very important in many real-life situations and in the economics of labor markets, education, and industrial organization. We mention and discuss briefly some of the issues arising in such contexts, but choose to illustrate general insights in the context of economic growth models, framing most of our discussion in terms of dynamic accumulation interactions.

We also stop very much short, however, of covering all aspects of models of growth and distribution. In particular, we do not model endogenous demographics, and typically refer to decision makers as "individuals" or "households" interchangeably. And while linkages between distribution and growth are crucial to growth-oriented policy issues, we only briefly address political economy issues. All of the models where distribution plays a role can serve as a platform for politico-economic analysis, but a careful discussion of all institutional issues lies outside this book's scope. We offer little more than a sketch regarding processes through which policy preferences may be aggregated into policy choices: readers may find in Persson and Tabellini (2000) and Drazen (2000) insightful treatments focused on those mechanisms, at a technical level and in a style similar to those of our book.

STRUCTURE

In our baseline framework of analysis, aggregate and individual income dynamics depend endogenously on the propensity to save rather than consume currently available resources and on the rate at which accumulation is rewarded by the economic system. In turn, the distribution of resources across individuals and across accumulated and non-accumulated factors of production determines the volume and the productivity of savings and investment. We consider increasingly complex formulations of this web of interactions, always aiming at isolating key insights and preserving tractability: treading a path along the delicate trade-off between tractability and realism, our models of inequality's macroeconomic role necessarily focusing on specific causal channels within a more complex reality.

The material is organized around a few methodologically useful simplifications of reality. The models discussed in part 1 assume away all uncertainty and rely on economy-wide factor markets to ensure that all units of accumulated factors are rewarded at the same rate. This relatively simple setting isolates a specific set of interactions between factor remuneration and aggregate dynamics on the one hand, which depend on each other through well-defined production and savings functions; and personal income distribution on the other hand, which is readily determined by the remuneration of aggregate factor stocks and by the size and composition of individual factor bundles. We assume that families have identical savings behavior (savings propensities, intertemporal objective functions) so that differences in actual savings outcomes arise either from differences in factor ownership or from differences in factor rewards across families. Chapters 1 to 3 of part 1 outline how, under suitable functional form assumptions, macroeconomic accumulation interacts with the distribution of income, consumption, and wealth distribution when savings are invested in an integrated market. In an economy where all intra- and intertemporal markets exist and clear competitively, savings are rewarded on the basis of their marginal productivity in a well-defined aggregate

production function. In that "neoclassical" setting, all distributional issues are resolved before market interactions even begin to address the
economic problem of allocating scarce resources efficiently, and the dynamics of income and consumption distribution have no welfare implications. In other models, however, the functional distribution of aggregate
income is less closely tied to efficiency considerations, and is quite relevant to both personal income distribution and aggregate accumulation.
If factor rewards result from imperfect market interactions and/or policy
interventions, aggregate accumulation need not maximize a hypothetical representative agent's welfare even when it is driven by individually
optimal saving decisions. Chapter 4 outlines interactions between distribution and macroeconomic accumulation when accumulated and non-
accumulated factors are owned by groups of individuals with different
saving propensities, and factor rewards may be determined by politico-
economic mechanisms so that distributional tensions, far from being resolved ex ante, work their way through distorting policies and market interactions to bear directly on both macroeconomic dynamics and income
distribution. The relevant insights are particularly simple in balanced-
growth situations, where factor shares are immediately relevant to the
speed of economic growth and, through factor ownership, to the distribution of income and consumption across individuals. In the appendix of
chapter 4 we review interactions between distribution and capital accumulation in a two-sector model where consumption and investment goods are
distinct. We proceed to explore links between distribution and macroeconomic accumulation when the scope of financial markets is limited by
finite planning horizons. Chapter 5 studies the dynamics of the income
distribution when individuals have finite lifetimes, and chapter 6 discusses
the role of taxation and the implications of non-competitively determined
factor shares for long-run growth in the context of overlapping generation
models.

The interactions between inequality and growth reviewed in part 1
arise from factor-reward dynamics, and from heterogeneous sizes and
compositions of individual factor bundles. Models where individual savings meet investment opportunities in perfect and complete *intertemporal*
markets, however, do not explain what (other than individual life cycles)
might generate such heterogeneity in the first place, and strongly restrict
the dynamic pattern of cross-sectional marginal utilities and consumption
levels.

The models reviewed in part 2 recognize that individual consumption and saving choices are only partially (if at all) interconnected by
financial markets within macroeconomies. Then, ex ante investment opportunities and/or ex post returns differ across individuals. We study
the implications of self-financing constraints imposing equality between

savings and investments at the individual rather than aggregate level, and of imperfect pooling of rate-of-return or labor income risk in the financial market. Studying in isolation different specifications of these phenomena offers key insights into real-life interactions between distribution and macroeconomics. In general, both the structure of financial markets and the extent of inequality are relevant to macroeconomic outcomes and to the evolution of income inequality. Financial market imperfections also make it impossible to characterize macroeconomic phenomena on a representative individual basis. Under appropriate simplifying assumptions, however, it is possible to highlight meaningful linkages between resource distribution and aggregate dynamics when investment opportunities are heterogeneous.

Chapter 7 analyzes the role of self-financing and borrowing constraints, which are clearly all the more relevant when income distribution is unequal. In an economy populated by identical representative individuals, in fact, no borrowing or lending would ever need to take place. If the rate of return on individual investment is inversely related to wealth levels, then inequality tends to disappear over time—and reduces the efficiency of investment. If instead large investments (made by rich self-financing individuals) have relatively high rates of return, then inequality persists and widens as a subset of individuals cannot escape poverty traps—and unequal wealth distributions are associated with higher aggregate returns to investment.

Next, we turn to consider how idiosyncratic uncertainty may affect the dynamics of income distribution and of aggregate income. In chapter 8 we discuss how a complete set of competitive financial markets would again make it straightforward to study aggregate dynamics on a representative individual basis, and deny any macroeconomic relevance to resource distribution across agents. While financial markets can be perfect and complete in only one way, however, they can and do fall short of that ideal in many different ways. The second part of chapter 8 is devoted to models where returns to individual investment are subject to idiosyncratic uncertainty which might, but need not, be eliminated by pooling risk in an integrated financial market. Imperfect pooling of rate-of-return risk certainly reduces ex ante welfare, but (depending on the balance of income and substitution effects) need not be associated with lower aggregate savings and slower macroeconomic growth. Chapter 9 discusses the impact of financial market imperfection for savings, growth, and distribution in the complementary polar case where all individual asset portfolios yield the same constant return, but non-accumulated income and consumption flows are subject to uninsurable shocks and lead individuals to engage in precautionary savings.

In part 3 we turn to a different set of generalizations to the simplest single-good, representative consumer macroeconomic models. We outline how recent modeling techniques may be used to represent situations where many different goods, produced by firms with monopoly power, exist within a given macroeconomic entity. We focus in particular on two families of models where income distribution affects the demand curves for the various products available in the economy: chapters 10 and 11 deal with the role of income distribution when growth is driven by the introduction of new or better products; chapters 12 and 13 study the implications of "hierarchic" preferences that imply different consumption patterns for differently rich consumers.

In Chapter 10 we study the relationship between distribution and growth in standard models of innovation and growth. These models typically assume that consumers have homothetic preferences and rule out any impact of distribution on growth. However, market power of firms is a constituting element of the new growth theory, and the extent of this power has important implications for the distribution of income between workers and entrepreneurs. While neutrality of distribution derives by assumption from homothetic constant elasticity of substitution (CES preferences), income distribution becomes important for growth as soon as we allow for variable elasticities of substitution (VES preferences). In that case demand elasticities differ between rich and poor consumers and the elasticity of market demand, and hence the firms' market power depends on the distribution of economic resources across households.

In chapter 11 we explore the implications of indivisibilities in consumption. Indivisibilities are not only empirically highly relevant but also theoretically interesting as they provide a simple tool to generate differences in consumption patterns between rich and poor consumers. Typically, poor consumers will consume a smaller range of products and/or will consume the various goods in lower qualities than richer consumers. Our framework of analysis provides a simple and easily tractable way to study interactions between distribution and innovation incentives.

Whether and to which extent new products are demanded on the market depends not only on whether they are technologically feasible but also on whether they satisfy sufficiently urgent needs. In chapter 12 we present a general framework of "hierarchic preferences" that captures the idea that goods are hierarchically ranked according to their priority in consumption. Without relying on indivisibilities, hierarchic preferences imply that consumption patterns vary with the level of a consumer's income, and some goods are consumed only by relatively rich individuals. This framework is useful to understand issues of structural change and long-run growth and how these processes may interact with the distribution of income.

Finally, in chapter 13 we study interactions between distribution and growth in the more general case, when the various products differ both with respect to their desirability and with respect to their production technologies. In general, increases in income change not only the relative demands for the various products but also the derived demands for production factors and the corresponding factor rewards. Hence the ex ante distribution of income affects not only long-run growth but also the patterns of technical progress and factor accumulation—and hence the ex post distribution of income. By using very stylized and simple assumptions, models in chapter 13 highlight various potentially important mechanisms by which growth may feed back to distribution through such dynamic interaction between demand and supply conditions.

ABOUT THE BOOK

The models outlined and discussed here are based on our own and others' recent and less recent research. The resulting book aims to be useful as a textbook as well as a research monograph. As a textbook, it can be used for advanced courses on growth and distribution, and on more general financial and macroeconomic topics. As a research monograph offering some nontrivial extensions and a new organization of existing results, it can offer a novel perspective and practical guide to both specialist and nonspecialist researchers in economics and other social sciences. Each chapter focuses on specific substantive and technical insights. Most chapters are sufficiently self-contained to be read in isolation, and frequent cross-references may help readers navigate the book without necessarily reading it sequentially. Our treatment is focused on technical and methodological insights, and many exercises make it possible for interested readers and students to develop their intuition and practice their research skills. The introductory section of each chapter, however, briefly reviews the historical and empirical aspects that motivate each of the steps in our journey through a complex set of substantive and technical issues. At the end of each chapter, extensive annotated references offer a guide to the literature, and outline directions of past and future research.

This book initially grew out of extended teaching notes based on G. Bertola, "Macroeconomics of Distribution and Growth" (in A. B. Atkinson and F. Bourguignon, eds., *Handbook of Income Distribution*, 2000). Additional material includes class notes and exam questions for courses at the European University Institute (Florence, Italy), the Institute for Advanced Studies (Vienna, Austria), the University of Zurich (Switzerland), and Università di Torino (Italy). For comments, and discussions over the years on various topics relevant for this book, we are grateful to Daron Acemoglu, George-Marios Angeletos, Anthony B. Atkinson, Antoine d'Autumne, Johannes Binswanger, François Bourguignon,

Giorgio Brunello, Johann K. Brunner, Michael Burda, Daniele Checchi, Avinash Dixit, Hartmut Egger, Josef Falkinger, Oded Galor, Peter Gottschalk, Volker Grossmann, Rafael Lalive, Lars Ljungqvist, Chol-Won Li, Kiminori Matsuyama, Giovanna Nicodano, Manuel Oechslin, and Gilles Saint-Paul. We are grateful for comments and guidance from several anonymous reviewers and from Richard Baggaley, and for thorough copyediting by Joan Gieseke. We benefited a lot from interactions with our students, who forced us to rethink the material by raising critical questions and who suffered many of the exercises as exam questions. Very special thanks to Tobias Würgler and Tanja Zehnder for their excellent research assistance, in particular in compiling answers to various exercises.

PART ONE

Aggregate Growth and Individual Savings

CHAPTER ONE

Production and Distribution of Income in a Market Economy

THE AIM OF THIS BOOK is to study the implications of economic interactions between heterogeneous individuals, both for macroeconomic outcomes and for the evolution of the income and wealth distribution. As these interactions are extremely complex, we organize our analysis around several key simplifications.

First, we will assume throughout that there are *two factors of production*: an "accumulated" factor and a "non-accumulated" factor. We will frequently refer to the former as "capital" and to the latter as "labor." As we discuss below, however, the important point is that the economy's (as well as the households') endowment with the former is endogenously determined by savings choices, whereas the economy's endowment with the latter is exogenously given.

Second, we will assume throughout that *all individuals have the same attitude toward savings*, i.e., *that any two individuals would behave identically if their economic circumstances were identical.* This is not to say that heterogeneity in preferences between present and future consumption is unimportant in reality. Allowing for systematic differences across individuals along this dimension, however, would tend to yield tautological results: one might, for example, find that the poor are and remain poor due to their low propensities to save. It is much more insightful to highlight other sources and effects of large differences in incomes across individuals: we will highlight the role of macroeconomic phenomena (such as capital accumulation and associated changes in factor prices, market imperfections, and economic policies) for the dynamics of the distribution of income and wealth and their feedback to the long-run process of economic development. Heterogeneous propensities to save are clearly of some importance in reality, but will not induce a systematic bias in our results if they are random and unrelated to economic circumstances.

Third, in many of our derivations we will assume that only *one good* is produced in the economy and can be used for either consumption or investment. Investment then coincides with forgone consumption, to be understood broadly as leisure choices are subsumed in consumption choices. The single-good assumption is adopted throughout part 1 (with the exception of the appendix to chapter 4) and part 2. In part 3, we relax it and consider the interrelation between distribution and growth when there are many goods and when the structure or consumption differs between rich and poor consumers.

As a further general principle, we will apply standard tools of modern macroeconomic analysis, formulating all models in formally precise and consistent terms. Even as we strive to take individual heterogeneity into account when studying macroeconomic phenomena, we will often find it useful to refer to situations where some or all of the implications of heterogeneity are eliminated by appropriate, carefully discussed assumptions, so that a representative agent perspective is appropriate for some or all aspects of the analysis. Specifying and carefully discussing deviations from these assumptions will make it possible to highlight clearly problems of heterogeneity and distribution, as well as their interaction with macroeconomic phenomena.

This first chapter sets the stage for our analysis. We introduce notation and set out basic relationships both at the level of the family and at the aggregate, making the important distinction between accumulated and non-accumulated income sources. Then, we analyze the relationship between distribution and the efficiency of production in a "neoclassical" setting of perfect and complete markets. Firms maximize profits and take prices as given, all factors of production are mobile, there is complete information, and all economic interactions are appropriately accounted for by prices (there are no externalities). In that setting we discuss in some detail the conditions under which macroeconomic aggregates do not depend on income distribution and on technological heterogeneity, so that production and accumulation can be studied as if they were generated by decisions of "representative" consumers and producers. As is often the case in economics, the model's assumptions are quite stringent, so we discuss briefly conceptual problems arising when certain tractability conditions are not met. In particular, if factors of production cannot be reallocated, aggregation becomes very problematic unless stringent conditions are met regarding the character of technological heterogeneity. This qualifies, but certainly does not eliminate, the usefulness of stylized models as a benchmark when assessing the practical relevance of deviations from the neoclassical assumptions.

1.1 ACCOUNTING

Consider an economy with many households endowed with two types of production factors: accumulated and non-accumulated. By definition, *accumulated* factors are inputs whose dynamics are determined by microeconomic savings decisions. At the aggregate level, these decisions affect both the distribution of accumulated factors across individuals and the dynamics of macroeconomic accumulation. In contrast, *non-accumulated* factors are, by definition, production factors that evolve exogenously (or, for simplicity, remain constant) in the aggregate. We will frequently refer to the accumulated factor as "capital" and to the non-accumulated factor as "labor." However, the simple capital/labor distinction may be misleading. For instance, an individual's human capital is essential for the efficiency of its "labor" but clearly affected by an individual's savings choices. In contrast, incomes from real estate ("land") as well as non-contestable monopolies are often counted as part of capital income but are, according to our definition, part of non-accumulated factors' rewards.

While here we take the evolution of non-accumulated factors as given, it is important to note that, in reality, the economy's supply with these factors is subject to households' supply choices. Here we abstract from the endogeneity of the supply of their non-accumulated factors and from endogenous fertility behavior. We subsume labor/leisure choices under the consumption choice.

A family or household i is endowed with $k(i)$ units of an accumulated factor and $l(i)$ units of a non-accumulated factor. In general, households differ in endowments k and l. Moreover, factor rewards may also differ between households, hence $r = r(i)$ and $w = w(i)$. However, when there are perfect factor markets, all households get the same returns and r and w no longer depend on individual endowment levels but are determined by their aggregate counterparts.

The models reviewed below can be organized around a simple accounting framework. The income flow y accruing to a family also depends on endowments k and l and equals

$$y(i) = w(i) \cdot l(i) + r(i) \cdot k(i).$$

The dynamic budget constraint, at the household level, is given by

$$\Delta k(i) = y(i) - c(i), \text{ or } \Delta k(i) = r(i)k(i) + w(i)l(i) - c(i), \tag{1.1}$$

where $c(i)$ denotes the consumption flow of a household who owns accumulated factor k and non-accumulated factor l in the current period. The change in the family's stock of the accumulated factor, denoted $\Delta k(i)$, coincides with forgone consumption (income not consumed). Income $y(i)$ is measured *net of depreciation* of the accumulated factor, and $r(i)$ is the *net return* of this factor. Consumption c, income y, and savings Δk are, in general, heterogeneous across individuals. This heterogeneity may be due to two sources: households own different baskets of factors $(k(i), l(i))$, and they may earn different rewards $r(i)$ and/or $w(i)$.

There are two important assumptions implicit in the above formulation. The first is that there is only one consumption good, and the second is that consumption is convertible one to one into the accumulated factor. We will stick to these assumptions throughout most of parts 1 and 2 of this book. In part 3 we will relax the first assumption: we will study conditions under which differentiating output by different consumption purposes becomes relevant for distribution and growth. In appendix 4.6 we will address the latter assumption. There a model with two sectors is presented where the accumulated factors and consumption goods are produced with different technologies.

Any of the variables on the right-hand sides of the expressions in (1.1) may be given a time index, and may be random in models with uncertainty. In (1.1), $\Delta k(i) \equiv k_{t+1}(i) - k_t(i)$ is the increment of the individual family's wealth over a discrete time period. In continuous time, the same accounting relationship would read

$$\dot{k} = y - c = rk + wl - c, \qquad (1.2)$$

where $\dot{k}(t) \equiv dk(t)/dt = \lim_{\Delta t \to 0} \left[\left(k(t + \Delta t) - k(t) \right) / \Delta t \right]$ is the rate of change per unit time of the family's wealth.

The advantage of a continuous-time formulation is that it frequently yields simple analytic solutions, and it is not necessary to specify whether stocks are measured at the beginning or the end of the period. The advantage of discrete time models is that empirical aspects and the role of uncertainty are discussed more easily in a discrete-time framework. We will use the continuous-time formulation in some chapters, the discrete-time formulation in others.

Aggregating across individuals leaves us with the macroeconomic counterparts of income, consumption, and the capital stock. We allow the distribution to be of discrete or continuous nature. In the former case, $p(i)$ denotes the population share of group i, with n different groups in the population, we have $\sum_{i=1}^{n} p(i) = 1$. If distribution is continuous, $p(i)$ denotes the density, and with a population distributed over the interval $[0, 1]$ we have $\int_0^1 p(i)di = 1$. For the sake of compact notation we use the Stjelties integral, which encompasses both the discrete and the continuous case. The measure $P(\cdot)$, where $\int_{\mathcal{N}} dP(i) = 1$, assigns weights to subsets of $\mathcal{N}$, the set of individuals in the aggregate economy of interest. To gain more intuition with the weight function $P(\cdot)$ consider the special case where $\mathcal{N}$ has n elements (of equal population size). Then, the weight function $P(i) = 1/n$ defines Y as the arithmetic mean of individual income levels $y(i)$.

With continuous distribution, the relative size or weight $P(A)$ of a set $A \subset \mathcal{N}$ of individuals is arbitrarily small, and conveniently lets the idiosyncratic uncertainty introduced in chapter 8 average to zero in the aggregate.

We use the convention to write uppercase letters for the aggregate counterpart of the corresponding lowercase letter. Hence aggregate income is denoted by Y and equals

$$Y \equiv \int_{\mathcal{N}} y(i) dP(i), \tag{1.3}$$

where $\mathcal{N}$ denotes the set of families. For the most part, we take $\mathcal{N}$ as fixed. However, when we want to study issues like population growth, finite lives, or immigration, we will allow $\mathcal{N}$ to be variable over time.

Recall that heterogeneity of the non-accumulated income flow wl may be accounted for by differences in w and/or l across individuals. We take l as exogenously given. Hence we sum up and get

$$L \equiv \int_{\mathcal{N}} l(i) dP(i), \tag{1.4}$$

where L denotes the amount of non-accumulated factors available to the aggregate economy.

Recall from (1.1) that we assumed the relative price of c and Δk to be unitary. This allows us to aggregate families' endowments with the accumulated factor. The aggregate stock of the accumulated factor K is measured in terms of forgone consumption

$$K \equiv \int_{\mathcal{N}} k(i) dP(i). \tag{1.5}$$

The definitions in (1.3), (1.4), and (1.5) readily yield a standard aggregate counterpart of the individual accumulation equation (1.1):

$$\Delta K = \int_{\mathcal{N}} \Delta k(i) dP(i) = \int_{\mathcal{N}} (y(i) - c(i)) \, dP(i) \tag{1.6}$$
$$= Y - C = RK + WL - C.$$

Corresponding to its individual counterpart we define $Y = RK + WL$, where R and W denote the aggregate rate of return on the accumulated and non-accumulated factor, respectively. The definition directly implies that R and W are weighted (by factor ownership) averages of their heterogeneous microeconomic counterparts,

$$R = \int_{\mathcal{N}} r(i) \frac{k(i)}{K} dP(i), \qquad W = \int_{\mathcal{N}} w(i) \frac{l(i)}{L} dP(i). \tag{1.7}$$

Interestingly, the economic interpretation of these aggregate factor prices is not straightforward in a world where inequality plays a role. In the models discussed in part 1, all units of each factor are rewarded at the same rate. In this case $r(i) = R$ and $w(i) = W$, which denotes an economy-wide interest rate and wage rate (or land rent), respectively. In the more complex models of part 2, however, unit factor incomes may be heterogeneous across individuals. This introduces interesting channels of interaction between distribution and macroeconomic dynamics. At the same time, such heterogeneity also makes it difficult to give an economic interpretation to aggregate factor supplies and remuneration rates.

Finally, note that the individual-level budget constraint (1.1) features net income flows, and so does (1.6). Hence, the aggregate Y flow is obtained subtracting capital depreciation, say δK, from every period's gross output flow, say $\tilde{Y}$, and (1.6) may equivalently be written

$$\Delta K = \tilde{Y} - \delta K - C.$$

In order to economize on notation and obtain cleaner typographical expressions, from now on we abstain from making explicit the indexing of (lowercase) individual-level variables. A convention we adopt throughout the book is the use of *lowercase letters* to denote variables relating to *individuals* and *capital letters* for variables relating to the *aggregate economy*.

Before proceeding it is important to note that we use the term "inequality" as a relative concept. More inequality can therefore be characterized by a shift in the Lorenz curve, which clearly is measured in relative terms. For example, the Lorenz curve for income depicts the relative share of total income of the poorest x percent of the population where the population percentages are on the horizontal axis. Obviously, we could also be interested in absolute differences in income. However, most of our discussions will not depend on details of such definitions. The interested reader is referred to Cowell (2000).

1.2 The Neoclassical Theory of Distribution

Let production take place in firms that rent factors of production from households, and use these factors in (possibly heterogeneous) production functions. (Now lowercase letters refer to a particular firm rather than a household.) A firm produces $y = f(k, l)$ units of output, takes as given the (possibly heterogeneous) rental prices r and w of the factors it employs, and maximizes profits as in

$$\max_{k,l} \left(f(k,l) - rk - wl \right). \tag{1.8}$$

If technology is convex, i.e., $f(\cdot,\cdot)$ is a concave function, the first-order conditions

$$\frac{\partial f(k,l)}{\partial k} = r, \quad \frac{\partial f(k,l)}{\partial l} = w \tag{1.9}$$

are necessary and sufficient for solution of the problem (1.8). Note that $f(\cdot,\cdot)$, r, and w may, in general, be different by firms.

Now assume that there are perfect factor markets. If factors can be costlessly relocated between production units, then, in equilibrium, the same factor must be rewarded at the same rate, irrespective of the particular firm where it is employed. Otherwise, arbitrage opportunities would exist, and reallocation meant to exploit them would eliminate all marginal productivity differentials.

It is easy but instructive to show that an equilibrium where, for all firms, $w = W$ and $r = R$ maximizes the aggregate production flow obtained from a given stock of the two factors. Formally the equilibrium allocation solves the problem

$$F(K,L) \equiv \max_{\{l(j),k(j)\}} \int_{\mathcal{F}} f^{(j)}(k(j),l(j)) \, dQ(j) \tag{1.10}$$

$$\text{s.t.} \quad \int_{\mathcal{F}} l(j) \, dQ(j) \leq L, \quad \int_{\mathcal{F}} k(j) \, dQ(j) \leq K,$$

where j indexes firms, $\mathcal{F}$ denotes the set of all firms, j is a firm index, and $Q(j)$ is the distribution function of firms. The first-order conditions of (1.10) are necessary and sufficient due to the same concavity assumptions that make (1.9) optimal at the firm level.

$$\frac{\partial f^{(j)}(k(j),l(j))}{\partial l(j)} = \lambda_L \quad \text{if } l(j) > 0 \tag{1.11}$$

$$\frac{\partial f^{(j)}(k(j),l(j))}{\partial k(j)} = \lambda_K \quad \text{if } k(j) > 0.$$

The optimality conditions (1.11) say that marginal products across firms have to be equalized whenever this factor is employed at firm j in positive amounts. This condition is exactly met by the firms' optimality conditions (1.9), because $r(j) = R$ and $w(j) = W$ for all j holds in equilibrium. Then, the factors' unit incomes coincide with the shadow prices λ_L and λ_K of the two aggregate constraints in (1.10),

$$w = W = \lambda_L = \frac{\partial F(K,L)}{\partial L}, \qquad r = R = \lambda_K = \frac{\partial F(K,L)}{\partial K}, \qquad (1.12)$$

and (1.10) defines an aggregate production function $F(\cdot,\cdot)$ as the maximum aggregate production obtainable from any given set of factors.

Hence we can state a central result: if markets are *perfect*, all factors are *mobile*, and firms choose inputs to *maximize profits*, aggregate production is at its efficient frontier. Under our assumptions of a single output good, efficiency means that aggregate output reaches its maximum level. Under neoclassical conditions, it is possible to abstract from distributional issues and technological heterogeneity. The allocation of resources and the distribution of income among factors of production can be viewed as if they were generated by decisions of representative consumers and producers. The *distribution across families* of production factors has no effect on productive efficiency, since factors can be reallocated across firms so as to equalize marginal products. Clearly, the initial distribution of endowments with factors of production does matter for the size distribution of income across families. The *distribution of technological knowledge* across firms plays no role for the existence of a well-defined aggregate production function for a similar reason. The mobility of production factors equalizes their marginal product across production units, hence the effect on aggregate output of increasing the aggregate stock of a factor by one unit is well defined. Aggregate output can thus be represented as a function of the aggregate stock of production factors. Clearly, the functional form of the aggregate production function $F(\cdot,\cdot)$ does reflect the heterogeneity of technologies, and the size distribution of firms will mirror the technological differences: firms with a better production technology will produce at a larger scale. In cases where no misunderstandings are possible, we will not explicitly index firms in what follows.

1.2.1 Returns to Scale

When all individual production functions have constant returns to scale, so does the aggregate production function. In that case, aggregate factor-income flows coincide with total net output by Euler's theorem:

$$F(K,L) = \frac{\partial F(K,L)}{\partial L}L + \frac{\partial F(K,L)}{\partial K}K = WL + RK \qquad (1.13)$$

The irrelevance of distribution and technological heterogeneity for the macroeconomic equilibrium does not hinge upon the assumption of constant returns: decreasing returns to scale at the firm level can be accommodated by including any fixed factors in the list of (potentially) variable factors. The rents accruing to these fixed factors are part of aggregate income. Obviously, the presence of decreasing returns in production with respect to k and l leaves the above central result unchanged. Marginal products of k and l are still equalized across production units. Similarly, factor-ownership inequality does not affect aggregate output, and a well-defined aggregate production function $F(K, L)$ exists despite technological heterogeneity across firms.[1]

Equation (1.13) states how income is distributed to the factors of production. According to (1.12), factors are paid their marginal product. In this neoclassical setting, each factor is paid according to its contribution to output. Equation (1.13) shows further that perfect factor markets and a competitive reward of factors can only exist if returns to scale are non-increasing. Were the technology to exhibit increasing returns to scale (*non-convexities*), the factor rewards $(\partial F(K, L)/\partial L) L + (\partial F(K, L)/\partial K) K$ would more than exhaust the total value of production. Consequently, at least one factor has to be paid less than its marginal product, implying that the respective market is not competitive. In other words, the neoclassical analysis has to rule out increasing returns.[2]

1.2.2 *Mobility of Production Factors*

The above discussion suggests that the mobility of production factors is crucial. It is therefore interesting to ask what happens if one factor is immobile. Consider, for instance, the case where the non-accumulated factor is firm-specific: a firm's production may involve use of a peculiar natural resource, or of its owner's unique entrepreneurial skills, and may therefore increase less than proportionately to employment of factors that are potentially or actually mobile across firms in the economy considered. It turns out that, when technologies are homogeneous across production units, factor-price equalization is still ensured. Since the marginal products of the mobile factor must be equal, the homogeneity of technologies implies that all firms produce with the same factor intensity.

---

[1]In general, an aggregate of the (immobile) fixed factor does not exist. While aggregate production function depends only on the stock of K and L, it will depend on the distribution of the fixed factors across production units just like the functional form $F(\cdot, \cdot)$ depends on the distribution of technologies.

[2]Note that, by the accounting conventions of section 1.1, both firm-level and aggregate production functions are defined net of capital depreciation. This has no implications for this argument: if the gross production function is concave and has constant returns to scale, so does net production as long as, as is commonly assumed, a fixed portion of capital in use depreciates within each period.

We also note that, if the non-accumulated factor is immobile and technologies are homogeneous, the distribution of production is determined by the distribution of l. The following exercise proves this claim formally.[3]

EXERCISE 1 Assume each firm is endowed with a fixed amount l of labor. Instead, k is mobile. All firms use the same CRS technology: $y = F(k, l)$. (Note this implies that the production function for a firm is the same as the aggregate production function.) Show that the reward of the immobile factor w is equal across firms and that the firm output is proportional to the endowment l of the immobile factor.

1.2.3 Heterogeneous Technologies and Immobile Factors

In the general case, with heterogeneous technologies and immobile factors, serious aggregation problems arise. As shown by Fisher (1969) and Felipe and Fisher (2001), aggregation is only possible under very restrictive assumptions on technological heterogeneity. Translated into our context, Fisher's aggregation result states that an aggregate production function exists *if and only if* technological heterogeneity is restricted to augmenting differences in the immobile factor. This means that if technological heterogeneity takes the form

$$f(k, l) = F(k, b\tilde{l})$$

there exists a well-defined measure for the aggregate stock of the immobile non-accumulated factor and aggregate output can be represented as $F(K, L)$. Of course, the appropriate aggregate measure of the immobile factor is then $L = \int b(j)\tilde{l}(j)dQ(j)$, and coincides with definition (1.4) if the (exogenously given) immobile factor is sensibly measured in efficiency units.

The following exercises show that mobility of some factors may suffice to ensure factor-price equalization if all firms have the same technology, and that some technologies remain unused if different firms have access to different technologies and factors are mobile.

---

[3]Obviously, when both factors are immobile no interaction takes place. There exists a collection of family firms that produce and consume in isolation, which differ not only in their ownership of productive factors, but also in the incomes earned by each unit of their factors. There is no macroeconomic equilibrium in such a situation: each family firm constitutes its own "macroeconomy."

EXERCISE 2 Discuss factor rewards and equilibrium allocation across two firms with production function

$$f^{[1]}(k,l) = A_1 k^\alpha l^\beta + A_2 k$$
$$f^{[2]}(k,l) = B_1 k^\gamma l^\delta + B_2 k$$

For what values of the parameters are these functions strictly concave? Suppose there is a total amount K of factor k, mobile across the two firms: is its employment positive at both firms if $A_2 = B_2$ and if $A_1 = B_1 = 0$? If l is immobile, are there parameter configurations such that its marginal productivity is equalized by mobility of k only?

EXERCISE 3 (a) For what parameter values are returns to scale constant in the functional forms proposed in exercise 2? (b) Discuss the form of the relevant aggregate production functions when $A_2 = B_2$. (Hint: Determine first whether both firms produce in equilibrium or not.)

The macro models of distribution reviewed in later chapters give up the neoclassical framework and study systematically deviations from these assumptions. The literature reviewed in chapters 4 and 6 studies models with increasing returns and treats distribution as exogenously given, and discusses the consequences of distribution for growth. Models in part 2 in which capital market imperfections play a central role typically feature technological heterogeneity and immobile factors of production ("human capital") in which aggregation conditions are clearly not satisfied. Models in part 3 study the consequences of distribution for macroeconomic outcomes when there are imperfections in product markets and the distribution of income among factors of production is affected by the heterogeneity in the families' initial endowments.

CHAPTER TWO

Exogenous Savings Propensities

IN THIS CHAPTER WE FOCUS on the evolution of inequality. Under neoclassical conditions, when each unit of a production factor is rewarded at the same rate, distributional dynamics are determined by savings choices. We proceed to study situations where macroeconomic variables influence the extent and evolution of inequality, but there is *no feedback from distribution to macroeconomic developments*. Even when relationships between macroeconomic aggregate variables do not depend on distribution, incomes and accumulated wealth may well be unequally distributed and the corresponding distributions may change over time.

All models that help us to understand why rational agents are willing to hold wealth (rather than consume it) also help us to understand how the distribution of economic resources will change during the process of capital accumulation. Analyzing and discussing alternative assumptions on savings behavior, we will see that such assumptions bear importantly on the dynamics of the income and wealth distribution. In the present chapter we consider the simplest case when savings behavior is not determined by optimizing behavior of households but by a simple ad hoc rule that postulates some exogenous relationship between individual savings on the one hand, and current income and current wealth on the other hand. In chapter 3 we will analyze the macroeconomic and distributional implications of a situation where infinitely lived households choose optimal levels of savings so as to smooth consumption over time and thus maximize lifetime utility. In chapter 4 we discuss implications of differential savings rates by income source (so that workers have lower savings rates than capital owners). And in chapter 5 we will study other savings motives such as savings for old age (when agents can only derive income from accumulated factors) and savings that arise from "warm-glow" bequest motives.

This chapter starts out with a situation where savings behavior derives from some exogenous relationship between the level of savings and the level of current income and wealth. We will focus on a situation where this exogenous relationship is linear, and discuss more complicated savings rules only briefly. A focus on linear specifications of individual savings functions recommends itself for a number of reasons.

First, the linear consumption and savings function has a long tradition in macroeconomic analysis, both in the theory of business cycles and in the analysis of economic growth and capital accumulation. In his *General Theory*, Keynes (1936) discussed savings propensities in terms of a "fundamental psychological law, . . . that men are disposed, as a rule and on average, to increase their consumption as their income increases but not by as much as the increase in income." Growth theorists such as Harrod (1939), Domar (1946), and Solow (1956) also postulated savings rates proportional to current income. Given the central role of constant savings rates in macroeconomics, it is interesting to look at the distributional implications of such savings behavior.

A second reason to focus on linear relationships between savings, income, and wealth is the resulting separation of aggregate capital accumulation and distributional issues, in that the distribution of income and wealth is irrelevant for the determination of aggregate variables. To study the dynamics of the income and wealth distribution, we have to account for the evolution of aggregate variables, in particular, the evolution of factor prices. Under neoclassical assumption, this can be done simply in the context of the Solow (1956) growth model: distribution is affected by accumulation, but the opposite is not true.

A third reason why it is interesting to focus on linear savings rates is its tractability. This analysis highlights some mechanical relationships between savings and current incomes that are potentially important also in more complex models. Just as the simplicity of Solow's (1956) model helps us to understand important basic principles of aggregate capital accumulation, the simplicity of linear savings functions highlights basic mechanisms that govern the dynamics of the income and wealth distribution and helps us to understand those dynamics in more complicated environments.

A final motivation for linear savings functions can be empirical. Empirical work on the evolution of the income and wealth distribution started with the work of Simon Kuznets. Based on long-run historical time series data for various (now developed) economies, Kuznets found that the extent of inequality follows an inverse U, also known as the Kuznets curve. Several subsequent studies including Paukert (1973), Ahluwalia, Carter, and Chenery (1976), and Barro (2000) confirmed such evidence.[1] At the end of this chapter we discuss briefly some relevant recent evidence. Here, we note that long-run cross-sectional relationships between savings rates, income levels, and income distribution are not easy to document empirically. The neutrality of distribution for aggregate savings, implied

---

[1] Kuznets (1955) argued that the movement of factors from a low-paying traditional sector to a high-paying modern sector leads to such an inverse U. In contrast to the neoclassical explanation based on capital accumulation presented in this chapter, Kuznets's explanation drew on mobility barriers and market imperfections.

by linearity, seems to be a meaningful first-order approximation to the aggregate cross-country data. In a comprehensive analysis that replicates previous studies with new and better data, Schmidt-Hebbel and Serven (2000) find that the neutrality of distribution is robust to measurement problems, econometric specifications, and conceptual issues. In micro-household data, however, interesting patterns can be detected (see e.g., Dynan, Skinner, and Zeldes 2004), and can motivate the more sophisticated savings models of later chapters in this book.

The analysis presented in this chapter, first undertaken by Stiglitz (1969), delivers the important message that accumulation implies a tendency toward equality in the distribution of income and wealth when the (exogenously given) distribution of the *non*-accumulated factor is relatively equal. There will be absolute convergence when all families are equally endowed with the non-accumulated factor. It is further interesting to note that this simple model of linear savings functions provides a theoretical underpinning for a relationship between inequality and capital accumulation as emphasized by Kuznets and his followers. At initial stages in the process of capital accumulation the distribution of income and wealth becomes more unequal, but after sufficient wealth has been accumulated (so that wages have sufficiently grown and investment returns have sufficiently fallen), the wealth and income distribution equalizes.

2.1 A LINEAR CONSUMPTION FUNCTION

A natural starting point for studying the implications of accumulation on distributional dynamics is a consumption function that is linear in current income. Moreover, we assume that all individuals have the same savings behavior, meaning that the relevant parameters in the consumption function are given constants across individuals. This avoids the tautological result that different consumption propensities would result in trivial distribution dynamics, as those with a high propensity to consume will tend to become poor relative to those who save more. Identical savings behavior together with the linearity of the consumption function ensures that inequality does not affect aggregate savings.

We assume that individual consumption takes the following form

$$c = \bar{c} + \hat{c} y + \tilde{c} k, \tag{2.1}$$

where $\bar{c}$, $\hat{c}$, and $\tilde{c}$ are constant parameters. Hence consumption depends linearly on current income y and also on the current stock of the accumulated factor k ("accumulated wealth"). $\hat{c}$ and $\tilde{c}$ denote the marginal propensities to consume out of income and accumulated wealth, respectively. If $\bar{c} \geq 0$, this parameter may be naturally interpreted as subsistence consumption.[2] Aggregating (2.1) and inserting it into the economy's accumulation constraint we obtain the dynamics of aggregate capital stock

$$\Delta K = (1 - \hat{c})\, Y - \tilde{c} K - \bar{c}, \tag{2.2}$$

which are independent of distribution of income and capital across households. If the propensity to consume out of income y and wealth k is constant, aggregate consumption and savings do not depend on the distribution of those variables across individuals. Hence aggregate dynamics only depends on aggregate income and parameters that are given and constant across individuals. Note that this result hinges entirely upon the assumption of constant marginal propensities to consume. Below we will discuss an example where these propensities depend on the levels of family income and wealth. We will see that then the aggregate savings rate varies with income, and distribution has an impact on the aggregate dynamics of the economy.

How does the distribution of wealth change in the accumulation process? With a consumption function linear in income and wealth aggregate dynamics are unrelated to the distribution, but the converse need not be true. The dynamic evolution of individual income and wealth depends endogenously on the parameters of individual savings functions, on the character of market interactions, and on the resulting aggregate accumulation dynamics.

2.1.1 Equal Endowments of Non-accumulated Factors

To study the dynamics of the income and wealth distribution in a neoclassical economy we assume that the non-accumulated factor l is exogenously given and (for simplicity) constant. We assume further that all individuals own the same amount $l = L$ of the non-accumulated factor, so that all income and consumption inequality is due to heterogeneous wealth levels. In the next subsection we will discuss the case when l is heterogeneous. Using (2.1) in (1.1), the dynamics of a household's wealth obey

$$\Delta k = (1 - \hat{c})y - \tilde{c}k - \bar{c} = (1 - \hat{c})\,(Rk + WL) - \tilde{c}k - \bar{c}. \tag{2.3}$$

---

[2]Note that our formulation encompasses the savings behavior assumed in the Solow (1956a) growth model as a special case. In that model, savings equal a constant fraction s of *gross* income. Since gross income $\tilde{y}$ is given by $\tilde{y} = y + \delta k$ where δ is the rate of depreciation, consumption of the average family can be written as $c = (1 - s)y + (1 - s)\delta k$. Hence savings behavior in the Solow model is the special case of the model analyzed in the text where $\bar{c} = 0$, $\hat{c} = 1 - s$, and $\tilde{c} = (1 - s)\delta$.

In an economy where R, W, and L are the same for all individuals, the individual wealth level k is the only possible source of income and consumption heterogeneity, and all such heterogeneity tends to be eliminated if higher wealth is associated with slower accumulation. Dividing (2.3) by k we get

$$\frac{\Delta k}{k} = (1 - \hat{c})R - \tilde{c} + \frac{(1 - \hat{c})WL - \tilde{c}}{k},$$

and find that higher wealth levels grow slower if $(1 - \hat{c})WL - \tilde{c} > 0$. Hence, there is convergence toward more equality if the economy satisfies the condition

$$(1 - \hat{c})WL > \tilde{c}. \tag{2.4}$$

Wealth inequality is reduced by savings behavior if savings out of non-accumulated factor income $(1 - \hat{c})WL$ is larger than the (subsistence) consumption flow $\tilde{c}$ that is independent of income and wealth. To see why, we can consider the limit case of an individual with no wealth in equation (2.3). Such an individual's wealth will increase above $k = 0$ if (2.4) holds, but will otherwise decline further (and become negative: since the model lacks an explicit budget constraint, it cannot address the obvious issue of whether the resulting debt will ever be repaid). The simple derivations above establish that, for similarly mechanical reasons, poor individuals tend to become relatively richer starting from positive wealth levels too.

In the following chapters' utility-maximizing framework, we will find it insightful to refer to such relationships between saving propensities, income sources, and income convergence. But do qualitatively realistic specifications of linear consumption functions in the form of (2.1) satisfy the condition (2.4) for the poor to become relatively richer? An interesting special case is the familiar Solow-Swan growth model, which assumes that savings are a constant fraction s of income flows: with $\tilde{c} = 0$ and $1 - s = \hat{c} < 1$, condition (2.4) is satisfied because $WL > 0$. Thus, a constant average savings propensity unambiguously tends to equalize wealth, income, and consumption across individuals. Of course, the tendency toward equality would be even stronger if $\tilde{c} < 0$, i.e., if the average savings rate were higher for poorer individuals.

EXERCISE 4 **Different savings propensities from accumulated and non-accumulated factors.** Consider a Solow-Swan economy with heterogeneous k and l endowments. Assume that individuals have an exogenous propensity to consume $c_l < 1$ for labor income and $c_k < 1$ for capital income. Moreover, there is a subsistence level $\tilde{c}$ of consumption, and a fraction $\tilde{c}$ of the capital stock is consumed. Thus, the consumption function is given as:

$$c = \bar{c} + c_l Wl + c_k Rk + \tilde{c}k$$

a. Does distribution matter for accumulation?
b. Show in which case there is divergence (convergence) in the individual capital stock.
c. With a standard neoclassical production function, does the economy have a unique stable steady state?

The more interesting and perhaps most empirically relevant case is that where $\bar{c} > 0$, to imply that richer agents have a higher average propensity to save or bequeath wealth. Note that $\bar{c} > 0$ is also the standard assumption concerning consumption in textbook Keynesian macroeconomic models. If $\bar{c}$ is so large as to violate the inequality in (2.4), i.e., "subsistence consumption" is very high, wealthier agents save a larger proportion of their income and, for *given* R and W, wealth inequality would tend to increase over time.

However, factor prices vary over time and depend endogenously on aggregate accumulation. In particular, when the marginal product of capital is falling, the marginal product of labor and wage rate W increases as more capital is accumulated: $\partial W / \partial K = \partial^2 F(K, L) / \partial L \partial K > 0$. The following exercise asks you to prove this (quite intuitive) property formally.

EXERCISE 5 Show that wages increase in the accumulation process if there are diminishing marginal returns to capital.

As wages increase with rising aggregate wealth, the condition for convergence $(1 - \hat{c})WL > \bar{c}$ may be fulfilled once wages have risen enough. In an economy that starts with $(1 - \hat{c})W(0)L < \bar{c}$ one would observe a Kuznets curve: rising inequality first and decreasing inequality thereafter. Indeed, in steady state the condition for convergence $(1 - \hat{c})WL > \bar{c}$ is always fulfilled. To see this, consider figure 2.1, where output Y and net aggregate savings ΔK are plotted as a function of capital. The three panels of the figure illustrate the implications of linear consumption functions whose intercept $\bar{c}$ is respectively zero, negative, and positive; along each panel's horizontal axis, arrows pointing to the right or left represent the sign of aggregate accumulation from (2.2),

$$\Delta K = Y - C = (1 - \hat{c})F(K, L) - \tilde{c}K - \bar{c}. \qquad (2.5)$$

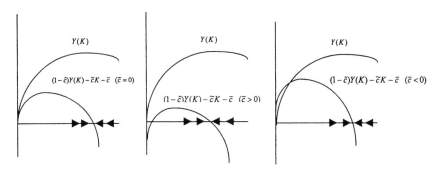

Figure 2.1 Capital accumulation with exogenous savings propensities

The aggregate economy to tend toward a stable steady state where $\Delta K = 0$. In the neighborhood of this steady state we must have $\Delta K > 0$ if K is below the steady-state level and vice versa. This implies that the ΔK curve (the net savings schedule) has a negative slope near the steady state. Inserting this stability condition $\partial(\Delta K)/\partial K < 0$ in (2.5) yields

$$(1 - \hat{c})\frac{\partial F(K, L)}{\partial K} - \tilde{c} < 0.$$

The stability condition is satisfied at points where arrows converge in the figure. When $\tilde{c} > 0$, as in the middle panel of figure 2.1, there is also an unstable steady state. If the economy starts at the left of this steady state, net savings are always negative and K diverges to zero. The economy is captured in a poverty trap.

If the economy converges to the steady state that features a positive output, all individual wealth levels also converge to each other, and to the economy's *per capita* steady-state capital stock identified by the intersection of the accumulation schedule with the horizontal axis. To see this, note that since factor markets are perfect, $\partial F(K, L)/\partial K = R$. Hence, the economy's stability condition reads

$$(1 - \hat{c})R - \tilde{c} < 0 \tag{2.6}$$

around a stable steady state where

$$\begin{aligned} \Delta K &= (1 - \hat{c})(RK + WL) - \tilde{c}K - \tilde{c} \tag{2.7} \\ &= [(1 - \hat{c})R - \tilde{c}]K + (1 - \hat{c})WL - \tilde{c} = 0. \end{aligned}$$

At a stable steady state, and in its neighborhood, (2.6) and (2.7) both hold, and together imply that the condition for cross-sectional convergence (2.4) is fulfilled by (2.7),

$$(1 - \hat{c})WL - \bar{c} = -[(1 - \hat{c})R - \check{c}]K,$$

which is a positive quantity. Hence a neoclassical economy that converges to a stable steady state also features cross-sectional convergence,
and eventual full equality, of individual wealth levels. Wealth levels converge not only in relative but also in absolute terms. To see this, note that
from (2.3) and (2.7) it follows

$$\Delta k|_{SS} = [(1 - \hat{c})R - \check{c}]k + (1 - \hat{c})WL - \bar{c}$$
$$= [(1 - \hat{c})R - \check{c}](k - K) >, =, < 0 \text{ if } k <, =, > K.$$

In steady state, every individual with wealth level $k > K$ will decumulate
and every individual with wealth below average will increase wealth. At
the end, everyone owns the same amount of capital. What is the intuition
behind this astonishing result? To answer this question, interpret $(1 -
\hat{c})R - \check{c}$ as net savings propensity out of wealth. Since diminishing returns
cause R to fall in the accumulation process and $\hat{c}$ and $\check{c}$ remain constant,
the net savings propensity is negative in steady state. This causes the result
of absolute convergence. The falling rate of return R exerts a further
equalizing force because this is especially harmful for the wealthy people.
   This result is very interesting but it does rely on all of the standard
model's assumptions, as we will see in the next chapter and as the following exercise shows by considering a slightly different consumption
function.

EXERCISE 6 Individual consumption is given by

$$c = \bar{c} + \hat{c}y + \check{c}k + \alpha C,$$

where C denotes aggregate consumption and $\alpha < 1 - \hat{c}$ is a constant
parameter.

   a. Give an interpretation for this consumption function.
   b. Markets are competitive so that $r = R$ and $w = W$. Does the distribution
      of the accumulated factor (k) have an impact on the accumulation of the
      aggregate of that factor?
   c. How does the individual distribution of k change over time? In particular,
      what are the conditions for convergence (divergence)?

2.1.2 Unequal Endowments of Non-accumulated Factors

So far, we have assumed that l is identical across individuals. In that case, there is a tendency toward absolute equality in the economy. However, this result no longer holds in the more general case when families are heterogeneous with respect to their endowment with the non-accumulated factor. It turns out that, if the endowment of l differs across families, in the limit all wealth heterogeneity will, in some form, depend on the exogenously given distribution of l. Moreover, whether or not the distributional dynamics imply divergence or convergence of wealth levels depends crucially on the initial distribution of the non-accumulated factor relative to the distribution of the accumulated factor.

To make this precise we consider first the special case in which $\bar{c} = 0$. The distributional dynamics of wealth in this case is given by the relation

$$\frac{\Delta k}{k} = (1 - \hat{c})R - \tilde{c} + \frac{(1 - \hat{c})Wl}{k}.$$

Obviously, whether or not a family's wealth level grows faster or slower than the wealth level of another household does not depend on the absolute stock it owns of factor k, but on *relative* ownership of the two factors, k/l. Families who own a large k/l have a low growth rate of k and vice versa. Given the macroeconomy is in steady state (i.e., when W remains unchanged and $(1 - \hat{c})R - \tilde{c} + \left[(1 - \hat{c})WL\right]/K = 0$), it is straightforward to characterize the dynamics of the wealth distribution. If, initially, the factor l is more unequally distributed than the factor k, there is divergence in the distribution of k. Conversely, if k is more unequally distributed, the distribution of k becomes more equal. Whatever the initial distribution of k, the long-run (ergodic) distribution of k is characterized by a situation where all households own the two factors in the aggregate K/L proportion. The resulting income and wealth inequality is identical to the exogenously given distribution of l.

When $\bar{c} > 0$ the distributional dynamics of k are only slightly more complex. Consider again the situation where the macroeconomy is in the steady state. The ergodic distribution of k is again such that $\Delta k = \left((1 - \hat{c})R - \tilde{c}\right)k + (1 - \hat{c})Wl - \bar{c} = 0$ in which case we get

$$k = -\frac{(1 - \hat{c})Wl - \bar{c}}{(1 - \hat{c})R - \tilde{c}}.$$

Recall that the steady-state value is characterized by $(1 - \hat{c})R - \tilde{c} < 0$. Hence, with $\bar{c} > 0$ the ergodic distribution of k is *more unequal* than the exogenous distribution of l. The ergodic distribution may even be characterized by negative values of k for families very scarcely endowed with the non-accumulated factor such that $(1 - \hat{c}) Wl - \bar{c} < 0$. In other words, such a steady state has a destitute class of borrowers.

We finally note that in the (perhaps less realistic) case where $\bar{c} < 0$ all individuals own positive wealth levels in the limit and the ergodic distribution of k is *less unequal* than the exogenous distribution of l.

2.1.3 Nonlinear Consumption Functions

Finally, let us briefly discuss the impact of nonlinearities in the consumption function. In that case the personal distribution of income is then directly relevant to *aggregate* savings since marginal savings propensities differ across individuals. Assume that the consumption function is concave in income or accumulated wealth. In that case, any given average levels of income or accumulated wealth are associated with a larger average consumption flow whenever these variables are more equally distributed. Formally, this is a consequence of Jensen's inequality. Intuitively, if poorer individuals have a higher marginal propensity to consume than richer ones, then redistributing income toward the former and away from the latter (i.e., considering a more equal distribution) will tend to increase consumption.

As an example, suppose that the consumption function is given by

$$c = \bar{c} + \hat{c} y + \check{c} y^2.$$

Then,

$$C = \bar{c} + \hat{c} Y + \check{c} \int_{\mathcal{N}} [(y - Y) + Y]^2 \, dP(y) = \bar{c} + \hat{c} Y + \check{c} \left[var(y) + Y^2 \right].$$

When the individual consumption function is quadratic, income inequality has aggregate implications: specifically, higher variance of the income distribution is associated with lower consumption if $\check{c} < 0$, because in this case the marginal propensity to consume $\partial c / \partial y = \hat{c} + 2 \check{c} y$ is a decreasing function of income, hence lower for the richer individuals who receive a larger proportion of aggregate income when the distribution is more unequal.

We saw above that macroeconomic equilibrium conditions play an important role in establishing income distribution convergence properties when the consumption function is linear. Similar interactions between individual behavior and equilibrium prices are relevant when there are nonlinearities in the consumption function. Furthermore, while the accumulation process is affected by distribution when consumption functions are non-linear, the steady state may be invariant to distribution: if the consumption function is convex ($\check{c} > 0$ in the example above), it is easy to show that there exists a unique stable steady state. In addition, the steady state is characterized by absolute convergence if non-accumulated income is distributed equally across families. The intuition behind this convergence result is simple. Absolute convergence already obtains if the consumption function is linear, and there is even more convergence if consumption is a convex function of income (and wealth), to imply that the rich accumulate less wealth. Hence in steady state all individuals have the same wealth, and the steady state is unique because a concave savings functions implies that ΔK is a concave function of K not only through decreasing returns to accumulation but also through saving behavior. As in the case illustrated by figure 2.1, therefore, there are at most two intersections between that function and the horizontal axis, and only the higher positive-output steady state is stable.

If the consumption function is concave, however, things become much more complicated. Intuitively, convergence may not obtain when the rich have the higher propensity to save. Bourguignon (1981) shows that, under some weak assumptions concerning the savings function, there may exist two steady states with persistent inequality as well as a steady state with full equality. The inegalitarian steady states are characterized by a two-class equilibrium, where the two groups differ in their amount of the accumulated factor. In addition, and surprisingly, the unequal steady states are Pareto dominant vis-à-vis the egalitarian steady state: income and capital of both groups are higher in the inegalitarian steady states compared to the egalitarian one. This is because the convexity of the savings function increases savings and capital accumulation in a more unequal society, and the wage income of poorer individuals is bolstered by the higher capital intensity of the steady state reached from a more unequal starting point. We will have occasion in what follows to discuss other situations where the higher income of some individuals in more unequal situations "trickles down" to poorer ones and, through dynamic feedbacks, eventually makes them better off than they would be in initially more egalitarian societies.

In light of this discussion the potential relevance of consumption-function nonlinearities is obvious. It is hard, however, to draw precise implications from it in the absence of theoretical foundations for individual behavior: does the nonlinearity of the consumption function reflect invariant characteristics of each microeconomic unit's tastes, or does it depend on features of the environment in which they operate? The next chapter discusses how an optimizing approach to the study of saving behavior may help address such issues.

2.2 REFERENCES AND FURTHER ISSUES

Stiglitz (1969) also discusses the qualitative implications of nonlinear consumption functions. The empirical and theoretical relevance of the idea that a more equal distribution of permanent income may be associated with higher aggregate consumption is explored by Blinder (1974) and Carroll (2000). Its macroeconomic implications are studied in more detail by Bourguignon (1981) cited above. A positive correlation between income levels and savings propensity can be rationalized in that and other contexts by consumption smoothing in the face of income fluctuations; we will come back to that important issue in part 2. Based on introspection, earlier writers such as Fisher (1930) and Keynes (1936) argued that the savings propensity rises with income, but the evidence from long-run aggregate data is not clear-cut and casts doubt on the validity of a mechanical link of inequality to the level of per capita income. For instance, Bourguignon and Morrisson (1998) found that the inverted-U hypothesis was probably valid in the 1970s; in later periods when additional countries were added to the sample, such a relationship no longer showed up in the data. Other studies, including Anand and Kanbur (1993), showed that the relationship strongly depends on the particular indicator by which inequality is measured. In their survey Adelman and Robinson (1989) showed that first generation studies agree in one respect: early industrialization is associated with an increase in inequality. However, it is unclear whether a subsequent decrease in inequality is brought about by increases in income or by a matter of policy choice.[3]

A second generation of studies emerged with the availability of new data. Rather than relying on pure cross-sectional data, these studies used repeated observations for single countries. Fields and Jakubson (1993) and Fields (2001) pointed to a particular flaw in cross-country data. Latin American countries had both high inequality and middle income levels, thus generating the inverted-U shape in cross sections. Using panel data, they found quite different outcomes across countries. Deininger and Squire (1996) compiled a new and better comparable data set on income inequality. In cross-sectional data, they typically find the inverted U (see also Barro 2000). Using first (decadal) differences, however, it turns out that the results are both statistically less significant and quantitatively less important. Studies, such as Lindert and Williamson (1985), focusing on

---

[3]The Kuznets research program has also been pursued by economic historians: see in particular Williamson (1991) and his references.

evolution of inequality in historical (very long-run) context, however, find support for an inverted U even in panel data.

A third generation of studies looks at the long-term evolution of the income distribution in particular countries. These studies, pioneered by Piketty (2003) focusing on France, Piketty and Saez (2003) on the United States, and Atkinson (2003) on the United Kingdom, construct long time series of top income shares over the twentieth century. Top incomes not only comprise a substantial share of total income but can also be traced over long time periods by using tax statistics. These studies consistently show a dramatic decrease in inequality throughout the first half of the twentieth century. In both France and the United States, at the beginning of the twentieth century the top 1 percent tax unit earned close to 20 percent of total income; by the end of the 1970s this share had fallen to about 8 percent in both countries. These studies have been replicated for a number of other countries, such as the Netherlands, Canada, and Switzerland. While the initial fall in top income shares seems to be present in all countries, the recent experience is quite diverse across countries. In some countries, such as France, the Netherlands, and Switzerland, no change took place over the last decades. However, in Anglo-Saxon countries top income increased. Piketty and Saez (2003) document that the increase in U.S. top income shares has been particularly dramatic. Within less than two decades, from 1980 to 1998, the 1 percent (0.1 percent) top income shares almost doubled (more than tripled) reaching again levels close to those at the early twentieth century. There was also an increase in Canada and the United Kingdom, albeit on a lower level. Saez (2004) provides a survey of this recent literature. It is also interesting to note that this pattern in the evolution of inequality is not necessarily confined to rich countries. Banerjee and Piketty (2003) look at top incomes in India and find a rather similar shape of the evolution of income distribution over the twentieth century: a decrease in the top 1 percent income share from the early 1920s up to the early 1980s, followed by a disproportionate increase in top incomes over the past two decades.

A further related strand of the recent empirical literature is concerned with the evolution of the worldwide income distribution. Bourguignon and Morrisson (2002) and Sala-i-Martin (2002) find that worldwide inequality has been decreasing in recent decades *between* countries (mainly because average incomes in China and India moved closer to the world mean income), while the *within*-country component of inequality has been increasing. Over the longer term since the early nineteenth century, Bourguignon and Morrisson (2002) find that the relative importance of inequality has shifted from *within*- toward *between*-country inequality. At the beginning of the nineteenth century, almost all income differences were due to inequalities within countries. At the beginning of the twenty-first century, worldwide inequality can be decomposed to roughly 60 percent due to differences in per capita income between countries and 40 percent due to unequal distribution of income within countries. This does not mean that the evolution of within-country inequality has become less relevant or interesting. It points to the fact that economic growth may change the picture quite strongly. Furthermore, inequalities within countries may affect country-specific growth outcomes, as we will discuss later.

CHAPTER THREE

Optimal Savings

We have seen in the last chapter that, when all consumers have the same constant marginal savings rate, the distribution of wealth will eventually converge toward the (exogenous) distribution of non-accumulated factors. When the marginal propensity to consume out of current income and wealth is constant and identical across households, wealthy people consume so much that, in steady state, all wealth differences—beyond those implied by non-accumulated factors—will eventually vanish. The ad hoc consumption functions considered earlier usefully highlight some important mechanic interactions between distribution and macroeconomic growth. It produces clear predictions about the dynamics of the distribution of wealth. Hence the assumption that savings choices depend only on current income and wealth levels makes the analysis particularly simple and provides a useful benchmark. Of course, as emphasized by Modigliani and Brumberg (1954) and Friedman (1957) and subsequent literature, that simple assumption is theoretically unsatisfactory if savings are motivated by a desire to smooth consumption over time: then, rational savings choices should be based on households' *permanent* (rather than *current*) income levels.

In this chapter we will assume that households make savings choices so as to maximize utility subject to a budget constraint. Assuming that maximization problem to have an infinite time horizon, we study the dynamics implied for distribution and accumulation by savings decisions. If preferences are such that savings depend linearly on lifetime resources, then the economy's aggregate dynamics are those of the standard "Ramsey-Cass-Koopmans" growth model, commonly used to study long-run growth and development issues. Savings motives, however, turn out to be crucial for the dynamics of distribution. While in the previous chapter growth was typically associated with income and wealth convergence, when households' savings choices are based on intertemporal utility maximization over an infinite horizon the distribution of lifetime wealth may well become increasingly unequal in a growing economy. This is the case when consumption-smoothing motives lead poorer consumers to choose a flatter consumption path in order to ensure the satisfaction of a minimum consumption standard: if subsistence consumption is important, poor households cannot afford to save, while wealthier ones choose steeper consumption paths and accumulate relatively more wealth.

Linearity of the consumption function again plays a crucial role, albeit in terms of "lifetime income" (the current stock of wealth, including its current returns, plus the current and discounted future non-accumulated income flows) rather than current income and accumulated wealth. As before, linearity ensures that aggregation is unaffected by the distribution of income. When all consumers have the same marginal propensity to consume from lifetime income, the distribution of lifetime income is irrelevant for aggregate accumulation, and aggregate dynamics can be viewed as if generated by the behavior of a "representative" agent. Regarding *macroeconomic aggregates*, all results from the Ramsey-Cass-Koopmans model are applicable. In this respect the present analysis resembles the one of the previous chapter where we could apply the results from the Solow-Swan growth model. Just like in the previous chapter, distributional issues can be discussed separately from the evolution of aggregate outcomes.

The analysis in the present chapter not only yields different implications as to the evolution of inequality, but also goes beyond the previous one in another important respect. An optimizing framework makes it possible not only to characterize the distribution of economic resources but also, thanks to an explicit formulation of individual utility, to address welfare issues. We will discuss the evolution not only of relative wealth but also of relative welfare, finding that the dynamics of the two can be really very different when, as we assume, perfect and complete intertemporal financial markets exist. In all respects other than individual consumption behavior, our previous assumptions remain valid. In particular, factor rewards are determined on perfect markets and all agents have the same preferences.

3.1 THE OPTIMAL CONSUMPTION PATH

We assume that all individuals maximize the following intertemporally additive utility function

$$v(\{c_{t+s}\}) = \sum_{s=0}^{\infty} \left(\frac{1}{1+\rho}\right)^s u(c_{t+s}), \tag{3.1}$$

The time horizon is infinite, hence we focus on a situation where the decision makers take into account the welfare of future generations, so we have a setting of perfect and complete markets. Inter alia this implies that all individuals face the same interest rate R_{t+1} between periods t and $t + 1$. The rate of time preference $\rho \geq 0$, and the increasing and concave period utility function $u(\cdot)$ are the same across individuals. The optimal consumption path satisfies the Euler equation

$$u'(c_t) = \frac{1 + R_{t+1}}{1 + \rho} u'(c_{t+1}), \tag{3.2}$$

which states that the families' optimal policy is to equalize marginal utilities over time (up to differences between rates of interest and time preference). Moreover, the transversality condition

$$\lim_{T \to \infty} \frac{k_T}{\prod_{l=1}^{\infty}(1 + R_{t+l})} = 0.$$

states that individuals cannot spend more (and will not spend less) than their lifetime income. In continuous time, the corresponding conditions are

$$\dot{c}(t) = -\frac{u'(c(t))}{u''(c(t))}(R(t) - \rho) \quad \text{and} \quad \lim_{T \to \infty} k(T) \exp\left(-\int_0^T R(s)ds\right) = 0.$$

In chapter 2 we saw that aggregate savings are independent of the resource distribution if and only if consumption is a linear function of current income and wealth. When consumption behavior is modeled in terms of optimal savings decisions subject to an intertemporal budget constraint, it is not *current* income but *lifetime* income that matters. In analogy to the discussion of the previous chapter, aggregate consumption, savings, and accumulation will be independent of distribution if and only if current consumption is an affine linear function of the present value of income flows resulting from one's ownership of production factors.

We now proceed to characterize the class of preferences that guarantees such linearity in consumption functions. The value added of such a procedure should be obvious. In the previous chapter, we have studied distributional dynamics in an economy that behaves like the Solow economy in the aggregate. We now show that, by assuming an appropriate specification of preferences, we are able to discuss distributional dynamics in an economy that behaves just like the Ramsey-Cass-Koopmans economy in the aggregate. Once we have characterized the class of preferences that allows for such easy aggregation, we proceed by deriving and discussing the properties of the consumption functions implied by such preferences.

3.1.1   The Euler Equation with HARA Preferences

In this subsection we establish the following result: if and only if preferences belong to the class of "quasi-homothetic" utility functions or, equivalently, display "hyperbolic absolute risk aversion" (HARA), then

current and future consumption levels are linearly related at the individual level. This linearity implies that current and future levels of *aggregate*
consumption levels are also linearly related. This eventually implies linearity in the individual consumption function and, hence, no impact of
distribution on the dynamics of macroeconomic accumulation.

With HARA preferences, the marginal utility of consumption is proportional to a power of a linear function of the consumption level

$$u'(c) = \left(\frac{\beta c}{\sigma} - \bar{c}\right)^{-\sigma},\tag{3.3}$$

where β, σ, and $\bar{c}$ are preference parameters. The parameter β is always
positive. The functional form (3.3) includes as special cases the constant
relative risk aversion (CRRA) utility functions, if $\sigma > 0$ and $\bar{c} = 0$; the
constant absolute risk aversion (CARA) utility function, if $\sigma = -\infty$ and
$\bar{c} = -1$; and many other utility functions commonly specified in applications, including the quadratic. The appendix to this chapter discusses
the characteristics of some widely used utility functions that belong to the
HARA class.

Now consider aggregation. The important property of the HARA class
(3.3) is a linear relationship between current and future consumption
that is implied by the intertemporal Euler condition. With HARA preferences (3.3), we can write $u'(x) = f(g(x))$ where $f(\cdot)$ is a power function and $g(\cdot)$ is an affine (constant slope) function. Using this in the
Euler equation $u'(c_t) = u'(c_{t+1})(1 + R_{t+1})/(1 + \rho)$, we get $f(g(c_t)) =
f(g(c_{t+1}))(1 + R_{t+1})/(1 + \rho)$. Applying the inverse function $f^{-1}(y)$ to
both sides,

$$g(c_t) = f^{-1}\left(\frac{1 + R_{t+1}}{1 + \rho}f(g(c_{t+1}))\right).$$

Power functions (and only power functions) have the property that the
function of a product of two terms equals the product of the function
applied to each of the two terms. Hence $f(kx) = f(k)f(x)$ and, since
the inverse of a power function is also a power function, $f^{-1}(kx) =
f^{-1}(k)f^{-1}(x)$ for all k and x such that these expressions are well defined.
Thus, we can write

$$g(c_t) = f^{-1}\left(\frac{1 + R_{t+1}}{1 + \rho}\right)f^{-1}\left(f(g(c_{t+1}))\right) = f^{-1}\left(\frac{1 + R_{t+1}}{1 + \rho}\right)g(c_{t+1})$$

or, defining $1/\xi_{t+1} \equiv f^{-1}((1 + R_{t+1})/(1 + \rho))$,

$$g(c_t) \equiv \frac{1}{\xi_{t+1}}g(c_{t+1}).$$

Rearranging and applying the $g^{-1}(\cdot)$ inverse function to both sides we obtain

$$c_{t+1} = g^{-1}\left(\xi_{t+1}g(c_t)\right). \tag{3.4}$$

The function on the right-hand side of this expression is linear in c since the slope of $g(\cdot)$, and of its $g^{-1}(\cdot)$ inverse, is constant. To see this, suppose $g(c) = a + bc$, so $g^{-1}(y) = (y - a)/b$: consumption levels at time $t + 1$ and t are then linked by the relationship

$$c_{t+1} = \left(\xi_{t+1}\left(a + bc_t\right) - a\right)/b,$$

which is linear with slope ξ_{t+1}. This establishes our result: *For utility functions such that $u'(\cdot) = f((g(\cdot))$ with $f(\cdot)$ a power function and $g(\cdot)$ an affine function as in (3.3), the Euler relationship (3.2) implies a linear relationship between each individual's consumption levels in adjoining periods.*

An important corollary of this result is that the same Euler equation that holds for the individual also holds in the aggregate. Recall that all individuals have the same preferences and interact on a single financial market. Hence, ρ and R_{t+1} are the same for all individuals, and the term ξ_{t+1} is the same for all individuals. Thus, the individual Euler equation can be aggregated simply by replacing the individual consumption levels (which enter linearly) with their aggregate consumption counterparts $C \equiv \int_N c(i)dP(i)$ at t and $t + 1$, to obtain from (3.4) $C_{t+1} = g^{-1}\left(\xi_{t+1}g(C_t)\right)$ or $g\left(C_{t+1}\right) = \xi_{t+1}g(C_t)$. Applying the functions $f(\cdot)$ to both sides, and recalling the definition of ξ_{t+1}, we have $f\left(g\left(C_{t+1}\right)\right) = f(g(C_t))\left(1 + \rho\right)/\left(1 + R_{t+1}\right)$. Since $f(g(\cdot)) \equiv u'(\cdot)$, rearranging this expression recovers the Euler equation with aggregate (average) consumption as the argument of marginal utility functions at times t and $t + 1$.

When the return to investment is the same for all agents and preferences are homogeneous and in the HARA class, heterogeneous consumption levels simply scale equation (3.2) multiplicatively. The linearity that affords aggregation of individually optimal consumption programs into the optimal program of a representative individual derives from the same properties of utility that guarantee linearity of consumption expansion paths over time in any two periods (see Pollack, 1971): linear income expansion paths imply that consumers have HARA preferences.[1] To

---

[1]In continuous time, $\dot{c}(t)$ must be a linear function of $c(t)$ when the income expansion path is linear. To show our claim in the text, one has therefore to solve the differential equation

$$-\frac{U'(c)}{U''(c)}(r - \rho) = ac + b$$

for r, ρ, a, and b given constants. The general solution is indeed equation (3.3).

illustrate the implications of the HARA assumption from this perspective, figure 3.1 considers two individuals earning different lifetime incomes. As factor returns are equalized, the slope of the budget constraint is the same for the rich and the poor individual. Optimal consumption choices are located where the individual's lifetime budget constraint touches the respective indifference curve. Connecting the tangency points yields consumption tomorrow c_{t+1} as an affine linear function of consumption today c_t. Note that the income expansion path (IEP) traced for consumption levels by considering different resource levels need not go through the origin: this happens only if $\bar{c} = 0$.

3.1.2 Consumption and Lifetime Wealth

It is readily verified that (3.3) and (3.2) imply not only a linear relationship between c_{t+1} and c_t, but also a linear relationship between consumption levels and lifetime income. Inserting (3.3) into the individual optimality condition (3.2) yields

$$\left(\frac{\beta c_t}{\sigma} - \bar{c} \right)^{-\sigma} = \frac{1 + R_{t+1}}{1 + \rho} \left(\frac{\beta c_{t+1}}{\sigma} - \bar{c} \right)^{-\sigma},$$

which can be rewritten as

$$c_{t+1} = \left(1 - \xi_{t+1} \right) \frac{\sigma}{\beta} \bar{c} + \xi_{t+1} c_t, \text{ where } \xi_{t+1} \equiv \left(\frac{1 + R_{t+1}}{1 + \rho} \right)^{1/\sigma}. \qquad (3.5)$$

It is then straightforward to show that equation (3.5) implies a linear relationship between consumption and lieftime income. Since the relationship (3.5) holds in every period we can iterate this equation forward and get

$$c_{t+j} = \left(1 - \Xi_{(t,j)} \right) \frac{\sigma}{\beta} \bar{c} + \Xi_{(t,j)} c_t \qquad (3.6)$$

where, for $m \geq t$, and $\Xi_{(t,j)} \equiv \prod_{m=1}^{j} \xi_{t+m} = \prod_{m=1}^{j} [(1 + R_{t+m}) / (1 + \rho)]^{1/\sigma}$. Similarly, iterating the individual accumulation constraint (1.1) forward from t to ∞, and using the transversality condition, we get the individual's intertemporal budget constraint

$$c_t + \sum_{j=1}^{\infty} \frac{c_{t+j}}{\prod_{m=1}^{j}(1 + R_{t+m})} = (1 + R_t)k_t + W_t l + \sum_{j=1}^{\infty} \frac{W_{t+j} l}{\prod_{m=1}^{j}(1 + R_{t+m})}. \qquad (3.7)$$

Hence, the intertemporal budget constraint says that the present value of consumption equals wealth at the end of period t plus the present value of income flow of the non-accumulated factor.

34 • Chapter 3

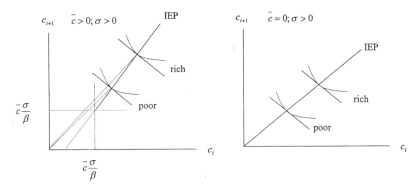

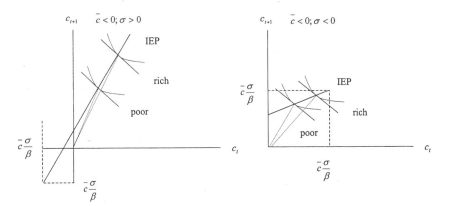

Figure 3.1 Implications of HARA preferences (with $R > \rho$)

Using (3.6) in (3.7), we can express c_{t+j} in terms of c_t, for all j. Solving the lifetime budget (3.7) for c_t shows that, under the HARA assumption, current consumption c_t is a linear function of lifetime income $(1 + R_t)k_t + h_t$

$$c_t = \bar{\bar{c}}_t + \hat{c}_t \left((1 + R_t)k_t + h_t\right), \tag{3.8}$$

where

$$\hat{c}_t = \left(1 + \sum_{j=1}^{\infty} \prod_{m=1}^{j} \left(\frac{(1 + R_{t+m})^{(1-\sigma)/\sigma}}{(1 + \rho)^{1/\sigma}}\right)\right)^{-1}, \tag{3.9}$$

$$\bar{\bar{c}}_t = \sum_{j=1}^{\infty} \left(\frac{\prod_{m=1}^{j}[(1 + R_{t+m})/(1 + \rho)]^{1/\sigma} - 1}{\prod_{m=1}^{j}(1 + R_{t+m})}\right) \hat{c}_t \frac{\sigma}{\beta} \bar{c}.$$

where b_t denotes the present value of the income flow from the non-accumulated factor

$$b_t = \sum_{j=0}^{\infty} \frac{(1 + R_t)W_{t+j}l}{\prod_{m=0}^{j}(1 + R_{t+m})}.$$

By equation (3.8) we see that individual consumption depends linearly on wealth. This implies that the marginal propensity to consume is constant across families and resource levels. Hence, if all families have (identical) HARA preferences, maximize utility over an infinite horizon, and face the same factor returns, the distribution of income and wealth has no effect on aggregate consumption and accumulation.

The savings behavior resulting from the ad hoc consumption function of the previous chapter and the savings behavior resulting from optimal savings decisions in the present chapter both imply that distribution does not affect aggregate savings and investment. The two approaches, however, are different in three important respects. First, optimal savings behavior relates individual variables with coefficients that are the same across all individuals but, unlike those of the previous chapter's assumed consumption functions, are not constant over time. In fact, $\hat{c}_t$ and $\bar{\bar{c}}_t$ generally depend not only on the preference parameters but also on the sequence of rates of return $\{R_j\}$, which do vary along the economy's transition toward the steady state. The marginal propensity to consume $\hat{c}_t$ is independent of R only if $\sigma = 1$, in which case (see the appendix) preferences are a logarithmic function of a linear function of consumption. And for rates of return to be irrelevant to current consumption choices, it must also be the case that $\bar{c} = 0$. Only in that case the income and substitution effects of the rate of return R exactly offset each other at all consumption levels, and consumption's relationship to lifetime resources is independent of the economy's aggregate dynamics.

Second, while the ad hoc savings function in (2.1) had accumulated wealth and current income as its two distinct arguments, optimal savings decisions attach the same propensity to consume to accumulated wealth, k_t, and to the present value of the non-accumulated income flow b_t. When it is possible to borrow and lend against future non-accumulated income flows, consumption decisions are forward looking and based on permanent income. The propensity to consume non-accumulated income is high when income is currently low relative to its future discounted path. Instead, the ad hoc consumption function studied in the previous chapter viewed consumption as a function of current income and accumulated wealth, disregarding future income from non-accumulated factors. This explains why the source of income (accumulated and non-accumulated factor) was important in determining consumption behavior in the section before. With optimal savings, the relative importance of accumulated and non-accumulated factors in an individual's resources does not affect consumption.

Third, we also note that the sequence of rates of return $\{R_j\}$ matters even when income and substitution effects offset each other, that is when $\sigma = 1$ (preferences are logarithmic) and when $\bar{c} = 0$ (no subsistence consumption). This is because individuals base their consumption decision on total resources that are available to them at a given date. These resources include all future income flows from non-accumulated factors, the present value of which depends on the sequence of rates of return $\{R_j\}$. These (human) wealth effects imply that sequences of high interest rates tend to depress the value of human wealth and hence the level of current consumption. Wealth effects will play an important role when considering models with finite (rather than infinite) planning horizons and endogenous (rather than exogenous) growth.

3.2 THE DYNAMICS OF ACCUMULATION AND DISTRIBUTION

Having solved optimal savings decisions at the individual level, we can now look at how the level of a household's wealth evolves during the process of capital accumulation. The present section proceeds in two steps. We first briefly review the aggregate accumulation dynamics implied by the individual Euler equations (3.6). In other words, we first look at the aggregate evolution of the accumulated factor (1.6) and its implication for factor rewards. We then focus on the evolution over time of the resources of (initially) heterogeneous households.

3.2.1 The Accumulation of Capital

Before we come to characterize the evolution of wealth distribution, it is necessary to look at aggregate dynamics and the implied changes in factor rewards along the transition path toward a steady state. For HARA preferences, the distribution of factor endowments across households does not matter for aggregate savings and accumulation. Thus, aggregate dynamics are familiar from standard Ramsey-Cass-Koopmans models with a representative agent. We briefly discuss them referring to figure 3.2. This figure plots the aggregate income available for consumption or net investment as a hump-shaped function of K (whose decreasing portions reflect capital depreciation); the vertical axis of figure 3.2 measures consumption, and since $\Delta K = Y - C = F(K, L) - C$ by (1.6), points along the net production function imply $C = F(K, L)$ and $\Delta K = 0$. Since we abstract from technical progress, aggregate consumption is constant if

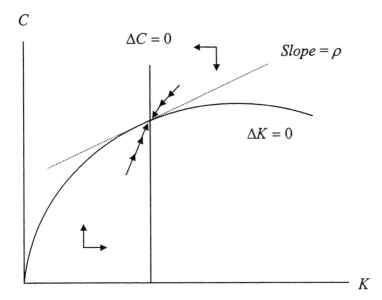

Figure 3.2 Neoclassical growth with optimal savings and consumption choices

$R_t = \rho$; see equation (3.2). Under neoclassical assumptions, factors earn their marginal product, therefore $R = \partial F(K, L)/\partial K$. This means that the locus of points where $\Delta C = 0$ is a vertical line, and is determined by

$$\frac{\partial F(K, L)}{\partial K} = \rho. \tag{3.10}$$

The dynamics of the aggregate economy is characterized by the saddlepath in figure 3.2, which does not depend on distribution. The macroeconomy is growing toward the steady state if $R_t > \rho$ and shrinking if $R_t < \rho$.

3.2.2 Evolution of the Wealth Distribution

Just like in the case of ad hoc savings behavior studied in the previous chapter, under optimal savings choices macroeconomic aggregates also have an impact on the dynamics of distribution. Since utility is derived from consumption, we can directly assess the evolution of *consumption inequality*: dividing an individual household's Euler equation (3.5) through by c_t we find that consumption growth,

$$\frac{c_{t+1}}{c_t} = (1 - \xi_{t+1}) \frac{\sigma}{\beta} \frac{\bar{c}}{c_t} + \xi_{t+1}, \tag{3.11}$$

is independent of current consumption if $\bar{c} = 0$ or $\xi_{t+1} = 1$. Recall that

$$\xi_{t+1} \equiv [(1 + R_{t+1}) / (1 + \rho)]^{1/\sigma},$$

so $\xi_{t+1} = 1$ and (potential) consumption inequalities persist when the economy has reached its steady state and $R_{t+1} = \rho$. For other parameter configurations, the consumption growth rate is different across individuals: it is faster or slower for higher consumption levels depending on whether the first term on the right-hand side of (3.11) is negative or positive.

We proceed by characterizing the evolution of lifetime resources over time. To economize notation we denote lifetime resources by

$$a_t \equiv (1 + R_t)k_t + h_t$$

and will henceforth refer to a_t as a household's "wealth" including both "accumulated wealth" $(1 + R_t)k_t$ and "non-accumulated wealth" h_t. Part of these resources are consumed, so at the end of period t, the household's wealth is given by $a_{t+1} = (1 + R_{t+1}) (a_t - c_t)$. Recall that consumption is given by (3.8). We can insert this in the previous equation, and divide both sides by a_t to obtain

$$\frac{a_{t+1}}{a_t} = (1 + R_{t+1}) (1 - \hat{c}_t) - \frac{(1 + R_{t+1})\bar{\bar{c}}_t}{a_t}. \tag{3.12}$$

The first term of equation (3.12) is identical for all individuals. (Recall that $\hat{c}_t$ is a time-varying parameter of the household's consumption function that depends only on the sequence of interest rates and the rate of time preference.) Hence it is the second term in (3.12) that determines the evolution of the wealth distribution. Since $(1 + R_{t+1})$ and a_t are strictly positive, it depends on the sign of $\bar{\bar{c}}_t$ whether the wealth distribution converges or diverges in the economy's transition toward the steady state.

To interpret the meaning of $\bar{\bar{c}}_t > 0$ or $\bar{\bar{c}}_t < 0$, consider the special case where preference parameters in (3.3) satisfy $\beta = \sigma > 0$. We will refer to this subclass as "generalized Stone-Geary preferences." In that case marginal utility is $u'(c) = (c - \bar{c})^{-\sigma}$. This functional form implies that utility and marginal utility have constant elasticity with respect to the excess of consumption c over some critical level $\bar{c}$. A positive $\bar{c}$ can be interpreted as the subsistence level of consumption (note that utility is ill defined if $c < \bar{c}$). Less realistically we could also imagine that $\bar{c}$ is negative, representing a situation where consumers derive well-defined utility even if they do not consume anything. Our discussion will focus on the former case.

In a *growing* economy we have $R_t > \rho$. It is straightforward to verify from (3.9) that $\bar{\bar{c}}_t > 0$ if $\bar{c} > 0$. In that case, equation (3.12) tells us that the growth factor a_{t+1}/a_t is higher the higher the initial wealth level a_t. Hence we reach the following result: *When a household's preferences require a minimum consumption level to be well defined, the distribution of lifetime wealth diverges along the transition path toward the economy's steady state.*

In fact, the elasticity of intertemporal substitution

$$-\frac{u'(c)}{u''(c)c} = \frac{c - \bar{c}}{\sigma c} \equiv \varepsilon(c)$$

is increasing in c if $c > \bar{c} > 0$. Thus the rich are more inclined toward intertemporal substitution. A higher elasticity implies a steeper consumption path, i.e., consume less today to enjoy higher consumption tomorrow: hence the rich save relatively more than the poor. The lower elasticity of intertemporal substitution of the poor is due to the positive subsistence level $\bar{c} > 0$, which forces them to start with relatively high consumption and relatively low savings.

Things are only slightly different in a *shrinking* economy. When the economy approaches the steady state from above, we have $R_t < \rho$. This implies from (3.9) that $\bar{\bar{c}}_t < 0$ if $\bar{c} > 0$. As the poor have a higher propensity to smooth consumption they will choose a flatter consumption path. This means they save more and consume less at the start. The result is *convergence* in the distribution of lifetime incomes.

Finally, when the economy has reached its *steady state*, that is when $R_t = \rho$, we see directly from (3.9) that $\hat{c}_t = [1 + \sum_{j=1}^{\infty} (1 + \rho)^{-j}]^{-1} = \rho/(1 + \rho)$ and $\bar{\bar{c}}_t = 0$. Savings decisions reproduce the current state forever as the growth rate of a_t is zero for all individuals, that is, $a_{t+1}/a_t = (1 + \rho)[1 - \rho/(1 + \rho)] = 1$. In the steady state, everyone follows a flat consumption path equal to his or her permanent income. Together with the constant reward rates R and W for the production factors, this implies that the distribution does not change over time. Hence when the macroeconomy has reached its steady state, the distribution has also reached its ergodic state, which is characterized by persistent inequality.

The above discussion was confined to the HARA subclass where $\sigma > 0$ and $\bar{c} > 0$. The discussion of the other subclasses is done quickly by considering how the elasticity of intertemporal substitution varies with consumption (see also figure 3.1). Consider first the case $\beta = \sigma > 0$ and $\bar{c} = 0$, the familiar CRRA specification with homothetic preferences and constant elasticity of intertemporal substitution. Homotheticity implies that saving rates do not depend on resource levels. Hence, all individuals save the same proportion of their income, and any initial distribution persists. If $\sigma > 0$ and $\bar{c} < 0$, or if $\sigma < 0$ and $\bar{c} < 0$, the utility function exhibits increasing relative risk aversion. (For $\sigma < 0$, $\bar{c} < 0$ the utility function exhibits even increasing *absolute* risk aversion.)[2] Hence, the rich face a lower rate of intertemporal substitution and will choose the flatter consumption path. This means, for all HARA utility functions—*other than the generalized Stone-Geary with $\bar{c} > 0$*—there is convergence (divergence) in the distribution of lifetime income in a growing (shrinking) economy. This also becomes clear if we again look at figure 3.1: if $\bar{c} >$ ($<$)0 the c_{t+1}/c_t ratio is higher (lower) for the rich than for the poor. To sum up, as compared to the generalized Stone-Geary with $\bar{c} > 0$ studied above, the results change sign when $\bar{c} < 0$.

In summary, we have:

	$R_t > \rho$	$R_t = \rho$	$R_t < \rho$
$\bar{c} > 0$	*Divergence*	*Persistence*	*Convergence*
$\bar{c} = 0$	*Persistence*	*Persistence*	*Persistence*
$\bar{c} < 0$	*Convergence*	*Persistence*	*Divergence*

The dynamics of distribution are quite different from those resulting from the ad hoc specification of savings analyzed in the previous chapter. In that case, all inequality arising from differences in k vanished in the limit. With optimal savings, however, this can never be the case, and for certain parameter values the optimal savings model predicts *divergence* of lifetime incomes. And even when there is convergence of lifetime income and consumption levels, this is only in relative rather than absolute terms. Equalization of marginal utilities and the absence of shocks imply that any initial ordering of wealth levels will persist over time. If family i is richer than j in period t, it will also be richer in all future periods. Full convergence (as is the case with ad hoc savings) or leapfrogging (that is, social mobility) can never occur.[3]

The analysis of the dynamics of consumption and lifetime resources provided clear and interesting predictions. However, inequality is also measured in terms of *current income* or *accumulated wealth* holdings. To determine the dynamics of the accumulated factor k, note that $\Delta k_t = W_t l + R_t k_t - c_t$. Having determined the dynamics of k, the dynamics of income $y = rk + wl$ then follow immediately. Obviously, in steady state there is persistent inequality not only in total wealth but also in the *composition* of accumulated and non-accumulated wealth across in-

---

[2] For completeness note that if $\sigma = -\infty$ and $\bar{c} = -1$, the utility function exhibits constant absolute risk aversion, which obviously also faces increasing relative risk aversion.

[3] This "non-convergence" result is very general and does not hinge on the assumption of time-separable HARA preferences. As shown by Bliss (2004) it holds for Koopmans preferences.

dividuals. We showed that in steady state individual lifetime resources are constant; this implies that k must also be constant. In the transition process things are much more complicated, so we can only do a qualitative analysis. Using (3.8) we can replace consumption to get $\Delta k_t = W_t l + R_t k_t - \left(\bar{\bar{c}}_t + \hat{c}_t((1 + R_t) k_t + h_t)\right)$. The growth rate of k_t then is given by

$$\frac{\Delta k_t}{k_t} = \frac{W_t l - \hat{c}_t h_t - \bar{\bar{c}}_t}{k_t} + (1 - \hat{c}_t) R_t - \hat{c}_t.$$

Divergence occurs if $W_t l - \hat{c}_t h_t - \bar{\bar{c}}_t < 0$. Three conceptually distinct factors play a role in this condition:

1. The condition is more likely to be satisfied in a growing economy if $\bar{c}$ is large, because in this case $\bar{\bar{c}}_t > 0$.
2. Divergence will occur when $\hat{c}_t$, the propensity to consume out of wealth, is high. The marginal propensity to consume $\hat{c}_t$ is higher (lower) than in steady state, when $\sigma > (<) 1$. Intuitively, a lower intertemporal rate of substitution implies that individuals want to have a high level of consumption today when they face higher income of the non-accumulated factor in their future. If non-accumulated income takes a large share of their total income, this effect will be very strong, and those individuals will save less today. Hence, k_t is more likely to diverge if σ is high.
3. It remains to discuss the relation between $W_t l_t$ and h_t, given $\hat{c}_t$ There are two effects. On the one hand, with wages growing over time, h_t is high compared to $W_t l$. On the other hand, in a growing economy future wage income is discounted more strongly because $R_t > \rho$. Which effect dominates depends on technology and on the growth rate of the economy (which in turn is determined by technology and preferences).

3.3 WELFARE DISTRIBUTION IN COMPLETE MARKETS

The "neoclassical" models discussed in the previous chapters characterize interactions between cross-sectional income and consumption distribution on the one hand, and aggregate dynamics on the other. In that setting, however, distribution of consumption and its dynamic evolution have little economic relevance, for two reasons.

First, the same functional form assumptions that make it possible to characterize aggregate dynamics imply that the speed of aggregate growth depends only on aggregate variables, not on their distribution across individuals. With HARA preferences, as in (3.3), macroeconomic dynamics can be interpreted in terms of representative agent savings choices even as the economy features persistent and variable heterogeneity of individual consumption paths.

Second, the dynamics of consumption distribution have no substantive welfare implications: if all individuals' savings earn the same rate of return, relative welfare remains constant over time even though, as discussed above, relative consumption levels may diverge or converge. To see this, consider that equations in the form (3.2) hold for all individuals, and take ratios of their left- and right-hand sides for different individuals: for any $i, j \in \mathcal{N}$ and all t we may write

$$\frac{u'(c_t^i)}{u'(c_t^j)} = \frac{u'(c_{t+1}^i)}{u'(c_{t+1}^j)} \equiv \frac{\omega^j}{\omega^i} \qquad (3.13)$$

where ω^i differs from ω^j if individuals i and j enjoy different consumption flows, but neither ω^i nor ω^j depend on time. It turns out that conditions in the form (3.13) are necessary and sufficient for maximization of a weighted sum of individual welfare functions in the form (3.1) under an aggregate resource constraint.

Denote by $v(\{c_t^i\})$ the level of lifetime welfare of individual i that enjoys consumption flow $\{c_t^i\}$. Formally, the market allocation of the neoclassical economy under consideration solves the social planning problem $\max \int_{\mathcal{N}} \omega^i v(\{c_t^i\}) dP(i)$ subject to the resource flow constraint $\int_{\mathcal{N}} c_t^i \, dP(i) \leq F(K_t, L) + K_t - K_{t+1}$, for all t. To characterize the solution of this problem and its relationship to market phenomena, suppose for simplicity that individuals are identical within each of two groups, $\mathcal{N}^1$ and $\mathcal{N}^2$, and consider the social planning problem

$$\max \quad \left[\omega^1 P(\mathcal{N}^1) v(\{c_t^1\}) + \omega^2 P(\mathcal{N}^2) v(\{c_t^2\}) \right] \qquad (3.14)$$
$$\text{s.t.} \quad c_t^1 P(\mathcal{N}^1) + c_t^2 P(\mathcal{N}^2) \leq F(K_t, L) + K_t - K_{t+1}, \forall t \geq 0,$$

where $P(\mathcal{N}^i)$ is the number of individuals in group i, $\omega^i > 0$ is the Pareto weight assigned to their welfare, and $L \equiv l^1 P(\mathcal{N}^1) + l^2 P(\mathcal{N}^2)$ is the constant aggregate endowment of non-accumulated factors of production. To form the Lagrangian of the social planning problem, a sum of shadow-price-weighted constraints in the form

$$\sum_{t=1}^{\infty} \lambda_t \left(F(K_t, L) + K_t - K_{t+1} - (c_t^1 P(\mathcal{N}^1) + c_t^2 P(\mathcal{N}^2)) \right) \qquad (3.15)$$

may be added to the discounted utility objective function in (3.14). If $F(\cdot, L)$ and $v(\cdot; t)$ are concave, first-order conditions are necessary and sufficient for maximization of (3.14). Differentiating with respect to c_t^1

and c_t^2 yields

$$\omega^1 P(\mathcal{N}^1)\frac{\partial v(\{c_t^1\})}{\partial c_t^1} = \lambda_t P(\mathcal{N}^1), \quad \omega^2 P(\mathcal{N}^2)\frac{\partial v(\{c_t^2\})}{\partial c_t^2} = \lambda_t P(\mathcal{N}^2), \quad \forall t, \quad (3.16)$$

where λ_t denotes the Lagrangian multiplier assigned to the resource constraint at time t. These conditions can be rearranged in two insightful ways. Eliminating λ_t from (3.16) yields

$$\omega^1 \frac{\partial v(\{c_t^1\})}{\partial c_t^1} = \omega^2 \frac{\partial v(\{c_t^2\})}{\partial c_t^2}, \quad \forall t: \quad (3.17)$$

in a social optimization problem like (3.14), resources are allocated in order to keep the ratio of marginal welfare effects constant at ω^1/ω^2. If all individuals have the same preferences, consumption flows are equalized in each period if $\omega^1 = \omega^2$; if $\omega^1 > \omega^2$, then the consumption flow allocated to individuals in group 1 must be so much larger as to appropriately reduce its marginal effect on the concave $v(\cdot)$ welfare function.

Alternatively, taking term-by-term ratios of the left- and right-hand sides of (3.16) evaluated at different times, one may eliminate ω's and obtain

$$\frac{\partial v(\{c_t\})}{\partial c_t} = \frac{\lambda_t}{\lambda_{t+1}}\frac{\partial v(\{c_{t+1}\})}{\partial c_{t+1}}, \quad \forall t. \quad (3.18)$$

The ratio of marginal utilities across different time periods is the same for all individuals, as it depends only on the ratio of the aggregate Lagrangian multipliers λ_t and λ_{t+1}. To characterize this ratio, one should note that all capital levels except the initial K_1, which is exogenously given to the social optimization problem, are endogenously determined by consumption and accumulation choices. Hence, along an interior optimal trajectory the derivative of the Lagrangian expression with respect to K_t must vanish for each $t \geq 2$ (note that each K_t appears in two constraints), to imply that

$$\frac{\lambda_{t-1}}{\lambda_t} = 1 + \frac{\partial F(K_t, L)}{\partial K_t}.$$

If markets are perfectly competitive within each period, then $\lambda_t/\lambda_{t+1} = 1 + R_{t+1}$ for all t. This sequence of relationships is easily interpreted as no-arbitrage requirements when written in the form

$$\lambda_t = \left(1 + \frac{\partial F(K_{t+1}, L)}{\partial K_{t+1}}\right)\lambda_{t+1}.$$

From the social planner's point of view, it is always possible to increase savings and decrease aggregate consumption by one unit at time t; this changes the objective function by λ_t at the margin, and yields one additional unit of K and $\partial F(K_{t+1}, L)/\partial K_{t+1}$ additional units of output at time $t + 1$, when resources are worth λ_{t+1} in terms of the planner's objective function. Thus, the planner should take advantage of arbitrage opportunities (and would not be optimizing) if the two terms of the above equation were not equal.

Thus, the "social" optimality condition (3.18) coincides with the "private" one in (3.2) if preferences have the standard form (3.1) and

$$\frac{\partial v(\{c_t\})}{\partial c_t} = \left(\frac{1}{1+\rho}\right)^t u'(c_t)$$

for all households at all times. Not only the static but also the dynamic aspects of individual optimal choices are Pareto efficient: the sequence of reward rates $\{R_t\}$ on which intertemporal financial market transactions are based appropriately reflects the economic scarcity of reproducible (= accumulated) factors of production, or "capital," whose aggregate supply can only be increased by forgoing consumption at earlier dates.

In market equilibrium, relative consumption levels are determined by factor ownership, since

$$c_t = Rk_t + W_t l + k_t - k_{t+1} = F(k_t, l) + k_t - k_{t+1} \qquad (3.19)$$

in each period. Given identical preferences, only different factor bundles can imply different consumption streams and welfare levels, and different Pareto weights in the social planner interpretation of the competitive market equilibrium.

In an economy with complete competitive markets, macroeconomic phenomena and distribution are conceptually separate. Macroeconomic growth is a dynamic phenomenon and, if preferences are such as to allow aggregation, completely independent of distribution. Distribution, in turn, is viewed as an issue to be resolved once and for all (hence, statically) at the beginning of time, where claims to current and future production flows are allocated to individuals.

The characterization (3.16) of complete market allocations suggests an important qualification to the distributional dynamics results discussed above. Recall that if preferences lend themselves nicely to aggregation, then macroeconomic dynamics can be interpreted in terms of representative agent savings choices even as the economy features persistent and variable heterogeneity of individual consumption paths. The observed dynamics of consumption distribution have little economic significance under complete markets, however, because the apparent dynamics of inequality are just a by-product of efficient once-and-for-all allocation of a maximized welfare "pie." The same HARA assumptions that allow aggregation of individual actions in representative agent terms make it easy to discuss the cross-sectional dynamics of consumption levels. In competitive equilibrium, dynamics are such as to keep marginal utilities proportional to each other across individuals: for example, in the case $\beta = \sigma > 0$ we have

$$\left(c^j - \bar{c}\right)^{-\sigma} = \frac{\omega^i}{\omega^j} \left(c^i - \bar{c}\right)^{-\sigma},$$

where $\omega^j > \omega^i$ (individual j is relatively well endowed, and receives a higher weight in the social planner's objective function). If $\bar{c} = 0$, this implies that the two individuals' consumption levels should remain forever proportional to each other. When $\bar{c} > 0$, however, we may write

$$c_t^j = \left(1 - \left(\frac{\omega^j}{\omega^i}\right)^{1/\sigma}\right)\bar{c} + \left(\frac{\omega^j}{\omega^i}\right)^{1/\sigma} c_t^i.$$

Since $\left(\omega^j/\omega^i\right)^{1/\sigma} > 1$, the consumption level of the richer individual has larger-than-unitary slope and a negative intercept when written as a function of the poorer individual's (see figure 3.3). Hence, if both consumption levels grow, the larger one grows faster. This cross-sectional perspective is of course consistent with the dynamic one discussed above: whether consumption grows or declines over time, however, depends on whether R is larger or smaller than ρ, a fact that is determined at the aggregate level in an economy where all individuals have access to the same rate of return.

EXERCISE 7 Can the two individuals' consumption levels ever be found within the shaded area in the figure?

Such divergence of cross-sectional consumption rates simply reflects the fact that individuals who are privileged in the initial allocation must remain so in all future periods. Since an efficient allocation of resources should keep marginal utilities aligned as in (3.18), individuals who are farther from the required consumption level $\bar{c}$ need to receive larger consumption increases to ensure a similar proportional fall in marginal utility: relative consumption dynamics just compensate the impact of different consumption levels on the degree of concavity of individual utility functions. The same qualitative irrelevance of observed consumption

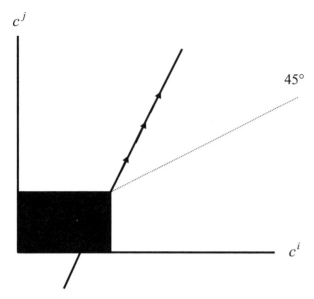

Figure 3.3 Relative consumption levels in a socially planned allocation.

dynamics would characterize more general specifications where preferences are not such as to allow a representative individual interpretation of aggregate consumption.

3.4 References and Further Issues

Lucas and Stokey (1984) present and describe the general conditions for a solution of the optimal growth problem within a neoclassical economy where consumers are heterogeneous. They also consider the case of unequal discount rates. The results on the implications of optimizing consumption choices for observable distribution dynamics are due to Chatterjee (1994). In Caselli and Ventura (2000) unequal consumers have HARA preferences with heterogeneous $\bar{c}$ (which they interpret as publicly provided goods). When taste heterogeneity enters in this linear form, inequality still does not affect savings. Steger (2000) shows that incomes across countries may diverge when preferences take a Stone-Geary form with a subsistence level in consumption. For further discussion of the HARA preferences class, see Merton (1971) and Gollier (2001a).

In models where the non-accumulated factor is identified with labor, its individual and aggregate supply should depend endogenously on current and expected wage rates, on financial wealth, and on the structure of preferences. For a discussion of how models of labor/leisure choices may yield analytically convenient and realistic aggregate models under appropriate simplifying assumptions, see Rebelo (1991) and his references.

3.5 APPENDIX: HARA PREFERENCES

The purpose of this appendix is to show which commonly used utility functions are special cases of our HARA function (3.3) assumed in the text. First, we must determine what values the parameters of the utility function characterized by $u'(c) = (\beta c / \sigma - \bar{c})^{-\sigma}$ can take. Note that $u''(c) = -\beta (\beta c / \sigma - \bar{c})^{-\sigma - 1}$, which must be nonpositive (due to the law of declining marginal utility). Hence, β is always positive and can be interpreted as a scaling factor. It is also evident that the combination $\sigma < 0$, $\bar{c} \geq 0$ is impossible, since the term in brackets has to be positive and the utility function defined for nonnegative consumption levels only. The different branches of the utility function can then be analyzed by looking at the behavior of absolute risk aversion (ARA). It is given by

$$ARA = -\frac{u''(c)}{u'(c)} = \frac{\beta}{\beta c / \sigma - \bar{c}}$$

$$\frac{\partial ARA}{\partial c} = -\frac{1}{\sigma} \left(\frac{\beta}{\beta c / \sigma - \bar{c}} \right)^2 \quad \begin{array}{l} < 0, \text{ if } \sigma > 0 \\ = 0, \text{ if } \sigma \to -\infty \\ > 0, \text{ if } \sigma < 0. \end{array}$$

We identify three groups of preference specifications according to the parameter values: decreasing (DARA), constant (CARA), and increasing (IARA) absolute risk aversion.[4]

$\sigma > 0$ *(Generalized Stone-Geary, DARA).* Setting our scaling parameter $\beta = \sigma > 0$, we can write the marginal utility function $U'(c) = (c - \bar{c})^{-\sigma}$. If $\bar{c} > 0$ this parameter can be interpreted as a subsistence level in consumption as marginal utility goes to infinity if consumption c approaches $\bar{c}$ from the right. In that case, the utility function also exhibits decreasing *relative* risk aversion (DRRA). Instead, for $\bar{c} < 0$, it exhibits increasing relative risk aversion (IRRA). This utility function— where marginal utility is finite even at zero consumption—may be applied in a situation where the individual also gets a minimum utility out of non-market activities such that it may survive even if consumption c equals

---

[4]Of course, there are also other utility functions whose risk aversion is not HARA that also belong to the DARA or IARA class.

zero. Finally, if $\bar{c} = 0$, we get the most general homothetic function, which is still additively time separable, the famous constant relative risk aversion (CRRA) utility function. All HARA functions exhibit linear income expansion paths but only for the CRRA the path goes through the origin. (If $\sigma = 0$, the utility function is linear.)

$\sigma \to -\infty$, $\bar{c} = -1$ *(CARA)*. To get the constant absolute risk aversion utility set $\bar{c} = -1$ and define $\theta \equiv -\sigma/(\beta c)$. When $\sigma \to -\infty$, we get $\lim_{\sigma \to -\infty} (\beta c/\sigma - \bar{c})^{-\sigma} = \lim_{\sigma \to -\infty} (1 + \beta c/\sigma)^{-\sigma} = \lim_{\theta \to \infty} (1 - 1/\theta)^{\theta \beta c} = e^{-\beta c} = u'(c)$. The coefficient of absolute risk aversion is then equal to β. The CARA function is extensively used in applications concerning risk and uncertainty. With CARA, risk premia do not differ among rich and poor agents. This feature makes it easy to analyze dynamic investment problems with uncertainty (see chapter 9).

$\sigma < 0$, $\bar{c} < 0$ *"Saturation" (IARA)*. We set the parameter $\beta = -\sigma > 0$ and we define a saturation level $s \equiv \bar{c}\sigma/\beta = -\bar{c} > 0$. This implies $U'(c) = (\beta c/\sigma - \bar{c})^{-\sigma} = (s - c)^{\beta}$. This class is perhaps the most unfamiliar one, as it exhibits increasing absolute risk aversion, which seems totally at odds with casual evidence. But the quadratic utility function, which is often used in finance and consumption theory, is a special case of the saturation class, with $\beta = -\sigma = 1$.

3.6 Review Exercises

Exercise 8 **Toward the *AK* Model** Consider an economy populated by L infinitely lived individuals, with perfectly competitive markets. There is a single good, so output can be consumed or used as capital in the next period. Capital does not depreciate.

a. Each individual owns one unit of labor, and can use it with k units of capital to produce $f(k) = k^{\alpha} + Ak$ units of output. Show that the aggregate production function is $F(K, L) = K^{\alpha} L^{1-\alpha} + AK$, regardless of who owns the capital stock. Discuss the dynamics of aggregate output and the evolution of consumption and capital inequality in steady state when utility is logarithmic.

b. Now assume that, in addition to the technology in a., it is possible to operate another technology that uses only capital, and yields B units of output for each unit of k. What is the form of the aggregate production function? Show that if a constant proportion of output is saved, then this economy will grow indefinitely as long as $B > 0$.

EXERCISE 9 Consider the model presented in this chapter. Suppose the utility function takes the CARA (constant absolute risk aversion) form

$$V(\{c_{t+s}\}) = \sum_{s=0}^{\infty} \left(\frac{1}{1+\rho}\right)^s \left(-e^{-\gamma c_{t+s}}\right),$$

where ρ and γ are positive parameters.

a. Write the Euler condition: is it satisfied by aggregate consumption levels at all times t and $t+1$ if it is satisfied by each individual? Does the consumption of the rich grow faster than the consumption of the poor?

b. Now suppose individuals choose consumption in continuous time to maximize

$$\hat{V}(\{c(s)\}) = \int_t^\infty e^{-\hat{\rho}(s-t)} \left(-e^{-\gamma c(s)}\right) ds,$$

and let $\hat{R}$ be the instantaneous per-period interest rate, which is assumed to be constant over time. Write the Euler condition: is it satisfied by aggregate consumption levels if it is satisfied by each individual? In this continuous-time setting, under what conditions is proportional consumption inequality increasing over time? Suppose individuals own $k(0)$ of wealth at time zero, and never earn anything else than capital income $\hat{R}k(s)$ at any time s. Write the budget constraint, and solve for individual i's optimal consumption path.

c. We know that decentralized equilibria can be equivalent to a social planning problem, where a weighted sum of individual utility functions is maximized subject to a resource constraint on total consumption. In the case of a constant rate of return, and only capital income, how are the social planner's weights ω^i and ω^j for individuals i and j related to those individuals' initial wealth $k^i(0)$ and $k^j(0)$ in the decentralized markets version of the same equilibrium? Suppose instead the economy has no productive capital, just an endowment of non-accumulated income flows: individual i earns $W(s)l^i$ at time s, l^i is constant over time, and $W(s) = W(0)e^{\vartheta s}$. Discuss: the equilibrium interest rate in this economy; consumption distribution dynamics; and the relationship of the social planner's weights ω^i and ω^j for individuals i and j to l^i and l^j.

d. Negative consumption flows are rather unrealistic; however, for the utility function proposed nothing prevents the optimal consumption levels from being negative. Discuss how imposing the constraint $c \geq 0$ might change the answers above.

EXERCISE 10 **Nonconstant marginal propensity to consume (PTC)**
Assume that the marginal utility function of the individual i at date
t is $u'(c) = (c^\alpha - \bar{c})^{-\sigma}$, where α and σ are positive constants.

a. Does this function belong to the HARA class? (Hint: Check the form of
absolute risk aversion formula $-u''(c)/u'(c)$.)
Now consider a two-period model. Individual i receives an exogenous
endowment of k_i. The interest rate is exogenously set to R, and the rate
of time preference is given by ρ. The individual does not work.

b. Write down the utility maximization problem of i, define the relation
between individual consumption in t and $t + 1$ (Euler equation), and find
an implicit expression for initial consumption at t.

c. Now assume that: $\alpha > 1$. How does the marginal propensity to consume depend on capital k_i? (Hint: Reinsert c_{t+1} in the marginal PTC
expression.)

d. Draw the implicit income expansion path in a chart with c_t and c_{t+1} on
the axes. Is it linear? How does distribution affect accumulation?

CHAPTER FOUR

Factor Income Distribution

THE MODELS OUTLINED IN THE PREVIOUS CHAPTER studied the distribution of income, wealth, and consumption across individuals whose preferences were such as to avoid any direct relevance of distribution for the aggregate savings rate. In the "neoclassical" market economy we were considering, each individual is entitled to a portion of aggregate output on the basis of factor ownership, and each unit of every factor is compensated according to marginal productivity. In this chapter we relax the latter assumption, recognizing that imperfect market interactions, and taxes or subsidies, may well distort factor incomes away from the theoretical marginal productivity benchmark. We still let all individuals access an integrated financial market, but we focus on how macroeconomic growth and personal income distribution are shaped by the distribution of income across factors of production.

In fact, the distribution of income across factors of production was the central topic of classical writers in economics. The focus of Adam Smith's "Order according to which its Produce is naturally distributed among the different Ranks of the People" was primarily a question of the distribution of income across social classes: workers, capitalists, and landowners. For David Ricardo, the problem of how production is divided among the three classes of the community was the central question of economic analysis. In his words: "To determine the laws which regulate this distribution is the principal problem in Political Economy."

Against this background, the role of the factor distribution in the process of economic development is per se a question of interest. In this chapter we briefly review the role of factor shares in various theories of economic growth since the work of Harrod (1939) and Domar (1946), who provided the first systematic formal analysis of economic growth. The Harrod-Domar framework explicitly focused on factor shares, and the condition for steady growth that is central to their analysis turns out to be more generally useful as an organizing framework for growth theories. Post-Keynesian theories suggested that factor shares are endogenously given by the investment behavior of firms. In a full employment equilibrium, if investment demand increases then the resulting increase in total aggregate demand raises prices and profit margins. Hence the share of profits (that is, the income share of owners of accumulated factors of production) depends on the investment-output ratio. We will see that, in a steady growth equilibrium, where income and output capacity grow at the same rate, this investment output ratio is determined by the aggregate savings rate and the (technologically given) capital-output ratio.

Neoclassical growth theory took a route different from that of post-Keynesian theories. Central to neoclassical growth (Solow 1956a) is the possibility of technological substitution of factors of production. Hence the capital-output ratio is endogenously determined by the aggregate savings rate and by technological factors. The reward of factors reflects their contribution to aggregate output. Pasinetti (1962) and Samuelson and Modigliani (1966), however, study the interesting case in which savings occur only out of accumulated factor income, whereas all income from non-accumulated factors is consumed. There is a simple rationale that makes such an assumption meaningful in the context of an analysis of the role of factor shares. Families that own accumulated factors must have saved in the past, whereas families that do not own such factors did not save. Hence assuming that only owners of accumulated factors have a positive savings propensity is consistent with a strong relation between wealth levels and further accumulation. When there is such a relationship between income sources and factor shares, this heterogeneity persists over time.

More recent theories of economic growth turned the question of factor shares and economic growth upside down. Rather than asking how the distribution of incomes across factors of production may adjust so as to support technologically determined growth, they ask the opposite question: how does the distribution of income across factors (whatever its determinants) affect the rate of accumulation and growth?

In a complete-market setting, factor-income distribution and aggregate dynamics are jointly rather than causally determined by the underlying allocation problem. In reality, however, the distribution of income across factors of production does not always reflect efficiency considerations. On the one hand, real-life market interactions are not necessarily based on the price-taking behavior assumed in chapters 1 to 3 (a behavior which, as noted there, relies on constant returns to scale in order to yield an efficient aggregate equilibrium). On the other hand, the distribution of resources and welfare across individuals need not be implemented by lump-sum instruments, i.e., by the attribution of property rights on factors followed by efficient market allocation. Rather, politico-economic interactions often use distortionary instruments, which alter the distribution of income across individuals by changing the rewards rather than the ownership of factors of production. When rewards change, individual incentives are affected, opening interesting channels of interaction between income distribution and macroeconomic phenomena.

In the main text of this chapter, we focus on one-sector models where a single produced good may be either consumed or invested. The production of different goods by different sectors, however, was central to many classical models of long-run growth and value determination. In fact, in multi-sector models with many output goods relative prices, income distribution, and aggregate dynamics may be jointly determined. The appendix to this chapter outlines how such insights may be gained from a model with consumption and capital goods.

4.1 FACTOR SHARES AND SAVINGS IN EARLY GROWTH MODELS

This chapter studies how macroeconomic dynamics depend on income distribution (however determined) across accumulated and non-accumulated factors of production. To focus such issues in the simple two-factor setting of the derivations above, it will be convenient to let γ denote the fraction of consumable income Y that is paid to owners of L, the non-accumulated factor of production. The remaining $(1 - \gamma)$ fraction of aggregate resources is paid to owners of accumulated factors of production. The two factors are remunerated according to

$$W = \gamma \frac{Y}{L}, \qquad R = (1 - \gamma)\frac{Y}{K}, \tag{4.1}$$

where all quantities and the factor shares themselves may in general be variable over time.

"Neoclassical" models of personal savings pay little attention to issues of factor-income distribution not only because factor incomes do not have an obvious distributional role when they are viewed as a by-product of efficient market allocation of available resources, but also because shifting income across accumulated and non-accumulated factors of production has complex and ambiguous effects on optimal savings. A higher rate of return R on savings makes it optimal to plan faster consumption growth, but also lets it be financed by a smaller volume of savings: the net effect on savings depends on the balance of these substitution and income effects. The factor composition of income flows, and the rate at which accumulated and non-accumulated factors are rewarded, also influence consumption and savings through a wealth effect: a higher rate of discount decreases the present value, the term h_t^i in (3.8), of the future stream of non-accumulated income.

4.1.1 The Harrod-Domar Growth Model

To understand the role of factor shares in various growth models, one has to go back to the starting point of growth theory. The first formal treatment of ongoing growth was that of Harrod (1939) and Domar (1946): earlier studies of savings and accumulation, dating back to David Ricardo, focused on mechanisms tending to choke growth, but the Harrod-Domar models identified a knife-edge condition for steady growth that will be useful in the following discussion of relationships between factor shares, saving propensities, and steady growth rates.

Central to the growth analyses of Harrod (1939) and Domar (1946) was the proposition that a steady-state growth rate was feasible only under very special circumstances. These papers were written under the impression of the highly unstable economic development, deriving by the contrast between the fin de siècle economic prosperity and the Great Depression of the 1930s. Hence an important concern of these authors was to explain why the capitalist system was inherently unstable. After the Second World War, a long period of full employment and high growth rates in most modern industrial countries shifted attention away from the knife-edge growth condition, and led growth economists to formulate different conceptual frameworks suitable for analysis of steady growth paths.

The instability result of Harrod and Domar was based on three main assumptions. First, the technology was assumed to be one with fixed coefficients: to produce one unit of output a fixed amount of labor and a fixed amount of capital are necessary. This implies that the capital output ratio K/Y is a technologically given constant. Second, Harrod and Domar assumed that a fixed proportion of income is saved, so that the aggregate savings rate s is also a constant. Third, technological improvements lead to growth in output per worker. Hence the growth factor $\theta = \frac{Y_{t+1}}{Y_t}$ is also exogenously given.

In this setting, it is straightforward to describe the equilibrium growth path of the economy along which savings have to equal investment. By assumption, a constant fraction of income is saved, so savings are sY. With a technologically fixed capital output ratio K/Y and a change in output ΔY, an aggregate investment of $K/Y \cdot \Delta Y$ is necessary to generate that output. Equating savings and investment and solving for the growth rate of output $\Delta Y/Y$ yields the "warranted rate of growth" $s\frac{Y}{K}$. At the same time we have growth in effective labor units as a result of technical change (and possibly population growth) given by the "natural rate of growth" $\theta - 1$. Obviously, only when effective labor units grow at the same rate as output and capital is full employment of both factors of production possible. Hence the steady growth path is given by the condition

$$\theta - 1 = s\frac{Y}{K}. \tag{4.2}$$

In the Harrod-Domar framework θ, s, and Y/K are exogenously given constants, so equation (4.2) is satisfied only by chance. If $\theta - 1 < sY/K$, then capital grows faster than labor. The result is that there will be more and more idle capacity, whereas labor is fully employed. If instead $\theta - 1 > sY/K$, effective labor units expand more quickly than capacity. The result is ever-increasing unemployment of labor, while the capital stock is fully utilized.

Harrod and Domar's knife-edge condition does not yet say anything about the relationship between the growth rate and distribution of income among factors of production. But what if we suppose that owners of the non-accumulated factors consume all of their income, while the propensity to save is positive for owners of accumulated factors of production? This assumption, taken literally, is of course far from realistic. In particular, it would prevent the economy from lifting itself out of an initial zero-capital situation. But it can be potentially appropriate when studying situations of ongoing growth, and it is internally consistent: if some individual owns more accumulated wealth than others, it may well be the case that this was due to relatively high saving propensity in the past, and whatever determines such heterogeneity may well persist over time. And, like any assumption, it can be judged in the light of its implications. If savings occur only from accumulated factors, whereas all income from the non-accumulated factors is consumed, the aggregate savings rate s can be written as $s = s^p(1 - \gamma)$ where s^p is the savings rate out of accumulated factor income and γ is the share of income that goes to non-accumulated factors. Harrod and Domar's knife-edge condition (4.2) can then be rewritten as

$$\theta = 1 + s^p(1 - \gamma)\frac{Y}{K}. \tag{4.3}$$

Ceteris paribus, a larger accumulated factor share $(1 - \gamma)$ tends to raise the aggregate savings rate and raises the growth rate of capacity.

Equation (4.3) is useful because it highlights the approaches of various growth theories to modeling equilibrium steady growth paths. Since that equation *has* to be satisfied, any theory of balanced growth must view some of its variables as endogenously determined. Growth theorists of the 1950s and 1960s took essentially two different approaches to address the instability problem. First, post-Keynesian theory (Kaldor

1955; Pasinetti 1962) assumed that the factor share $(1 - \gamma)$ was endogenously determined: appropriate variations in this share guaranteed an aggregate savings rate that was consistent with equilibrium. The second approach was the development of the neoclassical growth model (Solow 1956) in which Harrod and Domar's assumption of fixed factor inputs was replaced by the possibility of technological substitution between production factors, that is, Y/K became endogenous. Cass (1965) and Koopmans (1965) further endogenized the savings rate s^p by assuming that the individuals were optimizing over an intertemporal utility function (the Ramsey model). A third approach was taken in the 1980s when, starting with Romer (1986), new theories of growth began to focus on the "natural" rate of growth as the important endogenous variable.

4.1.2 Growth and Distribution in Post-Keynesian Models

In post-Keynesian models of growth and distribution, aggregate savings are endogenous and determined by the rate of investment. Kaldor (1955) assumed that savings propensities are different between workers and capitalists. For simplicity we assume here that workers earn only wage income and capitalists earn only capital income.[1] The aggregate savings rate is

$$s = s^w \frac{WL}{Y} + s^p \frac{RK}{Y}$$
$$= s^w \gamma + s^p (1 - \gamma).$$

By definition of equilibrium we must have equality of savings and investment. In short-run post-Keynesian models, with idle capacities and given prices and wages, real wage and labor productivity are constant, hence the functional distribution of income is given. Note, however, that in a standard short-run Keynesian model with fixed prices and idle capacities, the I/Y ratio is *endogenously* determined because Y is endogenous: $Y = (1/s)I$.[2] However, in the state of full employment (or a long-run state with a constant utilization rate of labor resources), prices and wages are flexible, whereas full employment output is exogenous. Hence not only I but also the investment-output ratio I/Y is exogenously given and determines the capitalists' income share. To see this

---

[1]See Pasinetti (1962) for analysis of the case where workers also earn capital income and capitalists also earn wage income, and saving propensities differ across the two groups. Kaldor thought, instead, that savings propensities are different by income source rather than class affiliation: "Savings propensities are attached to profits as such not to capitalists as such."

[2]In a standard short-run Keynesian model with fixed prices and idle capacities the I/Y ratio is *endogenously* determined because Y is endogenous: $Y = \frac{1}{s}I$. In a state of full employment, however, both I and Y are given. To ensure equality of savings and investment s has to adjust.

formally, note that the equality of savings and investment can be written as $I = \left[s^w \gamma + s^p (1 - \gamma) \right] Y$. Solving for the income share of capitalists yields

$$1 - \gamma = \frac{1}{s^p - s^w} \frac{I}{Y} - \frac{s^w}{s^p - s^w}.$$

An increase in the investment-output ratio, and thus in total demand, will raise prices more than wage. Hence profit margins increase and the real wage falls, causing a redistribution of income from wages to profits, i.e., a decrease in γ. In other words, equilibrium is a decrease restored by an adjustment in the aggregate savings rate s. Because the (exogenously given) propensity to consume from wages $1 - s^w$ is higher than the (exogenously given) propensity to consume from profits $1 - s^p$, the shift in the functional distribution of income in favor of profits reduces aggregate consumption. With full employment, this implies higher aggregate savings, and in the new equilibrium, the equality between savings and investment is restored.

In the long-run steady-state equilibrium, in which the Harrod and Domar knife-edge condition is satisfied (capacity and effective labor force grow at the same rate), we have $\Delta K / K = \Delta Y / Y = \theta - 1$. Hence, in the long-run full employment equilibrium we must have

$$\frac{I}{Y} = \frac{\Delta K}{K} \frac{K}{Y} = (\theta - 1) \frac{K}{Y},$$

and the share of capital income is given by

$$1 - \gamma = \frac{1}{s^p - s^w} (\theta - 1) \frac{K}{Y} - \frac{s^w}{s^p - s^w}.$$

In the Kaldorian golden age, income distribution is thus determined not only by the savings behavior of workers and capitalists, but also by the natural rate of growth rate θ (which itself is determined by technical progress and population growth) and the technologically (i.e., exogenously) given capital-output ratio K/Y.

4.2 Factor Shares in the Neoclassical Growth Model

In this section we study neoclassical models where factor ownership is a determinant of individual savings behavior. As above, we let individuals be entitled to portions of the economy's aggregate income flow on the basis of factor ownership and, for simplicity, we continue to view consumption and income in terms of a single, homogeneous good. The owner of each unit of capital receives a return R and, as in (4.1), each unit of the non-reproducible factor L entitles its owner to W units of income. The factor(s) denoted by L may include land and other natural resources as well as labor. It is unnecessary to disaggregate L along such lines, however, if none of the income flows accruing to non-reproducible factors are saved.

If, as assumed here, savings behavior depends on income sources, then aggregate accumulation is straightforwardly related to income distribution. If $(1 - s^p)$ denotes the portion of capitalists' income that is consumed *and* all depreciation is reinvested, the aggregate capital stock evolves according to

$$\Delta K = s^p R K = s^p (1 - \gamma) Y, \tag{4.4}$$

where (4.1) is used to express R in terms of the accumulated factor share $(1 - \gamma)$. Recall that, according to our accounting convention, R is the return on the accumulated factor net of depreciation. Equation (4.4) then states that aggregate accumulation is the product of the (exogenously given) savings propensity s^p, the income share of accumulated factors $1 - \gamma$, and aggregate output Y.

Factor shares, however, depend in turn on the economy's aggregate dynamic equilibrium behavior, as they did in chapter 1. In what follows we normalize to unity the economy-wide supply of non-accumulated factors $(L = 1)$ and omit L as an argument of the production function $F(\cdot)$. The economy's net income per worker is thus given by $Y_t = F(K_t) = G(K_t) - \delta K_t$, where $G(K_t)$ denotes the *gross* output per worker and $\delta > 0$ is the rate of depreciation. We assume that the gross production function $G(K_t)$ satisfies the Inada condition $\lim_{K \to \infty} G(K) = 0$, so the net marginal product of the accumulated factor tends to $-\delta$ as more capital is accumulated:

$$\lim_{K \to \infty} \frac{\partial G(K)}{\partial K} = 0, \quad \text{hence} \quad \lim_{K \to \infty} \frac{\partial F(K)}{\partial K} = -\delta < 0. \tag{4.5}$$

We continue to assume that factors are rewarded their marginal productivities, like in the neoclassical model of chapter 1. Maintaining these assumptions will be useful for the purpose of highlighting the implications of factor ownership–based saving behavior. Under these conditions the factor rewards are given by

$$R_t = G'(K_t) - \delta, \quad \text{and} \quad W_t = G(K_t) - G'(K_t) \cdot K_t$$

and the shares of the accumulated and the non-accumulated factors in aggregate income at time t equal

$$\gamma_t = \frac{G(K_t) - G'(K_t) \cdot K_t}{G(K_t) - \delta K_t} \quad \text{and} \quad 1 - \gamma_t = \frac{(G'(K_t) - \delta) K_t}{G(K_t) - \delta K_t}.$$

Since the owners of such factors are assumed to save nothing, the economy tends to settle in a stationary state where gross savings just suffice to reproduce the existing stock of accumulated factors. The steady-state capital stock K^* has the following properties:

$$\Delta K^* = 0 \;\Rightarrow\; s^p (1 - \gamma) (G(K^*) - \delta K^*) = s^p \left(G'(K^*) - \delta\right) K^* = 0.$$

The steady-state level of the accumulated factor K^* satisfies $G'(K^*) = \delta$.[3] Because the savings propensity $s^p > 0$ is a strictly positive number and also net income is positive $G(K) - \delta K > 0$, a situation where the capital stock remains unchanged $\Delta K^* = 0$ is only possible if the share of the accumulated factor in (net) income $1 - \gamma$ becomes zero. The reason is that there are diminishing returns to the accumulated factor: increasing capital intensity is associated with ever smaller increases in output and also with larger scarcity rents for the non-accumulated factor.

The savings propensity s^p, while determining the speed at which the steady state is approached, is irrelevant in such a steady state. Again, the reason is that diminishing returns drive the marginal productivity of the accumulated factor and hence accumulated factor income to zero.

4.2.1 Exogenous Productivity Growth

The above reasoning has two unsatisfactory features: the irrelevance of the savings propensity for the steady-state level of output and the absence of output growth in the long run. Both may be amended by allowing for exogenous growth in the economy's effective supply of the non-accumulated factor. We now assume that the contribution of the non-accumulated factor L to aggregate production varies over time according to the constant returns-to-scale gross production function $F(K_t, A_t L) + \delta K_t$ where A_t measures the level of technological knowledge in the economy that augments non-accumulated factors. We continue to set $L = 1$,

---

[3] Hence our assumption on savings behavior is equivalent to assuming that the steady-state stock of the accumulated factor reaches its golden rule level. To see this, recall that the golden stock of the accumulated factor is realized if the gross savings rate equals the accumulated (gross) factor share. Gross savings equal depreciation plus a fraction s^p of accumulated factor income (net of depreciation). In the steady state, all gross accumulated factor income is used to replace the depreciated capital stock, hence the gross savings rate equals the gross accumulated factor share.

so that Y_t is also net output per worker and Y_t/A_t is net output per effective unit of labor. In what follows, we denote the *gross* output per effective unit of labor, $Y_t/A_t + \delta K_t/A_t$, by

$$G(K_t/A_t) \equiv F(K_t, A_t)/A_t + \delta K_t/A_t. \tag{4.6}$$

The function $G(\cdot)$ satisfies analogous Inada conditions as before, and production factors are rewarded their respective marginal products, which are now given by $R_t = G'(K_t/A_t) - \delta$, and

$$W_t = A_t \left(G(K_t/A_t) - G'(K_t/A_t) \cdot (K_t/A_t) \right).$$

Hence, the income shares are

$$\gamma_t = \frac{W_t L}{Y_t} = \frac{G(K_t/A_t) - G'(K_t/A_t) \cdot (K_t/A_t)}{G(K_t/A_t) - \delta(K_t/A_t)}$$

for non-accumulated factors, and

$$1 - \gamma_t = \frac{R_t K_t}{Y_t} = \frac{(G'(K_t/A_t) - \delta)(K_t/A_t)}{G(K_t/A_t) - \delta(K_t/A_t)}$$

for the accumulated factors.

If there is continuous exogenous technical progress, we have $A_{t+1}/A_t \equiv \theta > 1$ at all times. The economy converges to a path of "balanced" growth where the aggregate stock of the accumulated factor measured in efficiency units of the non-accumulated factor remains constant $K_t/A_t = (K/A)^*$ and the aggregate variables K and Y grow at the same rate $\theta - 1 = (K_{t+1} - K_t)/K_t = (Y_{t+1} - Y_t)/Y_t$.

If capitalists save a given portion s^p of their net income (and reinvest all depreciated inputs out of gross income) and other agents' savings are negligible, then along a balanced growth path, equation (4.4) implies $R = (\theta - 1)/s^p$ and the direct, linear relationship (4.4) between the economy's growth rate and capital's factor share.

The important message of the above analysis is that the relationship (4.4) between the propensity to save from accumulated factor income, the economy's rate of balanced growth, and aggregate share of accumulated factors of production is consistent with "neoclassical" distribution. From that perspective, the inverse of the capital-output ratio Y/K and the factor share $(1 - \gamma)$ are endogenously determined by technology and competitive market forces. We find that the balanced-growth condition determines the economy's steady-state capital intensity as functions of s^p

and θ,

$$\frac{\theta - 1}{s^p} = G'((K/A)^*) - \delta,$$

from which it follows that the steady-state capital stock $(K/A)^*$ is determined by the savings rate and the growth rate

$$(K/A)^* = \kappa(s^p, \theta; \ldots)$$

with $\partial \kappa / \partial s^p > 0$ and $\partial \kappa / \partial \theta < 0$. Consequently, the long-run output level $(Y/A)^* = G((K/A)^*) - \delta(K/A)^*$ is also a function of s^p and θ. Hence, if there is productivity growth in the economy, the savings rate no longer plays the passive role that it had above. Productivity growth implies that the workforce has to be equipped with machines, maintaining a high marginal product of capital. These investments are, by assumption, financed out of the net returns from capital. Hence the accumulated income share has to be positive along a balanced growth path with $\theta > 1$.

Using the above equation we immediately see that technical progress prevents the capital share from reaching zero in the long run. The net return to capital is $(\theta - 1)/s^p > 0$, and is increasing in the rate of technical progress, decreasing in the savings rate. Fast technical change and a low savings rate both imply a low capital intensity along the balanced growth path. This is associated with a high marginal product of capital and a correspondingly high net return for the accumulated factor. The steady-state factor share $1 - \gamma^*$ also depends on the savings rate and the rate of technical change in the following way:

$$1 - \gamma^* = \frac{\theta - 1}{s^p} \cdot \frac{\kappa(s^p, \theta)}{G(\kappa(s^p, \theta)) - \delta\kappa(s^p, \theta)}.$$

EXERCISE 11 Suppose that $c = \bar{c} + \hat{c}y + \check{c}k$, as in (2.1). Show that if $\check{c} = (1 - \hat{c} - s^p)R$ and $\bar{c} = 0$, then the aggregate saving function is similar to that studied above, but features a possibly non-zero saving propensity $s^w = 1 - \hat{c}$ for non-capital income. Characterize the balanced-growth relationship between factor shares, growth rates, and capital intensity!

EXERCISE 12 Let the economy's production function have Leontief form,

$$Y_t = \min\{K_t\alpha, A_t L\beta\},$$

and let $A_{t+1} = \theta A_t$ for all t. If aggregate savings are a portion s^p of capital income $(1 - \gamma)Y_t$, what must be the value of the capital's share

γ to sustain a full employment balanced-growth equilibrium? Is it in any way related to capital's marginal productivity?

4.2.2 Bounded Marginal Product of the Accumulated Factor

Even under constant returns, however, we need not have a situation where the long-run state of the macroeconomy features a situation where diminishing marginal products are necessarily associated with increasing income shares of non-accumulated factors. Consider a situation where the supply of the effective labor force is normalized to unity $A_t L = 1$ at all times, denote with $G(K_t) = F(K_t, 1) + \delta K_t$ the gross production function, and suppose

$$\lim_{K \to \infty} G'(K) = B > \delta > 0, \quad \text{hence} \quad \lim_{K \to \infty} G'(K) - \delta K = B - \delta > 0. \quad (4.7)$$

This means that the gross marginal product of the accumulated factor is bounded from below by $B > 0$. The implications of $B > \delta$ are similar to those of a negative depreciation rate: the passage of time leads capital to more than reproduce itself, no matter how large the capital stock, if the marginal productivity of K is larger than the depreciation rate.

In that case it is straightforward to show that the accumulated factor share attracts all income in the limit, despite the fact that as a result of growth the accumulated factor incomes also increase in absolute value. To see this, note that we can write

$$1 - \gamma_\infty = \lim_{K \to \infty} \frac{(G'(K) - \delta) K}{G(K) - \delta K} = \lim_{K \to \infty} (G'(K) - \delta) \cdot \lim_{K \to \infty} \frac{K}{G(K) - \delta K}$$

$$= (B - \delta) \cdot \frac{1}{B - \delta} = 1.$$

While $B < \delta$ would imply that the income share of accumulated factors would tend to zero if accumulation continued forever (and also prevent that from occurring), in the case $B > \delta > 0$ where accumulation can continue forever the income share of the accumulated factor tends to unity and γ_∞ must be zero.

Note also that, under such circumstances, the savings rate plays an important role, not only for the level of accumulation but also for the long-run growth rate of the economy. To see this, write

$$\Delta Y / Y_t = R_{t+1} \Delta K / Y_t + \Delta R K_t / Y_t + \Delta W L / Y_t$$

$$\approx \partial F(K_{t+1}, L) / \partial K_{t+1} \cdot \Delta K / Y_t$$

(the approximation, due to neglecting changes in factor returns, would vanish in continuous time). The net marginal product of the accumulated factor is $\partial F(K_{t+1}, L)/\partial K_{t+1} = G'(K_{t+1}) - \delta$ and, under our assumptions, the net savings ratio is $s^p \cdot (1 - \gamma_t)$. Thus, the growth rate approaches

$$\lim_{K \to \infty} \frac{\Delta Y}{Y_t} = \lim_{K \to \infty} \left(G'(K_t) - \delta \right) \cdot s^p \cdot (1 - \gamma_t) = (B - \delta) \cdot s^p.$$

Hence we reach the result that, in a single-sector model where returns to scale are constant in the aggregate and returns to accumulation are bounded away from zero, non-accumulated factors of production earn a vanishing share of aggregate production if they are rewarded at marginal productivity rates.

EXERCISE 13 The aggregate gross production function is $K^\alpha L^{1-\alpha} + BK$. Show that the net income share of the accumulated factor increases in the capital intensity K/L if the capital productivity parameter B is larger than the depreciation rate δ and decreases otherwise.

4.3 OPTIMAL SAVINGS AND SUSTAINED GROWTH

So far in this chapter we have considered economies where savings occur out of capital income (or savings propensities from capital income are higher than those from labor income) by assumption. Of course, this is unsatisfactory from a theoretical point of view. It is therefore interesting to take a closer look at the savings behavior that arises when it is endogenously determined by individuals seeking to maximize their lifetime utility. An important maintained assumption in what follows is that capital accumulation does not drive investment returns to zero, and sustained endogenous growth is therefore possible.

The focus of the first subsection below will be on optimal savings choices along the balanced growth path. Balanced growth may arise either because technology grows exogenously letting investment returns not be depleted, or because technology is such that investment returns cannot fall below a certain limit. In either case, the economy tends toward a state where the economy grows at a constant rate. Without further specifying how steady growth is sustained (and how factor shares are determined), we ask what determines the savings behavior of individuals out of incomes earned from accumulated and non-accumulated factors. Our result will be an interesting one: provided there is sustained growth, it is optimal to consume all non-accumulated income inasmuch as that income flow grows at the same rate as desired consumption. All savings occur from incomes accruing to the accumulated factor. This result is interesting because it provides a theoretical rationale for the ad hoc assumption on savings behavior studied in the previous sections of this chapter.

In the second subsection below, we explore the role of factor shares and savings behavior as determinants of endogenous long-run growth. The relationship is symmetric to that of post-Keynesian and neoclassical models, studied above, that treat the rate of growth as an exogenous determinant of endogenous functional income distribution. An important strand of the recent growth literature, starting with Romer (1986) and Lucas (1988), has instead focused endogenous determination of the growth rate. We study the simplest case that generates endogenous growth, the "*AK* model," and taking the functional distribution of income as exogenously given we study how changes in factor shares affect the economy's long-run growth rate.

4.3.1 Optimal Savings Along the Balanced Growth Path

In chapter 3 we have studied the optimal savings behavior that arises from utility functions that belong to the HARA class. In particular, we have studied the evolution of inequality both in lifetime resources and consumption when individuals have positive required consumption levels $\bar{c} > 0$. This assumption had a crucial role in determining the dynamics of distribution. Minimum required consumption levels lead to high propensities for poor individuals, and higher average savings propensities of richer individuals reinforce initial inequality.

In that model, the economy finally reached a steady state with persistent inequality, in which nothing was saved out of net income. In many interesting models, however, the economy is capable of sustaining endless growth—because of exogenous technological progress, as in (4.6), or because capital accumulation does not endogenously deplete returns to investment, as in (4.7). If aggregate consumption does tend to grow at a proportional rate in the long run, relative-consumption dynamics must eventually become irrelevant, as a finite "required" consumption level constitutes an ever lower proportion of each individual's total consumption. Asymptotically, a growing economy behaves as if there was no required consumption, hence

$$U'(c) = c^{-\sigma}. \tag{4.8}$$

When preferences are of the form (4.8), the growth factor of consumption

$$\frac{c_{t+1}}{c_t} = \left(\frac{1+R}{1+\rho}\right)^{\frac{1}{\sigma}}, \tag{4.9}$$

is constant not only over time but also across individuals faced by the same R. Equalization of marginal utilities implies equalization of consumption levels for the functional form in (3.17). Hence, savings behavior in perfect capital markets perpetuates whatever heterogeneity may exist across consumption and income levels.[4]

Along a balanced growth path, output and capital grow at the same rate as consumption,

$$\frac{K_{t+1}}{K_t} = \frac{Y_{t+1}}{Y_t} = \frac{C_{t+1}}{C_t} = \left(\frac{1+R}{1+\rho}\right)^{\frac{1}{\sigma}} \equiv \theta.$$

Optimal savings choices associate a larger rate of return R with faster consumption and output growth. The growth rate can be written as the product of the savings rate and the inverse of the capital-output ratio (which is constant in balanced growth),

$$\theta - 1 \equiv \frac{\Delta Y}{Y} = \frac{\Delta K}{Y} \frac{Y}{K}.$$

By (4.1), the rate of return R is higher if Y/K is larger and/or if capital receives a larger share of aggregate output. Hence faster output growth is either associated with a larger savings propensity or with a larger impact of accumulation on output. When larger returns to investment result from a larger income share for accumulated capital, rather than from a lower capital-output ratio, a larger R and smaller W both make the human wealth expression smaller in (3.7), and are associated with a lower consumption level and hence higher savings. In addition to such wealth effects, a larger R also has income and substitution effects: as we have seen in the discussion of (3.8) above, the balance of these depends on the substitution parameter σ, and investment returns stimulate or lessen individuals' propensity to consume out of total lifetime resources depending on whether that parameter falls short of or exceeds unity.

When preferences are in the form (4.8) and all savings yield the same rate of return R, the growth rate of consumption is constant across individuals. Constant marginal utility ratios, as in (3.18), imply that the ratio of consumption levels between a rich and a poor individual remains forever constant. Along the path of balanced long-run growth, savings behavior perpetuates whatever heterogeneity may exist across consumption and income levels.

---

[4]If labor supply were not constant over time, and consumption choice were not separable from leisure choices, then marginal welfare equalization need not imply proportional consumption levels, unless the utility function is appropriately separable. Space prevents us from exploring this issue in detail.

Optimal savings choices imply that a larger rate of return R goes hand in hand with faster consumption growth. Even when income effects dominate so that a higher R leads to lower savings, a higher rate of return allows higher future consumption. In light of (4.1), balanced growth at a constant rate is associated with a constant income share $(1 - \gamma)$ for accumulated factors, and a larger factor share for capital is associated with faster growth. This is qualitatively similar to the relationship between the two in (4.4), and reflects a similar relationship between income sources and savings propensities.

Consider, in fact, the budget constraint

$$\sum_{j=0}^{\infty} c_{t+j} \left(\frac{1}{1+R} \right)^j = k_t(1+R) + \sum_{j=0}^{\infty} W_{t+j} l \left(\frac{1}{1+R} \right)^j \qquad (4.10)$$

of an individual who owns k_t units of wealth and l units of the non-accumulated factor of production at time t. The latter is compensated by a wage rate W_t, and the former by a constant rate R. The fact that R is constant over time implies a constant growth rate for both wages and individual consumption; hence we may insert $c_{t+j} = c_t \theta^j$ and $W_{t+j} = W_t \theta^j$, and we may write

$$c_t \sum_{j=0}^{\infty} \left(\frac{\theta}{1+R} \right)^j = k_t(1+R) + W_t l \sum_{j=0}^{\infty} \left(\frac{\theta}{1+R} \right)^j. \qquad (4.11)$$

The infinite series in (4.11) converges to $(1 - \theta/(1 + R))^{-1}$ as long as $\theta < 1 + R$. Solving for the consumption level yields

$$c_t = W_t l + (1+R) \left(1 - \frac{\theta}{1+R} \right) k_t = W_t l + (1 + R - \theta) k_t. \qquad (4.12)$$

Equation (4.12) reveals an important result. Across individuals, any difference in the amount of non-accumulated income $W_t l$ is reflected one-for-one in different consumption levels. *The propensity to consume non-accumulated-factor (or "labor") income is unitary and all savings occurs out of accumulated factor income.* This is just as in the simple models outlined above, which imposed by assumption that aggregate savings all accrue from accumulated factors only. In the simple optimal savings model we are considering, however, it arises endogenously from the households' optimal savings choices. In fact, it is unnecessary (and would be suboptimal) to save any portion of the income flows accruing to non-accumulated factors of production when their wages grow at the same rate as each individual's optimal consumption, as is the case along a path of balanced growth. Any individual who happens to own only the non-accumulated factor l and nothing from the accumulated factor k enjoys a stream of income that grows at the same rate as desired consumption. To maximize lifetime utility, all current income has to be spent for consumption, as deviating from that rule would violate (4.9).

By contrast, and again consistently with the ad hoc behavioral assumptions made in the previous sections, a positive share of capital income must be saved. Individuals who own only accumulated factors earn current income Rk_t. By constancy of R, income can only grow when k_t gets larger. In other words, absent any further accumulation, it would not be possible for owners of the accumulated factors to keep up with the individually optimal consumption paths implied by (4.9). Savings by an individual who owns factor of production in amounts k_t and l are given by

$$Rk_t + W_t l - c_t = (R - (1 + R - \theta)) k_t = (\theta - 1)k_t, \qquad (4.13)$$

hence directly proportional to wealth and to accumulated factor income. An individual who is a pure "capitalist," i.e., happens to own only an amount k_t of the accumulated factor of production, needs to save the amount $(\theta - 1)k_t$ so as to let his or her wealth and income increase at the same rate θ as optimal consumption.

There is a further interesting analogy between the optimal savings model discussed above and the simple models with exogenous factor ownership–based saving rates discussed in the previous sections. This analogy concerns the implied relationship income share γ of non-accumulated factors and the economy's growth rate along the balanced growth path. Under a logarithmic specification of the utility function, the model based on optimal savings choices implies the relationship between growth and capital-output ratios given by

$$\theta = \frac{1 + (1 - \gamma)\frac{Y}{K}}{1 + \rho}.$$

This relationship is linear, just like the one that is implied by models with exogenous (factor ownership–based) savings propensities: normalizing (4.4) by the capital stock, in fact,

$$\theta = 1 + s^p(1 - \gamma)\frac{Y}{K}. \qquad (4.14)$$

Individual savings indeed depend on factor ownership in both models. Owners of the accumulated factor have to save a portion $s^p = (\theta - 1)/R$ of the income flow accruing to them to ensure desired consumption growth θ. The whole economy's savings rate is a weighted (by factor-income shares) average of the two groups' savings propensities:

$$\frac{\Delta K}{Y} = \gamma \cdot 0 + (1 - \gamma)\frac{\theta - 1}{R} = (1 - \gamma)\frac{\theta - 1}{(1 - \gamma)Y/K} = \frac{K}{Y}(\theta - 1).$$

Since savings behavior perpetuates any initial heterogeneity in the factor composition of income, the economy can feature a stable class structure, and the functional and personal distribution of income are strictly related to each other and to the economy's growth rate. We note further that savings propensities are attached to factor-income flows rather than to class affiliation, and the rate at which "profits" are saved is endogenous to preferences and distributional parameters.

EXERCISE 14 Discuss the relationship between factor-income distribution, savings propensities, and growth when the elasticity of marginal utility is not unitary ($\sigma \neq 1$). Is that relationship linear in the discrete-time specification studied in the text? And in its continuous-time counterpart? How does the propensity to save capital income depend on ρ and σ?

Any balanced-growth path under optimal savings features relationships similar to (4.14) among factor-income distribution, aggregate growth, and the capital-output ratio. Both the cross-sectional distribution of relative income levels and the pattern of factor ownership remain constant if total labor income grows at the same rate as aggregate income. Since the aggregate savings which are necessarily associated with positive (endogenous or exogenous) aggregate growth rates are all performed by owners of capital, any "class" structure tends to persist over time in such an economy. Hence the endogenous outcome under optimal savings is identical to the one that was *assumed* in the ad hoc models where saving rates from capital income were exogenously determined.

This optimization-based relationship between factor-income sources and savings behavior throws some new light on the distributional dynamics analyzed above. As mentioned when discussing equation (2.4), linear saving functions fail to yield convergence to a stable egalitarian steady state if $\bar{c} = 0$ and $\hat{c} = 1$ (the savings propensity out of non-wealth income is zero). As it turns out, this is the case if savings are modeled as the result of individually optimal decisions in an economy that does feature sustained steady growth. Furthermore, it is irrelevant whether the growth rate is exogenously or endogenously determined. Any inequality of consumption and income levels will persist indefinitely, and so will any heterogeneity in the factor composition of individual income flows. In this situation, optimal savings behavior establishes a direct link between the *factor* distribution of income, the aggregate rate of growth, and the capital-output ratio.

4.3.2 Factor Shares and Long-Run Growth

In optimization-based models discussed above, various causal relationships among factor shares, savings propensities, and growth are possible. In equation (4.14) the growth rate θ, the capital-output ratio K/Y, and the capital-income saving propensity s^p may all be endogenously determined by the economy's technology, preferences, and market structure. For instance, if factor markets are cleared by price-taking behavior of economic agents, and if returns to accumulation are decreasing, exogenous growth of the economy's effective labor endowment AL is the only source of long-run growth. In that case, equations like (4.14) simply determine the endogenous steady-state capital-output ratio.

Interactions between factor-income distribution and macroeconomic phenomena are more complex and interesting in models when returns to accumulation do not go to zero but have a positive upper bound. Such models typically specify the economy's technology and its market structure in such a way that returns to aggregate accumulation are constant in the steady state. In the simplest case, the AK model, the aggregate production function, in its reduced form, can be written as $F(K, L) = A(L)K$. The returns to accumulation, in a reduced form, are then given by

$$\partial F(K, L)/\partial K = A(L). \tag{4.15}$$

The marginal product of capital A depends on L if non-accumulated factors have a productive role. However, it is constant with respect to K. If aggregate output is $F(K_t, L) = A(L)K_t$, the capital-output ratio, for given L, is also independent of K. The proportional growth rate of output is constant if the aggregate savings rate and $A(L)$ are constant:

$$\frac{\Delta Y}{Y} = \frac{\Delta K}{K} = \frac{Y - C}{K} = A(L)\frac{Y - C}{Y} = s^p (1 - \gamma) A(L) = \left(\frac{1 + (1 - \gamma)A(L)}{1 + \rho}\right)^{\frac{1}{\sigma}}. \tag{4.16}$$

If non-accumulated factors have a nonnegligible role in production, and accumulation does not encounter decreasing returns, aggregate returns to scale are not constant but increasing, and markets cannot be perfect and complete. If the income share going to the non-accumulated factor is constant and given by γ, the individual factor rewards are given by

$$W_t = \gamma A \frac{K_t}{L}, \text{ and } R = (1 - \gamma)A. \tag{4.17}$$

Note that the private return to capital $R = (1 - \gamma)A$ must be *lower* than its social return $\partial Y / \partial K = A$ whenever the share of the non-accumulated factor is different from zero.

For the present purpose of analyzing interactions between distribution and aggregate growth, the most relevant and general feature of this class of endogenous growth models is the simple fact that, if the economy's production possibilities feature increasing returns, then intertemporally efficient allocations cannot be decentralized in complete, competitive markets. Since the sum total of marginal productivities exceeds aggregate production, the private remuneration of one or more factors of production must differ from its "social" counterpart. When the microeconomic structure of markets and production cannot be such as to guarantee that market equilibria are efficient, then, as in class-based models of savings, the distribution of income flows across factors is obviously relevant to aggregate dynamics and, if factor ownership is heterogeneous, to resource distribution across individuals. Hence, in a developed economy capable of steady endogenous growth, it is natural to let the growth rate and distribution depend on policies, institutions, and politics as well as on the technological features emphasized by the neoclassical approach.

EXERCISE 15 (Golden Rule) Show that if the capital stock is such as to maximize per capita consumption in a constant-returns competitive economy with exogenous balanced growth, then aggregate consumption coincides with wages, and aggregate investment coincides with capital income. Show that this result follows (for a zero discount rate) from that, discussed in the text, pertaining to the savings propensity of workers and capitalists when aggregate savings can be interpreted in terms of individual maximization of discounted logarithmic utility in balanced growth. What does the result imply when the exogenous growth rate is zero, and the steady state is only identified because capital depreciates?

4.4 POLICY AND POLITICAL ECONOMY

In a neoclassical economy with complete competitive markets, one-time redistributions could and should resolve any distributional issues without compromising the efficiency of macroeconomic outcomes. Appropriate lump-sum redistribution instruments, however, are not available in reality: taxes, subsidies, and market imperfections alter the way economic welfare is shared among individuals. At the same time they decrease the size of the economic "pie" available to a hypothetical representative individual (or to a social planner with access to lump-sum redistribution).

Hence, distribution and macroeconomics interact not only through the channels surveyed in the previous sections, but also by influencing the extent to which distortionary policies are implemented in politico-economic equilibria.[5]

The point is relevant to any model where policy is allowed to play a role, but perhaps most relevant when taxes and other relative price distortions can affect an economy's endogenous rate of growth. In that case they alter private incentives to allocate resources to the sector or sectors where a "core" of accumulated factors can reproduce itself without encountering decreasing returns (Rebelo 1991). Since many such models feature increasing returns, missing markets, or imperfectly competitive market interactions, policy interventions meant to offset laissez-faire inefficiencies and distortions play a prominent role in this context. Accordingly, widely recognized work (also surveyed by Bénabou 1996c; and Persson and Tabellini 1998) has focused on the growth implications of distributional tensions.

4.4.1 Political Sources of Distortionary Taxation

It is of course far from surprising to find that taxing the income of an endogenously supplied factor, like k_{t+1} in this simple model, decreases private supply incentives and has negative effects on macroeconomic efficiency. Such effects would be present even in a representative individual macroeconomy when all agents are equally endowed with accumulated and non-accumulated factors, or $k = K$ and $l = L$ for all individuals. We now discuss how such outcomes may come about, despite being clearly undesirable from a representative individual's point of view. This requires explicit consideration of the redistributive motives of heterogeneous individuals. Such heterogeneity is potentially very important in understanding the politico-economic process that presumably underlies policy choices in reality. Bertola (1993) and Alesina and Rodrik (1994) study policy determination in models of endogenous growth. Distortionary redistribution can be a political equilibrium outcome only if individual agents' endowments are cross-sectionally heterogeneous. In fact, identical individuals— like a hypothetical social planner—would never want to decrease

---

[5]Related incentive mechanisms may also be relevant in other contexts. Even selfish individuals may be concerned with inequality when it is so wide as to make predatory activities preferable to market participation for poor individuals, and costly defensive activities necessary for richer individuals; Grossman and Kim (1996) and their references analyze in detail the microeconomic determinants and macroeconomic implications of predatory activity. Distributional issues are also directly relevant when individuals' relative standing bears on their economic welfare and their savings decisions, as in the model of Cole, Mailath, and Postlewaite (1992).

economic efficiency. These models, like the one outlined in the previous section, feature balanced paths of endogenous growth with no transitional dynamics.

Assume the same setup as in the previous section. Growth is directly related to the private rate of return on savings and investment decisions, hence to the portion of aggregate production accruing to accumulated factors of production. The reduced-form parameters γ and A in this simple model reflect the institutional and technological structure of property rights and production in the economy. The underlying structure is left implicit but may be determined by market imperfections and/or by an explicit role of government expenditures allowing for constant returns to accumulation and, if labor plays a productive role, for increasing returns to scale at the aggregate level.

In such a framework, policy intervention would generally be desirable even from a representative individual's point of view. If ownership of accumulated and/or non-accumulated factors of production is not evenly spread across all individuals, the factor-income distribution affects not only the aggregate growth rate but also the distribution of income and welfare across individuals. This opens up a new channel of interaction between distribution and macroeconomics: heterogeneity matters because political interactions between agents introduce policies that distort individual behavior. Hence heterogeneity affects macroeconomic outcomes even when the functional form of individual objective functions would, in principle, allow interpretation of macroeconomic phenomena in terms of a representative agent's choices and behavior. In other words, within such a framework, a hypothetical agent still represents the economy's reaction to policy and to exogenous factors. But that agent's welfare need not be what is maximized when policies are formulated and implemented through political interactions among agents that are different from each other as well as from the representative agent.

We proceed to illustrate these insights in the context of the previous section's AK endogenous growth model. Assume that capital income is taxed at rate τ so the after-tax rate of return equals $R(1 - \tau)$. If there is a subsidy on capital income τ will be negative. The resulting tax revenues are redistributed through a subsidy S (or financed through a lump-sum tax if $\tau < 0$), the same for all individuals. When individuals aim at maximizing logarithmic utility flows discounted at rate ρ over an infinite horizon, savings implies that all consumption flows grow according to

$$\frac{c_{t+1}}{c_t} = \frac{1 + R(1 - \tau)}{1 + \rho} \equiv \theta \tag{4.18}$$

and the level of individual welfare can be written as

$$\sum_{j=0}^{\infty} \left(\frac{1}{1+\rho}\right)^j \ln(\theta^j c_t) = \frac{1+\rho}{\rho^2} \ln\theta + \frac{1+\rho}{\rho} \ln c_t \qquad (4.19)$$

as of time t. At date t, the optimal level of an individual's consumption is given by

$$c_t = W_t l + (1 + R(1 - \tau) - \theta)k_t + S_t \qquad (4.20)$$

for an individual who owns a constant number l of units of the non-accumulated factor (each earning W_t at time t) and k_t units of the accumulated factor at time t (earning a constant gross rate of return $1 + R(1 - \tau)$). As technology and the factor rewards are the same as in the last section, we have $W = \gamma A K_t / L$ and $R = (1 - \gamma)A$, and, by the government's budget constraint, $S_t = \tau(1 - \gamma)AK_t$. Substituting this into (4.20) yields

$$c_t = \left(\gamma A \frac{1}{L} + \frac{\rho}{1+\rho}(1 + (1 - \gamma)(1 - \tau)A)\frac{k_t}{K_t} + \tau(1 - \gamma)A\right) K_t. \qquad (4.21)$$

Consequently, it possible to write individual welfare as a function of the capital income tax rate τ. Replacing θ and c_t in equation (4.19) by the expressions (4.18) and (4.21), respectively, allows us to write individual welfare as a function of the capital tax rate τ. Disregarding irrelevant constants, and the level of the aggregate capital stock K_t (which affects all welfare levels equally), we can express individual welfare as

$$V(\tau) = \frac{1}{\rho} \ln(1 + (1 - \gamma)(1 - \tau)A) \qquad (4.22)$$
$$+ \ln\left(\gamma A \frac{l}{L} + \frac{\rho}{1+\rho}(1 + (1 - \gamma)(1 - \tau)A)\frac{k_t}{K_t} + \tau(1 - \gamma)A\right).$$

Welfare levels are affected by the capital income tax through two different channels. On the one hand, a higher capital income tax affects the growth rate. This is shown by the first term of equation (4.22). The growth effect of a smaller τ is unambiguously positive. Above we have seen that all savings come from capital income. Lowering the capital income tax τ implies that a larger share of aggregate output is paid to accumulated factors of production, which increases savings and investment. This, in turn, increases the growth rate of output and consumption. Hence, the growth effect of a lower capital income tax τ benefits all individuals.[6]

Faster investment-driven growth must be financed by lower consumption levels, however, and the impact of a smaller τ on initial consumption depends on the factor composition of individual income sources. This is shown by the second term of equation (4.22). Let us consider the extreme cases. The "representative consumer" owns factors in proportions that equal the aggregate economy's relative factor endowments. When $l/L = k/K \equiv 1$, maximizing equation (4.22) with respect to τ yields a preferred tax rate $\tau^{RA} = -\gamma/(1-\gamma)$. Note that this implies a negative income tax on capital income so that the representative individual's after-tax capital income is equal to

$$R(1 - \tau^{RA})K = \frac{RK}{1-\gamma} = AK = Y.$$

In other words, the representative individual prefers a (after-tax) factor-income distribution such that all income is earned by accumulated and none by the non-accumulated factor. As long as after-tax income that accrues to non-accumulated factors cannot become negative, all individuals with relative factor endowments such that $k/l > K/L$ will also prefer a tax that equals the representative individual's preferred rate. Individuals with relative endowments $k/l < K/L$, however, will be in favor of higher after-tax income for non-accumulated factors. The following exercise asks you to calculate the preferred tax rates conditional on a household's characteristics.

EXERCISE 16 Suppose the median voter owns the average amount of non-accumulated factors, so that $l = L$. For which level of k does that voter prefer a tax rate of $\tau^{RA} = -\gamma/(1-\gamma)$?

The above model provides an explanation of why owners of non-accumulated factors may wish to depress the returns to investment and the economy's growth rate. If a household's k/l ratio is lower than the aggregate ratio K/L, it will gain more than the average individual from a larger non-accumulated income share. And a household that happens to own only non-accumulated factors would clearly not be pleased if the growth rate were the one that maximizes welfare of the average individual, but is supported by zero income for the non-accumulated factor. More

---

[6] If the individuals live only for two periods and work only in the first period of life, savings accrue from labor income only. In such an OLG model, higher capital taxation (rebated to the workers) tends to *increase* growth. We will discuss this issue in section 6.1.1.

generally, households whose income accrues from non-accumulated factors prefer functional distributions that give them a larger income level, even though reducing returns to accumulation depresses their own (and the whole economy's) growth rate.

At this point, it is again worth mentioning that the factor "raw labor" is not the only factor one should identify as a "non-accumulated" factor. The income share that goes to natural resource owners (and noncontestable monopolists) should be viewed as being part of the share that goes to non-accumulated factors. At the same time, part of the income share that goes to "labor" results from investments in workers' education and training, which should be viewed as part of accumulated factor income.

The above setup also provides a simple politico-economic mechanism through which the *personal* income distribution affects growth. In a democratic one-person, one-vote system, the median voter's preferred tax rate is decisive. When the median voter is scarcely endowed with accumulated factors, he or she will tend to vote for a tax system that favors non-accumulated factor income. As noted by Persson and Tabellini (1994), realistic skewness of income distribution associates higher inequality with a higher percentage of relatively poor individuals. Hence, a democratic one-person, one-vote political process will generally result in redistribution-motivated distortions, because the median voter is capital poorer than the average (representative) individual. Applied to our example above, high inequality in the personal distribution implies that the tax rate in the political outcome will be far above $-\gamma/(1-\gamma)$.

Empirical evidence, however, does not support the notion that redistribution is the reason why unequal economies grow slowly. The empirical observation that less unequal countries grow faster over the long run may well reflect joint causation by underlying country characteristics. Perotti (1996a, 1996b) finds that there is no statistically significant impact of (ex ante) inequality on taxes and transfers, and there is very little evidence that redistribution lowers growth.[7]

A reason why this mechanism could fail might be that especially in unequal societies the median voter is not decisive. There is evidence that political power is positively correlated with income (see Bénabou 1996d; and Mueller and Stratmann 2003). If the capital owners exert higher political power, the relationship between inequality and tax rate does not

---

[7]Perotti (1996b) argues that the redistribution-growth mechanism is difficult to test. If redistribution occurs through investment subsidies, for example, there will be a positive relationship between transfers and growth.

have to be monotonic anymore.[8] If the distribution of political influence is correlated with accumulated and non-accumulated factor endowments, uneven political power will affect the growth rate of the economy. This may have been important in many historical instances. For instance, in feudal times political power was strongly concentrated among landowners. The diverging growth performances of Europe and the United States in the nineteenth century (Gordon 2004) could be attributed to more evenly spread political power in the United States. This may have favored policies conducive to capital accumulation, whereas the political culture in many European countries was still more strongly influenced by a landowning aristocracy with less interest in policies favoring capital owners.[9]

4.4.2 The Menu of Policies

The general insight from the above discussion is that distributional tensions can have macroeconomic effects when they result in distortionary policies. The results, of course, hinge on the details of politico-economic interactions on the one hand, and on the specific distortionary instrument used for redistributive purposes on the other. In models where distribution-motivated policy interventions unavoidably distort incentives, individuals trade their preference for a large share of the social pie against the size of the latter. Of course, to obtain interior politico-economic equilibria, it is generally necessary to limit the extent and character of heterogeneity across agents in such a way as to ensure that preferences over packages of different policy instruments are well behaved (single-peaked).

In practice, more than one instrument is generally available to pursue distributional objectives and, like imperfect and incomplete financial markets, political interactions can be specified in many different ways. While the simple illustrative models above can characterize sharply the

---

[8] Glaeser, Scheinkman, and Shleifer (2002) describe this as "King John redistribution." The rich may redistribute from the poor by designing the legal or regulatory institutions in their favor. The redistribution from the rich to the poor described in our previous model is labeled "Robin Hood redistribution."

[9] The median voter may favor low taxes because he takes into account that he could become richer in the future because of social mobility. In the model of Bénabou and Tirole (2004), the latter depends endogenously on tax policy. When individuals can manipulate their beliefs and they are myopic due to hyperbolic discounting, Bénabou and Tirole (2004) show that there is a complementarity between individuals' beliefs about mobility and desired tax levels. This gives rise to multiple political equilibria. One is characterized by a "belief in a just world" and laissez-faire policy, and the other by a pessimistic view about social mobility and a generous welfare state.

distortionary effects of political interactions by focusing on simple policy instruments, more complex models recognize that many different policies may be (separately or simultaneously) implemented in reality.

While in the simple model outlined above distributional tensions clearly reduce aggregate efficiency, redistribution can have beneficial effects on representative agent welfare when it substitutes missing markets—for example, when time horizons are finite (see section 6.1.1). The formation of human capital is another example which is perhaps more obvious. Human capital accumulation is most likely to be distorted by self-financing constraints and uninsurability, and is often targeted by policy interventions (see Glomm and Ravikumar [1992] for a simple model of the implications of private or public education schemes for growth and distribution). We will discuss in chapter 7 models where self-financing constraints prevent relatively poor agents (and the aggregate economy) from taking advantage of high returns from investment in their own education. In that setting, since inefficient investment patterns are unanimously disliked, politico-economic interactions will display more of a tendency toward efficiency. Similarly, Bertola (1993) finds that capital-poor individuals would obviously vote against policies that increase the growth rate of the economy by reducing their share of aggregate income, but would favor policy packages that restore growth rate efficiency by subsidizing investment. In general, existing distortions and a wider menu of potentially distortionary policy instruments make it easier for redistribution-motivated policy interventions to preserve efficiency, and bring macroeconomic outcomes closer to those that would be realized if distributional issues could be resolved by lump-sum instruments.

4.5 References and Further Issues

The first part of this chapter offers a simple formal treatment of a vast literature spanning Physiocratic tableaus, Ricardian theory, and post-Keynesian growth models. Asimakopoulos (1988) offers a more extensive review of this material. Levine (1988) discusses Marxian theories of the distribution of surplus (the portion of net income in excess of what is necessary to reproduce the economy's capital and labor force).

The models implicit in the work of Ricardo did feature multiple goods, and in particular a distinction between luxuries and basic consumption goods. The relationship of simpler post-Keynesian single-good macro models to Ricardian theory is discussed in, e.g., Kaldor (1956, sec. 1) and Pasinetti (1960, fn. 24). In part 3 we will discuss the important new issues that arise in the interaction of distribution and macroeconomic phenomena when we consider heterogeneous consumption goods.

At the theoretical level, the assumption that workers never save any portion of their resources may be rationalized by the classical notion of a "natural" wage rate which barely suffices to let the labor force subsist and reproduce but leaves no room for savings. A subsistence approach to wage determination makes it natural for classical theories to suppose that wage payments precede production flows. Thus, wages are a portion of the economy's working capital, and the notion of "organic" composition of capital plays an important role in Marxian studies of factor-income distribution (see Roemer [1981] for a critical review and formal results in this field). For simplicity—and consistently with Marglin (1984), Kaldor (1956), and Sraffa (1960)—the timing of wage outlays is the same as that of accumulated-factor income flows in the simple formal models of this chapter. A wage level higher than the "subsistence" one that would let the labor force reproduce itself may lead to faster population growth, implying that no rents accrue to labor in the long run (Pasinetti 1960; Casarosa 1982). Through Malthusian population dynamics, labor is an accumulated factor of sorts in a classical economy: while no part of workers' income is saved in the form of capital, faster population growth when wages exceed subsistence levels does contribute to extend the economy's production possibilities. The role of endogenous population dynamics in modern growth models is surveyed by Nerlove and Raut (1997). No such mechanism restrains the inframarginal rents paid to factors in fixed supply ("land").

The idea that decreasing returns and increasing rents would prevent capitalists' savings from endlessly fueling accumulation could be acceptable to nineteenth-century economists who had not experienced prolonged periods of economic development. The model of exogenous technological progress outlined in the text entered the mainstream literature when long-run growth at approximately constant rates achieved "stylized fact" status (Kaldor 1961). Our treatment outlines the post-Keynesian, income distribution–based solution to the (Harrod-Domar) knife-edge property of balanced-growth accumulation.

A preference-based class structure can also feature a non-zero propensity to save out of labor income. Pasinetti (1962) lets a relatively low (but strictly positive) savings propensity apply to both the accumulated and non-accumulated income flows accruing to individuals belonging to the working class, and shows that the exact value of their propensity to save is irrelevant in the long run as long as it is lower than the aggregate one. Samuelson and Modigliani (1966) argue that it is more realistic and insightful to attach different savings propensities to income sources rather than recipients. In his comments, Kaldor (1966) acknowledges that high savings propensity "attaches to profits as such, not to capitalists as such" (310). See also Bertola (1994a, 1994b) for a review of this literature.

The possibility of unceasing accumulation-driven growth under constant returns was already recognized by Solow (1956a), and recently modeled by Jones and Manuelli (1990). Models of endogenous growth based on increasing returns were studied by Arrow (1962) and others, and more recently by Romer (1986). Grossman and Helpman (1991) and Aghion and Howitt (1998) offer extensive reviews of these and other microeconomic foundations of endogenous growth. Since it is always conceptually possible to increase production by proportionately increasing all inputs or "replicating" identical microeconomic production units, decreasing returns to aggregate inputs can be ruled out on a priori grounds (Solow 1956a). Replication arguments do not rule out increasing returns, however: as in Romer (1986, 1989, 1990), such *non-rival* factors as know-how, software, and other determinants of an economy's technological progress can be simultaneously used in an arbitrary number of production units or processes, and need not increase in proportion to rival inputs to yield proportionately larger output at the aggregate or at the firm level. This makes it possible to rationalize increasing returns from first principles in many qualitatively realistic ways, and to model growth as endogenous to the economy's preferences, technology, and market structure. Intratemporal markets prices and factor payments for given K may be determined by competitive interactions if increasing returns are external to firms, as in Arrow's (1962) learning-by-doing model and Romer (1986). Inputs that are non-rival but excludable, such as patent-protected knowledge, imply increasing returns within each firm, and are naturally associated with market power in the models of Romer (1987), Grossman and Helpman (1991), and others. Externalities and other market imperfections play an essential role in other multi-sector growth models, such as those of product and quality innovation proposed by Grossman and Helpman (1991) where growth is driven by production of K (which represents "knowledge" in these models) in a research and development sector which employs and compensates only labor, a non-accumulated private factor of production. As we will see in part 3, isoelastic functional forms for technology and demand lead to AK reduced form functions, which satisfy (4.15) when aggregate flows are measured as a price-weighted index of heterogeneous goods.

Our analysis was confined to single-sector models. Multi-sector models in which relative prices, income distribution, and aggregate dynamics may be jointly determined were not considered. The appendix to this chapter outlines how similar insights may be gained from such models. Production of different goods by different sectors was central to many classical models of long-run growth and value determination, and the relevant issues may to some extent be analyzed abstracting from capital accumulation (as in Pasinetti 1993). As pointed out by Rebelo (1991), efficient market interactions between accumulated and non-accumulated factors of production can support endogenous balanced growth in multi-sector growth models, as long as a "core" of accumulated factors reproduces itself without encountering decreasing returns. Like in single-sector models of growth, savings propensities of individuals who happen to own accumulated and non-accumulated factors in different proportions depend on income sources along such economies' balanced-growth paths because, again, an individual who owns no capital never needs or wants to accumulate any wealth. While aggregation of heterogeneous goods into homogeneous "capital" and "output" measures may be difficult from an accounting point of view (unless production functions satisfy separability conditions, as in Solow 1956b), relative prices are unambiguously defined and easily interpreted as long as perfect, competitive markets support an efficient allocation (Dixit 1977). Along the balanced-growth equilibrium paths of multi-sector economies, taxes or other distortions which introduce wedges between factor incomes and marginal productivities affect the economy's growth rate, factor shares, and the relationship between the former and the latter in much the same way as in the simpler single-good models outlined above. Recent work on models of suboptimal endogenous growth under a variety of market imperfections has rekindled interest in distributional issues. If the distribution of income across factors owned by different individuals is allowed to play a substantive economic role, it unavoidably affects relative prices. It may be interesting to note that factor-income distribution also affects the relative prices of capital and consumption in ways that are somewhat reminiscent of the Sraffa (1960) problem of how savings, investment, and "capital" might be measured in models where multiple capital goods are used in production and reproduction, and relative prices and the value of the aggregate stock of capital in terms of consumption generally depend on factor-income distribution. Marglin (1984) and especially Kurz and Salvadori (1995) offer recent extensive treatments of these matters.

We already made in the main text many references to the literature on inequality and political economy, so we are keeping the review short here. The recent empirical work on inequality and growth working via politico-economical channels starts with Persson and Tabellini (1994), Perotti (1996a, 1996b), and Alesina and Rodrik (1994). Good summaries of the empirical studies can be found in Bénabou (1996c), Persson and Tabellini (1998), and Drazen (2000, chap. 11). Early studies of politico-economic issues in an endogenous growth context include Bertola (1993), Persson and Tabellini (1994), Alesina and Rodrik (1994), and Bénabou (1996c). A complementary politico-economical channel is presented by Alesina and Perotti (1996), who argue that inequality is bad for growth because it may lead to sociopolitical unrest or revolutions.

4.6 APPENDIX: FACTOR SHARES IN A TWO-SECTOR GROWTH MODEL

Factor-income distribution and aggregate accumulation are closely related in the models of balanced growth discussed in this chapter. This appendix briefly reviews that same relationship in an economy where different sectors produce investment and consumption goods. As pointed out by Rebelo (1991), multi-sector growth models where a "core" of accumulated factors reproduces itself without encountering decreasing returns can simultaneously feature endogenous balanced growth, constant returns to scale, and efficient market interactions between accumulated and non-accumulated factors of production.

The total capital stock available by K can be employed either in the consumption or in the investment sector. We denote by K_k the stock of accumulated factors used in the investment sector, and by K_c the corresponding stock used in the consumption sector. The output flow of the investment sector is equal to the change in the aggregate capital stock (there is no depreciation) and produced with only capital as an input factor

$$\dot{K} = AK_k. \tag{4.23}$$

Assume that non-accumulated factors have no productive role in producing investment goods and that markets are competitive. As the production function of investment goods has constant returns to scale, this implies that the factor reward to capital has to be equal to the marginal product of capital which, when measured in units of the investment good, is equal to A; and that total output is exhausted by this reward to capital.

The remaining $K_c \equiv K - K_k$ units of capital are employed, along with non-accumulated factors ($=$ "labor") L, to produce consumption goods. The consumption goods sector's technology has constant elasticity to the two factors (to ensure that growth is balanced),

$$C = L^\alpha (K_c)^{1-\alpha}. \tag{4.24}$$

As the consumption sector technology also has constant returns, perfect markets imply that factor rewards equal the marginal products and the income paid to both factors exhausts total output. Measured in units of the consumption good, the marginal product of labor in the consumption sector is $\alpha(K_c/L)^{1-\alpha}$ and that of capital is $(1-\alpha)(L/K_c)^\alpha$. The relative price of capital and consumption is neither constant nor unitary, as in chapter 1.1, but must be such as to make owners of the accumulated factor K indifferent to allocating it to K_k or K_c. Additional capital in the investment sector yields A units of capital, while a marginal increment of

K_c yields $(1-\alpha)(L/K_c)^\alpha = (1-\alpha)(L)^\alpha((1-\kappa)K)^{-\alpha}$ units of consumption. In the absence of taxes and distortions on this margin, the two income flows must be equal. Hence the price of consumption in terms of capital is given by

$$p_k = \frac{1-\alpha}{A}(L/K_c)^\alpha = \frac{1-\alpha}{A}\left(\frac{L}{(1-\kappa)K}\right)^\alpha. \tag{4.25}$$

Clearly, when L is constant, and the aggregate capital stock increases over time, the relative price of capital in terms of consumption goods decreases over time. This is not surprising as (labor-intensive) consumption firms have to reward the relatively scarce factor labor at an increasing wage rate. From equation (4.25) we immediately see that p_k decreases at a rate α times the growth rate of the aggregate capital stock.

Taking consumption goods as the numéraire, aggregate output can be measured by summing up over output in the consumption sector and output in the investment sector, weighted with the relative price of investment goods in terms of consumption output $Y = C + p_k \Delta K$. Now consider a balanced growth path, where both the value of output in the consumption sector C and the value of output in the investment sector $p_k \Delta K$ grow at the same rate. Along such a balanced growth path the allocation of total capital across sectors $K_k/K \equiv \kappa$ is constant and capital grows at a proportional rate

$$\frac{\dot{K}}{K} = A\kappa \equiv \theta_K, \tag{4.26}$$

and aggregate income measured in terms of consumption can be expressed as a Cobb-Douglas function of aggregate capital and can be written as

$$Y = C + p_k\dot{K} = L^\alpha K^{1-\alpha}(1-\kappa)^{-\alpha}[1-\alpha\kappa]. \tag{4.27}$$

Like the growth rate of capital, the level of output in consumption terms depends on the proportion κ of capital employed in the investment sector. Suppose we are on a balanced growth path and the capital stock grows at rate θ_K. Since L and κ are constant, it is immediately clear from equations (4.24) and (4.27) that the growth rate of consumption and total output (when measured in terms of the consumption good) are given by

$$\theta_C = (1-\alpha)\theta_K = (1-\alpha)\dot{K}/K = (1-\alpha)\kappa A.$$

Nothing prevents us from measuring aggregate output in terms of investment (rather than consumption) goods. We get aggregate output in terms of the investment good Y_K by dividing equation (4.27) by expression (4.25); output in terms of capital (or of investment) is given by

$$Y_K = C/p_K + \dot{K} = L^\alpha K^{1-\alpha}(1-\kappa)^{-\alpha}[1-\alpha\kappa]\left(\frac{1-\alpha}{A}\left(\frac{L}{(1-\kappa)K}\right)^\alpha\right)^{-1}$$

$$= \frac{1-\alpha\kappa}{1-\alpha}AK.$$

(4.28)

Along a balanced-growth path κ is constant, so output (when measured in terms of investment) also grows at the rate θ_K and at the slower rate $(1-\alpha)\theta_K$ if measured in terms of consumption. Aggregate consumption (measured in terms of the investment good C/p_K) also grows at rate θ_K if κ is constant. The rate of increase of the consumption price of capital is

$$-\alpha\dot{K}/K = -\alpha\kappa A.$$

Since returns are constant within each sector, factors can be compensated according to their marginal productivity. The competitive shares of the two factors are constant if κ is constant. In terms of consumption, the aggregate stock of capital earns

$$A\kappa Kp_k + (1-\alpha)L^\alpha(1-\kappa)^{1-\alpha}K^{1-\alpha} = p_kAK = (1-\alpha)K^{1-\alpha}L^\alpha(1-\kappa)^{-\alpha}, \quad (4.29)$$

hence its share of total output in consumption terms is

$$1-\gamma = \frac{(1-\alpha)(1-\kappa)^{-\alpha}}{(1-\kappa)^{-\alpha}[1-\alpha\kappa]} = \frac{1-\alpha\kappa}{1-\alpha};$$

the non-accumulated factor L gets the complementary share.

Factor shares are independent of the units in which production is measured at each time: capital's $1-\alpha$ share of the consumption sector's output amounts to

$$\frac{\partial(C/p_K)}{\partial K} = \left((1-\alpha)L^\alpha((1-\kappa)K)^{1-\alpha)}\left[\frac{1-\alpha}{A}\left(\frac{L}{(1-\kappa)K}\right)^\alpha\right]^{-1}\right) = (1-\kappa)KA$$

in terms of capital or investment. Adding the output of the investment sector (all of which accrues to capital) and dividing by (4.28), capital's share in aggregate output is again

$$\frac{A\kappa K + (1-\kappa)KA}{\frac{1-\alpha\kappa}{1-\alpha}AK} = \frac{1-\alpha}{1-\alpha\kappa}.$$

(4.30)

As in single-sector models, faster growth (a large κ) is associated with a larger factor share of capital. To close the model, κ is determined by optimal consumption and savings decisions. Given the stock of L, the growth rate of consumption must satisfy an optimality condition in the form

$$\frac{\dot{C}}{C} = (R - \rho)\left[-\frac{Cu''(C)}{u'(C)}\right]^{-1}, \qquad (4.31)$$

where R is the consumption-terms rate of return on savings and differs from $(1 - \gamma)Y/K$ because p_K is not unitary and decreases over time.

The proportional rate of decline of capital's consumption price is $\alpha A\kappa$ if, as is the case in balanced growth, the fraction κ of capital employed in reproduction is constant. Hence, the rate of return on consumption-term loans is $A - \alpha A\kappa$, i.e., the rate of interest in capital terms (which equals A in both sectors in the absence of arbitrage opportunities) adjusted for capital loss.

If the rate of utility discount is ρ and the elasticity of marginal utility is a constant σ, the optimal rate of consumption growth is

$$\frac{\dot{C}}{C} = \frac{A - \alpha A\kappa - \rho}{\sigma}.$$

The optimal aggregate consumption growth must equal the realized rate of consumption growth, $\theta_C = 1 - \alpha)A\kappa$. Setting $\frac{\dot{C}}{C} = \theta_C$ we can solve for the equilibrium allocation of capital across consumption and investment sector

$$\kappa = \frac{A - \rho}{A\left[(1 - \sigma)\alpha + \sigma\right]}.$$

Inserting the equilibrium value of κ in expression (4.30), we obtain the factor share of capital as a function of the model's preference and technology parameters

$$1 - \gamma = \frac{1 - \alpha}{1 - \alpha A \frac{A - \rho}{(1 - \sigma)\alpha + \sigma}}.$$

The derivatives of this expression with respect to ρ and σ are both negative (and that with respect to A is positive) as long as $\alpha < 1$ and $A - \rho > 0$. Hence we see that the *features of preferences (and of technology) that are associated with slower growth are also associated with a smaller share of capital in aggregate output.*

Along this economy's balanced-growth path, the income flow paid to each unit of the non-accumulated factor L grows at the same rate as output (since both L and its factor share are constant) in terms of consumption; and both aggregate and all individuals' consumption grow at that same rate. Hence, the savings propensities of individuals who happen to own accumulated and non-accumulated factors in different proportions depend on their income sources: like in single-sector models of growth, an individual who owns no capital never needs or wants to accumulate any wealth.

Since the model's technology has constant returns to scale, factor incomes may be determined by complete competitive markets. It is interesting, however, to let taxes or other distortions introduce wedges between factor incomes and marginal productivities, as in Rebelo (1991), and examine their effects on the economy's growth rate, on factor shares, and on the relationship between the former and the latter. Suppose all capital income (in both sectors) is taxed at rate τ_k and the revenue is used to subsidize labor income. The rate of return on investment is then $(1 - \tau_k)A < A$ in terms of capital. Since capital income is taxed uniformly in both sectors, the relative price implied by the absence of arbitrage opportunities is still given by (4.25), and still declines as the capital stock increases in the consumption sector. If $\tilde{\kappa}$ is the constant proportion of aggregate capital allocated to the investment sector, capital's consumption-terms price grows at rate $-\alpha\tilde{\kappa}A$.

To determine $\tilde{\kappa}$, we equate the actual growth rate of aggregate consumption,

$$(1 - \alpha)A\tilde{\kappa},$$

to the growth rate of consumption,

$$\frac{(1 - \tau_k)A - \alpha\tilde{\kappa}A - \rho}{\sigma},$$

that is optimally chosen by individuals whose preferences feature a rate of discount equal to ρ and an elasticity of marginal utility equal to σ, and who are faced by a consumption-terms rate of return $(1 - \tau_k)A - \alpha\tilde{\kappa}A$ on their savings. Solving for $\tilde{\kappa}$ yields

$$\tilde{\kappa} = \frac{(1 - \tau)A - \rho}{(1 - \sigma)\alpha + \sigma}.$$

Taxation of capital income slows down growth. Retracing the steps that led to (4.29) or to (4.30), we find that, for given $\tilde{\kappa}$, the share of capital is reduced proportionately by capital taxation and labor-income subsidization. Hence, net capital income amounts to a fraction $1 - \tau_k$ of the share found above,

$$\tilde{\gamma} = (1 - \tau_k) \frac{1 - \alpha}{1 - \alpha \tilde{\kappa}} \tag{4.32}$$

of aggregate output. Since a higher value of $\tilde{\kappa}$ is associated with a smaller value of $\tilde{k}$, redistributing aggregate income away from capital unambiguously reduces both its factor share and the economy's growth rate.

Taxes and other distributional distortions, however, leave the growth rate unchanged if they leave the private return to investment unchanged. Suppose that (as a result of redistribution or of distorted market interactions) the shares of L and K_c in the consumption sector are γ and $1 - \gamma$ rather than α and $1 - \alpha$. This is equivalent to a tax on consumption (Stokey and Rebelo 1995). The dividend earned by each of the K_c units of capital employed in the consumption-goods sector amounts to

$$\frac{(1 - \gamma)C}{K_c} = (1 - \gamma)L^\alpha (K_c)^{-\alpha}$$

units of consumption. If all of the investment sector's output is still paid to capital, then, to prevent arbitrage, this consumption-terms income must be equal to A units in terms of capital. Thus, the relative price of capital is given by

$$p_k = \frac{1 - \gamma}{A}(L/K_c)^\alpha = \frac{1 - \gamma}{A}\left(\frac{L}{(1 - \kappa)K}\right)^\alpha \tag{4.33}$$

rather than by (4.25): for any given κ, a smaller share of capital in the consumption-goods sector quite intuitively reduces the price of capital in terms of consumption.

Since the rate of change of this relative price still equals $-\alpha\theta_K$, and the growth factor of aggregate capital is again $\theta_K = \kappa A$, the rate of return on savings is again approximately $A - \alpha\kappa A$, and the equilibrium value of κ is determined as above by equating aggregate consumption growth and the optimal growth rate of the typical individual's consumption flow. The factor share γ in the consumption-goods sector plays no role in this derivation. Hence, κ and the economy's growth rates are not affected by redistribution within the consumption-goods sector, which, however, does change both the net income share of capital—computed as in (4.32) at the laissez-faire value of κ—and the level of aggregate output in consumption terms,

$$L^\alpha K^{1-\alpha}(1 - \kappa)^{-\alpha}[1 - \gamma\kappa].$$

Since non-accumulated factors earn a constant share of aggregate income in the resulting equilibrium, W grows at the same rate as desired consumption and, as before, no part of the economy's non-accumulated income flow is saved.

In the balanced growth equilibrium of a multi-sector economy, any deviation of factor-income shares from the perfect-competition baseline affects not only the share κ of resources allocated to reproduction rather than consumption and the economy's rate of endogenous growth, but also the relative price of capital and consumption-terms output, and the aggregate capital-output ratio. Such phenomena are reminiscent of the Sraffa (1960) problem of how savings, investment, and "capital" might be measured in models where multiple capital goods are used in production and reproduction, and relative prices and the value of the aggregate stock of capital in terms of consumption generally depend on factor-income distribution. Solow (1956b) and Dixit (1977) extend the national-income accounting concepts of "savings" and "investment" to many-capital-goods settings. Relative prices are always unambiguously defined and easily interpreted from an efficiency standpoint, and aggregation of heterogeneous goods into homogeneous "capital" and "output" measures on an accounting basis yields economically meaningful measures if production functions satisfy regularity conditions. If distributional issues could be resolved by lump-sum instruments, there would be no reason to contemplate deviations from the static and intertemporal allocations characterized by neoclassical models, or indeed to allow for any distortionary taxation at all. But recent work on models of suboptimal endogenous growth has rekindled interest in politico-economic distributional issues. If the distribution of income across factors owned by different individuals is allowed to play a substantive economic role, it unavoidably affects prices and "values" even when preferences are homogeneous across individuals.

CHAPTER FIVE

Savings and Distribution with Finite Horizons

IN THE PREVIOUS CHAPTER we have discussed the relationship between factor shares and long-run growth. In this chapter we focus more closely on the determinants of personal income and wealth distribution across individuals, beginning with a summary of previous chapters' perspectives and of relevant empirical evidence.

In chapter 3 we studied optimal savings choices when the economy's households have an infinitely long time horizon and no additional households enter the economy. In that perfect world markets are complete, as all currently alive households can participate in perfect and integrated financial markets. Such a setup, together with the assumption of HARA preferences and the associated linear consumption functions, led to strong results concerning the evolution of inequality in the distribution across households of both current consumption levels and lifetime resources. First, whether there is convergence or divergence in the distribution of available resources depended only on preference parameters and was unrelated to technological conditions in the economy. Second, inequality changes monotonically and increases during the process of capital accumulation when savings choices are subject to minimum required consumption levels.

Clearly, the empirical evidence briefly does not provide much support for uniform divergence. Dollar and Kraay (2002) find that, in a panel of countries, per capita income growth is tightly associated with the growth rate of the incomes of the poor. In other words, poor and rich individuals benefit equally (in relative terms) from faster growth. Ravallion (2001) points to the importance of looking at differences in country experiences. Drawing on a data set—compiled by Chen and Ravallion (2001)—consisting of 297 national sample surveys spanning eighty-eight developing countries, he finds that growth episodes were associated with increases in inequality in about 50 percent of the cases and decreases in inequality in the other 50 percent of the cases. Similarly, episodes of contractions were associated with increases in inequality in 30 percent of the cases and decreases in inequality in 70 percent of the cases. In other words, while *on average across countries* no Kuznets-type relationship emerges, this does not imply that there are no important linkages from growth to inequality. In sum, the empirical evidence seems to suggest that infinite horizon models—while certainly providing a useful theoretical benchmark—fail to reproduce the general picture provided by the empirical evidence.

In this chapter, we drop the assumption of infinite horizons and look at optimal savings behavior when consumers have finite horizons. In such a context, it is interesting to look not only at the evolution of *overall* inequality but also at the evolution of inequality *within and between cohorts*. Empirical evidence suggests that inequality of a given cohort increases with age. For instance, Deaton and Paxson (1994) studied repeated cross-sectional household data from the United States, the United Kingdom, and Taiwan. They found that the extent of inequality for a given cohort was monotonically increasing in age. This result turned out to be quite robust, holding for all three countries and for both income and consumption inequality. For more recent evidence, see, for instance, Storesletten, Telmer, and Yaren (2004a). While much of the theoretical literature to explain the empirical patterns observed in the data relies on uninsurable income risks, we show in the present chapter that such a pattern may arise during a process of capital accumulation from the life cycle savings behavior of individuals even when future incomes are certain.

Postponing the discussion of uncertainty to chapters 8 and 9, in the present chapter we begin to analyze more complex patterns of personal income distribution, first in overlapping generations (OLG) models (sections 5.1 and 5.2), then in a simple model where consumers live for one period and derive utility from a (warm-glow) bequest motive, but otherwise do not care about their offspring (section 5.3). In the simplest OLG production economy, proposed by Diamond (1965), individuals live only for two periods. More complex dynamics arise when individual lifetimes are finite but uncertain. In the perpetual youth model (Blanchard 1985) lifetimes are exponentially distributed and incomes from non-accumulated factors decrease over time (to capture the idea that individuals' labor productivity decreases with age). It will turn out that the divergence results in chapter 3 rest upon the specific assumptions on savings behavior. As soon as we drop these assumptions much richer and more complex dynamics arise. In particular, we will see that accounting for within-cohort heterogeneity in the two-period OLG model may lead to complex dynamics of the distribution of population-wide consumption. In the continuous-time OLG model and the model with bequest, a Kuznets curve—rising inequality in early stages and falling inequality in later stages of development—may arise. Put in different terms, extending widely used standard macroeconomic models for individual heterogeneity produces quite different implications as far the distributional dynamics are concerned. In what follows, we aim at making this general insight precise.

5.1 Distribution and Growth in the Two-Period OLG Model

In the well-known model of Diamond (1965), individuals live for two periods. They work in the first period and retire in the second period. A newborn generation is endowed with raw labor but does not inherit any wealth.[1] Hence young individuals earn only labor income, and old individuals, being no longer capable of working, earn only income from factors they have accumulated during their working life.

In this section, we proceed as follows. In the first subsection we look at individual savings choices of young individuals and briefly discuss aggregate dynamics. In subsection 5.2.2 we look at the dynamics of inequality within cohorts. To study this issue we extend the Diamond (1965) model assuming that a newborn generation is unequally endowed with labor. In the absence of bequests, differences in labor endowments are the only source of within-generation inequality. We assume further that the distribution of labor endowments is stationary: labor endowments of a generation born at some date t are distributed in exactly the same way as the labor endowments of a generation born at some other date. Focusing on the savings functions resulting from the households' optimal choices allows us to study how the extent of inequality in savings (and hence accumulated factors) changes during the process of capital accumulation. It also allows us to focus on consumption inequality within cohorts, both over the life cycle for a given cohort, and how within-cohort inequality changes during the process of capital accumulation.

In subsection 5.2.3 we discuss heterogeneity between cohorts. Unlike in the quasi-representative agent models studied in chapter 3, in OLG models aggregate and individual dynamics do not coincide as households differ in age. Clearly, such heterogeneity arises even if all individuals within a new cohort are identical. To understand the evolution of inequality that arises along the between-cohort dimension, it is important to focus on factor shares. This is because young individuals derive only income from labor, whereas old individuals derive only income from accumulated capital.

In what follows we continue to assume HARA preferences, hence (within-cohort) inequality does not affect aggregate outcomes, and macroeconomics dynamics follow the standard OLG framework. The utility function is given by

$$\tilde{u} = \frac{1}{1-\sigma}\left(\frac{\beta c_{1t}}{\sigma} - \bar{c}\right)^{1-\sigma} + \frac{1}{1+\rho}\frac{1}{1-\sigma}\left(\frac{\beta c_{2t+1}}{\sigma} - \bar{c}\right)^{1-\sigma} \tag{5.1}$$

---

[1] In this context, the non-accumulated factor may only be interpreted as raw labor. Obviously, the assumption that non-accumulated factors yield no returns in the second period is very unrealistic when the non-accumulated factor is land.

where c_{1t} and c_{2t+1} are the levels of consumption of an agent when young and when old. Future is discounted at rate ρ and, just like before, σ, β, and $\bar{c}$ are exogenous preference parameters.

In the first period the agent decides how much to save and consume out of labor income $W_t l_t$. The part of the income that is consumed in the first period is c_{1t} and savings are $W_t l_t - c_{1t}$. It follows that consumption in the second period is given by $c_{2t+1} = (1 + R_{t+1}) (W_t l_t - c_{1t})$, where R_{t+1} denotes the interest rate. The intertemporal budget constraint can be written as

$$W_t l_t = c_{1t} + \frac{1}{1 + R_{t+1}} c_{2t+1}.$$

The optimal savings decision of agent i satisfies the Euler equation

$$\left(\frac{\beta c_{1t}}{\sigma} - \bar{c} \right)^{-\sigma} = \frac{1 + R_{t+1}}{1 + \rho} \left(\frac{\beta c_{2t+1}}{\sigma} - \bar{k} \right)^{-\sigma}. \qquad (5.2)$$

Inserting the budget constraint into this latter equation allows us to solve for savings $s_t^i = W_t l_t^i - c_{1t}^i$ in the first period

$$
\begin{aligned}
s_t(W_t, R_{t+1}) = {} & \frac{(1 + R_{t+1})^{\frac{1-\sigma}{\sigma}}}{(1 + \rho)^{\frac{1}{\sigma}} + (1 + R_{t+1})^{\frac{1-\sigma}{\sigma}}} W_t l_t \\
& - \bar{c} \frac{\sigma}{\beta} \frac{(1 + R_{t+1})^{\frac{1}{\sigma}} - (1 + \rho)^{\frac{1}{\sigma}}}{(1 + R_{t+1})^{\frac{1}{\sigma}} + (1 + \rho)^{\frac{1}{\sigma}} (1 + R_{t+1})}.
\end{aligned}
\qquad (5.3)
$$

Equation (5.3) shows that individual savings (and consumption) are a linear function of an individual's income $W_t l_t$. Linearity ensures that distribution plays no role for aggregate accumulation.

For our discussion of the role of savings to generate inequality, it will be instructive to draw the relationship (5.3) in a diagram (figure 5.1). This graph draws a household's savings as a function of labor income $W_t l_t$, and shows how a falling interest rate R_t affects the savings schedule. The graph is drawn for a positive minimum required consumption level $\bar{c}\sigma/\beta > 0$ and for a situation where the interest rate R is larger than the rate of time preference ρ. In that case the savings schedule intersects the horizontal axis in the positive domain of $W_t l_t$. Hence there is a minimum income level necessary to generate positive savings. For simplicity, we will refer to this point as the "savings threshold." The threshold depends on preference parameters $\bar{c}\sigma/\beta$ and ρ as well as on the interest rate R.

Just as in previous chapters, we consider only families that, at all times, can afford at least a consumption level of $\bar{c}\sigma/\beta$. In terms of figure 5.1, for utility to be well-defined incomes have to be sufficiently far to the right of

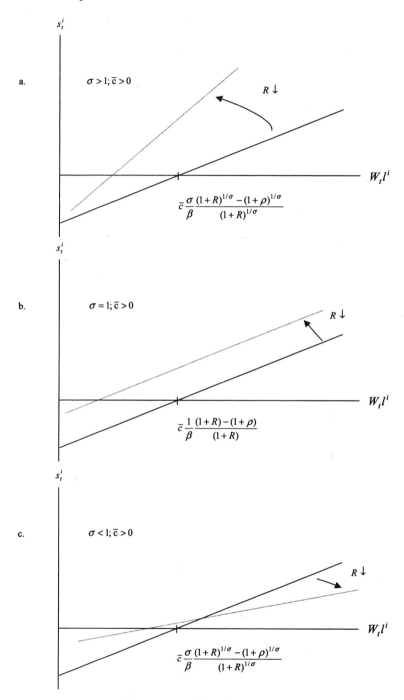

Figure 5.1 Savings in the OLG model (with $R > \rho$)

the savings threshold, i.e., the intersection point of the savings line with the horizontal axis.[2]

Ceteris paribus, a higher labor income $W_t l_t$ increases a household's savings. A change in the interest rate is a priori less clear as it affects both the slope and the intercept of the savings schedule. When $\sigma > 1$ (see panel a), the substitution effect is not particularly strong and is always dominated by the substitution effect. Hence a falling interest rate unambiguously increases savings. When $\sigma < 1$ (see panel c), the relative size of income and substitution depends on the level of labor income. When incomes are relatively small, the income effect still dominates (due to the minimum required consumption level), whereas at sufficiently high labor incomes the substitution effect may outweigh the income effect. When $\sigma = 0$ (see panel b), a reduction in the interest rate leads to a parallel upward shift in the savings schedule and an unambiguous increase in savings at all income levels. We note further that, as a result of an increasing interest rate, the savings threshold shifts to the left, irrespective of the size of σ.

5.1.1 Capital Accumulation and the Steady State

To study the aggregate dynamics of this model we have to look at the evolution of the aggregate capital stock that arises from the savings behavior studied above. We get the aggregate capital stock that is available at time $t + 1$ from aggregating both sides of equation (5.3) across the young generation. By linearity of (5.3) aggregation is independent of the distribution of income within a generation. Since aggregate production is given by the constant returns to scale (CRS) production function $F(K_t, L_t)$ and normalizing the aggregate amount of labor to unity $L_t = 1$ we have $R_{t+1} = F'(K_{t+1})$ and $W_t = F(K_t) - K_t F'(K_t)$ (where $F'(K_t)$ denotes the derivative of the production function with respect to the first argument). The aggregate capital stock can be written as

$$K_{t+1} = \frac{(1 + F'(K_{t+1}))^{\frac{1-\sigma}{\sigma}} \left[F(K_t) - K_t F'(K_t) - \bar{c}\frac{\sigma}{\beta} \right] + \bar{c}\frac{\sigma}{\beta} (1 + \rho)^{\frac{1}{\sigma}} (1 + F'(K_{t+1}))^{-1}}{(1 + \rho)^{\frac{1}{\sigma}} + (1 + F'(K_{t+1}))^{\frac{1-\sigma}{\sigma}}}.$$

(5.4)

Equation (5.4) implies a complex relationship between the present capital stock and the capital stock in the next period. Despite that fact that, under our assumption on the felicity function, distribution does not play any role for aggregate accumulation, this simple model may exhibit quite

---

[2]Note that during the process of capital accumulation the interest rate falls and the wage rate increases. This implies that the intersection point shifts to the left and the relevant labor income distribution shifts to the right. Hence, when all labor incomes are sufficiently far to the right in the initial period, they will be (even more) to the right in all subsequent periods.

94 • Chapter 5

complex dynamics. For instance, the model may generate multiple steady
states depending on how factor shares evolve over time. When savings
are negatively related to interest rates, multiple equilibria ("sunspots")
may arise. In this latter case, there are multiple levels of K_{t+1} that, given
K_t, satisfy equation (5.4). We do not go into the details of aggregate dynamics of the model. We refer the interested reader to the comprehensive
treatment by Galor and Ryder (1989) and to the more accessible textbook
discussions in Romer (1996) or Barro and Sala-i-Martin (1997).

Instead we concentrate our discussion on the relationship between income distribution and capital accumulation. Rather than allowing for
multiple equilibria, sunspots, and so on, we study the evolution of the
income distribution during the process of capital accumulation and characterize the distribution when the economy has reached a stationary state.
In this subsection we illustrate the issues by way of a simplified specification using a Cobb-Douglas production function $Y_t = K_t^\alpha L_t^{1-\alpha} - \delta K_t$ that
features constant factor shares in gross income (as discussed above), and
also a simplified specification of preferences $u(c) = \ln(c - \bar{c})$, with $\bar{c} > 0$.
The latter belongs to the HARA class (the case when $\sigma = \beta = 1$) and
$\bar{c} > 0$ implies decreasing relative risk aversion. The capital accumulation
equation (5.4) can then be rewritten as

$$K_{t+1} = \frac{1-\alpha}{2+\rho}K_t^\alpha - \bar{c}\frac{\alpha K_{t+1}^{\alpha-1} - \delta - \rho}{\left(1 + \alpha K_{t+1}^{\alpha-1} - \delta\right)(2+\rho)}. \tag{5.5}$$

Figure 5.2 shows the capital accumulation equation (5.5) of this simple special case of the model. If $\bar{c}$ is high enough, the model exhibits
two steady states, where only the higher steady state is a stable one. In
addition, at low levels of K, the capital accumulation equation is compatible with two values of K_t, i.e., the economy exhibits sunspots. Sunspots
may arise because the intertemporal elasticity of substitution of our utility function $u(c) = \ln(c - \bar{c})$ is less than one. This implies that reductions
in the interest rate stimulate savings. (The income effect dominates the
substitution effect.) This is a necessary condition for sunspot equilibria
to arise. The intuition is this: if individuals expect a high (low) interest
rate, they are willing to save only little (a lot), so the capital stock tomorrow will be low (high) and the interest rates will be high (low), making
expectations fulfill themselves.[3]

---

[3]The non-homotheticity of the Stone-Geary utility implies that this effect may be rather
strong—in particular when the capital stock is still small. This becomes clear if we compare
these results with an OLG model where utility is CRRA (and production is Cobb-Douglas).
One can show (e.g., in Barro and Sala-i-Martin 1997) that the steady state will always be
unique even when the elasticity of substitution is less than one.

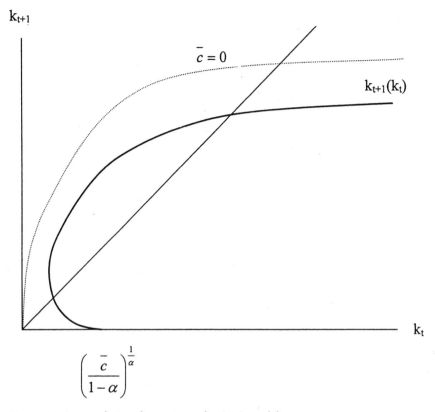

k_{t+1}

$\bar{c} = 0$

$k_{t+1}(k_t)$

k_t

$$\left(\frac{\bar{c}}{1-\alpha} \right)^{\frac{1}{\alpha}}$$

Figure 5.2 Accumulation dynamics in the OLG model

We will see below that, for characterizing the dynamics of the income distribution, it may be quite relevant whether the steady-state interest rate R^* exceeds or falls short of the rate of time preference ρ. From (5.5) it is obvious that the numerator of the $\bar{c}$–term is positive when $R_{t+1} = \alpha K_{t+1}^{\alpha-1} - \delta > \rho$. As we have $\bar{c} > 0$ the steady-state interest rate is bounded from below: $R^*|_{\bar{c}>0} > R^*|_{\bar{c}=0} > \rho$. Instead, if $R^* < \rho$, the interest rate with $\bar{c} > 0$ will be even lower: $R^*|_{\bar{c}>0} < R^*|_{\bar{c}=0} < \rho$. It is straightforward to see from (5.5) that

$$R^*|_{\bar{c}=0} = \frac{\alpha}{1-\alpha}(2+\rho) - \delta.$$

Hence a sufficient condition for a steady state in which the interest rate exceeds the rate of time preference is $(2+\rho)\alpha/(1-\alpha) \geq \rho + \delta$.

As far as the aggregate dynamics are concerned, one major difference between the infinite horizon models of chapter 3 and the overlapping generation model discussed here concerns welfare issues. As is well known, the equilibrium in the two-period OLG model may be Pareto inefficient (dynamically inefficient). Obviously, this economy is dynamically inefficient if the steady-state (net) interest rate R^* becomes negative. In light of the discussion above, a sufficient condition for dynamic inefficiency is $\frac{\alpha}{1-\alpha}(2+\rho) \leq \delta$ if $\bar{c} > 0$ because then $R^*|_{\bar{c}>0} < R^*|_{\bar{c}=0} \leq 0 < \rho$. Dynamic inefficiency arises because markets are incomplete, i.e., the young must save on their own for the time when they will not work, in the second period. A social planner could overcome the dynamic inefficiency by redistributing resources from the young to the old. Everybody is better off because the next generation of young is also forced to do the same in the next period.

5.1.2 Savings Choices and Within-Generation Inequality

As mentioned above, the basic OLG framework suggested by Diamond (1965) does not consider inequality within generations. However, Diamond's model can be easily extended to allow for such heterogeneity. By assumption, the age of an individual determines its economic position. Young individuals are endowed with labor, but have no capital. Old individuals own the capital stock, but are no longer capable of working. The extent of inequality *within* a generation is exogenously given at birth. Heterogeneity among young individuals is given by differences in labor endowments, and this is assumed exogenous. Moreover, we assume that this distribution is stationary so that, irrespective of the date of birth, the extent of inequality among the newborn remains constant over time. The households' savings behavior determines whether these exogenously given initial differences are amplified or attenuated over the life cycle. Hence the households' savings behavior is crucial for the determination of *wealth* inequality.

Studying the households' savings behavior allows us to discuss various interesting issues. First, we can ask how does inequality within a cohort change when households get old? Or, put in a different way: Are labor incomes (the incomes of the young) more or less unequally distributed than incomes from capital (the incomes of the old)? Empirical evidence clearly suggests that aggregate wealth—and the returns on wealth—are much more unequally distributed than labor incomes that arise due to such endowment differences (for recent empirical evidence see Davies and Shorrocks [2000] or Wolff [1994]). The second interesting question relates to the dynamic evolution of wealth inequality. Savings increase the aggregate capital stock, and hence it is interesting to ask whether such inequality increases or decreases as the economy grows. Finally, from a welfare point of view it is interesting to look at consumption inequalities that arise from the savings choices. As we did before, we will assume positive required consumption levels $\bar{c}\sigma/\beta > 0$ and focus the discussion on a situation where $R_t > \rho$. At the end of this subsection, we briefly discuss the $R_t < \rho$ case.

By our assumption (5.1) on preferences, savings are linear in income and the distribution of endowments with non-accumulated factors at birth does not affect the evolution of the economy in the aggregate. However, even though the marginal savings rate is constant across households, that fraction of income that a household saves, the *savings ratio*, depends on how rich a household is. From (5.3) the savings ratio is smaller for a poor household and larger for a rich household, as long as there is positive required consumption $\bar{c}\sigma/\beta > 0$ and as long as $R_t > \rho$. Our discussion assumes these two conditions are satisfied. We comment at the end of this subsection what happens if $R_t \leq \rho$.

We can now immediately answer the first question raised above, the evolution of within-cohort inequality over the life cycle. As positive required consumption levels imply that the savings ratio of the poor is lower than the one of the rich, hence endowment differences at birth are amplified through the households' savings choices. Current savings are equivalent to wealth levels $s_t = k_{t+1}$ and proportional to available resources next period, $(1 + R_{t+1})k_{t+1}$. As the rich have a higher savings ratio than the poor, the distribution of resources among the old generation (wealth and capital incomes) will have a larger spread than the labor incomes. This observation allows us to make two interesting statements. First, *for any given cohort*, income inequality is relatively low during the first period of life and relatively high during the second period of life. Second, *at any given period*, labor incomes are less unequally distributed than capital incomes (and wealth levels). This latter result follows from the stationarity of the labor income distribution and the fact that, for any cohort, capital incomes are more unequally distributed. We note that this latter result is in line with empirical evidence.

The second question raised above concerns the changes in the wealth distribution during the process of capital accumulation. During this process wages rise and interest rates fall. Both changes lead to lower relative savings and hence let the distribution of wealth and capital income among the old population become more equal over time. To see this consider figure 5.1. The increase in wages raises the savings ratios of rich and poor families, but increases the latter more strongly than the former. As a result, the gap in wealth levels between rich and poor households decreases. The reduction in interest rates works in the same direction. In figure 5.1, a reduction in the interest rate shifts the savings threshold to the left. This is sufficient to generate a lower gap in savings between rich and poor families. To see this consider the linear function $s = -a + by$ with a and b as positive constants, and s and y as the savings and the income level, respectively. The intersection point on the horizontal axis (the savings threshold) is given by a/b. Consider two income levels $y_1 > y_0$ generating savings $s_1 > s_0$. It is straightforward to show that, as long as $0 < a/b < y_0 < y_1$,

$$\partial \left(s_1/s_0 \right) / \partial \left(a/b \right) = \left(y_1 - y_0 \right) / \left(-a/b + y_0 \right)^2 > 0$$

Hence the degree of inequality in savings, $s_1/s_0 > 1$, *decreases* when the saving threshold a/b *falls* (which happens to be the case when the interest rate falls—see equation [5.3]).

While both increases in wages and falling interest rate both lead to savings decisions that result in more equality among the old population, there are subtle differences between wage and interest rate effects. On the one hand, increases in wages generate a pure income effect and lead to increases in savings that, in relative terms, are stronger for the poor so the wealth levels of the poor catch up. On the other hand, decreases in the interest rate cause both an income and a substitution effect. In the bottom panel of figure 5.1 the substitution effect is strong ($\sigma < 1$). A lower gap in savings between rich and poor may come from *lower* savings by the richest consumers, whereas the savings of the poorer consumers are higher. (As long as the economy grows, which we assume here, the aggregate capital stock K has to increase. Lower savings by the richest consumers have to be offset by higher savings of poorer consumers.) Clearly when the substitution effect is weak ($\sigma > 1$), as in the top panel of figure 5.1, the income effect dominates which implies higher savings for all consumers. Similarly, when the substitution parameter $\sigma = 1$ the marginal savings rate remains unchanged and there is a parallel shift in the savings schedule implying the same absolute increase in savings for all consumers, irrespective of their income.

Finally, let us look at consumption inequality. How does consumption inequality evolve over the life cycle? We know that savings are more unequally distributed than labor incomes. From that it follows directly that consumption *at young ages is less unequally* distributed than labor incomes. Moreover, as consumption levels of the old are proportional to their savings, it follows that consumption *at old ages is more unequally* distributed. In other words, consumption inequality increases with age— and it increases more strongly than corresponding inequalities in income. Note also that diverging consumption levels among the young and converging consumption levels among the old imply that, *at each date*, consumption inequality is higher among the currently old than among the currently young.

It is worth emphasizing at this point that the above discussion was confined to a situation where the interest rate exceeds the rate of time preferences. However, nothing prevents the steady-state level of the capital stock to reach a level so that the steady-state interest rate falls short of the rate of time preference, $R^* < \rho$. Clearly when this happens the savings threshold is negative, i.e., the savings schedule intersects the horizontal axis in the negative domain of labor incomes. In that case it is easy to see that the distribution of savings becomes *less unequal* than the distribution of labor incomes. (Recall that the labor income distribution is stationary.)

In sum, the evolution of savings and wealth inequality may be quite complex. When the economy starts with a low capital stock so that $R_0 > \rho$, savings and wealth levels will converge. However, as soon as the interest rate falls short of the rate of time preference $R_t \leq \rho$, wealth levels continue to converge and wealth inequality must become lower than wage inequality. However, there is a further subtle point here. When $R_t \leq \rho$, the savings threshold becomes negative: the isolated effect of an increase in labor incomes causes the savings ratios of both rich and poor consumers to *decrease*, but they decrease the ratio of the poor more strongly than for the rich, causing divergence in savings and wealth levels. The isolated effect of an increase in interest rates, however, has qualitatively the same effect as before, i.e., it increases the savings ratio of the poor more strongly than the one of the rich. As capital accumulation is now associated with two effects that go in opposite directions, it is no longer clear whether savings and wealth inequality is increasing or decreasing as the economy moves toward the steady state. However, when $R_t \leq \rho$, the extent of wealth inequality must remain *lower* than wage inequality.[4]

5.1.3 The Evolution of Inequality between Generations

Above we have extended Diamond's (1965) model to allow for within-generation inequality. We have not yet discussed inequality *between* generations. Inequality is already present in the basic two-period OLG model, as there are young and old individuals the endowment of whom with factors of production is different. We do not allow for within-generation inequality but compare the average young household to the average old household.

The extent of inequality between young and old generations is determined by two crucial variables: (1) the factor share and (2) the savings

---

[4]Above we have argued that the empirically relevant case is a situation where wage inequality is smaller than wealth inequality. Does this mean we should consider a situation where $R_t < \rho$ empirically less relevant? Certainly not. The reason is that the model is still highly stylized abstracting from many features, such as uncertainty, market imperfections, and many other relevant issues. Adding these elements to the above model may well result in limit distributions of wealth that are more unequal than labor incomes. See part 2 for an extensive discussion of issues of capital market imperfections and uncertainty.

rate. The factor share determines how much of current output accrues to labor and capital, and the savings rate determines how much wealth will be accumulated. Moreover, the resources available to the old consist of capital income and, in addition, also depend on the amount of accumulated wealth (unless capital fully depreciates). Clearly, the latter is determined by how much the currently old generation has saved during its working life.

To illustrate the point, it suffices to look at the simplest case, where the production function is Cobb-Douglas and given by $Y_t = A K_t^\alpha L^{1-\alpha}$ with A as a positive constant. For simplicity assume there is no depreciation and normalize the population size of a cohort to unity, $L = 1$. Preferences are logarithmic and given by $u_t = \ln c_{1t} + [1/(1 + \rho)] \ln c_{2t+1}$. Under these assumptions, the savings rate (from labor income) is s, and the fraction of output that goes to labor is $1 - \alpha$, both constant over time. The aggregate capital stock evolves according to $K_{t+1} = [1/(2 + \rho)] (1 - \alpha) A K_t^\alpha$.

How do the relative available resources between generations evolve over time? Abstracting from within-cohort inequality we have $l = L = 1$ for all young individuals and $k = K$ for all old individuals. Denote, in analogy to the previous chapter, by a_{1t} and a_{2t} the available resources to a member of, respectively, the young and the old generation at date t. The ratio of available resources between old and young generations can be written as

$$\frac{a_{2t}}{a_{1t}} = \frac{R_t K_t + K_t}{W_t} = \frac{\alpha + K_t^{1-\alpha}/A}{1 - \alpha}, \tag{5.6}$$

which is increasing in K. From this equation it is easy to check under which conditions the old are richer or poorer than the young. When $\alpha \geq 1/2$, the old will always be richer, irrespective of the accumulated capital stock. However, the more relevant case is perhaps a situation where $\alpha < 1/2$ (as a rough estimate, it is often assumed that $\alpha = 1/3$). In that case, and with a sufficiently small capital stock such that $K_t < [(1 - 2\alpha)A]^{1/(1-\alpha)}$, it may be the young who dispose of more resources.

The steady-state level of the capital stock K_∞ can be straightforwardly calculated and is given by $K_\infty = [(1 - \alpha)A/(2 + \rho)]^{1/(1-\alpha)}$. Knowing the steady-state capital stock allows us to characterize the evolution of inequality across cohorts. In a growing economy, K_t approaches K_∞ from below in the transition process toward the steady state. When the inherited capital stock $K_0 < [(1 - 2\alpha)A]^{1/(1-\alpha)} < [(1 - \alpha)A/(2 + \rho)]^{1/(1-\alpha)}$ we have a situation where initially the young are richer than the poor, but once the capital stock reaches a critical size, the old start to become relatively richer. In any case, the ratio a_{2t}/a_{1t} increases during the accumulation process. In such a situation we have first decreasing inequality (because initially the old are poorer, but capital accumulation lets them catch up) but then increasing inequality (because later on the old overtake the poor and relative incomes start to increase). Clearly depending on parameter values, any relationship between inequality and growth is possible. When the steady-state value of the capital stock is small (e.g., because the savings ratio is small), we might have $K_0 < [(1 - \alpha)A/(2 + \rho)]^{1/(1-\alpha)} < [(1 - 2\alpha)A]^{1/(1-\alpha)}$. In that case, the old remain relatively poor but growth is associated with higher between-generation inequality. But when the inherited capital stock is relatively large so that $[(1 - 2\alpha)A]^{1/(1-\alpha)} < K_0 < [(1 - \alpha)A/(2 + \rho)]^{1/(1-\alpha)}$, the old are richer already when the transition process starts and we observe a monotonically positive correlation between growth and inequality.

The above discussion was undertaken under the simple case of logarithmic preferences and a Cobb-Douglas production function. It is straightforward to see that the constancy of the savings rate resulting from the former assumption does not change our discussion concerning the evolution of inequality between generations. (It does affect the level of the steady-state capital stock and may affect the nature of aggregate dynamics, though.) However, as long as a steady state exists and as long as the inherited capital stock falls short of this steady state, the above discussion is fully relevant.

The assumption of a Cobb-Douglas production function implies that (gross) factor shares remain unchanged during the accumulation process. In general, however, it may well be that factor shares depend on the stage of development. In other words the production elasticity of capital α is a function of the capital stock K, so $\alpha = \alpha(K)$. It is straightforward to see that, when $\partial\alpha/\partial K > 0$, the above discussion remains qualitatively unchanged, but the positive impact of capital accumulation on the ratio a_{2t}/a_{1t} is reinforced by the increase in capital share that favors the old generation. However, things become ambiguous when $\partial\alpha/\partial K < 0$, as the increase in the capital stock is counteracted by a decreasing share in output that accrues to the old. The following exercise elaborates on this point by assuming a CES production function that allows for changes in factor shares.

EXERCISE 17 Show for a CES production function

$$Y = F(K, L) = (\alpha K^\eta + (1 - \alpha)L^\eta)^{\frac{1}{\eta}}$$

how the functional distribution income evolves over time in an OLG growing economy with no within-cohort inequality and a constant saving rate at the household level. Also discuss how personal income distribution depends on the beginning of period capital-labor ratio, the savings rate, and the rate of population growth.

While there is the theoretical possibility of changing factor shares, this case is perhaps empirically less relevant. There is no clear trend in factor shares in most industrialized countries over long time periods. For instance, the U.S. evidence presented in Piketty and Saez (2003) shows no trend (and even very little fluctuation) in the capital share in the U.S. corporate sector throughout the twentieth century. European evidence is less clear (see Bentolila and Saint-Paul [2003] or Giammarioli et al., [2003]), although the observed changes in factor shares in the postwar period are more likely related to institutional changes (such as changes in union power) and less likely to be driven by technology.

So far, our discussion was confined to inequality between cohorts with respect to *available resources*. Such a comparison, while potentially interesting as such, may erroneously indicate that the young are "better off" than the old. However, the young have to allocate these resources over two periods, whereas the resources available to the old generation can be fully consumed in the current period. In other words, from a welfare point of view, we should look at relative *consumption levels* (that determine the utility levels at date t). To do so, we take up our above discussion, and stick to the assumption that technology is Cobb-Douglas so that factor shares remain unchanged over time. However, for consumption inequality, the households' savings behavior plays a critical role.

Since the level of consumption of consumers who are old at date t is equal to $c_{2t} = a_{2t}$, the level of consumption of young consumers is $c_{1t} = a_{1t} - s_t = (1 - \alpha)(1 - s_t/W_t)K_t^\alpha$. As a result we can use (5.6) to express relative consumption levels as

$$\frac{c_{2t}}{c_{1t}} = \frac{R_t K_t + K_t}{W_t} = \frac{\alpha + K_t^{1-\alpha}/A}{(1 - \alpha)(1 - s_t/W_t)}. \tag{5.7}$$

Equation (5.7) tells us that relative consumption levels depend on accumulated capital but—unlike in the case of relative wealth levels—the evolution of relative consumption levels is less clear and depends on how the savings ratio s_t/W_t evolves over time. When capital accumulates, wages W_t increase and the interest rate R_t falls. The former effect increases the savings ratio (because the marginal savings rate is positive and the intercept of the savings schedule in figure 5.1 is negative). The latter effect, however, is less clear and depends on the parameter σ. When $\sigma \geq 1$ figure 5.1 shows that s_t/W_t increases for all labor incomes beyond the savings threshold. Even when $\sigma < 1$, it could well be that s_t/W_t increases. It is not only the income effect of a reduction in R but also the (direct) income effect from the increase in W that works in this direction. Only when the substitution effect is very strong (thus dominating the income effects) does the savings ratio decrease.

How will relative consumption levels evolve over time? The numerator of the right-hand side of equation (5.7) increases in K_t and the denominator decreases in K_t (unless the σ is very small), so that s_t/W_t increases with the aggregate capital stock. In sum, c_{2t}/c_{1t} will increase during the process of accumulation and growth. Whether this implies an increase or a decrease in the consumption inequality between generations depends on the initial capital stock. If the initial capital stock is small, consumption of the old is small and the young save relatively little, both implying that $c_{2t}/c_{1t} < 1$, so that growth implies a decrease in inequality between generations. However, if the steady-state features $R^* > \rho$ it must be that, in steady state, $c_2^*/c_1^* > 1$. This follows from the Euler equation (5.2). In other words, the dynamics of inequality between generations is U-shaped if the economy is initially poor: it first decreases and then increases again once consumption levels of the old have taken over. Of course, if the initial capital stock is already so large as to ensure that $c_{20}/c_{10} > 1$, inequality is monotonically related to income levels.

It is worth noting that our discussion has assumed a steady state with $R^* > \rho$. Suppose instead the steady-state capital stock satisfies the knife-edge condition $R^* = \rho$. In that case we would have decreasing inequality and we would approach a state of perfect equality in consumption levels between generations. Things become more complex once we assume that $R^* < \rho$. In that case growth has an ambiguous effect on the savings ratio (when $R_t < \rho$ the saving threshold in figure 5.1 becomes negative, and the effect of wage increases and falling interest rates on the savings ratio will in general go in opposite directions). Then it is unclear whether consumption inequality increases, decreases, or remains constant along the transition path. The steady state, however, features $c_2^*/c_1^* < 1$ because, ceteris paribus, households prefer a decreasing consumption path when the interest falls short of the rate of time preference.

The above discussion has put emphasis on the situation where income effects from falling interest and increasing wage rates dominate the substitution effect. Hence accumulation is characterized by increasing savings ratios.[5] The following exercise asks you to discuss in more detail the role of the substitution parameter σ for consumption inequalities (for the special case of a CES utility function—where the saving threshold always passes through the origin and changes in savings ratio come about only through changes in the marginal savings rate).

---

[5] Laitner (2000) discusses empirical evidence that shows that, over very long time horizons, savings ratios have been increasing. His explanation, however, relies on valuation of assets (not considered in national income products accounts) rather than a change in actual savings behavior.

EXERCISE 18 Discuss differences in consumption levels between cohorts. Assume that the production function is Cobb-Douglas and given by $Y_t = AK_t^\alpha L_t^{1-\alpha}$. Assume there is no population growth and normalize population size to unity, so $L_t = 1$. Assume further that preferences are given by $u = \frac{c_{1t}^{1-\sigma}}{1-\sigma} + \frac{1}{1+\rho}\frac{c_{2t+1}^{1-\sigma}}{1-\sigma}$. Assume that $R_{t+1} > \rho$.

So far, we have focused, separately, on inequality among households of the same generation and on the differences in average old and young households. In this respect, the discussion here is not directly comparable to the last chapter where individuals had infinite horizons and no age differences between households did exist. The discussion there was devoted to an analysis of inequality among the *entire population*. In analogy to the infinite horizon model, we could focus on the distribution of lifetime resources that are available to currently alive individuals. For young individuals, these resources consist of their labor income; for old individuals, these resources are given by the value of accumulated wealth plus the capital income that accrues from it during the second period of life. Just like in the infinite horizon model, the overall distribution is shaped by savings decisions. Unlike in the infinite horizon model, however, only savings decisions of currently old (= previously young) individuals are relevant for the current distribution.

5.2 INEQUALITY IN A PERPETUAL YOUTH MODEL

The two-period OLG model studied above has the advantage of a very simple age and population structure that allows us to discuss distributional dynamics in a tractable way. However, tractability comes at the cost of a constant time horizon. This is important, however, because many issues in macroeconomics, such as the steady-state interest rate, depend crucially on the time horizon of agents. Moreover, comparing the results in chapter 3 to those in section 5.1 of the present chapter, it is obvious that the agents' time horizon also plays a crucial role for distributional dynamics under neoclassical conditions. In this chapter we study distributional dynamics in a slightly more complex but also more realistic setting. Our analysis elaborates Blanchard's (1985) continuous-time OLG model that allows us to study the importance of finite horizons for the distribution of income and wealth across agents (within and between cohorts).

Consider an economy populated by agents who face, throughout their life, a constant instantaneous probability of death p. This implies a life expectation of $\int_0^\infty tpe^{-pt}dt = 1/p$ and $1/p$ can be taken as the horizon index. The instantaneous probability of death is the same constant p for every currently alive individual. At each date t there is entry of new cohorts of size p. Taken together the assumption on birth and mortality rates implies that a cohort born at date 0 has size pe^{-pt} at some later date t. It also implies that aggregate population is kept constant and the size of the population at date t is given by $\int_{-\infty}^{t} pe^{-pt} dt = 1$.

Our aim is to study the implications of heterogeneity in the labor endowment distribution on the dynamics of inequality in this economy. In particular, we assume that an individual born at date s is endowed with $l(s,s)$ units of labor but inherits no wealth, so $k(s,s) = 0$. This is because individuals leave no bequests. Any wealth accumulated by individuals i at later dates comes from savings out of their own labor income.

We assume that individuals differ in their initial labor endowment. The distribution of labor endowment of each newborn is assumed to be stationary and has mean $\bar{l}$. It depreciates at rate α to capture the idea that, at old ages, it is increasingly difficult for a household to generate labor income. Hence the motive to save arises from caring for old age. The depreciation of labor endowment implies that the mean labor endowment of cohort s at date t is $\bar{l}e^{-\alpha(t-s)}$ and also that relative endowments between any two individuals stay constant over time. Normalizing average labor endowment of all currently alive individuals L we must have $L = \int_{-\infty}^{t} p\bar{l} \exp((\alpha + p)(s - t)) ds$. Hence the average labor endowment of a newborn population $\bar{l}$ and average labor endowment of all currently alive individuals L are related by $\bar{l} = \frac{p+\alpha}{p} L$.

The assumption that each individual's labor supply $l(s,t)$ declines at rate α approximates a life cycle where individuals' earnings capacity is high when young and becomes (close to) zero at older ages ("after retirement"). The resulting model usefully highlights the time horizon for the savings decisions. In particular, the model encompasses the infinite horizon model as the limit case where $p = \alpha = 0$. While the model does not exactly encompass the two-period lifetime models introduced above, a situation with a short life expectation $1/p$ and a high labor endowment depreciation rate α is a close approximation.

Individuals in this economy allocate their income to consumption and savings so as to maximize a time-separable objective function, defined over consumption paths $\{c(\cdot)\}$,

$$\tilde{u}(t) \equiv E_t \left(\int_t^{\tilde{t}} u(c(s, \tau)) e^{-\rho(\tau - t)} d\tau \right), \tag{5.8}$$

where $\tilde{t}$ denotes the time of the individual's death, and the expectation is taken over the probability distribution of residual life length. (Note that by assumption of a constant mortality rate per unit time, the density of residual life length is exponential and age-independent.[6]) Evaluating the expectation in (5.8) yields

$$\tilde{u}(t) = \int_t^\infty e^{-(\rho+p)(\tau-t)} u(c\,(s,\tau))\,d\tau. \tag{5.9}$$

A household maximizes (5.9) subject to his budget constraint. A household's return on (positive or negative) financial wealth equals $R(t) + p$: private remuneration of capital $R(t)$, plus the annuity premium paid (or received) by zero-profit insurance companies for the right to appropriate the individual's wealth (or the obligation to repay his debts) upon his death. At date t, an agent born at date s is endowed with $k(s,t)$ units of financial wealth and $l(s,t)$ units of labor. There are no bequests, so for a newborn individual we have $k(s,s) = 0$ (at date s). The dynamic budget constraint is given by

$$\dot{k}(s,t) + c(s,t) = (R(t) + p)k(s,t) + l(s,t)W(t). \tag{5.10}$$

To prevent agents from going infinitely into debt, we need the condition

$$\lim_{v\to\infty} k(s,v) \exp\left(-\int_t^v (R\,(\tau) + p)\,d\tau\right) = 0.$$

Taking this transversality condition into account, the budget constraint can be rewritten as

$$\int_t^\infty c\,(s,v)\,e^{-\int_t^v (R(\tau)+p)d\tau}\,dv = k(s,t) + h\,(s,t). \tag{5.11}$$

The right-hand side of the previous equation denotes lifetime wealth. This consists of accumulated wealth $k\,(s,t)$ and "human wealth" $h\,(s,t)$. The latter is the present value of the labor income flow as of date t for an individual born at date s. It is straightforward to calculate human wealth as

$$h\,(s,t) = \int_t^\infty W(v)l(s,s) \exp(-\alpha(t-s)) \exp\left(-\tilde{R}\,(v) - (\alpha+p)(v-t)\right) dv.$$

(Here the cumulative discount factor between the current date t and some future date v is given by $\tilde{R}(v) = \int_t^v R(\tau)d\tau$.)

---

[6]Exponentially distributed lifetimes are not fully realistic, of course, but recommend themselves on grounds of algebraic simplicity. If we assumed that agents have a deterministic life span of n years, for example, aggregate relationships would involve polynomials of order n in discrete time and transcendental equations in continuous time.

Now consider the agents' intertemporal decision problem. (For convenience we drop cohort indices.) Optimality requires agents choose a consumption path that satisfies the Euler equation $\dot{c} = (R - \rho) / [-u''(c)/u'(c)]$. To ensure that income distribution does not matter directly for accumulation, the contemporaneous utility function has to be of the HARA class. In that case marginal utility is $u'(c(t)) = [(\beta/\sigma)c(t) - \bar{c}]^{-\sigma}$ and the Euler equation is given by

$$\dot{c}(t) \left(\frac{c(t)}{\sigma} - \frac{\bar{c}}{\beta} \right)^{-1} = R(t) - \rho. \tag{5.12}$$

Appendix 5.5 shows that the solution to this differential equation can be written as a consumption function that is linear in lifetime wealth

$$c(s,t) = \bar{\bar{c}}(t) + \hat{c}(t) \left[k(s,t) + h(s,t) \right]. \tag{5.13}$$

The (time-varying) propensity to consume out of lifetime wealth $\hat{c}_t$ is given by

$$\hat{c}(t) = \left(\int_t^\infty \exp(\frac{(1 - \sigma)\tilde{R}(v) - \rho(v - t) - \sigma p(v - t)}{\sigma}) dv \right)^{-1}, \tag{5.14}$$

which is the same for all individuals, and the (also time-varying) intercept of the consumption function $\bar{\bar{c}}(t)$ is given by

$$\bar{\bar{c}}(t) = \frac{\sigma \bar{c}}{\beta} \left(1 - \hat{c}(t) \int_t^\infty \exp(-\tilde{R}(v) - p(v - t)) dv \right), \tag{5.15}$$

which is also identical across individuals. We note the formal equivalence of the above consumption function to the solution of the infinite horizon model discussed in chapter 1. In fact, when $p = 0$ the solutions $\hat{c}(t)$ and $\bar{\bar{c}}(t)$ derived here are the continuous-time counterparts of that model. As all individuals are alike with respect to their time horizon (which, at any date t, is given by $1/p$, and independent of their age), consumption depends only on the level of lifetime resources. The composition of these resources (human wealth or accumulated wealth) plays no role.

5.2.1 Aggregate Dynamics

Now look at aggregate dynamics. Because the individual consumption function (5.13) is linear in individual lifetime wealth $k(s,t) + h(s,t)$, aggregate consumption is independent of the distribution and a linear function of aggregate wealth

$$C(t) = \bar{\bar{c}}(t) + \hat{c}(t) (K(t) + H(t)), \qquad (5.16)$$

where, as hitherto, $K(t)$ is the aggregate capital stock and $H(t)$ is the aggregate value of human wealth (i.e., the present value of lifetime labor income, aggregated over all currently alive individuals). Note that, unlike in the infinite horizon case, the dynamics of individual and aggregate consumption do not coincide. The reason is that, in each period, some agents disappear and new households come along. Hence the aggregate economy does coincide with a representative agent's behavior. To calculate the change in aggregate consumption, differentiate the expression for $C(t)$ with respect to t. It is straightforward, albeit somewhat tedious, to calculate the change in aggregate consumption as[7]

$$\dot{C}(t) = \left(\alpha + \frac{R(t) - \rho}{\sigma}\right) C(t) - \hat{c}(t) (p + \alpha) K(t) - \alpha \bar{\bar{c}}(t) - \frac{\bar{c}}{\beta} (R(t) - \rho).$$
$$(5.17)$$

The dynamics of the aggregate capital stock can simply be written as the difference between (net) aggregate output (net of depreciation) and aggregate consumption

$$\dot{K}(t) = F(K(t), L) - C(t).$$

In the steady state we have $\dot{C} = \dot{H} = \dot{K} = 0$. The steady-state system can be reduced to two equations. The first equation, the $\dot{K} = 0$ locus, states under which conditions the aggregate capital stock remains unchanged and is given by

$$C = F(K, L).$$

The second equation, the $\dot{C} = 0$ locus, describes values of C and K such that aggregate consumption remains unchanged and is given by[8]

$$C = \frac{(p + \alpha) [(\sigma - 1) (R(K) + p) + (\rho + p)] K}{\alpha\sigma + R(K) - \rho} + \frac{\sigma\bar{c}}{\beta} \frac{(R(K) - \rho) (\alpha + R(K) + p)}{(R(K) + p) (\alpha\sigma + R(K) - \rho)}.$$

---

[7]Note that we have to take account of the fact that $H(t) = \int_t^\infty W(\tau) L \exp(-\tilde{R}(\tau) + (\alpha + p)(\tau - t)) d\tau$, so that the change in aggregate human wealth is $\dot{H}(t) = (R(t) + p + \alpha) H(t) - W(t)L$. The change in the aggregate capital stock is $\dot{K}(t) = -pK(t) + \int_{-\infty}^t \dot{K}(s, t) pe^{p(s-t)} ds$, where the first term is the capital stock of those who die and the second term is the capital stock of those alive. ($K(s, t)$ is the capital stock, at date t, aggregated over all individuals born at date s.)

[8]In steady state, the interest rate is constant, and $\hat{c}(t) = [(\sigma - 1) R + \rho + \sigma p] / \sigma$ and $\bar{\bar{c}}(t) = (\bar{c}/\beta) (R - \rho) / (R + p)$. Inserting these expressions into the equation for the dynamics of consumption yields the steady-state level of consumption.

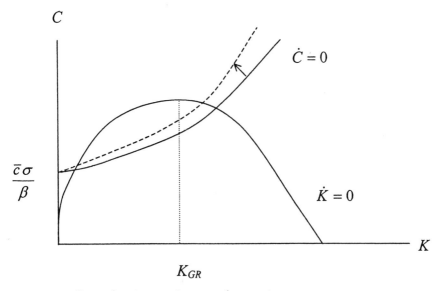

Figure 5.3 Effects of an increase in p or a decrease in α

It is convenient to analyze this system graphically in a phase diagram (figure 5.3). The $\dot{K} = 0$ locus is a concave function that starts at the origin and reaches a maximum at K_{GR}. The $\dot{C} = 0$ locus starts at the minimum required consumption level $\sigma \bar{c}/\beta$ (note that $R(0) = \infty$) and is finally upward sloping with a slope increasing in K. (The figure is drawn such that this slope is always positive but, if σ is sufficiently below one, it may be negative at small levels of K.) The steady-state levels C^* and K^* are determined by the intersection of the two curves. The dynamics of C and K over time are given by a monotonically increasing saddle path (not shown in figure 5.3).

The slope of the $\dot{K} = 0$ locus at the point of intersection gives the steady-state interest rate $R^* = R(K^*)$. As the dynamics of the wealth distribution will depend crucially on the steady-state interest rate, let us study how crucial parameters affect this variable. Figure 5.3 shows how the steady state is affected by the parameters α and p. For a given α, a larger p increases the aggregate propensity to consume out of the current capital stock, and decreases the equilibrium capital stock. We note further that, if $\alpha = 0$ but $p > 0$, the steady-state level of capital is lower than in the model with infinite horizon, so $\alpha > 0$ is a necessary condition for a steady-state interest rate that is below ρ. Hence, a state of dynamic inefficiency (a negative steady-state interest rate) can only occur when agents' labor endowment falls sharply with age. In that case, they are forced to save a large portion of their current income flow to ensure a smooth consumption path even at old ages when labor income gets small. When this motive to save for old age is sufficiently strong, aggregate "over-saving" may occur.

Consider next the impact of the preference parameters σ and $\bar{c}$ on the steady-state interest rate. With a larger $\bar{c}$, the Euler equation (5.12) implies that consumption growth at the individual level will fall as long as $R > \rho$. Hence, with a larger $\bar{c}$, the interest rate must be larger in steady state to ensure that aggregate consumption is constant. In terms of figure 5.4, the $\dot{C} = 0$ locus will shift to the right in the neighborhood of the steady state. However, if the steady-state interest rate is below the discount rate or is even negative the opposite, signs reverse. An increase in $\bar{c}$ shifts the $\dot{C} = 0$ locus to the left, decreasing the steady-state capital stock (see figure 5.4). The mechanism is similar to the one that is also at work in the simple two-period OLG model studied above. A higher $\bar{c}$ or a higher σ is associated with a lower elasticity of intertemporal substitution. As long as $R > \rho$, the resulting stronger preference for a flat consumption path reduces savings today.

5.2.2 The Evolution of Population-Wide Inequality

In Blanchard's (1985) OLG model studied above, individuals have a finite but (potentially) very long time horizon. An important assumption of this model is that all currently alive individuals have the same time horizon. Individuals are "perpetually young" in the sense that the probability of death is independent of age. An important implication of this assumption is that age has no direct effect on consumption and savings. More precisely, two individuals who differ in age, but have the same income and lifetime resources, will have exactly the same levels of consumption and savings. Because remaining life expectancy is identical for all currently alive individuals, an individual's age affects neither the marginal propensity to consume nor the intercept in the consumption function (5.13).

We start out by looking at the distribution of lifetime resources across the *entire population*. Savings occur out of total lifetime resources (and not just from labor income as in the simple two-period model). To economize on notation we define lifetime resources as $a(s, t) \equiv k(s, t) + h(s, t)$. How $a(s, t)$ changes over time depends on the change in the endowment with the accumulated factor $k(s, t)$ and present value of the labor income $h(s, t)$. Note first that $\dot{k}$ is given by

$$\dot{k}(s, t) = [R(t) + p]k(s, t) + W(t)l(s, t) - c(s, t)$$

and that $\dot{h}$ is given by

$$\dot{h}(s, t) = [R(t) + p]h(s, t) - W(t)l(s, t).$$

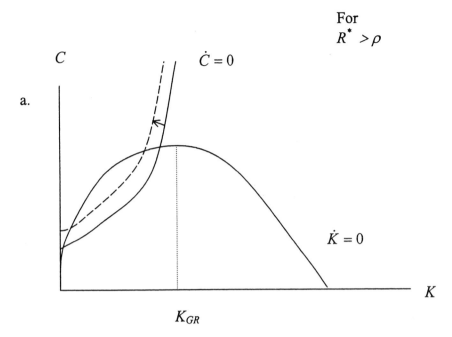

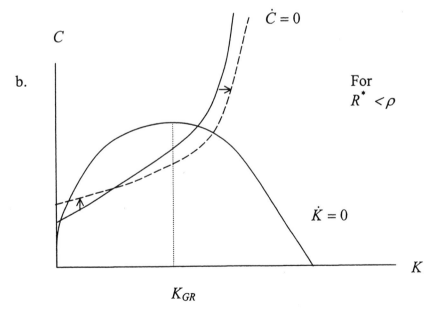

Figure 5.4 Effects of an increase in $\bar{c}$ or σ

To see how the extent of inequality in $a(s,t)$ changes over time we calculate growth rates of lifetime wealth $\dot{a}/a$ and ask in which way it depends on the level of a. Using $\dot{a}(s,t) = \dot{k}(s,t) + \dot{h}(s,t)$, and the consumption function (5.13) it is straightforward to calculate the rate of growth of $a(s,t)$ as

$$\frac{\dot{a}(s,t)}{a(s,t)} = R(t) + p - \hat{c}(t) - \frac{\bar{\bar{c}}(t)}{a(s,t)}. \qquad (5.18)$$

Does the distribution of $a(s,t)$ converge or diverge as the economy grows? Just like in the infinite horizon model, the answer to this question depends on the sign of the intercept $\bar{\bar{c}}(t)$ in the consumption function (5.13). If $\bar{\bar{c}}(t) > 0$ there is divergence in the distribution of lifetime resources: individuals with a high level of $a(s,t)$ will experience the higher growth rates of their lifetime resources and vice versa.

From equation (5.15) we see that $\bar{\bar{c}}(t) > 0$ when $R(t) > \rho$ and when $\bar{c} > 0$.[9] What does it economically mean when $\bar{\bar{c}}(t)$ is larger than zero? To answer this question we have to consider how the elasticity of intertemporal substitution varies with the level of consumption. Denoting this elasticity by $\varepsilon(c)$, our assumption of HARA preferences implies that $\varepsilon(c)$ is given by

$$\varepsilon(c) = -\frac{u'(c)}{u''(c)c} = \frac{c - \bar{c}\sigma/\beta}{\sigma c}.$$

When required consumption levels $\bar{c}\sigma/\beta$ are positive (which requires that also $\sigma > 0$) the agents with high lifetime income exhibit a higher elasticity of intertemporal substitution. This implies a rich household will be more willing to shift consumption due to changes in interest rates, and will therefore follow a steeper consumption path. Hence a rich household will save relatively more than a poor household. The poor have a low elasticity of intertemporal substitution as the positive subsistence level forces them to start with a relatively high level of consumption and a correspondingly low amount of savings. As a result, the economy will experience *divergence in the distribution of lifetime income*.

Hence our analysis yields results that are very similar to the infinite horizon model studied in chapter 3. For instance, equation (5.13) derived

---

[9]To see this, note that

$$\bar{\bar{c}}(t) = \frac{\sigma\bar{c}}{\beta}\left(1 - \left(\int_t^\infty e^{\left[\bar{R}(v) - \rho(v-t)\right]/\sigma - \bar{R}(v) - p(v-t)}\,dv\right)^{-1}\int_t^\infty e^{-\left(\bar{R}(v) + p(v-t)\right)}\,dv\right).$$

When $R(t) > \rho$ we have $\int_t^\infty e^{\left[\bar{R}(v) - \rho(v-t)\right]/\sigma - \bar{R}(v) - p(v-t)}\,dv \geq \int_t^\infty e^{-\left(\bar{R}(v) + p(v-t)\right)}\,dv$, from which the claim $\bar{\bar{c}}(t) > 0$ follows immediately.

above is akin to the consumption function (3.8) derived for infinitely lived households in chapter 3. As a result, the evolution of the population-wide distribution of lifetime incomes is qualitatively the same as in the infinite horizon case.[10]

It is important to note at this point that, unlike in the infinite horizon setting, preference parameters alone do not determine the evolution of the distribution of lifetime wealth. Our discussion so far has assumed that the interest rate exceeds the rate of time preference $R(t) > \rho$. In the transition toward the steady state, this will always be the case in the infinite horizon model studied in chapter 3 (as long as the economy grows, i.e., approaches the steady state from below). However, in the finite horizon model, depending on parameter values, the steady-state interest rate may well be smaller than the rate of time preference. Provided the economy starts with a sufficiently low aggregate capital stock K, the transition process can then be characterized as follows. Initially the interest rate is large and exceeds the rate of time preference. Once capital accumulation has proceeded for a sufficiently long period, the interest rate may fall short of the rate of time preferences. As long as $R(t) > \rho$ the distribution of lifetime incomes diverges, but as soon as $R_t \leq \rho$ signs reverse. All households find it optimal to choose a falling consumption path. Because of their smaller elasticities of intertemporal substitution, poor agents choose a flatter consumption path than the rich and, as a consequence, they save more and let consumption fall less quickly. This leads to *convergence in the distribution of lifetime wealth*.

In sum, inequality may initially be small; then increase during the process of capital accumulation; fall again when the capital stock has reached a critical level; and settle at a low level as the economy reaches its steady state. In other words, the Blanchard (1985) OLG model may feature a situation where inequality follows an inverted U, i.e., a Kuznets curve. Note that a dynamically inefficient economy will always have such a transition path as, in that case, $R^* < 0 < \rho$. However, dynamic inefficiency is only a sufficient but not a necessary condition for an inverted U, as we may have $0 < R^* < \rho$.

Finally, note that our discussion has concentrated on HARA preferences that have a minimum required consumption level $\bar{c} > 0$ and $\sigma > 0$. This implies that the elasticity of intertemporal substitution is an increasing

---

[10]The question may arise why the changing composition of population (some households die, new households come along) has no impact on the population-wide distribution of lifetime resources. The reason is that in steady state the distribution of disappearing households' wealth—new households have no wealth—is constant over time. Of course, should the birth or death rate change, wealth and income inequality would both change along demographic transitional paths.

function of the consumption level. When $\bar{c} < 0$ the opposite is the case. For all HARA utility functions—other than those where $\bar{c} > 0$—there is *convergence* (*divergence*) in the distribution of lifetime resources in an economy where $R(t) > (<)\rho$. The transition path either converges or follows a U. We have not focused on this case because it features increasing absolute risk aversion, behavior that is not particularly realistic from an empirical point of view.

5.2.3 Distribution of Wealth within and between Generations

In our version of Blanchard's (1985) OLG model there is heterogeneity between households for two reasons. On the one hand, households are different at birth. Some are "rich," i.e., endowed with a high amount of labor; others are "poor," i.e., endowed with only a little labor. While individuals are endowed with no capital at birth, saving for old age lets them accumulate wealth—which may or may not amplify innate inequalities. On the other hand, currently alive households differ in age. Young individuals are endowed with labor but inherit no capital. Old individuals own capital. This raises the issue of inequalities that may arise as a matter of age.

Let us first study the evolution of inequality *within a generation.* Clearly, at birth the extent of inequality is determined by the (exogenously) given distribution of labor endowments. So let us consider two individuals of the same generation who differ in their labor endowment. At date of birth, both individuals own zero amount of the accumulated factor, hence the distribution of lifetime resources is given by the distribution of the non-accumulated factor. The distribution of human wealth h is persistent over time, since the l endowments decline at the same rate α for all individuals; therefore l and h are proportional. Whether or not there is convergence or divergence depends on who has the higher growth rate of assets. The answer to this question is the same as in the previous subsection. There, divergence occurs as long as $R > \rho$ (when the utility function has $\bar{c} > 0$). In that case inequality within generations increases over time. Put differently, at a given point in time, older cohorts have a more unequal distribution. Furthermore, we note that consumption inequality (at a given point in time) is determined entirely by the wealth inequality, since the consumption function (5.13) is linear in wealth. Hence within-cohort consumption inequality will rise over time. This follows immediately from the Euler equation (5.12).

It remains to study the dynamics of inequality *between generations.* Obviously, generations with higher average wealth will exhibit a higher growth rate as long as there is divergence in the wealth distribution. Since all generations have the same time horizon, the dynamics of wealth distribution within and between cohorts must remain the same over time. However, we cannot tell whether the old cohorts have higher wealth than the young. On the one hand the young generation owns little capital; on the other hand they have a higher endowment of the non-accumulated factor (on average). In particular, if α is very high, the lifetime resources of the old may be lower. Note that lifetime resources may even decrease in a generation's lifetime although the consumption path has a positive slope (if $R > \rho$), since the coefficients $\bar{\bar{c}}(t)$ and $\hat{c}(t)$ of the consumption function (5.13) change over time.

As in the simple two-period OLG model, the steady state is also characterized by social mobility, i.e., by a situation where individuals change their position in the distribution of lifetime wealth. When the steady-state interest rate exceeds the rate of time preference $R^* > \rho$, within-generation inequality increases over time (both in consumption and in lifetime resources) as long as $\bar{c} > 0$. Furthermore, in the steady state we can also make a clear statement as to how between-generation inequality evolves over time. Since $\bar{\bar{c}}$ and $\hat{c}$ are constant in steady state, the consumption function (5.13) also implies that higher consumption must be associated with a higher level of wealth over time. Hence, as long as $R^* > \rho$, older cohorts have a higher growth rate of wealth than the young cohorts.

5.3 One-Period Lifetimes and Bequests

Overlapping generation models feature the important motive of saving for old age. Both models of the last two sections have assumed away any other motive that may lead individuals to sacrifice current consumption. While this highlights the consequences of one important saving motive for the dynamics of the income and wealth distribution, it abstracts from a savings motive that is at least equally important for understanding such dynamics: inheritance and bequests.

In this section we analyze a different and also very tractable class of simple dynamic models in which savings are determined on the basis of optimal behavior of non-overlapping generations linked by bequests. As we are not interested in life cycle savings, we simply assume that individuals are active only for one period. Newborn individuals are endowed with l units of the non-accumulated factor. l may differ between individuals but is assumed to stay constant over time. In contrast to the standard OLG models discussed above, we assume that now newborn individuals also inherit a bequest of amount k_t from their parents. During their active period they earn labor income $W_t l$ and capital income $R_t k_t$. Lifetime resources then are equal to $W_t l + (1 + R_t)k_t$. At the end of their life individuals consume c_t and leave a bequest k_{t+1} to their heirs.

This decision problem can be written as

$$\max_{c_t} \left\{ u(c_t) + \frac{1}{1+\rho} v\left(k_{t+1}\right) \right\} \text{ s.t. } k_{t+1} = (1 + R_t)k_t + W_t l_t - c_t, \quad (5.19)$$

where $v(\cdot)$ represents the utility from bequeathing resources to their offspring.

There are essentially two different ways to think about the intergenerational links represented by the function $v(\cdot)$. First, as in Barro (1974), parents may directly care about the welfare of their children; $v\left(k_{t+1}\right)$ then is defined by

$$v\left(k_{t+1}\right) = \max_{c_{t+1}} \left\{ u(c_{t+1}) + \frac{1}{1+\rho} v\left(k_{t+2}\right) \right\} \quad (5.20)$$

$$\text{s.t. } k_{t+2} = (1 + R_{t+1})k_{t+1} + W_{t+1} l - c_{t+1}. \quad (5.21)$$

Iterating this relationship forward, the problem boils down to the infinite horizon optimal-savings problem discussed in chapter 1. If $v(\cdot)$ directly accounts for the utility of the children, it can be interpreted as the value function of an infinitely lived individual's problem, which indeed has to satisfy a recursive Bellman equation in the form (5.20). Intergenerational links are strongest in this case and very wide-ranging because children care about the welfare of their own children and the parents care about the welfare of their children, the parents also care about their grandchildren, and so on. Hence, when the objective function of each generation is a weighted average of their own utility from consumption and their offsprings' utility from consumption, the above argument suggests that generations are perfectly intertemporally linked and parents—though only active for one period—optimize on behalf of the whole as yet unborn dynasty. This specification of the bequest motive (somewhat ironically in the context of the present chapter's focus on finite lifetimes) provides a microfoundation of the infinite horizon optimal-savings model.

The other polar case is the interpretation of $v(\cdot)$ as "warm glow" (see Andreoni 1989), whereby parents enjoy giving bequests to their children and draw utility directly from the size of the bequest. Note that, with a pure warm-glow motive, parents do not care about the income of their children: what matters is the size of k_{t+1}.

The following exposition concentrates on this pure warm-glow motive of savings. To keep the analysis simple and tractable, it is useful to assume that $v(\cdot)$ takes—up to an affine linear transformation—the same form as

$u(\cdot)$.[11] To ensure that aggregate savings are independent of the income and wealth distribution, we again assume that preferences satisfy the HARA properties. Furthermore we allow different minimum levels $\bar{c}$ and $\bar{k}$ for consumption and bequests, respectively. The utility function is then given by

$$u(c_t) + v(k_{t+1}) = \frac{1}{1-\sigma}\left(\frac{\beta c_t}{\sigma} - \bar{c}\right)^{1-\sigma} + \frac{1}{1-\sigma}\frac{1}{1+\rho}\left(\frac{\beta k_{t+1}}{\sigma} - \bar{k}\right)^{1-\sigma}.$$

Individuals seek to maximize this objective function subject to the lifetime budget constraint

$$W_t l + (1 + R_t)k_t \geq c_t + k_{t+1}.$$

The first-order condition to this problem is then given by

$$\left(\frac{\beta c_t}{\sigma} - \bar{c}\right)^{-\sigma} = \frac{1}{1+\rho}\left(\frac{\beta k_{t+1}}{\sigma} - \bar{k}\right)^{-\sigma}.$$

Inserting this latter expression into the lifetime budget constraint yields the optimal levels of consumption c_t and bequests k_{t+1}. They are given by

$$c_t = \frac{(1+\rho)^{\frac{1}{\sigma}}}{1+(1+\rho)^{\frac{1}{\sigma}}}\left[(1+R_t)k_t + W_t l\right] + \frac{\sigma}{\beta}\frac{\bar{c} - (1+\rho)^{\frac{1}{\sigma}}\bar{k}}{1+(1+\rho)^{\frac{1}{\sigma}}} \qquad (5.22)$$

$$k_{t+1} = \frac{1}{1+(1+\rho)^{\frac{1}{\sigma}}}\left[(1+R_t)k_t + W_t l\right] - \frac{\sigma}{\beta}\frac{\bar{c} - (1+\rho)^{\frac{1}{\sigma}}\bar{k}}{1+(1+\rho)^{\frac{1}{\sigma}}}.$$

Equation (5.22) shows the familiar result that the optimal consumption level c_t is linear in lifetime income and, consequently, aggregate savings do not depend on the distribution of lifetime resources across families. We also see that the propensity to consume out of lifetime resources depends only on the rate of time preference ρ and the elasticity of marginal utility σ. Most notably, the propensity to consume is independent of the interest rate. When there is a sufficiently large (positive) required consumption level $\bar{c}$, individual (and aggregate) consumption functions have a positive

---

[11]A slightly different formalization of the "warm-glow" motive also exists, used e.g., in Galor and Zeira (1993). They assume that $V(k_{t+1}) = u((1 + R_{t+1})k_{t+1})$, i.e., the parents care how much the children may consume with the bequest. In some sense, this formulation is between the "pure" warm-glow and the welfare motive. However, it is arbitrary to let parents care about their offsprings' utility from capital income but not about the income of the non-accumulated factor $W_{t+1}l$.

intercept. The optimal bequest levels k_{t+1} (being the residual of lifetime resources) mirror the optimum consumption choice.

Comparing these solutions with the OLG model above, we see two important differences: first, in the standard OLG individual consumption choices are independent of the current interest rate R_t. This is because individuals do not inherit accumulated factors when they are born, hence the initial capital stock k_t and accumulated factor income $R_t k_t$ equal zero irrespective of the current interest rate. This is different in the present model where lifetime resources consist not only of the income flow that results from the non-accumulated factor endowment $W_t l$ but also of inherited wealth and the resulting income flow $(1 + R_t) k_t$.

Second, in the standard OLG model, the next period's interest rate R_{t+1} determines the consumption choice via income and substitution effects. This is because consumption possibilities depend on tomorrow's value of today's savings $c_{t+1} = (1 + R_{t+1}) s_t$. In contrast, in the present model the future interest rate does not play a role for consumption and savings. This would only be the case if the parent's objective function did not depend directly on forgone consumption k_t but only on the value of the bequest including its return next period. Such a return-inclusive formulation of the bequest motive would imply that the bequest part of the objective function becomes $v\left[(1 + R_{t+1})k_{t+1}\right]$. Such an assumption implies somewhat stronger intergenerational links: parents do not only enjoy bequeathing as such, but also care about the increase in the *level* of lifetime resources available to their heirs as a result of the bequest. Hence such determinants of lifetime utility parents maximize

$$u(c_t) + v\left[(1 + R_{t+1})k_{t+1}\right] = \frac{1}{1 - \sigma}\left(\frac{\beta c_t}{\sigma} - \bar{c}\right)^{1-\sigma}$$
$$+ \frac{1}{1 - \sigma}\frac{1}{1 + \rho}\left(\frac{\beta(1 + R_{t+1})k_{t+1}}{\sigma} - \bar{k}\right)^{1-\sigma}$$

subject to the budget constraint specified above. The following exercise asks you to show that, with such a "return-inclusive" specification of the bequest motive, the optimal savings problem closely resembles the optimal savings solution in the two-period OLG framework.

EXERCISE 19 Show that, when $\bar{c} = \bar{k}$, the resulting optimal levels of consumption c_t and savings (bequests) k_{t+1} are given by

$$s_t = \frac{(1+R_{t+1})^{\frac{1-\sigma}{\sigma}}}{(1+\rho)^{\frac{1}{\sigma}} + (1+R_{t+1})^{\frac{1-\sigma}{\sigma}}} \left[W_t l + (1+R_t)k_t \right]$$

$$- \bar{c} \frac{\sigma}{\beta} \frac{(1+R_{t+1})^{\frac{1}{\sigma}} - (1+\rho)^{\frac{1}{\sigma}}}{(1+R_{t+1})^{\frac{1}{\sigma}} + (1+\rho)^{\frac{1}{\sigma}}(1+R_{t+1})}.$$

Compare this solution to the one in the two-period OLG model.

We further note that whether or not the parents' objective function includes the value of the bequest at the end of the parents' life or the end of their heirs' life is irrelevant if preferences are logarithmic ($\sigma = 1$ and $\bar{c} = \bar{k} = 0$). With logarithmic utility, the interest rate R_{t+1} plays no role for the savings decision as income and substitution effectively cancel each other.

There is a further nice analogy here. Note that, using the definitions $y_t = W_t l + R_t k_t$ we can rewrite (5.22) to get

$$c_t = \frac{\sigma}{\beta} \frac{\bar{c} - (1+\rho)^{\frac{1}{\sigma}} \bar{k}}{1 + (1+\rho)^{\frac{1}{\sigma}}} + \frac{(1+\rho)^{\frac{1}{\sigma}}}{1 + (1+\rho)^{\frac{1}{\sigma}}} \left[y_t + k_t \right].$$

The model studied presents a simple microfoundation of the ad hoc consumption function $c^i = \bar{c} + \hat{c} y^i + \tilde{c} k^i$, with

$$\bar{c} = \frac{\sigma}{\beta} \frac{\bar{c} - (1+\rho)^{\frac{1}{\sigma}} \bar{k}}{1 + (1+\rho)^{\frac{1}{\sigma}}} \quad \text{and} \quad \hat{c} = \tilde{c} = \frac{(1+\rho)^{\frac{1}{\sigma}}}{1 + (1+\rho)^{\frac{1}{\sigma}}}.$$

The marginal propensities to consume out of income and wealth are equal because the agent lives only one period. The limited time horizon provided by the simple bequest motive induces individuals' consumption to follow actual rather than permanent income. (The period, of course, is long: one lifetime.) If the parents care about the welfare of their offspring instead, we saw above that consumption is determined by forward-looking behavior, that is by the present value of lifetime income of all members in the dynasty.

Before discussing the evolution of the distribution of accumulated wealth in this model, it is necessary to describe the evolution of factor rewards W_t and R_t. To perform this task, we first derive the aggregate capital accumulation equation, and then characterize the steady state. From (5.22) it is straightforward to derive the aggregate capital stock K_t. Note that the aggregate size of the non-accumulated factor L is normalized to one.

$$K_{t+1} = \frac{1}{1+(1+\rho)^{\frac{1}{\sigma}}} [(1+R_t)K_t + W_t L] - \frac{\sigma}{\beta} \frac{\bar{c} - (1+\rho)^{\frac{1}{\sigma}}\bar{k}}{1+(1+\rho)^{\frac{1}{\sigma}}} \quad (5.23)$$

$$= \frac{Y_t + K_t}{1+(1+\rho)^{\frac{1}{\sigma}}} - \frac{\sigma}{\beta} \frac{\bar{c} - (1+\rho)^{\frac{1}{\sigma}}\bar{k}}{1+(1+\rho)^{\frac{1}{\sigma}}}.$$

The steady state exists[12] (and is stable) if $(\partial Y_t/\partial K_t + 1)/(1+(1+\rho)^{\frac{1}{\sigma}}) <$ 1, or, equivalently, $R_t - (1+\rho)^{\frac{1}{\sigma}} < 0$.

It remains to determine the dynamics of the individual capital stock k_t. We calculate from (5.22) $\Delta k_{t+1} = k_{t+1} - k_t$ and divide by k_t to get the growth rate of accumulated wealth by a family

$$\frac{\Delta k_{t+1}}{k_t} = \frac{R_t - (1+\rho)^{\frac{1}{\sigma}}}{1+(1+\rho)^{\frac{1}{\sigma}}} + \frac{W_t l - \frac{\sigma}{\beta}\left[\bar{c} - (1+\rho)^{\frac{1}{\sigma}}\bar{k}\right]}{1+(1+\rho)^{\frac{1}{\sigma}}} \cdot \frac{1}{k_t}. \quad (5.24)$$

For reasons mentioned above, these dynamics of the distribution of the non-accumulated factor k_t closely resemble those derived in the model with exogenous savings propensities. However, when the economy approaches steady state, wages will rise such that there will be convergence. To see this, multiply both sides of (5.24) by k_t, aggregate across individuals' set and use the fact that, by definition of the steady state, $\Delta K = 0$. This yields

$$WL = \left[(1+\rho)^{\frac{1}{\sigma}} - R\right]K + \frac{\sigma}{\beta}\left[\bar{c} - (1+\rho)^{\frac{1}{\sigma}}\bar{k}\right]. \quad (5.25)$$

As we have seen that in the steady state $R - (1+\rho)^{\frac{1}{\sigma}} < 0$, it follows that $WL > \frac{\sigma}{\beta}\left[\bar{c} - (1+\rho)^{\frac{1}{\sigma}}\bar{k}\right]$ in steady state. Hence, if $l = L$, the same for all individuals, there will be *absolute* convergence of the accumulated factor k in steady state.

When the economy is still far away from the steady state, there may be (relative) divergence at low levels of K_t even if the non-accumulated factor is equally distributed. To see this, note that for low levels of the capital stock K_t wages W_t are small and we may have $W_t L < \frac{\sigma}{\beta}\left[\bar{c} - (1+\rho)^{\frac{1}{\sigma}}\bar{k}\right]$. This inequality, of course changes its direction for larger levels of K_t. Hence, just like in the model with exogenous savings propensities studied

---

[12] Of course, the subsistence level $\bar{c}$ must be bounded if $\beta = \sigma > 0$, otherwise no steady state with a positive level of capital exists.

in chapter 2, the distribution of income and wealth may follow an inverted U, i.e., a Kuznets curve, during the transition toward the steady state.

Furthermore, when there is perfect equality in endowments with the non-accumulated factor, the economy converges toward perfect equality. To see this, consider a situation where the aggregate economy has reached its steady state, so $R_t = R$ and $W_t = W$. Multiplying (5.24) by k_t and inserting the relationship for WL from equation (5.25) above yields

$$\Delta k_{t+1} = \frac{(1+\rho)^{\frac{1}{\sigma}} - R}{1 + (1+\rho)^{\frac{1}{\sigma}}} \left[k_t - K \right] + \frac{W}{1 + (1+\rho)^{\frac{1}{\sigma}}} \left[l - L \right].$$

In steady state $R - (1+\rho)^{\frac{1}{\sigma}} < 0$. Hence, if we compare two individuals with the same l but different k_t, the richer individuals will save less in absolute terms than the poorer and the dynasty must end up with the same k. Inserting $\Delta k_{t+1} = 0$ into (5.24) allows us to solve for the ergodic distribution of k, which is determined by the distribution of l only.

$$k = \frac{W}{(1+\rho)^{\frac{1}{\sigma}} - R} l - \frac{\sigma}{\beta} \frac{\bar{c} - (1+\rho)^{\frac{1}{\sigma}} \bar{k}}{(1+\rho)^{\frac{1}{\sigma}} - R}.$$

We finally note that not all bequests have to driven by an altruistic motive such as the warm-glow motive we have studied above. The following exercise discusses the resulting wealth distribution when there is no warm-glow bequest motive but where instead all bequests accrue only because the previous generation died suddenly. We will see that qualitative results are very similar to the case with intended bequests discussed in this chapter.

EXERCISE 20 **Accidental Bequests** *(following Laitner [2002])* Consider the following framework. Every individual is born with differing earning abilities and lives at most two periods. In the first period the individual starts as a child, then starts working as an adult and raises a child itself. In the second period the adult retires and consumes its savings. The child leaves home as the adult retires. But there is uncertainty about being alive in the second period.

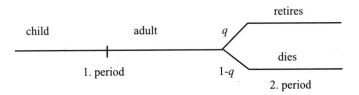

If the individual dies, savings $s(1 + R) = k$ are bequeathed to the child. If the individual is still alive in second period, the bequest is 0. The adult has no utility from bequeathing, so the bequest is purely accidental. The household's probability of being alive in the second period is q. We focus on steady-state equilibria, so factor prices remain constant $(R_t = R; W_t = W)$, but the interest rate need not equal ρ. An individual with inheritance k solves:

$$\max_s U = u(k + Wl - s) + \frac{q}{1 + \rho} u(s(1 + R))$$

a. Let the utility function belong to the HARA class and calculate individual consumption in first period c_{1t} and individual savings s_t. (Hint: The uncertainty of being alive in the second period has the same impact as an increase in the discount rate. Therefore we may interpret the term $\frac{q}{1+\rho}$ as $\frac{1}{1+\hat{\rho}}$, whereas $\hat{\rho} > \rho$.)

b. Make the following further assumptions: Production is Cobb-Douglas and takes the form $Y_t = K_t^\alpha L_t^{1-\alpha}$, there is no technical progress, no population growth, and normalize the cohort population size to unity $L_t = 1$. For simplicity assume that utility is logarithmic $(\sigma = 1)$ and $\beta = 1$. Give an expression for aggregate savings and state a condition for convergence (divergence) in the distribution of accumulated wealth.

c. Determine the individual wealth distribution in the steady-state when $l = \bar{L}$, $\sigma = \beta = 1$, and $\bar{c} = 0$.

5.4 References and Further Issues

The basic two-period OLG model is due to Samuelson (1958) and Diamond (1965). Galor and Ryder (1989) give a comprehensive discussion of existence, uniqueness, and stability in the OLG model. Auerbach and Kotlikoff (1987) use simulation techniques to study more realistic (multi-period) overlapping generations models. The two-period Diamond model has been extended to account for intragenerational inequality, primarily to study issues of optimal taxation and/or social security issues. Ordover and Phelps (1979), Pirttilä and Tuomala (2001), and Brunner (1996) introduce intragenerational inequality in the two-period OLG model and show that no Pareto-improving transition from a pay-as-you-go to a fully funded system is possible when only distortionary taxes can be imposed.

The continuous-time overlapping generations model of Blanchard (1985) has been elaborated by Weil (1989) to allow for entrance of infinitely lived households. His analysis shows that, for most results concerning aggregate dynamics, the entrance of new households (rather than the time horizon) is crucial.

Kotlikoff and Summers (1981) point to the high importance of bequests for capital accumulation. See also the surveys by Laitner (1997, 2002) and Piketty (2000). Gokhale et al. (2001) present a calibrated model with bequests to investigate the intergenerational transmission of U.S. wealth inequality. Brunner (1997) discusses optimal inheritance taxes when bequests and labor endowments are correlated. For a recent survey of issues of optimal taxation in models with bequests, see Cremer and Pestieau (2003).

The important contribution of Barro (1974) puts forth the argument that bequests can be explained because parents care about the utility of their children. Classic papers that analyze the implications of bequest behavior for wealth and earnings distributions are Laitner (1979b) and Loury (1981). Andreoni (1989) discusses the realism of imperfectly altruistic motives for interpersonal transfers. Zilcha (2003) studies the evolution of intragenerational inequality when parents have more than one bequest motive and transfer both physical and human capital to their offspring. Baranzini (1991) proposes and solves several simple models of life cycle savings where a "capitalist" class leaves bequests, while "workers" may perform life cycle savings but never care for their children.

A related empirical literature is concerned with how different savings motives affect the dynamics of the wealth distribution. For recent empirical evidence on the United States see the discussion "Bequests, Saving, and Wealth Inequality" in *AER Papers and Proceedings 2002* and Bernheim (2000). An important question related to this debate is the extent to which wealth inequality is shaped by bequests, life cycle savings, or other types of heterogeneity, like inequality in skills. A literature that is closely related to the issues raised in this chapter is concerned with the question of how different savings motives affect the dynamics of the wealth distribution in connection with uncertain future incomes. De Nardi (2004) studies implications of both bequest motives (accidental versus voluntary) and shows that the observed concentration of wealth requires a sufficiently strong voluntary bequest motive and/or earnings persistence within families, whereas the model of Castaneda, Diaz-Gimenez, and Rios-Rull (2003) relies on a combination of life cycle savings, bequests, and uninsurable income shocks. Quadrini (2000) shows that wealth concentration may be due to savings behavior of individuals with unequal opportunities to start up a business. In Krusell and Smith (1998), agents must have heterogeneous discount rates to generate the extent of wealth inequality observed in the data. Storesletten, Telmer, and Yaron (2004a) provide evidence that the earnings and consumption inequality increases with age. However, and different from the deterministic setup in this chapter, they argue that the results are due to persistent idiosyncratic shocks that individuals face. We will tackle these issues in chapters 8 and 9.

5.5 Appendix: Consumption in the Perpetual Youth Model

In this appendix we sketch the derivation of the individual and aggregate consumption. We get the individual consumption function (5.13) by finding the solution to (5.12)

$$
\frac{\dot{c}(t)}{\frac{c(t)}{\sigma} - \frac{\bar{c}}{\beta}} = R(t) - \rho
$$

$$
\Longleftrightarrow \int_t^v \frac{dc}{\frac{c(s,\tau)}{\sigma} - \frac{\bar{c}}{\beta}} = \int_t^v (R(\tau) - \rho)\, d\tau
$$

$$
\Longleftrightarrow \sigma \ln\left(\frac{c(s,v)}{\sigma} - \frac{\bar{c}}{\beta}\right) = \tilde{R}(v) - \rho(v - t) + B
$$

$$
\Longleftrightarrow \frac{c(s,v)}{\sigma} - \frac{\bar{c}}{\beta} = be^{\sigma^{-1}(\tilde{R}(v) - \rho(v-t))}
$$

$$
\Longleftrightarrow c(s,v) = \sigma b e^{\sigma^{-1}(\tilde{R}(v) - \rho(v-t))} + \sigma \frac{\bar{c}}{\beta}
$$

where B is a constant, $b = e^B$, and

$$
\tilde{R}(v) = \int_t^v R(\tau)\, d\tau.
$$

Replacing $c(s,v)$ in the budget constraint (5.11) we get

$$
\int_t^\infty \sigma \frac{\bar{c}}{\beta} e^{-\int_t^v (R(\tau)+p)d\tau}\, dv + \sigma b e^{\sigma^{-1}(\tilde{R}(v) - \rho(v-t))} e^{-\int_t^v (R(\tau)+p)d\tau}\, dv = k(s,t) + h(s,t).
$$

If $t = v$: $c(s,t) = \sigma \frac{\bar{c}}{\beta} + \sigma b e^{\sigma^{-1}\left(\tilde{R}(v)-\rho(v-t)\right)} = \sigma \frac{\bar{c}}{\beta} + \sigma b$. Replacing σb by $c(s,t) - \sigma \frac{\bar{c}}{\beta}$ gives

$$
\int_t^\infty \left(c(s,t) - \frac{\sigma \bar{c}}{\beta}\right) e^{\sigma^{-1}(\tilde{R}(v)-\rho(v-t))} e^{-\int_t^v (R(\tau)+p)d\tau}\, dv
$$

$$
= k(s,t) + h(s,t) - \int_t^\infty \sigma \frac{\bar{c}}{\beta} e^{-\int_t^v (R(\tau)+p)d\tau}\, dv
$$

$$\Longleftrightarrow c(s,t) = \frac{k(s,t) + h(s,t)}{\int_t^\infty e^{\frac{\bar{R}(v)-\rho(v-t)}{\sigma} - \bar{R}(v)-p(v-t)} dv}$$

$$+ \frac{\sigma \bar{c}}{\beta} \left(1 - \frac{\int_t^\infty e^{-\int_t^v (R(\tau)+p)d\tau} dv}{\int_t^\infty e^{\frac{\bar{R}(v)-\rho(v-t)}{\sigma} - \bar{R}(v)-p(v-t)} dv} \right)$$

$$\Longleftrightarrow c(s,t) = \bar{\bar{c}}(t) + \hat{c}(t) \left[k(s,t) + h(s,t) \right].$$

Hence we get the coefficients $\bar{\bar{c}}(t)$ and $\hat{c}(t)$ that were defined in the text (5.15) and (5.14).

We turn to the aggregate consumption function. Note that $\bar{\bar{c}}(t)$ is given by (5.15). Inserting this into (5.16) in the main text, we get the change in aggregate consumption (5.17)

$$C = (K + H)\hat{c}(t) + \frac{\sigma \bar{c}}{\beta}(1 - \hat{c}(t)) \int_t^\infty e^{-(\bar{R}(v)+p(v-t))} dv).$$

Define $\Delta(t) = 1/\hat{c}(t)$ and differentiate aggregate consumption with respect to time

$$\dot{C}(t) = \frac{\dot{K}(t)\Delta(t) - K(t)\dot{\Delta}(t)}{(\Delta(t))^2} + \frac{\dot{H}(t)\Delta(t) - H(t)\dot{\Delta}(t)}{(\Delta(t))^2}$$

$$- \frac{\sigma \bar{c}}{\beta} \frac{1}{(\Delta(t))^2} \left(\left(\int_t^\infty e^{-(\bar{R}(v)+p(v-t))} dv(R(t)+p) - 1 \right) \Delta(t) \right.$$

$$\left. - \int_t^\infty e^{-(\bar{R}(v)+p(v-t))} dv \dot{\Delta}(t) \right)$$

where

$$\dot{\Delta}(t) = -1 - \sigma^{-1} \left[(1-\sigma)(R(t)+p) - (\rho+p) \right] \Delta(t)$$

$$\dot{H}(t) = (R(t)+p+\alpha)H(t) - W(t)L$$

$$\dot{K}(t) = R(t)K(t) + W(t)L - C(t).$$

Hence

$$
\begin{aligned}
\dot{C}(t) &= \left(\alpha + \frac{R\,(t) - \rho}{\sigma}\right) C(t) - (p + \alpha)\,(\Delta(t))^{-1}\,K(t) \\
&\quad - \sigma \frac{\bar{c}}{\beta}\left(\alpha - \alpha \int_{t}^{\infty} e^{-\left(\tilde{R}(v) + p(v-t)\right)} dv\,(\Delta(t))^{-1} + (R\,(t) - \rho)\,/\sigma\right) \\
&= \left(\alpha + \frac{R\,(t) - \rho}{\sigma}\right) C(t) - \hat{c}(t)\,(p + \alpha)\,K(t) - \alpha \bar{\bar{c}} - \frac{\bar{c}}{\beta}\,(R\,(t) - \rho).
\end{aligned}
$$

CHAPTER SIX

Factor Shares and Taxation in the OLG Model

IN CHAPTER 5 WE HAVE STUDIED the dynamics of distribution when consumers have finite time horizons. In particular, we have explored the role of entrance of new households, of savings for old age (or falling labor incomes as consumers grow old), and of a bequest motive. Throughout this chapter we have assumed that factor rewards are determined on competitive markets. In such a neoclassical framework diminishing investment returns lead to a state of stagnation in the long run. Again, we have studied the case of HARA preferences to ensure aggregate neutrality of the endowment distribution. Just like in the models studied in chapters 2 and 3, we could separate the process of accumulation from the dynamics of distribution. However, while the process of (transitional) growth remained unaffected by the distribution of income, the accumulation of capital affected the factor rewards and income levels, hence changing savings behavior and affecting the dynamics of households' wealth holding.

In chapter 4 we have seen that abandoning diminishing returns to accumulation in favor of a simple AK technology not only allows us, in a very simple way, to determine the growth rate endogenously, but also yields interesting insights on the impact of factor shares on economic growth. In chapter 4 where consumers had infinite horizons we have seen that a higher labor share is detrimental for growth. This is in perfect accordance with conventional wisdom according to which capital taxation should be low to allow for a high capital stock and accordingly high incomes and consumption possibilities. We have also seen in chapter 4 that, along the balanced growth path, owners of non-accumulated factors have no need to save. Along this path, their optimal rate of consumption growth coincides with the economy-wide growth rate and the return to non-accumulated factors ("wages") $W_t L$ also grows at this rate. Hence it is optimal to consume all income from non-accumulated factors rate. In contrast, aggregate income from accumulated factors RK_t can only keep up with aggregate income and consumption when capital owners save. In other words, all savings accrued from capital income, whereas all labor income was spent on consumption. Obviously, under such conditions, redistributing income from capital to labor (for instance, by taxing capital incomes) lets the economy end up with less income out of which to save. The result is a lower growth rate.

The aim of this chapter is to study whether this implication is robust with respect to alternative assumptions on the savings behavior of households. In particular, we will study simple endogenous growth (AK) variants of the OLG models in chapter 5. Interestingly, we will see that impact of factor shares on the growth rate depends crucially on the particular assumptions on savings behavior. In this sense, the conventional wisdom mentioned above is not a theoretically robust insight. For instance, introducing an AK technology into the simple two-period OLG model of chapter 4 shows that, under plausible parameter values, capital taxation may be beneficial rather than harmful for growth. The basic intuition is simple: in the OLG model all savings accrue from young individuals who earn only labor income. Raising the labor share (for instance, by means of capital taxation) lets the economy end up with *more* income out of which to save. The result is—most likely—a higher growth rate. We will study in some detail the conditions that generate this result, and we will see that the size of wealth effects and the length of the time horizon play a crucial role. To make the interesting issues precise, we use an AK version of the continuous-time OLG model of chapter 5. This model is particularly useful as it includes the infinite horizon model in chapter 4 as a special case and, by focusing specific parameter values, is able to approximate the simple two-period OLG model rather closely.

We then return to the political economy issues of chapter 4. The thought experiment is to let government tax capital and redistribute tax revenues lump-sum to the households. More precisely we will study the conflicts of interest among households that differ in their labor endowment labor at birth. An obviously interesting issue is to study the preferred tax rate of the median voter and the possible distortions that arise by implementing such policies.

6.1 Factor Shares in the Two-Period Model

We again turn to the AK model with increasing returns. As we saw in chapter 5, overlapping generations models are not just simpler versions of their infinite horizon counterparts. When individuals have finite lifetimes within an infinite horizon economy, aggregate income flows are distributed between generations as well as between factors and individuals. The dynamics of the distribution of wealth and consumption may be quite different when households have finite horizons. To underline the explanatory importance of OLG models for economic growth, note that we can imagine—as in Persson and Tabellini (1994)—that each generation's initial resources, denoted $W_t l$ in the derivations below, depend on the previous generation's savings decisions through external effects. Then, the simple insights afforded by the two-period savings decision carry over directly to aggregate dynamics. In subsection 6.1.1 we therefore take up the point of section 4.4 and turn to political economy. A higher level of exogenous inequality will be associated with more intense redistributive tensions and, in situations where distortionary taxation is used for redistributive purposes, with slower growth. Persson and Tabellini (1994) offer evidence in support of this simple and realistic insight. Further and more detailed empirical work (see the references, further issues) is less supportive, and other theoretical models also suggest more complex linkages between inequality, redistribution, and economic performance.

For the same reason as in chapter 4, we assume that the agents' utility function is CRRA. When the economy experiences sustained growth any required consumption levels become small relative to the current consumption levels. In that case relative consumption levels stay constant over time. However, unlike in chapter 4 we consider the implication of finite lives and start with a simple setup where individuals live for only two periods. Their lifetime utility is given by

$$U = \frac{c_{1t}^{1-\sigma}}{1-\sigma} + \frac{1}{1+\rho}\frac{c_{2t+1}^{1-\sigma}}{1-\sigma}. \tag{6.1}$$

Recalling the results from chapter 5, we get the level of savings in the first period (5.3) by setting $\bar{c} = 0$ and $\beta = 1$

$$s_t = \frac{(1+R_{t+1})^{\frac{1-\sigma}{\sigma}}}{(1+\rho)^{\frac{1}{\sigma}} + (1+R_{t+1})^{\frac{1-\sigma}{\sigma}}} W_t l. \tag{6.2}$$

Equation (6.2) shows that individual savings (and consumption) are proportional to the household's labor income $W_t l$. This is the total amount of resources available to a young household, as there are no bequests. In that context, the distribution of income among production factors does matter for aggregate accumulation. Just as in the standard two-period OLG economy studied in chapter 5, all labor income is earned by the young generations and all savings are made by the young households. Instead, old individuals consume not only all of their capital income but also their stock of wealth. Aggregating (6.2) across all young individuals yields aggregate savings which determines the capital stock next period

$$K_{t+1} = \frac{(1+R_{t+1})^{\frac{1-\sigma}{\sigma}}}{(1+\rho)^{\frac{1}{\sigma}} + (1+R_{t+1})^{\frac{1-\sigma}{\sigma}}} W_t L. \tag{6.3}$$

To study the implications of this simple insight for macroeconomic dynamics, it is necessary to specify how the capital-output ratio and the share γ that accrues to the non-accumulated factor are determined by the economy's markets, policies, and technology. We again consider a simple endogenous growth economy where $Y_t/K_t = A(L)$ is constant. The interest rate is also constant and given by $R_{t+1} = (1 - \gamma) A$. Non-accumulated income is then $W_t L = \gamma A K_t$. Using these relations in equation (6.3) allows us to express the growth factor of aggregate capital (and output) as

$$\frac{K_{t+1}}{K_t} = \frac{(1 + (1 - \gamma) A)^{\frac{1-\sigma}{\sigma}}}{(1 + \rho)^{\frac{1}{\sigma}} + (1 + (1 - \gamma) A)^{\frac{1-\sigma}{\sigma}}} \gamma A. \tag{6.4}$$

Equation (6.4) reveals that a higher labor share γ affects growth via two channels. On the one hand, there is a direct effect of a higher γ as more income accrues to those households who save. This tends to increase growth. On the other hand, there is an indirect effect of a rise in γ that works via the savings rate. A higher γ lowers the interest rate. Whether the savings rate falls or rises depends on the relative strength of income and substitution effects. If $\sigma \geq 1$ (which seems the more relevant situation from an empirical point of view), the income effect dominates and a higher labor share raises the savings rate. In that case, the direct effect of higher labor incomes is reinforced by an increase in the savings rate. If $\sigma < 1$ the savings rate decreases and the impact of the labor share on growth becomes ambiguous. Still, unless the substitution effect is very strong, outweighing not only the income effect but also the direct effect of the increase in labor income, growth and the labor share are positively related.

It is worth noting at this point that relationship (6.4) turns the results we reached in chapter 4 upside down. In chapter 4 we found that a higher labor share had an unambiguously negative effect on growth (see equation [4.14]). In that model households had an infinite horizon, and earned a labor income flow that grew at the same rate as optimal consumption. As a result, it was optimal not to save at all, and to consume the entire labor income. All savings had to be raised from capital income. A higher labor share γ was bad for growth because it left the households with *less* income out of which to save. In the present framework, exactly the opposite is the case. A higher labor share γ is good for growth. As all savings are made from labor income, a higher labor share leaves the households with *more* income out of which to save.

We note that just like in the endogenous growth economies of chapter 4, the long-run growth path features dynamic efficiency, as the marginal productivity of capital is independent of accumulation. In other words, a situation where lower savings raises consumption of all individuals in the long run (as would be the case in a dynamically inefficient economy) is not possible in the present context. A higher savings rate translates directly into higher long-term growth of consumption. Furthermore, just like in the endogenous growth models of chapter 4, production factors are not rewarded their marginal product. With the simple AK technology assumed above capital has to be paid below its marginal product in order to leave income for labor. In the present context, the economy would starve if capital were paid its marginal product. Egoistic old households would earn all income and consume this income in addition to the entire capital stock, leaving no income and wealth for young households and hence no income for subsequent consumption and savings.

The following exercise asks you to consider this issue in the context of example (4.7). Non-accumulated factors must then earn a vanishing share of aggregate production if returns to accumulation are asymptotically constant. Neoclassical markets assign an ever smaller share of aggregate production to labor at the same time as the economy accumulates an increasingly large stock of capital, and it must eventually become impossible for young capital-poor individuals to purchase with their savings an ever-increasing aggregate capital stock from older, about-to-die individuals.

EXERCISE 21 Consider an economy where aggregate gross output and capital accumulation are described by

$$Y(t) = F(K_t, L) = L + K_t, \qquad \Delta K = Y_t - C_t - \delta K_t,$$

where L is a given constant. Markets are complete and competitive. Can this economy grow forever if a constant proportion $\tilde{s} > 0$ of net output is saved? What if aggregate savings are modeled using a standard overlapping generations structure with logarithmic utility functions?

6.1.1 Capital Taxation

As in section 4.4, we want to study the macroeconomic impact of distortionary policies and the political mechanisms linking distributional tensions to equilibrium distortions. There, we considered the introduction of capital taxation in an AK model where individuals have infinite horizons (and work forever). Here, we study the same problem in our OLG economy with AK production discussed above where individuals only work in the first period of their life. Importantly, we will have to specify to whom the tax revenues are rebated. Depending on who gets the subsidy, we will get exactly contrary predictions about the efficiency effect of capital taxation.

Capital returns are taxed at rate τ. The revenues are distributed as a lump-sum subsidy. Both τ and S can, in principle, be negative (to represent an investment subsidy financed by lump-sum taxes). Assume for now that the subsidy S is paid to the old individuals only: every individual living in the second period of life receives the same subsidy. A household's first- and second-period consumption levels are then given by

$$c_{1t} = W_t l - k_{t+1}, \quad c_{2t+1} = [1 + (1 - \tau)R]\, k_{t+1} + S_{t+1},$$

where the labor income $W_t l$ and the amount k_{t+1} saved out of this income are individual-specific. The net return on savings equals $(1 - \tau)\, R$, the same for all individuals.

Furthermore, we simplify the optimization problem by supposing that utility is logarithmic (a CRRA specification, with unitary elasticity). Crucially, the individual takes both τ and S_{t+1} as given when choosing how much to save. The individually optimal consumption choice is

$$c_{1t} = \frac{1 + \rho}{2 + \rho} \left(W_t l + \frac{S_{t+1}}{1 + (1 - \tau)R} \right), \tag{6.5}$$

whereas the individual's level of savings is

$$k_{t+1} = \frac{W_t l}{2 + \rho} - \frac{1 + \rho}{2 + \rho} \frac{S_{t+1}}{1 + (1 - \tau)R}. \tag{6.6}$$

With a logarithmic utility function, the lower net rate of return implied by a higher tax rate τ has offsetting income and substitution effects on the savings rate. The subsidy, however, unambiguously increases first-period consumption, to an extent that depends on the wealth effect of the tax-determined rate of return.

The individual choice problem does not take into account the government's budget constraint: this is appropriate as long as the individual saving decision has a negligible impact on the amount of the subsidy, i.e., if there are many individuals. At the aggregate level, however, the two policy instruments are related to each other: the per capita subsidy is financed by taxing the income RK_{t+1} of capital in the second period, so

$$S_{t+1} = \tau R K_{t+1}, \tag{6.7}$$

where K_{t+1} is the aggregate capital stock when the considered individual is old. Aggregating equation (6.6) across all individuals yields the aggregate capital stock at date $t + 1$. Taking account of the government's budget constraint (6.7) the aggregate capital stock can be written as

$$K_{t+1} = \frac{\gamma A K_t}{2+\rho} - \frac{1+\rho}{2+\rho}\frac{\tau(1-\gamma)AK_{t+1}}{1+(1-\tau)(1-\gamma)A}.$$

Solving for the equilibrium growth factor K_{t+1}/K_t, we find that

$$\frac{K_{t+1}}{K_t} = \frac{(1+(1-\tau)(1-\gamma)A)\gamma A}{(1+(1-\gamma)A)(2+\rho)-\tau(1-\gamma)A}.$$

From this equation it is straightforward to check that a higher tax rate τ on capital unambiguously reduces the growth

$$\frac{\partial}{\partial\tau}\left(\frac{K_{t+1}}{K_t}\right) = \frac{-(1+\rho)[1+A(1-\gamma)](1-\gamma)A^2\gamma}{[(1+(1-\gamma)A)(2+\rho)-\tau(1-\gamma)A]^2} < 0$$

in the second period, which is the same result as in section 4.4. Indeed, the insight is more general than the simple model considered here. Rate of return taxes only have substitution effects when their revenues are redistributed lump-sum to the same group of agents from where the tax has been taken. Any homothetic objective function leads to individual savings choices that yield the same qualitative results as in the logarithmic case considered here (Persson and Tabellini 1994).

It is obvious that, for the individual with the average labor income, the policy package has only a substitution effect. This is because the income effect of a lower rate of return is exactly compensated by the rebate. The more general message is that a positive tax rate on investment returns, together with a lump-sum consumption subsidy, makes savings less attractive. This kind of redistribution allows each individual to rely on taxation of others' savings to finance his of her own future consumption. In equilibrium, individuals free ride on each other's choices to postpone consumption. As a consequence less capital is accumulated.

To see the conflicts of interest among individuals with different labor endowment, let us focus on the welfare of an individual as a function of the capital tax rate τ. This allows us to calculate how the preferred tax rates differ across individuals. Furthermore, after having identified the critical voter, this also allows us to determine the political equilibrium. We know that, for each individual, consumption levels today and tomorrow are related by the Euler equation which, under our assumptions, is given by

$$c_{2t+1} = \frac{1+(1-\tau)R}{1+\rho}c_{1t}.$$

Inserting (6.5) and (6.7) into (6.1), and neglecting irrelevant constants, we get the following expression for individual welfare

$$V(\tau) = (2 + \rho) \ln \left(W_t l + \frac{S_{t+1}}{1 + (1 - \tau)R} \right) + \ln \left(1 + (1 - \tau)R \right). \qquad (6.8)$$

Each individual's welfare is increased by the tax and subsidy package's impact on the two consumption levels, represented by the first term on the right-hand side of (6.8). Differentiating this term, it is easy to show that the welfare effect of a higher τ is more positive for small values of $W_t l$. Intuitively, individuals who are poor—that is, endowed with little labor l—are subsidized by taxing the higher savings of richer individuals. Individuals' welfare is also decreased by the distorted intertemporal pattern of consumption, represented by the last term in the above expression. This distortion affects all individuals alike.

Differentiating both terms on the right-hand side of equation (6.8) shows that these two marginal effects offset each other if $W_t l = W_t L$. In other words, if the above welfare function refers to the "representative" individual's welfare, such an individual would prefer not to be taxed at all (and getting no subsidy). For individuals with $W_t l < W_t L$, however, the level effect is larger than the slope effect at $\tau = 0$, and welfare is maximized at a positive τ. Poorer individuals prefer larger tax rates because for them, the benefits of redistribution more than offset the welfare loss from a distorted intertemporal consumption pattern. Conversely, for those endowed with more resources than the representative individual ($W_t l > W_t L$) a policy of investment subsidization and lump-sum taxes would be preferable to the laissez-faire outcome.

EXERCISE 22 Show the above result formally (by differentiating equation [6.8]).

The situation is very different if we assume that the subsidy is rebated to the *young* individuals. In that case individual i's first- and second-period consumption levels are given by

$$c_{1t} = W_t l + S_t - k_{t+1}, \quad c_{2t+1} = (1 + (1 - \tau)R)k_{t+1}, \text{ where } S_t = \tau R K_t$$

This implies for the aggregate capital stock next period

$$K_{t+1} = \frac{1}{2 + \rho} (\gamma + \tau (1 - \gamma)) A K_t.$$

Higher taxes τ unambiguously increase the capital accumulation. With logarithmic preferences, the propensity to save out of wealth does not depend on the after-tax interest rate because the income and substitution effects cancel. Hence, higher taxes leave the savings rate unaffected. By (6.7) higher taxes imply higher subsidies to the young workers. Since the savings rate is constant and all savings are out of first-period income— because individuals work only in the first period—aggregate savings must rise. In other words, taxing the capital owner and rebating the revenues to the young workers decreases the factor share paid to capital, and we can apply the result from section 6 where we showed that a higher labor share (γ rises) increases growth, as long as the substitution effect is not too strong (which holds if $\sigma = 1$).

6.1.2 Bequests

Above we have assumed that households have a finite horizon in a particular sense. They are egoistic and do not care what happens after the period when they have passed away. However, in reality households do bequeath to their children, so let us ask whether the positive role of the labor share for growth is due to the (unrealistic) assumption that households are complete egoists.

Let us assume that households derive utility from leaving resources to their offspring. When the bequest can be described by such a "warm-glow" motive, all elements of the two-period OLG model studied above are still in place. In particular, the time horizon that underlies agents' savings decisions is still finite: they do not care what happens after their second period of life. (Things would be different when households did care for the *utility of their children* rather than the size of the bequest to their children, as in Barro [1974]. In that case, the model would translate into the infinite horizon model of chapters 3 and 4.) We also keep the assumption that households do not work during their second period of life. Note that this setup is different from the one-period lifetime models analyzed in section 5.3; individuals here are also alive in the second period.

Let us assume the simplest case where utility is logarithmic and given by

$$u_t = \ln c_{1t} + \frac{1}{1+\rho} \left[(1-\beta) \ln c_{2t+1} + \beta \ln b_{2t+1} \right], \tag{6.9}$$

where b_{2t+1} is the bequest that an old household leaves for his offspring. As each household is now endowed not only with labor l (assumed constant over time) but also with the bequest $b_{2t+1} = b_{1t+1}$, the budget constraint is given by

$$c_{1t} + \frac{1}{1+R} c_{2t+1} + b_{2t+1} = W_t l + (1+R) b_{1t}. \tag{6.10}$$

Each household decides how much to consume today c_{1t}, how much to bequeath b_{2t+1}, and how much to save for second-period consumption $s_{1t} = c_{2t+1}/(1 + R)$. Maximization of (6.9) with respect to (6.10) yields

$$c_{1t} = \frac{1+\rho}{2+\rho} \left[W_t l + (1+R)b_{1t} \right]$$

$$b_{2t+1} = \frac{\beta}{1+\rho} c_{1t}$$

$$s_{1t} = \frac{1-\beta}{1+\rho} c_{1t}.$$

The aggregate capital stock is the sum of savings and bequests. We get

$$K_{t+1} = b_{2t+1} + s_{1t}$$

$$= \frac{1}{2+\rho} \left[W_t l + (1+R)b_{1t} \right].$$

Comparing the values of b_{2t+1} and K_{t+1} we see that $b_{2t+1}/K_{t+1} = \beta$. This must hold in all periods, hence $b_{1t} = \beta K_t$. Insert this into the equation above to receive

$$K_{t+1} = \frac{1}{2+\rho} \left[W_t l + \beta(1+R)K_t \right]$$

$$= \frac{1}{2+\rho} \left[\beta + (\beta + \gamma (1-\beta)) A \right] K_t.$$

We still get the result that a lower labor share γ decreases growth. To understand the intuition consider a tax on capital. When capital of both young and old is taxed, and rebated to labor, the young gain on net (they get the tax revenues paid by the old, whereas their own taxes are rebated one for one). However, the effects are smaller than without bequests.

6.1.3 Income, Substitution, and Wealth Effects

Before we extend the time horizon to multiple periods, we want to examine the role of factor shares for long-run economic growth in more detail. Our previous arguments in chapter 4 and in the present chapter lead to two opposite results as to how the functional distribution (by taxing capital and redistribution of the returns to labor) affects growth. When people have infinite horizons and always work, a lower capital share is harmful for growth. In contrast, in the simple model studied above where consumers have a finite horizon, exactly the opposite result emerged.

Of course, the result of the OLG model is due to the fact that individuals live only for two periods and are not capable of working in the second period. They must save in the first period in order to dispose of the necessary resources to finance their consumption in the second period. How robust is this result? To shed light on this question we proceed in two steps. In the present subsection, relax the assumption that individuals are no longer able to work in the second period. Thus we allow for wealth effects. In the next section we will study longer time horizons. More precisely, we will assume that time horizons are finite but potentially very long, allowing wealth effects to be very strong. We will see that both a long time horizon and a sufficiently high working capacity at higher ages are ingredients that break the positive impact of a higher labor share.

Let us consider first the situation when agents' life cycle consists of two periods, but they work not only when young but also in the second period of their life. When households expect to earn future labor income at the date when savings are decided, *wealth effects* play a role. A higher interest rate discounts future incomes more strongly and lets households consume less and save more in the current period. Suppose agents are endowed with l_2 units of labor in the second period of their life, in addition to the l_1 units in the first period. Assume for simplicity that utility is logarithmic ($\sigma = 1$). Then, consumption of the young is given by

$$c_{1t} = \frac{1+\rho}{2+\rho}\left(W_t l_1 + \frac{W_{t+1} l_2}{1 + R_{t+1}}\right). \qquad (6.11)$$

A once-and-for-all change in the functional income distribution in favor of capital decreases W in all periods. Even when the utility function is logarithmic (and income and substitution effects offset each other), a higher R tends to decrease consumption and increase savings via wealth effects, that is, because the present value of future wages is smaller.

What is the effect of the non-accumulated factor share γ on growth in this case? With production given by $Y_t = AK_t$ the factor shares are

$$\gamma = \frac{W_t L}{Y_t} = \frac{W_t(L_1 + L_2)}{Y_t}, \quad 1 - \gamma = \frac{R_t K_t}{Y_t},$$

where L_1 and L_2 are the aggregate labor endowments of, respectively, the young and the old generation. Denoting by C_{1t} the aggregate consumption of the young generation, the aggregate savings rate is given by

$$\frac{W_t L_1 - C_{1t}}{Y_t} = \frac{W_t L_1}{Y_t} - \frac{1+\rho}{2+\rho} \frac{(W_t L_1 + W_{t+1} L_2/(1 + R_{t+1}))}{Y_t}$$

$$= \frac{1}{2+\rho} \frac{L_1}{L} \gamma - \frac{1+\rho}{2+\rho}\left(1 - \frac{L_1}{L}\right)\frac{\gamma}{1 + (1 - \gamma)A}.$$

The dynamics of capital accumulation are slower when individuals are still working when old. The reason is that part of their consumption when old can be financed out of the income of the non-accumulated factor earned at old age. Hence, the wealth effect per se tends to decrease the savings rate.

What is the impact of a change in the non-accumulated factor share γ? When income and substitution effects exactly offset each other, as is the case in the log utility specified above, a higher non-accumulated factor share stimulates aggregate savings even when individuals work at old age, unless L_1/L is not (much) smaller than $L_2/L = 1 - L_1/L$. So our analysis has shown that, while letting individuals work in the second period, and thus allowing for wealth effects of changing interest rates, does weaken the positive impact of the labor share on the growth rate, such wealth effects are too weak to overturn the result. We will come back to this issue below and we will see that what is crucial for wealth effects to become dominant is the length of the time horizon.

6.2 FACTOR SHARES AND GROWTH IN THE PERPETUAL YOUTH MODEL

The above analysis has shown that when households have a finite horizon and are not fully capable of working during old age, a redistribution from labor to capital most likely results in lower growth and may imply that a higher labor share is favorable for long-run growth. Both of these elements lead households to save out of labor income. However, the above model is very stylized and, as such, serves as an interesting example. However, it is not clear what drives this result. In the last subsection we have seen that allowing for wealth effects weakens but does not offset the positive effect of the labor share on growth.

To study the effects of different time horizons and different working patterns more precisely, and in a setting that has the infinite horizon case as a limit, it is convenient to turn to the perpetual youth model discussed in the previous chapter. Again, we assume that the utility function is CRRA and the technology is given by $Y(t) = A(L)K(t)$. The objective function is

$$u(t) = \int_t^\infty e^{-(\rho+p)(\tau-t)} \frac{c(\tau)^{1-\sigma} - 1}{1 - \sigma} \, d\tau,$$

where p again denotes the constant death probability. The individual growth rate of consumption then is given by the Euler equation

$$\frac{\dot{c}(t)}{c(t)} = \frac{(R+p) - (\rho+p)}{\sigma} = \frac{(1-\gamma)A - \rho}{\sigma} \equiv \nu. \tag{6.12}$$

The consumption growth rate v is common across individuals and constant over time since $R = (1 - \gamma)A$. Each individual satisfies the same Euler equation that would be implied by the choices of a representative individual. However, no such individual can be defined in an economy where lifetimes are finite, and aggregate consumption (as we have seen in chapter 5 and briefly see below) does not satisfy (6.12). Convergence of the objective function requires $\rho + p > (1 - \sigma)v$ or, in terms of the model's parameters,

$$\sigma p + \rho > (1 - \sigma)(1 - \gamma)A. \tag{6.13}$$

6.2.1 Savings Choices and the Aggregate Growth Rate

The aggregate level of consumption is the sum of individual consumption levels, which depend on individual factor ownership as well as on factor rewards. While individuals may differ in their factor endowments, all households earn the same rates of return $W(t)$ and R on their endowments. We assume the labor force L and the labor share γ are constant over time, hence equation (4.17) implies that the wage earned by each unit of labor $W(t) = \gamma Y(t)/L$ grows at the same rate as aggregate income $Y(t)$, while each individual is endowed with labor l at birth, which declines at rate α throughout his or her lifetime.

Denoting with ϑ the rate of balanced growth, and recalling from (6.12) that individual consumption grows at rate v, we may write the intertemporal budget constraint

$$c(t) \int_t^\infty e^{-(R+p-v)(\tau-t)} d\tau = k(t) + W(t)l \int_t^\infty e^{-(R+p+\alpha-\vartheta)(\tau-t)} d\tau$$

which allows us to solve for individual consumption in t

$$c(t) = (R + p - v)\left(k(t) + \frac{W(t)l}{R + p + \alpha - \vartheta}\right). \tag{6.14}$$

The first term in parentheses on the right-hand side of (6.14) is the propensity to consume out of wealth. Using equation (6.12) we can write $R + p - v = [\sigma p + \rho - (1 - \sigma)(1 - \gamma)A]/\sigma$ which is positive by (6.13). At date t, wealth consists of $k(t)$ units of accumulated factors and the present value of the labor income flow. At birth $k(t) = 0$, whereas labor earnings are $W(t)l = \gamma AK(t)l/L$. Current labor earnings change at rate $\vartheta - \alpha$ (which may be positive or negative), and have to be discounted at rate $R + p$. The parameters must, of course, be such that the present value of labor income is bounded, or that

$$R + p + \alpha > \vartheta. \tag{6.15}$$

Integrating (6.14) across individuals, using $R = (1 - \gamma)A$, we get aggregate consumption

$$C(t) = [(1 - \gamma)A + p - v]\left[1 + \frac{\gamma A}{(1 - \gamma)A + p + \alpha - \vartheta}\right]K(t). \tag{6.16}$$

The right-hand side of (6.16) is an increasing function of the (as yet undetermined) endogenous growth rate ϑ (as long as $\gamma > 0$). If there exists a wage income flow, which individuals take as given and independent of their own accumulation decisions, we see from (6.14) that faster wage growth lessens the incentive to save. This is an effect that translates into the aggregate. Such (human) wealth effects are key to understanding the impact of income distribution across accumulated and non-accumulated factors on the economy's long-run rate of growth.

6.2.2 Equilibrium Growth and Factor Shares

We are now able to solve for the equilibrium growth rate in this economy. To close the model, we use the accumulation equation $\dot{K}(t) = Y(t) - C(t)$ and note that in balanced growth capital, output, and wages grow at the same rate ϑ which is given by

$$\vartheta = \frac{\dot{C}(t)}{C(t)} = \frac{\dot{Y}(t)}{Y(t)} = \frac{\dot{K}(t)}{K(t)} = \frac{Y(t) - C(t)}{K(t)}, \tag{6.17}$$

or, since $Y(t) = AK(t)$,

$$\frac{C(t)}{K(t)} = A - \vartheta. \tag{6.18}$$

The economy is in dynamic equilibrium when ϑ satisfies (6.16) as well as (6.18). Equating the right-hand sides of these equations yields a quadratic equation in ϑ. Its smaller root is

$$\vartheta = \frac{1}{2}\left(A + v + \alpha - \sqrt{(A - v - \alpha)^2 + 4(p + \alpha)((1 - \gamma)A + p - v)}\right), \tag{6.19}$$

and it is straightforward to see that the other solution of the quadratic equation violates (6.15). Hence, the expression in (6.19) is the equilibrium growth rate of this overlapping generations economy. Having a closed-form solution for the average growth rate, it is instructive to compare it to the growth rate in models where savings decisions are taken by perpetual dynasties. If all agents have infinite planning horizons and no new individuals are ever born, the death and birth intensity p is zero; for wages to grow at the same rate as aggregate income when γ is constant, the labor force L must be constant: hence, $p = 0$ implies $\alpha = 0$ as well. With $p = \alpha = 0$, the expression in (6.19) yields $\vartheta = v$: aggregate and individual consumption growth each satisfy the Euler condition (6.12). In that special case, the economy behaves exactly as in the standard infinite horizon growth model studied in chapter 4. In that case, aggregate dynamics are not affected by composition effects across a heterogeneous population.

When the time horizon is finite, however, these composition effects play a role. When p and/or α are positive, the growth rate ϑ of the aggregate economy may be larger or smaller than the growth rate v of individual agents' consumption. Shorter lifetimes reduce the households' incentive to save, hence a larger p increases the aggregate propensity to consume out of the current capital stock and decreases the equilibrium growth rate. For any given p, however, a larger α induces individuals to save a larger portion of their current income flow. This appropriately smooths their consumption flow in the face of a smaller old-age labor income.

We turn to the initial question of whether the growth rate ϑ increases or decreases with a larger labor share γ. Differentiating (6.16) with respect to γ, holding ϑ constant, we find that a larger γ increases the economy's consumption-capital ratio and decreases its balanced growth rate if

$$(\sigma - 1)(\vartheta - \alpha) + p + \rho > 0. \tag{6.20}$$

Assume that $\sigma < 1$. Equation (6.15) then implies that $(\sigma - 1)(\vartheta - \alpha) > (\sigma - 1)(r + p)$. The convergence condition (6.13) further implies that $(\sigma - 1)(r + p) > -(p + \rho)$. Hence, the condition (6.20) necessarily holds. This is not surprising. A larger γ, or a lower interest rate, increases the marginal propensity to consume out of wealth, which is given by $(\sigma - 1)(1 - \gamma)A/\sigma + p + \rho/\sigma$. When $\sigma < 1$ the substitution effect dominates the income effect if $\sigma < 1$.

We note at this point that the continuous-time OLG model leads us to a different result from the simple two-period model studied in the previous section of this chapter. In the two-period model $\sigma < 1$ is a necessary but not a sufficient condition to overturn any positive impact of the labor share on growth. How does this difference in results come about? To see the point more clearly, consider the ratio of aggregate human wealth plus aggregate financial wealth relative to the capital stock. From (6.16) we see that this ratio is given as $1 + \gamma A/[(1 - \gamma)A + p + \alpha - \vartheta]$, which is an increasing function of γ. A higher γ increases the current wage level $W(t) = \gamma K(t)l/L$ and decreases the interest rate $R = (1 - \gamma)A$. This raises the value of wealth for two reasons. First, the future labor income flow evolves at a higher level *and* second, the rate at which these higher future wages have to be discounted is now lower. Both of these (human) *wealth effects* are absent in standard two-period lifetime models where all labor income accrues at the beginning of life.

The above analysis holds for a situation where the substitution effect outweighs the income effect. For the labor share γ to have a positive impact on growth, the income effects must be sufficiently dominant so that they outweigh not only the substitution effects but also the wealth effects discussed above. Differentiating (6.19) with respect to γ, and assuming that $\sigma > 1$, we see that the labor share γ has still a negative impact on growth, that is, we still have $\partial \vartheta / \partial \gamma < 0$, if the following condition holds:

$$\alpha\sigma(\sigma - 1) + p\sigma(\sigma - 2) - \rho < A(\sigma - 1). \qquad (6.21)$$

The inequality in (6.21) holds true for all admissible parameter values in the infinite horizon case (where $p = \alpha = 0$),[1] while positive values of p and α may lead to a reversal of the inequality's direction. Smaller investment rewards can lead to faster growth in a continuous-time model if $\sigma > 1$, so that income effects dominate substitution effects, and p and α are such as to make (human) wealth effects relatively small. Interestingly, shorter planning horizons need not make it less likely that larger interest rates speed up growth: a larger p tends to relax the inequality in (6.21), for fixed values of the other parameters, if $1 < \sigma < 2$. Conversely, a larger α (a steeply declining endowment of raw labor) and a larger σ (less intertemporal substitution in consumption) unambiguously make it more difficult for (6.21) to hold.

6.2.3 Discussion

The results in this and the previous section have shown that the result on the impact of the accumulated factor share on the economy's growth rate is not robust to the extension of the basic infinite horizon model studied in chapter 4 to an OLG framework where individuals' time horizon is finite and they do not earn (as much) labor income when old as in young ages. However, while the results of the simple two-period OLG model suggest that, under realistic parameter values, a higher labor share unambiguously *increases* growth, we have shown in the present section that this result hinges strongly upon the absence (or weakness) of wealth effects.

---

[1] Since labor force is assumed to be constant, α must equal zero when $p = 0$.

In the standard two-period OLG model, wealth effects are ruled out by the setup of the model, whereas in the continuous-time OLG model presented in the current section, such wealth effects are important. Clearly these effects are most important when individuals' labor income does not decrease very strongly over the life cycle. In that case, the income effect of higher investment returns leads not only to a substitution effect but also to a wealth effect that dominates the negative income effect. In that sense, the two-period OLG model, while being of analytical interest, may be misleading when evaluating the effect of factor shares on long-run growth.

Hence, in a more realistic setup where wealth effects are strong, higher investment returns increase the economy's growth rate and the political economy issues discussed in chapter 4 may still be relevant. The OLG structure of the present model enriches this analysis by accounting for the age structure of the population. Younger agents with higher labor incomes prefer higher taxes on capital incomes. However, as Saint-Paul (1992a) demonstrates, it may be that even the youngest agents prefer a negative tax rate on capital incomes, thus leaving room for policy intervention in the laissez-faire situation.

Whether or not such Pareto-improving interventions are possible, there are distributional tensions between owners of labor and capital incomes for the same reasons as in the infinite horizon model discussed in chapter 4. However, the analysis of distributional issues is different from the infinite horizon case. Owners of labor save a constant fraction of their income, which leads to a change in the factor composition over the life cycle. In other words, not only do distributional tensions arise between capital and labor, but preferences over such policies also change over an individual's life cycle.

6.3 REFERENCES AND FURTHER ISSUES

The implications of the two-period lifetime overlapping generations model for the relationship between factor shares and growth are discussed in Uhlig and Yanagawa (1996). There, and in the text, factor shares in net income are viewed as the result of tax-and-transfer government policies. A similar mechanism is at work when an infinite number of market participants lets asset prices deviate from their fundamental values (Grossman and Yanagawa 1993). Like public debt or unfunded Social Security, asset bubbles transfer resources from the (saving) young to the (dissaving) old. As each generation finds it less necessary to rely on productive capital for consumption-smoothing purposes, investment-driven economic growth slows down. The result that an endogenously growing economy must be dynamically efficient can be found in Saint-Paul (1992a).

Jones and Manuelli (1992) and Boldrin (1992) show that standard discrete-time overlapping generations models cannot feature both complete competitive markets and endogenous growth. Jones and Manuelli also show that an overlapping generations economy can experience unbounded endogenous growth if, as is possible in multi-sector models, the price of capital in terms of consumption and wages declines steadily over time. The growth effects of policy interventions that redistribute income toward the early stages of individual lifetimes are similar to those outlined above, and can even make endogenous growth possible for an economy whose income would reach a stable plateau under laissez-faire markets. Once again, however, such growth-enhancing policies affect intergenerational distribution, and a Pareto improvement is impossible in this respect.

The perpetual youth model presented here draws on Bertola (1996). Similar models of lifetime savings are applied to endogenously growing economies by Saint-Paul (1992a), Alogoskoufis and van der Ploeg (1990), Buiter (1993), and Engel and Kletzer (1992), among others. These contributions analyze the role of public debt, unfunded Social Security, and bubbles, finding that these features have much the same effect in continuous-time OLG models as in a more conventional Diamond (1965) setting. Issues of factor-income distribution are addressed by Buiter (1993) and Saint-Paul (1992b), who discuss the growth effects of capital income taxation, and by Engel and Kletzer (1992), who stress the distinction between "labor" and other non-reproducible but infinitely lived factors of production. The experiment performed by increasing γ coincides with that considered by Saint-Paul (1992a), who evaluates the welfare effects of a profit subsidy financed by labor income tax, and is symmetric to that of Uhlig and Yanagawa (1996), who shift the tax burden of financing a given amount of government expenditure from labor to capital; in terms of the present paper's reduced-form relationships, such policies move γ away from its (unspecified) laissez-faire value. An increase in the capital income share γ is also related to the exercise considered by Buiter (1993, 85–86), where the revenue of capital income taxes is rebated lump-sum to all agents, regardless of what factor bundles they own. Uhlig and Yanagawa's analysis is framed in terms of two-period OLG models, while Saint-Paul's experiment assumes logarithmic utility in a Blanchard-Weil model. As in Uhlig and Yanagawa's and Buiter's analysis, allowing for low intertemporal elasticity of substitution (or $\sigma > 1$) has important implications for the general equilibrium effects of income distribution across accumulated and non-accumulated factors of production.

PART TWO

Financial Market Imperfections

CHAPTER SEVEN

Investment Opportunities and the Allocation of Savings

IN ALL THE MODELS REVIEWED SO FAR it was assumed that agents have access to fully integrated financial markets. By ruling out arbitrage, such markets offer the same rate of return to all individuals. In this chapter, we take the extreme opposite route and rule out access to financial markets altogether. Hence, investment must equal savings not only at the aggregate but also at the *individual* level. This extreme assumption gives inequality a new and important role in determining aggregate phenomena. Since identical agents would not trade with each other even when allowed to do so, in the absence of inequality the aggregate economy's accumulation path would simply resemble the accumulation path of each individual regardless of whether financial markets are open. But if individuals have heterogeneous resources and cannot interact in the financial market, it is no longer possible to represent aggregate savings, investment, and production dynamics in terms of a representative individual's utility maximization problem.

The extent of inequality then matters directly for macroeconomic phenomena: more pronounced inequality would imply more intense financial market trade, and magnifies the inefficiencies implied by ruling out such trade. The models reviewed below predict that inequality may have important *implications for investment and growth*. In particular we will see that how inequality affects investment opportunities in the presence of self-financing constraints depends crucially on the extent of initial inequality on the one hand, and technological conditions in the economy on the other hand.

The role of income and wealth inequality for investment and growth has received much attention in the recent empirical literature. Perotti (1996a) emphasizes the role of financial market imperfections as one of the most plausible channels behind the observed negative impact of income inequality on subsequent long-run growth rates. Using more reliable and better comparable inequality data, Deininger and Squire (1998) point to the importance of wealth (rather than income) inequality for investment and growth. This evidence is further supported by the studies of Castello and Domenech (2002) and Deininger and Olinto (2001). They find that inequality in both the distribution of land as well as the distribution of human capital has a significant negative impact on long-run growth rates.

While the empirical discussion (briefly reviewed at the end of this chapter) is clearly not yet settled, the evidence points to potentially very important feedback effects from inequality to long-run growth and investment rates.

The absence of trading opportunities that tend to smooth some of the economy's heterogeneity also has implications for the *dynamics of income distribution*. When investment returns are heterogeneous, the dynamics of relative resources depend on rates of return as well as savings differences. It can be the case that relatively wealthy individuals earn relatively low returns. Then, inequality will tend to disappear for reasons different from those studied earlier in the book, where convergence of relative incomes could occur as a consequence of a negative relationship between income levels and saving rates. We know, however, that for certain specifications of individual preferences, a common rate of return could be associated with increasing inequality. Similarly, the relationship between income levels and rates of return can also imply divergent inequality when relatively rich individuals have access to better investment opportunities.

In order to focus clearly on the role of self-financing constraints, we abstract from uncertainty and do not discuss more detailed financial market imperfections, such as the availability of collateral. Self-financing constraints are broadly realistic if investment is embodied in individuals, as is the case for human capital accumulation (educational investments, occupational choices). No collateral can be offered to lenders when loans finance education. And investment returns accrue to heirs who are not legally bound to honor debts incurred by their parents. Hence, we discuss the real-life relevance of the simple insights offered in this chapter with references to the microeconomic determinants and macroeconomic implications of educational choices.

In section 7.1 we assume that all individuals have access to a conventional technology that exhibits constant returns to scale and decreasing investment returns. Under such conditions, self-financing constraints imply that the poor can realize only low investment levels (with high returns at the margin), whereas marginal investment returns of the rich are small. Sections 7.2 and 7.3 allow for indivisibilities in the investment technology. Self-financing constraints imply that low wealth levels restrict access to investment opportunities. Such situations may or may not lead to a segregated ("class") society in the long run, and we analyze the process and steady-state equilibria that will lead to one or the other situation.

7.1 Decreasing Returns to Individual Investment

In this section we start our discussion by considering the implications of the standard technological structure introduced in chapter 2 where output is produced with an accumulated factor k and a non-accumulated factor l using the CRS production function $y = f(k, l)$.[1] The next section deals with issues that arise when there are non-convexities in the available technology.

Given that all individuals have access to the same production technology, competitive factor markets would imply linear budget constraints at the individual level, $\Delta k = [\partial F(K, L)/\partial K] \cdot k + [\partial F(K, L)/\partial L] \cdot l - c$, where $\partial F(K, L)/\partial K \equiv R$ and $\partial F(K, L)/\partial L \equiv W$ are determined at the aggregate level and taken as given by each individual. (Recall that, in general, the aggregate production function $F(K, L)$ and individually available production technologies $f(k, l)$ will be different between firms.)

Before starting our discussion of situations where the returns are *not* equalized by factor markets, it is useful to note explicitly that, when different individuals have different wealth and savings levels (or different technologies), investment returns are *shared* when the capital market efficiently allocates the aggregate volume of savings across all investment opportunities. Some people invest in other people's projects or, equivalently, those who can efficiently perform a volume of investment larger than their savings borrow from those for whom the opposite is true. The result is that investment returns are equated at the margin, as individuals with high capital endowments have an incentive to invest in the technology of other individuals endowed with little capital that yields high returns. Hence the market mechanism, by providing inframarginal gains from trade, equalizes investment returns across all individuals.

Equalization of investment returns also implies that the returns to the non-accumulated factor are equalized as well, irrespective of whether or not this factor is mobile (see discussion in section 1.2). In fact, the implicit assumption in the last paragraph was that each individual has his or her own "investment project," meaning that the non-accumulated factor of production is immobile. The following example takes up this point and asks you to examine the individual accumulation constraint when the production function is Cobb-Douglas.

EXERCISE 23 Let the production function have Cobb-Douglas form and let capital depreciate completely between periods, so that net production at the individual level is $y = k^\alpha l^{1-\alpha} - k$. If investment and savings are reallocated across individuals to ensure that unit factor incomes are equalized, what are r and w in the standard form of the budget

---

[1] When finitely lived individuals face a smooth trade-off between time spent in education and working time, educational investment opportunities may be modeled directly by such a standard decreasing-returns production function $f(k, l)$ with $f_j(., .) > 0$, $f_{jj}(., .) < 0$, $j = k, l$. The non-accumulated factor l may be interpreted as natural ability or talent, and the accumulated factor k, human capital, is measured as cumulative sacrificed consumption.

constraint, $\Delta k = rk + wl - c$? Would r be equalized if l, but not k, is traded on an integrated factor market?

When markets efficiently allocate savings across investment opportunities, all individuals face the same factor rewards. Then, the linear budget constraints introduced in section 1.1 are valid, in the form $\Delta k = Rk + Wl - c$. The dynamics of individual wealth, consumption, and welfare levels are those illustrated in part 1, and the overall efficiency of the economy's allocation does not depend on the extent of inequality.

7.1.1 Self-Financing Constraints

Assume now, to the contrary, that there are no factor markets at all. Not only are individuals unable to borrow and lend capital to each other, but there is also no opportunity to equate the returns to investment by trading the services of labor. For simplicity, assume further that all individuals have access to the same constant returns-to-scale production technology $F(k, l)$. (Due to the absence of technological heterogeneity, this technology has the same properties as, under neoclassical assumptions, would have the aggregate production function.) When factor markets are closed and each production unit can use only a given individual's factor bundle, the individual accumulation constraint takes the form

$$\Delta k = \frac{\partial F(k, l)}{\partial k} k + \frac{\partial F(k, l)}{\partial l} l - c.$$

The factor remuneration rates $\partial F(k, l)/\partial k \equiv r$ and $\partial F(k, l)/\partial l \equiv w$ then obviously depend on individual factor endowments k and l.

EXERCISE 24 As in the previous exercise suppose net production at the individual level is $y = k^\alpha l^{1-\alpha} - k$. Show that the individual accumulation constraint can be written in the form $k_{t+1} = k_t^\alpha l^{1-\alpha} - c$ when each individual can only use factors he or she owns (there are no factor markets). What are the implicit wage and rate of return in that accumulation constraint?

A constant savings rate. What does the complete absence of factor markets imply for the dynamics of distribution? Individual wealth dynamics are most simply illustrated by assuming that a constant proportion of current resources is saved. Hence let us assume that $s \in (0, 1)$ is the constant savings rate, the same for all individuals. We also assume that all individuals have access to the same technology and the production function $F(k, l)$ satisfies the neoclassical assumptions. To be consistent with a human capital interpretation of the accumulated factor k, we let the accumulated factor completely depreciate after one period, hence $F(k,l) = G(k,l) - k$ where $G(k,l)$ denotes gross production. Furthermore, let all households own the same endowment of the non-accumulated factor and normalize $l = 1$. For notational convenience we suppress the second argument in the production function and write $G(k)$ for individual gross production. With a constant savings rate, the individual accumulation constraint is given by

$$k_{t+1} = G(k_t) - c_t = sG(k_t).$$

Relative wealth dynamics implied by this equation are straightforward. The assumptions of decreasing returns to the accumulated factor and of constant savings rates imply that wealth levels of rich individuals grow less quickly than that of poorer ones. In such a setting, wealth levels converge toward a state of perfect equality where all households own wealth k_∞ given by $k_\infty = sG(k_\infty)$.

Figure 7.1 illustrates the situation for a Cobb-Douglas technology $G(k_t) = (k_t)^\alpha$ in terms of relative wealth levels $k_t^i/k_t^j \equiv x_t$ of two individuals, i and j. Relative wealth levels are given by $x_{t+1} = (x_t)^\alpha$, and strictly decreasing returns to accumulation imply convergence to a single steady state for each individual's wealth. In turn, this implies cross-sectional convergence of the wealth distribution if all individuals are identical in all respects other than initial wealth levels.

If parameters of individual accumulation problems are heterogeneous, the model implies "conditional" convergence. For instance, if households differ in their endowment with the non-accumulated factor l, then all households converge to the same k/l-distribution. (There is convergence in levels if, initially, the factor k is more unequally distributed than l.)

Endogenous savings propensities. The above result of absolute convergence is more general and is not confined to constant savings rates. When factor markets do not exist, there is no interaction among households and, in fact, the economy consists of many atomistic (household) economies. If these households face identical technological possibilities and are equally endowed with the non-accumulated factor, all converge to the same steady-state level of wealth if this steady state is unique. With a *unique* steady state, it is obvious that the above convergence result holds irrespective of the particular assumption on savings behavior. The only requirement is that all households, whatever their initial wealth endowment, have the same intertemporal objective function. Note that, if there are *multiple* steady states, e.g., because non-homothetic preferences imply that very poor households do not bequeath at all (as in Galor and Moav 2004), we would get the analogous result as in the Solow-Stiglitz

x_{t+1}

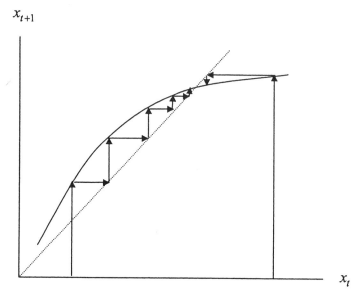

x_t

Figure 7.1 Wealth dynamics under self-financed investment

model in chapter 2 with positive subsistence consumption: households starting with wealth below the unstable steady state will end up with zero wealth—as long as there are no spillovers between households.

If the economy consists of many dynasties (each of which being a sequence of families), the optimal savings problem in such optimizing models can be specified as follows:

$$\max \quad u(c_t) + v(k_{t+1}, \ldots) \qquad (7.1)$$
$$\text{s.t.} \quad k_{t+1} = G(k_t) - c_t,$$

where $v(k_{t+1})$ is the value function that captures (discounted) future utility that depends on k_{t+1}.

In chapters 3 and 5 we have discussed the implications of various optimal savings models for the dynamics of distribution when factor markets are perfect. In the extreme opposite situation considered here, where no factor markets exist at all, atomistic families coexist next to each other, but no economic interaction takes place between them. In infinite horizon models discussed in chapter 3, the stationary solution features a unique steady state. As all individual households have access to the same technology and own the same amount of non-accumulated factors, each such household eventually converges to the same stationary state. The extent of inequality during the transition process is determined by initial conditions.

Similarly, in the OLG models or the one-period lifetime models with bequests of chapter 5, all dynasties will eventually converge to that same stationary steady state provided that a unique stationary solution exists. If this is the case, there will be full convergence also in the absence of capital markets. Note, however, that in finite horizon models, steady states are not necessarily unique. Uniqueness requires that the savings rate $s(k_t) = \left(G(k_t) - c_t\right)/G(k_t)$ does not depend so strongly and positively on individual wealth levels as to imply that richer individuals save so much more than poorer ones as to have higher wealth growth rates. With decreasing returns to individuals' investments, a situation where savings rates (strongly) increase with individuals' wealth is equivalent to a situation where savings rates (strongly) decrease in individual rates of investment returns. In other words, as long as the substitution effect of a higher return is not (too strongly) dominated by the income effect, the above convergence result also holds in more elaborate models where savings propensities are endogenously determined.

In the absence of any market interaction between individuals in the present setup, no solution of a complicated aggregation problem is required. Hence there is no need to restrict preferences as in (3.3) above. To focus on the crucial role of investment efficiency (rather than savings volume) in the study of financial market imperfections, however, it is convenient to study simple logarithmic functional forms for $u(\cdot)$ and $v(\cdot)$. These imply that savings rates are independent of returns to investment, and the convex technology implies convergence in wealth levels in the absence of factor markets. This is because decreasing returns to accumulation let rich individuals earn lower returns than poor individuals.

EXERCISE 25 (a) If $u(c_t) = \ln c_t$, $v(k_{t+1}) = [1/(1+\rho)]\ln k_{t+1}$, and $k_{t+1} = (k_t)^\alpha - c_t$, what are the dynamics of the individual wealth accumulation process? (b) Discuss under which conditions there is convergence if $u(\cdot), f(\cdot)$, and $v(\cdot)$ are increasing and strictly concave functions.

Alternatively, one might interpret $v(\cdot)$ as the value function of an infinite horizon optimization model. When the $v(\cdot)$ function is the value function of an infinite horizon model, then the dynamics converge to a unique steady state under the same conditions that would yield a well-defined competitive equilibrium for a neoclassical macroeconomy faced by the same problem as the individual considered (see, e.g., Chatterjee 1994). Of particular interest in the present context is the fact that all households converge to a unique steady state under the same conditions that would yield a well-defined competitive equilibrium for a neoclassical macroeconomy faced by the same problem as the individual considered. Under self-financing constraints, aggregate dynamics break down in a collection of side-by-side individual problems similar to that facing the representative individual or social planner of a neoclassical aggregate economy.

Decreasing returns to individual investment are intimately related to the condition determining whether growth may or may not be sustained by capital accumulation at the aggregate level. In neoclassical models where returns to investment decline toward zero, aggregate accumulation histories always converge to the same steady-state level. If instead returns to the accumulated factor are constant, or remain sufficiently large, the economy will not settle in a state of stagnation but on a long-run growth path with the growth rate being endogenously determined by technology and behavioral variables like the savings rate. Under such circumstances the reason for convergence in the wealth distribution—heterogeneous factor rewards—disappears. If returns to accumulation are constant and all individuals have the same technological possibilities, all individuals face the same rates of return and any initial cross-sectional inequality in individual wealth levels persists.

In sum, the absence of any market interaction implies that individuals can be viewed as a population of atomistic and independent producer-consumers. As long as technology and preferences are identical for all agents, all individuals will converge to the same steady state—as long as a unique steady state exists. The steady state is unique when individuals have an infinite time horizon (as in the standard Ramsey-Cass-Koopmans model). When the time horizon is finite (as in a standard overlapping generations economy), uniqueness is guaranteed by a positive (or only weakly negative) relationship between individuals' savings rates and individuals' rates of investment returns. Hence, the convergence result is (weakly) robust to particular assumptions on savings behavior. What is essential for convergence, however, is the assumption of decreasing investment returns. We will see in the next section that distributional dynamics may be completely different when there are increasing returns and/or indivisibilities in investment projects. Before we turn to this issue we will study how the extent of inequality may affect aggregate dynamics and growth rates of an economy when individuals' investment returns are decreasing.

7.1.2 Inequality, Inefficiency, and Growth

When savings are not allocated efficiently to investment opportunities by an integrated financial market, the level and dynamics of aggregate output are a function of all individual wealth levels $\{k\}$ rather than of the aggregate stock K only. Interactions between distribution and aggregate dynamics can be analyzed in a parsimonious way if the form of individual production functions and of the wealth distribution is appropriately restricted.

Consider the simple setup that is inspired by Bénabou (1996d). Assume that individuals live for one period and, at birth, all individuals are endowed with one unit of the non-accumulated factor so that $l_t = 1$. They also inherit wealth b_t ("bequest") and have access to their own "project" (a human capital investment, own firm, ...) that yields gross output $G(k_t, 1)$ where the function $G(\cdot, \cdot)$ is a CRS production function and k_t is the amount of the accumulated factor invested in the project. (The investment decision is discussed below.) For ease of notation we again suppress the second argument of the production function and denote an individual's gross output by $G(k_t)$ with $G' > 0$ and $G'' < 0$.

An individual enjoys utility from his or her own consumption and from a bequest that is left to his or her offspring. Hence, at the beginning of the period an investment decision has to be made; and at the end of the period the choice between consuming and bequeathing has to be made. To keep things simple we assume that utility of an individual born at date t is logarithmic and given by $u_t = (1 - s) \ln c_t + s \ln b_{t+1}$ with $s \in (0, 1)$. This implies that a fraction s is left as a bequest for the next generation, and the remaining fraction $1 - s$ is consumed. It is also assumed that capital fully depreciates at the end of the period, so consumption is $c_t = (1 - s) G(k_t)$ and $b_t = sG(k_t)$.

Now consider investment and savings decisions by the various households at the beginning of the period. Assume first that there is a *perfect capital market*. The total capital stock in the economy consists of the sum of all wealth that the previous generation has left for the newborn, hence $\int_i b_t dP(b_t) = K_t$. If the capital market is perfect, individuals invest their inherited wealth into their own project as long as the return of this investment does not fall short of the interest rate on the perfect capital market. With an integrated capital market the interest rate is given by $R_t = G'(K_t)$. Individuals with wealth $b_t < K_t$ will invest all their inherited wealth and borrow in addition $K_t - b_t$ on the capital market at interest rate R_t. Individuals with wealth $b_t > K_t$ invest an amount K_t in their own project and $b_t - K_t$ in the capital market. Thus poor people become borrowers and rich people become lenders. As production yields gross output $G(K_t)$ for each project, $R_t (K_t - b_t)$ has to be paid by the borrower (or received by the lender), $c_t = (1 - s) \left[G(K_t) - R_t (K_t - b_t) \right]$ is consumed, and $b_{t+1} = s \left[G(K_t) - R_t (K_t - b_t) \right]$ is transferred as a bequest to the offspring.

The above discussion makes it clear that with an integrated capital market, an individual's savings (that is, the amount transferred to the next generation b_{t+1}) does not have to be equal to the next generation's individual investments k_{t+1}. Of course, investments must equal savings at the aggregate level where obviously $\int b_{t+1} dP(b_{t+1}) = \int k_{t+1} dP(b_{t+1}) = K_{t+1}$. Since all individuals invest the same amount K_t in their own project aggregate output is $\int_{\mathcal{N}} G(K_t) dP(b_t) = G(K_t)$, and since all households have the same savings rate s, the aggregate capital stock evolves according to

$$K_{t+1} = sG(K_t).$$

Now consider the case where *no capital markets* exist, and individual investments are constrained by wealth endowments b_t. This means that investment has to equal savings not only at the aggregate but also at the individual level, $b_t = k_t$. Aggregate output is then equal to

$$\int_{\mathcal{N}} G(k_t) dP(k_t) = E\left[G(k_t)\right] < G(K_t),$$

where the last inequality follows from Jensen's inequality and the fact that $G(k_t)$ is concave. Individual accumulation dynamics are described by $k_{t+1} = G(k_t) - c_t = sG(k_t)$ and aggregate dynamics are given by the equation

$$K_{t+1} = s \int_{\mathcal{N}} G(k_t) dP(k_t) = sE\left[G(k_t)\right] < sG(K_t).$$

In general, the output loss due to inefficient allocation across decreasing-returns investment opportunities is an increasing function of the degree of heterogeneity across individuals. It is possible to formalize this insight in simple and realistic fashion by adopting functional forms that make analytical aggregation possible.

Linear combinations of normal random variables are normally distributed (other finite variance distributions do not have this property!). For this property to be useful in our context, we need to make suitable assumptions regarding both the distribution of k_t and the functional form of $G(\cdot)$.

So we let the gross production function take the Cobb-Douglas form $G(k_t) = (k_t)^\alpha$, and we suppose that $\ln k_t \sim N(m_t, \Sigma_t^2)$ so that initial wealth is lognormally distributed. Then, $\ln\left((k_t)^\alpha\right) \sim N(\alpha m_t, \alpha^2 \Sigma_t^2)$. The properties of the lognormal distribution imply $K_t = E[k_t] = e^{m_t + \Sigma_t^2/2}$, from which it follows that $K_t^\alpha = e^{\alpha m_t + \alpha \Sigma_t^2/2}$. This allows us to express aggregate output as a function of the average endowment with the accumulated factor, K_t, and the extent of inequality in accumulated factor endowments, as measured by the variance Σ_t^2:

$$K_{t+1} = sE[(k_t)^\alpha] \qquad (7.2)$$
$$= se^{\alpha m_t + \alpha^2 \Sigma_t^2/2} = se^{\alpha m_t + \alpha \Sigma_t^2/2 - \alpha \Sigma_t^2/2 + \alpha^2 \Sigma_t^2/2}$$
$$= sK_t^\alpha e^{-\alpha(1-\alpha)\Sigma_t^2/2}.$$

As long as $\alpha < 1$, less inequality (a lower value of Σ_t) reduces the extent to which self-financing constraints are binding, and increases output. We have seen above that, if a well-functioning financial market exists, there would be no reason for inequality to reduce the economy's efficiency. However, when the extent of inequality is large, output is far from its efficient level. In the last subsection we have seen that the growth process is converging toward an egalitarian steady state. Hence, in an economy that is far from its steady state, inefficiencies arising from absent capital markets are strongest. In contrast, an economy that has reached its steady-state level has also reached equality.

The aggregate expression in (7.2) makes it straightforward to study the dynamics of aggregate consumption and/or of its distribution. To illustrate the point in the present context, let the specification of individual accumulation constraints feature an aggregate knowledge spillover, as in

$$k_{t+1} = s(k_t)^\alpha A K_t^{1-\alpha}, \qquad (7.3)$$

where A is a sufficiently positive constant.[2] Then the aggregate dynamics represented by (7.2) read

$$\frac{K_{t+1}}{K_t} = Ase^{-\alpha(1-\alpha)\Sigma_t^2/2}. \qquad (7.4)$$

The aggregate growth rate is independent of the aggregate capital stock K_t, hence does not tend to decline as production grows. The growth rate may vary, however, as the distribution of accumulated factor endowments converges over time. In the simple model developed above, the economy moves toward a steady state of cross-sectional equality. Hence the growth rate increases over time and approaches $As - 1$ in the limit.

The above discussion has abstracted from uncertainties and random shocks that may cause individuals' returns and/or endowment levels to differ both in cross section and over time. In chapters 8 and 9 we will discuss how exogenous shocks and endogenous accumulation dynamics interact to determine the equilibrium level and dynamics of inequality.

---

[2] A has to be sufficiently large to ensure that the growth rate in (7.4) is positive.

7.2 Increasing Returns and Indivisibilities

In the neoclassical model of section 1, factor remuneration on the basis of marginal productivity was a logical possibility only if production functions had non-increasing returns. It was then natural to let the marginal productivity of capital be decreasing in the capital intensity of production, and possibly so strongly decreasing as to imply that endogenous growth must eventually cease. However, returns can be increasing (in a range) at the level of production units, to imply that each investment opportunity has a specific efficient scale. Locally increasing returns are realistic when an investment only pays off once a given amount of resources is devoted to it: for example, again focusing on education, learning only twenty-five of a twenty-six-letter alphabet is pointless, and learning the twenty-sixth letter is really useful.

We now study the implications of such investment non-convexities and indivisibilities and their interaction with a missing financial market. The setup is closely related to the seminal paper by Galor and Zeira (1993). Consider an economy where households are endowed with a unit of a non-accumulated factor, "labor" $l_t = 1$ (inelastically supplied), that yields income w_t at the end of the period; and of inherited wealth k_t that parents have left as a bequest for the next generation.

The available technology exhibits a non-convexity. Inherited wealth k_t at time t can earn an exogenous net rate of return R in the financial market. Alternatively, part of it may be allocated to an indivisible investment opportunity. It is insightful and realistic to think of investment in human capital, so that the yield of such an investment represents higher future labor income. Against payment of (at least) x, purchase of education ensures that labor income in the next period is $w_{t+1} = W^S$, the wage of a skilled worker. When this human capital investment is not undertaken, the household receives labor income $w_{t+1} = W^N$, the wage of a non-skilled worker. This specification assumes that educational investments have increasing returns, and lets the structure of returns be highly nonlinear: if less than x is invested in education, the return is zero, as is realistic if completion of an educational program is essential to give it market value. In terms of the educational example, learning less than twenty-six letters of the alphabet yields a return of zero; learning all twenty-six letters yields a return that is higher than the return of any other possible investment in the economy.

Clearly, the indivisible educational opportunity is relevant only if it offers higher returns than financial investment,

$$\frac{W^S - W^N}{x} - 1 \equiv R_h > R. \tag{7.5}$$

In other words, there are two ways to accumulate wealth in this model: a financial investment that yields a return R, or an investment in human capital that yields a (net) return $R_h \equiv \left(W^S - W^N\right)/x - 1$. Clearly, the problem is economically interesting only if the human capital investment yields the higher return, so that $R_h > R$. Otherwise self-financing constraints would be irrelevant (as nobody has an incentive to become a skilled worker). When $R_h > R$, however, it would be efficient to educate all individuals provided that aggregate resources suffice to do so, that is if aggregate savings are larger than the aggregate investment necessary to educate all workers $s(K_t + RK_t + W_tL) \geq x$ where s is the aggregate savings rate. Even when domestic savings fall short of x, educating all workers would still be efficient if the economy can borrow from the outside world at the rate of return $R < R_h$.

To keep things simple, suppose that the individual savings rate is a constant. Hence individual and the aggregate savings rate are both equal to s. At time t, an individual consumes a fraction $1 - s$ of available resources and leaves the remainder for his or her offspring. If the educational investment is undertaken, the family's resources evolve according to

$$a_{t+1} + w_{t+1} = (1 + R)\left[s(a_t + w_t) - x\right] + W^S, \qquad (7.6)$$

where $a_{t+1} = (1 + R)k_{t+1}$ denotes the value of one unit of financial wealth at the end of the period (including its rate of return).

In the efficient solution everyone would become educated and, provided that neither the savings rate nor the return on financial investment is too large, so that $(1 + R)s < 1$, the economy converges to an egalitarian steady state, $a_t + w_t = a_{t+1} + w_{t+1} = a_{ss} + w_{ss}$, in which all individuals have access to end-of-period resources

$$(a_{ss} + w_{ss})^S = \frac{W^S - x\,(1 + R)}{1 - s(1 + R)}. \qquad (7.7)$$

EXERCISE 26 What technological structure can be consistent with such individual budget constraints? In particular, can capital and labor be imperfectly substitutable to each other?

7.2.1 Self-Financed Indivisible Investment

Distribution does matter when access to financial markets is prohibited and investments must be self-financed. In that case it may be that, for some households, savings fall short of the amount required to undertake the high-return human capital investment. More precisely, if $s(a_t + w_t) < x$ for some households, then such households are too poor to undertake the indivisible investment. Their accumulation constraint takes the form

$$a_{t+1} + w_{t+1} = (1 + R)s(a_t + w_t) + W^N. \tag{7.8}$$

When financial market imperfections make it impossible to reap the fruits of investment in others' education, then the economy's resources are not allocated efficiently. When the required investment level x stays constant over time and when $(1 + R)s < 1$, the wealth paths of individuals who always earn different wages converge to heterogeneous steady states. In the case of poor individuals who cannot afford education and earn only w^N, wealth follows the dynamics in (7.8) and may always remain too low to afford education. In that case, the end-of-period resources available to them are equal to

$$(a_{ss} + w_{ss})^N = \frac{W^N}{1 - s(1 + R)}.$$

Symmetrically, the wealth of individuals who are initially rich enough to afford education may always suffice to make education affordable for them. Thus, there exist configurations of parameters such that all individuals with initial resources below the critical level x/s never purchase education and, if their wealth is initially above the steady-state level, become increasingly poor over time, while individuals whose resources are even only marginally higher than x/s follow a path of increasing wealth and consumption.

7.2.2 Optimal Savings

The distributional dynamics outlined above can be embedded in more complex and realistic models of macroeconomic dynamics. The study of individual and aggregate dynamics is more complex if savings are modeled in terms of optimal choices but, as usual, only slightly more complex if the objective function is logarithmic and concerns about each saver's own future is summarized by a "warm-glow" bequest function.

A simple formal model may let savings decisions be aimed at solving a problem similar to the one studied in section (5.3) above. Assume the household solves the problem

$$\max_{c_t, \chi_t} \ln(c_t) + \frac{1}{1 + \rho} \ln(a_{t+1} + w_{t+1})$$
$$\text{s.t. } a_{t+1} = (1 + R)(a_t + w_t - c_t - \chi_t),$$
$$w_{t+1} = \begin{cases} W^N & \text{if } \chi_t < x, \\ W^S & \text{if } \chi_t \geq x, \end{cases} \tag{7.9}$$

where χ_t denotes the amount invested in human capital. Note that the objective function in problem (7.9) is not quite the warm-glow objective function (5.19) in section (5.3). In that case, parents' utility depended only on the size of the bequest. In contrast, in the objective function of (7.9) parents care about the resources that their heirs have at the end of the heirs' life (that is, the bequest including the returns that accrue to their children). Future resources—whether in the form of financial capital or in the form of earnings—increase the saver's utility according to a "warm-glow" logarithmic bequest function, as in section 5.3. Forgone consumption at time t yields a gross return R if invested in the financial market; but if at least x units of forgone consumption are invested in education, then the next period's wage is W^S instead of W^N. Again, this is qualitatively realistic for many educational investments. The nonlinear (indivisible) character of this investment opportunity and the associated self-financing constraints are crucial in determining the dynamics and efficiency implications of the cross-sectional resource distribution.

Figure 7.2 illustrates the relevant (non-convex) budget sets for three individuals—poor, medium, and rich—with different initial levels of financial wealth and/or earnings (obviously, only the sum of the two matters in the present context). If it were possible to finance education by borrowing at rate R, then it would be optimal to do so. Future wages would be equal to W^S for all individuals, no matter how poor initially, and the budget set would be convex, as shown by the dashed lines in figure 7.2. The budget set is non-convex as long as the borrowing rate on educational loans is higher than (one plus) the internal rate of return of education, $(W^S - W^N)/x$.

Figure 7.2 also illustrates the properties of optimal choices. If borrowing is prohibitively expensive for poor individuals, their optimal choice entails investing only in financial assets (if at all), as at point P. When $w_{t+1} = W^N$ the first-order condition of the problem (7.9) is given by $a_{t+1} + W^N = [(1 + R) / (1 + \rho)] \cdot c_t$. When no educational investment is undertaken $\chi_t = 0$, in which case the budget constraint in problem (7.9) is given by $c_t = a_t + w_t - a_{t+1}/(1 + R)$. Taken together, this yields an equation mapping total resources at time t, $a_t + w_t$, into future resources

$$a_{t+1} + w_{t+1} = \frac{1 + R}{2 + \rho} \left(a_t + w_t + \frac{W^N}{1 + R} \right), \tag{7.10}$$

In contrast, a sufficiently rich individual will invest $\chi_t = x$ in education and a positive amount in the financial market, as at point R. The first-order condition is similar to that above, but with W^S instead of W^N, and, with $\chi_t = x$, the budget constraint is given by $c_t = a_t + w_t - x - a_{t+1}/(1 + R)$. As $w_{t+1} = W^S$ when the educational investment is under-

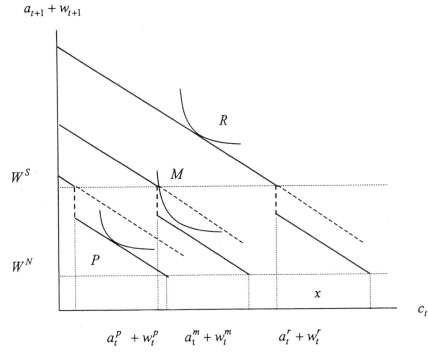

Figure 7.2 A two-period saving problem with indivisible, high-return investment

taken, resources at time $t + 1$ depend on resources at time t according to

$$a_{t+1} + w_{t+1} = \frac{1 + R}{2 + \rho}\left(a_t + w_t + \frac{W^S}{1 + R} - x\right). \tag{7.11}$$

The recursions (7.10) and (7.11) have the same slope, $(1 + R)/(2 + \rho)$, and both converge to a fixed point if the slope is below unity (see figure 7.3). Because we have assumed that investment in human capital has the higher return $\left(W^S - W^N\right)/x - 1 \equiv R_h > R$, however, the present value of resources across the two periods considered is higher if it is possible to take advantage of the educational investment's high internal rate of returns, and so is the optimally chosen value of future resources. Hence, the intercept of the recursion and its fixed point is larger for individuals who do invest in education. In fact, it is straightforward to calculate the differences in available resources between skilled and unskilled households. From equations (7.10) and (7.11) it is easy to verify that, in the transition toward the steady state where $a_t + w_t = a_{t+1} + w_{t+1} = a_{ss} + w_{ss}$, the

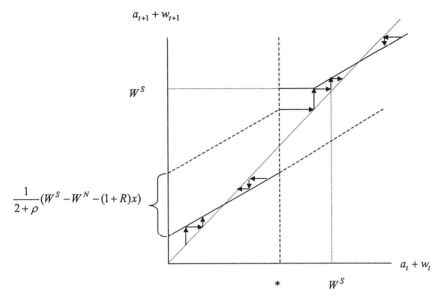

Figure 7.3 Dynamics of financial wealth and earnings when non-convex investment opportunities are self-financed

available resources of an *unskilled* household converge to

$$(a_{ss} + w_{ss})^N = \frac{W^N}{1 + \rho - R},$$
(7.12)

whereas the corresponding steady-state value of resources available to a skilled household is given by

$$(a_{ss} + w_{ss})^S = \frac{W^S - (1 + R)x}{1 + \rho - R}.$$
(7.13)

Equations (7.12) and (7.13) imply that the difference in available resources between a skilled and an unskilled household is proportional to the difference in the returns of the two types of investments, and inversely related to educational investment costs, as $(a_{ss} + w_{ss})^S - (a_{ss} + w_{ss})^N = (R_h - R) / [x (1 + \rho - R)]$. Clearly, this result takes factor rewards as exogenously given. Things are more complicated when factor prices change during the accumulation process because production factors are imperfectly substitutable. We will discuss these issues in the next section.

It is clear from figure 7.3 that only a sufficiently high level of *initial* resources makes it feasible and optimal for an individual to invest in education. At point M, $c_t = a_t + w_t - x$ and $a_{t+1} + w_{t+1} = W^S$, investment in education yields utility

$$\ln(a_t + w_t - x) + \frac{1}{1+\rho} \ln(W^S)$$

and is barely preferable to investment in financial assets only, which would yield utility

$$\ln\left(\frac{1+\rho}{2+\rho}\left(a_t + w_t + \frac{W^N}{1+R}\right)\right) + \frac{1}{1+\rho} \ln\left(\frac{1+R}{1+\rho}\left(a_t + w_t + \frac{W^N}{1+R}\right)\right).$$

Equating the two expressions identifies (albeit not in closed form) the critical level of initial resources, $(a_t + w_t)^*$, marked by a star in figure 7.3, that induces an individual to invest in education. If a skilled wage level suffices to finance investment in education even at zero levels of financial capital, then all the children of skilled workers will be skilled. (This case is shown in figure 7.3.) Otherwise, the children of skilled workers who are sufficiently poor at the initial time will be unskilled. As long as, initially, some unskilled families are too poor to finance their children's education, they will remain segregated in the low-education stratum of the population.

The above analysis shows that the prediction—established in the last section—that equality is associated with better efficiency and faster growth under self-financing constraints can be overturned if investment projects yield increasing returns and/or are indivisible. In the context of the simple example above, if the aggregate economy is too poor, an egalitarian allocation of resources would make self-financing constraints binding for all individuals. In that case, inequality increases aggregate production, as at least a few rich families are able to invest in education. Since the speed of further aggregate development depends on the initial distribution of resources under these circumstances, macroeconomic dynamics are generally path-dependent and may feature multiple equilibria.

Note further that the simple model presented above does not feature growth. However, savings decisions and distributional dynamics can be combined with standard specifications of aggregate technology to model growth. For example, an AK technology (with spillovers) and constant factor shares yield a constant R, as above. In the resulting model, the proportion of individuals who are in a position to invest in education will, in general, depend on the distribution of any given initial stock of wealth. If aggregate growth is positive, any fixed x becomes asymptotically irrelevant, and growth can "trickle down" to poorer individuals. Poverty traps do not disappear, however, if the fixed cost of education grows in step with aggregate income and wages, as is realistic if it is specified in terms of labor.

7.3 ENDOGENOUS FACTOR PRICES AND "TRICKLE-DOWN" GROWTH

In the model presented above, the dynamics of educational investments are very simple. Individuals who, initially, own sufficient wealth to educate their children will converge toward the high-income steady state, whereas households who are too poor will converge toward the low-income steady state. These simple dynamics result, inter alia, from the assumption that factor prices are exogenously given and constant over time. In general, however, factor rewards will change during the process of capital accumulation, and this may have important implications for economic efficiency in the long run. In this section we look at the interaction between distribution and growth that arises through this macroeconomic channel.

In this section we study a simple model where self-financing constraints continue to be important. Moreover, just like in the previous section, we focus on the interaction between minimum investment level and self-financing constraints. Compared to the previous section, we make two important changes. First, rather than assuming a technology with perfect substitution in production (as is implicitly assumed in the previous section's model), we assume that (human) capital and unskilled labor are imperfect substitutes in production. As labor is mobile and as all firms have the same production technology, all firms will choose the same factor intensity and get the same reward for capital. Second, we assume access to the production technology is costly. Specifically, there is a minimum investment level below which this investment is useless and yields no return whatsoever. Investments above this minimum level yield access to the production technology, and the returns to that investment are then determined by a conventional production function with constant returns to scale. This investment could be in human capital, like in the previous section's interpretation, and provide workers with skills necessary to operate the production technology. More conventionally, one could also imagine this investment to represent some fixed cost necessary to set up a production unit. In that interpretation, the investor is an entrepreneur who hires workers on a perfect labor market and uses his own labor.[3] In what follows we will refer to the conventional entrepreneur-worker interpretation.

Apart from the minimum investment level, the production technology has constant returns. Hence the assumed technology features decreasing returns at the aggregate level despite the fact that there are increasing returns (over some range) at the individual level. Just like in the standard

---

[3] By assumption, all households are endowed with one unit of (raw) labor at birth. In the model, an entrepreneur employs her own labor and that of workers who did not become entrepreneurs.

neoclassical model, wages will increase during the process of capital accumulation as increasing relative scarcity will drive up the returns to labor during the process of capital accumulation.

In the setting described above the distributional dynamics are more complex but also more interesting. In particular, the analysis yields additional insights into how severe capital market imperfections will be during the process of development, and how such constraints will shape the income and wealth distribution in the long run. For instance, the fraction of agents who can overcome the minimum investment threshold will, in general, change over time. This is different from the simple model discussed in the last section, where this fraction is entirely determined by the initial wealth distribution. Two types of steady states exist. First, the distribution of capital may be egalitarian. This will be the case if the minimum investment level is low, when the economy starts with a high amount of capital (which allows for the "trickle-down" mechanism because wages are high and an increasing proportion of individuals can overcome the minimum investment), or when a large share of agents has enough capital to finance minimum investment already at the beginning. Second, there may exist inegalitarian steady states where a constant (but endogenous) fraction of the population remains at a capital level too low to overcome the minimum investment level.

7.3.1 An Egalitarian Steady State

We consider a similar model setup as in section 7.2. Agents live for one period. At the beginning of the period, the household receives a bequest k_t from their parents and is endowed with raw labor l (which is inelastically supplied). Aggregate labor supply L therefore equals 1 in every period.

At the beginning of the period the household makes an investment decision. A sufficiently rich household will pay the fixed costs and get access to an efficient production technology. Otherwise the household has to invest his funds into a linear storage technology that, for simplicity, yields zero net returns. At the end of the period, the household decides how to distribute the available resources between consumption and bequests. Utility is assumed to be logarithmic in own consumption and bequests (as specified by a conventional warm-glow motive)

$$u(c_t, k_{t+1}) = \ln c_t + \frac{1}{1+\rho} \ln k_{t+1}, \qquad (7.14)$$

where k_{t+1} denotes the bequest transferred to the household's offspring.

The economy produces a single numéraire good, which can be either consumed or invested. Again we assume that capital markets do not exist. However, the labor market is competitive. Technology is non-convex. In particular we assume that a minimum level of investment Φ is required to set up a firm and start production. If an entrepreneur employs l_t workers, the resulting output is given by the following neoclassical production function with constant returns to scale (see also figure 7.4):

$$y_t = \begin{cases} 0 & k_t < \Phi \\ F(k_t, l_t) & k_t \geq \Phi \end{cases} \tag{7.15}$$

Again, all individuals have access to the same technology, i.e., production function is the same for all firms. Note that the production function (7.15) contains the convex technology as a special case: simply set $\Phi = 0$. The budget constraint is given by

$$k_{t+1} = y_t - c_t.$$

Every agent with wealth $k_t \geq \Phi$ will become an entrepreneur. Agents whose wealth falls short of this limit $k_t < \Phi$ can store their capital but earn no returns. (The gross interest rate equals unity.) As investment returns are strictly positive, an agent sufficiently rich to become an entrepreneur will invest all of his or her wealth into the project. This lets investments and bequests coincide and allows us to denote both variables by k_t. Finally, recall that the labor market is competitive, hence each firm takes the wage rate W_t as given. The entrepreneur maximizes

$$\max_{l_t} F(k_t, l_t) - W_t l_t.$$

This is solved for a unique k_t/l_t ratio. Hence an entrepreneur that has twice as much wealth as some other entrepreneur sets up a firm that is twice as large.

The resulting *wealth of an entrepreneur* at the end of the period amounts to $W_t + (1 + R_t) k_t$ (recall that each entrepreneur also supplies one unit of labor). Note that, under our assumptions, investment returns R_t are identical for all entrepreneurs. This is because $F(k_t, l_t)$ exhibits CRS and is identical across firms. Our results from section 1.2 imply that, when all other factors of production are mobile and the technology is the same for all firms, the marginal product of the fixed factor, which in our application is k_t, will be equalized across firms. Now consider the *wealth level of workers*. As they inherit an amount of wealth such that $k_t < \Phi$, they have to become workers. Absent the option to invest their wealth into a productive technology, they simply store their wealth. Therefore, the wealth of a worker equals $W_t + k_t$ at the end of the period.

With logarithmic utility (7.14) the agents choose to bequeath a share $1/(2 + \rho) \equiv s$ of their end-of-period wealth. The bequest dynamics

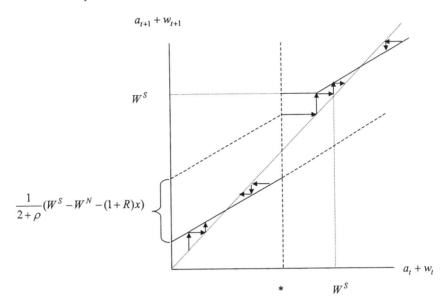

Figure 7.4 A production function with minimum investment

therefore read as follows:

$$k_{t+1} = \begin{cases} s\left[W_t + (1+R_t)\,k_t\right] & \text{if } k_t \geq \Phi \\ s\left[W_t + k_t\right] & \text{if } k_t < \Phi \end{cases} . \tag{7.16}$$

Figure 7.5 illustrates equation (7.16).

The dynamics of accumulation within a family is linear and has a slope of $s(1+R_t)$ for individuals who have become entrepreneurs, and the slope is s for the workers. Clearly, when the economy grows so that the aggregate stock of capital invested in the efficient technology increases, then wages W_t increase and investment returns R_t decrease. In terms of figure 7.5, rising wages imply that the intercept of accumulation dynamics of both entrepreneurs and workers (7.16) shifts upward. It is straightforward to infer from figure 7.5 that an egalitarian steady state will emerge if the economy is capable of accumulating, at some future period, a capital stock K^{eg}, which solves $F(K^{eg}) - K^{eg}F'(K^{eg}) = \Phi s/(1-s)$. In terms of figure 7.5, this generates a situation where the relevant segment of the workers' accumulation constraint has shifted upward to such an extent that no intercept with the $45°$ line exists anymore.

Aggregate capital in t is the sum of all capital units that are invested in the efficient (rather than the storage) technology. Let $P_t(k)$ denote the distribution function of bequests (or capital) across individuals, and

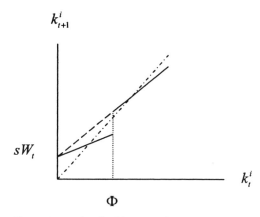

Figure 7.5 Individual bequest dynamics

$\beta_t \equiv 1 - P_t(\Phi)$ the *share of entrepreneurs* in the population. Moreover, let $\bar{K}_t$ be the average capital for agents who inherited more than or equal to Φ. Thus $\beta_t \bar{K}_t$ is equal to the aggregate capital stock K_t. Therefore, β_t and $\bar{K}_t$ determine the wage rate and the interest rate:

$$W_t(\beta_t) = F(\beta_t \bar{K}_t) - F'(\beta_t \bar{K}_t) \cdot \beta_t \bar{K}_t, \text{ and} \qquad (7.17)$$

$$R_t(\beta_t) = F'(\beta_t \bar{K}_t). \qquad (7.18)$$

In the egalitarian steady state the wealth distribution is degenerate as all households own the same of wealth. In that egalitarian steady state all households are rich enough to become employers $(\beta_{ss} = 1)$.[4] Thus we have $k_{ss} = K_{ss} > \Phi$ for all individuals in the population. Similarly, all agents supply exactly one unit of labor for the same wage rate W_{ss}. Thus all households converge to the same level of wealth, which is given by $W_{ss} + (1 + R_{ss})K_{ss}$.

Therefore workers will escape from poverty and catch up with the employers in the long run. This implies that the wage rate must increase over time, otherwise a household that inherited $k_0 < \Phi$ will never become an employer. An increasing wage rate also enables the working class to become an employer and therefore inequality disappears. Aggregating (7.16) gives

$$\beta_t \bar{K}_{t+1} = s\left[W_t L \beta_t + (1 + R_t)\beta_t \bar{K}_t\right].$$

---

[4]When initially no household is able to invest in the efficient technology, no firms exist and the wage rate is zero. In that case, the economy is not viable in the long run and approaches a state where all agents own $k_t = 0$.

Note that in the steady state $k_{t+1} = k_t$ and $\beta_{ss} = 1$. Thus the aggregate capital stock in the long run is given by

$$K_{ss} = \frac{s W_{ss}}{1 - s(1 + R_{ss})} \tag{7.19}$$

EXERCISE 27 Assume that the production technology is Cobb-Douglas $F(k, l) = k^\alpha l^{1-\alpha}$. Calculate the steady-state capital stock. Show how (and why) the steady-state capital stock differs from the one realized in the standard Solow model when the rate of depreciation equals unity (and growth of population and productivity equals zero).

7.3.2 A Class Society

It is easy to see that the egalitarian steady state is not the only one in this economy. An alternative steady state features an unequal distribution of wealth across households and a *class society*. There is a class of entrepreneurs, each member of which is rich enough to invest in the efficient technology and set up a firm. And there is a class of individuals who are not capable of setting up a firm because they are too poor and missing capital markets prevent them from raising the necessary funds from outside.

In that steady state, the fraction of entrepreneurs, β_{ss}, and the fraction of workers, $1 - \beta_{ss}$, are endogenously determined. Aggregating (7.16) gives for the entrepreneur,

$$K_{t+1} = s[W_t \beta_t + (1 + R_t) K_t].$$

In the steady state we have $K_{t+1} = K_t = K_{ss}$ and the last equation becomes

$$K_{ss} = \frac{s W_{ss} \beta_{ss}}{1 - s(1 + R_{ss})}.$$

If $\beta_{ss} = 1$ the expression collapses to equation (7.19) and is identical to that relevant to an egalitarian steady state, where each household's wealth converges to the same level. A higher number of employers means a larger aggregate capital stock of the economy.

The aggregate (storage) capital that is accumulated by the workers as a class, K_t^P, can be calculated from aggregating equation (7.16). This yields

$$K_{t+1}^P = s[W_t(1 - \beta_t) + K_t^P].$$

In the steady state we have $K_{t+1}^P = K_t^P = K_{ss}^P$, where K_t^P stands for the aggregate capital of the workers,

$$K_{ss}^P = \frac{s W_{ss} \left(1 - \beta_{ss}\right)}{1 - s}.$$

Note that this capital stock of the poor cannot be invested and serves only as stored wealth that can be costlessly transferred between generations. Obviously, the wealth level owned by a typical working-class household, $K_{ss}^P / \left(1 - \beta_{ss}\right)$, will fall short of Φ.

Under which conditions will the steady state be characterized by an egalitarian steady state, and when will a class society arise? Just like in the previous section, what matter is the size of the investment and the initial distribution of wealth. However, while the steady-state fraction of households was entirely determined by the initial distribution and stayed constant forever, the fraction of entrepreneurs in the present model is endogenously determined. Suppose that, initially, a fraction of households can afford to invest in the efficient technology. Suppose further their initial wealth is only slightly above the threshold. In that case the available resources that are saved and transferred to the next generation are larger than the ones they have inherited themselves—which causes the aggregate capital stock to increase. This, in turn, raises wages and induces households that were previously too poor to set up a firm and become an entrepreneur. In other words, *growth trickles down to the poor.* In the egalitarian steady-state equilibrium, this trickle-down process is so strong as to make all individuals invest and become entrepreneurs (each working in their own firm).

However, when the steady state features a class society, in the long run, the population is polarized into a rich bourgeoisie and a poor proletariat. Regardless of the initial distribution of wealth, such an outcome is more likely if the required investment cost is very high. In such a steady state, the very rich (whose income consists predominantly of capital income) maintain a high level of wealth, partly because of the inability of the poor to invest. This keeps the aggregate capital stock low and the returns to such investment high. Note that there is a continuum of inegalitarian steady states which depends on the initial distribution of wealth. (With each distribution, a different steady state is associated.)

Still, the model predicts steady states, each of which is characterized by a two-point distribution. Clearly, this result is an artifact of the assumption that no individual is subject to random shocks, that is, can become rich (or poor) by having luck (or misfortune). The analysis of the implications of uncertainty when there are incomplete financial markets is the subject of the next two chapters.

7.4 REFERENCES AND FURTHER ISSUES

The treatment of cross-sectional heterogeneity in terms of lognormal distributions follows Bénabou (1996c, 1996d). For a model where cross-sectional convergence occurs within an endogenously growing macroeconomy, see Tamura (1991). Convergence can occur within subeconomies, or neighborhoods, if the nonmarket interactions that allow aggregate growth to proceed forever occur within such units. Bénabou (1996a, 1996b), Durlauf (1996), and others propose and study models of endogenous neighborhood choice and discuss their implications for the dynamics of distribution and of aggregate variables.

The model outlined in section 7.2 follows the seminal work of Galor and Zeira (1988, 1993). To make its key point it is very simplified in that each individual's accumulation proceeds independently of all others and factor prices are exogenous. This may be rationalized by a linear production function or by access to external financing opportunities. Galor and Zeira (1993) interpret the model as a small open economy, where the rate of return on financial investment is given at the world level. They discuss possible interactions across individual problems in the case where the wage paid to unskilled workers depends on the amount of labor supplied to a sector that uses no internationally mobile capital. Banerjee and Newman (1993) propose a related model with capital market imperfections and occupational choice (instead of human capital investment), but they allow wages to be endogenous. A survey of the early literature on inequality and capital market imperfections is outlined in Aghion and Bolton (1992). Other models focusing on the incentives to invest in human capital include Bénabou (1996a), Galor and Tsiddon (1997), Moav (2002), Galor (2000), and Galor and Moav (2002). The latter two argue that inequality may be good for growth when investments in physical capital are more important than human capital accumulation. In particular, inequality promotes accumulation if preferences are non-homothetic and the nonnegativity constraints of bequests are binding. This savings channel may be so strong (see Grossmann 2004) that inequality increases the aggregate stock of human capital although there are decreasing marginal returns to human capital. Moav (2002) demonstrates that non-homothetic preferences, where the poor do not save at all, may generate a poverty trap even without relying on indivisibilities in technology. The dynamic interactions among individual-level savings and investment problems are investigated also in Aghion and Bolton (1997). In their model interest rates are determined endogenously, and a "trickle-down" mechanism is present by which aggregate growth eventually brings all individuals to take advantage of the more favorable opportunities afforded by their non-convex investment sets. Bourguignon and Verdier

(2000) study the dynamics of inequality in the presence of capital market imperfections when education is both the engine of growth and a determinant of political participation.

In the context of the simple model in section 7.2 above, any fixed x would similarly become irrelevant if aggregate wages grew along with aggregate capital. The poverty traps would not disappear, however, if the cost x_t of education grows in step with aggregate income and wages, as might be realistic if it is specified in terms of labor (e.g., wages paid to teachers). The point is relevant in the context of the model analyzed by Acemoglu and Zilibotti (1997), who abstract from distributional issues by assuming that all individuals are identical within each generation, and in many other models where individual returns are increasing in the size of investment, such as those proposed by Banerjee and Newman (1993) and Perotti (1993). In the latter two models, individual-level increasing returns interact with complex and realistic financial market imperfections and endogenously determined redistributive policies. Ghatak and Jiang (2002) consider a non-stochastic (and, hence, greatly simplified) version of the Banerjee and Newman (1993) model. Garcia-Penalosa (1996) studies the inequality-growth relation in a framework where the cost of education is endogenously determined.

The model presented in section 7.3 draws on Matsuyama (2003); see also Matsuyama (2000a). His analysis models explicitly the financial market imperfections and shows combinations of financial market imperfections and minimum investment levels that lead to the rise (and fall) of class societies. Similar setups are discussed in papers by Mookherjee and Ray (2002, 2003). They analyze models in which, despite convex technologies and no other externalities, credit constraints imply that poor agents have less incentive to save and poverty traps emerge, so that the society is polarized into two classes with no interclass mobility. In the model of Bernhardt and Lloyd-Ellis (2000) growth is determined by the supply of entrepreneurial skills. When these skills are scarce, credit constraints may lead to economic cycles; see also Lloyd-Ellis (2000). Freeman (1996) presents one of the first models on endogenous inequality arising from capital market imperfections.

We motivated this chapter with empirical evidence that analyzes the role of (initial) inequality on long-run (subsequent) growth rates. Only part of the relevant empirical work analyzes issues of self-financing constraints and investment opportunities, but these and other capital market imperfections are crucial to a vast body of literature, which we proceed to briefly (hence selectively) review here. Among the more recent papers that identified the extent of inequality as a potentially important determinant of macroeconomic outcomes other than aggregate savings was a paper by Berg and Sachs (1988), who were interested in explaining the likelihood of a country's debt rescheduling during the 1980s. Subsequent papers started to analyze the impact of initial inequality on subsequent growth rates. Two path-breaking papers were Persson and Tabellini (1994) and Alesina and Rodrik (1994), who both find that initial inequality has a negative impact on subsequent long-run growth rates. These findings were replicated and confirmed for different time periods, countries, and inequality indicators in studies by Birdsall, Ross, and Sabot (1995), Clarke (1995), and Benhabib and Spiegel (1994). In his 1996 survey Bénabou (1996c) notes the consistent result that inequality is harmful for growth. Furthermore, Perotti (1996a), who tries to distinguish between various channels by which inequality may affect growth rates (such as fiscal policy and capital market imperfections), also finds strong and significant effects of inequality on long-run growth rates. In his 1996 survey Bénabou (1996) notes the consistent results that inequality is harmful for growth.

This initial result was challenged by Deininger and Squire (1996). They compiled better comparable and more reliable data on measures of income inequality. While still finding a negative point estimate between inequality and growth, their results are no longer statistically significant. These studies typically used cross-sectional country data and regress the growth rate over long time periods (such as 1960–1990) on some inequality measure at the beginning of the sample period (around 1960), to assess whether inequality causally affects the long-run growth rate.[5] Subsequent studies used larger data sets and considered not only the cross-sectional but also the time-series dimension of inequality and growth. Barro (2000) uses pooled time-series cross-section estimates to assess the relationship between initial inequality and subsequent (decadal) growth rates. He finds that the negative relationship is confined to poor countries, whereas in rich countries, low inequalities are associated with lower subsequent growth rates. Forbes (2000) uses panel data on five-year growth episodes and finds an overall positive relationship between inequality and growth, a result also found in the study of Li and Zou (1998). The study by Banerjee and Duflo (2003) finds that changes in the distribution of income (in either direction) have a negative impact on growth.

Other studies have used regional data within large countries. Partridge (1997), using state-level data for the United States for the period 1960–1990, finds a positive relationship between the Gini coefficient subsequent state per capita income growth, but also a positive correlation between the income share of the third quintile (middle-class) income share and subsequent growth rates. Panizza (2002), replicating Partridge's study using improved measures of income inequality and focusing on a larger time

---

[5]While Deininger and Squire (1996) improved the data quality and comparability, serious problems of data quality remain; see Atkinson and Brandolini (2001).

span, 1920–1990, however, finds no evidence for a negative correlation. While not robust in all cases, there seems to be a positive relationship between inequality and long-run growth rates across U.S. states. Two further interesting studies focus on regional variation in growth and inequality in India. Ghosh and Pal (2004), using panel data for Indian states, find that the correlation between inequality and growth tends to be negative. Moreover, the relationship seems to be stronger for rural than for urban areas. In a related study, McKay and Pal (2004) examine the interrelationships between average *consumption* growth and inequality in Indian states. Their findings point to a strong negative effect of initial inequality on subsequent growth.

While the relationship between the distribution of income and economic growth has received the most attention in the literature, studies on the impact of wealth and asset inequality are more scarce. The reason is data availability, not lack of theoretical arguments. However, a few studies have documented that asset inequality plays a potentially important role in determining long-run growth. Deininger and Squire (1998) find that, in a cross section of countries, long-run growth rates are negatively affected by the distribution of land. Ravallion (1998) looks at the inequality-growth relationship in rural China and finds that asset inequality in the area of residence has a harmful effect on subsequent consumption growth rates. Castello and Domenech (2002) point to the importance of the distribution of human capital rather than physical or financial wealth, and find that measures of inequality in education levels have a robust negative impact on long-run growth rates. This result is confirmed by Deininger and Olinto (2001), who use both land inequality and human capital inequality as a determinant of an economy's growth rates. Analyzing cross-country data they find that inequality in the distribution of assets—unlike inequality in incomes—has a robust negative impact on long-run growth rates, both in cross section and in panel data.

Bourguignon (2004), reviewing the empirical evidence on the relationship between inequality and long-run growth rates, concludes that the available evidence is inconclusive. Even if one is willing to conclude that the majority of studies points to a negative relationship between inequality and long-run growth rates, nothing can be said about the direction of causality in this relationship, as there may be common unobserved determinants of both variables. The difficulty is finding convincing instruments to correct for the resulting endogeneity bias. The study by Lundberg and Squire (2003) supports the hypothesis that endogeneity bias may be a serious problem and inequality and growth may not be considered independently of each other.

Few studies have come up with a convincing instrument. An interesting argument comes from Engermann and Sokoloff (1994, 2002), who argue that the origins of inequalities in (North and South) American countries date back to European colonization. Several South American countries started out with an extremely unfavorable income distribution and developed institutional structures that greatly advantaged members of elite classes and disadvantaged the majority. In contrast, North American countries managed to develop institutions that benefited a larger part of the population and hence were more conducive to favorable long-run development. One important argument is that, in North America, land endowments lent themselves to commodities (wheat, corn) grown on family farms, whereas in South America land endowments favored large plantations (sugar cane, precious metals) exploiting economies of scale and slave labor. Galor, Moav, and Vollrath (2003) analyze the importance of land inequality for the evolution of institutions that favor the accumulation of human capital. Easterly (2002) borrows the idea that a country's commodity endowments may be a valid instrument for inequalities in postwar data for developing countries. He finds that inequality is a large and statistically significant independent source of long-run prosperity of a country.

Apart from searching for appropriate instrumental variables, several studies have looked for more disaggregate data to check the empirical relevance of various microeconomic arguments by which inequality may work its way. Such estimates could then be used to get some rough estimate of the likely aggregate effect on growth of various types of redistribution. Banerjee, Mookherjee, and Ray (2001), looking at sugar cooperatives in the Indian state of Maharashtra, find that larger heterogeneity in landownership (and control rights) is associated with lower levels of cooperation among farmers, leading to lower sugarcane prices and output. Other studies, such as Bourguignon, Ferreira, and Leite (2003), have shown that "smart transfer" programs were successful in increasing school enrollment rates and health conditions of low-income families, pointing to the importance of liquidity constraints and capital market imperfections.

Theoretical and empirical work has brought the insights outlined in this chapter to bear on politico-economic interactions. When the status quo cross-sectional allocation of savings is distorted by self-financing constraints, a more equal distribution improves the efficiency of investment allocation, and is associated with higher output levels (or faster growth). If there are many political instruments available, such as it is possible to target both efficiency and distribution separately, then aggregate outcomes are much less likely to be affected by inequality, and distributional issues can be separated from macroeconomic performance in much the same way as in the complete markets case. Most relevantly, investment efficiency can be preserved by appropriately targeted subsidies even as politico-economic determination of tax rates pursues distributional objectives. Human capital accumulation is most likely to be distorted by self-financing constraints and uninsurability, and is often targeted by policy interventions (see Glomm and Ravikumar [1992] for a simple model of the implications of private or public education schemes for growth and distribution). Efficiency can be pursued by education subsidies (or by state-financed education) as well as by progressive taxation schemes, and individual agents, regardless of their income level, all benefit from better efficiency: this objective does not interfere with heterogeneous incentives to redistribute income when the latter can be pursued by a separate instrument, and redistribution can have beneficial effects on representative-agent welfare when it substitutes missing markets.

As the efficiency benefits of redistribution depend on the extent of inequality, but only the relatively poor ones gain from the redistributive aspects of investment subsidies, political support for such redistributive policies as education subsidies is generally not a monotonic function of status quo inequality. In the models proposed by Bénabou (1996c, 1996d), which introduce tractable specifications of tax and subsidy schemes in log-linear budget constraints, the relative importance of efficiency-enhancing and redistributive effects in political interactions depends on the dispersion and skewness of income distribution, and on the distribution of political power across income levels. Moreover, since policies that affect ex post inequality feed back into their own political sustainability in a dynamic environment, multiple equilibria are possible: at relatively low levels of inequality, political equilibrium entails efficiency-enhancing redistribution and smaller income dispersion increases future political support for more redistribution, while symmetric reinforcing effects can be featured by high-inequality, low-redistribution dynamic trajectories.

7.5 REVIEW EXERCISES

EXERCISE 28 Consider an overlapping generations economy where individuals live for two periods, have no wealth at birth, and work in both periods. All generations consist of a constant number of individuals, normalized to unity. In each generation, $y/2$ individuals are endowed with $1 - x$ units of labor when young and $1 + x$ units of labor when old; $y/2$ other individuals are endowed with $1 + x$ units of labor when young, and $1 - x$ units of labor when old; the remaining $1 - y$ individuals are endowed with 1 unit of labor in each period of their lives. The exogenous parameters x and y, which index the extent of labor heterogeneity, satisfy $0 \leq x \leq 1$ and $0 \leq y \leq 1$. All individuals aim at maximizing an undiscounted logarithmic utility function of consumption when young (c_{1t}) and when old (c_{2t+1}),

$$\ln c_{1t} + \ln c_{2t+1},$$

subject to an appropriate budget constraint. We denote aggregate output with Y_t, aggregate wealth with K_t, and we treat the factor income share of labor γ as a parameter. All units of labor earn the same wage $W_t = \gamma Y_t/2$ (there are 2 units of labor in each period). Suppose all individuals can lend and borrow at the same rate $R_t = (1 - \gamma)Y_t/K_t$.

a. Does the economy's equilibrium depend on x and y?
b. Suppose further that $Y_t/K_t = A$ is a given constant, independent of t. Write an expression for aggregate savings by young individuals, recognize that it must be equal to the next period's aggregate wealth, and write the growth factor K_{t+1}/K_t as a function of the parameters.
c. Does a larger γ increase or decrease the economy's growth rate?
d. Show that x can be so large that some individuals need to borrow in the first period. Suppose this is not possible because they cannot be forced to repay their debt when old: discuss the impact on aggregate savings and growth of this financial market imperfection.
e. Suppose legislation is proposed that would actually force debts to be repaid (and therefore allow those who would like to borrow to obtain credit). Among individuals who are alive in this economy in each period, who would be in favor of it?

EXERCISE 29 People live two periods. In the first period they have w and consume c_1; in the second period they consume a function $c_2 = f(w - c_1)$ of their savings. There are two groups, the poor with $w_P = 1$ and the rich with $w_R = 2$.

a. Suppose $f(x) = (1 + R)x$.

   i. If all individuals want to maximize

$$\ln(c_1 + 1) + \ln(c_2 + 1)$$

   does consumption inequality increase or decrease between periods 1 and 2 when $R > 0$? How does your answer change if $R = 0$?
   ii. How does the intertemporal elasticity of substitution depend on consumption for the this utility function? Which general result is illustrated by this exercise (recall our results from chapter 3)?

b. Now suppose that

$$f(x) = \begin{cases} x & \text{for } x < 1 \\ 2x - 1 & \text{for } x \geq 1. \end{cases}$$

What difference does this make to the dynamics of consumption inequality?

CHAPTER EIGHT

Risk and Financial Markets

IN THIS AND THE FOLLOWING CHAPTER we study how uncertainty affects the relationship between distribution and growth. In all previous chapters, the dynamics of individual and aggregate income, consumption, and wealth levels were deterministic. In reality, however, random shocks are clearly relevant, both to the evolution of aggregate resources and to the evolution of their distribution. There are several reason why this is the case. First, random shocks imply there are winners and losers. In other words, luck and misfortune per se (in addition to initial conditions and individual choices) become a source of inequality. Second, depending on how resources are distributed, exposure to random shocks affects savings choices at the individual level and thus the accumulation of capital in the aggregate. We will see that, when individuals cannot fully insure themselves against such shocks, a likely outcome will be nonlinear consumption functions. Third, random shocks imply social mobility so that a currently poor agent may become rich and vice versa. The deterministic models above did not generally allow for such income mobility through savings decisions. For instance, in the infinite horizon model of chapter 3, the relative position of an individual in the lifetime income distribution is given by initial conditions and remains unchanged forever. Also in the overlapping generations models studied in chapter 5, social mobility occurs only in a very restricted sense: either because of a changing earnings capacity with age or because new households that own no accumulated factors enter the economy. In reality, however, income mobility due to luck or misfortune is clearly important, so the introduction of random shocks adds an important aspect of economic inequality to our analysis of the relationship between income distribution and growth. At a more fundamental level, the results from the deterministic models studied above leave open the question of the origins of wealth heterogeneity. Idiosyncratic shocks can provide an obvious answer to that question, but need to be taken into account when modeling individual decisions and market interactions.

Chapter 7 analyzed the investment behavior under alternative assumptions on the production function (convex versus non-convex technologies) when financial markets do not exist. In this and the following chapter, we assume throughout that technology is convex. In this chapter we introduce and characterize financial market interactions, first reviewing briefly the basic tools and concepts for intertemporal optimization under uncertainty and characterizing the equilibrium of perfect and complete financial markets. In such a stylized world, it turns out that only aggregate risks, not individual-level or "idiosyncratic" uncertainty, affect aggregate accumulation. In the absence of aggregate risks, exchanging contingent securities in perfect and complete financial markets makes it possible for individuals to smooth consumption not only over time, as in the models of part 1, but also across different realizations of exogenous random events. Consumption levels are affected by shocks if there is aggregate uncertainty but, if preferences are in the HARA class extensively discussed in part 1, the marginal propensity to consume is constant and identical across consumers—implying that inequality has no effect on aggregate variables. This result is analogous to the deterministic one discussed in chapter 3 and, as was the case there, the outcome is always efficient.

Financial markets do not allow all idiosyncratic rate-of-return risk to be traded, especially (but not only) across countries (see e.g., Obstfeld [1994] for an extensive discussion of international financial interactions). Accordingly, we proceed to discuss interactions between distribution and efficiency under incomplete markets, and set the stage for a discussion of labor income risk (and distributional dynamics) in the next chapter.

8.1 OPTIMIZATION UNDER UNCERTAINTY

Following the standard literature, originated by Arrow (1964) and Debreu (1959), uncertainty can be represented by allowing factor returns to depend on the *state of nature*. Common knowledge is that there exists an exhaustive set of S states in the world but at date t only one state s_t will realize. Ex ante, the individuals only know the probabilities $\pi(s_t)$ of state $s = 1, \ldots, S$ at date $t = 1, \ldots, \infty$.

A *state-contingent claim*, or "Arrow-Debreu security" as it is also called, yields one unit of consumption (or capital) at date t in state s. A risky *asset* can be simply defined as an investment yielding different returns in different states. Hence, an asset is a linear combination of different state-contingent claims. It is now possible that an asset that an individual holds yields very low returns in some states. A risk-averse individual will insure herself against these unfavorable outcomes by purchasing Arrow-Debreu securities (or corresponding assets). If markets are complete such Arrow-Debreu securities exist for all states and points in time, so individuals can perfectly plan their future consumption $c(s, t)$ $\forall s, t$ by buying and selling such state-contingent claims. In other words, when markets are complete, the financial market provides full insurance for all individuals.

In reality, assets available to each individual may yield idiosyncratic (i.e., individual-specific) random returns, and the risk associated with investment in individual-specific assets may be uninsurable.[1] The most important example is human capital and non-accumulated factor (i.e., labor) income. Its returns are highly idiosyncratic, and full insurance is difficult for obvious (moral hazard) reasons. However, when full insurance is not possible (because the payoffs associated with the assets traded on financial markets cannot isolate individual consumption from idiosyncratic events), uncertainty about future non-accumulated income will affect savings decisions. The individual then tries to provide self-insurance by accumulating *precautionary* savings. We will discuss this in subsection 8.1.2 and we will elaborate the macroeconomic consequences in section 8.2 and chapter 9.

In general, the individual savings choice has to be made under uncertain returns to endogenously accumulated wealth, borrowing constraints, and/or random flows of non-accumulated factor income. The dynamic accumulation constraints can still be written in the form (1.1)

$$k_{t+1} - k_t = r_t k_t + w_t l_t - c_t, \tag{8.1}$$

The factor rewards in equation (8.1) may be individual-specific (recall our convention to denote with lowercase letters variables that may vary between households and capital letters for aggregate variables). In particular, as in chapter 7, the return r_t on the savings of a given individual may depend on the size of his or her own investments. In the presence of uncertainty, both r_t and $w_t l_t$ may also depend on exogenous random events. In general, the composition as well as the size of an individual's investment are relevant to the dynamics of individual wealth.

The individual consumer maximizes expected utility over an infinite horizon where we again assume that all individuals share identical preferences (and beliefs about the state probabilities). The individual's planning horizon starts at time t and goes to infinity, and time is indexed by τ. The consumer's consumption and savings choices may be subject to several liquidity constraints in future periods: $k_\tau \geq \bar{k}_\tau$. For example, if borrowing is not allowed at all, $\bar{k}_\tau = 0$. In addition, future returns from labor income w_{t+1} may be uncertain.

We assume further that there are different assets in which the individual capital stock k_t can be invested. This assumption adds one additional choice problem for the consumer: the portfolio choice. For ease of exposition we assume that there are only two assets. One asset is risk-free

---

[1] *Ex constructione* the realized state s_t is the same for all individuals, but some agents may be worse off in that state compared to the others.

and yields a constant return $\bar{R}_{t+1}$ at every state at date $t + 1$, the same for all consumers. The second asset is risky, with returns equal to $r_{t+1}(s_{t+1})$ which depend on the state of nature. We will let s_{t+1} be implicit in what follows, if there is no confusion. Moreover, we define the return-inclusive wealth

$$a_t \equiv \left((1 + \bar{R}_t)\varphi_t + (1 + r_t)(1 - \varphi_t) \right) k_t$$

where φ_t denotes the share invested in the risk-free asset.

To solve this problem we introduce the value function $v_t(a_t, l_t w_t, ..)$ which is defined as follows:

$$v_t(a_t, l_t w_t, ..) = \max_{\{c_\tau, \varphi_{\tau+1}\}} E_t \left[\sum_{\tau=t}^{\infty} \beta^{\tau-t} u(c_\tau) \right]$$

$$\text{s.t. } a_{\tau+1} = \left[(1 + \bar{R}_{\tau+1})\varphi_{\tau+1} + (1 + r_{\tau+1})(1 - \varphi_{\tau+1}) \right] \left[a_\tau + w_\tau l_\tau - c_\tau \right],$$

$$\text{and } k_{\tau+1} = a_\tau + w_\tau l_\tau - c_\tau \geq \bar{k}_{\tau+1},$$

where $\beta \equiv (1 + \rho)^{-1}$ denotes the discount factor (in this strand of literature it is more common to work with discount factors instead of discount rates). The value function v_t is the discounted value of expected utility evaluated along the optimal consumption (and optimal portfolio) path. It depends on the end-of-period asset value a_t, the non-accumulated factor income $w_t l_t$, and on the joint distribution of (uncertain) future wages and interest rates.

The tool of dynamic programming reduces this difficult multiperiod problem to a sequence of two-period problems. In particular, the value function can be expressed recursively by the Bellman equation:

$$v_t(a_t, l_t w_t, ..) = \max_{c_t, \varphi_{t+1}} \left\{ u(c) + \beta E_t \left[v_{t+1}(a_{t+1}, l_{t+1} w_{t+1}, ..) \right] \right\} \tag{8.2}$$

$$\text{s.t. } a_{t+1} = \left[(1 + \bar{R}_{t+1})\varphi_{t+1} + (1 + r_{t+1})(1 - \varphi_{t+1}) \right] \left[a_t + w_t l_t - c_t \right],$$

$$\text{and } \bar{k}_{t+1} \leq a_t + w_t l_t - c_t.$$

The first-order condition for the maximization on the right-hand side of (8.2) is given by

$$u'(c_t) = \beta E_t \left[\left[(1 + \bar{R}_{t+1})\varphi_{t+1} + (1 + r_{t+1})(1 - \varphi_{t+1}) \right] \frac{\partial v_{t+1}}{\partial a_{t+1}} \right] + \mu_t, \tag{8.3}$$

$$0 = E_t \left[(\bar{R}_{t+1} - r_{t+1}) \frac{\partial v_{t+1}}{\partial a_{t+1}} \right],$$

where the Kuhn-Tucker shadow price μ_t is positive if the borrowing constraint is binding, and zero otherwise. Along an optimal consumption-saving program, the marginal utility from immediate consumption coincides with the marginal value of a unit of accumulated resources available at date $t + 1$ (provided that the liquidity constraint is not binding so that $\mu_t = 0$). Instead, if the liquidity constraint is binding, $\mu_t > 0$, consumption today is reduced, hence marginal utility of immediate consumption must exceed the marginal value of additional resources available at date $t + 1$.

When the liquidity constraint does not bind ($\mu_t = 0$), the marginal value of wealth can be expressed in terms of the marginal utility of consumption at date t. If we differentiate both sides of (8.2) with respect to a_t, taking into account the budget constraint (8.1), we get

$$\frac{\partial v_t}{\partial a_t} = \beta E_t \left[\frac{\partial v_{t+1}}{\partial a_{t+1}} \left[(1 + \bar{R}_{t+1})\varphi_{t+1} + (1 + r_{t+1})(1 - \varphi_{t+1}) \right] \right],$$

$$\frac{\partial v_t}{\partial a_t} = u'(c_t),$$

where the second equality follows from the first-order condition of consumption (8.3). In the optimum, the marginal value of wealth equals the marginal utility of consumption. This is just another application of the envelope theorem. As long as the borrowing constraint is not binding, this relationship holds for every period. This allows us to rewrite the second equation of (8.3):

$$E_t \left[\left(\bar{R}_{t+1} - r_{t+1} \right) u'(c_{t+1}) \right] = 0$$

or

$$\left(1 + \bar{R}_{t+1} \right) E_t \left[u'(c_{t+1}) \right] = E_t \left[(1 + r_{t+1}) u'(c_{t+1}) \right]. \tag{8.4}$$

This is the optimality condition that has to be fulfilled if the individual chooses to invest in both the risky and the risk-free asset. The condition says that expected returns—with marginal utilities in the corresponding states as weights—must be equalized. For example, if the risky asset has high returns when consumption is high and marginal utility is low, high realizations of r_{t+1} go together with low values of $u'(c_{t+1})$. Hence, the expected return of the risky asset must be higher than that of the risk-free asset, as otherwise (8.4) would be violated. On the contrary, an asset that yields high returns in bad states where consumption is low serves as an "insurance." The individual will hold the asset in his or her portfolio although the expected return is lower. Put in other terms, he or she is willing to pay a price for the insurance for an asset with lower expected returns.

With (8.4) and the relationship $\partial v_t(\cdot)/\partial a_t = u'(c_t)$ we can also rewrite the first equation of (8.3) to get a familiar Euler equation in the case of uncertainty:

$$u'(c_t) = \beta E_t \left[(1 + r_{t+1}) u'(c_{t+1}) \right]. \tag{8.5}$$

Analogously, we could have written the Euler equation in terms of the risk-free return $\bar{R}_{t+1}$.

8.1.1 Complete Markets

We now study the optimal consumption path when markets are complete. Recall that this means that all intertemporal and intratemporal (across states) markets exist, allowing individuals to finance their future consumption $c(s_t) \; \forall \; s, t$ with appropriate sales and purchases of state-contingent securities. Since all markets are competitive, if technology is neoclassically convex the equilibrium allocation under complete markets can be interpreted in terms of a social planning problem, as in section 3.3. If we write out the expectation in terms of the state probabilities $\pi(s_t)$, the expected utility can be written as

$$E\tilde{u}^i = \sum_{\tau=t}^{\infty} \beta^{\tau-t} \left(\sum_{s_\tau=1}^{S} \pi(s_\tau) u(c^i(s_\tau)) \right).$$

Denote ω_i the individual i's weight in the social welfare function. These weights again depend on the individual i's endowment of factors of production. To capture the uncertainty about resources the aggregate production function depends on the specific state s_t. The social planner's problem can then be written as follows:

$$\max_{\{c_i(s_\tau)\}} \int_{\mathcal{N}} \omega^i \sum_{\tau=t}^{\infty} \beta^{\tau-t} \left(\sum_{s_\tau=1}^{S} \pi(s_\tau) u(c^i(s_\tau)) \right) dP(i)$$

$$\text{s.t. } 0 \leq F(K_t, L; s_t) + K_t - K_{t+1}(s_{t+1}|s_t) - \int_{\mathcal{N}} c^i(s_t) dP(i) \; \forall s, t.$$

The social planner's problem implies

$$u'(c^i(s_t))\omega^i = \lambda(s_t) \tag{8.6}$$

as the necessary and sufficient first-order condition; here, as in (3.16), $\lambda(s_t)$ represents the Lagrangian shadow value of resources available for aggregate consumption at time t divided by the realization probability

π (s_t), and ω^i the weight assigned to individual i's utility in the social planner's objective function. The value of λ (s_t) depends on aggregate variables only. This is a central result: the exchange of state- and time-contingent claims in financial markets ensures that different individuals' marginal utilities always remain proportional, as in (3.18). Taking this result into account, what do individual consumption plans look like? To answer this question, it is instructive to differentiate between idiosyncratic and aggregate risk.

Idiosyncratic uncertainty. If there is only individual-level uncertainty but no aggregate uncertainty, the individual endowments depend on s but the aggregate amount of resources is constant at date t. In that case the shadow value λ is independent of the particular state. Condition (8.6) then implies that individual consumption is constant at a given point in time because marginal utility of consumption must be constant in all states at t. Note the similarity of this result with equation (3.18) in section (3.3). The intuition is the same as in the certainty case: an efficient allocation of resources should keep marginal utilities aligned. Moreover, distribution cannot affect economic outcomes (at a given point in time) if there is only idiosyncratic uncertainty. Intuitively, with no aggregate uncertainty, all idiosyncratic risk is made irrelevant by financial market interactions, as risk-averse individuals optimally choose "full insurance" (which is possible as markets are complete) and equalize consumption across states at a given point in time.

Aggregate uncertainty. Since idiosyncratic uncertainty plays no role with perfect and complete markets, let us consider the other polar case, i.e., that there is only aggregate uncertainty. If there is aggregate uncertainty only, output (and factor rewards) tomorrow are uncertain but all individuals will get the same factor rewards with idiosyncratic uncertainty. The individuals could choose full insurance, i.e., to smooth consumption perfectly, as markets are complete. However, if all individuals chose this option, the aggregate resource constraint would be violated. Hence, in equilibrium, the prices of the state-contingent claims that pay off in the bad states must be higher. Consequently, the individuals will optimally choose to consume less in the bad states where prices are higher.

The open question is how much individuals will consume and save, i.e., how resources are allocated intertemporally. In particular—following the arguments of chapter 1—we ask when will distribution have an effect on accumulation.

From the deterministic case, we know that aggregate dynamics can be modeled as optimal choices by a representative agent if and only if utility has HARA form. Provided markets are complete, it is easy to show that this result also holds under uncertainty. From (3.3) we know that HARA preferences can be expressed by the form $u'(c) = (\gamma c/\sigma - \bar{c})^{-\sigma}$ with $\gamma > 0$. From (8.6) it is easy to derive a relationship between $c(s_{t+1})$ and $c(s_t)$:

$$\beta \left(\frac{\gamma c(s_{t+1})/\sigma - \bar{c}}{\gamma c(s_t)/\sigma - \bar{c}} \right)^{-\sigma} = \frac{\lambda (s_{t+1})}{\lambda (s_t)}. \tag{8.7}$$

Analogously to (3.5), equation (8.7) can be rewritten as

$$c(s_{t+1}) = (1 - \xi (s_t, s_{t+1})) \frac{\sigma}{\gamma} \bar{c} + \xi (s_t, s_{t+1}) c(s_t),$$

$$\text{where } \xi (s_t, s_{t+1}) \equiv \left(\beta \frac{\lambda (s_{t+1})}{\lambda (s_t)} \right)^{-1/\sigma}. \tag{8.8}$$

Since $\xi (s_t, s_{t+1})$ is the same for all individuals, equation (8.8) can be easily aggregated across individuals. The linearity of (8.8) at the individual level implies that also aggregate consumption in $t + 1$ depends linearly on the consumption in t. Put differently, aggregate consumption growth does not depend on the distribution of income and wealth. Combining (8.8) with the intertemporal budget constraint, it is easy to show that, in analogy to the problem in the absence of uncertainty studied in chapter 3, the optimal individual consumption levels under uncertainty depend linearly on expected lifetime income. Hence not only aggregate consumption growth but also the level of aggregate accumulation are independent of the distribution of income and wealth across households.

It is interesting to note that, provided that markets are complete, we get the same welfare results as in the certainty case studied in section 3.3. Equation (8.7) implies that the ratio of marginal utilities over time is the same for all agents. But then the optimality condition (8.6) implies that the ratio of marginal utilities *between* agents must also remain constant over time. Hence, relative welfare levels of two unequally endowed individuals remain constant over time, which is the identical result as in the certainty case.

The close analogy regarding efficiency and welfare to the deterministic case analyzed in chapter 3 is easily explained. Remember that, given complete markets, any individual can perfectly plan his or her future consumption $c(s_t)$ ∀ s, t by buying and selling state contingent claims. The completeness of markets implies that (1) they can fully insure against idiosyncratic events and (2) aggregate uncertainty only matters for them because the prices of the contingent claims will be higher in bad states.

Due to the close analogy with the deterministic case it is straightforward to characterize the *dynamics of distribution* when there is uncertainty but complete markets. Idiosyncratic uncertainty has no effects, since everyone is fully insured against it. Aggregate uncertainty hurts everyone in the same proportions, measured in marginal utility terms. With positive required consumption levels, $\bar{c} > 0$, *consumption levels diverge* over time in a growing economy. However, *relative welfare levels stay constant*, as the ratio of marginal utilities does not change. These results are identical to those derived in chapter 3. The difference is that, under uncertainty, market participants own portfolios of contingent claims, rather than just bundles of production factors. Of course, the former are much more difficult to measure.

8.1.2 Implications of Market Incompleteness

We have explored the role of uncertainty in the context of complete markets. In what follows we deviate from the assumption that all inter- and intratemporal markets exist and study how this affects the relationship between inequality and aggregate outcomes. Just like in previous chapters, we are again interested in the dynamics of inequality and whether, and how, inequality affects efficiency and growth.

In the previous chapter we have already seen that, when different people had different investment opportunities (e.g., due to borrowing constraints), marginal utilities failed to be efficiently aligned. Moreover, we know from our analysis above that equalization of marginal utilities is a central condition for (1) efficiency and (2) stable welfare dynamics. Hence, if people cannot freely borrow or lend *and* endowments are unequally distributed, the equilibrium allocation is, in general, characterized by inefficiency. For example, poor agents may not make indivisible education investments (because of borrowing constraints), although it would have been desirable from a social planner's point of view. Concerning the welfare dynamics, we saw in the models above that the distribution will not remain constant when there are borrowing constraints.

In what follows, we focus on the *implications of idiosyncratic uncertainty* for savings behavior, aggregate accumulation, and inequality. We will disregard aggregate shocks, relying on the fact that in an economy populated by many small individuals, idiosyncratic events cancel out in the aggregate. In the remainder of this chapter we examine the aggregate and distributional implications of rate-of-return risks: we let non-accumulated income be certain—and, for simplicity, equal to zero—while returns to accumulation are partly or wholly individual-specific. In the next chapter we will study the implications of non-accumulated factor income risk by symmetrically supposing that returns to accumulation are constant, but other sources of income are subject to idiosyncratic shocks. In each case, we consider the role of uncertainty in individual savings decisions and then discuss the consequences for aggregate outcomes and the dynamics of inequality. We will see that uninsurable risks make aggregation much more complex. Outside of the certainty and/or complete markets framework, assuming HARA preferences does not guarantee that aggregate accumulation is independent of distribution. Idiosyncratic but uninsurable risks have macroeconomic effects, and market incompleteness implies that the consumption function becomes concave even when preferences are HARA. Hence, inequality affects efficiency and macroeconomic phenomena unless more restrictive (and less realistic) assumptions are made.

8.2 RATE-OF-RETURN RISK

In this section we study the macroeconomic effects of idiosyncratically uncertain investment returns when the returns to non-accumulated factors (i.e., labor income) are certain. Realized returns to accumulation may be heterogeneous across individuals not only because capital-market imperfections require partial or complete self-financing of investments. Heterogeneous returns may also arise because it is difficult or impossible to avoid exogenous rate-of-return risk. Idiosyncratic rate-of-return risk may arise in many situations: An investor buys an asset (e.g., a firm). However, at the time of the purchase he does not know whether some of the firm's projects will turn out to be profitable or not. The success of a project is determined by many uncertain factors: preference shifts, macroeconomic shocks that have asymmetric effects on the different sectors (e.g., cyclical versus non-cyclical industries), own luck (especially in R&D projects), luck of the other competitors. By its very own nature, such idiosyncratic risk can only be partially insured (or pooled among agents). In addition, "labor income" may also be subject to rate-of-return risk when we think of returns to education or, more generally, human capital. Undiversifiable investment risks are not only important in the developing world. Moskowitz and Vissing-Jørgensen (2002) point out that U.S. entrepreneurs face an extreme dispersion in returns. When rich households and entrepreneurs control a large fraction of savings and investment in the economy, as Angeletos and Calvet (2003) summarize, undiversifiable risks are potentially important for macroeconomic performance.

What are the effects of uninsurable rate-of-return risk on the savings behavior of the individuals? We know that income and wealth heterogeneity is neutral to macroeconomic outcomes whenever the consumption function is linear in (lifetime) income and wealth. In the absence of uncertainty and/or when markets are complete, linearity is ensured if preferences are

HARA. However, with incomplete markets, this is no longer the case. We will see that linearity is only ensured under the more restrictive assumption of CRRA preferences. Furthermore, we will also see that increasing risk may or may not increase the volume of savings, depending on the curvature of the utility function. In the simplest case where preferences are logarithmic, the volume of savings is independent of investment returns. Hence increasing the spread of those returns affects neither individual nor aggregate savings.

In addition, we study a simple portfolio problem with two assets. When preferences are logarithmic, the share of the risky asset with higher expected returns is higher when idiosyncratic risk is reduced. Therefore, when returns are pooled, which decreases the risk an individual has to bear, high (idiosyncratic) risk assets with high returns get a larger share of the aggregate economy's portfolio. This simple but important fact is illustrated with an equally simple model in section 8.3.

In the following we consider the case where the investor cannot be insulated from idiosyncratic shocks. To keep things simple, we consider the case where there is no non-accumulated income. Hence we are assuming that "capital" is the only factor of production and (non-accumulated) factors, such as raw labor, do not play a productive role. Each individual can invest into a single asset that offers stochastic constant returns. Apart from this asset, no other investment possibilities are available. The stochastic investment return is given by r_{t+1} with expectation $E_t r_{t+1} = R_{t+1}$, i.e., the individuals face the same investment opportunities ex ante but are subject to noninsurable idiosyncratic risk ex post.[2] Returns on savings are then given by

$$a_{t+1} = (a_t - c_t)(1 + r_{t+1}),$$

where $a_t = (1 + r_t)k_t$ again denotes return-inclusive wealth. The assumption that all individuals face the same investment opportunities ex ante but are subject to noninsurable idiosyncratic risk ex post implies that the return r_{t+1} is independent of wealth and investment levels. Hence the discussion here is under the assumption that self-financing constraints (if any) would not affect distributional and aggregate dynamics through the mechanisms reviewed in chapter 7.

In (8.5), the extent to which investment risk influences individual-specific returns and consumption growth depends on the degree of fi-

---

[2]Note that the definition of the average interest rate R is consistent with the definition of aggregate factor rewards introduced in chapter 1 (see equation [1.7]). As individuals face the same investment opportunities ex ante, r and k are uncorrelated, hence $R = E[\int_N r \cdot k/KdP(k)] = [\int_N k/KdP(i)]Er = Er.$

nancial market completeness on the one hand, and on the proportion of individual savings channeled through risky assets on the other. When a "stock market" is open, access to less risky (hence more favorable) investment opportunities may or may not increase the savings rate, depending on the balance of "income" and substitution effects. The point can be illustrated simply in the case where non-accumulated or "labor" income is absent.

Assume that preferences are CRRA, $u'(c_t) = c_t^{-\sigma}$, and the consumers have an infinite time horizon. Now assume further that returns are stationary:

$$E_t\left[\int_N (1 + r_{t+1}) k_t/K_t dP_t(k_t)\right] = 1 + R. \tag{8.9}$$

We conjectured that the consumption function is linear in income and wealth. Hence, we guess that the optimal solution is of the form: $c_t = \hat{c}a_t$ where $\hat{c}$ is a constant to be determined. Consumption tomorrow then must equal $c_{t+1} = \hat{c}a_{t+1} = \hat{c}(1 - \hat{c})(1 + r_{t+1})a_t$. In the optimum the Euler equation (8.5) must hold

$$c_t^{-\sigma} = \beta E_t\left[(1 + r_{t+1}) c_{t+1}^{-\sigma}\right]$$
$$(\hat{c}a_t)^{-\sigma} = \beta E_t\left[(1 + r_{t+1})(\hat{c}(1 - \hat{c})(1 + r_{t+1})a_t)^{-\sigma}\right]$$
$$1 = \beta E_t\left[(1 + r_{t+1})^{1-\sigma}\right](1 - \hat{c})^{-\sigma}.$$

This can be solved for $\hat{c}$ and we get

$$\hat{c} = 1 - \left(\beta E_t\left[(1 + r_{t+1})^{1-\sigma}\right]\right)^{1/\sigma}. \tag{8.10}$$

This confirms our initial claim: the parameter $\hat{c}$ is indeed constant as long as returns are stationary and the time horizon is infinite. If one (or both) of these two simplifying assumptions do not hold, the consumption function is still linear, i.e., $\hat{c}$ is independent of a_t, but the marginal propensity to consume depends on calendar time. For our purposes it is further interesting to note that $\hat{c}$ does not depend on wealth. This is due to the homothetic CRRA preferences.

The assumption (8.9) of stationary returns is reasonable if capital is the only factor of production, or if its ratio to other factors has settled down in steady state. The results established here, however, do not hinge on that assumption, as the following exercise asks you to show.

EXERCISE 30 Consider the model discussed above. Derive the optimal consumption when returns are not stationary and depend on time:

$E_t \left[\int_{\mathcal{N}} (1 + r_{t+1}) k_t / K_t dP(k_t) \right] = 1 + R_{t+1}$. Compare the solution with the optimal consumption rule in the certainty case (chapter 3).

8.2.1 Rate-of-Return Risk and Long-run Growth

Since the savings rate satisfying (8.10) is the same for all individuals faced by the same ex ante investment opportunity set and realized returns are uncorrelated to individual wealth levels, aggregating across individuals yields

$$C_t = \hat{c} \int_{\mathcal{N}} a_t dP(k_t) = \hat{c} \int_{\mathcal{N}} (1 + r_t) k_t dP(k_t) = \hat{c}(1 + R) K_t.$$

As the consumption function is linear, it is straightforward to describe the dynamics of the aggregate capital stock. Recall that we abstracted from labor income. As there is no aggregate uncertainty, the income equals RK_t.

$$\Delta K_t = RK_t - C_t = \left(R - \hat{c}(1 + R) \right) K_t.$$

At this point, it is interesting to ask whether savings will be higher or lower when the agent faces idiosyncratic rate-of-return risk. At a first glance one would expect savings to be higher with complete markets where agents can fully insure and individual returns are no longer uncertain. However, equation (8.10) tells us that this is not clear. If $\sigma > 1$, we have $E\left[(1 + r)^{1-\sigma} \right] > (1 + R)^{1-\sigma}$ by Jensen's inequality. Hence, if there is a second-order stochastically dominating shift of the r-distribution, $\hat{c}$ will be lower and the savings rate higher. Roughly speaking, higher risk exhibits an "income" and a "substitution" effect. When the rate-of-return risk is higher, the expected utility of an additional unit of savings is smaller because the expected return remains constant while it is more uncertain. This may be called substitution effect. On the other hand, the possibility of very low returns is higher because returns have a higher variation; this induces the agent to save more if marginal utility is convex ($u''' > 0$). This is the usual precautionary effect, which may be called "income" effect. The size of the precautionary effect depends on the coefficient of relative prudence, which is $-cu'''(c)/u''(c)$ in general and $1 + \sigma$ with CRRA preferences. With σ high, the coefficient of relative prudence will be high and the "income" effect dominates. It can be shown that the precautionary effect dominates if $-cu'''(c)/u''(c) > 2$. Hence, the individuals will save more with more rate-of-return risk when $\sigma > 1$.[3] With logarithmic

---

[3]It is imprecise to say that individuals will save more with higher rate-of-return risk if they are more risk-averse. They will save more if they are more prudent. For a detailed discussion of precautionary savings and prudence see Gollier (2001a, 237).

preferences instead ($\sigma = 1$), the two competing effects cancel: the saving rate does not depend on the interest rate and $\hat{c}$ equals $1 - \beta^{1/\sigma}$. Thus, if utility is logarithmic, (increased) idiosyncratic rate-of-return risk has no effect on individual savings. Finally, if relative prudence is smaller than 2 ($\sigma < 1$), the "substitution" effect dominates and increased rate-of-return risk decreases savings.

8.2.2   Dynamics of the Wealth Distribution

The evolution of the individual capital stock is easily derived

$$a_{t+1} = (a_t - c_t)(1 + r_{t+1})$$
$$\frac{a_{t+1}}{a_t} = (1 - \hat{c})(1 + r_{t+1}).$$

Note that r_{t+1} follows a random walk. Hence, the growth rate of individual assets follows a random walk. This implies that the distribution is not stationary, a result we will encounter again in section 9.2. The nonstationarity stems from the fact that the consumption function is linear in wealth: rich and poor consumers exhibit the same saving rates. If an individual enjoys a positive rate of return shock, his wealth a_{t+1} will be higher than expected. With constant savings rates, the agent will maintain—in expectation—his higher wealth level. There is no mean-reverting mechanism. Like the probability distribution of a random-walk process, the cross-sectional distribution of consumption and welfare levels tends to widen.[4]

To sum up, the presence of uninsurable idiosyncratic risk has macroeconomic effects. If $\sigma > 1$, an economy without financial markets produces a larger amount of aggregate resources—even as it distributes it more unevenly across its consumers/investors. However, individual welfare is lowered ex ante by consumption volatility. Welfare is lower as the rise in savings (and growth rates) is only due to uncertainty.[5] Moreover, we saw that inequality does not affect aggregate savings provided that utility is CRRA. For more general HARA preferences, instead, Carroll and Kimball (1996) show that the poor will exhibit a higher propensity to consume

---

[4]Such lack of mean reversion in relative consumption and welfare levels is a general feature of efficient allocations under private information, which prevents full insurance but still makes it desirable for individuals to smooth consumption (and hence to equalize expected marginal utilities) over time. The same efficiency considerations that imply stability of relative marginal utilities in the first-best setting of section 8.1.1 imply unpredictability of marginal utility shocks.

[5]Due to this argument, Devereux and Smith (1994) point out that output is a quite imperfect welfare measure. In their work, they compute and discuss alternative welfare measures.

than the rich, hence the consumption function becomes concave. Therefore, and in contrast to the complete markets case, distribution affects accumulation for HARA preferences.

8.2.3 Portfolio Choice

The model with only one risky asset provided interesting insights into how the volume of savings reacts to a change in idiosyncratic uncertainty. The assumption that there is one and only one risky asset means that households tackle any such risk by appropriate savings choices. However, in reality there are both high- and low-risk assets and households can react to idiosyncratic risks by choosing an appropriate portfolio.

In this section we study this intuition by assuming there are two assets, a risk-free asset that yields a low return and a risky asset with high expected returns. In this subsection we study the impact of risk on the households' portfolio choice. In particular, assume there exist both a risky asset with expected return $E_t r_{t+1} = R_{t+1}$ as above and, additionally, a riskless asset yielding return $\bar{R}_{t+1} < R_{t+1}$. Just like before, we assume there is no aggregate risk so that both R_{t+1} and $\bar{R}_{t+1}$ are exogenously given. Implicitly, we are assuming that aggregate production is undertaken by two different AK technologies $Y_t^0 = R_t K_t^0$ and $Y_t^1 = \bar{R}_t K_t^1$. Both produce the same homogeneous good that can be used as both a consumption and an investment good, hence aggregate output can be written as $Y_t = Y_t^0 + Y_t^1 = \bar{R}_t \varphi_t K_t + R_t (1 - \varphi_t) K_t = C_t + \Delta K_{t+1}$.

To look at the portfolio problem per se we choose a setup such that the volume of savings is independent of the extent of uncertainty. In the last section we have seen that uncertainty does not have an impact on aggregate savings if income and substitution effects of investment returns offset each other. This is the case with a logarithmic utility function. Hence assuming logarithmic utility allows us to look at the impact of risk on aggregate growth that works via the households' portfolio choice (rather than their savings behavior).[6]

We have already stated the first-order conditions for this problem: they are given by (8.4) for the portfolio choice and by (8.5) for the intertemporal consumption choice. The consumption function is given by

$$c_t = \hat{c} a_t \text{ where } \hat{c} = \rho / (1 + \rho). \tag{8.11}$$

---

[6]As a simple exercise note that we could reintroduce wage income. The consumption function would still remain linear as there exists a riskless bond (if a storage technology does not exist the net holding of the riskless bond is zero). If for some reason there is no risk-free asset, as in the preceding section, the consumption function would become concave even with logarithmic preferences. The problem lies in the fact that it is a nontrivial task to discount wage income when the rate of return is uncertain (see also Koo 1999).

Not surprisingly, this is the same form as above. Consumption tomorrow then equals

$$c_{t+1} = \hat{c}a_{t+1}$$
$$= \left[(1 + \bar{R}_{t+1})\varphi_{t+1} + (1 + r_{t+1})(1 - \varphi_{t+1})\right]\hat{c}(1 - \hat{c})a_t.$$

Inserting into (8.4) we get

$$E_t\left[\left(\bar{R}_{t+1} - r_{t+1}\right)u'(c_{t+1})\right] = 0 \qquad (8.12)$$
$$E_t\left[\left(\bar{R}_{t+1} - r_{t+1}\right)\left[1 + \left(\bar{R}_{t+1} - r_{t+1}\right)\varphi_{t+1}\right]^{-1}\right] = 0.$$

It is easy to check that $\left(\bar{R}_{t+1} - r_{t+1}\right)\left[1 + \left(\bar{R}_{t+1} - r_{t+1}\right)\varphi_{t+1}\right]^{-1} \equiv g(\varphi_{t+1}, r_{t+1})$ is decreasing and concave in r_{t+1}. Thus, if the distribution of r_{t+1} is perturbed by a second-order stochastic dominant shift (so that there is more rate-of-return risk), the expression $E_t\left[g(\varphi_{t+1}, r_{t+1})\right]$ decreases for a given φ_{t+1}. As $E_t\left[\partial g(\varphi_{t+1}, r_{t+1})/\partial \varphi_{t+1}\right] > 0$, the first-order condition (8.12) implies a higher value of φ_{t+1}. Thus, the share of the risky asset, $1 - \varphi_{t+1}$, is lower if the idiosyncratic risk is higher. Note further that φ_{t+1} does not depend on wealth. This is due to the homotheticity of logarithmic preferences. The portfolio choice problem therefore depends on the risk/return characteristics of the two assets but does not change with the household's wealth level due to the homothetic utility function.

EXERCISE 31 Redo the derivations above for a CRRA utility function. Show that the share of the high yield assets decreases with more risk, if σ is not too high.

As the consumption function (8.11) is a special case of the one defined by (8.10) above, the aggregate dynamics are very similar to the one-asset case studied above.

8.3 PORTFOLIO CHOICE AND RISK POOLING

In the previous section we have discussed conditions under which the share of the risky asset in the agent's portfolio decreases with the associated level of risk. An obvious way to reduce idiosyncratic risk is to pool risk. If two agents pool their risks, individual risk will be reduced as long as the idiosyncratic shocks are not perfectly correlated between the agents. With many agents pooling risks, it is even possible to fully diversify the risk, as long as there is no aggregate uncertainty. Obviously, if we allow for risk pooling, there will be trade in financial assets—provided that risks are not perfectly correlated. When the number of involved agents grows, the outcome must resemble more and more that of complete markets. In that view, risk pooling is an intermediate institutional setting between the "perfect" world of complete markets and the full absence of financial trade discussed above.

The important message here is that pooling risk can increase efficiency. Risky investments must be more productive (on average) than riskless investments if they are ever undertaken. Hence increasing the share of risky assets increases aggregate productivity. In the last section we have seen that, when preferences are logarithmic and there is only one risky asset, pooling risk will increase welfare but the volume of savings will not be affected. In the present section we have seen that, when agents can choose between a risk-free and a risky asset, pooling risk will increase the optimal share of the risky asset. Pooling risk decreases the idiosyncratic uncertainty that agents must bear. Hence, in the aggregate, agents will invest more in risky projects. In other words, aggregate productivity is higher and, ceteris paribus, growth is faster when risk pooling makes it individually optimal to invest a higher fraction of resources in risky investments. Obviously, in the absence of aggregate uncertainty, reducing idiosyncratic risk increases efficiency.

In addition, and interestingly, these mechanisms predict a positive relationship between efficiency and equality. If we compare no insurance and full insurance, in the latter case inequality is obviously lower (as idiosyncratic risk can be fully diversified) and aggregate output is higher (because there is more intense investment in risky, high-return opportunities). Of course, a correlation between inequality and efficiency should not be given a causal interpretation, since for a given degree of market completeness a single underlying factor—the intensity of idiosyncratic risk— may simultaneously drive inequality and inefficiency in the same direction.[7]

8.3.1 Redistributive Policies

From an institutional point of view, pooling need not only be done by financial markets. Government policies also offer collective redistribution schemes, for example in the form of Social Security or the unemployment insurance systems. Ex ante, these redistributive systems represent an insurance vehicle for the individuals: a main advantage of the welfare state may be that it reduces the variance of lifetime incomes. To the extent

---

[7]For intermediate levels of idiosyncratic risk it is a priori not clear whether increased pooling possibilities imply more equality in equilibrium, as the implications for equality of better insurance opportunities are generally offset by the fact that riskier projects will be implemented.

that these policies mimic (missing) financial markets, however, they can also improve efficiency. Sinn (1995) emphasizes that the welfare state is an insurance device that may increase risk taking and increase aggregate productivity. Relatedly, Barsky, Mankiw, and Zeldes (1986) argue that individuals are better insured against future (idiosyncratic) risks when government expenditures are financed by bonds instead of taxes: uncertainty tomorrow is reduced since future income taxes will be higher. Binswanger (2002) points out that such a policy induces individuals to perform riskier high yield investments that are socially desirable.

From the politicol-economic point of view discussed at the end of chapters 4 and 7, efficient implementation of risk-sharing schemes should, at least ex ante, be unanimously agreeable to all agents. While once-and-for-all choices from a wide menu of policies can in principle minimize the distortionary consequences of politically desirable redistribution, the kind of one-time redistribution that would support the textbook separation of efficiency and distribution is hardly feasible in realistic dynamic settings. If the menu of available policies indeed included a lump-sum redistribution instrument, nothing should in principle prevent macroeconomic efficiency, but since each individual would simply want to appropriate as large a share of aggregate resources as possible, it would be impossible to characterize interior political equilibria. In reality, only distortionary instruments are available: in any situation where binding, complete intertemporal contracts are not available, in fact, "lump-sum" redistribution is generally feasible only at the beginning of time, and can hardly be discussed or implemented in real time. Like capital income taxation in the simple models of sections 4.4 and 6.1.1, threats of "one-time" expropriation in an ongoing dynamic environment and lax enforcement of property rights loosen the link between individual supply decisions and individual consumption levels and, in the models proposed by Tornell and Velasco (1992), Benhabib and Rustichini (1996), and others, slow down capital accumulation. When taxation is decided ex post, or when predatory activity is made possible by imperfect protection of property rights, then the rational expectation of redistributive pressure affects incentives to save and invest even when all agents face identical problems and no redistribution takes place ex post. Distributional tensions are present and distortionary even when agents are and remain homogeneous, for the simple *fear* of ex post expropriation tends to remove incentives to save and invest. Symmetrically, when taxation and redistribution policies are decided before the realization of exogenous income inequality is known, the observed intensity of ex post fiscal redistribution may mimic that which would be implied by intertemporal contingent contracts. In reality, of course, imperfect insurance reflects incomplete or asymmetric information and, unless tax-based redistribution can exploit superior sources of information, ex post redistribution meant to shelter individual consumption from undesirable fluctuations should generally worsen the economy's allocative efficiency at the same time as it reduces ex post cross-sectional inequality.

As an example of how policy-based redistribution may improve laissez-faire efficiency, consider maximization of

$$\ln c_t + \beta \ln c_{t+1},$$

under the constraints

$$c_t = W_t - k_t, \quad c_{t+1} = (1 - \tau)W_{t+1} + (1 + r_{t+1}(1 - \tau) + S)k_t, \qquad (8.13)$$

where r_{t+1} is idiosyncratically random as of time t. If for some reason individuals find it impossible to stipulate insurance contracts, or if such contracts are even slightly costly to write and enforce, all would unanimously agree that $\tau = 1$, $S = E_t[r_{t+1}]k_t$ is a welfare-increasing set of taxes and investment subsidies. Less benign but qualitatively similar implications for the role of redistribution can be drawn from models where individuals are not ex ante identical. If $E_t[r_{t+1}]$ is heterogeneous across individuals in (8.13), then those individuals who expect relatively large returns to the accumulated factor will be opposed to complete equalization of second-period incomes. As long as their rate of return is uninsurably uncertain, however, even the richest individuals will favor at least partial redistribution. In politico-economic equilibrium, the extent and character of redistribution will then depend not only on the dynamics of status quo inequality, but also on the aggregate economy's dynamics. As in the model of Wright (1996), in fact, the insurance properties of ex post redistributive taxation may be made more or less desirable by faster growth of average labor income endowments. Since future taxes and subsidies play the role of otherwise nonexistent financial investment opportunities in this type of model, the sign of growth effects—as in section 8.2.1—depends on whether the coefficient of relative prudence is larger or smaller than two. If $\sigma > 1$ with CRRA preferences, then faster growth is associated with less ex post redistribution in a politico-economic equilibrium. In this case, when $\sigma > 1$, a non-random second-period consumption would eliminate precautionary savings and higher welfare would be associated with slower aggregate consumption growth.

8.3.2 Pooling and Risk Taking

We now illustrate the basic insight that risk pooling makes it individually optimal to increase the share of high-return risky assets by a simple model.[8] Suppose there are two assets, two agents, and two states of the world, each occurring with probability 1/2. There is only one period. Suppose that, for agent 1, the first asset yields $1 + r$ units of consumption in the first state of the world and zero in the second state. The second asset yields zero in the first state of the world and $(1 + r)f$ units of resources in the second state. If $f < 1$, the second asset has lower expected returns, and risk-neutral investors would not want to hold it in positive amounts. Risk-averse investors, however, are willing to hold some of the lower-return asset for hedging purposes. Provided that the portfolio return plus the principal can be identified with consumption, the share φ of wealth invested in the second (lower-return) asset is determined so as to solve the problem

$$\max_{\varphi} \left[\frac{1}{2} u \left((1 - \varphi)(1 + r) \right) + \frac{1}{2} u \left(\varphi(1 + r)f \right) \right]. \tag{8.14}$$

The first-order condition is

$$(1 + r)f u' \left(\varphi(1 + r)f \right) = (1 + r)u' \left((1 - \varphi)(1 + r) \right), \tag{8.15}$$

and if the marginal utility function has constant elasticity σ, the optimal value of φ conveniently simplifies to

$$\varphi = \frac{f^{(1-\sigma)/\sigma}}{1 + f^{(1-\sigma)/\sigma}} = \frac{1}{1 + f^{(\sigma-1)/\sigma}}. \tag{8.16}$$

The portfolio share of the lower-return asset is equal to half if utility is logarithmic or if $f = 1$ (so that there is no risk/return trade-off). It may otherwise be lower or higher than half, depending on whether the income or substitution effect is stronger. However, it is always positive as long as $f u'(0) > u'(1 + r)$, i.e., if the investor is sufficiently risk-averse and the inferior asset project has not too low returns (the parameter f should not be too far from 1) and if the rate-of-return uncertainty is purely idiosyncratic across the two types of individuals.

Now assume that asset returns of the agents are *perfectly negatively correlated*. This means that, for agent 2, the first asset is the one with

---

[8] What follows is inspired by Saint-Paul (1992b). Obstfeld (1994) and Devereux and Saito (1997) also formulate and solve models where this effect has a role. Similarly, a well-developed financial market lets savings be allocated more efficiently when new capital takes time to become productive and, as in the model proposed by Bencivenga and Smith (1991), individual portfolios are biased to more liquid but less productive assets when financial institutions ("banks") are not available to smooth liquidity risk across heterogeneous individuals; see also Greenwood and Smith (1997).

lower returns and yields $(1 + r)f$ in the first state and zero otherwise. Asset 2 yields $1 + r$ units in the second state. The extreme assumption of a perfectly negative correlation implies that two agents suffice to eliminate aggregate risk.

Consider now the best case where the two agents are able to perfectly pool their risk. Obviously, aggregate returns would be $(1 + r)/2$ with certainty: each of the two individuals could undertake the higher expected return investment and nobody would go into the inferior project. In equilibrium, everyone could draw on each other's realized returns so as to stabilize future consumption completely. On the other hand, if there is no pooling, aggregate returns are lower because sufficiently risk-averse agents will invest a positive amount into the inferior project. The expected return in the autarchic investment portfolios is then given by

$$\frac{1+r}{2}\left[(1 - \varphi) + f\varphi\right] < \frac{1+r}{2}.$$

8.4 References and Further Issues

We studied a general equilibrium model with rate-of-return risk in a simple AK model and abstracted from labor income. Angeletos and Calvet (2003) provide a closed-form solution for a model with investment risk and neoclassical technology where individuals have CARA preferences. In a similar setup, Angeletos (2004) obtains an explicit solution for CRRA preferences when entrepreneurs face constant returns to scale such that the expected (but uncertain) rate-of-return is constant among firms. Quantitative implications of rate-of-return risk on macroeconomic variables are explored in Heaton and Lucas (1996).

As mentioned in the introduction to this chapter, models where returns to accumulation are idiosyncratically uncertain rationalize ex post inequality over any finite horizon. In infinite-horizon models, we saw that inequality would simply increase without bounds if returns to investment were continuously perturbed by idiosyncratic shocks, and were unrelated to wealth levels. Models like Bénabou's (1996c, 1996d) feature uncertain returns to investment, but also self-financing constraints, which generate mean-reverting wealth dynamics as in Tamura (1991). In general, financial markets offer better insurance against idiosyncratic income and consumption uncertainty, and a more efficient allocation of aggregate savings across investment opportunities. Cochrane (1991) presents evidence that individual consumption is insured against some idiosyncratic shocks but not for others, such as involuntary job losses. For developing countries

Bekaert, Harvey, and Lundblad (2004) provide some empirical support that liberalization of financial markets decreases consumption volatility.

Across economies at different levels of financial development, accordingly, higher production and faster growth should be associated with more stable inequality. Recent work brings this insight to bear on time-series developments, allowing the evolution of financial markets to be endogenously related to growth and wealth dynamics. Greenwood and Jovanovic (1990), Saint-Paul (1992b), and other models surveyed by Greenwood and Smith (1997) let it be costly for individuals to access an intermediated financial market. The implications of costly access to the favorable investment opportunities offered by organized financial markets depend on distribution as well as on the level and expected growth rate of income, and are similar to those of the indivisibilities and fixed costs in individual investment opportunity sets reviewed in section 7.2. The model of Acemoglu and Zilibotti (1997), for example, features better diversification in a more developed economy because investment projects are indivisible, rather than because of assumptions regarding financial market setup costs. Depending on the distribution of resources, a more or less large fraction of the population may be able to afford participation when its costs are partly fixed at the individual level. Since relative welfare levels are completely stabilized across those individuals who do participate in the financial market, the dynamic paths of aggregate output and cross-sectional inequality are jointly determined, as in the simpler setting discussed in section 7.2. In addition, fixed participation costs may become irrelevant if growth "trickles down" such that, eventually, all individuals can enter the financial market. The Greenwood and Jovanovic (1990) model predicts convergence to a stable distribution of welfare (and, since utility is logarithmic, of consumption and wealth). Some individuals' wealth levels may never become high enough to induce them to enter the financial market. Even in that case, however, all of the economy's wealth is asymptotically invested in the financial market, for individuals may remain out of it only if their wealth becomes negligible in relative terms.

As we have seen, pooling risk has wonderful efficiency and equality implications, so the question is why are they not all pooled? The main reason lies in information problems: there is a huge literature we do not want to cover in detail which discusses moral hazard (hidden action), adverse selection, and/or enforcement problems. Let us consider the moral hazard problem because it is the most intuitive for our purposes. Assume that the success of a project depends on the investor's effort, which is assumed not to be observable. Only the success of the project can be observed. However, effort is costly for the investor as it consumes time and resources. If the investor is fully insured against a bad outcome of the project ex ante, there is no reason to undertake effort as it is costly and the resulting investor's income is the same whether the project succeeds or fails. Of course, the agent offering the insurance takes these considerations into account and anticipates the low effort of the investor. Hence, the price for the insurance will be very high, or there will be no insurance contract at all. Models where such asymmetric information problems are central and where interesting interactions between inequality and investment/growth are studied include Aghion and Bolton (1997), Piketty (1997), and Freeman (1996).

Obviously, the moral hazard problem gets even more severe for human capital and individual labor market decisions in general. As a consequence, we never observe full insurance on the labor market. For example, it would be very difficult for a private company to offer unemployment insurance. There is not only the problem of moral hazard, i.e., an unemployed agent exhibits little effort to find a new job, but also problems of adverse selection: agents who have private knowledge that they are likely to lose their job will choose a high amount of unemployment insurance. Therefore, unemployment insurance is only offered by governmental authorities who can force the agents to join the insurance system. However, the government also faces the moral hazard problem. Hence, existing unemployment insurance always offers only partial insurance. From this discussion the reader should be motivated to study the effects of uninsurable endowment risks in the next chapter.

8.5 REVIEW EXERCISE

EXERCISE 32 (Borrowing constraints, overlapping generations, pooling) Consider an economy populated by L infinitely lived individuals, with a single good that may be either consumed or accumulated as (nondepreciating) capital.

a. Suppose each individual owns one unit of labor, and can use it with k units of capital to produce $f(k) = k^\alpha + Ak$ units of output. Recall that if the economy has perfectly competitive markets for factors in each period, then the aggregate production function is $F(K, L) = K^\alpha L^{1-\alpha} + AK$, regardless of who owns the capital stock. Suppose individuals maximize the present value of $\ln c$ discounted at rate ρ. At the beginning of time, there exist $K_0 = 2L$ units of capital; a group of $L/2$ individuals owns only one unit of capital each, the other $L/2$ own three units of capital each. Discuss the dynamics of the income (consumption, wealth) distribution: first, if all individuals can borrow and lend at the same market interest rate, then if neither borrowing nor lending is possible; what are the dynamics of aggregate output in the latter case?

b. Now consider the different technological setup where each of L individuals can combine his unit of labor with k units of capital and obtain k^α units of output; also, it is possible to operate a technology that uses only capital, and yields $\tilde{A}$ units of output for each unit of k. Suppose individual lifetimes last two periods, and there is no population growth. Each individual maximizes

$$(c_{1t})^{0.5} + (c_{2t+1})^{0.5}$$

and earns only labor income in the first period, only capital income in the second period. What levels of output are consistent with a standard market structure where all factors are paid their marginal product and young agents buy the capital stock from the old?

c. Suppose that the linear technology is random: if individual i invests k^i units in it, production is A^H or $A^L < A^H$ with equal probability. There are infinitely many individuals and all risk is idiosyncratic, but the financial market is imperfect: investors earn the random return of their individual project rather than the aggregate return $\tilde{A} = (A^H + A^L)/2$, which is not random. Discuss the implications of this for savings, investment, and distribution.

CHAPTER NINE

Uninsurable Income Shocks

As we discussed at the end of the previous chapter, the need to elicit effort limits the scope for risk sharing in investment projects. Moral hazard problems are perhaps even more important for (non-accumulated) labor income; so, it is difficult to obtain insurance against bad luck in the labor market. Bad luck is obviously possible in the form of involuntary unemployment, yet unemployment insurance is hardly provided by private companies—and public unemployment insurance schemes face challenging efficiency problems, also due to imperfect information, which we review briefly in the concluding section of this chapter. There we also discuss the empirical importance of idiosyncratic labor market shocks: the volatility of sector-specific wages is obviously higher than that of the aggregate wage bill and, empirically, both sector-level and individual-level wage and employment shocks bear importantly on individual consumption levels, confirming that labor market risk is not traded on well-functioning financial or insurance markets.

In this chapter we study how this noninsurable endowment risk interacts with savings and distribution. We assume that the individual faces shocks on the non-accumulated factor, i.e., his labor endowment.[1] To make the point most clearly, we abstract from rate-of-return risk, hence there exists only one investment project that yields a deterministic return. First, we introduce the two key concepts that will come up in this chapter: *liquidity constraints* and *precautionary savings*. This will be done in a simple two-period problem in partial equilibrium where factor prices are given. We then discuss that borrowing constraints and precautionary savings are indeed related: they have similar welfare implications and they imply similar predictions about consumption and savings behavior. Interestingly, it will turn out that the consumption function may become concave, i.e., the marginal propensity to consume will decrease with the level of wealth, even when all individuals have the same constant degree of relative risk aversion.

---

[1]Instead of assuming that endowments are shocked we could assume that wages are risky. We chose this to make a clear difference from the rate-of-return risk on savings. It is obvious that the results would be quite similar, as it is the wage income Wl that matters for the individual's consumption.

We discuss the dynamics of distribution, and then turn to general equilibrium. Focusing on steady states, we determine the factor prices in the macroeconomic equilibrium and discuss how aggregate and individual capital stocks evolve. We characterize the endogenous wealth distribution for both the CARA and the CRRA case. As in the previous chapter, the realization of the uncertain endowments creates inequality endogenously. Idiosyncratic uninsurable shocks imply a tendency for consumption inequality to increase over time, but their effects on the amount of savings and the equilibrium rate of return of accumulated factors (which is lower than the rate of utility discount in steady state) are such as to imply a degree of long-run convergence.

The models reviewed are concerned with consumption-savings and portfolio choices. However, other decisions will also be affected in the presence of noninsurable idiosyncratic risk. In the final section we present a model where the presence of idiosyncratic risks affects labor market outcomes. In that model, *mobility* choices are costly and only workers who happen to be rich enough can take advantage of high wages in alternative jobs and only the behavior of rich workers determines wage differentials. This implies that risk-neutral behavior in the labor market approximates aggregate outcomes. As in Krusell and Smith (1998) and related studies, self-insurance will be very powerful, and uninsurable idiosyncratic shocks have potentially minor implications for aggregate phenomena.

9.1 A Two-Period Characterization

Before we start our analysis of the implications of idiosyncratic shocks on non-accumulated factor incomes for savings behavior, we focus on implications of liquidity constraints when labor incomes are certain. This is interesting for at least two reasons. First, liquidity constraints are certainly of great importance in practice, so it is interesting per se how such constraints do affect savings behavior. Second, we will see that, analytically, there are strong similarities between a situation of certain incomes flows but potentially binding liquidity constraints, and a situation where labor incomes are uncertain but not insurable.

In the first part of this section we focus on liquidity constraints. Intuitively, future liquidity constraints force individuals to save more today to escape this constraint. The result is that the consumption function is concave. Rich individuals will save more (at the margin) than poor individuals. In the second part of this section we then discuss the implication for savings of noninsurable income risks, that is, the case of precautionary savings. We will see that, just like in the presence of liquidity constraints, the consumption choices are no longer linear in income but concave.

The present section treats factor prices as exogenous, thus working in the context of general equilibrium analysis. In the following sections we then focus on the aggregate consequences of noninsurable endowment risk for aggregate savings and the aggregate capital stock. In doing so, we extend our analysis to a macroeconomic general equilibrium framework.

9.1.1 Liquidity Constraints

Consider a standard two-period situation in which individuals earn certain (labor) income in both periods and decide on consumption in order to maximize lifetime utility. The rate of return R is not random. Consumption in the second period is given by

$$c_{2t+1} = (W_t l_{1t} - c_{1t})(1 + R) + W_{t+1} l_{2t+1}, \qquad (9.1)$$

where l_{1t} denotes the labor endowment of individuals who are young at time t, and l_{2t+1} that of the same individual when old, at time $t + 1$. Consumption choices satisfy (8.5), with $v(\cdot) = \frac{1}{1+\rho} u(\cdot)$:

$$u'(c_{1t}) = \frac{1 + R}{1 + \rho} E_t \left[u' \left((W_t l_{1t} - c_{1t})(1 + R) + W_{t+1} l_{2t+1} \right) \right] + \mu_t, \qquad (9.2)$$

where $\mu_t > 0$ if a borrowing constraint is binding.

Assume, for simplicity, that utility is CRRA, which implies that $u'(c) = c^{-\sigma}$. Then, it is easy to verify that $W_t l_t^i - c_{1t}^i > 0$ (savings are positive) if

$$\frac{W_{t+1} l_{2t+1}}{W_t l_{1t}} < (\beta(1 + R))^{\frac{1}{\sigma}} \equiv \xi. \qquad (9.3)$$

Clearly, the direction of the inequality in (9.3) depends on the lifetime pattern of labor endowments l_{1t}, l_{2t+1} and on the taste parameters ρ, σ, but also on the rate of return on savings R and on the growth rate of wages W_{t+1}/W_t. The condition is trivially satisfied if $l_{2t+1} = 0$, as in the standard overlapping generations model (5.19).

In more general models, however, the growth rate of wages may exceed the desired growth rate of consumption, at least in early stages (or other parts) of an individual's life. If the inequality in (9.3) is reversed, the young individuals would wish to borrow. When this is not possible, the liquidity constraint becomes binding. In (9.2), this implies that $\mu_t > 0$. The obvious consequence is that first-period consumption is smaller than it would be in the absence of borrowing constraints.

EXERCISE 33 Assume that an individual lives for two periods with labor income $W_t l_{1t}$ and $W_{t+1} l_{2t+1}$ in the first and second period, respectively.

The individual cannot run into debt. For simplicity set $R = \rho = 0$. Characterize the optimal consumption path and show that the consumption function is concave in $W_t l_{1t}$.

Figure 9.1 illustrates optimal (and possibly constrained) choices. Even if labor incomes are known with certainty, figure 9.1 shows that strongly increasing labor incomes may make liquidity constraints binding. Note that this implies the consumption function becomes nonlinear (as was to be shown in the simple exercise above). Obviously, the marginal propensity to consume of constrained individuals equals unity, whereas the marginal propensity of unconstrained agents is necessarily below unity. This holds true for any preferences and follows directly from the desire to smooth consumption over time. Thus, in the presence of binding borrowing constraints, the aggregate savings of a heterogeneous population are larger than in the absence of such constraints. Although binding constraints increase aggregate savings, welfare is necessarily reduced. This can be directly inferred from figure 9.1. A constrained individual would be better off if he or she could consume more today. Finally, a more unequal distribution of endowments l_{1t} increases savings when such redistribution occurs between individuals who face the borrowing constraint and individuals who do not. Even without uncertainty, liquidity constraints make the consumption function concave, which implies that more inequality increases savings.

The following simple exercise asks you to derive this result in an economy populated by identical two-period-lived agents.

EXERCISE 34 Consider a population of two equally sized groups of young and old agents in each period, and let $\sigma = 1$ (logarithmic utility). Let $l_{2t+1} \equiv l_2$ be constant over time, and similarly let $l_{1t} = l_1$ for all t. Assume that wages grow at a constant rate $W_{t+1}/W_t = \theta > 1$ for all t, with certainty. Show that aggregate savings are larger when young agents would like to borrow, but cannot.

9.1.2 Precautionary Savings

Above we have seen that the presence of liquidity constraints affects aggregate savings even under certainty, provided there are liquidity constraints and initial labor incomes are relatively low. We now show that very similar consequences may arise when future labor incomes are uncertain (but individuals can freely borrow at a certain interest rate). The resulting increase in aggregate savings that arises from such uninsurable labor income risk is called "precautionary savings."

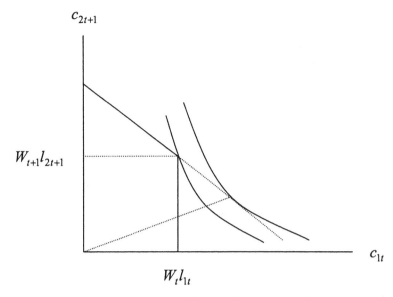

Figure 9.1 A two-period saving problem with increasing labor income and liquidity constraints

Assume that non-accumulated income is random and noninsurable. To make the problem as simple as possible, suppose that both interest rate and rate of time preference are equal to zero, so $R = \rho = 0$. Furthermore let us assume that, in each period, the individual expects the same labor income $\bar{y}$, so we can write

$$\bar{y} = W_t l_{1t} = E_t W_{t+1} l_{2t+1}.$$

Obviously, in the absence of labor income risk, the individual would consume the same amount in each period, $c_{1t} = c_{2t+1} = \bar{y}$. Hence in the absence of uncertainty the individual would not save at all but just consume his or her (permanent) income flow. This need no longer be the case when future income is uncertain. In that case, the level of consumption may be written as $c_{1t} = \bar{y} - s_t$ where s_t tells us by how much consumption under uncertainty deviates from consumption in the absence of uncertainty. In other words, s_t is the level of precautionary savings. The individual can set aside an (additional) amount s_t in the first period and consume it in the second period (in addition to the random income received then), so we can rewrite the Euler equation as

$$E_t \left[u' \left(y_{t+1} + s_t \right) \right] = u' (\bar{y} - s_t). \tag{9.4}$$

If $u'(\cdot)$ is convex—or equivalently $u'''(\cdot) > 0$—expected marginal utility is larger than the marginal utility of expected income, $E_t[u'(y_{t+1})] > u'(\bar{y})$. Hence the optimal amount of savings is $s_t > 0$ such as to fulfill equation (9.4). When the utility function exhibits a positive third derivative, this is called *prudence*.

Like the borrowing constraints discussed above, the uninsurable endowment risk tends to both decrease welfare and increase savings for given factor returns. Although the individual would like to equalize consumption across periods, as the interest rate equals the discount rate, expected consumption growth is positive. This is done as to self-insure against the labor income risk in the second period.

9.1.3 Liquidity Constraints, Precautionary Savings, and Self-Insurance

It is important to see that the basic reason for precautionary savings lies in the presence of a borrowing constraint or—more generally—a solvency constraint. In the two-period setting studied above, the agent cannot die with negative wealth. Hence consumption in period 2 would follow income pari passu when there were no savings. In a multiperiod setting, liquidity constraints may affect the actual consumption level, even if they do not bind today but they might bind in future periods. As a result, individuals who are liquidity constrained or might be liquidity constrained will save more today to reduce the probability that the constraint will bind in the future. Hence, the individuals accumulate wealth to acquire *self-insurance* against future negative events that may cause the borrowing constraint to be binding. The reason why liquidity constraints can induce precautionary saving is quite intuitive. Carroll and Kimball (2001) point out that constrained agents—with less self-insurance—have less flexibility in responding to shocks because the effects of the shocks cannot be spread out over time. Thus risk has a bigger negative effect on expected utility for constrained agents than for unconstrained agents. The precautionary saving motive is strengthened by the desire to make the liquidity constraint less likely to bind.

More formally, we saw above in equation (9.4) that *prudence*—$u'''(\cdot) > 0$—induces precautionary saving. Carroll and Kimball (2001) proved that when a liquidity constraint is added to a standard optimization problem, the resulting value function exhibits *"increasing prudence"* around the level of wealth where the constraint becomes binding, i.e., the third derivative of the value function becomes (more) positive. This means that liquidity constraints can induce "precautionary behavior" even when the utility function does not exhibit a positive third derivative (i.e., quadratic utility functions) because the value function gets a positive third derivative. Of course, with infinite horizons the utility function must have a positive third derivative, otherwise the utility function must exhibit a bliss point: as Ljungqvist and Sargent (2004, 557) point out, for high consumption levels (which are possible with many periods when there are idiosyncratic shocks to income) the assumption of positive marginal utility is violated for high consumption levels when marginal utility is non-convex.

To sum up, precautionary savings only occur because the agent must fulfill a solvency constraint. With finite horizons, (possible) debts must be repaid when the life ends. With infinite horizons, the transversality condition must hold. If there were no solvency constraint, there would be no reason for the agent to save for precautionary reasons, as negative shocks could be financed by going (possibly infinitely) into debt. We will take up this issue again in section 9.3.

9.2 General Equilibrium: The CARA Case

Here we study the macroeconomic outcome of a model with endowment uncertainty. We assume consumers have CARA preferences, where $-u''(c)/u'(c) = \eta > 0$ is the constant coefficient of absolute risk aversion. Then, the utility function in each period is an exponential function

$$u(c_t) = -\frac{1}{\eta}e^{-\eta c_t}. \tag{9.5}$$

For such a *constant absolute risk aversion*, CARA, utility function the coefficient of *absolute prudence*, $-u'''(c)/u''(c) = \eta$, is also constant. This implies that amount of precautionary savings does not depend on wealth.

Suppose that the economy is in a stationary steady state. Hence, the interest rate and the aggregate wage bill are constant: $R_{t+1} = R = (1 - \gamma)A$ and $W_t = W$. There is no aggregate risk. However, individuals face idiosyncratic shocks on their labor endowment l_t, so individual labor income is given by Wl_t where l_t is an random i.i.d. shock, with finite support and unitary mean. With total population normalized to unity it follows that the aggregate labor endowment also equals unity, as there is no aggregate risk. (The simplest case of independently and identically distributed labor endowments is perhaps adequate if the "period" is taken to represent a generation.)

We turn to a household's utility maximization problem. The modified Bellman equation (8.2) is given by

$$v_t(k_t, W_t l_t) = \max_{c_t} \left\{ -\frac{1}{\eta}e^{-\eta c_t} + \beta E_t \left[v_{t+1}(k_{t+1}, W_{t+1}l_{t+1}) \right] \right\} \tag{9.6}$$

$$\text{s.t. } k_{t+1} = (1 + R)k_t + W_t l_t - c_t.$$

Moreover, assume that the transversality condition holds.[2] We guess the value function takes the following form:

$$v_t(k_t, Wl_t) = -\frac{B}{\eta}e^{-\eta A\left[(1+R)k_t + Wl_t\right]} \tag{9.7}$$

where A and B have to be determined. We insert the flow budget constraint for k_{t+1} in the value function for $t+1$ and we rewrite the problem (9.6) using our guess (9.7)

$$v_t(k_t, Wl_t) = \max_{c_t}\left\{-\frac{1}{\eta}e^{-\eta c_t} - \beta\frac{B}{\eta}e^{-\eta A(1+R)\left[(1+R)k_t + Wl_t - c_t\right]}E_t e^{-\eta AWl_{t+1}}\right\}$$

Recall that the expectation $E_t e^{-\eta AWl_{t+1}}$ is independent on time as l_{t+1} is i.i.d. We have to take a factor out of the maximization problem on the right-hand side such that the problem itself does not depend on calendar time. Define $x_t \equiv c_t - z_t$. The "factor" z_t can be determined by the condition that $c_t - z_t = -\left[(1+R)k_t + Wl_t - c_t - z_t/(A(1+R))\right]$ or

$$z_t = \left[(1+R)k_t + Wl_t\right]A(1+R)/\left[A(1+R)+1\right].$$

Hence we can write

$$v_t(k_t, Wl_t) = -\frac{1}{\eta}e^{-\eta z_t}\max_x\left\{e^{-\eta x} + \beta Be^{\eta A(1+R)x}E_t e^{-\eta AWl_{t+1}}\right\},$$

where we omitted the time index for x because the reduced maximization problem does not depend on time. We see that the value function indeed takes a CARA form, confirming our guess. Comparing $e^{-\eta z_t}$ with the exponent in (9.7) shows that $A = R/(1+R)$. Maximizing over x and reinserting into the original value function to determine B allows us to find an expression for consumption c_t. The following exercise asks you to do that.

EXERCISE 35 Derive the optimal consumption (9.8) in the CARA case.

We get an intuitive result where $h_t = Wl_t + W/R$ is the expected present value of the individual's labor income.

$$c_t = R\left[k_t + \frac{h_t}{1+R}\right] - \frac{1}{\eta R}\ln\left[\beta(1+R)\right] - \frac{1}{\eta R}\ln E_t e^{-\eta\frac{R}{1+R}W(l_{t+1}-1)}. \tag{9.8}$$

---

[2]We do not impose a further borrowing constraint explicitly because the CARA utility allows for negative consumption as the marginal utility at zero is finite.

CARA preferences allow for an explicit solution of the optimal consumption problem with uncertain labor income. The level of consumption is determined by three terms. The *first* component, $R(k_t + h_t/(1 + R))$, is analogous to the definition of permanent income. In particular, the marginal propensity to consume out of lifetime resources does not depend on income. This is an important result: with CARA preferences, the consumption function is linear if there is only labor income risk. This implies that aggregate savings are not affected by the distribution of economic resources. Furthermore, the propensity to consume out of wealth does not depend on the discount rate ρ. Again, this is a particular feature of CARA preferences.[3]

The *second* component, $-\ln\left[\beta\left(1 + R\right)\right]/\eta R$, represents the usual intertemporal substitution effect (which does not affect the marginal propensity to consume from permanent income). If the interest rate R exceeds the discount rate, the agent is relatively patient. Thus, consumption today is lower.

Finally, the *third* component, $-(\ln E_t e^{-\eta \frac{R}{1+R} W(l_{t+1}-1)})/\eta R$, captures the precautionary motive. By Jensen's inequality, $\ln E_t e^{-\eta \frac{R}{1+R} W(l_{t+1}-1)} > E_t \ln\left(e^{-\eta \frac{R}{1+R} W(l_{t+1}-1)}\right) = 0$, hence the precautionary term is negative. If the income process is more uncertain, $E_t e^{-\eta \frac{R}{1+R} W(l_{t+1}-1)}$ will be higher, because e^x is a convex function. Hence the precautionary savings must rise. Perhaps surprisingly, this term is the same for all individuals. The reason for this result is that all households face the same labor income risk and that the amount of the precautionary savings does not depend on wealth. This is specific to CARA preferences where absolute prudence is constant and does not depend on wealth. To get further intuition on the precautionary motive, note that we can express expected consumption growth from (9.8) as

$$E_t c_{t+1} - c_t = \frac{1}{\eta} \ln\left[\beta\left(1 + R\right)\right] + \frac{1}{\eta} \ln E_t e^{-\eta \frac{R}{1+R} W(l_{t+1}-1)}.$$

In the absence of uncertainty the (absolute) change in consumption is (approximately) given by $\ln\left[\beta\left(1 + R\right)\right]/\eta \approx (R - \rho)/\eta$. In the presence of uncertainty, the increase in consumption is larger than $(R - \rho)/\eta$. In other words, individuals consume less today and more tomorrow, which is just another way to describe the precautionary motive.

---

[3]This can be easily checked by referring to the results derived in chapter 3. From equation (3.9), the marginal propensity to consume from financial wealth, in the stationary steady state with $R < \rho$, is given by $\partial c_t/\partial k_t = 1 + R - \left(\frac{1+R}{1+\rho}\right)^{\frac{1}{\sigma}}$. With CARA preferences we analyze the special case where the HARA parameter $\sigma \to \infty$. Hence we get $\partial c_t/\partial k = R$.

9.2.1 The Steady-State Interest Rate

As the consumption function is linear in wealth, it is easy to derive aggregate consumption, the aggregate capital stock, and the corresponding interest rate in the steady state. Aggregate income equals $RK_t + W$ as the endowment risk is idiosyncratic and there is no aggregate risk. Denote $\ln E_t e^{-\eta \frac{R}{1+R} W (l_{t+1}-1)} \equiv \Phi > 0$. The capital stock then evolves according to the following equation:

$$\Delta K_t = RK_t + W - C_t \tag{9.9}$$

$$= RK_t + W - R(K_t + \frac{W}{R}) + \frac{1}{\eta R} \left(\ln \left[\beta \left(1 + R \right) \right] + \Phi \right)$$

$$= \frac{1}{\eta R} \left(\ln \left[\beta \left(1 + R \right) \right] + \Phi \right).$$

We consider a stationary steady state, with a constant interest rate and constant (average) consumption and wages. In that case we have $\Delta K_t = 0$. As $\Phi > 0$, the product $\beta (1 + R)$ has to be smaller than one, or the interest R must be below the rate of time preference ρ. If $\beta (1 + R) = 1$ or $R = \rho$ the presence of risk would imply a growing consumption path because individuals are prudent. Hence, it must be the case that $R < \rho$ just so as to compensate the precautionary motive and lead all agents to expect constant consumption. The steady-state interest rate can be easily derived from (9.9) setting $\Delta K_t = 0$:

$$R^* = e^{-\Phi}(1 + \rho) - 1$$

which is smaller than ρ as $\Phi > 0$.[4] To self-insure against the idiosyncratic risks, prudent individuals still choose—in expectation—an increasing path of consumption and assets when the discount rate equals the interest rate. Therefore the presence of risk implies that the aggregate savings and the resulting steady-state capital stock are higher and the *interest rate is lower* than in an economy with certainty.

9.2.2 The Dynamics of the Wealth Distribution

With these results it is straightforward to characterize the dynamics of inequality in a steady state. The evolution of individual assets is given by

---

[4]Note that the income process must not be too risky. More precisely, it must hold that $e^{\Phi} < 1 + \rho$ as to ensure that $R^* > 0$.

the following relationship

$$k_{t+1} = k_t + Rk_t + Wl_t - \frac{R}{1+R}((1+R)k_t + Wl_t + W/R)$$

$$\Delta k_t = \frac{1}{1+R}(Wl_t - W) = (l_t - 1)\frac{W}{1+R}.$$

As the random variable l_t is i.i.d. with mean one, individual assets follow a random walk. Hence the distribution is *not stationary* as in section 8.2. The agents consume all their capital income. If there is a positive income shock, their assets rise but will not be reduced thereafter. There would only be a tendency for wealth to mean-revert if the propensity to consume were larger than R.

There are two basic problems with the CARA assumption. First, the nonstationarity of the distribution implies that some consumption levels eventually become negative. Because the CARA utility function exhibits a finite marginal utility at zero, negative consumption levels are a possible solution of this optimization problem. If we imposed nonnegativity explicitly, no closed-form solution would be possible anymore. However, the distribution would become stationary if the propensity to consume out of financial wealth exceeds the interest rate. If we stick to CARA preferences this is the case if the time horizon of the agents is finite. For HARA preferences where absolute risk aversion is declining, the propensity to consume out of wealth is larger than the interest rate when ρ exceeds R. In particular, this is the case for CRRA (constant relative risk aversion) preferences. This example will be discussed at length in the next section.

A second problem with the CARA assumption is the fact that only stationary steady states can be studied. If the economy exhibits exogenous or endogenous productivity growth, consumption must grow. But this implies that steady states are no longer feasible because, under the CARA assumption, the elasticity of intertemporal substitution is not constant. As is well-known, the only utility function that is compatible with balanced growth paths is again the CRRA where the elasticity of substitution is constant. Hence, constant interest rates (which is the case in steady state) go along with constant consumption growth.

9.3 General Equilibrium: The CRRA Case

In this section we perform the analogous analysis as above for the case when the household's *relative* (rather than absolute) risk aversion is constant. When preferences are CRRA, both absolute risk aversion and absolute prudence are decreasing. Hence with CRRA preferences—and unlike in the CARA case—the precautionary savings motive is less pronounced for the rich than for the poor. In fact, we show by means of simulations that in the presence of idiosyncratic labor income risk the consumption function becomes nonlinear. Richer people are less hurt by uncertainty, so they have to save less for precautionary reasons. Their consumption path will be similar to the certainty case. Instead, poor people exhibit a tendency to go to a "buffer stock" of savings. If a poor individual faces a negative labor income shock, he or she will reduce consumption more than a rich individual. Such behavior provides the reason why—in contrast to the CARA case analyzed in the previous section—the steady-state wealth distribution is stationary.

An interesting feature of the model presented in this section is that it rationalizes a consumption function that is concave in available resources in a cross section of households and, at the same time, does *not* feature a trend in the aggregate savings rate. In other words increasing marginal savings rates are not due to ad hoc assumptions on the functional form of utility that would, unrealistically and in contradiction with empirical evidence, imply an increase in aggregate savings rates as per capita incomes rise. The assumption of CRRA preferences allows us to analyze an economy with balanced growth because the homotheticity of the utility function guarantees a constant saving rate in a growing environment.

To take the simplest possible case, we assume that growth setup as in chapter 4 where aggregate output is given by $Y_t = AK_t$. According to equation (4.1), the rewards to the accumulated and non-accumulated factor read $W_t = \gamma Y_t$ and $R_t = (1 - \gamma)Y_t/K_t = (1 - \gamma)A$, where γ is an exogenous parameter determining the functional distribution. These assumptions imply that output, capital stock, and wages grow by a constant factor which we denote by θ.[5] The growth factor θ is determined by aggregate savings but it is exogenous for the individuals. The unit wage rate at date τ is therefore given by $W_\tau = W_t\theta^{\tau-t}$. Apart from technology and preferences the model is identical to that analyzed in the previous section. In particular, agents have free access to a risk-free asset that yields a constant return R and face idiosyncratic shocks on their labor endowment l_t, which is an i.i.d. random variable, with finite support and unitary mean. This setup implies that individual labor income $W_t l_t$ is exposed to uninsurable risk. Just like in the previous section, variability of labor endowment is exogenous to the model and there is no aggregate risk.

We first turn to the individual's problem. To prevent the individual from obtaining infinite utility by rolling over an infinitely negative debt,

---

[5] Recall that the AK model may also be interpreted as the reduced-form representation of almost any linear endogenous growth model's technology, where a fixed output-capital ratio A indexes the economy's efficiency in using forgone consumption as a productive factor.

a lower bound on accumulated wealth must be imposed. For simplicity, we impose for the derivations below a "liquidity" constraint $\bar{k}_t \geq 0$. Although simplifying,[6] this is appropriate if no part of future labor income can be used as collateral and, in particular, if a time period is taken to represent a generation (where utility of the offspring enters the parents' utility function) and negative bequests are realistically disallowed.

The modified Bellman equation (8.2) is given by

$$v_t(k_t, W_t l_t) = \max_{c_t} \left\{ \frac{c_t^{1-\sigma}}{1-\sigma} + \beta E_t \left[v_{t+1}(k_{t+1}, W_{t+1} l_{t+1}) \right] \right\} \qquad (9.10)$$

$$\text{s.t. } k_{t+1} = (1+R)k_t + W_t l_t - c_t,$$

$$\text{and } 0 \leq (1+R)k_t + W_t l_t - c_t.$$

Note that, given i.i.d. realizations of the labor endowment l_{t+1}, the conditional expectation on the right-hand side of (9.10) is independent of l_t. Further note that the interest rate $R = (1-\gamma)A$ is constant. The Euler condition is, as usual,

$$c_t^{-\sigma} = \beta(1+R)E_t \left[c_{t+1}^{-\sigma} \right] + \mu_t. \qquad (9.11)$$

Given CRRA utility, constant return on savings, and i.i.d. distributed labor endowments, it is easy to show for $\sigma \neq 1$ that the value function is CRRA, i.e., it is homogeneous of degree $1 - \sigma$ in wealth and labor income. Guess that the value function takes the CRRA form so that

$$v_t(\lambda k_t, \lambda W_t l_t) = \lambda^{1-\sigma} v_t(k_t, W_t l_t), \quad \forall t, \forall \lambda > 0. \qquad (9.12)$$

We insert the flow budget constraint for k_{t+1} in the value function for $t+1$ and we rewrite the problem (9.10) using our guess (9.12):

$$v_t(\lambda k_t, \lambda W_t l_t) = \max_{c_t} \left\{ \frac{c_t^{1-\sigma}}{1-\sigma} + \beta E_t \left[v_{t+1}((1+R)\lambda k_t + \lambda W_t l_t - c_t, \lambda W_{t+1} l_{t+1}) \right] \right\}$$

$$= \lambda^{1-\sigma} \max_{x_t} \left\{ \frac{x_t^{1-\sigma}}{1-\sigma} + \beta E_t \left[v_{t+1}((1+R)k_t + W_t l_t - x_t, W_{t+1} l_{t+1}) \right] \right\}$$

$$= \lambda^{1-\sigma} v_t(k_t, W_t l_t)$$

$$\text{s.t. } 0 \leq (1+R)k_t + W_t l_t - x_t$$

and our guess is confirmed. Note that we defined $x_t \equiv c_t/\lambda$. As a corollary, we see that individual consumption is homogeneous of degree one in

---

[6]If labor income is bounded below by a strictly positive amount, negative finite wealth does not necessarily imply insolvency.

wealth and labor income because the optimal solution c_t/λ is constant and does not depend on λ. Finally, in the logarithmic case ($\sigma = 1$), the right-hand side also features the additive term $\ln[\lambda]/(1 - \beta)$, which is constant with respect to the individual's control problem and irrelevant to the optimal program.

EXERCISE 36 Show that $v_t(\lambda k_t, \lambda W_t l_t) = v_t(k_t, W_t l_t) + \ln[\lambda]/(1 - \beta)$ if utility is logarithmic.

In equation (9.15) below we will see that, in fact, an agent who starts out with scaled-up wealth and wage income, and maximizes a homothetic function of the consumption stream, chooses a proportionately scaled-up state-dependent consumption path. Such scaled-up behavior affects the value function by an irrelevant additive constant in the logarithmic case, and by a multiplicative factor if $\sigma \neq 1$.

The property in (9.12), and the time-independent labor endowment process, make it possible to analyze the individual's consumption problem in terms of a single state variable. As the homogeneity property (9.12) holds for any positive constant λ we may set λ equal to the growth factor θ. The value function for period $t + 1$ in (9.10) can then be written as

$$v(k_{t+1}, W_{t+1} l_{t+1}) = \theta^{1-\sigma} v\left(\frac{k_{t+1}}{\theta}, \frac{W_{t+1}}{\theta} l_{t+1}\right) \qquad (9.13)$$

(plus $\ln[\theta]/(1 - \beta)$ if $\sigma = 1$). The homogeneity property of (9.13) allows us to detrend the variables such that the program can be written as a function of stationary variables. Obviously, the value function v is then also stationary so we can omit the time index. Denoting $\tilde{k}_t \equiv k_t$, and $\tilde{k}_{t+1} \equiv k_{t+1}/\theta$, $\tilde{c}_t \equiv c_t$, and $\tilde{W} \equiv W_t = W_{t+1}/\theta$, the recursive relationship (5.20) may be rewritten in the form

$$v\left(\tilde{k}_t, \tilde{W} l_t\right) = \max_{\tilde{c}_t} \left\{ \frac{\tilde{c}_t^{1-\sigma}}{1 - \sigma} + \beta \theta^{1-\sigma} E_t\left[v\left(\tilde{k}_{t+1}, \tilde{W} l_{t+1}\right)\right] \right\} \qquad (9.14)$$

$$\text{s.t. } \tilde{k}_{t+1} = \left((1+R)\tilde{k}_t + \tilde{W} l_t - \tilde{c}_t\right)/\theta, \ \tilde{k}_{t+1} \geq 0.$$

(Again, the logarithmic case requires additive rather than multiplicative scaling and has the additive constant $\ln[\theta]/(1 - \beta)$ on the right-hand side, irrelevant for the individual's problem.) This time-independent functional relationship is defined on geometrically detrended exogenous and endogenous variables, the detrending factor being the growth factor θ.

The value of the program can also be written as a function of current consumable resources ("cash in hand") $(1+R)\tilde{k}_t + \tilde{W} l_t$, because $\tilde{W}$ is constant over time and $E_t l_{t+\tau}$ with $\tau \geq 1$ is independent of l_t. Therefore, the optimal consumption policy function $c(\cdot)$ is also a function of cash in hand at date t. We showed above that the consumption policy function $c(\cdot)$ responds linearly to a rescaling of both accumulated and non-accumulated income,

$$c(\lambda(1 + R)k_t + \lambda W l_t) = \lambda c((1 + R)k_t + W_t l_t), \quad \forall \lambda > 0. \tag{9.15}$$

Moreover, along the optimal program, detrended consumption satisfies the Euler equation implied by the recursion (9.14). Again, the detrended Euler equation does not depend on calendar time because of the constant elasticity of substitution and the constant growth rate. Taking (9.11) and (9.15) together, the Kuhn-Tucker multiplier, reflecting the value of relaxing the borrowing constraint, equals $\mu_t(\lambda) = \lambda^{-\sigma} \mu_t(1)$, hence it decreases in λ at a constant rate. Thus the detrended Kuhn-Tucker multiplier, $\tilde{\mu}_{t+\tau} \equiv \theta^{\sigma\tau} \mu_{t+\tau}$, does not depend on calendar time, $E_t \tilde{\mu}_{t+\tau} = \tilde{\mu}_t$, but it may change over time due to shocks. The detrended Euler equation (9.11) reads

$$(\tilde{c}_t)^{-\sigma} = \beta(1 + R)\theta^\sigma E_t \left[(\tilde{c}_{t+1})^{-\sigma} \right] + \tilde{\mu}_t. \tag{9.16}$$

9.3.1 The Household's Consumption Function

The solution of the $v(\cdot)$ recursion can only be determined numerically: here, we simply outline the character of the solutions rather than doing simulations ourselves. (The interested reader is referred to the relevant literature discussed at the end of this chapter.) Figure 9.2 illustrates the qualitative character of consumption choice in partial equilibrium, i.e., for a given rate of growth θ and a given rate of return R. General equilibrium issues will be discussed in the next subsection.

In figure 9.2a, gross savings are measured by the vertical distance between the dotted 45° line and consumption, plotted as a solid line against consumable resources. While consumption exhausts all available resources when labor income is low and accumulated wealth is zero, an increasing proportion of available resources is saved when the consumer is richer. By (9.15), in fact, the individual's propensity to consume is constant with respect to proportional scaling of both currently consumable resources and of the labor income process; but if (the distribution of) future labor income is kept fixed, as in the figure, then the propensity to consume is smaller for larger wealth levels, because the consumption afforded by higher current wealth is optimally smoothed over the current and future periods. While a perfectly insured consumer would have constant propensity to save out of current resources if the period utility

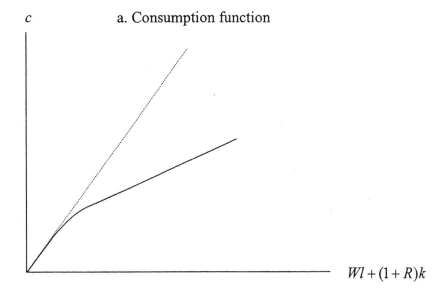

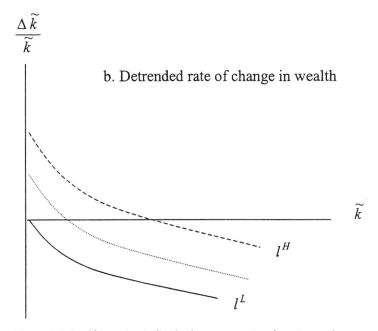

Figure 9.2 A self-insuring individual's consumption function and consumption and wealth dynamics

function $u(\cdot)$ is CRRA, savings are "luxuries" if labor income is uncertain (see Proposition 3 in Laitner 1979a).

Hence, this class of models can rationalize an increasing income elasticity of savings without resorting to ad hoc assumptions on the form of utility. Such assumptions are undesirable because they imply increasing rates of accumulation and growth in a growing economy where all agents become richer over time.

Consumption is an asymptotically linear function of total available resources in figure 9.2a. The (i.i.d.) distribution of detrended labor income is kept fixed along the horizontal axis of the figure; hence, labor income becomes a smaller and smaller fraction of total consumable resources as they (and consumption) become larger and larger. Hence the individual is better able to self-insure against its fluctuations. Consequently, the variance in *relative* consumption must go to zero when wealth k_t goes to infinity. This observation allows us to determine the asymptotic slope of the consumption function, which is given by the consumption growth of an individual with infinite wealth. To see this, use equation (9.12) to write the optimization problem as follows:

$$v_t(k_t, W_t l_t) =$$
$$k_t^{1-\sigma} \max_{z_t} \left\{ \frac{z_t^{1-\sigma}}{1-\sigma} + \beta E_t \left[v_{t+1}((1+R) + W_t l_t/k_t - z_t, W_{t+1} l_{t+1}/k_t) \right] \right\}$$

$$v_t(1, W_t l_t/k_t) =$$
$$\max_{z_t} \left\{ \frac{z_t^{1-\sigma}}{1-\sigma} + \beta E_t \left[v_{t+1}((1+R) + W_t l_t/k_t - z_t, W_{t+1} l_{t+1}/k_t) \right] \right\}$$

where $z_\tau \equiv c_\tau/k_t$. For $k_t \to \infty$, the maximization problem becomes deterministic as $W_{t+1} l_{t+1}/k_t$ approaches zero. In that case, the problem reduces to that of consumer owning an initial wealth of $1 + R$ but earning no future labor income. The optimal growth of z_t is then given by the usual Euler equation $z_{t+1}/z_t = (\beta(1+R))^{1/\sigma}$. Inserting this into the intertemporal budget constraint yields

$$\lim_{k_t \to \infty} z_t \sum_{\tau=0}^{\infty} \left(\beta^{1/\sigma} (1+R)^{(1-\sigma)/\sigma} \right)^\tau = 1 + R.$$

We solve for $\lim_{k_t \to \infty} c_t/k_t$ to get

$$\lim_{k_t \to \infty} \frac{c_t}{k_t} = 1 + R - [\beta(1+R)]^{1/\sigma}$$

or in terms of the consumption function (we omit time indices)

$$\lim_{k \to \infty} \frac{c((1+R)k + Wl)}{(1+R)k + Wl} = 1 - \beta^{1/\sigma}(1+R)^{(1-\sigma)/\sigma}. \qquad (9.17)$$

As we expected, both the slope of the consumption function and consumption growth are equal to the deterministic case when $k \to \infty$.

Let us turn to the dynamics of the accumulated factor. Figure 9.2b displays the detrended wealth transition functions obtained by inserting the consumption function of figure 9.2a in the dynamic budget constraint: the vertical axis measures $\Delta \tilde{k}/\tilde{k} \equiv \left(\tilde{k}_{t+1} - \tilde{k}_t\right)/\tilde{k}$, which is related to the current accumulated wealth level on the horizontal axis by

$$\frac{\Delta \tilde{k}}{\tilde{k}} = \frac{1}{\theta}\left(1 + R + \frac{\tilde{W}}{\tilde{k}}l - \frac{\tilde{c}}{\tilde{k}}\right) - 1. \qquad (9.18)$$

In figure 9.2b it is assumed that the i.i.d. labor endowment may take only two values: l^L and l^H with equal probability. The solid line plots the amount of capital carried into the next period by an individual whose current labor income is low, $l = l^L$, as a function of the amount of capital carried into the current period from the previous one (without knowing, of course, that labor income would turn out to be low). The liquidity constraint binds for an individual who enters the period with no capital and experiences a low draw of labor income. Hence, the solid line passes through the origin: such an individual consumes all that is available to him or her, and carries zero wealth into the next period. The dashed line plots the corresponding wealth transitions conditioned on high income draws $l = l^H$. This line has a positive intercept: when labor income is high, even the poorest individual accumulates some wealth so as to distribute the newly available resources across future periods' consumption. The average of these wealth transition functions represents expected net accumulation, before labor income's realization, for each wealth level. Plotted as a dotted line in the figure, it slopes downward and crosses the horizontal axis at a "target" wealth level.

To summarize, with CRRA preferences savings propensities depend in intuitive and realistic ways on both the level and the factor composition of individual and aggregate income flows. The propensity to consume out of wealth is higher for richer individuals, who are less concerned with (heavily discounted) future consumption volatility; the propensity to consume out of non-accumulated income depends, in accordance with permanent income theory, on whether the current flow is above or below its long-run expected level. This class of models can rationalize an increasing income elasticity of savings without resorting to ad hoc assumptions on the form of utility, which would imply increasing rates of accumulation and growth in a growing economy where all agents become richer over time.

9.3.2 Implications for the Distribution of Wealth

Temporary labor income fluctuations have persistent effects on individual consumption and wealth, because optimal consumption policies tend to smooth over time their consumption impact by accumulation and decumulation of wealth. Hence, the cross-sectional distribution of wealth is realistically predicted to be more unequal than that of labor income by this class of models. Moreover, the approximate constancy of consumption (and wealth) growth rates in the setting considered implies that the distribution of wealth is skewed to the right, and features a mass of very poor individuals if liquidity constraints are binding. These are also qualitatively realistic features in light of available evidence: there is an empirical consensus that the wealth distribution follows a Power law (Pareto distribution), at least at its right tails, which implies a highly skewed wealth distribution. For a survey see Persky (1992) or Davies and Shorrocks (2000), and for recent evidence see Levy and Solomon (1997).[7]

The evolution of individual wealth can be obtained from (9.17) and (9.18). Using (9.17) we obtain, for large k, the following approximation:

$$\frac{\Delta \tilde{k}}{\tilde{k}} \approx \frac{1}{\theta} \left(\frac{\tilde{W}}{\tilde{k}} l - [\beta(1+R)]^{1/\sigma} \right) - 1. \tag{9.19}$$

When the condition

$$\theta > ((1+R)\beta)^{1/\sigma} \tag{9.20}$$

holds, the process (9.19) has increasingly negative drift for larger and larger values of $\tilde{k}$. Condition (9.20) states that the growth factor must be larger than the one in the certainty case. We will argue below—when the growth factor θ is determined endogenously—that this must hold in steady state. As the independently distributed innovation $\tilde{W} l_t / \theta$ of the process has bounded support, there exists a finite level $k^{max} < \infty$ of detrended wealth that is large enough to imply decumulation even when current labor income is high. All $\tilde{k}$ levels larger than k^{max} form a transient set: if the individual happened to be richer than that, detrended wealth would be decumulated with probability one and would certainly fall below k^{max} in finite time. As the opposite transition is impossible,

---

[7]Levy and Solomon (1997) analyze data from the 1996 Forbes 400 list of the richest people in the United States. Their results confirm that wealth is distributed according to a power law at its right end.

$[0, k^{\max}]$ is the support of the long-run distribution of wealth, whose existence and uniqueness is proved by Laitner (1979a, 1979b) under the assumptions made here. If condition (9.20) were not satisfied, the dashed line would remain indefinitely above the horizontal axis of figure 9.2b and the dynamics of detrended wealth would be nonstationary. Regardless of current wealth, the consumer would always choose to carry forward an even larger amount of detrended wealth when experiencing a favorable labor income draw. In the long run, this positive drift would make uncertain labor income an infinitesimally small proportion of the individual's resources, and complete self-insurance would be reached with probability one.

Therefore condition (9.20) is necessary and sufficient for uninsurable uncertainty to matter for long-run consumption/saving choices (see Proposition 4 in Laitner 1979b). Intuitively, it imposes that the mean growth rate of labor income be larger than the desired consumption growth rate under certainty. As the resulting desired consumption path is flatter than the labor income profile, individuals would like to decumulate wealth and possibly go into debt whenever labor income is below its long-run "permanent" discounted level, planning to finance future consumption and repay any debts when labor income will be (exogenously) higher. If (9.20) holds, however, this behavior would lead accumulated wealth, driven by a cumulation of stationary labor income realizations, to follow a nonstationary process with negative drift and to reach minus infinity with probability one. If unbounded debt is disallowed—as it must be, for otherwise it would be optimal to incur it immediately—then consumption cannot be forever sheltered from labor income uncertainty. Knowing that labor income uncertainty will sooner or later destabilize the consumption path, the consumer is led to "precautionary" or "buffer stock" savings, and the consumption path is steeper.

The model's parameters have intuitive implications for aggregate and disaggregated outcomes. Regarding factor income distribution, a higher wage rate increases proportionally the consumption propensity at all levels of resources. By linear homogeneity of the policy function (9.15), in fact,

$$c(\lambda \tilde{W} l + \tilde{k}) = \lambda c(\tilde{W} l + \tilde{k}/\lambda).$$

Hence, the transitions in (9.18) are rescaled by λ: when the wage rate is $\lambda \tilde{W}$, the relationship between $\Delta \tilde{k}/\lambda$ and $\tilde{k}/\lambda$ is the same as that between $\Delta \tilde{k}$ and $\tilde{k}$ when the wage rate is $\tilde{W}$. As a consequence, the stable distributions of accumulated wealth are related by $F(\tilde{k}; \tilde{W}) = F(\lambda \tilde{k}; \lambda \tilde{W})$. Symmetrically, a higher return on accumulation increases the desired growth rate of consumption and reduces the propensity to consume at every level of resources and accumulated wealth: this, and the direct effect of $\tilde{R}$ in

(9.18), induces faster accumulation at every wealth level and widens the ergodic distribution of detrended wealth. As to the parameters of labor incomes' dynamic processes, higher volatility of labor income makes the consumption-smoothing individual more reluctant to allow accumulated wealth to decline: consumption is a flatter function of more volatile resources, so as to reduce undesirable consumption volatility, as the stronger "precautionary" saving motive makes self-insurance more attractive. As a result, wealth is predicted to be more unequal. Faster labor income growth has the opposite effect since, as long as the liquidity constraint is not binding, an individual who expects fast growth of labor income finds it optimal to consume more of whatever current resources may be available, and to rely on future exogenous income to finance future consumption. A stronger trend tends to make detrended wealth decline faster (on average) until liquidity constraints bind: in combination with the optimal consumption policy, this implies that the long-run distribution of normalized wealth is more strongly concentrated near zero, and the liquidity constraint is more likely to bind.

9.3.3 The Extent of Risk and the Rate of Growth

We turn to the characterization of the steady-state equilibrium. Note first that the microeconomic behavior characterized above interacts with the dynamics of macroeconomic equilibria. As each individual attempts to self-insure against idiosyncratic risk, aggregate accumulation is more intense for any given rate of return and expected accumulation rate. Because the marginal return of wealth accumulation is constant, the higher propensity to accumulate capital increases the average growth rate of consumption and of (expected) non-accumulated factor incomes θ. Higher growth of labor income in turn restores the equilibrium as a larger expected flow of future incomes makes it less necessary for individuals to rely on accumulation to boost future consumption levels.[8]

The equilibrium value of the growth factor θ can only be computed by numerical simulations as there exists no explicit solution for the individuals' concave consumption function either. However, the steady-state outcome has intuitive qualitative properties. In a growing economy where labor income uncertainty is uninsurable, the R and θ parameters which the microeconomic problem took as given must always be such in steady-state equilibrium that (9.20) holds true. In turn, this implies that liquid-

---

[8]As a digression, note that we could also have assumed a neoclassical technology as in Laitner (1979b) or Aiyagari (1994). In this case higher precautionary savings—due to more idiosyncratic risk—result in a higher aggregate wealth-to-output ratio. The steady-state equilibrium then is restored by the decline of the rate of return on savings.

ity constraints are relevant to the consumption-savings problem of every individual, no matter how wealthy, since all (detrended) wealth levels reach zero with positive probability in finite time and never return above $k^{\max}$. Hence, a stationary long-run distribution of detrended wealth exists and is unique. Given that labor income uncertainty is idiosyncratic, the cross-sectional distribution of wealth is similarly well defined and bounded in the long run.

Precautionary motives increase individuals' propensity to save, and liquidity constraints increase the aggregate saving rate. If the economy's long-run growth rate is exogenous, then the resulting higher capital intensity reduces the rate of return R. And of course uninsurable uncertainty increases the growth rate of the economy when growth is endogenous. As to wealth distribution, consumption-smoothing individuals who can access (noncontingent) borrowing/lending markets save part of unusually favorable income flows, and dissave in the face of unfavorable income shocks. As a result, individual incomes' factor composition and size evolve endogenously over time, and the cross-sectional distribution of accumulated wealth and of the resulting income flows (or "capital income," for short) tends to become more dispersed than that of "labor" income. Such dispersion is limited, however, because liquidity constraints are endogenously binding in an economy like that considered here: precautionary savings raise the economy's rate of investment-driven growth (or its steady-state capital stock) above the one that would obtain in an equivalent economy without uninsurable uncertainty. In the dynamic equilibrium of the infinite horizon economy considered here, the expected growth rate of labor income exceeds the desired mean growth rate of individual consumption, so that there are incentives for individuals to dissave, and any lower bound on wealth binds with positive probability when the output-capital ratio is fixed, and the rate of balanced growth adjusts to ensure that all existing capital markets clear. As the relative wealth levels of the economy's individuals cannot diverge without bound, the process followed by $\tilde{k}$ must have a limiting distribution and (9.20) must hold true. Hence, the economy grows *faster* than it would if it were possible to insure against labor income fluctuations—though, of course, a faster growth rate is not associated with higher welfare. It is not difficult to see whence faster growth originates. If the growth rate were the same as in the certainty case, the inequality in (9.20) would be violated, and liquidity constraints would tend to become irrelevant in the long run of each individual's microeconomic problem. For any initial wealth distribution, however, precautionary savings would still imply a smaller propensity to consume and, inasmuch as a higher saving propensity implies faster growth, the economy experiences faster growth—leading to binding liquidity constraints in equilibrium.

9.4 Application: Uninsurable Risk in the Labor Markets

We argued in the previous sections that financial markets offer neither the unbounded lending and borrowing opportunities that would insulate consumption levels from exogenous earnings fluctuations, nor the state-contingent financial assets that would rationalize risk-neutral mobility choices in the face of idiosyncratic risk. We then saw that the presence of (idiosyncratic) risk affects the consumption-savings (and portfolio) decision and makes it depend upon distribution unless the sources of risk and the utility function take a special form. However, other decisions, e.g., labor supply, education, may also be affected by idiosyncratic risk. Hence, distribution can matter for labor market outcomes (not only for savings and growth).

In this section we therefore study an interesting application, namely how inequality affects the mobility of workers across industries when workers face uninsurable idiosyncratic risk. Similar to the results in the sections above, inequality does not alter labor market behavior if preferences display constant absolute risk aversion (as assumed by, e.g., Flemming [1978] and Acemoglu and Shimer [1999]). Instead, if preferences are CRRA, distribution will affect labor market outcomes. However, and again analogous to the CRRA section above, the implications of imperfect insurance for labor allocation are muffled by the fact that those among workers who are richer and more nearly risk-neutral are more readily inclined to arbitrage away mobility opportunities. In particular, we will consider an equilibrium labor market setting where only workers who happen to be rich enough to finance their own job mobility can react to wage incentives in the way called for by aggregate output maximization. Put in other terms, the behavior of richer, well self-insured people is that which determines wage differentials. This implies that risk-neutral behavior in the labor market approximates aggregate outcomes. As in Krusell and Smith (1998) and their references, self-insurance will be very powerful, and uninsurable idiosyncratic shocks have potentially minor implications for aggregate phenomena.

9.4.1 Consumption and Mobility Choices

Consider an economy with homogeneous workers, who may differ in their wealth only. The supply side consists of a continuum of decreasing-returns production sites, representing different industries, geographical locations, or occupations. We focus on steady state.

Each worker supplies the same quantity of homogeneous labor to a specific production site. The worker takes the wage rate as given. Total labor employment at site j is denoted by l_j. We assume that labor's marginal revenue product at site j is a constant-elasticity function of its employment level l_j,

$$MPL(l_j, \alpha_j) = \alpha_j l_j^{-\beta}, \ 0 < \beta < 1, \tag{9.21}$$

where α_j is an exogenous productivity parameter following a Markov chain process over the states α_g ("good state") and $\alpha_b < \alpha_g$ ("bad state"). Transitions are idiosyncratic and occur with symmetric probability p. Formally,

$$Pr\left[\alpha_{j,t+1} = \alpha_g \middle| \alpha_{j,t} = \alpha_b\right] = Pr\left[\alpha_{j,t+1} = \alpha_b \middle| \alpha_{j,t} = \alpha_g\right] = p.$$

Put in other terms, the probability that the production sector finds itself in the same state tomorrow equals $1 - p$. Since the sites are modeled as a continuum and the Markov process is symmetric, in steady state half of the sites are in each of the two states.

In the steady-state equilibrium, employment is uniquely determined by each site's current labor demand state, i.e., $\alpha_{j,t} = \alpha_g$ implies that $l_{j,t} = l_g$ and $\alpha_{j,t} = \alpha_b$ implies that $l_{jt} = l_b$. Employment and labor demand determine the marginal revenue product of individuals working at site j, and their wage.[9] Hence, employment and wage are constant, given the site's state. The labor market's allocation be indexed by a single variable, namely the fraction P denotes the fraction of total labor employed by high-demand sites. We normalize the total measure of sites to twice that of the labor force, then the employment level of a good site is $l_g = P$ and that of a bad site is $l_b = 1 - P$. In steady-state equilibrium,

$$W_g = MPL(P, \alpha_g), \qquad W_b = MPL(1 - P, \alpha_b), \tag{9.22}$$

and the differential between the two wage levels is a decreasing function of P.

Obviously, if the labor market were perfect, i.e., labor were mobile, workers would move to the sites with high labor demand such that $l_g > l_b$ and the wages $W_g = \alpha_g l_g^{-\beta}$ and $W_b = \alpha_b l_b^{-\beta}$ would be equalized. Upon realization of site-specific negative labor demand shocks, some of the employees in sites finding themselves in a bad state move toward sites that have simultaneously experienced a positive labor demand shock.

---

[9] As in Lucas and Prescott (1974), Topel (1986), and other standard competitive models, the laissez faire wage coincides with marginal products if a competitive spot market for labor clears at each production site. If each of the model's production sites is populated by only one potential employer, then mobility costs may endow employers with monopsony power. See Pissarides (2001) for a characterization of wage bargaining under imperfect insurance.

In reality, of course, mobility across sectors, occupations, and geographical locations is *costly*. Technological switching costs or the loss of specific human capital are possible examples, and labor mobility may also entail utility terms costs, as in the continuous-time model of Dixit and Rob (1994).

For simplicity, we assume the following time structure. In a single period, individuals observe the labor demand shocks of all sites and each site announces the wage it will pay (depending on employment l_g or l_b, respectively, which is constant in steady state, however). Then the worker decides whether to move to a "good" production site and earn the high wage W_g in this period. If she does so, she has to pay a fixed mobility cost $\gamma \geq 0$, measured in the same units as wages and subtracted from the worker's disposable income W_t. All these events happen in one period.

Workers aim at maximizing, over an infinite planning horizon, a standard time-separable objective function with constant elasticity of substitution,

$$V(\cdot) \equiv \max E_t \left[\sum_{\tau=t}^{\infty} \beta^{\tau-t} \frac{c_\tau^{1-\sigma}}{1-\sigma} \right], \tag{9.23}$$

subject to the sequence of budget constraints

$$k_{t+1} = (1+R)k_t + W_t - c_t - m_t \gamma \tag{9.24}$$

where k_t again denotes financial wealth at the beginning of the period. The constant rate of return on noncontingent borrowing and lending is denoted by R. To ensure solvency and satisfy the transversality condition, wealth can never be more negative than the lowest possible realization of discounted labor income. The implications of any tighter noncontingent lower bound on wealth are qualitatively similar; for simplicity, let borrowing limits take the form $k_t \geq 0$ for all t. In the dynamic budget constraint (9.24), the binary choice variable m_t equals zero if the worker holds the same job at time t and at time $t-1$, while the $m_t = 1$ mobility option subtracts k from the period's wage flow.

At the beginning of each period, workers learn the wage available at the job held during the previous period. On the basis of that information and of available assets, they decide whether to move ($m_t = 1$) or stay at the previous period's job ($m_t = 0$), and choose the consumption flow (c_t) during the period. Since mobility takes workers to sites that just experienced a positive labor demand shock, the period's wage flow W_t equals W_g for workers who move to a good job, and may otherwise equal W_g or W_b depending on their employer's realization of $\alpha_{j,t}$.

The worker's consumption and mobility choices depend on at least two state variables: the wealth level k at the beginning of each period, and the wage available in the absence of job mobility. In general, the future evolution of the worker's budget set would also be relevant, and would depend on the evolution of the distributions of workers across sites and of assets across the worker population.[10] In the steady-state equilibrium we are focusing on, however, both distributions are stable, and wages equal W_g or W_b, respectively, and are constant. This section characterizes consumption and mobility policies for a typical worker in such a steady-state equilibrium, taking the two wages and the interest rate (discussed in the next section) as parametrically given.

Let $\omega_t \in \{W_b, W_g\}$ denote the wage available to the worker in the absence of mobility, and recall that, with probability p, it differs from the wage $w_{t-1} \in \{W_b, W_g\}$ earned by the worker in the previous period. Utility is CRRA. The problem's policy variables are then $m_t \in \{0, 1\}$ and $c(t) \in [0, k_t(1+R) + w(\omega_t, m_t) - m_t \gamma]$, where $w(\omega_t = W_b, 1) = W_g$. The Bellman equation for the optimal contingent policy's value function $V(k, \omega)$ reads

$$
V(k_t, \omega_t) = \max_{c,m} \left[\frac{c_t^{1-\sigma}}{1-\sigma} + \beta E \left[V \left(k_{t+1}, \omega_{t+1} \right) \mid w(\omega_t, m_t) \right] \right]
$$
$$
\text{s.t. } k_{t+1} = k_t(1+R) + w(\omega_t, m_t) - c - m_t \gamma, \tag{9.25}
$$
$$
c \leq k_t(1+R) + w(\omega_t, m_t) - m_t \gamma.
$$

In two extreme special cases, the characterization of the optimal solution for problem (9.25) is straightforward. If workers are risk-neutral ($\sigma = 0$), then they should move whenever doing so increases the expected present value of their labor income net of mobility costs: as in e.g., Bertola and Rogerson (1997), for given W_b mobility is a matter of indifference if the good wage is

$$
\hat{W}_g = W_b + \frac{2p + R}{1 + R} \gamma. \tag{9.26}
$$

EXERCISE 37 Derive formula (9.26)

If $W_g > \hat{W}_g$, moving is strictly preferred, and smaller values imply that accepting employment at the low wage w_b (and waiting for a positive shock) is strictly preferred to paying the mobility cost γ. Note that the wage differential needed $\hat{W}_g - W_b$ is smaller than the mobility cost γ

---

[10] See Gomes, Greenwood, and Rebold (2001) and Krusell and Smith (1998) for characterization of off-steady-state dynamics.

when $p < 1/2$. With $p < 1/2$, moving to a good site implies that the probability of working in a good site tomorrow is higher compared to staying in the present site, which suffers from adverse shock. Hence, there are two gains from moving: (1) the worker earns a higher wage today and (2) the present value of future wages increases when $p < 1/2$. Linearity of the utility function implies that labor income fluctuations have no welfare impact, and that the timing of consumption is immaterial if $R = \rho$ (and unrealistically concentrated at the beginning or end of time otherwise). Individual economic agents, of course, are averse to risk and intertemporal substitution; hence, only access to complete state-contingent financial markets could possibly rationalize risk-neutral behavior in the labor market.

An opposite and perhaps no less unrealistic special case is that where workers cannot even access financial markets on the noncontingent basis allowed for in the accumulation constraint (9.24). If the rate of return is such as to prevent wealth accumulation ($R = -100\%$), then the workers' consumption-saving program simply equates consumption to labor income net of mobility costs. Then, mobility choices are based on a comparison of simple utility streams: mobility is optimal if, for given W_b, the good wage is at least as large as the $\hat{W}_g$ level satisfying the no-arbitrage equation

$$\left(\hat{W}_g\right)^{1-\sigma} = (W_b)^{1-\sigma} + (1 + \beta\,(2p - 1))\left(\left(\hat{W}_g\right)^{1-\sigma} - \left(\hat{W}_g - \gamma\right)^{1-\sigma}\right), \quad (9.27)$$

which coincides with that in (9.26) if $p = 1/2$ or $\sigma = 0$,[11] but exceeds it if $p < 1/2$ and $\sigma > 0$.

EXERCISE 38 Assume that the individuals are risk-averse, i.e., the utility function is strictly concave. Show that—for a given wage differential— the allowed mobility costs with no capital markets are lower compared to the case with complete capital markets whenever $p < 1/2$.

The intuition of the result shown in the exercise is easy to grasp. When $p < 1/2$ the mobility cost γ will be higher than the present wage differential $\hat{W}_g - W_b$. Because there are no capital markets, the incurred mobility cost translates directly into consumption. Hence, consumption today will be lower—compared to staying in a bad site—when the worker decides

---

[11]Note that the interest rate R with complete capital markets equals ρ, the rate of time preference, as the economy is in a stationary steady state. (See Bertola [2004] or the solution of the exercise in the text for analytical proofs applicable to more general utility functional forms.)

to move. Because of the declining marginal utility this is relatively more valued than the future gains from higher wages; hence the worker will move less than with complete capital markets.

We know from section 9.3.1 that the consumption function is concave when preferences are CRRA and the agent faces noninsurable labor income risk. Hence, for the general intermediate cases with $\sigma > 0$ and $R > -100\%$ but incomplete financial markets only numerical solutions are available. Figure 9.3 illustrates the qualitative character of the solution where lump-sum mobility cost γ has the same order of magnitude as the W_b flow and wage differentials lie between those identified by (9.26) and (9.27).

Figure 9.3 plots, as functions of accumulated wealth, the consumption levels contingent on the two possible realizations of the wage ω_t at the previous period's job. The wealth level above which all workers choose to switch their location when experiencing a bad wage offer is denoted by $\tilde{k}$. Obviously, at any given asset level, consumption is higher when W_g may be earned without moving than when the employer has received a negative labor demand shock, and the worker must choose between earning W_b and $W_g - \gamma$. Also intuitively, $c(k, W_g) = c(k + \gamma, W_b)$ for all values of k such that $m(k) = 1$. In other words, as long as the worker's optimal reaction to a bad wage is mobility toward a good job, the consumption and value functions contingent on a bad wage coincide with those contingent on a good wage and the lower wealth level implied by financing the mobility cost γ.

At the wealth level $\tilde{k}$, where the worker is indifferent to move, consumption of a worker observing a bad wage is a discontinuous function of wealth. If he decides to switch the location, his consumption today will be strictly lower because he incurs the mobility cost γ. The worker is willing to consume less today when he is compensated by higher expected wages in the future, which is the case for $p < 1/2$.

The consumption functions in figure 9.3 are increasing and concave, except around the point $c(\tilde{k}, W_b)$. This means that the current level of assets affects consumption strongly when it is low, but higher levels of accumulated assets allow the worker to smooth consumption and enjoy a high degree of self-insurance over the relevant planning horizon. Thus, as wealth increases, consumption becomes a flatter function of available assets and the impact of labor income fluctuations on consumption is reduced. In the limit, an unboundedly rich worker would behave according to the permanent income hypothesis, and simply consume the annuity flow equivalent of his wealth and expected discounted labor income. Hence, the slope of both consumption functions approaches $R/(1 + R)$ asymptotically, and the vertical difference between them approaches $R\gamma/(1 + R)$.

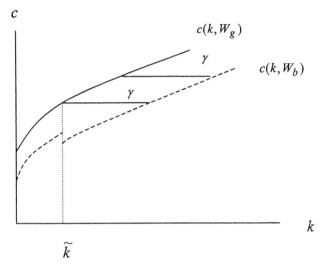

Figure 9.3 Consumption and mobility policies

The shape of the consumption functions has important implications for workers' inclination to engage in costly mobility. As in (9.27) and in the more general analysis of Bertola (2004), mobility is less attractive for workers who find it impossible to smooth consumption through financial market access: the future wage gains afforded by mobility investments need to be large for mobility to be optimal if its costs are large in terms of marginal utility. Consumption is a steep function of available assets when wealth is low, and has high utility value. Hence, for low wealth levels, the $m = 0$ choice of remaining in the current job at wage W_b is preferable in figure 9.3, even though mobility would have positive returns if its payoffs could be valued on a constant marginal utility basis, i.e., the present value of wage gains would exceed the mobility cost γ. Instead richer agents are self-insured because they have a larger buffer stock of assets to pay the mobility cost without incurring a high probability that the liquidity constraint might bind in future periods. So it is optimal for them to switch to the good industry. To sum up, poor workers can hardly afford to invest in a job that is good today *and* exhibits better future perspectives when it needs a relatively high investment γ today.

To gain further intuition on the mobility choice note that the forward-looking decision to forsake current consumption in exchange for a higher (on average) future wage and consumption stream is akin to purchasing a risky asset, and the needed wage gain that makes such an investment attractive is an increasing function of the worker's risk aversion. Intuitively, marginal utility functions that are more steeply declining in consumption associate a larger loss with earning (and consuming) even less than the low wage W_b, and smaller welfare gains with consuming W_g rather than W_b in the future. Hence, large $\hat{W}_g$ values are required to trigger forward-looking mobility decisions by poor workers who finance mobility out of current consumption rather than out of accumulated assets. As wealth increases, however, self-insurance isolates the worker's consumption path from labor income fluctuations, and the $\hat{W}_g(k)$ functions quickly approach the recurring good wage (9.26) that would trigger mobility under risk neutrality.

9.4.2 The Distribution of Assets and the Allocation of Labor

We are now ready to discuss the steady-state distribution of wealth and wages. We saw above that, by solving problem (9.25), workers aim at reducing the likelihood of down-and-out combinations of low wealth, low wages, and low and volatile consumption by saving a larger share of consumable resources when poor than when rich. The extent to which the optimal saving policy achieves a good degree of self-insurance in the long run depends essentially on the rate of return R offered by financial assets. We already noted that wealth accumulation is impossible if $R = -100\%$, but becomes easier as R increases toward the rate of utility discount ρ.[12]

In the model considered here, the dynamics of labor income and financial wealth are endogenously determined by mobility choices, as well as by savings. Formally, the dynamics of the worker's wealth depend on the state variables k and ω through the consumption and mobility policy functions and the accumulation constraint (9.24). If $\omega_t = W_g$ and the worker does not even need to consider moving to a different job, then

$$k_{t+1} = k_t(1 + R) + \omega_t - c(k_t, \omega_t), \tag{9.28}$$

where $c(\cdot)$ is the consumption policy characterized in figure 9.3; if instead the previously held job pays $\omega_t = W_b$ and the worker may or may not be able to afford to move out of the bad job, then

$$k_{t+1} = k_t(1 + R) + W_b\left(1 - m(k_t, W_b)\right) + (W_g - \gamma)m(k_t, W_b) - c(k_t, \omega_t), \tag{9.29}$$

for $m(k, \omega)$ the optimal mobility indicator function.

When faced by a low wage at the current job, the worker depletes his assets to maintain a relatively smooth consumption path and/or to finance mobility toward a good job (which implies a discretely lower new wealth

---

[12]Infinite wealth accumulation would be optimal if $R \geq \rho$ (which would be the case in a growing economy). See, e.g., Laitner (1979b), Deaton (1991), and their references.

level across the boundary of the region where it is optimal for the worker to invest γ in exchange for more favorable future wage prospects). When a good wage is available instead, the worker takes advantage of a high labor income flow to accumulate wealth as well as to consume. As in the CRRA case discussed above (with completely exogenous wage uncertainty), as long as the interest rate R is smaller than the rate of utility discount ρ, sufficiently rich workers will dissave: consumption smoothing over time implies a declining consumption path, and "life cycle" dissavings dominate the precautionary savings motive when the worker is so rich as to discount heavily the consumption instability induced by labor income uncertainty at low wealth levels. Hence, for any $R < \rho$ there exists a bounded wealth level $\bar{k}$ such that if $k_t > \bar{k}$ then $k_{t+1} < k_t$ with certainty and the wealth distribution is stationary.

We discussed that larger wealth is associated with a higher propensity to exploit mobility opportunities, and with higher earnings in cross section. In this section we discuss the implications of these qualitatively simple insights for aggregate equilibria.

Note first that the long-run incidence of low wages (observed at the beginning of periods) would be $pP + (1 - p)(1 - P) < 0.5$ where $P = \left[1 + (\alpha_b/\alpha_g)^\beta\right]^{-1} > 0.5$ if workers always moved toward good jobs, and would be 0.5 (the ergodic probability distribution of a symmetric Markov chain) if mobility were never optimal. To derive the former result note that $l_b = (\alpha_b/\alpha_g)^\beta l_g$ in an equilibrium with perfect mobility ($\gamma = 0$). In realistic intermediate cases, the long-run fraction of bad wages lies between these two extremes, because workers move out of bad jobs only when wealthy enough.

Recall that, in the extreme cases of perfect or impossible access to financial market, supporting equations (9.26) and (9.27), respectively, all workers have identical attitudes toward mobility, and all employees of downsizing firms should be indifferent to it in equilibria with positive mobility and positive low-wage employment. For intermediate cases instead, we saw that poorer workers (whose marginal utility is higher) are less inclined toward mobility (or retraining) than richer ones. Hence, the richer among the employees of a downsizing site prefer mobility to accepting the low wage W_b; others, unable to smooth out the consumption impact of mobility costs, strictly prefer to stay. In the steady-state equilibrium of interest, the mobility option is exercised by $l_g - l_b = 2P - 1$ among the $l_g = P$ workers who used to be employed by a typical high-productivity site receiving a negative shock. (Thus the total number of changers is given by $p(2P - 1)$.) Hence, the cumulative wealth distribution must be such that $(2P - 1)/P = 2 - 1/P$ of all workers who are earning good wages (and may be called to take a mobility decision) are rich enough to afford mobility at the end of the period.

Interactions between wealth accumulation and labor mobility are intricate, but for any given R it is possible to characterize graphically the labor allocation P that satisfies all of the model's long-run equilibrium conditions. The extent to which workers can indeed achieve wealth levels that are consistent with mobility depends on the rate of return on savings. As R approaches ρ, a higher degree of long-run self-insurance becomes optimal. When R is much smaller than ρ, conversely, optimal saving behavior implies that a high fraction of agents will hold low wealth levels.

Even when the allocation of labor is driven by the risk-neutral behavior of the richer self-insured agents, since wages and wealth levels are positively correlated in the model's long-run equilibrium, increasing wage dispersion and volatility imply even wider dispersion of consumption and economic *welfare*. Hence inequality (in welfare) is far from irrelevant, and institutions and policies that implement state-contingent transfers from well-diversified employers (or the representative agent) to uninsured employees with high marginal utility can increase the level and reduce the inequality of workers' welfare.

9.5 REFERENCES AND FURTHER ISSUES

We encountered at many positions in this chapter that individuals use savings to self-insure against income fluctuations in the presence of borrowing constraints as full insurance is not available with incomplete markets. Ljungqvist and Sargent (2004, chap. 16) provide a comprehensive treatment of the self-insurance mechanism. Self-insurance occurs in the models of Laitner (1979a, 1979b, 1992), Atkeson and Lucas (1992), Aiyagari (1994), Aiyagari and McGrattan (1998), Huggett (1993, 1997) and others who study wealth accumulation in general equilibrium settings with CRRA preferences and exogenous or endogenous growth.

Incomplete markets with rate-of-return risk and labor income risk, respectively, are studied in Heaton and Lucas (1996). In a calibrated model they evaluate the effects of idiosyncratic risks on (macro)economic variables such as the equity premium. Our exposition in section 9.2 draws on Caballero (1991), Irvine and Wang (1994), and Wang (2003) who explore the general equilibrium implications of pure endowment risk when preferences are CARA. For a pure exchange economy, results can also be derived for more general preferences. Gollier (2001b) shows how the risk-free rate and the equity premium changes with wealth inequality when preferences are not HARA, i.e., the absolute risk tolerance is not linear in wealth. Zeldes (1989), Deaton (1991), Carroll (1992, 1997), and others discuss precautionary savings behavior at the individual level. Ljungqvist (1993, 1995) and Jappelli and Pagano (1994) explore the growth implications of precautionary savings in overlapping generations settings. When endogenous growth is driven by productivity spillovers, then liquidity constraints may improve every individual's welfare if the distortion of consumption patterns over each generation's lifetime is more than offset by the faster consumption growth induced by external effects. Besides distorting intertemporal consumption patterns relative to what would be optimal for the given private rate of return on savings, in fact, liquidity constraints also reduce individual borrowing, hence increase aggregate savings. To the extent that each generation's savings affect its own wages through external effects (and the social return on savings is higher than the private one, as is plausible in an endogenous growth model), higher savings may bring each generation closer to the truly optimal life cycle pattern of consumption. De Gregorio (1996) studies the interaction of such welfare-enhancing effects of financial market imperfections with the investment distortions implied by self-financing constraints. One of the models that Devereux and Smith (1994) specify and solve in an international framework of analysis is isomorphic to a macroeconomic model where infinitely lived individuals can neither borrow nor lend, and can only use self-financed investment for consumption-smoothing purposes. Like in the overlapping generations model of Jappelli and Pagano (1994), precautionary savings induced by additive ("labor income") uninsurable shocks can accelerate endogenous growth to the point that welfare is higher under financial autarchy than under perfect insurance.

Atkeson and Lucas (1992) characterize patterns of increasing inequality in an endowment economy with intertemporal transfers, but without insurance. Finite individual lifetimes or planning horizons, of course, limit the extent to which wealth and welfare levels can drift randomly away from each other. Deaton and Paxson's (1994) empirical work supports the implication that consumption inequality should be increasing with age within consumer cohorts. Building on this, Storesletten, Telmer, and Yaron (2004a) show empirically that inequality in earnings increases with age because of persistent idiosyncratic shocks. Furthermore, they argue that other reasons (such as heterogeneity in skills together with nonseparable preferences over consumption and leisure) cannot explain the rise in earnings inequality in the life cycle. The macroeconomic implications of savings "precautionary" cushions against idiosyncratic bad luck are typically studied by numerical methods. The empirical realism of the infinite horizon models can be enhanced in a variety of ways, most notably allowing for realistic life cycle patterns of labor earnings and wealth as in Laitner (1992). All results and numerical procedures could be straightforwardly adapted to handle more general stationary stochastic processes, such as the first-order autoregressive process considered by Aiyagari (1994). While this earlier work usually adopts models with infinite horizons (as we did in the text), recent work by Castaneda, Diaz-Gimenez, and Rios-Rull (2003), De Nardi (2004), and Storesletten, Telmer, and Yaron (2004a) develop models with finite horizons and investigate their quantitative predictions. We discussed this literature also in the references to chapter 5.

The implications of binding liquidity constraints are in many ways similar to those of finite lifetimes in overlapping generations models (Laitner 1979a). Tighter bounds on consumption and wealth dynamics than those required by simple solvency may reflect nonnegativity constraints on bequests, limited possibilities to use future labor income as collateral, and/or welfare lower bounds implied by redistribution policies (Atkeson and Lucas 1995). We noted in our references to chapter 2 that introspection and casual empiricism suggest that richer agents have a higher propensity to save or bequeath, even though it may be hard to document by hard econometric evidence: see, e.g., Williamson (1991, 71) and his references. Moreover, we learned in chapter 3 that—in a certainty setting—an increasing wealth elasticity of savings could be rationalized by the Stone-Geary period utility function. Precautionary savings provide a better rationale for wealth-dependent savings rates than the positive $\bar{c}$ required consumption levels studied above in a certainty setting, since any finite $\bar{c}$ would become asymptotically irrelevant in a growing economy (unless required consumption is specified in relative terms). Rebelo (1992), Atkeson and Ogaki (1996), and their references formulate and solve models of this type and assess their empirical relevance. Uzawa (1968) assumed that the discount rate ρ is an increasing function of current utility (and wealth). However, this has the unintuitive implication of a decreasing wealth elasticity of savings, yet it is often adopted in macroeconomic applications where asymptotic stability of wealth accumulation is needed. Heterogeneous discount rates (or intertemporal substitution) do not imply a degenerate distribution in the presence of idiosyncratic uncertainty and liquidity constraints—rather, they will increase the dispersion of wealth. Krusell and Smith (1997, 1998) and other recent contributions point out that the preference heterogeneity we abstract from in this book appears necessary for calibrated self-insurance models to match wealth inequality evidence.

The empirical relevance of uninsurable labor market shocks is corroborated by evidence of increasing consumption volatility and inequality during the recent period of increasing wage inequality in the United States and the United Kingdom: see, e.g., Cutler and Katz (1991), Blundell and Preston (1998), Attanasio et al. (2002), and Krueger and Perri (2003) for relevant insights and evidence. Our discussion was confined to a steady-state growth setting; Storesletten, Telmer, and Yaron (2004b) assess empirically the extent to which labor market risk varies cyclically.

In many countries, labor market institutions decrease the inequality and volatility of wages, and generous unemployment benefits further shelter workers' consumption. Unemployment, however, is of course higher and more persistent when wages cannot fall so low as to ensure full employment and/or the same information incompleteness that prevents private markets from providing insurance leads unemployed workers to exert low search effort. In certain circumstances, a declining pattern of benefits can induce workers to search intensely initially, and reduce the duration of unemployment even as the relatively high initial level of benefits affords the same overall insurance as a lower constant level would (Shavell and Weiss 1979). More generally, however, the characteristics of efficient insurance provision schemes depend on detailed features of labor market interactions.

PART THREE

Many Goods

CHAPTER TEN

Distribution and Market Power

IN PARTS 1 AND 2 OF THIS BOOK we have focused on the role of savings behavior and/or financial market imperfections to understand potentially important channels which link an economy's growth rate to the distribution of income and wealth, and vice versa. Throughout parts 1 and 2, we made the simplifying assumption that the economy's output consists of a single good. In the last part of this book we relax this assumption and allow for multiple commodities.

The assumption of a single output good allowed us to focus on various potentially important channels that link income distribution to growth without getting lost in complications that arise from distributional effects on the composition of demand and the industrial structure of output. Our previous assumption of a single output good can be rephrased in terms of a "composite commodity" that can represent the thousands of different goods and services that are available in reality. If the relative quantities and relative prices of the goods remained unchanged over time, the growth in output would be perfectly represented by such a composite. With growing incomes households simply purchase more of the existing goods and the changes in the aggregate quantity of the composite commodity leave the composition of output and the structure of production unchanged.

Reality, however, is much more complicated. Over time, the content of produced output changes as new and better goods are brought to the market. Increases in incomes lead to relative shifts in demand toward luxurious goods (i.e., goods with an income elasticity greater than unity), whereas necessities (goods with lower income elasticities) lose weight. Changes in demand will lead to changes in prices with potentially important feedback effects on the allocation of resources across sectors of production. The changes in demand that occur during the process of growth may also lead to changes in the supply of production factors. Consider, for instance, a situation where new goods (with a high income elasticity) are produced with a capital-intensive technology. This will raise the demand for accumulated factors and increase investment returns. Clearly this will affect the incentive to save and the supply of production factors. Furthermore, the changes in investment returns not only will affect aggregate accumulation but may also have important effects on the distribution of income and wealth across households.

In the third part of this book we will address several of these channels but, just like in the previous parts, we do not attempt to present a comprehensive analysis of all relevant issues. Instead we focus, separately, on three potentially important mechanisms relating distribution and growth in a multi-good economy. The starting point of our analysis is the fact that income distribution may have an effect on the demand curve for the various products. In chapters 10 and 11 we ask how income distribution interacts with the process of innovation and growth. When growth is driven by innovations and the incentives to conduct industrial R&D, as has been emphasized by Schumpeter (1939), income distribution may have an effect on the incentive to innovate if it has an effect on the firm's *market power*. When income distribution affects the demand curves of monopolistic firms, marginal revenues are affected by the income distribution, as will equilibrium quantities *and* prices.

In chapter 10 we first review the relationship between distribution and growth in standard models of industrial R&D which are based on the assumption of a constant elasticity of substitution between products. By this assumption of *homothetic preferences*, any impact of income distribution on the various products' demand curves is assumed away. We then show how distribution may affect demand and market power, when we allow for variable elasticities of substitution. In chapter 11 we present models in which the various goods are indivisible. This implies that poor consumers cannot consume the same number of products (or the same qualities) as rich consumers. In other words allowing for indivisibilities is a simple and tractable way to allow for *non-homothetic preferences*. We will present both static models in which income distribution affects prices and the industrial structure of the economy and dynamic models which give a direct role for distribution to economic growth.

In chapter 12 we emphasize the role of preferences and income distribution for two important phenomena that characterize the growth process. At the micro level, the composition of consumer demand shows a clear pattern, as the budget share for food is decreasing as households experience a growth in their income. This relationship has become famous as "Engel's law," after the German statistician Ernst Engel (1857), and is certainly one of the most robust empirical findings in economics (Houthakker 1987). At the macro level, the process of growth is associated with huge structural transformation away from goods with low income elasticities—agricultural goods—toward goods with high income elasticities such as services (see e.g., Maddison 1987). Chapter 12 presents a framework that allows us to address these issues in a tractable way. Our analysis is based upon the assumption of "hierarchic preferences." In our framework of analysis we highlight the assumption necessary to generate balanced growth equilibria despite the fact that preferences are non-homothetic. At each point in time, there are goods with high and low income elasticities generating structural change, i.e., coexistence of sectors with expanding, stagnating, and contracting output and employment shares.

In chapter 13 we address issues that may arise when heterogeneities between products arise not only from the demand side but also from differences in technology. Unlike in chapters 10, 11, and 12, changes in relative demand may affect the supply of production factors. Production factors that are intensively used in expanding sectors will experience an increase in demand and in returns. This generates potentially important dynamic interactions between demand and supply that are transmitted via the distribution of income. We illustrate these issues by two simple models. The first emphasizes the importance of learning-by-doing for "trickle-down" growth. When the learning potential is highest in the luxury goods sector, a more unequal distribution of income concentrates more demand in that sector and increases technical progress. This may lead to a situation where growth trickles down from the rich to the poor. The second model shows that, when the luxury good technology is intensive in the accumulated factor, existing inequalities may be reinforced. In that case, economic growth will increase the demand for accumulated factors and raise their returns. When accumulated factors are predominantly owned by rich consumers, the growth process favors the rich.

10.1 Growth through Expanding Product Variety

This section sets the stage of our analysis of the relationship between distribution and growth in the context of recent R&D-driven models of innovation and growth. The basic idea behind these models dates back to Schumpeter (1939) who emphasized the important role of innovative activities and industrial R&D as a main driving force behind technical progress. The recent endogenous growth literature starting with Romer (1987), Aghion and Howitt (1992), and Grossman and Helpman (1991) presented models in which incentives to conduct industrial R&D and innovative activities are essential for long-run growth. An important ingredient of these models is that firms have market power and the resulting profit flow provides the incentives to incur any initial R&D costs.

From the perspective of distribution and growth, there are basically two questions of interest in this context. First, when growth is driven by innovations, what are the implications for the distribution of incomes among factors of production? In other words, how are the social gains from an innovation distributed between "entrepreneurs" (who acquire property rights—e.g., a "patent"—for a successful idea) and "workers" (who conduct both the research effort and the production work necessary to transform the idea into a flow of sales). And how does the resulting distribution depend on the fundamental parameters of the economy?

In the present section, we concentrate on that first issue. We will present a model in which distribution does not affect long-run growth, but the growth process has an impact on the distribution of income between workers and entrepreneurs. Note that this question is very similar to the one we posed in chapter 1 of this book, where we have concentrated on the distribution of income between owners of non-accumulated and accumulated factors in an economy where a single output good is supplied on a perfect output market. Here we focus on many differentiated products (giving rise to market power of the various suppliers) in which the "accumulated factors" are property rights (ownership in firms) that result from previous R&D investments. Unlike in chapter 1, here the technology exhibits increasing returns to scale, so perfect competition in all markets is impossible and factors of production have to be paid below their marginal product. The fact that firms have market power leads to a situation where, in equilibrium, real wages are lower than the marginal product of labor—as firms charge a price that is above marginal cost. In our model, market power arises because consumers have a preference for product variety. Unlike in the perfect competition model, a firm that raises its prices does not lose all of its customers, as no perfect substitute for its product exists. The extent to which consumers love variety determines the scope for price setting.

The second basic question relates to the role of income distribution for the demand for innovative products. When is the existence of a rich class necessary to stimulate R&D activities? When is the purchasing power of lower classes instead conducive to innovation and growth? We abstract from such issues in the present section. As in standard R&D-driven growth models, we assume homothetic preferences and, by that assumption, rule any impact of the distribution of income on the demand function of innovators. In the next section, we will relax this assumption and study how distribution—by affecting innovators' demand curves—may determine market power. We will see this has important implications not only for the distribution of income, but also for the incentive to conduct R&D, hence for long-run growth.

10.1.1 Prices, Mark-ups and Consumption Choices

Consider the following setup. Firms produce consumer goods using labor as the single production factor. At date t, $1/a(t)$ units of labor are required to produce one unit of a consumer good, the same for all goods. However, before production can take place, an "innovation" has to take place. The firm has to incur a setup cost to create the blueprint for a new good. The creation of the blueprint requires $F(t)$ labor units, the same for all new goods. We assume that innovations drive growth. This implies that productivities of production labor, $a(t)$, and R&D labor, $1/F(t)$, are positively related to the number of previous innovations. This is justified to the extent that innovations create new knowledge that is applicable in all industries. The knowledge created by an innovation is a non-rival good: all firms can apply it once it exists. Others can be excluded from making use of this knowledge, by patent protection, but it is assumed that there is only imperfect excludability—in other words, there are spillover effects from innovations that cannot be appropriated by the innovator. As a result, other firms become more productive during the innovation process. For simplicity, we assume that $a(t) = aN(t)$ and $F(t) = F/N(t)$.[1]

Consumers' preferences are represented by the following utility function:

$$u(t) = \int_0^\infty \frac{c(j,t)^{1-\alpha}}{1-\alpha} dj,$$

where $u(t)$ denotes a consumer's instantaneous utility at date t, and the index j refers to products. There are several assumptions implied by such a specification. First, we have assumed *separability* in the various goods. The subutility function takes the form $c^{1-\alpha}/(1-\alpha)$ and the parameter $1 > \alpha \geq 0$ determines the substitutability between the various products, the elasticity of substitution being $1/\alpha$. When $\alpha = 0$ this substitutability is perfect among all products and decreases as α becomes larger. Second, note that the utility integral is defined over an *infinitely large product space*. This assumption is needed because we want to study a balanced growth path along which the number of available products grows at a constant rate. Third, we have assumed *symmetry* among the various products. This assumption primarily simplifies the analysis. Finally note that the parameter α has to be strictly smaller than 1, otherwise the

---

[1]Note that we deviate here from the assumption made, for instance, in Grossman and Helpman (1991). They assume that knowledge spillovers arise only with respect to $F(t)$ but not with respect to $a(t)$. In their model productivity in the production of final output stays constant over time. This implies that, along the balanced growth path, the total units of consumer-produced consumer goods stay constant over time but are spread out over an expanding variety of products. As consumers love product variety, such innovation leads to a growing utility of consumers. Here, we do not insist on the Dixit-Stiglitz specification of preferences. With more general preferences, it turns out that a balanced growth path may no longer exist when the elasticities of substitution between products are no longer constant. An easy way to resolve this issue is to assume that $a(t)$ increases in previous innovations.

utility integral would diverge, as $\lim_{c \to 0} v(c) = c^{1-\alpha}/(1-\alpha) = -\infty$ when $\alpha > 1$.[2]

With preferences characterized by a constant elasticity of substitution (CES) between products, the demand curve of an individual is defined by the first-order condition $\lambda p(j) = c(j)^{-\alpha}$ (we omit time indices to ease notation). This implies an individual demand for good j given by

$$c(p(j)) = \lambda^{-\frac{1}{\alpha}} p(j)^{-\frac{1}{\alpha}}, \qquad (10.1)$$

which may differ across households as the marginal utility of income λ varies with the level of income. Aggregating individual demand curves horizontally yields firm j's market demand curve

$$x(p(j)) = p(j)^{-\frac{1}{\alpha}} \int_i \lambda_i^{-\frac{1}{\alpha}} dP(i). \qquad (10.2)$$

Firms set prices to maximize profits, given the demand function (10.2). In other words, firms can vary $p(j)$ but take the term $\int_i \lambda_i^{-\frac{1}{\alpha}} dP(i)$ as a constant. Profits are given by $\pi(p(j)) = p(j) \cdot x(p(j)) - (W/a) \cdot x(p(j))$ and the price $p(j)$ which maximizes profits is given by

$$p(j) = \frac{1}{1-\alpha} \frac{W}{a}, \qquad (10.3)$$

the same for all products j. The mark-up factor pa/W is determined only by the preference parameter α and independent of the distribution of income. The reason is that all individual demand functions (10.1) exhibit the same constant price elasticity of demand. Hence the price elasticity of market demand is also constant and independent of the distribution of income.

To see the role of income distribution more clearly, let us take a look at how the demand curve of a typical firm, that is the term $\int_i \lambda_i^{-\frac{1}{\alpha}} dP(i)$ in equation (10.2), is determined in the general equilibrium. Because consumers value all goods equally and because prices are the same for all goods, households allocate an equal amount of expenditures to each product. Using equations (10.1) and (10.3), equilibrium expenditures per variety are given by $p(j)c(j) = \lambda^{-\frac{1}{\alpha}} \left[\frac{1}{1-\alpha} \frac{W}{a} \right]^{1-\frac{1}{\alpha}}$, the same for all j. Plugging

---

[2] Why is this no problem in a standard infinite horizon model? Because in that model there must be positive consumption in every period in order to keep the utility integral from diverging. Here, however, not every "period" (= every good) is consumed in positive amounts. Only for $j \in [0, N(t)]$ we can have $c > 0$; for all $j \in (N(t), \infty)$ we are constrained by $c = 0$.

this into the households' constraint yields

$$e = \int_0^N p(j)c(j)dj = N\lambda^{-\frac{1}{\alpha}} \left[\frac{1}{1-\alpha} \frac{W}{a} \right]^{1-\frac{1}{\alpha}} \tag{10.4}$$

where e denotes total expenditures of a household. We can solve the budget constraint (10.4) for $\lambda^{-1/\alpha}$, and plug this and the equilibrium price (10.3) into the market demand function (10.2). This allows us to express $\int_i \lambda_i^{-\frac{1}{\alpha}} dP(i)$—which determines the position of a firm's demand curve—in terms of the distribution of expenditures across consumers as

$$\int_i \lambda_i^{-\frac{1}{\alpha}} dP(i) = \left(\frac{1-\alpha}{W/a} \right)^{1-\frac{1}{\alpha}} \frac{1}{N} \int_i e_i dP(i) = \left(\frac{1-\alpha}{W/a} \right)^{1-\frac{1}{\alpha}} \frac{E}{N}.$$

This expression says that, what matters for the position of the demand curve of the typical firm is the *aggregate* level of expenditures $E = \int_i e_i dP(i)$. *The distribution of expenditures across consumers is irrelevant.* Clearly, this results from the assumption of CES preferences. CES preferences are homothetic, implying an income elasticity of unity for all products. In other words, when poor consumers enjoy an increase in their income they allocate this additional income in the same way across the available products as rich consumers.

The equilibrium level of demand can now be easily calculated using (10.2) and (10.3):

$$x = \left(\frac{1-\alpha}{W/a} \right) \frac{E}{N}. \tag{10.5}$$

Hence CES preferences imply that not only the equilibrium monopoly price but also the equilibrium quantity of production is independent of the distribution of income.[3] In other words, any endowment inequality (that will ultimately lead to differences in consumption expenditures) will not matter in the allocation of any given amount of expenditures across sectors.

10.1.2 Growth and Factor Shares

Now consider the dynamics of the economy. Suppose growth is driven by innovations and that changes in productivity are the result of a firm's innovation activities. In other words, we assume that the productivity

---

[3] CES preferences are not the most general class of preferences that ensure that inequality has no impact on the firm's prices and the firm's equilibrium quantity. A subclass of the HARA preferences also has this feature. We will discuss this issue later.

parameters grow pari passu with the number of innovations, so that $1/F(t) = N(t)/F$ and $a(t) = aN(t)$ where a and F are positive constants. Along the balanced growth path, wages grow pari passu with productivity, so also $W(t)$ grow at the same rate as $N(t)$. As we are free to choose a numéraire we set marginal costs of production to unity $W(t)/a(t) \equiv 1$.

How is income distributed between entrepreneurs and workers? We have seen above that firms supply differentiated products allowing them to charge prices above marginal costs. These profits are necessary to provide an incentive to innovate: without the ability to reap the benefits of an innovation, no firm would be willing to incur the necessary R&D cost. Using equations (10.3) and (10.5) these profits are given by

$$\pi(t) = [p(t) - 1]x(t) = \alpha \frac{E(t)}{N(t)}, \tag{10.6}$$

where $E(t) = p(t)x(t)N(t)$ is the aggregate level of consumer expenditures. Aggregate income can be expressed as the sum of the total wage bill $W(t)L$ and the aggregate level of profits $N(t)\pi(t)$. The labor share γ can now be expressed as

$$\gamma = \frac{W(t)L}{N(t)\pi(t) + W(t)L} = \frac{aL}{\alpha \frac{E(t)}{N(t)} + aL}, \tag{10.7}$$

where we have used our productivity assumption $W(t) = a(t) = aN(t)$. Equation (10.7) says that the labor share is (not surprisingly) inversely related to the market power parameter α and positively related to the productivity parameter a. However, it also depends on the level of revenues per firm $E(t)/N(t)$.

The ratio $E(t)/N(t)$ can be determined from the consumers' choices of how to allocate total lifetime resources over time, i.e., from the savings decisions. Note that, at the individual level, we have $c(t) = e(t)/(N(t)p)$, constant over time. If we plug this into the instantaneous utility function, we get the indirect utility function $u(t) = \int_0^{N(t)} \frac{c(j,t)^{1-\alpha}}{1-\alpha} dj = \frac{e(t)^{1-\alpha} N(t)^\alpha}{(1-\alpha)^\alpha}$, where we have used $p = 1/(1 - \alpha)$.[4]

Consumers maximize utility over an infinite horizon. They are endowed with l units of labor (possibly different across households) and earn labor income $W(t)l$ at date t. Furthermore they own $k(t)$ units of an accumulated asset (also different across households) which yields a

---

[4]Note that we apply two-stage budgeting here. Due to the separability of the intertemporal utility function, we can treat the problem of allocation consumption expenditures across periods independently from the problem of allocating a given amount of expenditures at a given date across the various goods.

return $R(t)$ and we focus on a balanced growth path where the return to the accumulated asset is constant, so that $R(t) = R$. The intertemporal problem of the consumer can then be written as

$$\max_{\{e(t)\}} \int_0^\infty \frac{1}{1-\sigma} \left(\frac{e(t)^{1-\alpha} N(t)^\alpha}{(1-\alpha)^\alpha} \right)^{1-\sigma} \exp(-\rho t) dt$$

subject to

$$\int_0^\infty e(t) \exp(-Rt) dt \leq k(0) + \int_0^\infty W(t) l \exp(-Rt) dt.$$

The first-order condition to this problem is given by $e(t)^{-\alpha-\sigma+\sigma\alpha} N(t)^{\alpha(1-\sigma)}$ $(1-\alpha)^{\sigma\alpha+1-\alpha} e^{-\rho t} = \mu_0 e^{-Rt}$ (where μ_0 is the Lagrangian multiplier, i.e., the time-0 shadow value of wealth). Taking logs and the derivative with respect to time yields $(-\alpha - \sigma + \sigma\alpha) \dot{e}/e + \alpha(1-\sigma)g - \rho = -R$ where g denotes the growth rate of $N(t)$. Solving this equation for $\dot{e}/e$ yields $\dot{e}/e = (R-\rho)/(\alpha(1-\sigma)+\sigma) + g\alpha(1-\sigma)/(\alpha(1-\sigma)+\sigma)$. We know that prices remain constant. Moreover, quantities consumed of each good do not change on the balanced growth path, which is shown in the following exercise.

EXERCISE 39 Show that $\dot{e}/e = g$ on a balanced growth path.

Hence, expenditures grow at the same rate as variety, $\dot{e}/e = g$. Using this in the latter equation yields the familiar Euler equation

$$g = \frac{R-\rho}{\sigma}. \tag{10.8}$$

Since $W(t)$ grows at rate g, too, we can rewrite the budget constraint as

$$e(0) = W(0)l + [(\sigma - 1)g + \rho] k(0). \tag{10.9}$$

This equation says that, just like in the simple AK model of chapter 4, all labor income is consumed and all savings come from profit income. Each consumer wants to finance a consumption stream that grows at rate g. When endowed only with labor, he or she does not need to save as labor income grows also at rate g.

Note, however, that unlike in the AK model, the value of the accumulated assets $k(0)$ is endogenous and still needs to be determined. Assets in this economy consist of the profits that monopolist producers can earn. Hence accumulated assets consist of property rights in monopolistic firms. As shown in the solution of the above exercise, not only prices but also consumed quantities of a particular product stay constant over time. This implies that each firm earns the same constant flow profit $\pi(j,t) = \pi$. Since firms live forever and since the interest rate is constant, the value of a firm is given by π/R. There are $N(t)$ such firms at date t, hence the aggregate value of accumulated assets equals $K(t) = N(t)\pi/R$. Hence the value of the assets owned by the consumer is given by $k(0) = \theta N(0)\pi/R$ where θ is a distribution parameter that says how much assets a consumer owns, in relation to the per capita endowment of the economy.[5]

The value of a firm π/R is endogenous and is determined at the market for R&D. There is free entry into this market. The entry decision weights the costs of entry against its benefits—the value of an innovation. The required R&D costs are $W(t)F(t) = aF$ and constant over time. The value of an innovation is given by the present value of the flow profit that results from an innovation π/R. Due to free entry into the R&D market, the equilibrium will be a situation with zero profits (in present value). Using equations (10.8) and (10.6) the value of a firm can be rewritten as $\pi/R = \alpha E(t)/N(t)/(\sigma g + \rho)$, and let us express the R&D equilibrium condition as

$$aF = \frac{\alpha}{\sigma g + \rho} \frac{E(t)}{N(t)}. \tag{10.10}$$

In other words, the equilibrium value of an innovation is aF. As the flow profit remains unchanged over time, and as the firm stays on the market forever, the firm value also remains constant at aF. Hence the aggregate value of assets at date t is simply

$$K(t) = N(t)aF. \tag{10.11}$$

This allows us to determine both the growth rate of the economy and the labor share along the balanced growth path. Aggregating (10.9) and using (10.11) yields $E(t) = aN(t)L + [(\sigma - 1)g + \rho]N(t)aF$. We insert this expression into (10.10) and calculate the equilibrium ratio growth rate g as

$$g = \frac{\alpha L - (1 - \alpha)\rho F}{\sigma F - (\sigma - 1)\alpha F}.$$

As the denominator is positive, growth of variety is positive if $L/F > \rho(1 - \alpha)/\alpha$. The growth rate is independent of the productivity parameter

---

[5]Note that θ is determined by the savings behavior of individuals. However, when all individuals have the same preferences leading to the same linear expenditure function as in the main text, θ remains constant over time. Hence, in what follows, we treat θ as an exogenous parameter.

a. An increase in *a* not only increases productivity in production of final output but also increases the R&D cost. We can now also easily determine the level of consumption per variety along the equilibrium growth path, which is given by

$$\frac{E(t)}{N(t)} = \frac{a}{\alpha}\left[\sigma\frac{\alpha L - (1-\alpha)\rho F}{\sigma - (\sigma - 1)\alpha} + \rho F\right].$$

This finally allows us to express the labor share γ as

$$\gamma = \frac{aL}{\alpha\frac{E(t)}{N(t)} + aL} = \frac{L}{F(g\sigma + \rho) + L}$$

$$= \frac{L/F}{\sigma\frac{\alpha L/F - (1-\alpha)\rho}{\sigma - (\sigma - 1)\alpha} + \rho + L/F}.$$

Note that the labor share and the growth rate are inversely related. A higher growth rate is always associated with a lower labor share. Intuitively, the Euler equation of consumption requires that a higher growth rate goes together with a higher return on accumulated assets. This tends to increase the share that goes to entrepreneurs and lowers the labor share. Notice the crucial role of the mark-up parameter α. A higher α unambiguously increases the growth rate and hence lowers the labor share. Note the similarity of this result to the *AK* model studied in chapter 4. When individuals have infinite horizons we showed that the growth rate decreases in the labor share.

We also note that the functional distribution of income is independent of *a*, the productivity of labor in the production sector. The reason is that a higher *a* implies not only a higher wage rate but also higher income and demand. In the simple model presented above, both effects exactly offset each other. The exercise below asks you to discuss the effect of the remaining parameter L, F, σ, and ρ on the labor share.

EXERCISE 40

    a. Discuss how the parameters L, F, σ, and ρ affect the labor share. What is the intuition behind these effects?

    b. Discuss impact of taxes, respectively, on capital and labor income.

EXERCISE 41 What is GDP in the economy described in this section? Use all three ways of constructing GDP and carefully discuss each component of each aggregation. Show that all lead to the same result.

EXERCISE 42 Redo the same analysis as above for a Romer-style model (1990) with one final output good Y where research increases the variety of intermediate goods x. $Y = (L_Y)^\alpha \int_0^\infty x(j)^{1-\alpha} dj$ is the final good production function. Individuals can work either in the final good sector or in the research sector where new intermediate goods are invented. Intermediate good firms use η units of the final good to produce one unit, once they have acquired a blueprint. Assume, opposed to Romer, that the intermediate is not a capital good but used up in production. Use the final good price as numéraire and solve for the growth rate. Compare the results to those in the main text. Discuss the role of α and its effect on growth.

10.2 VARIABLE ELASTICITIES OF SUBSTITUTION

The monopolistic competition model presented above is attractive because of its simplicity. It has been widely applied to analyze the role of imperfect competition in product markets in a macroeconomic context. While the constant elasticity assumption makes the analysis very simple and thus very useful for many purposes, it is neither an innocent nor an empirically realistic assumption. In this section we will relax this assumption and allow for variable elasticities of substitution (VES) preferences. While the case of VES preferences has been emphasized already in Dixit and Stiglitz's (1977) paper, they did not discuss potential complications that might arise from allowing for an unequal distribution of income.

To gain intuition on how income distribution may affect price setting behavior, consider the following thought experiment. Suppose there are two groups in the population and consider a redistribution of income from the rich to the poor. How will market demand for the typical product be affected? Clearly, when preferences are CES the price elasticity of demand is constant, as it is for all consumers. When preferences are VES, however, the two groups will have different elasticities of demand and the market demand elasticity is a weighted average of individual demand elasticities. How the distribution of income affects the market demand elasticity is not completely obvious a priori. Consider, for instance, the case when the poor have a more price-elastic demand than the rich. Does a redistribution from top to bottom automatically imply that total market demand becomes more price elastic? Not necessarily. To gain intuition, the analogy with savings rates is helpful. In chapter 2 we saw that a redistribution of income from the rich to the poor lowers the aggregate savings rate if and only if the poor have a lower *marginal* savings rate. In the present context we deal with price elasticities of demand rather than savings rates, but the situation is perfectly analogous: when individual price elasticities of demand change in a nonlinear way with the level of a consumer's income, the market price elasticity of demand—and hence the mark-ups—is affected by the distribution of income.

In what follows we derive, in a general equilibrium context, the criteria under which higher inequality may increase (or decrease) prices and mark-ups in a monopolistically competitive economy. Understanding the relationship between income distribution and mark-ups allows us to take the analysis one step further and study the relationship between inequality and growth. As mark-ups are an important determinant for incentives to innovate, we can analyze conditions under which inequality may be an obstacle and when it may be beneficial for the incentive to innovate and hence for long-run growth.

10.2.1 Income Distribution and Mark-ups

All assumptions of the previous section are still valid. However, we now explore the implication of the more general functional form on (additive) preferences

$$u(t) = \int_0^\infty v(c(j,t)) \, dj.$$

Concerning the subutility function $v(\cdot)$ make the following assumptions: (1) $v' > 0 > v''$; (2) $v(0) = 0$; (3) $v'(0) = \infty$. Assumption 1 is standard. Assumption 2 is a normalization; it is needed to keep the above integral from diverging when the product space is infinite and the utility for the various products enters symmetrically and additively. Assumption 3 is crucial for what follows. It implies that consumers value the first unit of each product very highly. Hence every available good will be consumed by each consumer in positive amounts. In other words, assumption 3 implies that all consumers purchase all goods and nonnegativity constraints will not become binding. This assumption guarantees a *symmetric equilibrium*. (When assumption 3 is violated, nonnegativity constraints may become binding for poorer consumers and asymmetric equilibria will arise. We will discuss this in more detail in chapter 11.)

Obviously, assumption 3 implies that inequality works only via the intensive margin. Assumption 3 is still a crude simplification but is justified because it highlights the role of differences between rich and poor consumers in their reaction to price changes. With CES preferences these reactions are the same for all consumers: each individual's elasticity of demand is the same (given by $1/\alpha$). With VES preferences this elasticity varies with the level of consumption. In equilibrium, rich consumers have a higher level of consumption hence a different level of consumption of each product and hence a different demand elasticity. The elasticity of *market demand* is relevant for the monopolistic producers' price setting decisions. Hence the distribution of income will matter for the elasticity of market demand.

With this intuition in mind, we now go through the model. Just like in the previous section, let us assume that labor is the only production factor and there is a linear production technology with productivity $aN(t)$ and setup labor requirement $F/N(t)$. Aggregate supply of labor L is constant over time, and there are N_0 firms at date 0. Aggregate income is $Y(t) = W(t)L + RK(t)$. Let us, for simplicity, assume that each consumer has the same income composition ($k/l = K/L$). The income level of a randomly chosen consumer can then be written as $\theta\,[W(t)L + RK(t)]$ where θ is a random draw from the distribution which has support over the interval $[\underline{\theta}, \bar{\theta}]$, $0 < \underline{\theta} < \bar{\theta} < \infty$, and cumulative density $F(\theta)$.

We can now proceed analogously to the previous section. We first look at the static equilibrium and focus on the equilibrium levels of market demand (and production) and on the equilibrium prices and mark-ups. Doing this, we take the consumers' expenditure levels as given and take for granted that the distribution of expenditures will follow the distribution of endowments (which will be the case in equilibrium). Having established the static equilibrium, we discuss intertemporal choices of consumers and (R&D) firms. This will finally allow us to establish the relationship between inequality and growth. It will further allow us to establish the role of the endowment inequality for factor shares. (For ease of notation we suppress the product index j in what follows.)

In the static equilibrium, the optimal consumption of good j is given by the first-order condition

$$v'(c) = \lambda(\theta)p, \qquad (10.12)$$

where $\lambda(\theta)$ is the marginal utility of income for a consumer with endowment parameter θ. The first-order condition implicitly defines the optimal demand for product j as a function of its price and the endowment level θ. Let us denote the individual demand function of an individual with relative endowment θ by $c(p, \theta)$ and the equilibrium consumption level by $c(\theta)$. We can calculate the *individual* price elasticity at equilibrium from (10.12) which, evaluated at the optimal level of consumption $c(\theta)$, is given by $\eta(\theta) \equiv -\,[v'(c(\theta))]\,/\,[c(\theta) \cdot v''(c(\theta))]$. Clearly, the individual price elasticity of demand is determined by the curvature of the utility function $v(\cdot)$ and varies with the consumption level unless the elasticity of marginal utility is constant.

Market demand $x(p)$ can be calculated by horizontally aggregating individual demand curves $c(p, \theta)$. From equation (10.12), market demand is

$$x(p) \equiv \int_{\underline{\theta}}^{\bar{\theta}} c(p,\theta)dF(\theta). \tag{10.13}$$

Producers have monopoly power on their respective markets and set prizes to maximize profits, taking the prices of all other producers and the aggregate income level as given. Each monopolist solves the problem $\max_p (p - W/a) x(p)$. The solution to this problem can be expressed in terms of the familiar Lerner index

$$\frac{p - W/a}{p} = \frac{1}{\varepsilon(p)}, \text{ with } \varepsilon(p) = \int_{\underline{\theta}}^{\bar{\theta}} \frac{c(p,\theta)}{x(p)} \eta(c(p,\theta))dF(\theta). \tag{10.14}$$

where $\varepsilon(p)$ denotes the price elasticity of *market* demand. Equation (10.14) states that profits are maximized where the relation between the profit margin (price minus marginal cost) and the price, the "Lerner index," is equal to the inverse of the price elasticity of demand. This price elasticity is a weighted sum of the *individual* price elasticities, the weights being individuals' relative consumption levels $c(p,\theta)/x(p)$. Equation (10.14) allows us to shed light on the role of the endowment distribution. Suppressing the argument p in (individual and market) demand functions, we can rewrite equation (10.14) as

$$\frac{p - W/a}{p} = \int_{\underline{\theta}}^{\bar{\theta}} \frac{x}{c(\theta)} \frac{1}{\eta(c(\theta))} dF(\theta) = \int_{\underline{\theta}}^{\bar{\theta}} x \frac{1}{-v'(c)/v''(c)} dF(\theta). \tag{10.15}$$

Clearly, equation (10.15) says that the elasticity of market demand at equilibrium depends on the curvature of $-v'(c)/v''(c)$. When $-v'(c)/v''(c)$ is concave (convex) in c, a mean preserving spread of θ will decrease (increase) η and increase (decrease) the Lerner index. In other words, *when $-v'(c)/v''(c)$ is concave (convex) in c, more inequality in the distribution of endowments raises (reduces) monopoly prices and mark-ups*. It does not matter for the relationship between inequality and mark-ups whether—compared to the poor—the rich have a low demand elasticity and steep demand or vice versa: if we redistribute from a person with low elasticity of demand to a person with high elasticity, it does *not* follow that the elasticity of aggregate demand must increase. From (10.14) we see that the aggregate elasticity $\varepsilon(p)$ is a weighted average of individuals' elasticities. By redistribution, the individual weights change. The equation (10.15) instead states that it depends on the *change* of the slopes of the individuals' demand curves, i.e., whether the slope of individual demand is concave or convex in consumption.

Obviously, in the special case when $-v'(c)/v''(c)$ is linear in c, the distribution of θ does not affect the market demand elasticity. As we have mentioned above (see the appendix on HARA preferences in part 1), the only class of utility functions that features linearity of $-v'(c)/v''(c)$ is the HARA class where $-v'(c)/v''(c) = c/\sigma - \bar{c}/\beta$. In the even more special case when $\bar{c} = 0$, $-v'(c)/v''(c)$ is proportional to the consumption level c. This is the particular case of CES preferences.

10.2.2   Inequality and Long-Run Growth

The dynamics of the model are similar, although slightly more complicated, than in the CES monopolistic competition model. Just like before, we assume that growth occurs as a result of innovations. Again, we focus on a balanced growth path where (1) the range of products $N(t)$ grows at the constant rate g, where (2) wages grow at the same rate as $N(t)$, and where (3) the (nominal) rate of interest R is constant. The second balanced growth condition implies that the marginal cost of production $W(t)/a(t)$ stays constant over time. Just like in the previous section we chose the marginal cost of production as the numéraire, so $W(t)/a(t) = 1$. Assuming a constant elasticity of *intertemporal* substitution the objective function is given by

$$\max_{\{c_\theta(j,t)\}} \int_0^\infty \frac{[N(t)v(c_\theta(t))]^{1-\sigma}}{1-\sigma} e^{-\rho t} dt$$

subject to the intertemporal budget constraint

$$\int_0^\infty [N(t)p(t)c_\theta(t))]\, e^{-Rt} dt \leq \theta \left[K_0 + \int_0^\infty aN(t)Le^{-Rt} dt \right],$$

which yields the first-order condition $N(t)^{1-\sigma}v\,(c_\theta(t))^{-\sigma}\,v'\,(c_\theta(t))\,e^{-\rho t} = \mu_\theta N(t)p(t)e^{-Rt}$, where μ_θ is the (time-invariant) marginal value of lifetime wealth at date 0. Taking logs and the derivative with respect to time yields

$$(1-\sigma)g - \sigma\frac{v'\,(c_\theta(t)) \cdot c_\theta(t)}{v\,(c_\theta(t))}\frac{\dot{c}_\theta(t)}{c_\theta(t)} + \frac{v''\,(c_\theta(t)) \cdot c_\theta(t)}{v'\,(c_\theta(t))}\frac{\dot{c}_\theta(t)}{c_\theta(t)} - \rho = g + \frac{\dot{p}(t)}{p(t)} - R.$$

Guess that $\dot{c}_\theta(t)/c_\theta(t) = \dot{p}(t)/p(t) = 0$. Then we get the familiar Euler equation

$$g = \frac{R - \rho}{\sigma}.$$

Furthermore, because the expenditures of a consumer with endowments θ are given by $e_\theta(t) = N(t) \cdot c_\theta \cdot p$, $e_\theta(t)$ also grows at rate g. In equilibrium, consumption expenditures are given by

$$e_\theta(t) = N(t) \cdot c_\theta \cdot p = \theta \left[W(t)L + ((\sigma - 1)g + \rho) K(t) \right]. \tag{10.16}$$

This implies that a consumer with endowment θ consumes exactly θ times the per capita consumption level. As we have normalized population to unity, per capita consumption coincides with the market demand for a given variety x. Hence we have

$$c_\theta = \theta x. \tag{10.17}$$

The total labor supply L is employed either in the R&D sector, where employment is gF, or in the production sector, where employment is x/a. The resource constraint is exhausted if $L = gF + x/a$ from which we can derive the feasible per capita level of consumption per variety

$$x = aL - agF.$$

The above arguments can be used to rewrite the profit maximization condition (10.14) for the monopolist derived above. We can use this in

$$\frac{p}{p-1} = \int_{\underline{\theta}}^{\bar{\theta}} \frac{c_\theta}{x} \eta(c_\theta) dF(\theta) = \int_{\underline{\theta}}^{\bar{\theta}} \theta \eta(\theta x) dF(\theta) \tag{10.18}$$

$$= \int_{\underline{\theta}}^{\bar{\theta}} \theta \eta(\theta \cdot (aL - agF)) dF(\theta),$$

which is a first equation in p and g. Equation (10.18) shows values of p and g such that firms maximize profits. Hence we call this relationship the "*PM curve*" and present this curve in the (p, g)-space. (Moreover, to derive the *PM* curve we have used the economy's resource constraint.) How p and g are related depends on the curvature of the $v(\cdot)$-function. Suppose first that the individual price elasticity of demand $\eta(c) = -v'(c)/[cv''(c)]$ is non-increasing in c, so that $\eta(\theta \cdot (aL - agF))$ is *non-decreasing* in g. This implies that the right-hand side of equation (10.18) non-decreasing in g. As the left-hand side is decreasing in p, equation (10.18) yields a nonpositive relationship between p and g.

The intuition for such a negative relationship is straightforward. A high g implies low production in final output sectors. By assumption, lower consumption levels are associated with higher price elasticities of *individual* demands, so the price elasticity of *market* demand—the weighted average of individual price elasticities—will also be larger. The results are lower prices and a lower profit margin. The inverse of the Lerner index increases.

The above discussion assumed that the curvature of the $v()$-function is such that the price elasticity of demand $\eta(c)$ is decreasing in c. However, the opposite could also be the case. By the same arguments as above, this implies that low consumption levels—and hence a high growth rate g—are associated with low price elasticities of individual demands. So high growth rates go hand in hand with a low market demand elasticity, high mark-ups, and high prices. Hence, when $\eta(c)$ is increasing in c, the price level p and the growth rate g are positively related.

The second equation in p and g can be determined in a straightforward way. As there is free entry into the R&D market, the equilibrium will be characterized by a situation where the value of an innovation equals the cost of the innovation. We have discussed in the last section that the R&D equilibrium is given by $W(t)F(t) = \pi(t)/R = (p-1)x/(g\sigma + \rho)$, which, using the resource constraint, can be rewritten as

$$F = \frac{(p-1)(L-gF)}{g\sigma + \rho}.$$

This implies a positive association between p and g. A higher g reduces the value of an innovation for two different reasons. First, a higher g implies a lower output per variety x and hence a lower profit flow. Second, a higher g also implies a higher interest rate, so the profit flow is discounted more strongly, which decreases the value of an innovation. In sum, a higher growth rate requires higher prices, counteracting the depressing effects on the value of an innovation and restoring R&D equilibrium. We call this relationship the "*ZP curve.*"

We are now ready to discuss the impact of inequality on economic growth. Higher inequality does not affect the *ZP* curve. However, changes in endowment inequality shift the *PM* curve. The reason is that mark-ups are affected, which implies higher or lower prices for any given rate of growth. Whether, for example, an upward shift increases or decreases growth depends on how the two curves cross. This is shown in figure 10.1. If the *PM* curve is downward sloping (panel *a* in the figure), growth increases unambiguously. If the curve is upward sloping (panel *b* in the figure), the effect on growth is not a priori clear. If the *PM* curve crosses the *ZP* curve from above, growth increases, too. However, if the *PM* curve is upward sloping there may exist multiple equilibria (*PM2*). In panel *b* of figure 10.1 there are three equilibria, and comparative statics of the middle equilibrium indicate that growth may also fall as a result of higher inequality. Furthermore, the *PM* curve could never cross the *ZP* curve—in which case the only equilibrium is stagnation.

We still need to discuss whether the *PM* curve shifts upward or downward when inequality increases. The direction of the *PM* shift resulting

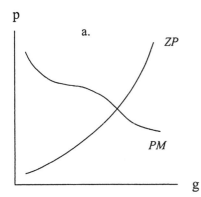
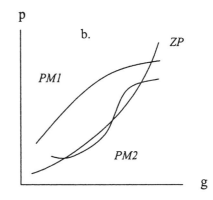

Figure 10.1 *PM* and *ZP* curves

from an increase in inequality depends on the curvature of the (income-weighted) demand elasticity. When $\theta\eta(\theta x) = -v'(\theta x)/v''(\theta x)$ is *concave* in θ, an increase in inequality raises mark-ups and prices. The *PM* curve shifts out, and the result is that an increase in inequality increases growth. When $\theta\eta(\theta x)$ is *convex* in θ, exactly the opposite is the case and inequality is beneficial for growth. An important point of reference is the HARA class of preferences where $\theta\eta(\theta x)$ is affine linear in c and the distribution of θ does not matter for mark-ups.

At this place, the analogy of the effects of income distribution on the aggregate saving rates, which we have discussed in chapter 2, is worth noting. In chapter 2 we have seen that the aggregate savings rate does not depend on the distribution of income if and only if the *marginal* savings rate does not change with the level of a consumer's income. In fact, neoclassical models of optimal savings in chapters 3 and 5 were analyzed under the provision that aggregate accumulation did not depend on the distribution of income. There we have seen that, under neoclassical conditions, income distribution does not have an impact on aggregate savings rates if and only if preferences are HARA. In the present case, the issue is not the marginal savings rate, but the *marginal* sensitivity of demand to price changes. Just like in the case of the savings rate, the aggregate slope of demand (and hence on mark-up and price level) is affected by the distribution of income if and only if preferences deviate from HARA. When the individual slope of demand is concave in income, an increase in inequality lowers the aggregate slope of demand—and increases prices and mark-ups. As higher mark-ups increase innovation activities, a relationship between income distribution and long-run growth is established.

It is also interesting to note that the above model predicts a relationship between the size distribution of endowments θ and the labor share γ. Just like in the simple CES monopolistic competition model the labor share is given by $\gamma = W(t)L/[W(t)L + RK(t)]$. The aggregate value of wealth $K(t)$ is given by the value of all currently existing firms. By the zero-profit condition, the value of the most recent innovator equals the cost of an innovation $W(t)F(t) = aF$ and, by symmetry, the value of all firms equals $N(t)aF$. From the Euler equation we know $R = \sigma g + \rho$, so that we get

$$\gamma = \frac{L}{L + (\sigma g + \rho) F},$$

where g is now potentially affected by the distribution of endowments. Interestingly, it is not a priori clear whether more inequality leads to a lower or a higher labor share. The question is whether inequality is good or bad for growth. When higher inequality raises the growth rate, the labor share will decrease. When higher inequality lowers the growth rate, however, the labor share will increase.

It is hard to say which scenario is the more plausible one. How changes in c affect the ratio $-v'(c)/v''(c)$ depends on higher-order derivatives of the v-function. What is important for our purpose is that, from a theoretical point of view, not much can be said about the role of endowment inequality for expanding product varieties. It is essentially an empirical question and both relationships are equally plausible. However, we could use criteria of plausibility outside the model. For instance, we might want to think that there is more product variety in an economy with higher inequality. Such a scenario would imply that there is more innovation when income is more unequally distributed. This is consistent with a situation where $-v'(c)/v''(c)$ is *concave* in c.

We need to make a couple of important qualifications. The above analysis has assumed that $v'(0) = \infty$. That assumption is very convenient for our purposes because it ensures that equilibria are always symmetric. Non-homotheticity of the $v()$ function implies that inequality has an effect on the shape of the market demand curves. However, the above assumption ensures that nonnegativity constraints never become binding. Even for the poorest consumer it is optimal to consume all goods supplied in the market. Hence all action arising from inequality takes place along the intensive margin. However, we might think that the most important difference in consumption behavior between rich and poor consumers is that the poor cannot "afford" certain goods that the rich can. In other words, binding nonnegativity constraints are very important to explain differences in consumption behavior between rich and poor countries. Such issues naturally arise in setups when consumer goods are indivisible.

In that case, consumers with very low incomes will not be able to afford all goods, so income distribution affects the relative size of the various markets. We explore such issues in the next chapter.

A second (closely related) qualification concerns our result that under HARA preferences income distribution does not affect growth in the above setup. Also this result hinges upon the assumption that nonnegativity constraints do not become binding. There are utility functions that belong to the HARA class where $v'(0) < \infty$. Two important examples are the Stone-Geary utility function $v(c) = \ln(c - \bar{c})$ with negative required consumption levels ($\bar{c} < 0$) where $v'(0) = -1/\bar{c} < \infty$ and the quadratic $v(c) = -(s - c)^2$ where $v'(0) = 2s < \infty$. When consumers have subutilities of this type, very poor consumers will not purchase all commodities. In other words, inequality will have an impact on macro outcomes, because demand will be asymmetrically distributed across firms. How the structure of demand and production looks like will be determined by the income distribution. We will come back to the role of asymmetric preferences and their implications for growth and structural change in chapter 12.

A third qualification relates to the types of goods that are available in the economy. In the present chapter we have studied a very stylized environment, in which all goods are symmetric and each monopolistic producer has the same market power. In reality, sectors with fierce competition coexist with other sectors where firms can exert a lot of monopoly power. Hence it may be interesting to consider models with both a monopolistic and competitive sector. Preferences over the two types of goods need not be homothetic, which opens up a further channel by which income distribution could affect macroeconomic outcomes. Furthermore when the various sectors contribute in different ways to technical progress—because, for instance, the monopolistic sector is innovative whereas the competitive sector is not—income distribution may affect long-run growth via its influence on the composition of sectors.

A fourth qualification relates to our specification of income distribution. For simplicity, we have assumed that each household has the same income composition. This greatly simplified our analysis, but it hardly meets empirical regularities. In reality, we typically observe that richer households also possess disproportionately more wealth, whereas many poor households do not have any wealth at all. Allowing for such differences in the composition of factor incomes would imply that changes in the distribution of endowments with production factors not only would change prices and mark-ups, but also would feed back to the size distribution of income. For instance, when a more unequal distribution of ownership in monopolistic firms leads to higher mark-ups, households with a small share of profit income lose, whereas households whose income consists largely of profits gain. Note, however, that such complications will not qualitatively change the basic mechanisms concerning the effects of distribution on mark-ups and growth.

A final qualification relates to product quality. We have assumed that each product is available in only one quality. The setup implies that rich and poor consumers purchase the same goods. The only difference is that the rich purchase more of each good than the poor. The reality certainly looks different. There are many consumption categories, starting from basic goods such as food and clothes to conveniences and luxuries such as cars, entertainment, medical care, and so on, that the rich demand in better qualities than the poor. Inequality may affect not only the horizontal but also the vertical differentiation of products in an economy. We come back to this issue in chapter 11.

10.3 FACTOR SHARES, TAXATION, AND POLITICAL ECONOMY

It is suggestive to ask which distributional tensions arise among different consumers in the presence of product market power. In the context of innovation and growth, conflicts of interest arise because consumers face unequal trade-offs between the static inefficiencies resulting from product market power and the dynamic efficiency gains from the process of R&D. Suppose there are two groups of households: workers (without any assets) and capitalists (owning the monopolistic firms). A redistribution of income by taxing capitalists' profits and redistributing the gains to workers would not only have effects on levels of income and consumption of the two groups. A lower after-tax profit flow will reduce the incentive to undertake R&D investments and discourage entry into the R&D sector. To establish equilibrium on the market for R&D, the interest rate has to decrease. With a lower interest rate, however, it is optimal to choose a flatter consumption path, i.e., to consume more today and (for capitalist households) accumulate less for the future. This result is very similar to the one we got in the simple model of section 4.3. The infinite horizon framework implies that in steady state all savings accrue from income generated from the accumulated factors. Redistributive policies in the R&D model studied here will reduce growth just as in the simple *AK* model studied in section 4.3.

How would our results change by allowing for finite time horizons in households' savings choices? In the simple two-period OLG model of chapter 6, all accumulation arises from savings choices of young, wage-earning households. Under such savings motives (and a simple *AK* technology), a redistribution from capital to labor would lead to *higher* accumulation and growth provided the propensity to smooth consumption over time is high enough. However, in the R&D models of the present chapter, taxing profits does not only imply a larger income source out of which savings occur. It also implies a lower return on investment, hence a lower incentive to undertake R&D investments. It is not a priori clear whether the net effect of such a redistribution implies higher or lower growth.

Of course, in practice the menu of redistributive policies is much broader than just taxing/subsidizing factor incomes, and the specific macroeconomic effects of various policies hinge upon the particular conflicts of interest and the policy instruments adopted to resolve such conflicts. In the context of innovation and growth, an interesting and widely used policy instrument are institutions that protect intellectual property rights. Patent policies protect successful innovators from being imitated and/or require potential innovators to produce not only something new, but also something that is sufficiently different from the existing products. Whatever the particular design of patent policies, they strengthen the monopoly position of successful innovators. This clearly has distributive consequences.

In our simple models presented above our assumption was that patent protection is infinite. We made this assumption because it simplified our analysis considerably. However, in reality patent protection is much more limited, and conflicts of interest about its optimal duration arise. To the extent that stronger patent protection implies a higher growth rate (which is always the case in the models discussed in this chapter, but need not be the case in others), patents have a positive impact on the welfare of all individuals.[6] On the one hand, patents change the distribution of income between owners of protected firms and all other individuals in society. Individuals whose income consists primarily of sources other than the monopoly profits due to patent protection will favor shorter patents. A shorter duration of patents enforces competition on a larger number of markets, which drives down prices and increases real incomes of non-protected production factors. Hence, depending on the household's particular income composition, conflicts of interest arise that are quite similar to those coming up in the context of factor income taxation. Saint-Paul (2004b) studies the interesting question of which policies should be adopted to achieve certain redistributive goals when both patent policies and traditional instruments (i.e., taxes and transfers) are the available policy instrument. He models the distributional conflict between (human) capitalists and workers that arises from protection of intellectual property and studies the implications for incentives to invest in human capital. When such human capital investments are a

---

[6]See, for instance, O'Donoghue and Zweimüller (2004) for the effects of various patent policies in the context of endogenous growth.

prerequisite for innovative activities, weaker patents are unlikely to be welfare improving, as they distort educational choices. Few people will take up the (educational) investments necessary to make them successful innovators. The standard redistributive tools of taxes and transfers, despite their efficiency costs, may be a more effective means to achieve redistributive goals.

A final message to take away from the analysis of this chapter is that not only the distribution of factor incomes but also the *size distribution* of income may have a direct effect on steady-state growth. We have shown that, when preferences over the various goods are not of constant elasticity, but characterized by variable elasticities of substitution, income distribution will, in general, have an effect on growth—even when all individuals have the *same* income composition of accumulated and non-accumulated factors. Policies that change the size distribution of income do have an impact on growth by their impact on market price elasticities and hence on mark-ups. Hence changes in the size distribution lead to endogenous changes in the factor income distribution, which in turn affects the incentives to undertake R&D investments.

10.4 REFERENCES AND FURTHER ISSUES

The monopolistic competition model is due to Dixit and Stiglitz (1977). This model was later extended to differentiated inputs in production by Ethier (1982). Judd (1985) and Grossman and Helpman (1989) studied dynamic models in which profit-maximizing firms introduce new goods. However, these models were not capable of sustaining long-run endogenously determined growth. The model of Romer (1987) was pathbreaking in the sense that it generated long-run growth through specialization, formalizing an old idea of Young (1928). Since then, the basic model of endogenous growth with an expanding variety of products has been extended in many directions. However, the issue of how income distribution determines long-run growth via its impact on the nature of monopolists' demand curves has received little attention. See Gancia and Zilibotti (2005) for a recent survey and insightful discussion of applications in contexts of growth and development.

The analysis of income distribution in the context of monopolistic competition dates back to the 1930s, where the work of Chamberlin (1933) and Robinson (1933) led foundations of the analysis of market power and the determinants of price setting behavior. Lerner (1934) showed the close relation between the price elasticity of demand and the "degree of monopoly" of an industry, and Kalecki (1938, 1954) explored the distribution of income in a macroeconomic context when industries are dominated by monopolistic firms.

Among the few recent papers that explore the role of income distribution for innovation and growth along the lines of the monopolistic competition model is Chou and Talmain (1996). In that model, households have (possibly non-homothetic) preferences for leisure on the one hand, and differentiated products (the latter being represented by CES preferences) on the other hand. Just like in the expanding variety model, growth is driven by innovations. However, unlike in that model, distribution affects growth because it determines the labor supply and hence the level of income of each individual. With a concave labor Engel curve, an unequal distribution decreases the rate of growth and Pareto-improving growth-enhancing wealth redistributions can be achieved.

The implications of VES preferences have not received much attention in the macroeconomic literature on monopolistic competition. In the second part of their seminal contribution, Dixit and Stiglitz (1977) were concerned with implications of variable elasticities of substitution for optimum product diversity. However, in their discussion consumer heterogeneity was not an issue. Our discussion of VES preferences allows for general subutility functions in which case inequality has distributional implications. The text elaborates the model of Foellmi and Zweimüller (2004a) who study the relationship between income distribution, factor shares, and product diversity in a static context. In Saint-Paul (2004a) consumers have quadratic preferences (which belong to the HARA class) and linear demand curves. He shows in a general equilibrium context that, holding the number of available products constant, an increase in labor productivity will increase mark-ups. The reason is that technical progress allows for higher consumption levels per available product. With linear demand curves, the price elasticity of demand falls along the demand curve, which leads to higher mark-ups and lower real wages in the new equilibrium. In other words, technical progress may lead to lower real wages in that context. However, as quadratic preferences belong to the HARA class, there is no direct impact of inequality on the mark-ups as long as all consumers purchase all goods. When there is "exclusion," i.e., poor consumers do not buy all goods, inequality will affect mark-ups even with HARA preferences. In such a context, Foellmi and Zweimüller (2003) show that higher inequality leads to higher mark-ups and more exclusion when consumers have quadratic preferences. More important, this recent strand of the literature explains how inequality affects factor prices when markets are imperfect, and it presents empirically testable hypotheses about the relationship between inequality and (macro)economic performance. The focus can be on imperfect product markets or on imperfect capital markets, as in Foellmi and Oechslin (2003).

CHAPTER ELEVEN

Indivisible Goods and the Composition of Demand

IN THE MODELS STUDIED in chapter 10, households earned unequal incomes and consumed unequal amounts of each product, but each household allocated the same expenditure share to each product. In other words, while there are differences in the consumed quantities, *the structure of consumption* does not differ across consumers, *and the composition of aggregate demand is unaffected by the income distribution.* The assumption of infinitely high marginal utilities for the first units of a particular good prevented consumers from concentrating their expenditure on a subset of the supplied commodities. This is clearly an unrealistic feature of these models. In reality, we observe that poor consumers cannot afford certain products. Not only do the rich consume the various goods in better quality, they can also afford to consume a greater variety of goods than the poor.

Casual observation and also empirical evidence suggest that there is a strong impact of income on the number of varieties purchased by households. Jackson (1984) provides evidence for both predictions using micro data from the Consumer Expenditure Survey of the Bureau of Labor Statistics (BLS). He finds that the richest income class consumed twice as many different products as the poorest class. Falkinger and Zweimüller (1996) present a similar analysis using aggregate cross-country data from the International Comparison Project of the UN on per capita expenditure levels on ninety-one different consumption categories. It turns out that both the level and the distribution of income are strong and significant predictors of the number of product categories consumed in significant amounts.

In this chapter we study models where consumers' consumption patterns vary with their level of income due to indivisibilities in consumption. Consumption indivisibilities provide a simple and tractable way to allow for differences in the composition of demand across consumers. Suppose there are N different products, each with price p, and the smallest quantity that can be consumed from each product is $\varepsilon > 0$. Clearly, consumers with income $y < Np\varepsilon$ cannot afford all goods. Indivisibilities in consumption are of enormous importance in reality. Durable consumption goods are typically indivisible so that the household consumption choice is a take-it-or-leave-it decision. For marketing and/or organizational reasons, even perfectly divisible products are often supplied in prepacked quantities (e.g., bottles of wine, packets of sugar). We also note that introducing indivisibilities in consumption bears a close analogy to models studied in chapter 7. There, investment opportunities differed across consumers as a high-return investment was indivisible and households with too little available resources were not able to undertake such investments. The reason for the exclusion of poor households from investment opportunities was *capital market imperfections*. A similar situation can arise in the context of indivisible consumption goods. Poor households may be excluded from certain consumption activities because *imperfect product markets* allow firms to charge high prices. Hence high monopoly prices may be the reason why the poor cannot afford certain goods—even though they would be purchased at competitive prices.

The key issue is the role of income distribution effects on the economy's industry structure and the firms' incentive to introduce new products. Indivisibilities in consumption add one important element to our analysis. The supplied products will differ by the *size of the market* even if all products have identical costs and are equally desirable. This results from the simple fact that poor consumers cannot purchase all goods when there are indivisibilities. For instance, when incomes are rather equally distributed, most markets will be large, whereas with a very unequal and highly concentrated distribution many markets will be small and then only a small number of consumers can afford to buy. Just like in section 10.2, the distribution of income also has an *effect on the prices* that monopolistic producers can charge. Prices and market sizes will be closely related. For instance, a very unequal distribution may lead to a situation where only very rich consumers purchase the most fancy new products and firms supplying those products may be able to realize very high prices.

The analysis of these issues is split into three sections. In section 11.1 we study a static model where consumers have the choice to either purchase a certain good or not to purchase it. In such a situation, the distribution of income will affect the structure of the economy even when all goods are symmetric with respect to preferences and technology. Income distribution will determine the extent of product diversity in the economy. Monopolistic price setting implies that distribution will also affect the structure of prices. Some sectors supply mass consumption goods at low prices, and other sectors supply exclusive goods at high prices that are purchased only by the rich. In section 11.2 we present a dynamic version of this model. Just like in chapter 10, innovations that expand the range of existing products drive growth, which allows us to inquire into the role of income distribution for innovative activities. In section 11.3 we explore a possible role of income distribution along the quality dimension. When firms supply different qualities the sufficiently unequal distribution of income will feature a situation where the distribution of income stratifies consumption patterns along the quality dimension. We study a simple setup where the rich buy goods in high qualities, whereas the poor purchase these goods in low qualities—and look at the implications of income inequality for innovation incentives and long-run growth.

11.1 INCOME DISTRIBUTION AND PRODUCT DIVERSITY

In this section we proceed in two steps. First, we study a static model of monopolistic competition in which consumers purchase indivisible goods. We show how income distribution affects an economy's industry structure and product diversity, and how it affects the structure of prices and relative consumption levels of rich and poor consumers. In order to highlight the importance of competition we also study a model where the scope for price setting of the monopolistic firms is limited by the existence of a competitive fringe that produces goods that are perfectly substitutable for the products supplied by monopolists. In the next step we study the relationship between inequality and growth. We show that when growth is driven by product innovations, a more unequal distribution is favorable for growth. The reason is that rich consumers are willing to purchase high prices for new products. We also show that, when there are limits to the price setting scope due to the presence of substitutable goods, the effect of inequality on market size becomes dominant. In that case, inequality may be an obstacle to growth.

11.1.1 Mass Consumption and Exclusive Goods

When goods are indivisible the levels of consumption are restricted to $c(j) \in \{0, 1\}$. Just like in the previous chapter, let us assume that the utility function is additive separable in the various products and that the subutility function is symmetric and given by $v(c)$, which, due to take-it-or-leave-it consumption, can only take two values $v(0)$ and $v(1)$. A consumer with marginal utility of income λ will purchase a particular good if the utility derived from purchasing the good $v(1) - v(0)$ exceeds the utility-adjusted price λp and will not purchase it when $v(1) - v(0)$ falls short of λp.

Concerning technology we stick to our assumption of the previous chapter. We assume that labor is the only production factor and all goods are produced with the same technology that requires a setup cost of F units of labor, which gives access to a linear production technology with productivity a.

To keep things as simple as possible we assume from now on that there are *two types of consumers*: rich, R, and poor, P. There are βL poor and

$(1 - \beta) L$ rich consumers. Inequality arises from different endowments with labor. Total labor supply is L. A poor consumer supplies $l_P = \theta < 1$ units of labor. This implies that total aggregate labor supply from the poor is $\beta\theta L$. The labor supply of a rich consumer is $l_R = (1 - \beta\theta) / (1 - \beta) > 1$, which implies that total aggregate labor supply from the rich is $(1 - \beta\theta) L$. Figure 11.1 draws the corresponding Lorenz curve on our assumption of inequality. The Lorenz curve is determined by the two inequality parameters β and θ. Inequality increases in β and decreases in θ.

With this simple setup a basic channel by which income distribution affects macroeconomic outcomes will become clear. When all consumers are identical, the outcome is necessarily symmetric. However, in the present setup, even very little inequality breaks the symmetry. To see this note that, when there are rich and poor consumers, all of which purchase all goods at the same price, expenditures of the rich are the same as those of the poor, whereas, per definition, incomes of the rich are higher than those of the poor. This means that the rich would not spend all of their income. The rich would have an infinitely large willingness to pay for some additional goods. Hence, it would be profitable for a firm to raise its price and only serve the rich. This discussion suggests what an *asymmetric* equilibrium will look like. There will be two types of goods: *mass consumption goods*, which will be purchased by all consumers and sold at relatively low prices, and *exclusive goods*, which will be purchased only by rich consumers and sold at relatively high prices. There are two variables, which characterize the asymmetry in the economy: (1) the size of the mass consumption sector (or, alternatively, the fraction of mass consumption goods in the whole economy) and (2) the structure of prices of mass consumption goods relative to exclusive goods. The distribution of income affects both of these variables.

Let us consider the equilibrium in the above model in more detail. The objective function of a consumer can be written as $u(N) = \int_0^N v(c(j)) \cdot dj = N$, where $c(j) \in \{0, 1\}$ is the consumption indicator and $v(c(j))$ is the utility index. We normalize $v(1) = 1$ and $v(0) = 0$. The budget constraint is given by $Wl = \int_0^N c(j)p(j)dj$ where $c(j) \in \{0, 1\}$. (This formulation of the budget constraint assumes that, for all firms, the zero-profit condition is satisfied. Hence all income accrues only from labor.) A consumer purchases good j, $c(j) = 1$, if his or her marginal utility of income $\lambda \leq 1/p(j)$.

The pricing decision of firms is very simple in the case of (0,1)-preferences with two groups of consumers. A firm has two strategies. The first is to charge a price that equals the willingness of the poor to pay, $p(j) = 1/\lambda_P$. In that case, both poor and rich consumers purchase the product and the firm makes profit $L(1/\lambda_P - W/a)$. (Just like before, W

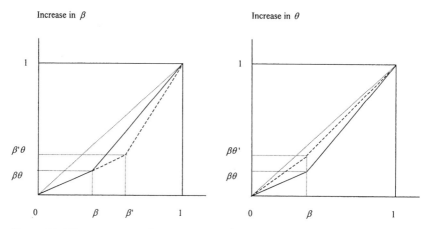

Figure 11.1 Lorenz curve: change in inequality

is the wage rate and W/a are the constant marginal costs of production.) Alternatively, the firm could charge a price that equals the willingness of the rich to pay, $p(j) = 1/\lambda_R$. In that case, only rich consumers purchase the product and the firm makes profit $(1 - \beta)\,L(1/\lambda_R - W/a)$. Adopting the former strategy implies that the firm supplies a "mass consumption good," whereas the latter strategy implies that the firm supplies an "exclusive good." In equilibrium, entry may not yield any profits and both strategies just break even. Hence we must have

$$WF = (1 - \beta)\,L(1/\lambda_R - W/a),$$
$$WF = L(1/\lambda_P - W/a).$$

Using $p(j) = 1/\lambda_P$ for mass consumption goods and $p(j) = 1/\lambda_R$ for exclusive goods, we can rewrite the budget constraint of poor consumers as

$$N_P/\lambda_P = W\theta$$

and of rich consumers as

$$N_P/\lambda_P + (N_R - N_P)/\lambda_R = W\,(1 - \beta\theta)\,/\,(1 - \beta)\,.$$

These are four equations in the five unknowns W, λ_R, λ_P, N_P, and N_R. We get the fifth equation from using one of the prices W, $1/\lambda_R$, and $1/\lambda_P$ as the numéraire, so let us set

$$1/\lambda_P = 1.$$

The above system of equations can be easily solved. Just like in the previous model that has studied symmetric outcomes, it is interesting to focus on how inequality affects product diversity N. *Equilibrium product diversity* is given by the number of products purchased by the rich N_R. The solution is

$$N = \frac{aL}{aF + L} \frac{aF + (1 - \beta\theta)L}{aF + (1 - \beta)L},$$ (11.1)

which is increasing in β and decreasing in θ. This implies that product diversity is unambiguously increasing in inequality. (Recall that inequality is increasing in β and decreasing in θ.)

Unlike in the previous model, the equilibrium is now asymmetric. Let us first focus on the equilibrium mark-ups. The *mark-up of mass consumption goods* is given by $[p(j) - (W/a)]/p(j) = 1 - W/a$. We know from the zero-profit condition of mass consumption producers $WF = L(1 - W/a)$ from which we can solve for the equilibrium wage rate $W = aL/(aF + L)$

$$1 - W/a = \frac{aF}{aF + L}.$$ (11.2)

While (due to the simple structure of this model) the mark-up of mass consumption producers is entirely determined by total market size and technology, the *mark-up of exclusive producers* depends on the distribution of income. Note first that we can write $[p(j) - (W/a)]/p(j) = 1 - \lambda_R W/a$. Using $W = aL/(aF + L)$, we can solve the no-entry condition for exclusive producers for the price of exclusive goods:

$$1/\lambda_R = [aF + (1 - \beta)L]/[(1 - \beta)(aF + L)] > 1.$$

It is straightforward to calculate the mark-up as

$$1 - \lambda_R W/a = \frac{aF}{aF + (1 - \beta)L}.$$ (11.3)

Finally, we can characterize the asymmetry in this economy by determining the fraction of sectors that set prices that the poor can afford defined by $n = N_P/N$. Obviously, $1 - n$ is the fraction of sectors from which the poor are excluded. Using the above discussion it is straightforward to determine n. From the budget constraint of poor consumers and the normalization $1/\lambda_P = 1$ we can calculate $N_P = \theta aL/(aF + L)$. Making use of equation (11.1) for N we can write

$$n = \frac{\theta[(1 - \beta)L + aF]}{(1 - \theta\beta)L + aF}$$ (11.4)

which is decreasing in β and increasing in θ. Hence the size of mass consumption industries decreases with income inequality.

The mark-up of exclusive producers only depends on the distribution parameter β. With higher inequality arising from a larger β, the market size for exclusive goods is smaller, suppliers of exclusive goods need to earn high profit margins, and the price ratio between mass consumption and exclusive goods must increase, otherwise excluding the poor from the market would not be profitable. The now higher prices of the exclusive goods can be paid by the rich because with a larger group of the poor β (but the same average endowment in the economy, equal to unity, and the same endowment of a poor consumer θ), we implicitly have a larger endowment of the rich. This is because $l_R = (1 - \beta\theta)/(1 - \beta)$ increases in β (holding the endowment of the poor θ constant). When the rich are more wealthy, the suppliers of exclusive goods can charge higher prices, hence the mark-up of these producers is also larger. It is also interesting to note that the profit margin does not directly depend on θ, the second distribution parameter. This appears surprising because the price of exclusive goods equals the willingness of rich consumers to pay. However, as can be seen from equation (11.4), a lower θ leads to a smaller fraction of firms that supply mass consumption goods. The larger income of the rich is spread across a larger number of exclusive goods with high prices, i.e., $1 - n$ increases. The prices of neither the exclusive nor the mass consumption good are affected by such an increase in inequality.

Clearly, the *dichotomy* rests upon the assumption that there are only *two* types of consumers. With n types of consumers there can be (up to) n groups of goods—and n different prices.

EXERCISE 43 Suppose the distribution of labor endowments θ is given by a general continuous distribution $G(\theta)$. Determine the structure of prices and production and the product variety in this economy.

EXERCISE 44 Assume again that there are two groups of consumers with $(0,1)$ preferences. Suppose there is a fixed set of N goods and there is no entry. How does this affect the structure of prices and production/exclusion? Show that, even if the wage rate falls to zero, labor demand will not increase sufficiently to exhaust the labor supply—so there is unemployment. How does inequality affect unemployment?

The above analysis has sketched models where income distribution affects mark-ups, prices, and/or patterns of consumption and production. We have assumed that production possibilities are given by a simple *increasing returns to scale (IRS)* production technology to which firms have free access. As not only technologies, but also preferences, were symmetric in an equilibrium where firms can enter freely, there will be no profits in equilibrium.

However, the assumption of symmetry was primarily made for analytical convenience and has allowed us to address the implications of income distribution for the patterns of production/exclusion and prices. What happens to the distribution of income if we introduce heterogeneity in preferences or technologies? The following exercise asks you to calculate profits when goods are asymmetric with respect to preferences.

EXERCISE 45 Still assuming $(0,1)$ preferences, now consider an objective function given by

$$u_i = \int_0^\infty v(c(j)) \cdot j^{-\gamma} \, dj,$$

where we still have $c(j) \in \{0, 1\}$ and $v(1) = 1$ and $v(0) = 0$. Denote the aggregate profits that accrue in equilibrium aggregate by Π. Assume that all individuals have the same income (wage/profit) composition and that there are two groups, rich and poor. The poor have income $y_P = \theta (wL + \Pi)/L$ and the rich have income $y_R = (1 - \beta\theta)/(1 - \beta)(wL + \Pi)/L$.

a. Discuss how prices change with the index j.
b. Calculate aggregate profits in this economy.

11.1.2 Inequality, Demand Composition, and Industrialization

The implicit assumption in the above analysis was that there is a unique technology with which the various goods can be produced. The long-run economic development of modern societies, however, is characterized by a process of industrialization where initially production takes place with a traditional technology, but over time more and more markets adopt mass production technologies. Abramovitz and David (2000) mention the important role of the income distribution to explain the extremely favorable economic performance of the United States as opposed to Europe in the second half of the nineteenth century. In the United States, manufacturers produced large quantities of rather simple versions of products, whereas in many European countries products satisfying similar wants were produced in high quality but with highly labor-intensive technologies to satisfy more fastidious standards of living of rich individuals. In the United States a rather equal distribution of land created the mass markets for such simple manufacturing products. In contrast, incomes and wealth in aristocratic Europe were still very unequally distributed before World War I, supporting demand for such handmade luxurious products. The more favorable distribution of income and wealth in the United States led to the adoption of mass production techniques and standardization. This has been an important reason for the high speed of U.S. industrialization in the nineteenth century. Clearly, the problem of industrialization and the development of mass markets has not only been important in certain historical episodes but is of central importance in many developing countries.

In the following section we discuss a simple model of technology adoption that is closely related to the framework of monopolistic competition developed earlier. Our discussion is also closely related to a paper by Murphy, Shleifer, and Vishny (1989) who have proposed a model of technology adoption that captures the historical development sketched above. Their analysis puts emphasis on the importance of increases in productivity in the agricultural sector that release resources to be employed in manufacturing. At the same time manufacturing production creates additional incomes that are directed toward goods of lesser priority. A larger demand for such products, in turn, supports a situation that allows the adoption of modern production technologies. Murphy, Shleifer, and Vishny then show that a rather even distribution of income fosters the creation of mass markets and allows industrialization, i.e., the adoption of modern production technologies.

Here we reproduce a simplified version of their model that captures the main intuition. Assume there are two technologies: a traditional (constant returns to scale, CRS) technology that requires $1/b$ units of labor to produce one unit of final output, and a modern (increasing returns to scale, IRS) technology that requires a fixed setup cost of F units of labor and $1/a$ units of labor to produce one unit of final output. We assume that $b < a$, which means that the modern technology is more productive than the traditional one. Consider again the simple case in which the population has size L and the distribution of income is given by the population share of the poor β and the poor's endowment parameter $\theta < 1$. The rich have endowment $\theta_R = (1 - \beta\theta) / (1 - \beta)$.

We take goods produced by traditional firms as the numéraire. When the traditional producers have positive demand, we can directly determine the wage rate. Prices in that sector equal the (marginal) costs of production, which are given by $W/b = 1$, by choice of the numéraire. A competitive labor market ensures that wages in the whole economy are given by the marginal product of the traditional sector, $W = b$.

Consider first the case when parameters are such that $bF > L(1 - b/a)$. In this "preindustrialization" stage, all output is produced by traditional CRS producers. The IRS technology does not break even as the setup costs bF are larger than the profits an IRS producer can earn from serving the entire market. Note that such a producer can charge at most a price of unity, which just keeps the competitive fringe from entering the market. Income distribution plays a passive role in that stage.

Next consider the case where $L(1 - b/a) \geq bF > (1 - \beta) L(1 - b/a)$. In that stage of early industrialization the size of the market L has sufficiently grown, and/or the IRS production technology has become sufficiently efficient (F low enough and/or a high enough). IRS firms will capture some markets and the fraction of IRS producers depends crucially on the income distribution. To see this, note that free entry implies the zero-profit condition for IRS producers $L(p - W/a) = bF$, which in turn implies that the prices p that IRS producers charge for their product must be $p \leq 1$. The above inequality implies that modern technologies break even only when the entire population is willing to purchase the product of an IRS firm. This depends on the income level of the poor, which is equal to θb. (Recall that no profits accrue in equilibrium, and all income comes from wage income. Poor consumers are endowed with θ units of labor and earn wage $W = b$.) Hence we must have $pN_P = \theta b$. From the zero-profit condition we can calculate $p = bF/L + b/a \leq 1$, so the number of sectors where the IRS technology breaks even is given by

$$N_P = \theta \frac{aL}{aF + L}.$$

Clearly, how many sectors can adopt the modern techniques of production depends on θ, which determines the income level of the relatively poor consumers. When incomes are very unequally distributed θ is low and the modern technology breaks even only in a smaller number of sectors. In this sense a more equal distribution of income fosters industrialization.

Finally, in the state of "full industrialization" we have $bF \leq (1 - \beta) L(1 - b/a)$. In that case, the size of the market for an IRS producer is (at least) $(1 - \beta)L$. In such a situation, the competitive fringe of traditional producers is no longer competitive. Inequality affects macroeconomic outcomes in exactly the same way as in our model studied in the previous subsection.

11.2 THE INTRODUCTION OF NEW PRODUCTS

In the previous section the analysis was confined to a static environment. However, income distribution not only affects prices, mark-ups, and the allocation of productive resources across sectors, but may also have an important effect on innovation incentives. These incentives will depend on whether or not there is a group of rich consumers willing (and able) to purchase a new product.

In this section we put the static framework discussed in the last section into a dynamic context. This allows us to study the role of income distribution in the light of recent approaches of endogenous growth where technical progress is driven by *industrial R&D* (Romer [1990]; Aghion and Howitt [1992]; Grossman and Helpman [1991]; and others). In particular, we can look at the role of income distribution for the incentives to conduct R&D. In the last section we have seen that, in a static context, income distribution gives rise to a market size effect and a price effect. In a growth context, we will see that the income distribution will affect the *dynamics of market size* and the *dynamics of prices*. Hence the model generates a product life cycle in which income distribution plays a crucial role.

To highlight the role of income distribution via demand and the product life cycle we will confine the analysis to the simplest structure. First we will assume, just like in the static framework, that there is no heterogeneity with respect to technology across products. (This assumption is for simplicity but not necessarily innocuous—income distribution, by affecting market size and the potential of learning by doing, may have important effects on the dynamics of technical progress within an industry—as demand varies across industries, the potential of learning by doing will differ by industries as well.) Second, we will confine the analysis to (0, 1)-preferences. This assumption keeps the analysis tractable and captures the fact that many consumption choices are discrete in nature. Third, we will concentrate on the case when there are two groups of consumers with an identical income composition, which allows us to get explicit solutions. Fourth, we will assume that consumers have identical (marginal) savings rates. Hence any impact of distribution on growth results from the way that consumers allocate their expenditures across goods. Finally, our discussion will be confined to steady-state equilibria.

We will see that, whether a more equal distribution of income is beneficial or harmful for growth depends crucially on the existence of close substitutes for the products of innovators. There are two effects at work. On the one hand, income distribution has a *market size effect*. A very unequal distribution means there are small markets for new products and those markets grow slowly. Clearly, the market size effect implies that a more equal distribution of income is favorable for innovation and growth. On the other hand, there is the *price effect*. A very unequal distribution implies that the richest consumers have a very high willingness to pay for new goods. The price effect implies that inequality tends to be beneficial for growth, as profit margins will be comparably high in the early phases of the product life. Obviously whether or not the price effect outweighs the market size effect depends on the scope of price setting of an innovator. If the new product faces competition from products that satisfy similar wants, the market power of an innovator will also be small and the market size effect will dominate. If, on the other hand, innovators open up completely new consumption possibilities their market power will be high and very rich consumers will be willing to pay very high prices. Under such conditions, the price effect will dominate, and inequality can be beneficial for growth.

11.2.1 Income Distribution, Profits, and the Incentive to Innovate

Let us first consider a simple setup where innovators supply completely new products. We assume that innovation activities are the source of technical progress so that, in a steady-state equilibrium, the innovation rate equals the rate of growth in the economy.

Before a certain good can be produced, there has to be an innovation. We model innovations in the simplest case possible. We assume that, in order to create the blueprint for a new good, $F(t)$ units of labor have to be employed. Thereafter, such a blueprint enables the innovator to produce the new good with a linear technology that uses only labor as a production factor and that has productivity $a(t)$. We assume that, at all dates t, $a(t)$ is the same for all goods.

To capture the idea that innovations are the source of technical progress, we assume that the technology parameters are linked to the number of previous innovations. Hence we have $F(t) = F/N(t)$ with $F > 0$ being a positive constant. This formulation implies that labor requirements for a new blueprint decrease with the number of previous innovations $N(t)$, an assumption that is typically made in growth models with expanding product variety (see Grossman and Helpman 1991). In other words, innovators can build upon knowledge of previous innovators, making it more easy to create a new blueprint. Similarly, we assume that productivity in production depends on previous innovations $a(t) = aN(t)$, with $a > 0$ being a technological constant, the same for all products. In other words, not only the research sector but also all existing production processes gain from a new innovation by technological spillovers.

Concerning preferences, we stick to the assumptions made in the previous section: instantaneous utility is represented by $(0, 1)$-preferences and, for simplicity, we assume that goods enter the utility function symmetrically. A consumer maximizes utility over an infinite horizon and chooses the time path of consumption all consumption goods j, $[c(j, t) \in \{0, 1\}]_{t=0}^{\infty}$, so as to maximize lifetime utility

$$u = \int_0^\infty \frac{1}{1-\sigma} \left[\int_0^\infty c(j, t)dj \right]^{1-\sigma} e^{-\rho t} dt$$

subject to the budget constraint

$$\int_0^\infty \left[\int_0^\infty p(j, t)dj \right] e^{-Rt} dt \le \theta \left[LW(t)/R + V(t) \right],$$

where $p(j,t)$ denotes the price of good j at date t. $W(t)$ is the wage, L is aggregate supply of labor, R is the interest rate (assumed to be constant over time), and $V(t)$ is the aggregate value of wealth (= the value of all monopolistic firms that are on the market at date t in the economy). $LW(t)/(R-g)$ is the present value of aggregate labor income. Aggregate wealth consists of the present value of the monopolistic firms' profits. For simplicity, we assume that all consumers have the same income composition, and that there are two groups, rich and poor. The lifetime income of a poor consumer is θ with $\theta < 1$, whereas a rich consumer earns lifetime income $[(1-\beta\theta)/(1-\beta)][LW(t)/(R-g)+V(t)]$.

Consumers know their lifetime income and the time path of prices for all goods $p(j,t)$. (Goods that have not yet been invented up to date t are not available at a finite price so $p(j,t) = \infty$.) Furthermore, note that we have assumed there are infinitely many goods. Due to symmetry (with respect to both preferences and technology) we are free to order goods by the sequence of introduction.

The first-order conditions are given by:

$$c_i(j,t) = 1 \qquad p(j,t) \leq N_i(t)^{-\sigma}/\lambda_i(t), \text{ and}$$
$$c_i(j,t) = 0 \qquad p(j,t) > N_i(t)^{-\sigma}/\lambda_i(t),$$

where $N_i(t)$ is the range of goods consumed by a consumer at date t and $\lambda_i(t) = \mu_i e^{-(R-\rho)t}$ (where μ_i denotes the Lagrangian multiplier of the above maximization problem). Now suppose the rich consume all products that are on the market at date t, hence we have $N_R(t) = N(t)$. Clearly, in the steady-state equilibrium, it must be that the number of products consumed by the poor $N_P(t) < N(t)$. Furthermore, the proportions $N_P(t)/N(t)$ and $\underline{p}/\bar{p}$, the price of a mass good to one of an exclusive, must remain constant. Let us denote the growth rate of varieties by g. We take the marginal production cost as the numéraire so $W(t)/a(t) = 1$. An equilibrium requires constant profit flows and hence constant prices since the interest rate R and the entry cost aF remain constant. Therefore, expenditures grow at the same rate as varieties which yields the following Euler equation:

$$g = \frac{R-\rho}{\sigma}, \qquad (11.5)$$

where g is the rate of growth of consumption expenditures.

A firm serving the whole market will charge a price that the poor are (just) willing to pay. Hence we must have $p(j,t) = N_P(t)^{-\sigma}/\lambda_P(t)$ for goods $j \in [0, N_P]$ and $p(j,t) = N(t)^{-\sigma}/\lambda_R(t)$ for goods $j \in (N_P, N]$. A single monopolist will never change his or her price, as long as the customer base remains the same. Switching from the exclusive to the mass market strategy implies a change in price from $\bar{p}$ to $\underline{p}$ (and vice versa). Furthermore, at each date t, $N(t)$ firms are on the market. Due to symmetry in demand and costs, the date t equilibrium must be characterized by a situation where a given firm j is indifferent between setting a high price and selling to the rich and setting a low price and serving the whole customer base. Hence in equilibrium the arbitrage condition containing the endogenous variables $\bar{p}$ and $\underline{p}$ must hold:

$$(\bar{p} - 1)(1 - \beta)L = \left(\underline{p} - 1\right)L. \qquad (11.6)$$

To determine the fraction of firms selling exclusively to the rich, and the corresponding fraction of firms supplying mass consumption goods, we consider the economy's resource constraint. The resource base of the economy equals its labor supply L. The demand for production labor is given by $L_N(t) = \int_0^{N(t)} (1/a(t)) \left[\beta Lc_p(j,t) + (1 - \beta)Lc_R(j,t)\right] dj$. Using $a(t) = aN(t)$ and denoting the fraction of mass consumption market by $n(t) = N_P(t)/N(t)$ we have $L_N = (1/a)[\beta Ln + (1 - \beta)L]$. Labor in R&D is $\dot{N}(t)F(t)$ where $\dot{N}(t)$ is the number of blueprints created at date t. Recalling our assumption on $F(t) = F/N(t)$ labor demand in the research sector is given by $L_R = F\dot{N}(t)/N(t) = Fg$. In a full employment equilibrium we have $L = L_N + L_R$, so the resource constraint can be written in terms of the endogenous variables g and n

$$L = \frac{1}{a}[\beta Ln + (1 - \beta)L] + gF. \qquad (11.7)$$

This implies a function $n(g)$ with $n'(g) < 0$.

R&D activities are deliberate choices of profit-seeking entrepreneurs that ultimately drive the technical progress in this economy. Apart from the resource constraint, we have to consider the entry decision into the R&D sector. Entry into this sector is free, so the equilibrium will be characterized by zero profits. R&D costs are $W(t)F(t) = aF$ and the value of an innovation is given by a flow profit equal to $(\bar{p} - 1)(1 - \beta)L = \left(\underline{p} - 1\right)L$, constant over time. Hence the equilibrium condition is given by an equation in the two endogenous variables g and $\bar{p}$:

$$aF = \frac{(1 - \beta)(\bar{p} - 1)L}{\sigma g + \rho}. \qquad (11.8)$$

Finally, consumers' budget constraints must be exhausted. The consumption expenditures of a rich consumer relative to those of a poor consumer can be written as

$$\frac{1 - \beta\theta}{(1 - \beta)\,\theta} = \frac{pn + \bar{p}(1 - n)}{\underline{p}n}, \tag{11.9}$$

noting that $N_P(t)$ and $N(t)$ grow at rate g one gets for a poor consumer

$$\int_0^\infty \left[\int_0^\infty p(j, t)dj \right] e^{-Rt}dt = \int_0^\infty \left[\int_0^{N_P(t)} \underline{p}\, dj \right] e^{-Rt}dt = \underline{p}N_P(0) \int_0^\infty e^{(g-R)t}dt$$

$$= \underline{p}n \frac{N(0)}{R - g};$$

similarly, for a rich consumer,

$$\int_0^\infty \left[\int_0^{N_P(t)} \underline{p}\, dj + \int_{N_P(t)}^{N(t)} \bar{p}dj \right] e^{-Rt}dt = \left[\underline{p}n + \bar{p}(1 - n) \right] \frac{N(0)}{R - g}.$$

To determine the equilibrium we are left with four equations (11.6, 11.7, 11.8, and 11.9) in the four unknowns g, $\bar{p}$, $\underline{p}$, and n. The following exercise asks you to solve for the equilibrium growth rate and to show that, under the assumptions of this model, inequality is beneficial for growth.

EXERCISE 46

a. Solve the model above for the equilibrium growth rate g and for the fraction of mass consumption markets n.
b. Show the conditions under which a unique equilibrium exists.
c. How do g and n depend on distribution parameters β and θ?

The above analysis provides us with an unambiguous result: *Higher inequality implies faster growth.* The result is intuitive in the sense that it captures the (partial equilibrium) intuition that a class of rich people is a necessary condition to foster innovation activities. When a lot of income is concentrated in the hands of rich consumers, innovation incentives are higher. Innovators will be able to charge higher mark-ups. Consider first an increase in inequality due to a lower level of θ. When the rich have higher incomes they are willing to pay even higher prices which, ceteris paribus, increases the value of an innovation. Moreover, also the mark-ups for mass consumption goods increase. The arbitrage condition implies that, ceteris paribus, higher prices for exclusive products will raise prices for mass consumption goods as well. In total, mark-ups are higher which makes entry into the R&D sector very attractive. High mark-ups imply high prices and lower consumption. Hence the resources are available to support an equilibrium with high innovation activities.

The role of the market size parameter β is slightly trickier. If the population share β increases, the size of the market for an innovator becomes smaller. This tends to *decrease* the value of an innovation. However, there is a price effect. An increase in β (holding θ constant) implies higher incomes of the rich as $\theta_R = (1 - \beta\theta) / (1 - \beta)$ is increasing in β. This results in higher prices and profit margins for exclusive goods. The solution to the exercise shows that the price effect always dominates the former effect: higher inequality due to a high β increases average mark-ups, the profit share, and hence the growth rate. The intuition can also be seen from the resource side when we look at the allocation of labor. A larger β decreases the demand for production labor: there are more poor people consuming a small number of goods, and less rich people consuming a large number of goods. This implies that more resources are available for research. As a result, innovation activities tend to increase.

11.2.2 *Industrialization as Replacement of Traditional Technologies*

So far we have assumed that only monopolistic firms supply the various products. No other producers were able to produce the good supplied by a given firm. In such a setup the scope of price setting for monopolistic producers is rather high. We have been considering a situation where a new innovation opens up the possibility to satisfy an entirely new want. Under such a situation, high inequality is favorable for growth because innovators are interested in consumers that have a very high willingness to pay. However, many innovations just replace producers that satisfy the same want with a less attractive (and perhaps more expensive) product. Alternatively, we could assume that innovators come along with a completely new technology that allows to produce exactly the same product with a more efficient technology—just as in section 11.1.2, where we studied the problem of technology adoption in a static context.

While this looks like a small change in the setup, it has important consequences for the impact of income distribution on the growth process. We will see that, under such a setup, a more unequal distribution of income will be harmful for innovation and growth. There are two main reasons for this. First, the new setup implies that the scope of price setting is more limited for innovators. It will be less relevant *how rich* potential consumers are, but more relevant *how many* consumers are willing to purchase a new good as innovators will have to charge the limit price. In other words, market size effects will become more important and price effects will become less important. Second, it becomes important how consumers distribute their expenditures across productivity-enhancing innovative producers and non-innovative competitive producers. When the competitive fringe does not contribute to productivity growth—a natural assumption as there are only production activities but no innovative activities in that sector—high demand for the competitive fringe implies less demand for innovators and a correspondingly lower incentive to innovate. On markets where demand is too small (because only rich people can afford those goods satisfying wants of very low priority), entry by innovative producers does not pay. Hence a large fraction of income concentrated in the hands of the rich implies that a lot of demand is directed toward markets where innovators have no incentive to enter. In this sense, too high inequality may lead to a lot of "unproductive" (i.e., not productivity enhancing) consumption.

To be more precise, suppose there is a competitive fringe able to satisfy all goods so that there are firms that supply goods to satisfy each want j using a (traditional, inefficient) CRS technology with productivity $b(t) = bN(t)$. ($N(t)$ is still the number of innovators but not necessarily the total number of goods supplied as the competitive fringe may have a positive market share.)

We take the goods produced by the competitive fringe as the numéraire so $W(t)/b(t) = 1$. (Note that, because in the steady state wages increase with productivity $N(t)$, the price of competitively produced goods remains constant over time.) Pricing decisions by the monopolistic producers are constrained by the marginal costs of the competitive fringe. Whenever a monopolistic producer charges a price above unity he loses all his customers.

Depending on parameter values there are three outcomes. First, when the rate of time preference is high and inequality is low, all agents consume all innovative goods and some traditional goods. In that regime monopolists' prices and profits are determined by the competitive fringe only and inequality plays no role. The costs of an innovation are bF, and the value of an innovation consists of a profit flow with discounted value $L(1 - \frac{b}{a})/R$, where from the Euler equation (3.2) of consumers' intertemporal choices $R = \sigma g + \rho$ is given. In equilibrium we must have $bF = L(1 - \frac{b}{a})/(\sigma g + \rho)$ from which the growth rate can be calculated

$$g = \frac{L(1 - \frac{b}{a})}{\sigma bF} - \frac{\rho}{\sigma},$$

which is independent of distribution.

The second (more interesting) regime arises if inequality is more pronounced and the costs to innovate or the rate of time preference is lower. All agents still consume all innovative goods, but only the rich buy traditional goods in addition. The monopolists cannot set their price equal to one anymore since the poor could not afford all innovative goods any-more.

$$g = \frac{L(\underline{p} - \frac{b}{a})}{\sigma bF} - \frac{\rho}{\sigma}$$

Define $m = N^R/N$. To do so we have to focus on the two additional con-ditions that characterize the general equilibrium: the consumers' budget constraints and the resource constraint. Using the same procedure as in the last section we can determine the relative expenditures of poor and rich consumers, which yields an expression in the two endogenous variables m and n

$$\frac{(1 - \beta)\theta}{1 - \beta\theta} = \frac{\underline{p}}{\underline{p} + m - 1}.$$

The resources in the economy are given by labor supply L, of which $gF = \frac{L(\underline{p} - \frac{b}{a})}{\sigma b} - \frac{\rho}{\sigma}F$ workers are employed in the R&D sector, $\frac{1}{a}L$ workers are employed to produce consumption goods in monopolistic firms (see last section), and $\frac{1}{b}[(1 - \beta)L(m - 1)]$ workers are employed in the compet-itive fringe. Here $m = N_R(t)/N(t) > 1$ is the number of products con-sumed by rich individuals, which in a steady state will be constant. (Note that demand for products supplied by the competitive fringe comes only from rich individuals. These products have the same price as exclusive goods—which poor consumers cannot afford.) This allows us to write the resource constraint in terms of the endogenous variables m and $\underline{p}$

$$L = \frac{L(\underline{p} - \frac{b}{a})}{\sigma b} - \frac{\rho}{\sigma}F + \frac{1}{a}L + \frac{1}{b}[(1 - \beta)L(m - 1)].$$

Combining the two equilibrium conditions it is easy to solve for $\underline{p}$

$$\underline{p} = b\frac{\sigma + \frac{\rho F}{L} + (1 - \sigma)\frac{1}{a}}{1 + \left(\frac{1}{\theta} - 1\right)\sigma}.$$

The solution for $\underline{p}$ gives us the condition when the second regime will be the equilibrium outcome. When $\underline{p}$ reaches unity—which is the case if θ is high—we end up in the first regime where inequality no longer plays a role. Instead, when $\underline{p}$ falls short of $(1 - \beta) + \beta\frac{b}{a}$ it becomes profitable for some monopolistic firms to sell exclusively to the rich and to charge the maximal price equal to unity, which yields profits $(1 - \beta)L(1 - \frac{b}{a}) = L(\underline{p} - \frac{b}{a})$.

The interpretation of this result is straightforward. When the poor become richer, the monopolists are able to set higher prices, which results in a higher growth rate. Hence, the price effect turns out to generate an exact opposite inequality growth relationship from what we derived above. Because of the competitive fringe the monopolists cannot exploit the purchasing power of the rich anymore. On the other side, they are hurt when the poor are "too poor" because they have to accommodate the low demand with low prices.

Finally, we shortly consider the regime with sufficiently high inequality where it becomes profitable for some monopolistic firms to sell exclusively to the rich. In equilibrium the poor consume less innovative goods than the rich, and since all firms are symmetric a monopolistic firm has to be indifferent between selling only to the rich and serving the whole market. This means from the equilibrium condition $(1 - \beta) L(1 - \frac{b}{a}) = L(\underline{p} - \frac{b}{a})$ we can solve for the price of mass consumption goods $\underline{p} = (1 - \beta) + \beta\frac{b}{a}$. Accordingly, the growth rate can be calculated

$$g = \frac{(1 - \beta) L(1 - \frac{b}{a})}{\sigma bF} - \frac{\rho}{\sigma}.$$

In this regime, the growth rate depends on the distribution parameter β only (i.e., with a larger population share of the rich $1 - \beta$) the value of an innovation increases and hence increases the amount of innovative activities g. Via this channel higher inequality is harmful for growth under the above conditions. We also note that the growth rate is independent of the parameter θ, which (together with the parameter β) determines the relative incomes between rich and poor individuals (as long as we stay in this regime, of course). So we cannot say how inequality is related to growth in this regime. This is because a smaller value of β implies higher inequality if we hold θ_R constant and implies lower inequality if we hold $\theta_P = \theta$ constant. (To see this, draw the Lorenz curve.)

The following exercise asks you to solve the model for the interesting variables $n = N^P/N$ and $m = N^R/N$. In the solution, m is larger and n smaller if income distribution is more unequal (measured in terms of θ).

EXERCISE 47 a. Calculate the equilibrium values of m and n. b. How do m and n change with the distribution parameters β and θ?

The above model has highlighted the important role of income distribution via *market size*, whereas the presence of a traditional sector offering perfect substitutable products prevented the monopolists from exploiting the purchasing power of rich consumers, which we labeled *price effect*. With this admittedly strong assumption we got the exact opposite result from that in the previous section: in a regime when the monopolists sell to all customers but there is sufficiently high inequality, the relationship between inequality and growth is negative. Since the poor are the "critical" consumers who can just afford to buy the innovative goods, a redistribution away from the poor hurts the monopolists and they have to lower their prices. Instead, as long as $\underline{p} \geq (1 - \beta) + \beta \frac{b}{a}$, selling to the rich only is no option for the innovators; the loss of market size incurred would be too large.

11.3 Inequality and Vertical Product Differentiation

The previous sections have considered the situation where rich consumers purchase more goods than poor consumers. However, richer consumers do not only purchase a wider range of goods, they also typically purchase these goods in better qualities. Hence the process of upgrading the quality of consumption goods is another important dimension along which the distribution of income can affect consumption behavior. In the present section we address the issue of how endowment inequality affects the incentive to engage in quality improvements in *existing* industries.

When richer consumers purchase better products than poorer consumers, firms segment the markets into niches that satisfy the wants of the particular groups in the society. While not only income but also taste differences could explain market segmentation according to product quality we concentrate our analysis on income distribution and abstract from taste differences, as we did in the previous chapters.

11.3.1 A Static Model of Vertical Product Differentiation

An easy way to allow for the possibility that richer consumers purchase better qualities and poorer consumers purchase lower qualities is to assume that products are indivisible (see Lancaster [1979] for a discussion of the important role of indivisibility of vertically differentiated products). We consider a situation where consumers enjoy utility when consuming two different products: a quality good denoted by q and a standardized good denoted by c. The consumer either purchases the quality good or does not purchase it. The standardized good is divisible and can be purchased in any amounts. At date t, a discrete number of qualities are available. Preferences are modeled as follows:

$$\ln u = \ln q + \ln c.$$

Utility is maximized subject to budget constraint which is given by

$$p(q) + p_c c = y,$$

where $p(q)$ is the price of quality q, p_c is the price of the standardized commodity, and y_i is the income level of consumer i.

We assume there is a discrete number N of potential quality producers which is exogenously given. Furthermore, suppose the various available qualities differ by a factor $k > 1$. The best available quality is k times better than the quality level of the second-best quality and k^2 times better than the quality of the third best quality, and so on. Without loss of generality we can normalize the weakest quality $q_1 = k$ so that the set of quality goods the consumer can choose from is given by $\{k, k^2, \ldots, k^N\}$. The corresponding prices are given by $\{p_1, p_2, \ldots, p_N\}$.

On the technology side, we make very simple assumptions. Labor is the only factor of production. It takes $1/a$ units of labor to produce one unit of the quality good (a is the same for all quality levels) and $1/b$ units of labor to produce one unit of the standardized commodity. W is the economy-wide wage rate, so the marginal cost of production in the quality sector is W/a and the marginal cost in the standardized sector is W/b. There are no entry costs in the quality sector.

To keep the analysis simple we assume there are two groups of consumers which differ in income: poor P and rich R, with population shares β and $1 - \beta$. Both types of consumers are assumed to have the same income composition. Hence the income level of a consumer of type $i = P, R$ is given by $y_i = \theta_i [W + \Pi]$ where W is the aggregate wage bill (which is equal to the wage rate—as aggregate employment/population is normalized to unity) and Π are aggregate profits. θ_i is an exogenously given distribution parameter that indicates how much a consumer earns in income relative to average income. All income goes to members of these two groups so we must have $\beta \theta_P + (1 - \beta) \theta_R = 1$.

Our setup implies that the important choice for a consumer is to select the quality level that maximizes utility. All residual income is spent on the standardized commodity. Hence a consumer who purchases the best quality expends $c_i(p_N) = y_i - p_N$ on the standardized commodity and p_N on the quality good. Consumer i will purchase the best quality N if the following inequality holds for all available qualities $j < N$

$$\ln(y_i - p_N) + \ln q_N \geq \ln(y_i - p_j) + \ln q_j. \tag{11.10}$$

(The weak inequality is due to our assumption that, in case of equal utilities, the consumer chooses the better quality.)

Let us now turn to the price setting behavior of firms. Suppose that $N = 2$. Due to his superior quality, the top-quality producer can always underbid the second-best producer and obtain positive demand. There are two different scenarios. In the first scenario the top-quality producer sets a price such that both rich and poor consumers are willing to purchase his product. In the second scenario the top-quality producer sells only to the rich and the second-best producer satisfies the demand of the poor. Let us begin with the first scenario. In that case the top-quality producer will choose a price such that the poor are just indifferent between purchasing the best or the second-best quality. This price can be easily obtained from equation (11.10). Setting $y_i = y_P$, letting both sides of the equation be equal, and solving for p_N yields

$$p_2 = y_P \frac{k-1}{k} + p_1 \frac{1}{k}. \tag{11.11}$$

This expression holds for any given price p_1 of the second-best producer. A pair of prices (p_1, p_2) is a Bertrand price equilibrium if neither of the two firms has an incentive to deviate from the chosen price. This is the case when $p_1 = W/a$ and $p_2 = y_P \frac{k-1}{k} + \frac{W/a}{k}$. (The second-best producer will never offer a price below marginal cost.) Note that p_2 is the price that keeps the poor indifferent between purchasing the best and the second-best quality. It depends positively on the income level of the poor y_P. In other words, the corresponding price that keeps the rich indifferent is strictly higher than p_2. This is to say that if the poor prefer just the best quality, the rich will strictly prefer the best quality.

From this simple outcome, we can already infer the aggregate consequences of endowment inequality for the functional distribution of income. Recall that $y_P = \theta(W + \Pi)$. As the aggregate wage bill is pinned down by the marginal product of labor in the standardized sector we have $W = b$. However, aggregate profits are endogenously determined by the endowment distribution. Replacing $y_P = \theta(W + \Pi)$ in equation (11.11) it is straightforward to calculate aggregate profits as

$$\Pi = \frac{(\theta - 1/a)(k-1)}{k - \theta(k-1)} W. \tag{11.12}$$

Hence, when endowments are unequally distributed (θ is low), aggregate profits will also be low. The reason is very simple. As long as the top-quality producer sells his product to both rich and poor consumers, the willingness of the poor to pay is decisive for price setting. When the poor do not own much resources, the top-quality producer will not be able to charge high prices and profit margins will remain low. Note also that our result does not depend on the existence of only two quality producers. The same result would obtain, for any given number of qualities, worse than the second-best quality. Just like the second-best quality, these producers are not competitive and kept out of the market by the pricing behavior of the top-quality producer.

Consider now the second possible scenario where the top-quality producer sells only to the rich and the second-best producer satisfies the demand of the poor. The most promising candidate for such an equilibrium is a situation where the second-best producer sets a price such that the poor are indifferent between purchasing the second-best quality at price p_{N-1} and purchasing the third-best quality at marginal cost W/a. By the same reasoning as above it is straightforward to calculate this price as

$$p_{N-1} = y_P \frac{k-1}{k} + \frac{W/a}{k}.$$

The top-quality producer would, in turn, set prices such that the rich are indifferent between purchasing the best quality at price p_N and purchasing the second-best quality at price p_{N-1}. It is straightforward to calculate this price as

$$p_N = y_R \frac{k-1}{k} + y_P \frac{k-1}{k^2} + \frac{W/a}{k^2}$$

equal to the willingness of the rich to pay. (It is obvious that any lower quality would be kept out of the market by such pricing behavior.) While, prima facie, such an equilibrium seems plausible, it turns out that this pair of prices does not constitute a noncooperative price equilibrium. Given p_N, the second-best producer has an incentive to underbid slightly and attract the rich as customers. In that case the top-quality producer could retaliate by using the limit price policy discussed above (i.e., setting a price that makes the poor indifferent between the best and second-best quality) and drive the second-best producer out of the market. Gabszewicz and Thisse (1982) argue that this instability should favor a kind of tacit agreement between the sellers. Such a tacit agreement supports what they call *entry equilibrium*. This is defined as a pair of prices $(\hat{p}_N, \hat{p}_{N-1})$ such that $\Pi_N(\hat{p}_N, \hat{p}_{N-1}) \geq \Pi_N(p_N, \hat{p}_{N-1})$ for all p_N such that $D_{N-1}(p_N, \hat{p}_{N-1}) > 0$; and $\Pi_{N-1}(\hat{p}_N, \hat{p}_{N-1}) \geq \Pi_{N-1}(\hat{p}_N, p_{N-1})$ for all p_{N-1} such that $D_N(\hat{p}_N, p_{N-1}) > 0$. In other words, the strategy space is restricted to prices where both producers have positive demand. In that case the unique entry equilibrium is given by prices of (p_N, p_{N-1}) as calculated above.

Given such an entry equilibrium, we can again look for the aggregate consequences of endowment inequality. Obviously, aggregate profits will now depend on the sum of profits of best and second-best producers. It is straightforward to calculate aggregate profits. The profits of the best and second-best producer are given by

$$\Pi_N = (1 - \beta)\left[y_R\frac{k-1}{k} + y_P\frac{k-1}{k^2} - \frac{W}{a}\frac{k^2-1}{k^2}\right]$$

$$\Pi_{N-1} = \beta\left[y_P\frac{k-1}{k} - \frac{W}{a}\frac{k-1}{k}\right].$$

Taken together, and recalling that $y_i = \theta_i(W + \Pi)$, yields us with an expression for aggregate profits

$$\Pi = \frac{W(k-1)}{k - \theta(1-\beta)(k-1)}(k + \theta(1-\beta) - \frac{1}{a}(k+1-\beta)).$$

Given that we are in the entry equilibrium, when endowments are equally distributed (θ is high), aggregate profits will also be high. On the other hand, less inequality could also be the result of a lower group share of the poor β. The smaller β the higher aggregate profits (at least when $\theta > 1/a$). More inequality therefore decreases profits.

However, we cannot draw an overall conclusion of how inequality affects profits. If we stay in the pooling equilibrium, where all buy the best quality, or in the separating equilibrium, where the poor buy the second-best products, more inequality decreases profits. However, if inequality increases and we move from the pooling equilibrium to the separating equilibrium, where the poor buy the second-best products, profits jump up. Hence, the overall relationship between inequality and profits is non-monotonic.

Clearly, in this static setting, the aggregate implications of endowment inequality may affect not only the distribution of aggregate income between wages and profits, but also the allocation of resources across sectors of production. In our simple framework, where (1) each consumer purchases one and only one unit of the quality good, and where (2) the amount of resources necessary to produce a quality does not depend on the quality level, there are no implications of endowment inequality for the allocation of resources across production sectors. However, it is clear that such implications arise in a straightforward way as soon as we deviate from those assumptions. Allowing marginal cost to increase with quality levels clearly implies that high inequality reduces the amount of resources employed in the quality sector. With high inequality, lower qualities will be on the market and in these segments fewer resources need to be employed to satisfy consumers' demand for quality goods. The standardized sector will be correspondingly larger.

11.3.2 Improving Product Quality through Industrial R&D

Recent theories of endogenous growth have emphasized not only the importance of new products but also the important role of improving the quality of existing products. Also with continuous upgrading of product quality, the distribution of income is potentially important due to its effects on market size and its effect on prices of the various qualities. The central question is thus very similar to the one studied in section 11.2.: Is the existence of a rich class necessary to stimulate R&D incentives, or is it a high purchasing power of the lower classes? According to the former view, high profits accruing from the rich—due to their higher willingnesses to pay for better goods—drive the incentives to conduct R&D. According to the latter, a high purchasing power of the lower classes creates large markets and consequently high innovation incentives.

We now want to study this question in the context of a Schumpeterian growth model à la Aghion and Howitt (1992), Grossman and Helpman (1991), or Segerstrom, Anant and Dinopoulos (1990). In these models, entrepreneurs conduct industrial R&D to improve the quality of existing products. Here we study the simplest case where a successful innovation increases the current best quality by a constant multiple $k > 1$, which is exogenously given.

Technology is modeled as simply as possible. There is only labor to produce output. Just like before we assume that, at a given date t, the costs of production are given by $W(t)/a(t)$ for the quality goods (the same for all qualities) and $W(t)/b(t)$ for the standardized commodity. To keep things simple we take the standardized good as the numéraire and assume there is no technical progress in that sector. Hence marginal cost $W(t)/b(t)$ is equal to unity and the real wage is constant over time and given by $W(t) = W = b$. Furthermore, we assume there is no technical progress in quality production either, so the marginal cost W/a in that sector is also constant.

There is perfect competition in the standardized sector but imperfect competition in the quality sector. It is assumed that one particular quality is produced by one single firm. The top-quality producer can exert market power in just the same way as we have studied in the last section.

We now assume that consumers maximize utility over an infinite horizon and, just like before, instantaneous utility is defined over a standardized commodity and a quality good, with preferences taking the log form

$$EU(t) = E \int_t^\infty \left[\ln c(\tau) + \ln q(\tau) \right] e^{-\rho(\tau-t)} d\tau.$$

The consumer makes consumption choices such as to maximize lifetime utility subject to the intertemporal budget constraint

$$\int_t^\infty \left[c(\tau) + p(\tau, q(\tau))\right] e^{-R(\tau)} d\tau \leq k(t) + \int_t^\infty W(t)l e^{-R(\tau)} d\tau,$$

where $k(t)$ is the consumer's initial wealth (not to be confused with the quality ladder factor k). We restrict ourselves to the analysis of balanced growth paths where $\dot{k}(t) = 0$ for all t. In that case we have $R = \rho$ and, for all t, instantaneous income is $Wl + Rk = c(\tau) + p(\tau, q(\tau))$. In other words, each consumer spends exactly $Wl + Rk$ each period and chooses c and q to maximize instantaneous utility. This allows us to use the solution to our static model above to characterize the instantaneous allocation of consumers' expenditures for given values of income $Wl + Rk$ for rich and poor consumers. Like in that static setting, the value of a consumer's wealth is endogenously determined. Unlike in the static case, however, the value of wealth consists of the present value of the profit flow accruing to firms (rather than only instantaneous profits that are relevant in the static case).

We assume there is perfect competition in the market for R&D. As a result, it turns out that the market leader in the quality industry will not conduct R&D. As in Aghion and Howitt (1992) and Grossman and Helpman (1991), it is more profitable to gain a one-step advantage than to extend a one-step advantage to a two-step advantage. Innovations are random and arrive according to a Poisson process with parameter ϕ. For the representative R&D firm, ϕ is a choice variable: to achieve R&D intensity ϕ, $F\phi$ workers have to be employed and R&D cost flow $WF\phi$ has to be incurred. $F > 0$ is a technological parameter that indicates the (in)efficiency of R&D labor. The flow of expected profits is $B\phi$ where B denotes the value of an innovation. As there is perfect competition in the market for R&D, the equilibrium will be characterized by zero profits in the sense that the cost of R&D equals the benefits of R&D, i.e., we must have $B = WF$. The value of an innovation B is the present value of the flow profit that accrues to a successful innovator.

A Monopoly Equilibrium

How is B determined? We first study the case where the most recent innovator serves the entire market and all producers of lower qualities do not have positive demand. Because of the stationarity of our problem—the only endogenous variable that changes over time in a steady-state equilibrium is the quality level—we can use the results derived for the static equilibrium in the previous section. In that case we have seen the price

level charged by the quality leader is given by $p_{N(t)} = \bar{p} = y_P\frac{k-1}{k} + \frac{W/a}{k}$.
In the present problem we have $y_P = Wl_P + Rk_P$. Let us assume, just like
before, that $y_P = \theta(W + RK/L)$ where K/L is the per capita value of
wealth and θ is the income level of the poor relative to per capita income.
In that case, the quality leader earn a flow profit $\bar{\pi} = L(\bar{p} - W/a) =
L\frac{k-1}{k}[\theta(W + RK/L) - W/a]$. Note that the profit level is constant over
time and independent of the quality level. This is due to our simplifying assumptions that (1) each innovator supplies a quality k times better
than the previous one and that (2) the marginal cost of production W/a
is independent of the quality level. These two assumptions ensure that
despite increasing qualities (and increasing welfare), prices do not change
(the price per unit of quality is decreasing over time).

We can now determine the value of an innovation and the R&D equilibrium. The most recent innovator earns a profit flow which has to be
discounted at rate $R = \rho$. It has to be further discounted by the rate at
which the current innovator gets displaced by the next innovation, which
happens at rate ϕ. It follows that the value of an innovation is given by
$B = \bar{\pi}/(R + \phi)$. Noting that $W = b$, the R&D equilibrium condition can
be written as

$$bF = \frac{\Pi}{R + \phi},\tag{11.13}$$

$$\text{where } \Pi = L[\theta(b + RK/L) - b/a]\frac{k-1}{k}.$$

Now consider the economy's resource constraint. Total supply is equal
to L. The amount of labor resources employed (1) in the R&D sector is equal to ϕF, (2) in the sector producing the quality good is equal
to L/a, and (3) in the sector producing the standard good is equal to
$[(1 - \beta)c_R + \beta c_P]L/b$. Hence the economy-wide resource constraint can
be written as

$$L = \phi F + L/a + [(1 - \beta)c_R L + \beta c_P L]/b.\tag{11.14}$$

We are left to determine aggregate expenditures on the standardized commodity. As $\bar{p}L$ are aggregate expenditures for the quality good and
$WL + RK$ is aggregate income, we get

$$(1 - \beta)c_R L + \beta c_P L = WL + RK - \left[[\theta(W + RK/L)]\frac{k-1}{k} + \frac{W/a}{k}\right]L$$

$$= (WL + RK)\left(1 - \theta\frac{k-1}{k}\right) + L\frac{W/a}{k}.$$

This allows us to rewrite the resource constraint as

$$L = \phi F + \frac{L}{a} + \left[(b + RK/L) \left(1 - \theta \frac{k-1}{k} \right) + \frac{b}{a} \right] \frac{L}{b}. \qquad (11.15)$$

Equations (11.13) and (11.15) are two (linear) equations in the two unknowns a and ϕ and can be easily solved. They determine the two aspects of interest here: the rate of innovation (monotonically related to the growth rate of consumer welfare) and the allocation of resources across sectors of production.

In the case when only the most recent innovator but not lower qualities have positive demand, we can easily get an explicit solution for the interesting endogenous variables, in particular for the innovation rate ϕ. Note that only the most recent innovator has a positive value. Hence aggregate wealth consists of the firm value of the most recent innovator. R&D equilibrium implies that this value is equal to the cost of an innovation, hence we have $K = B = bF$. Setting K in equation (11.13) equal to bF allows us to calculate the equilibrium innovation intensity explicitly as a function of the exogenous parameters of the model (recall that $R = \rho$)

$$\phi = \frac{k-1}{k} \left[\frac{L(\theta - 1/a)}{F} + \theta R \right] - R. \qquad (11.16)$$

This equation reveals three interesting aspects concerning the role of the distribution of income. *First*, and most important for our purpose, the above equation shows that the innovation intensity in the economy depends critically on the distribution parameter θ. When the quality leader sells to both rich and poor consumers, a more equal distribution of income enhances the incentive to innovate. The reason is intuitive and easy to grasp given the results of the last section. A more equal distribution raises the willingness to pay for quality goods for the poor consumers. Other things equal, this allows innovators to charge higher prices and profit margins, so innovation becomes more attractive. However, and in analogy to the static case analyzed above, the opposite is not true over the whole range. If θ decreases, growth will decrease but eventually the monopoly or pooling outcome will not be an equilibrium anymore. When inequality is very large, so that the expression (11.17) below is violated, the high-quality producers will find it profitable to sell only to the rich. The *second observation* from the above equation is that the innovation intensity does not depend on the second important distribution parameter β. The reason is that what matters for a potential innovator is the size of the market. When all consumers purchase the product of the market leader, the fraction of poor consumers does not play any role (it only matters for the distribution of output of standardized consumption goods between rich and poor consumers but is, in this scenario, an otherwise completely passive variable). The *third observation* of interest concerns the role of the wage rate $W = b$. Notice that ϕ is independent of the wage rate (which means independent of b, the inverse of the marginal product in standardized commodity production). There are two effects: On the one hand, a higher wage increases both the R&D cost and the marginal cost for the quality good, which tends to make innovation less attractive. On the other hand, the wage is also a factor of demand. A higher wage rate increases the willingness to pay for the quality good. In the case when only the quality leader has positive demand, the two effects exactly cancel out.

We also observe that the above equation reproduces the standard results that innovation intensity ϕ (which is monotonically related to the growth rate of the quality level and hence of welfare) increases in the step size k and the size of the market L. It decreases in the interest rate R, the cost of an innovation F, and the labor requirement in the production of quality a.

Finally consider the *allocation of resources across sectors* of production in the case when the quality leader serves the entire market. There is a constant fraction $1/a$ employed in the production of final output. But the R&D sector and the standardized sector are now competing for resources. Less inequality leads to a lower level of per capita consumption of the standardized commodity, resources that can be employed in R&D to improve the quality of final output.

A DUOPOLY EQUILIBRIUM

Similarly to the static case, it can be shown that an outcome where the top-quality producer serves the entire market is likely to arise in a situation where there are little differences in income between rich and poor consumers. To see this consider the extreme case when the incomes of "rich" and "poor" differ only by a tiny amount. In that case there is no reason for the market leader to leave part of the market to the second-best producer, and the equilibrium will be characterized by a situation described in the last subsection. However, with sufficient income disparities, such a monopoly outcome is unlikely as the quality leader will find it more profitable to sell only to the rich at high prices and leave the remaining market to the second-best producer. Hence, the occurrence of a new innovation does not mean that the previous innovator gets displaced but is still on the market because the second-best producer now serves the demand by the poor individuals.

Gabszewicz and Thisse (1982, Proposition 2) have shown that such a noncooperative price equilibrium arises if

$$\beta \le \frac{y_P}{y_R}$$

which, using $y_P = \theta(b + RK/L)$ and $y_R = [(1 - \beta\theta)/(1 - \beta)](b + RK/L)$, can be rewritten as

$$\theta \ge \frac{\beta}{1 - \beta + \beta^2}. \qquad (11.17)$$

This condition says that, if relative income θ is small, the group share of the poor β must be sufficiently small as well. Note that the right-hand side of the above condition is strictly increasing in β. This keeps relative income differences small (because $\theta_R = (1 - \beta\theta)/(1 - \beta)$ is increasing in β).

Once this condition is violated, we know that a noncooperative price equilibrium does no longer exist. Let us again discuss Gabszewicz and Thisse's (1982) "entry equilibrium" in which both the quality leader and the second-best quality have a positive market share. The quality leader sets a price that just attracts the rich (i.e., makes them indifferent between purchasing the best and the second-best quality; we assume in case of indifference between two qualities, the consumers always purchase the better one), and the second-best producer sets a price that just attracts the poor (i.e., makes them indifferent between purchasing the second- and the third-best quality, which is supplied at marginal cost b/a). The prices that, respectively, the quality leader and the second-best producer can charge are given by

$$p_P = y_P \frac{k-1}{k} + \frac{b}{ak}$$

$$p_R = y_R \frac{k-1}{k} + y_P \frac{k-1}{k^2} + \frac{b}{ak^2}$$

and the corresponding flow profits are

$$\Pi_R = (1 - \beta)L(p_R - ba)$$

$$= (1 - \beta)L\frac{k-1}{k}\left[\frac{1 - \beta\theta}{1 - \beta}(b + RK/L) + \theta(b + RK/L)\frac{1}{k} - \frac{b}{a}\frac{k+1}{k}\right]$$

$$\Pi_P = \beta L(p_P - b/a)$$

$$= \beta L\frac{k-1}{k}\left[\theta(b + RK/L) - b/a\right].$$

The value of an innovation is now given by the following expression:[1]

$$bF = \frac{1}{R+\phi}\Pi_R + \frac{\phi}{(R+\phi)^2}\Pi_P. \qquad (11.18)$$

We note that Π_R and Π_P are determined by the endogenous variable K and exogenous parameters (the returns to accumulated and non-accumulated factors are $R = \rho$ and $W = b$). Hence equation (11.18) contains only two unknowns: the innovation intensity ϕ and the per capita value of wealth K/L.

Unlike in the monopoly equilibrium, the aggregate value of wealth K is no longer trivially determined by the cost of an innovation. In the duopoly equilibrium, K depends on the sum of the present value of the profit flow that accrues to the quality leader (which, in the R&D equilibrium is equal to bF) *plus* the present value of the profit flow that accrues to the second-best producer (which is given by $\Pi_P/(R+\phi)$). From this equation we can calculate K as a function of ϕ

$$K = bF\frac{1 + \frac{\phi}{R+\phi}\frac{k-1}{k}\beta\left[\theta - 1/a\right]\frac{F}{L}}{1 - \frac{\phi}{R+\phi}\frac{k-1}{k}\beta\theta R}. \qquad (11.19)$$

From (11.19) it is easy to see that K is monotonically increasing in ϕ. (Note that we must have $\theta > 1/a$, which means that the poor can afford the quality good, i.e., they have an income sufficiently above the marginal cost of producing the quality good.) Note that we must also have

$$1 > \frac{\phi}{R+\phi}\frac{k-1}{k}\beta\theta R.$$

A second expression in the two unknowns ϕ and K can be obtained from the resource constraint. This is given by

$$L = \phi F + L/a + \left[(1-\beta)c_R L + \beta c_P L\right]/b.$$

---

[1] This equation uses the following calculations:

a. If the flow profit π is received *until* uncertain time t that has Poisson arrival rate ϕ, then it has expected value

$$\int_0^\infty \left(\pi\frac{1-e^{-\rho t}}{\rho}\right)\phi e^{-\phi t}\,dt = \frac{\pi}{\rho+\phi}.$$

b. If the payoff v is received *at* uncertain time t that has Poisson arrival rate ϕ, then it has expected value

$$\int_0^\infty \left(ve^{-\rho t}\right)\phi e^{-\phi t}\,dt = \frac{\phi}{\rho+\phi}v.$$

Note that the endogenous variables $c_i = \theta_i(b + RK/L) - p_i$, $i = P, R$. Prices for the quality good paid by, respectively, the poor and the rich (i.e., prices for the second-best quality and the best quality) are given by

$$p_P = y_P \frac{k-1}{k} + \frac{b}{ak}$$

$$p_R = y_R \frac{k-1}{k} + y_P \frac{k-1}{k^2} + \frac{b}{ak^2}.$$

Hence we get for the corresponding consumed quantities of the standardized commodity by the poor and the rich

$$c_P = \frac{\theta(b + RK/L) - b/a}{k}$$

$$c_R = \frac{1-\theta}{1-\beta} \frac{(b + RK/L)}{k} + \frac{\theta(b + RK/L)}{k^2} - \frac{b/a}{k^2}.$$

This means we can write the resource constraint as

$$L = \phi F + \frac{L}{a} + \frac{L}{k^2} \left[\frac{RK/L}{b} \left[k - (k-1)\theta(1-\beta) \right] \right.$$
$$\left. + k(1 - 1/a) - (k-1)(1-\beta)(\theta - 1/a) \right], \tag{11.20}$$

which is a (linear) equation in the two unknowns ϕ and K. Obviously, there is a (negative) relation between ϕ and A. The intuition is very simple: a higher amount of aggregate wealth implies there is more demand for the standardized commodity, hence more resources have to be employed in the standardized sector. As employment in the quality sector is fixed by aL, fewer resources are available for the R&D sector, so ϕ must be smaller.

Equations (11.19) and (11.20) are two equations in the two unknowns ϕ and A. In figure (11.2) the two relations are drawn in (ϕ, K) space. The R&D equilibrium condition is, over the relevant range, upward sloping. The intuition is also clear: a higher value of aggregate wealth A implies a higher willingness to pay for quality, for both the rich and the poor consumers. In that case innovation is more attractive; there is more entry into the R&D sector, which implies that ϕ increases. This higher ϕ drives down the return to an innovation and restores the R&D equilibrium.

We can again study the role of the income distribution. In contrast to the pooling equilibrium the role of θ is no longer clear. Higher θ shifts the resource constraint to the right (and makes it steeper). However, the zero-profit constraint shifts up and the net effect on ϕ is unclear. In the static model more inequality was bad for profits. In the dynamic setting, however, the profits selling to the poor accrue later in the life cycle and

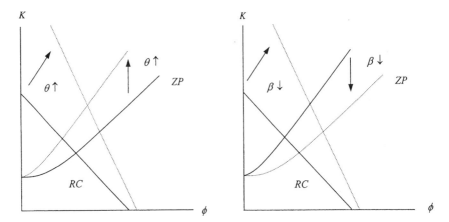

Figure 11.2 Effects of higher θ and lower β on growth

they are discounted. This is the same effect we encountered in chapter 10. Discounting implies that the demand of the rich counts more. Instead, a smaller group share of the poor (lower β) is clearly favorable for growth (as long as $\theta > 1/a$, as in the static case). A lower β shifts both the zero-profit constraint and the resource constraint to the right. Even though the relative income share of the rich $(1 - \beta\theta)/(1 - \beta)$ decreases, the income share of people who buy the high-quality products $(1 - \beta\theta)$ increases when β is lower. Intuitively, larger markets at early stages in product life cycle are good for innovators.

11.4 References and Further Issues

Models with indivisible consumption goods are a simple and tractable way to introduce non-homothetic preferences into the analysis. One of the first papers using such a setup is the influential paper by Murphy, Shleifer, and Vishny (1989). They show that a country can profitably industrialize when domestic markets are large enough. Industrialization in their model is driven by exogenous events. There is growth in leading sectors, such as agriculture or exports, that generates high demand for manufactures, and/or income generated in such sectors is rather evenly distributed, generating high demand for domestic manufactures. While Murphy, Schleifer, and Vishny (1989) conduct their analysis in a static environment, other applications have studied the implications of indivisible consumption goods and monopolistic competition in a dynamic context. They also assume a hierarchic order of preferences, an issue that we study in the next chapter. Falkinger (1990a) studies the introduction of indivisible products in a dynamic context and, in contrast to our analysis, assumes that rich consumers may face a demand constraint as the very rich would like to purchase more products than are actually available. In a related paper, Falkinger (1994) shows that when growth is driven by innovations, inequality is beneficial for growth, whereas when growth is stimulated by high levels of production in the various sectors (for example, because of learning effects), a more equal distribution is favorable for growth. In a dynamic context, demand changes over time, as new consumers become rich enough to afford new products. Falkinger (1990a, 1994) assumes that innovators survive only for one period, but lose their monopoly position thereafter. In contrast, Zweimüller (2000) assumes that innovators live infinitely long. Implications of such dynamics of demand are that profit flows of innovators may change over time and follow the size of the market. Innovation may be more profitable with a more equal distribution as markets develop more quickly into mass markets. Furthermore, there may be multiple equilibria due to a demand complementarity as high expected demand induces high innovation activities. When growth is driven by innovations, high R&D investments induce high growth in incomes, justifying optimistic demand expectations.

Indivisible consumption goods are also an essential ingredient in the model of Matsuyama (2000b) who develops a Ricardian model of North-South trade in which goods are indivisible and which aims to explain why the South specializes in goods with lower income elasticities of demand. Income distribution affects the sizes of the various markets, and the South's domestic income redistribution policy can improve its terms of trade. As a result every southern household may be better off. See also Falkinger (1990b) who explores the welfare implications of trade when consumers have non-homothetic preferences. Krishna and Yavas (2004) develop a model where indivisibilities in consumption interact with factor market distortions and monopoly power in the product market. They show that, as a result of complementarities in goods and labor markets, multiple equilibria may arise, one with high and the other with low equilibrium wages, incomes, and output. They also show that, even in a closed economy, growth may be immiserizing. In a related paper Krishna and Yavas (2005) show that similar issues arise in a trade context when labor market distortions interact with indivisibilities in consumption. The discussion in sections 11.1 and 11.2 draws on recent work by Foellmi and Zweimüller (2004c) who study the role of substitution and complementarity in R&D-driven growth models with an expanding product variety.

Models that address the issue of quality differentiation have been analyzed in a partial equilibrium (IO) context by Gabszewicz and Thisse (1979, 1980) and Shaked and Sutton (1982, 1983). The model discussed in section 11.3 is based on the static framework of Gabszewicz and Thisse

(1982). Gabszewicz et al. (1981) and Flam and Helpman (1987) study the issue of quality differentiation and income distribution in the context of international trade. See also Atkinson (1998, chap. 2) who uses variations of these models to study issues of poverty and social exclusion from consumption.

While income inequality (or an unequal distribution of consumer tastes) was an important ingredient in these partial equilibrium IO models, income inequality did not play a role in models that incorporate quality upgrading into the analysis of innovation and growth starting with Aghion and Howitt (1992) and Grossman and Helpman (1991). In these models homothetic preferences did not allow for any role of income distribution. The role of differences in consumer tastes was studied by Glass (2001). Li (2003) studies a model where consumers have identical preferences but differ in their labor endowments. It turns out that the equilibrium may be characterized by either a monopoly or duopoly regime and changes in the extent of inequality differ across the various regime. The discussion in the present chapter, section 11.3, is based on the models of Li (2003) and Zweimüller and Brunner (2005).

All the models analyzed in the present chapter were confined to possible interactions between distribution and growth when there are many *consumer goods*. It was argued that income distribution may have an impact not only on market size but also on relative prices. However, similar issues arise also for investment goods and/or intermediate inputs. A recent literature, started by Acemoglu (1998) and extended by Acemoglu and Zilibotti (2001) and Acemoglu (2003), studies a framework where R&D efforts are targeted toward new intermediate inputs, but where the direction of such R&D efforts are directed toward technologies that complement particular factors. Similar to the models studied in this chapter, a price and a market size effect determine the relative profitability of the different types of innovation. The price effect induces innovations in the more expensive goods (that is, in technologies using the more expensive factors). The market size effect targets the technologies that use the more abundant factor. When the relevant factors are high or low skills, it is the distribution of skills in the economy that determines the research investments in the various technologies. Koeniger (2004) analyzes a related model in the context of international trade and shows that high minimum wages induce more innovations complementary to unskilled labor, which may explain observed differences in wage differentials, trade volumes, and the sectorial composition across developed countries with different labor market institutions.

There is an empirical literature on the Linder (1961) hypothesis, i.e., the impact of non-homothetic preferences on trade. For recent papers on the impact of income distribution on trade, see Francois and Kaplan

(1996) and Dalgin, Mitra, and Trindade (2004). The earlier papers of Hunter and Markusen (1988) and Hunter (1991) provide evidence that tastes are non-homothetic without referring to inequality.

A recent empirical literature is concerned with the question of how market size affects innovation activities. Most research has focused on the pharmaceutical industry. Kremer (2001a, 2001b) has a number of papers on why research on vaccines for malaria, tuberculosis, and the strains of HIV is so minimal—despite the fact that many individuals in the Third World suffer from these diseases. His main explanation relies on the demand side: potential vaccine developers fear that they would not be able to sell enough vaccine at a sufficient price to recoup their research expenses. (An additional explanation for this result lies in the difficulty to enforce property rights on medicaments in developing countries.) Finkelstein (2004) also provides evidence that investment in vaccines research responds strongly to policy-induced changes in expected revenues. Acemoglu and Linn (2004) investigate the effect of potential market size on innovation of new drugs and find substantial effects of potential market size.

CHAPTER TWELVE

Hierarchic Preferences

SO FAR, WE HAVE ASSUMED that the various goods enter the utility function in a symmetric way. This assumption, which implies that all goods have the same priority in consumption, does not correspond well with actual consumer behavior. In reality, the different goods have different priorities and the consumption of a new good is considered only if the more urgent wants are already satisfied. In this chapter we focus on models that allow us to account for such hierarchic preferences. In particular we study the implications of income distribution for growth and patterns of structural change when consumers have hierarchic preferences. We will see that indivisibilities in consumption—while simple and realistic in many circumstances—are not a necessary ingredient to generate tractable and insightful interactions between distribution and growth.

The present chapter develops a general setup that allows us to study the aggregate implications of a hierarchic structure of preferences. In particular, it is simple enough to allow for solving the aggregation problem,[1] and generate a situation where there are necessary goods (those with low income elasticity) and luxury goods (with a high income elasticity). Our setup not only features important aspects of consumption patterns, but is also tractable enough to allow us to apply the methodological apparatus of macroeconomic dynamics. In particular, the model exhibits steady states, so all results from standard growth models can be applied while allowing, at the same time, for complex structural changes at the micro level. For instance, the model presented in the previous section 11.2 can, in principle, be viewed as a special case of this more general model of hierarchic (and non-homothetic) preferences.

The idea that consumption is hierarchically structured is a very old argument. Philosophers and classical economists have emphasized the importance of a hierarchic structure of preferences. Plato (Politeia, II. 369d) notes, "Now the first and greatest need is the provision of food for existence and life. The second is housing and the third is clothing and related things." Also Adam Smith (1776, 147) writes, "After food, clothing and lodging are the two greatest wants of mankind." The German statistician Ernst Engel (1857) was the first who systematically documented

---

[1] For a possible solution to this problem that does not rely on particular assumptions on preferences but on statistical regularities, see Hildenbrand and Kneip (1999). This is not the route taken up here.

how consumption patterns of individuals vary with the level of income. Engel's law—according to which the budget share of food decreases with income—has become one of the most robust empirical findings in economics (Houthakker 1987).

The result that consumption patterns change significantly with levels of income has strong empirical support (Deaton and Muellbauer 1980). The evidence shows up both in cross-sectional data, once we compare rich and poor individuals, and in aggregate time-series data, when all agents get richer. Furthermore, patterns of structural change (the huge reallocation of labor from agriculture to manufacturing and service sectors) have been explained by a hierarchical consumption structure (that is, by differences in income elasticities of the goods produced in the respective sectors).

Following the arguments put forth by classical writers and in line with empirical evidence, our basic setup starts from preferences that are characterized by a "hierarchy of wants." In economic terms, a hierarchy of wants can be viewed as a concept that extends the principle of declining marginal utility to a situation with many consumption goods: consumers with low incomes devote most of their expenditures toward basic needs. As incomes rise, individuals move on to needs of lower priority. In utility terms, the satisfaction of these lower priority needs gives less utility value than the basic needs, hence the marginal utility is falling. It is obvious that the patterns of aggregate consumption will depend on the distribution of income under such circumstances. For instance, the demand for lower priority (i.e., luxurious) goods will be higher when there is a class of very rich people.

We start by discussing our basic framework and the aggregation problem. Our basic setup continues to assume that all consumers have the same preferences. While it is obvious that not only an "objective" hierarchy of needs and wants but also differences in tastes determine actual demand patterns, prices, and allocations, there is little economic insight to be gained from assuming such taste differences. We then apply our setup to study growth and patterns of structural change in the simplest case when technological progress is exogenous. The hierarchy of wants gives a natural demand explanation for the observed patterns of structural change and income distribution and has important effects on the evolution of the industry structure.

12.1 A Basic Framework

As mentioned above, the approach taken here is putting enough structure on preferences in order to keep the analysis tractable and, at the same time, to capture those aspects of consumer behavior that match important empirical regularities. Such a setup implies that income distribution affects the market demand curve for the various products.

In this chapter we propose a general formulation of non-homothetic hierarchic preferences. The most important of such facts is, of course, Engel's law according to which the budget share for food decreases with income. However, many other goods have similar features. What is a necessary good and what is a luxurious good depend on the state of development of the economy. For instance, in a very poor society, a car, washing machine, or TV set may be a very luxurious product, whereas in a rich society consuming such products may be absolutely necessary for regular participation in the society. In that case, the aggregate structure of consumption will depend on the distribution of income.

We start from the general notion of preferences and identify critical assumptions needed to generate a hierarchical structure of preferences. In the first part of this chapter we focus on a static setup which allows us to remain fairly general in our choice of the (sub)utility function. The second part of the chapter shows which additional assumptions on the utility function and relative prices are needed to deal with dynamic problems. Under these assumptions the role of income distribution during the process of growth and structural change can be studied.

Consider an economy with infinitely many potentially producible goods ranked by an index j. A certain need j can be satisfied by consuming the corresponding good j. Put in other terms, a good represents a "technology" that satisfies a given need. A meaningful specification of hierarchic preferences then has to take account of three facts:

1. Needs are ordered.
2. Some goods may not be consumed, i.e., some needs remain unsatisfied because the consumers cannot afford it. Technically speaking, marginal utility at zero must be finite, at least for goods of lower priority.
3. If a consumer has additional income, he or she should spend it primarily on goods that have lower priority because the needs of higher priority are already saturated (at least in relative terms).

Therefore, we study the structure of consumption that is generated by preferences of the form[2]

$$u\left(\{c(j)\}\right) = \int_0^\infty \xi(j)v(c(j))dj, \tag{12.1}$$

---

[2]Earlier versions of hierarchic preferences can be found in Zweimüller (1998, 2000) and Foellmi (1999). Zweimüller (1998) is the first model with hierarchic preferences and a continuous range of goods where the consumption of a single good $c(j)$ is continuously variable. In particular, he assumed $v(\cdot)$ to be quadratic such that product demand is linear.

where $v(c(j))$ is an indicator for the utility derived from consuming good j in quantity c. The "baseline" utility $v(c(j))$ satisfies the usual assumptions $v' > 0$ and $v'' < 0$; and the *"hierarchy" function* $\xi(j)$ is monotonically decreasing in j, $\xi'(j) \leq 0$, hence low-j goods get a higher weight than high-j goods. It is important to note that we take three important assumptions or restrictions, respectively, at this stage. First, the marginal utility of good j only depends on $c(j)$ but does not depend on the consumption level of other goods. Thus, utility is assumed to be *additively separable*. This assumption seems rather innocuous for the questions we want to study. In addition, a deviation from this usual assumption would cause analytical complexity, since the goods space is modeled as a continuum (the number of goods is infinite). As a consequence, this utility function defined over different goods is formally analogous to additively separable intertemporal preferences defined over consumption at different points in time. Second, the utility of the goods only differs in the multiplicative factor $\xi(j)$. We will see below that this formulation is flexible enough to derive the patterns mentioned above. Third, all consumers have the same preferences. Hence, all differences in demand come from differences in endowments and not from differences in tastes. This assumption allows us to focus on the effects of different endowments alone. In addition, the assumption that the poor like to consume more bread, for example, would lead to tautological statements concerning the consumption structure and inequality.

The presence of a hierarchic weight $\xi(j)$ does not imply that the utility function $u(\{c(j)\})$ is non-homothetic. Whether $u(\{c(j)\})$ is homothetic or not depends on the form of the subutility function $v(\cdot)$ alone. Non-homotheticity implies that the expenditure shares of the different goods j differ or, equivalently, that the income elasticities of the different goods may differ from one. This will be the case whenever the elasticity of substitution $-\frac{v'(c)}{v''(c)c}$ varies with c. Put in other terms, preferences of the form (12.1) are homothetic if and only if $\frac{v'(c)}{v''(c)c}$ is constant.[3]

It will turn out below that the income elasticity for good j is proportional to $-\frac{v'(c)}{v''(c)c}$. To match the stylized fact that the income elasticity for a certain good declines with consumption/income we therefore assume that $-\frac{v'(c)}{v''(c)c}$ decreases in c. Hence, the elasticity of substitution between two goods should be falling. This assumption means that there is "relative" satiation in a single good. Having already consumed much of a good, an individual is increasingly less willing to consume more of that good in

---

[3] These are the CES (constant elasticity of substitution) preferences used, e.g., in Dixit and Stiglitz (1977).

exchange for a reduction of consumption of another good.[4] In addition we assume that the marginal utility of consuming good j in quantity zero, $\xi(j)v'(0)$, is finite for all $j > 0$.[5] This implies that consumers may not want to consume all goods—although they have the same preferences—because the *nonnegativity constraints may become binding*. If marginal utility at quantity zero were infinitely large, it would always be optimal to consume a (small) positive amount even when prices are very high and/or the budget is very low. Needless to say, nonnegativity constraints are incompatible with homothetic preferences. Every good must be consumed at all income levels or it is never consumed. To see this formally, the utility function in the standard monopolistic competition model uses homothetic preferences (Dixit and Stiglitz [1977]). In this model, the partial utility function is given by $v(c(i)) = \frac{1}{\alpha}c(i)^\alpha, \alpha < 1$, which implies a constant $\frac{v'(c)}{v''(c)c}$ and $v'(0) = \infty$. Thus in the standard monopolistic competition model all available goods are consumed in positive amounts.

The generalized version of Engel's law (as emphasized, for example, by Kindleberger [1989]) implies that *additional* income is spent primarily on low-priority goods (high income elasticity). This essential feature is caught by the formulation that the utility of consumption of different goods differs in the factor $\xi(j)$. As the hierarchy function $\xi(j)$ is decreasing in j the marginal utility of a high-priority good (low j) falls quickly. Optimal consumer behavior implies that additional income is spent primarily on the low-priority goods with slowly falling marginal utilities.[6]

12.1.1 Individual Demand

We turn to the consumer's static maximization problem. The total expenditures of a consumer are denoted by e, which are exogenous in the static problem. The consumer's objective function (12.1) will be maximized subject to the budget constraint $\int_0^\infty p(j)c(j)dj = e$ and the nonnegativity

---

[4]Trivially, this assumption is satisfied at points where there is full satiation: $v'(c) = 0$. However, it is not necessary that the utility function exhibits a bliss point. To see this, consider the utility function $v'(c) = (c + q)^{-\sigma}$ where $q, \sigma > 0$. It is easy to check that $-\frac{v'(c)}{v''(c)c}$ is monotonically falling in c.

[5]Note that the latter assumption implies that $\partial\left(-\frac{v'(c)}{v''(c)c}\right)/\partial c < 0$ at $c = 0$. Hence, the former and the latter assumption are compatible. In particular, if $\frac{v'(c)}{v''(c)c}$ is constant (homothetic case), marginal utility at zero $v'(0)$ necessarily equals infinity.

[6]Of course, the same consumption pattern could be generated by imposing a specific structure on prices. If the prices of the goods $p(j)$ would increase in j, consumption of low-j goods would be higher and their income elasticity lower as required when $\partial\frac{v'(c)}{v''(c)c}/\partial c > 0$. However, there is no clear evidence that such a cost pattern can be found on the production side.

constraints $c(j) \geq 0$ for all j. The optimality conditions then read

$$\xi(j)\, v'(c(j)) = \lambda p(j) \text{ if } c(j) > 0 \tag{12.2}$$
$$\xi(j)\, v'(c(j)) \leq \lambda p(j) \text{ if } c(j) = 0.$$

Equation (12.2) gives us the individual demand function: the consumer's optimal consumption of good j, $c(j)$, depends on its price $p(j)$ and the Lagrangian multiplier λ, the marginal utility of income of a consumer. It is immediately transparent that $c(j)$ and income e cannot be proportional. Very poor consumers with low E and high λ will choose not to consume good j. The nonnegativity constraint may become binding, since marginal utility at zero consumption is finite. It is instructive to consider how $c(j)$ varies with j, i.e., what the individual consumption profile looks like. Throughout the chapter we will assume that $\xi(j)/p(j)$ is decreasing. If the goods are ordered in such fashion, the model formalizes the notion of a "hierarchy of wants": loosely speaking, units of goods with low j indices yield higher utility, and consumers give priority to them when choosing the optimal consumption patterns. In that case the optimal quantity $c(j)$ decreases in j and the consumption range increases in income. Hence, a consumer will consume all goods $j < n$ where the critical good n is determined by the following condition:

$$\xi(n)\, v'(0) = \lambda p(n). \tag{12.3}$$

The consumption of the last good $c(n)$ equals zero as long as $\xi(j)/p(j)$ is continuous at $j = n$ (otherwise the consumption of good n is strictly positive). Importantly, condition (12.3) implies that consumption "follows the hierarchy." If an individual gets richer, he not only will consume more of the previous goods but also will consume more goods. A richer consumer exhibits a lower marginal utility of income λ, hence equation (12.3) is fulfilled by a larger n. Panel a of figure 12.1 shows the i's demand curve for a high j good and a low j good, respectively. Panel b shows the demand curve for the same good j of a rich and a poor consumer, respectively. Both pictures look very similar. This arises from the multiplicative formulation of the hierarchy factor $\xi(j)$.

To finish our discussion of the individual demand curve, calculate the price and the income elasticity of demand. By differentiation of (12.2) we get the (direct) price elasticity

$$\varepsilon(c(j)) \equiv \frac{dc(j)}{dp(j)} \frac{p(j)}{c(j)} = \frac{\lambda p(j)}{\xi(j)\, v''(c(j))c(j)} \tag{12.4}$$
$$= \frac{v'(c(j))}{v''(c(j))c(j)}.$$

a. Demand of 1 consumer
for different goods

b. Demand for a single good of
different consumers

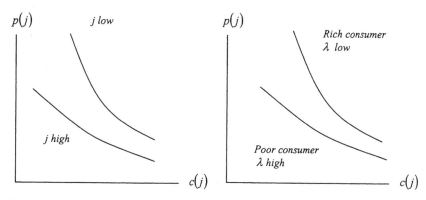

Figure 12.1 Demand patterns: *a*, demand of one consumer for different goods; *b*, demand for a single good of different consumers

The income elasticity can be derived by differentiating (12.2) and the budget constraint. Income *e* and its marginal utility are negatively related

$$de_i = \frac{d\lambda}{\lambda} \int_0^{n_i} p(j) \frac{v'(c(j))}{v''(c(j))} dj. \qquad (12.5)$$

The income elasticity then reads

$$\frac{dc(j)}{de} \frac{e}{c(j)} = \frac{v'(c(j))}{v''(c(j))c(j)} \frac{\int_0^n \xi(j)\, v'(c(j))c(j)dj}{\int_0^n \xi(j)\, v'(c(j))c(j)\frac{v'(c(j))}{v''(c(j))c(j)}dj} \qquad (12.6)$$

$$= \varepsilon(c(j)) \left(\int_0^n \eta_j \varepsilon(c(j))dj \right)^{-1},$$

where η_j denotes the expenditure share for good j, which is given by $\frac{p(j)c(j)}{\int_0^n p(j)c(j)dj}$. The income elasticity for a single consumer is proportional to $\frac{v'(c)}{v''(c)c} = \varepsilon(c)$. In particular, the income elasticity equals the direct price elasticity divided by an expenditure weighted average of the direct price elasticities.[7] Hence, the low j ("elementary") goods where consumption is higher exhibit a lower income elasticity than the high j ("luxury") goods. This is exactly the pattern required by Engel's law. In addition, the formula (12.6) suggests that richer individuals exhibit a lower income

---

[7]If $\frac{v'(c)}{v''(c)c}$ were constant, such that preferences are homothetic, the formula indeed shows that the income elasticity would equal unity for all goods j.

elasticity for a given good j than poorer individuals do. However, this relationship need not be strictly monotone without further assumptions on the price structure and/or preferences. In the special cases below, we are able to present a clear answer to that question. Finally, we note that there is a correlation between income and price elasticity of a certain good: goods with a low income elasticity also exhibit a low price elasticity in absolute value. This is due to the multiplicative manner that the hierarchy function $\xi(j)$ enters the utility function (see equation [12.1] and figure 2.1).

12.1.2 Market Demand Functions

We turn to our question of primary interest, how income distribution affects aggregate demand. We continue to assume that all consumers have equal preferences and are different only with respect to their expenditure levels (with respect to e). By assumption of equal preferences consumers are systematically different with respect to their marginal utility of expenditures (richer consumers have a lower marginal utility of income), and the distribution of the marginal expenditure utilities derives from the distribution of the individuals' budgets. Assume that individual incomes e are distributed according to the distribution function $G(e)$. In principle, we get the aggregate demand function by summing up the individual demands $c(j)$ from (12.2) and using the density $g(e)$ as weight. However, with general functional form $v(\cdot)$, no explicit solution for $c(j)$ is available. Nonetheless, we can derive the slope of aggregate demand and the price elasticity of aggregate demand. Denote aggregate demand by $C(j) = \int_{e^*}^{\infty} c(j) dG(e_i)$, where e^* is the minimum income level such that good j is consumed. The marginal utility of income λ^* of the marginal consumer is given by: $\xi(j) \, v'(0) = \lambda^* p(j)$. Since $de/d\lambda < 0$, the minimum income e^* depends negatively on $\xi(j)/p(j)$. Hence, for low-priority goods (with low $\xi(j)/p(j)$), the share of consumers buying this good will be small. The slope of aggregate demand can be written as follows:

$$\frac{dC(j)}{dp(j)} = \frac{1}{\xi(j)} \int_{e^*}^{\infty} \frac{\lambda}{v''(c(j))} dG(e)$$

$$= \frac{1}{p(j)} \int_{e^*}^{\infty} \frac{v'(c(j))}{v''(c(j))} dG(e).$$

It is instructive to look at which parameters determine the slope of aggregate demand $dC(j)/dp(j)$. The integral tells us that it is given by the average of the slopes of individual demands because the individual demand curves are aggregated horizontally. First, the slope depends on the hierarchy parameter $\xi(j)$. For high-priority goods, $dC(j)/dp(j)$ is very low or the demand curve is very steep. Second, it depends on the average of the λ's, the marginal utilities of income, of the consumers.[8] If good j is only consumed by a rich subset of the consumers who exhibit a low marginal utility of income, $dC(j)/dp(j)$ will be low (inelastic). To calculate the price elasticity of demand we use (12.2) to replace λ.

$$\frac{dC(j)}{dp(j)}\frac{p(j)}{C(j)} = \int_{e^*}^{\infty} \frac{v'(c(j))}{v''(c(j))}\frac{1}{C(j)}dG(e)$$

$$= \int_{e^*}^{\infty} \varepsilon(c(j))\frac{c(j)}{C(j)}dG(e).$$

We get the well-known result that the price elasticity equals a quantity weighted average of individual price elasticities. Ceteris paribus, aggregate demand is more elastic if more consumers choose to consume good j, i.e., if e^* is lower, and if the total quantity is lower. The former is due to the higher price elasticity of demand of poorer consumers. The latter comes from the fact that the individual demand becomes more inelastic when consumption rises, hence this holds also for aggregate demand.

12.1.3 Engel Curves with HARA Preferences

Assume that the subutility function $v(\cdot)$ is given by the HARA form (we omit the individual index i in what follows)

$$u(\{c(j)\}) = \int_0^{\infty} \frac{1}{\beta}\frac{\sigma}{1-\sigma}\xi(j)\left(\frac{\beta c(j)}{\sigma} - \bar{c}\right)^{1-\sigma} dj, \tag{12.7}$$

where $\beta > 0, \bar{c} < 0$, and $\sigma \in \Re$. The restrictions on the preference parameters guarantee that $-\frac{v'(c)}{v''(c)c}$ decreases in c. Again, the goods are arranged in such a way that the first n are consumed in positive amounts which must hold in equilibrium if $\partial\left(\xi(j)/p(j)\right)/\partial j < 0.$[9]

---

[8]The behavior of v'' is less clear since v''' may be either positive or negative. The second derivative v'' is constant if the partial utility function v is quadratic and demand is linear.

[9]To prevent divergence of the integral we need $\lim_{x\to\infty} -\int_N^x \frac{1}{\beta}\frac{\sigma}{1-\sigma}\xi(j)\left(-\bar{c}\right)^{1-\sigma} dj \equiv \Xi$. The limes exist if $\lim_{x\to\infty}\int_N^x \xi(j)dj$ converges, i.e., $\xi(j)$ goes to zero at a rate fast enough ("steep hierarchy"). If we want to study a "flat hierarchy" where the latter integral does not converge, we must normalize $v(c(j))$ such that $v(0) = 0$. In that case $\int_N^x \xi(j)v(0)dj = 0 \forall x$ and the normalized partial utility function is given by $\tilde{v}(c(j)) = \left(\frac{\beta c(j)}{\sigma} - \bar{c}\right)^{1-\sigma} - (-\bar{c})^{1-\sigma}$ (note that $\bar{c} < 0$). See also the discussion about finite utility in the next subsection.

The first-order conditions for an interior solution of individual consumption reads, by analogy to (12.2),

$$\xi(j) \left(\frac{\beta c(j)}{\sigma} - \bar{c} \right)^{-\sigma} - p(j)\lambda = 0, \forall i,$$

we obtain

$$c(j) = \frac{\bar{c}\sigma}{\beta} + \frac{\sigma}{\beta} (p(j)\lambda/\xi(j))^{-1/\sigma}. \tag{12.8}$$

This characterizes the solution if the maximization problem is convex. Since $\partial \left(\xi(j)/p(j) \right) / \partial j < 0$ the individual consumes the first n goods. Then, the budget constraint reads

$$\int_0^n p(i)c(i)di = e.$$

Inserting the consumption levels (12.8) in the budget constraint, we have

$$\int_0^n p(j) \left(\frac{\bar{c}\sigma}{\beta} + \frac{\sigma}{\beta} (p(j)\lambda/\xi(j))^{-1/\sigma} \right) dj = e,$$

hence

$$\lambda^{-1/\sigma} = \frac{\int_0^n p(j) \frac{\bar{c}\sigma}{\beta} dj - e}{\int_0^n p(j) \left(\xi(j)/p(j) \right)^{1/\sigma} dj}.$$

Thus, the (interior) consumption level of good j is given by

$$c(j) = \frac{\bar{c}\sigma}{\beta} + \frac{(\xi(j)/p(j))^{1/\sigma}}{\int_0^n p(j) \left(\xi(j)/p(j) \right)^{1/\sigma} dj} \left(e - \frac{\bar{c}\sigma}{\beta} \int_0^n p(j)dj \right) \tag{12.9}$$

for a consumer who is faced by prices $\{p(j)\}$ and spends an amount e on a set of measure n of the goods.

At this point, we note that if $0 > \sigma > -1$ (which implies $v'' > 0$) the allocation problem has a corner solution: the consumer should allocate his expenditure to the goods with the highest $\xi(j)/p(j)$ ratio and consumption of these goods equals $\frac{\bar{c}\sigma}{\beta} > 0$. As $\xi(j)/p(j)$ decreases, the consumer chooses $c(j) = \frac{\bar{c}\sigma}{\beta}$ for goods $j \in [0,n]$ and $c(j) = 0$ for goods $j \in (n, \infty)$ in the optimum. Obviously, this solution can also be derived by considering a consumer with utility $V(\{c(j)\}) = -\int_0^\infty \xi(j)c(j)dj$ where $c(j) \in \{0, 1\}$ and $\frac{\bar{c}\sigma}{\beta}$ is normalized to one. In the previous chapter we took advantage of this very convenient special case ("$0 - 1$ *preferences*").

From (12.9) the marginal propensity to consume good j can be derived.

$$\frac{\partial c(j)}{\partial e} = \begin{cases} \left(\frac{\xi(j)}{p(j)}\right)^{\frac{1}{\sigma}} \left(\int_0^n p(j) \left(\frac{\xi(j)}{p(j)}\right)^{\frac{1}{\sigma}} dj\right)^{-1} & j \in [0,n], \\ 0 & j \notin [0,n]. \end{cases}$$

The HARA assumption provides us with the required clear result. The marginal propensity to consume $\partial c_i(j)/\partial e$ is lower for richer agents because their n_i is higher. Hence, the Engel curve is strictly concave for $c_i(j) > 0$. This implication may seem restrictive because some empirical evidence suggests that the Engel curve takes a logistic shape. This would mean that for low levels of $c_i(j)$ the Engel curve is convex and for higher values it is concave. However, if we consider a range of goods and draw the corresponding Engel curve for this range, the curve takes indeed a logistic shape. The reason is that at low income levels only a subset of the given range will be consumed.

It is interesting to note how the derivative varies across goods taking expenditures e as constant. Note that $\partial c_i(j)/\partial e$ falls in j if $\sigma > 0$, which may seem somewhat unintuitive but follows from the fact that $\partial \frac{v'(c)}{v''(c)}/\partial c < 0$ if $\sigma > 0$. However, the increase is less than proportional for low-j goods since their income elasticity is below one. Put differently, although the consumption of "elementary" goods (low j) increases more strongly than that of "luxury" goods in absolute terms, the consumption of luxuries will always increase more strongly in relative terms even when $\sigma > 0$. For $\sigma \to -\infty$ where $v(\cdot)$ takes the CARA form, the propensity to consume is constant: $\partial c(j)/\partial e = 1/\int_0^n p(j)dj$. HARA preferences exhibit a bliss point if $\sigma < 0$; then $\partial c(j)/\partial e$ increases in j.

The income elasticity reads for goods where $c(j) > 0$:

$$\frac{dc(j)}{de}\frac{e}{c(j)} = \frac{e}{\frac{\bar{c}\sigma}{\beta}\left[\left(\frac{p(j)}{\xi(j)}\right)^{\frac{1}{\sigma}} \int_0^n p(j) \left(\frac{\xi(j)}{p(j)}\right)^{\frac{1}{\sigma}} dj - \int_0^n p(j)dj\right] + e}. \tag{12.10}$$

The income elasticity monotonically increases along the hierarchy, i.e., it is higher for goods of lower priority where $\xi(j)/p(j)$ is low (note that $\bar{c} < 0$). The value of the income elasticity allows us to give an intuitive condition of an "elementary" good. We define the goods with income elasticity below one as elementary. Therefore, good j is an elementary good if

$$\left(\frac{\xi(j)}{p(j)}\right)^{\frac{1}{\sigma}} > \int_0^n \frac{p(j)}{\int_0^n p(j)dj} \left(\frac{\xi(j)}{p(j)}\right)^{\frac{1}{\sigma}} dj \text{ for } \sigma > 0. \tag{12.11}$$

For $\sigma < 0$, the sign reverses. The formula tells us that good j is an elementary good if its utility-price ratio is higher than the weighted average of utility-price ratios of all goods the agent consumes. From this condition it also becomes clear that the notion "elementary" versus "luxury" is a *relative one*. A given good j may be an elementary good for a rich consumer, whereas it is viewed as a luxury from the viewpoint of a poor agent. Formally, for a rich individual who consumes a large range of goods, the weighted average of utility-price ratios is lower. Hence, the critical good j^*, where condition (12.11) holds with equality, is higher. The same pattern would arise if we looked at an economy with long-run growth, where the range of goods n expands over time (as each individual gets richer): a given good j would be a luxury good at low stages of development and then become an elementary good at a mature stage.[10]

12.2 Growth, Distribution, and Structural Change

Let us now consider the distribution of the aggregate output of consumption goods across the various sectors. Here we take prices $p(j)$ as given. Hence we can think of a long-run equilibrium where all markets are perfectly competitive and all goods are supplied at a price equal to the minimum average cost of production. Things are more complicated when firms have market power because, in such a situation, price depends on the income distribution.

We continue to assume that $\partial \left(\xi(j)/p(j) \right) /\partial j < 0$, which guarantees that consumption follows the hierarchy of wants. To study how the distribution affects demand we compare the derivatives of demand with respect to income across rich and poor consumers. From the income elasticity formula we can determine $\partial c(j)/\partial e$.

$$\frac{\partial c(j)}{\partial e} = \frac{v'(c(j))}{v''(c(j))} \left(\int_0^n p(j) \frac{v'(c(j))}{v''(c(j))} dj \right)^{-1}$$

The first general result is easily stated: *As long as prices for the various products are unchanged, more inequality increases the variety of goods consumed in the economy.* The result directly follows from (12.3). An increase in inequality (holding the average income constant) implies that the

---

[10]As already mentioned in the introduction, the relative notion of elementary versus luxury goods is illustrated by many examples: cars, vacuum cleaners, washing machines, TVs, and so on were luxuries when they were developed, and they were bought only by a small part of the population. Nowadays, these products are widespread among households. See chapter 13.

income of the richest consumer cannot fall. If the richest consumers' incomes rise, their marginal utility λ will be lower, hence their consumption range n is larger. The positive relationship between inequality and variety is due to our assumptions of a preference hierarchy $\xi(j)$ plus the fact that marginal utility is finite: $v'(0) < \infty$. (If $v'(0)$ were infinite, all consumers, irrespective of their income, would want to consume all products that are available as the first bit of each product yields extremely high utility.) In other words, with the preference hierarchy $\xi(j)$ and $v'(0) < \infty$, the love for variety is limited. The desired variety of products depends on income, and even rich consumers will not necessarily want to consume all goods that are available.

We know from the section above that, with this general function form for $v(\cdot)$, there is no clear statement whether $\partial c(j)/\partial e$ is higher for goods where $c(j)$ is lower. This depends on the sign of $\partial \frac{v'(c)}{v''(c)}/\partial c$, which may be positive or negative. In addition, when we compare two individuals, we cannot even say whether the marginal propensity to consume is lower for the rich person. For an experienced reader who is acquainted with intertemporal models and inequality, this should be no surprise. As mentioned above, an additively separable intertemporal utility function has, in principle, the same form as (12.1). The hierarchy parameter $\xi(j)$ plays the same role as it does in the discount rate intertemporal choice problems. There, the individual chose consumption levels at different points in time; here, the agent chooses the consumption levels at different "points" in the goods space. We have seen above that inequality has no effect on aggregate savings if and only if $v(\cdot)$ takes a HARA form. This is the only additive separable utility function that exhibits *linear* income expansion paths—as long as consumption is positive. Instead, if we allow $v(\cdot)$ to take a general form, the income expansion path could be convex or concave or both. Applying this to the problem at hand, it is not clear what happens when inequality changes unless we put more structure on the subutility function $v(\cdot)$.

With the above framework we can, by way of some simple examples, generate a balanced growth path, where (1) distribution affects the composition of demand in a nontrivial way and (2) there is structural change in the sense that goods coexist with different income elasticities of demand.

12.2.1 A Quadratic Subutility function

Assume that the subutility is quadratic

$$v(c) = -\frac{1}{2}(s - c)^2$$

and that the instantaneous utility is hierarchic with $\xi(j) = j^{-\eta}$, i.e., the hierarchic weight is a power function[11]

$$u(t) = -\frac{1}{2}\int_0^\infty (s - c(j,t))^2 j^{-\eta}dj. \qquad (12.12)$$

We want to show how aggregate demand is affected along the process of growth. For simplicity we assume that each good j is produced within an AK technology: $y(j,t) = Ak(j,t)$. All goods j are producible, but we will see that at date t only a range of $N(t)$ goods is actually produced. Aggregate output then is given by $Y(t) = \int_0^{N(t)} Ak(j,t)dj = AK(t)$. As usual the reward to accumulated factor is given by $R = (1 - \gamma)A$ and the non-accumulated factor yields $W = \gamma AK$. All goods j are supplied on competitive markets. We choose the goods price as numéraire, as the technology is symmetric and prices are the same for all products.

We will see that the savings motive plays no particular role here, so we simply assume that consumers have an infinite horizon. The intertemporal problem can then be written as

$$U = \int_0^\infty \left[-\frac{1}{2}\int_0^\infty (s - c(j,t))^2 j^{-\eta}dj \right] e^{-\rho t}dt \qquad (12.13)$$

subject to the intertemporal budget constraint

$$\int_0^\infty \left[\int_0^{n(t)} c(j,t)dj \right] e^{-Rt} \leq k(0) + \int_0^\infty W(t)le^{-Rt}dt. \qquad (12.14)$$

where $k(0)$ and l denote the individual endowments with the accumulated and non-accumulated factor, respectively. Note that $p(j,t) = 1$ for all t due to our choice of the numéraire. After rearranging, the first-order condition of this problem is given by

$$c(j,t) = s - \lambda(t)j^\eta \qquad (12.15)$$

where we defined $\lambda(t) \equiv \mu e^{(\rho - R)t}$.

To determine individual expenditures at date t note that a single agent will not consume all goods. As all goods have the same price, he will

---

[11] As individuals will only consume goods $j \in [0,n]$ in equilibrium, the utility integral diverges if the hierarchy parameter $\eta \geq 1$. To escape that problem we could work with a normalized utility function $\tilde{u}(t) = -\frac{1}{2}\int_0^1 (s - c)^2 j^{-\eta}dj + \frac{1}{2}\int_1^\infty [s^2 - (s - c)^2]j^{-\eta}dj$, which converges for all $\eta \neq 1$. As we only added the additive constant $\frac{1}{2}\int_1^\infty s^2 j^{-\eta}dj$, individual decisions are unaffected.

316 • Chapter 12

only consume goods $j \leq n$ where $c(n,t) = s - \lambda(t)n(t)^\eta = 0$. Note that the latter condition implies that $\lambda(t) = sn(t)^{-\eta}$, i.e., it allows us to express the marginal utility of income $\lambda(t)$ in terms of $n(t)$. We are ready to determine individual expenditures as a function of n

$$e(t) = \int_0^{n(t)} c(j,t)dj = sn(t) - \lambda(t)\frac{n(t)^{1+\eta}}{1+\eta} = s\frac{\eta}{1+\eta}n(t). \qquad (12.16)$$

We get a very nice result: the expenditures are proportional to the range of goods consumed. This feature, as can be shown, is due to the hierarchic power function $j^{-\eta}$ used, but it is not due to the quadratic subutility function. Taking into account that $\lambda(t) = sn(t)^{-\eta}$ and replacing $n(t)$ by (12.16) we can rewrite the demand function (12.15) in terms of expenditures

$$c^*(j) = s\left[1 - \left(\frac{\eta s}{1+\eta}\frac{j}{e}\right)^\eta\right] \text{ if } e \geq \frac{\eta s}{1+\eta}j. \qquad (12.17)$$

This is the (nonlinear) Engel curve. If $e < \frac{\eta s}{1+\eta}j$, the agent will not consume good j.

Reinserting (12.17) into the instantaneous utility function (12.12) renders us (after some calculations; see exercise 48) the indirect utility function u^*

$$u^*(t) = -\frac{1}{2}\int_0^\infty (s - c^*(j))^2 j^{-\eta}dj = \frac{\eta}{1+\eta}\left(\frac{1+\eta}{\eta s}\right)^{1-\eta}\frac{e^{1-\eta}}{1-\eta}. \qquad (12.18)$$

Indirect utility is CRRA in expenditures. This implies that the saving rate must be the same for the rich and the poor. Again, this convenient result is due to the hierarchic power function used. Moving along the hierarchy, marginal utility of additional products is proportional to $j^{-\eta}$.

EXERCISE 48 Derive the indirect utility function (12.18).

12.2.2 Steady Growth and Structural Change

The *AK* technology implies that income and capital grow at a constant rate θ:

$$\frac{\dot{Y}(t)}{Y(t)} = \frac{\dot{K}(t)}{K(t)} \equiv \theta$$

The indirect utility function is CRRA in expenditures and all individuals have access to same interest rate R. Hence the growth rate of expenditures is also constant and is given by rate $(R - \rho)/\eta$. The growth rate of expenditures must coincide with that of income. This allows us to express the economy-wide growth rate

$$\theta = \frac{R - \rho}{\eta}, \tag{12.19}$$

which is independent of personal distribution. This is due to the fact that both poor and rich have the same saving rate. We will return to this point below.

The level of individual expenditures can be derived from the intertemporal budget constraint (12.16) recalling that W grows at rate θ. We get

$$e(t) = (R - \theta)k(t) + W(t)l. \tag{12.20}$$

Having determined the steady-state growth rate of the model, it is very simple to analyze the patterns of structural change. The first thing to note is that structural change and (positive) growth are closely linked. If there were no growth there would be no structural change either. Therefore structural change will take place at a faster rate if the growth rate θ is higher. Second, we look at the evolution of a single sector j over time. Assume for an instant that there is no inequality, i.e., all agents have the same resources and therefore choose the same level of expenditures $E(t)$. The aggregate production of good j is then simply given by figure 12.2. At low levels of per capita income/expenditures, the sector is nonexistent and production equals zero. At the cutoff level $E = \frac{\eta s}{1+\eta} j$—where E is given by (12.20)—sector j starts production. With further growth, the production of good j increases but at a decreasing rate and converges to the saturation level s. As a consequence, the employment share (which is equal to the production share) of sector j will rise first and decline thereafter. In the growth process *each* sector will go through such a cycle of take-off, maturity, and then stagnation.

It is now straightforward to discuss how inequality changes the patterns of structural change. There are two main differences to the arguments outlined above. First, the take-off of a sector will take place earlier, at lower levels of average per capital income. Good j will already be in positive demand at per capita expenditure levels lower than $\frac{\eta s}{1+\eta} j$. As we see from (12.16), richer consumers spending larger amounts e will buy more goods than the "average" consumer. Hence, more inequality leads to more variety in the economy, as richer agents also cover needs of lower priority. Second, the take-off of a sector will not be as fast as suggested by figure 12.2. Instead, at the beginning only a few people will buy product

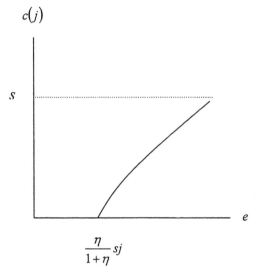

$c(j)$

s

e

$\dfrac{\eta}{1+\eta}sj$

Figure 12.2 Consumption of good j with representative agents

j, and even at the average expenditure level beyond $\frac{\eta s}{1+\eta}j$ not everyone will buy the product. Of course, with rising incomes more and more people will afford that product. This implies that the production curve in each sector as a function aggregate income takes an S shape, which is actually the form that empirical studies suggest. From figure 12.2 we see that more inequality increases the demand for good j in earlier stages of the product life cycle and decreases the equilibrium amount thereafter. Formally, the Engel curve is convex around $e = \frac{\eta s}{1+\eta}j$ and concave for higher levels of expenditures, and the claim follows by Jensen's inequality. The speed of structural change, however, remains unaffected as the growth rate is independent of distribution.

The surprising feature of this model is that although each industry undergoes structural change, aggregate expenditures grow at a steady rate over time. In equation (12.16) we see that the range of goods consumed and expenditures are proportional. Moreover, the proportionality factor is the same for the rich and the poor consumers, which implies that the saving rate is independent of income. Finally, the e/n ratio does not change over time, hence steady states with constant expenditure growth are possible (equation [12.19]). As can be shown (Foellmi 2005) this nice aggregation behavior is due to the fact that the hierarchic factor $j^{-\eta}$ is a power function. The quadratic subutility function $-(s - c(j,t))^2/2$ used in (12.13), however, is not essential. Every subutility function $v(c)$ with $v'(0) < \infty$ and $v'' < 0$ would also lead to the same qualitative results.[12]

The model outlined above has outlined the mechanics of structural change when individuals move along a hierarchy of needs. However, it would be interesting to ask how the picture changes when the various products are not available from the beginning, but must be invented first in a model economy similar to Romer (1990). Interestingly enough, an extended model would present a demand channel by which income distribution affects innovative activity and growth as inequality affects the demand for the different sectors. Intuitively, higher income inequality generates early demand for new products, but the market size remains small as only a subset of people can afford to buy that product. However, as profits are discounted, the former channel tends to dominate and inequality is good for growth (see Foellmi and Zweimüller [2002, 2004b, 2004c]).

12.3 References and Further Issues

As mentioned in the introduction to this chapter, the idea that preferences are hierarchically structured is an old argument. For interesting reflections on this argument see Robinson (1956, chap. 7) and Pasinetti (1981, chap. 4). For a review of the treatment of satiation and the structure of needs and desires in the history of economic thought, see Falkinger (1986). A basic framework of hierarchic preferences can be found in Foellmi (2005, chap. 2) on which our exposition in section 12.1 is based. For a treatment of consumption standards in relation to poverty and social exclusion, see Atkinson (1998).

From a technical point of view there are, of course, plenty of functional forms that can represent hierarchical preferences. In empirical work on the estimation of Engel curves flexible functional forms are used, which minimizes the risk of misspecifications in empirical applications. From a theoretical (macroeconomic) perspective, however, these functional forms are neither tractable nor particularly illuminating. Thus previous theoretical work based on hierarchic preferences typically imposes rather strong restrictions on preferences to illustrate possible implications of such consumer behavior.

Various studies have proposed models where differences in income elasticities of demand drive an economy's structural changes and economic

---

[12] Of course, with general subutility functions no explicit solution for the goods' demand (12.17) would be available.

growth. Kongsamut, Rebelo and Xie (2001) use a Stone-Geary type of utility over three types of products—agricultural goods, manufacturing goods, and services—with, respectively, positive, zero, and negative required consumption levels. Rather than using hierarchical weights they specify separate subutility functions for the various products. In order to generate balanced growth in these models, a further knife-edge assumption linking preferences and technology is needed to generate steady states. Echevarria (1997) follows a similar approach and studies structural change along the transition path to a steady state (of stagnation). In her model, a balanced growth path (where macro aggregates such as consumption and investment grow at a constant rate) does not exist. Zweimüller (1998) presents a first model where hierarchic preferences are studied in the context of a dynamic general equilibrium model. Foellmi and Zweimüller (2002) propose a model of hierarchic preferences with a continuum of goods where industries with high and low income elasticities exist along a balanced growth path. Also Murata (2004) studies a model of hierarchic preferences. In a static framework, he analyzes the introduction of new goods by focusing on the relative importance of desirability on the one hand and technological feasibility on the other hand. A further interesting approach to study a hierarchical structure of preferences are the models by Stokey (1988, 1991a, 1991b), which are based on the Lancaster (1979) characteristics approach.

An important special case of hierarchic preferences are lexicographic preferences. With such preferences, a consumer strictly prefers to consume a certain good to some other good at all relative prices. Lexicographic preferences are similar to a situation with hierarchic "0-1 preferences": a given need must be absolutely satiated before the consumer moves to the next in his or her hierarchy.

A possible formulation of lexicographic utility is given in Matsuyama (2002), which will be elaborated in the next chapter. Obviously, in such a case consumers will always consume along the hierarchy no matter what their prices are. Hence, and as we mentioned in the main text, lexicographic preferences present the most extreme form of a hierarchy. If there are only two goods, the same result can be obtained by Stone-Geary preferences. Therefore, the Stone-Geary type is very popular in models with two goods, see e.g., Matsuyama (1992). Other models that use non-homothetic preferences in two- or three-goods models include de Janvry and Sadoulet (1983), Flam and Helpman (1987), Baland and Ray (1991), and Chou and Talmain (1996). Stone-Geary is also common in (two-goods) models where the individuals decide how much to consume and bequeath (see section 5.3). Examples in the literature include Galor and Moav (2002, 2004) and Mani (2001). Eswaran and Kotwal (1993) and Laitner (2000) use lexicographic preferences in a two-goods model (agricultural and manufacturing goods).

CHAPTER THIRTEEN

Dynamic Interactions of Demand and Supply

SO FAR, ALL MULTIPLE GOODS MODELS studied have focused on the interaction of income distribution and consumer demand. In chapter 10 we have studied models where income distribution has an impact on prices and mark-ups because the nature of individual demand curves may change with the level of income. In chapter 11 our focus was on models where income distribution had an effect on market size as indivisibilities in consumption generated outcomes in which poor consumers could not afford all the goods supplied on the market. In chapter 12 we developed a general framework that allowed us to generate situations where products with different elasticities of demand coexist, so that empirically important features of the growth process, such as Engel's law and the huge structural changes of employment and production that are observed during the process of growth, could be captured.

In all these models assumptions on supply conditions and technologies were kept very simple. In particular, we have assumed identical technologies across the various sectors. As a result, any role of income distribution on macroeconomic outcomes was generated by interactions between income distribution on the one side and the demand for produced output on the other side. While this highlights an interesting channel by which income distribution may affect outcomes, it is clearly a simplification that leaves other potentially important mechanisms out of consideration. In this last chapter, we focus on situations where changes in relative demand across sectors—originating from hierarchic preferences—interact with technological conditions across sectors and feed back to the distribution of income.

Suppose there are two goods, a basic/agricultural good and a luxury/manufacturing good, and growth in income directs demand toward the manufacturing sector. When the two sectors produce with different technologies and/or have a different scope for technical progress, interesting channels of interaction between income distribution and growth arise. Suppose technical progress results from production experiences through a process of learning by doing. Suppose further there is a high learning potential in the manufacturing sector, but that this potential has been exhausted in the basic goods sector. Clearly, as the distribution of income determines the composition of output, inequality will have a crucial impact on dynamics of technical progress and the prices of goods produced in manufacturing. Issues that arise in such a context are illustrated in section 13.1.

Furthermore, when the production factors are used in different intensities, changes in relative demand will have an impact on the demand of production factors. Factors that are intensively used in the luxury sector will see an increase in relative demand pushing up their relative returns. This may have important implications for the supply of production factors as savings decisions and/or educational choices are determined by the respective investment returns. Hence changes in the composition of demand, triggered by the growth process, may feed back to distribution of income and the rates of factor accumulation. Section 13.2 elaborates on these issues.

13.1 LEARNING BY DOING AND TRICKLE-DOWN

In the model presented above income distribution becomes important for growth because of its role for the composition of consumer demand and the corresponding incentives for innovators. We have assumed that technical progress is driven by the introduction of new (consumer) goods. Technical progress was modeled in a very stylized way by simply assuming that the R&D necessary for designing, developing, and producing one additional good creates new knowledge that is valuable in other sectors and expands productivity in those sectors. No other forms of technical progress were allowed.

It is important to keep in mind, however, that an interaction between the speed of technical progress and the composition of consumers may take other forms. One such possible interaction relies on the fact that technical change results from a process of learning that takes place within industries. If such learning within industries is unbounded (because—even if learning within a given product is bounded—the industry may learn to produce new products from the production experiences of old products), there may be technical progress in various industries. Moreover, the speed of aggregate growth may depend on the distribution of income if the scope for technical progress is different in the various industries and if income distribution determines the level of demand in the various sectors.[1]

13.1.1 Trickle-Down

Consider the following setup. There are two different products: good 0 where no technical progress is possible, and good 1. We assume that

---

[1]The discussion in the next two subsections follows Matsuyama (2002).

good 0 is a divisible good that can be consumed in any quantity denoted by c. However, we assume there is a saturation level for good 0, which we normalize to unity. Good 1 is an indivisible good that is either consumed or not consumed: we denote the consumption indicator by x ($x = 1$ when the good is consumed and $x = 0$ when the good is not consumed). Consumers also may enjoy leisure ℓ. A consumer is endowed with l units of labor. We assume that labor income is the only source of income and take the wage rate as the numéraire. Hence a consumer's "total" income (including the value of leisure) is l and the consumer's actual income is $l - \ell$. Denoting by p_0 and p_1 the respective prices for goods 0 and 1, the consumer faces the budget constraint $p_0 c + p_1 x + \ell \leq l$.

Now suppose as in chapter 12 that preferences have a hierarchic structure: good 0 is a necessity and good 1 is a luxury good. For simplicity we assume that the hierarchy of needs takes an extreme—lexicographic—form: a consumer can enjoy the (luxury) good 1 and/or leisure only if the demand for good 0 is fully saturated. Under these assumptions, preferences can be represented by the following utility function:

$$u = c, \qquad\qquad \text{if } c < 1$$
$$u = 1 + x - \eta(l - \ell), \quad \text{if } c \geq 1.$$

where η denotes the weight of leisure in the utility function. We assume η to be sufficiently small, so that a consumer who can afford good 1 will always prefer consuming good 1 over enjoying leisure. This will be the case if $\eta p_1 < 1$. The solution to the consumers' problem is then straightforward: each consumer first expends his income l on the necessary good c up to a maximum of p_0, consumes the luxury good if he can afford it, and consumes the remainder of his full income in terms of leisure. Formally,

$$(c, x, \ell) = \begin{cases} (l/p_0, 0, 0) & l < p_0 \\ (1, 0, l - p_0) & p_0 \leq l < p_1 \\ (1, 1, l - p_0 - p_1) & l \geq p_1. \end{cases}$$

Consumers differ in their incomes but are otherwise identical. Let us consider only the simplest case, when there are two groups of consumers, rich and poor, and, following our previous convention, the distribution of endowments is determined by the distance and group share parameters θ and β. The labor endowment of a poor consumer is $l_P = \theta$ and the corresponding labor endowment of a rich consumer is $l_R = [(1 - \beta\theta)/(1 - \beta)]$, where β is the population share of the poor consumers. Population size is L. Hence, the aggregate labor endowment of the economy is L.

Now consider the available technologies to produce the two types of goods. We assume that the technology for good 0 does not change over time. To produce one unit of output of the c good, a_0 unit of labor are required in production. The technology of good 1, however, changes over time. Production experience in this sector triggers a learning process that decreases the costs of production. The labor requirement to produce one unit of good 1 is given by $a_1(Q(t))$ where $a_1()$ is a decreasing function. $Q(t)$ denotes discounted cumulative output of the (luxury) industry, which is given by

$$Q(t) = \delta \int_{-\infty}^{t} D(s)e^{\delta(s-t)}ds \leq L, \tag{13.1}$$

where $D(s)$ is the demand for good 1 at date s. Production takes place using only labor. Here the parameter δ can be interpreted as both the speed of learning in industry 1 and the rate of depreciation of learning experience in industry 1. Because there is depreciation, learning is bounded. To see this differentiate equation (13.1) with respect to t, which yields

$$\dot{Q}(t) = \delta\left[D(t) - Q(t)\right]. \tag{13.2}$$

Clearly, with only two groups of consumers and due to the indivisibility of good 1, $D(s)$ can only take three different values, $D(s) \in \{0, (1-\beta)L, L\}$. In a steady-state situation, where $\dot{Q}(t) = 0$, this implies that Q^* can also only take one of the three values 0, $(1-\beta)L$, or L. The corresponding steady-state levels for the unit labor requirements in the production of good 1 are then $a_1(0) > a_1((1-\beta)L) > a_1(L)$.

There is perfect competition in all markets and there are perfect knowledge spillovers within industries. As labor is the only production factor (taken as numéraire) and as there are constant marginal costs of production, the prices of goods 0 and 1 equal their unit labor requirements, $p_0 = a_0$ and $p_1 = a_1(Q(t))$.

Clearly, as production experience $Q(t)$ is determined by the distribution of endowments, the price structure of the economy is also determined by the distribution of endowments. In other words, if there is high demand for good 1, there will be much learning in this sector, which drives down prices. This, in turn, supports an equilibrium where poorer consumers can also afford the luxurious product. To see more clearly how the steady-state equilibrium can be characterized and also the dynamics toward the steady state, it is instructive to represent the situation graphically (see fig. 13.1).

We can now address the question of our primary interest: Is a more equal distribution good or bad for growth? To answer this question, suppose the economy inherits production experience Q_0, which implies a price $a_1(Q_0)$ for the luxury good. All consumers with income level $l_i \geq$

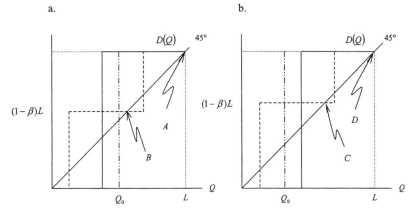

Figure 13.1 Income distribution and trickle-down

$p_0 + a_1(Q_0)$ can afford the luxury good and all consumers with income below that threshold cannot afford this good. Hence, the demand curve for the luxury good is given by $D(Q) = 1 - F(p_0 + a_1(Q))$, where $F(\cdot)$ is the (cumulative) distribution function of labor endowments l_i. In each panel of figure 13.1 the demand curve $D(Q)$ is drawn for an equal ($\theta = 1$) and an unequal ($\theta < 1$) distribution, respectively.

> EXERCISE 49 Assume the same setup as in the text, but now assume there is a continuous distribution of labor endowments, with cumulative distribution $F(l)$. How does this change the solution? How large is the fraction of consumers who can afford the luxury good (see also Matsuyama [2002])?

We have to consider two different scenarios. In the first case, depicted in panel a of figure 13.1, $a_1(Q_0)$ is such that a consumer whose income corresponds exactly to the per-capita income level of the economy can afford the luxury good. In the second case, depicted in panel b of figure 13.1, the mean income earner is not able to afford the luxury good.

As long as demand $D(Q)$ is above experience Q, there is a positive learning-by-doing dynamic because in such a case, equation (13.2) tells us that $\dot{Q} > 0$ and costs are decreasing. The economy reaches the steady state when $\dot{Q} = 0$ or $D(Q) = Q$, i.e., when the demand curve crosses the 45° line.

Consider the first case, panel a in figure 13.1. In that case all consumers can afford the luxury good if there is perfect equality (solid curve). As long as $Q_0 < L$, demand $D(Q)$ exceeds experience Q. Hence, by (13.2), there is learning from production experience and the economy will grow.

Because all consumers purchase the luxury good, the economy can realize the full learning potential and hence the highest possible rate of growth. It will converge to a steady state where productivity reaches its maximum (point A). Now consider an unequal distribution of endowments. If this spread is minor, the change in the income distribution will have no impact on the aggregate demand for the luxury good and only the composition of aggregate demand for leisure will be affected. In a intermediate case, when inequality is more substantial, the poorer consumers can no longer afford the luxury good. Production in this sector is then only $(1 - \beta)L$, which implies that learning occurs at a lower rate. If initially $Q_0 < (1 - \beta)L$ there will be learning, and, as long as only the rich but not the poor purchase the luxury good, the price will converge toward $a_1((1 - \beta)L)$. If the luxury reservation price of the poor is above this threshold, the economy will still converge to the same steady state as before (point A). Note, however, that the growth rate will initially be smaller due to less production and less learning in the initial phase, because it takes time until the poor can start to purchase the luxury. If the income distribution is even more unequal, and this is represented by the dashed line in the figure, the reservation price for the luxury good by the poor could fall short not only of the initial price $a_1(Q_0)$ but also of the price of $a_1((1 - \beta)L)$. In that case, we have a situation where growth stops prematurely. There are two possible steady states, and the economy will be trapped in the lower one (point B). This outcome may occur even when the poor could afford the luxury product when all would buy it. Formally, the "poverty trap" equilibrium arises when the reservation price of the poor $l_P - p_0$ is smaller than $a_1((1 - \beta)L)$ but it exceeds $a_1(L)$. Instead, if inequality is so high that $l_P - p_0$ is lower than $a_1(L)$, point B on figure 13.1 is the unique outcome and initial conditions play no role.

Now consider the second case, panel b in figure 13.1. In that case, the mean income earner is not able to purchase the luxury good. Assume again that Q_0 is sufficiently smaller than L, so that there is high learning potential in the luxury sector. In such a situation, with perfect equality (or little inequality) nobody will be able to purchase the product (solid curve). With a more substantial spread in the distribution, however, the rich will be able to purchase the product. The luxury sector learns from production and prices in that sector decrease toward $a_1((1 - \beta)L)$. Provided that the luxury reservation price of the poor is higher than $a_1((1 - \beta)L)$, the poor will sooner or later be able to purchase the luxury good and the economy converges to the highest steady state (point D). If the distribution is even more unequal (dashed line), however, such that the reservation price of the poor $l_P - p_0$ falls short of $a_1((1 - \beta)L)$, only the rich will be able to purchase the luxury good (point C). In other words, whether or not the technical progress "trickles down" to the poor depends critically on the distribution of income. If the distribution is too equal, the learning process does not start; if it is too unequal, the poor will not be able to participate in the growth process. Only for an intermediate degree of inequality will the poor, after some time, also be able to enjoy consumption of the luxury good. Of course, the two conditions could contradict each other and such "intermediate degrees of inequality" would never exist. The following exercise asks us to derive a condition on technology and distribution parameters such that trickling down is indeed possible.

EXERCISE 50 Derive a formal condition on technology and group shares β that allows for trickling down when θ is chosen appropriately.

The reader may note that the growth rate depends on the scale of the economy (a larger economy learns faster). But the threshold where people buy does not depend on the scale of the economy; it depends only on the mean income level. Hence, depending on the distribution of income, a large economy with an uneven distribution of income may not grow, whereas a small economy with an even distribution may grow.

13.1.2 Trickle-Up

We have seen that, depending on parameter values, a redistribution from the rich to the poor may have very different effects on the growth process of the economy. In particular, growth may trickle down from the rich to the poor, so that sooner or later, the poor may be better off after the redistribution than before.

An important discussion in the development literature has been on the question of whether a large enough middle class exists to foster industrialization and growth. We may use the above model to shed some light on this question. We change the model slightly and allow for three classes in the population: poor, middle class, and rich. Furthermore, we allow for three goods: a necessity, good c—a conveniency x_1 (again this good is indivisible and is either consumed or not; x_1 can only take values 0 or 1), and a luxury good x_2 (also indivisible). Again we assume that preferences are lexicographic. Consumers can enjoy good 2 only if good 1 is consumed, and they can enjoy good 1 only if the demand for good 0 is fully saturated. We also assume that leisure is of sufficiently low desirability, so that leisure absorbs the residual income (income that is left after all goods that one can afford have been consumed). This will be the case if $\eta p_1 < 1$ and $\eta p_2 < 1$. We assume there is learning potential in the sectors producing, respectively, the conveniency and the luxury. Just like before, there is no learning in the sector producing the necessary good.

With these slight changes in our setup we can again study the role of the distribution of income. Suppose that we have initially a situation where the rich consumers can afford only the necessity and the conveniency but not the luxury good. And the lower income classes can only consume the necessity but not the conveniency. Now consider a redistribution of income among the lower classes. This may change the situation. If the spread in the distribution of income is sufficiently large, the middle class may now become able to afford the conveniency. This starts a learning process in that sector that increases productivity and decreases prices in that sector. If prices decrease sufficiently this may, sooner or later, allow the rich to purchase the luxury good. Hence, even though the rich were not involved in the redistribution, they gain due to lower prices for conveniencies. The process of growth "trickles up" to the rich. Clearly, under our assumptions, the poor will definitely lose. Note, however, that we have assumed there is no learning spillover across industries. Once we allow for such spillover effects, the poor may also gain from such a redistribution.

13.2 DEMAND COMPOSITION AND FACTOR REWARDS

In the last section we have considered the implications of income distribution for economic growth that result from interactions between demand and asymmetric technical progress across industries. When the scope for technical progress differs across industries, income distribution affects not only the composition of output but also the nature of economic growth and the distribution of welfare increases that results from growth.

A related issue concerns the evolution of relative factor rewards. Consider our simple setup with two sectors, producing basic/agriculture and luxury/manufacturing goods. Assume there are two factors of production, skilled and unskilled labor, which are used in different intensities in the two sectors. When the luxury good is more skill-intensive than the basic good, economic growth will raise the relative demand for skilled labor—which tends to increase wage inequality between the two groups. Clearly, when relative factor intensities are reversed, exactly the opposite will be the case.

These arguments suggest that the increase in the demand for skilled workers, and the associated increase in wage differentials, may not be a pure supply phenomenon, triggered by a skill bias in technical change. With hierarchic preferences, growth will benefit owners of factors that are intensively used in the dynamic sectors of the economy. When owners of these factors are relatively richer in the first place (as are skilled workers relative to the unskilled), economic growth triggers a process where "inequality begets inequality" (see also the discussion in Ray [1998, chap.

7]). This intuition will be made precise in the model presented below. We proceed in two steps. We first consider a situation of exogenous technical progress, identical in both sectors, holding the supply of both factors constant and focus on the evolution of factor rewards. The second step is to allow for the endogenous accumulation of human capital and to show how the change in relative factor prices affects the decision to accumulate human capital. This allows us to represent the evolution of factor rewards as a race between the relative demand and the relative supply of production factors.

13.2.1 Growth and Factor Rewards

We consider the framework where the population consists of many families, each of which consists of a sequence of one-period lifetimes (similar to the model discussed in section 5.3—one period lifetimes with bequests). At birth, individuals are endowed with capital and labor which generates income.

Similar to the situation above, we assume there is a basic good c_0 and luxury good c_1 and preferences of consumers can be represented by

$$u = \begin{cases} c_0 & \text{if } c_0 < \bar{c}_0 \\ \bar{c}_0 + c_1 & \text{if } c_0 = \bar{c}_0 \end{cases}.$$

There are two factors of production, skilled labor H and unskilled labor L. One can think of human capital as the accumulated factor and unskilled labor as the non-accumulated factor. To capture a situation where the basic good is less skill-intensive than the luxury good we assume that the basic good is produced with a Cobb-Douglas technology $Y_0 = AH_0^\alpha L_0^{1-\alpha}$ using skilled labor H and unskilled labor L, whereas the luxury good is produced with skilled labor only, hence $Y_1 = AH_1$. (The latter assumption greatly simplifies the analysis. However, requiring unskilled labor in the production of the luxury good would yield qualitatively identical results as long as a factor intensity reversal cannot occur.) Obviously, full employment of both factors of production implies $L_0 = L$ and $H = H_0 + H_1$. The scaling parameter A captures the economy-wide stock of knowledge. There is neutral technological progress in the sense that an increase in A affects both the basic and the luxury sector alike.

Assume there is perfect competition on all markets and take the basic good as the numéraire, $p_0 = 1$. Factor prices are determined by

$$W_H = \frac{\partial Y_0}{\partial H_0} = \alpha A \left(\frac{L}{H_0}\right)^{1-\alpha} \quad \text{and} \tag{13.3}$$

$$W_L = \frac{\partial Y_0}{\partial L_0} = (1-\alpha)A \left(\frac{H_0}{L}\right)^\alpha, \tag{13.4}$$

where W_H and W_L are, respectively, the wage for skilled and for unskilled labor in terms of the basic good. The income of a skilled worker is $W_H H/(1 - \beta)$ because the economy-wide endowment with skilled labor is H and there are $(1 - \beta)$ skilled workers. To ease notation we define $h \equiv H/(1 - \beta)$ such that the skilled workers' income is given by $W_H h$. Analogously, the income of an unskilled worker is $W_L L/\beta \equiv W_L l$. Since there is perfect competition, the price for the luxury good in terms of the basic good is given by

$$p_1 = W_H/A = \left(\frac{L}{H_0}\right)^{1-\alpha}. \tag{13.5}$$

Equations (13.3), (13.4), and (13.5) are three equations in the four unknowns, p_1, W_H, W_L, and H_0. To determine H_0 we have to look at the composition of demand, that is, the demand for basic and luxury goods.

Case 1: Skilled and unskilled consume only basic goods. When the economy's stock of knowledge A is very low, the entire demand in the economy is directed toward the basic good. When does that happen? This outcome depends on the economy's relative endowments with skilled and unskilled labor. When only the basic good is produced we have $W_H = \alpha A(H/L)^{-(1-\alpha)}$ and $W_L = (1 - \alpha)A(H/L)^\alpha$. Clearly, for sufficiently low A a situation where both $W_H H/(1 - \beta) = W_H h < \bar{c}_0$ and $W_L L/\beta = W_L l < \bar{c}_0$ may arise. In such a situation, relative factor prices are entirely determined by endowments and technology. The demand side plays no role. More precisely, the relative income of the skilled is given by

$$\frac{W_H h}{W_L l} = \frac{\beta}{1 - \beta}\frac{\alpha}{1 - \alpha}.$$

Individuals endowed with skilled labor are richer than individuals endowed with raw labor only as long as $\alpha + \beta > 1$.

Case 2: Only skilled consume luxuries. Now consider more closely the situation when both the basic and the luxury sector have positive demand. Assume a sufficiently high A so that we have $W_H h = \alpha A(H_0/L)^{-(1-\alpha)}[H/(1 - \beta)] > \bar{c}_0$ for all $H_0 \leq H$. This implies that a skilled worker consumes the basic good at the maximum amount $\bar{c}_0$ and has a positive demand for the luxury good. The demand for the luxury good by a skilled worker can be found by considering the budget constraint $\bar{c}_0 + p_1 c_1^H = W_H h$. Solving the budget constraint for c_1^H yields

$$c_1^H = \frac{W_H h - \bar{c}_0}{p_1}.$$

The unskilled workers will not be able to consume luxury goods when their income $W_L l$ falls short of $\bar{c}_0$. In that case they use all their income for the basic good and have no demand for luxuries $c_1^L = 0$. The amount of skilled labor employed in the basic sector H_0 can now be easily determined from equating the supply $AH_0^\alpha L^{1-\alpha}$ in the basic sector to the level of demand in that sector $\beta [W_L L/\beta] + (1 - \beta)\bar{c}_0$. Using equation (13.4) we can solve for the equilibrium amount of skilled labor employed in the production of basic goods

$$H_0 = \left[\frac{(1 - \beta)\bar{c}_0}{\alpha AL^{1-\alpha}}\right]^{\frac{1}{\alpha}}. \tag{13.6}$$

It is obvious that H_0 is decreasing in A. Hence when the economy grows, there will be a reallocation of skilled labor from the basic to the luxury sector. We also see from equation (13.6) that a higher number of unskilled workers β decreases the amount of skilled labor employed in the basic sector. A higher β implies a lower number of skilled workers (population size is fixed and normalized to unity) and hence a lower number of workers who consume the basic good at its saturation point.

What does growth imply for relative wages and the distribution of incomes? Using equations (13.6), (13.3), and (13.4) it is straightforward to calculate relative factor prices as

$$\frac{W_H}{W_L} = \frac{\alpha}{1 - \alpha}\left(\frac{\alpha AL}{(1 - \beta)\bar{c}_0}\right)^{\frac{1}{\alpha}}.$$

The factor price differential increases when there is exogenous economic growth, i.e., an increase in A. As skilled workers are richer than the unskilled, and as the relative population size is constant, growth implies an unambiguous increase in inequality. The reason is that the luxury sector captures relatively more demand from the general increase in incomes. As this sector is skill-intensive, the demand for skilled labor increases and raises the relative wage. The welfare level of the poor is unaffected. To see this, note that combining (13.6) and (13.4) yields

$$W_L = \frac{1 - \alpha}{\alpha}\frac{(1 - \beta)\bar{c}_0}{L}.$$

Hence we end up in a situation where the increases in demand are totally appropriated by the rich. Note from this formula that the unskilled workers' income $W_L l$ is smaller than $\bar{c}_0$ if and only if $\alpha + \beta > 1$. This is the very same condition that guarantees that the skilled worker has more income in case 1 above. The equilibrium wage rate for skilled labor is

$$W_H = [\alpha A L^{1-\alpha}]^{\frac{1}{\alpha}} [(1 - \beta) \bar{c}_0]^{-\frac{1-\alpha}{\alpha}},$$

which increases more than proportionately with A. The result that only the rich gain from technical progress is clearly a corollary of our assumption that only skilled workers are demanded in the sector that produces luxury goods. However, as long as the luxury sector is more skill-intensive than the basic sector, growth will be skill-biased and lead to an increase in the gap between the wage of the skilled and unskilled workers (see exercise below).

Case 3: Both skilled and unskilled consume luxuries. The analysis above has assumed that unskilled workers will not consume luxury goods. The situation changes only slightly when we assume that unskilled workers also consume luxury goods. When not only the skilled but also the unskilled households can afford the luxury good, aggregate output in the basic sector equals $\bar{c}_0$ (a population equal to unity consumes $\bar{c}_0$ each). With Cobb-Douglas production and perfect competition, this implies that the unskilled wage bill in the basic sector (which coincides with the economy-wide wage bill) is equal to $(1 - \alpha)\bar{c}_0$. As there are β unskilled households in total, average income per unskilled worker is given by $(1 - \alpha)\bar{c}_0/\beta$. Hence the unskilled will consume luxuries whenever

$$1 - \alpha > \beta.$$

This condition should come as no surprise. It means that at low levels of A (case 1) the unskilled worker is richer than the skilled worker. If this condition did not hold, the skilled workers would reach the threshold to the luxury good first and the unskilled would thereafter stay at the same level (case 2). (Notice that this condition is independent of the productivity level A in the economy. The condition assumes that productivity is high enough that $\bar{c}_0$ is feasible, given productivity A and the economy's stock of resources H and L. We will not consider the case where only the unskilled consume the luxury good.) When the basic sector produces so much output as to provide every household with the saturation level for the basic good, we have $\bar{c}_0 = A L^{1-\alpha} \bar{H}_0^{\alpha}$, where $\bar{H}_0$ is the level of human capital that has to be employed in the basic sector in order to generate output $\bar{c}_0$. Solving for $\bar{H}_0$ yields

$$\bar{H}_0 = \left[\frac{\bar{c}_0}{A L^{1-\alpha}} \right]^{\frac{1}{\alpha}}$$

and the corresponding factor prices

$$W_H = \alpha A \left[\frac{AL}{\bar{c}_0} \right]^{\frac{1-\alpha}{\alpha}} \quad \text{and} \quad W_L = \frac{(1-\alpha)\,\bar{c}_0}{L}.$$

Obviously, the wage gap grows and the income distribution widens when there is technical progress. While technical progress occurs in both sectors, demand constraints limit the output in the basic sector. As a result, the wage for the skilled worker increases, whereas the wage for the unskilled stagnates. Clearly, the relative price between the basic sector and the luxury sector increases over time. Using $p_1 = W_H/A$, the relative price of the luxury good can be written as

$$p_1 = \alpha \left[\frac{AL}{\bar{c}_0} \right]^{\frac{1-\alpha}{\alpha}},$$

hence technical progress raises the price of the luxury relative to the basic good.

Interestingly, when the unskilled can consume the luxury good, it turns out that technical progress is *bad* for the unskilled. To see this, note that the income level of an unskilled household is $(1-\alpha)\,\bar{c}_0/\beta$, constant over time. The amount of expenditures devoted to the luxury good is given by $p_1 c_1^L = (1-\alpha)\,\bar{c}_0/\beta - \bar{c}_0$ so that consumption of an unskilled household is given by

$$c_1^L = \frac{(1-\alpha) - \beta}{\beta} \frac{\bar{c}_0}{p_1}.$$

This equation says that luxury consumption of an unskilled household changes with economic growth to the extent that growth affects the relative price of luxuries. When total factor productivity increases, p_1 increases and the luxury consumption of the unskilled decreases! As income increases, *growth is immiserizing* for workers who are not needed to generate the additional production. Higher production takes place in the luxury sector, but as the unskilled consume less of it, luxury consumption of the skilled must rise. There is leapfrogging: initially the unskilled enjoy the higher welfare, but at sufficiently high levels of A the skilled become the rich group.

EXERCISE 51 Assume that unskilled workers are also needed in the production of luxuries but the luxury sector is more skill-intensive than the basic goods sector. Assume further that both sectors use a Cobb-Douglas production technology where (as in the main text) production in the basic good sector is $Y_0 = AH_0^\alpha L_0^{1-\alpha}$ and production in the luxury sector is $Y_0 = AH_1^\delta L_1^{1-\delta}$ with $\delta > \alpha$.

    a. Is it still possible that the poor can never consume the luxury good?

    b. Is it still possible that growth is immiserizing for the unskilled workers?

EXERCISE 52 Assume the basic good is produced by unskilled labor only $Y_0 = AL_0$, whereas the luxury good is produced by a Cobb-Douglas technology $Y_1 = AHL_1$. Describe the distributional dynamics under the assumption that H and L are exogenous.

13.2.2   *Relative Factor Rewards: A Race between Supply and Demand*

Until now we have assumed that H and L are exogenously given. This is clearly a simplifying assumption. When there is productivity growth skill differentials increase without bound and hence there is a very strong incentive to acquire skills. It is interesting and insightful to study the importance of skill acquisition in the present context.

We assume that individuals are heterogeneous with respect to their (utility) cost of acquiring education. The utility function is now given by

$$u = c_0 - bx \qquad \text{if } c_0 < \bar{c}_0$$
$$u = \bar{c}_0 + c - bx \quad \text{if } c_0 \geq \bar{c}_0 \tag{13.7}$$

where x is the (exogenously given) disutility associated with an investment in skill and is a parameter that differs across individuals. We assume that skill acquisition is a discrete choice. The indicator variable takes value $b = 1$ when the individual acquires skills and $b = 0$ when he or she remains unskilled. The incomes of the skilled and unskilled are defined in the same way as in the section above. When an individual acquires skill, he or she gets income $W_H h$, the same for all skilled individuals. An individual that remains unskilled gets income $W_L l$, which is also the same for all unskilled individuals. Individuals maximize utility (13.7) subject to the budget constraint

$$W_H h = \bar{c}_0 + p_1 c_1, \text{ when } b = 1, \text{ and} \tag{13.8}$$
$$W_L l = \bar{c}_0 + p_1 c_1, \text{ when } b = 0.$$

Clearly, while these incomes are exogenous from the individuals' point of view, they are endogenously determined in the macroeconomic equilibrium. Under the present assumptions not only the demand for, but also the supply of, the two types of labor are relevant to determining factor prices and incomes. Denote by x^* the utility cost of getting educated for the individual who is indifferent between getting educated and remaining unskilled at the prevailing factor prices. Then all workers for whom $x < x^*$ find it optimal to become skilled, the aggregate stock of skilled labor is $H = F(x^*)h$, and the aggregate stock of unskilled labor is $L = [1 - F(x^*)]\, l$.

Case 2: The skilled but not the unskilled consume the luxury good. Let us first consider the case when the skilled but not the unskilled consume the luxury good. In that case it is straightforward to see that factor prices are given by

$$W_L = \frac{1 - \alpha}{\alpha} \frac{\bar{c}_0}{l} \frac{F(x^*)}{1 - F(x^*)}, \text{ and } W_H = (\alpha A)^{\frac{1}{\alpha}} \left[\frac{\bar{c}_0}{l} \frac{F(x^*)}{1 - F(x^*)} \right]^{-\frac{1-\alpha}{\alpha}}, \quad (13.9)$$

where we have used $\beta = 1 - F(x^*)$, $L = l\,[1 - F(x^*)]$, and $H = hF(x^*)$. It remains to determine the critical effort level x^* above which individuals do not find it optimal to get education. This critical level is determined by indifference between becoming skilled and remaining unskilled. The utility of a worker becoming skilled is $\bar{c}_0 + c_1^H - x = \bar{c}_0 + (W_H h - \bar{c}_0)/p_1 - x$, and the utility of a worker remaining unskilled is $c_0^L = W_L l$. The utility cost x differs across workers, and for the one who is indifferent we have $x = x^*$, which is given by

$$x^* = \bar{c}_0 + \frac{W_H h - \bar{c}_0}{p_1} - W_L l,$$

$$= \bar{c}_0 + Ah - \left[\frac{\bar{c}_0}{\alpha} \right]^{\frac{1}{\alpha}} \left[\frac{1}{Al} \frac{F(x^*)}{1 - F(x^*)} \right]^{\frac{1-\alpha}{\alpha}} - \frac{1 - \alpha}{\alpha} \bar{c}_0 \frac{F(x^*)}{1 - F(x^*)},$$

where we have used $p_1 = W_H/A$ and the wage expressions (13.9). This equation implicitly defines the critical x^*. Note that a unique solution exists since the right-hand side is monotonically falling in x^* and for $x^* = 0$ the right-hand side equals $\bar{c}_0 + Ah > 0$. Individuals with utility costs to acquire skills below x^* will invest in skills. Hence the fraction of the skilled population is given by $F(x^*)$.

We will proceed to analyze what happens to wages when there is exogenous growth, i.e. an increase in A. When the supply of H and L is exogenously given, which was the case in the last subsection, increasing productivity raises the relative demand for skilled workers. For an equilibrium, the relative wage of skilled workers, the skill premium, must unambiguously rise. Now the supply of H and L is endogenous, and the supply of skills increases, which dampens the need for a higher skill premium. In fact, the skill *premium* may even fall for a sufficient reaction of supply. This is possible since the incentive to acquire skills depends on the *difference* of wages, whereas the premium is a *ratio*. There is a race between supply and demand, which is visualized in figure 13.2. Panel *a* of the figure shows the exogenous case and panel *b* the endogenous case.

To see who wins the race, we differentiate the skill premium with respect to A:

$$\frac{d}{dA}\left[\frac{W_H}{W_L}\right] = \frac{\partial}{\partial A}\left[\frac{W_H}{W_L}\right] + \frac{\partial}{\partial(1-\beta)}\left[\frac{W_H}{W_L}\right]f(x^*)\frac{\partial x^*}{\partial A},$$

where the first term represents the demand effect and the second term the supply effect, respectively. The skill premium is given by

$$\frac{W_H}{W_L} = \frac{\alpha}{1-\alpha}\left[\frac{\alpha A l}{\bar{c}_0}\frac{\beta}{1-\beta}\right]^{\frac{1}{\alpha}}, \tag{13.10}$$

where we have used $F(x^*) = 1 - \beta$. We see that the skill premium rises in A and falls in $(1 - \beta)$, the supply of skilled workers. Whether the supply or the demand effect dominates critically depends on the magnitude of $f(x^*)$, the population density at the level where they are indifferent to acquire skills. The density $f(\cdot)$ of a continuous distribution may take values between zero and infinity. If $f(x^*)$ is very large, the supply effect would dominate and the premium would fall. However, if $f(x^*)$ is small, the skill premium rises due to an increase in the level of technological knowledge A, as demand for skilled workers increases more strongly than the supply of skilled workers does.

Case 3: Both skilled and unskilled consume the luxury good. Remember from the discussion in the last section that for this case $\alpha + \beta < 1$, respectively $\alpha < F(x^*)$, must hold. When both the skilled and the unskilled consume the luxury good, the factor prices are given by

$$W_H = \alpha A\left[\frac{A[1-F(x^*)]l}{\bar{c}_0}\right]^{\frac{1-\alpha}{\alpha}} \quad \text{and} \quad W_L = \frac{(1-\alpha)\bar{c}_0}{[1-F(x^*)]l}.$$

The indifferent individual has effort cost of education

$$x^* = Ah - \frac{1-\alpha}{\alpha}\left[\frac{1}{Al}\right]^{\frac{1-\alpha}{\alpha}}\left[\frac{\bar{c}_0}{1-F(x^*)}\right]^{\frac{1}{\alpha}}.$$

Again, whether the skill premium rises or falls depends on a supply and demand effect. Can growth still be immiserizing for the unskilled when the supply of factor is also endogenous? Look at consumption of the

a.

b.

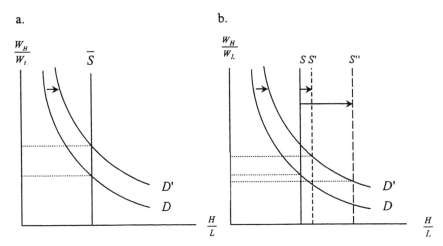

Figure 13.2 Race between relative supply and demand

luxury good of an unskilled worker:

$$c_1^L = \frac{W_L l - \bar{c}_0}{p_1} = \frac{\bar{c}_0}{\alpha} \left[\frac{1 - \alpha - \beta}{\beta} \right] \left[\frac{\bar{c}_0}{Al\beta} \right]^{\frac{1-\alpha}{\alpha}},$$

which falls in A and rises in $(1 - \beta)$. In this case, there is also a supply effect which counteracts the immiserizing effect discussed in the last section. As more workers get skilled when A rises, the wages of those who remain unskilled rise ceteris paribus. Hence, technological progress may or may not worsen the welfare of the unskilled.

13.3   REFERENCES AND FURTHER ISSUES

The importance of mass consumption as a characteristic of modern industrialized countries has been emphasized by Rostow (1960) who developed a theory of stages of economic growth in which the last of the five stages is "the age of high mass consumption." Katona (1964) emphasized the close relation of income distribution and demand patterns that characterize a mass consumption society. According to him, the participation of the broad masses in a large variety of consumption goods constitutes a mass consumption society. Most of the demand for the goods comes from the masses and demand levels follow an S shape where initially only rich consumers can buy and, gradually, the goods penetrate the whole society. The model discussed in the text is based on Matsuyama (2002).

Leonardi (2004) studies a model that is very similar in spirit to the one presented in section 13.2. Linking data from the UK Family Expenditure Survey and to industry data from the UK Labor Force Survey, he finds that skill-intensive industries have higher income elasticities of demand, giving empirical support to the demand-driven mechanisms of skill-biased technical change. Weiss (2004) provides a consumption-based explanation for relative factor-price dynamics that relies on complementarities between high- and low-tech goods.

A further interesting strand of the literature uses hierarchic preferences to study the structure of investment rather than consumption goods. Galor and Moav (2002, 2004) propose models in which households have non-homothetic preferences over a consumption good and bequests, implying that richer households have a higher savings rate. Their models show a complex interaction between the structure of investment (physical versus human capital). They show that in late stages of development, when the return to human capital increases due to capital-skill complementarity, human capital becomes the prime engine of growth and capital owners profit from workers' education as a well-educated workforce sustains high profit rates.

In section 13.2 we touched upon issues of wage inequality. While extremely important, these issues are not discussed elsewhere in this book, which focused on macroeconomic consumption and savings behavior in connection with imperfections in product or financial markets. Apart from chapter 7 and in this section, education, employment, and wages were not as prominent as would have been necessary in a comprehensive analysis of inequality. Readers can, of course, draw on the huge theoretical and empirical literature dealing with rising wage inequalities. Interesting theoretical frameworks are provided by Acemoglu (1998), Lloyd-Ellis (1999), and Eicher and García-Peñalosa (2001). Aghion (2002) discusses, in the context of an R&D-based growth model, the evolution of wage inequality both within and between educational groups.

A different though loosely related literature discusses situations where consumers demand not only consumption goods but also "status." In Fershtman, Murphy, and Weiss (1996) status is a luxury good, demanded predominantly by the rich. More emphasis on status may induce the wrong talents (i.e., low-ability children from high-income families) to get educated, thereby reducing economic growth. Cole, Mailath, and Postlewaite (1992) develop microfoundations for situations in which consumers derive utility from a higher position in the wealth distribution. Corneo and Jeanne (1999, 2001) discuss the relationship between inequality and growth transmitted via status preferences.

Solutions to Exercises

EXERCISE 1

The accumulated factor is exchanged on a competitive market, which must clear at a single price. Hence $r = R$. The non-accumulated factor l is immobile: thus firms solve the problem

$$\max_k lf(k/l, 1) - Rk - wl$$

with first-order conditions

$$\frac{\partial lf(k/l, 1)}{\partial k} = \frac{\partial lf(k/l, 1)}{\partial k}\frac{1}{l} = \frac{\partial f(k/l, 1)}{\partial k} \equiv f_k^* = R.$$

All firms use the same CRS technology, so all firms optimally choose the same factor intensity $[k/l]^* = \kappa^*$. This means that the marginal product of labor is equal across firms and given by:

$$\frac{\partial f(\kappa^*, 1)}{\partial l} = f_l^*.$$

What does this imply for the (firm-specific) return w? To answer this question note that, by Euler's theorem, we have

$$f(k, l) = f_k^* k + f_l^* l = (f_k^* \kappa^* + f_l^*)\, l,$$

where f_l^* is the same for all firms. Hence we have $w = W$. In other words, the return on the immobile factor is the same for all firms. We note that the distribution of output across firms is exactly proportional to the distribution of l endowments.

EXERCISE 2

Strict concavity requires $A_1 > 0, B_1 > 0$; $0 \leq \alpha < 1$ and similarly for the other exponents; $\alpha + \beta \leq 1, \gamma + \delta \leq 1$. Let l and k be the factors used at firm 1, and $K - k$ and $L - l$ the factors used at firm 2.

$$\frac{\partial}{\partial k} F^{[1]}(k, l) = A_1 k^{\alpha-1}\alpha l^{\beta} + A_2$$

$$\frac{\partial}{\partial (K - k)} F^{[2]}(K - k, L - l) = B_1 (K - k)^{\gamma-1} \gamma (L - l)^{\delta} + B_2$$

Equating the marginal productivity of k,

$$A_1 k^{\alpha-1} \alpha l^\beta + A_2 = B_1 (K-k)^{\gamma-1} \gamma (L-l)^\delta + B_2.$$

If $A_2 = B_2$, employment of k is positive in both firms as long as the production functions are strictly concave and $0 < l < L$. Allocation is such that

$$(K-k) = \left(\frac{B_1}{A_1} \frac{\gamma}{\alpha} (L-l)^\delta l^{-\beta} k^{1-\alpha} \right)^{\frac{1}{1-\gamma}}.$$

If instead $A_1 = B_1 = 0$ then the marginal productivity of k is only equalized if $A_2 = B_2$; otherwise, all capital should be in the firm where its average productivity is higher. Consider the marginal productivity of the other factor:

$$\frac{\partial}{\partial l} F^{[1]}(k,l) = A_1 k^\alpha l^{\beta-1} \beta$$

$$\frac{\partial}{\partial (L-l)} F^{[2]}(K-k, L-l) = \delta B_1 (K-k)^\gamma (L-l)^{\delta-1}$$

Mobility of k suffices to ensure equal marginal productivity of l if there are constant returns to scale and the production functions are identical, $\alpha = 1 - \beta = \gamma = 1 - \delta$.

EXERCISE 3

a. The conditions for constant returns to scale for the production functions named in exercise 2 are

$$\alpha > 0, \ \beta > 0; \quad \alpha + \beta = 1$$

$$\gamma > 0, \ \delta > 0; \quad \gamma + \delta = 1$$

b. When all individuals face a CRS production function then the aggregate production function is also CRS. However, only one of the two firms will produce in equilibrium for all parameter configurations, except for a knife-edge case. To see this note that the marginal costs of firm 1 are given by

$$min \left[(1/A_1) \alpha^\alpha (1-\alpha)^{\alpha-1} R^\alpha W^{1-\alpha}, (1/A_2) R \right],$$

where R and W denote the equilibrium factor prices of capital and labor, respectively. To ease exposition, let the firms' technologies have Cobb-Douglas form, i.e., suppose that the equilibrium factor prices are such that the linear component of each production function is inactive: $(1/A_2) R > (1/A_1) \alpha^\alpha (1-\alpha)^{\alpha-1} R^\alpha W^{1-\alpha}$

and that the analogous condition holds for the other firm. For an interior solution where both firms produce, marginal costs must be equal. This implies

$$(1/A_1)\,\alpha^{\alpha}(1-\alpha)^{\alpha-1}R^{\alpha}\,W^{1-\alpha} = (1/B_1)\,\beta^{\beta}(1-\beta)^{\beta-1}R^{\beta}\,W^{1-\beta}.$$

If we divide both sides by W it becomes clear that this equation has at most one positive solution for R/W.

However, the factor-price ratio R/W, equal to the rate of technical substitution, is uniquely determined by the resource constraint. To see this, consider the aggregate production function $F(K, L)$ with constant returns to scale. Let the intensive form be defined by $f(\kappa) \equiv F(K/L, 1)$ where $\kappa = K/L$. Then the factor-price ratio is given by

$$\frac{R}{W} = \frac{f'(\kappa)}{f(\kappa) - \kappa f'(\kappa)},$$

which is a monotonically decreasing function of the $K/L-$ ratio. Unless R/W is by chance such that the marginal costs are equal, the firms' costs differ. Hence, in general, only one of the two firms produces.

EXERCISE 4

a. Distribution does not affect accumulation, since the consumption function is linear. Formally,

$$\begin{aligned}
\Delta k &= y - c \\
&= Rk + Wl - \left(\bar{c} + c_l Wl + c_k Rk + \tilde{c}k\right) \\
&= [(1 - c_k)R - \tilde{c}]\,k + (1 - c_l)Wl - \bar{c}.
\end{aligned}$$

Aggregating yields

$$\Delta K = [(1 - c_k)R - \tilde{c}]\,K + (1 - c_l)WL - \bar{c}.$$

The individual growth rate of the accumulated factor reads

$$\frac{\Delta k}{k} = [(1 - c_k)R - \tilde{c}] + \frac{(1 - c_l)Wl - \bar{c}}{k}.$$

Hence, the individual capital stock diverges when $\bar{c} > (1 - c_l)Wl$ and diverges if the inequality goes the other way.

If the subsistence consumption $\bar{c}$ is larger than savings out of labor income, then poor individuals save little, as much of their income is needed to satisfy their subsistence consumption needs. In an economy where $\bar{c} > (1 - c_l)Wl$, wealth declines over time for individuals with little capital income. This leads to divergence.

c. If $\Delta K = 0$ holds, then the economy is in a steady state. The stability of the steady state is ensured if:

$$\frac{\partial(\Delta K)}{\partial K} = (1 - c_k)R - \tilde{c} + (1 - c_k)\frac{\partial R}{\partial K}K + (1 - c_l)\frac{\partial W}{\partial K}L$$
$$= (1 - c_k)R - \tilde{c} + (c_l - c_k)\frac{\partial R}{\partial K}K < 0,$$

where the second equality follows from $\partial W/\partial K = -(K/L)\partial R/\partial K$ (which holds with constant returns to scale). Considering the aggregate accumulation

$$\Delta K = [(1 - c_k)R - \tilde{c}]K + (1 - c_l)WL - \bar{c} = 0.$$

Hence, in the steady state $(1 - c_l)WL - \bar{c} > 0$ as long as $(c_l - c_k) \cdot K \cdot \partial R/\partial K$ is not too negative. From answer b above we know that this leads to convergence, for given $l(i)$. Recall that $(1 - c_l)R - \tilde{c}$ can be interpreted as the propensity to save $k(i)$. As R is decreasing during the accumulation process and c_l and $\tilde{c}$ are constant, this propensity may become negative. Hence, there is (conditional) convergence of the individual capital stocks. In particular, this holds if the marginal propensity to consume out of labor income is lower than the one of capital income. However, there will be divergence if c_l is sufficiently lower than c_k. A sufficient condition for divergence is $c_l = 0$ and $\tilde{c} > 0$.

To investigate the uniqueness of the steady state, rewrite the equation above:

$$\Delta K = (1 - c_k)Y - \tilde{c}K - \bar{c} - (c_l - c_k)WL = 0.$$

The steady state need not be unique. For example, if $c_l = 0$ and $c_k = 1$, capital accumulation reads $\Delta K = WL - \tilde{c}K - \bar{c}$. If the labor share increases with higher K, then labor income WL may be locally convex in K, and the economy features multiple steady states. If K is high, the labor share is high and the savings rate is also high, as only savings accrue from labor income. Instead, if K is low, the labor share and the savings rate will be low. Similar factor-share mechanisms have been studied in the context of overlapping generation models (see chapters 5 and 6), which feature accumulation equations similar to that assumed here.

EXERCISE 5

Under constant returns to scale, Euler's equation holds:

$$F(K; L) = \frac{\partial F(K; L)}{\partial K}K + \frac{\partial F(K; L)}{\partial L}L.$$

Differentiating both sides with respect to K we get:

$$\frac{\partial F(K; L)}{\partial K} = \frac{\partial^2 F(K; L)}{\partial^2 K}K + \frac{\partial F(K; L)}{\partial K} + \frac{\partial^2 F(K; L)}{\partial L \partial K}L.$$

Solving for $\partial^2 F(K; L)/\partial^2 K$,

$$\frac{\partial^2 F(K; L)}{\partial L \partial K} = -\frac{\partial^2 F(K; L)}{\partial^2 K} \frac{K}{L}.$$

With diminishing marginal return to capital we know that $\partial F(K; L)/\partial K \geq 0$, and $\partial^2 F(K; L)/\partial^2 K \leq 0$ implies that $\partial^2 F(K; L)/\partial L \partial K \geq 0$. Since $W = \partial F(K; L)/\partial L$,

$$\frac{\partial W}{\partial K} = \frac{\partial^2 F(K; L)}{\partial L \partial K} \geq 0.$$

EXERCISE 6

a. The parameter α indexes how much individual consumption is influenced by the average consumption and may capture "status consumption" effects: if aggregate consumption is higher, individuals consume more.

b. Aggregate consumption (and therefore accumulation) is independent of distribution because the individual consumption function is linear and its coefficients $(\bar{c}, \hat{c}, \tilde{c}, \alpha)$ are the same for all individuals. Hence aggregate consumption is given by

$$C = \bar{c} + \hat{c} Y + \tilde{c} K.$$

c. Under the assumption that $l = L$, differences in k across individuals are the only reason why consumption and income levels differ across individuals. In this exercise, $C = \bar{c} + \hat{c} Y + \tilde{c} K + \alpha C$, so aggregate consumption is

$$C = \frac{\bar{c} + \hat{c} Y + \tilde{c} K}{1 - \alpha}.$$

We can rewrite individual consumption as

$$c = \bar{c} + \hat{c} y + \tilde{c} k + \alpha \frac{\bar{c} + \hat{c} Y + \tilde{c} K}{1 - \alpha}.$$

Although accumulation is independent of distribution, distribution is affected by accumulation. Consider individual accumulation, $\Delta k = y - c$

$$\Delta k = (1 - \hat{c})(WL + Rk) - \tilde{c}k - \bar{c} - \alpha \frac{\bar{c} + \hat{c}\,(WL + RK) + \tilde{c}K}{1 - \alpha}$$

$$= \left[(1 - \hat{c})\,WL - \bar{c} - \frac{\alpha}{1 - \alpha}\,(\bar{c} + \hat{c}WL) \right] + \left[(1 - \hat{c})\,R - \tilde{c} \right] k - \frac{\alpha}{1 - \alpha}\,(\hat{c}R + \tilde{c})\,K$$

$$= \frac{1}{1 - \alpha} \left[(1 - \alpha)\,(1 - \hat{c})\,WL - (1 - \alpha)\,\bar{c} - \alpha \bar{c} - \alpha \hat{c}WL - \alpha \hat{c}RK - \alpha \tilde{c}K \right]$$
$$+ \left[(1 - \hat{c})\,R - \tilde{c} \right] k$$

$$= \frac{1}{1-\alpha} \big[(1 - \alpha - \hat{c}) \, WL - \bar{c} + [(1 - \alpha - \hat{c}) \, R - \tilde{c}] \, K$$
$$- (1 - \alpha) \big[(1 - \hat{c}) \, R - \tilde{c} \big] K \big] + \big[(1 - \hat{c}) \, R - \tilde{c} \big] k.$$

In steady state,

$$\Delta K = (1 - \alpha - \hat{c}) \, Wl - \bar{c} + \big[(1 - \alpha - \hat{c}) \, R - \tilde{c} \big] K = 0,$$

so

$$\Delta k \big|_{SS} = - \big[(1 - \hat{c}) \, R - \tilde{c} \big] K + \big[(1 - \hat{c}) \, R - \tilde{c} \big] k$$

or

$$\Delta k \big|_{SS} = \big[(1 - \hat{c}) \, R - \tilde{c} \big] \big[k - K \big].$$

If we divide this equation by k we get

$$\frac{\Delta k}{k} \bigg|_{SS} = (1 - \hat{c}) \, R - \tilde{c} - \big[(1 - \hat{c}) \, R - \tilde{c} \big] \frac{K}{k}.$$

Hence there is relative *convergence* if $(1 - \hat{c}) \, R - \tilde{c} < 0$. In this exercise, however, this is not necessarily implied by stability of the steady state, which requires $(1 - \alpha - \hat{c}) \, R - \tilde{c} < 0$ or

$$(1 - \hat{c}) \, R - \tilde{c} < \alpha R.$$

Parameter α was zero in the main text's standard derivation, but if $\alpha > 0$ then $(1 - \hat{c}) \, R - \tilde{c}$ may be positive, to imply absolute and relative wealth *divergence* in the steady state. When will this occur? The steady-state interest rate R is increasing in α, $\bar{c}$, $\hat{c}$, and $\tilde{c}$, because all these parameters decrease accumulation. Therefore, divergence is more likely if α and/or $\bar{c}$ are large. The effects of $\hat{c}$ and $\tilde{c}$, which also appear directly in the relevant condition, are ambiguous.

EXERCISE 7

No, because when the relative consumption line intersects the 45° line then $c^i = c^j = \bar{c}$: lower consumption levels would fall short of the "required" amount, and the utility functions would be ill-defined.

EXERCISE 8

a. In light of our discussion in chapter 2, the capital used with all individuals' labor units must have the same marginal productivity (and competitive pay), regardless of who owns the capital stock. Hence all individuals use the same amount

$k = K/L$ of capital and the efficient production function is $L((K/L)^\alpha + AK/L) = F(K, L)$ as was to be shown. Given log utility, each individual's consumption grows at rate $(1 + \partial F/\partial K)/(1 + \rho) - 1$, and so does aggregate consumption. The rate of return $\partial F/\partial K = \alpha(L/K)^{1-\alpha} + A$ is a decreasing function of K, bounded below by A. As more capital is accumulated, growth slows down: consumption and output converge to a finite asymptotic level if $A < \rho$. However, if $A > \rho$ growth proceeds forever at the asymptotic rate $(1 + A)/(1 + \rho) - 1$. Borrowing and lending is done at the interest rate $R(k) = \partial F/\partial K = \alpha k^{\alpha-1} + A$, where $k = K/L$ is the amount of capital used with each unit of labor; the wage is $w(k) = f(k) - R(k)k = (1 - \alpha)k^\alpha$. Due to log utility, all individuals' consumption is the same constant fraction of lifetime resources (capital plus present value of wages). Consumption grows at the same (slowing-down) rate for all individuals; if $A > \rho$ then initially poor individuals need to save more than rich ones, to provide for continuing consumption growth in the far future when wages become a small fraction of optimal consumption, so the k distribution becomes less unequal over time.

b. Again, the marginal productivity of all units of capital must be the same with complete markets. The marginal productivity of capital used with each unit of labor is $\alpha k^{\alpha-1}$; if it is equal to B then it means that $\bar{k} = (\alpha/B)^{1/(1-\alpha)}$ are in use with each of the L units of labor, the remaining $K - L\bar{k}$ produce B units of output, and the aggregate production function is linear in L and K:

$$F(K, L) = L\bar{k}^\alpha + B\left(K - L\bar{k}\right) = (\alpha/B)^{\alpha/(1-\alpha)}(1 - \alpha)L + BK$$

This is valid if the aggregate capital stock is large enough to equip all units of labor, $K \geq L\bar{k}$: otherwise, the linear technology is not used, and

$$F(K, L) = L(K/L)^\alpha.$$

This second (Cobb-Douglas) form, of course, holds for a larger range of K levels if B is small and always holds if $B = 0$. If a constant proportion of output is saved, then the economy grows at a decreasing rate if the capital stock is smaller than $L\bar{k}$, as in the Solow model. But when the capital stock exceeds that critical level the production function becomes linear and growth proceeds indefinitely at a constant rate:

$$\Delta Y = B \Delta K = B sY.$$

EXERCISE 9

a. The Euler condition of each individual is

$$\gamma e^{-\gamma c_t} = \frac{1 + R_{t+1}}{1 + \rho} \gamma e^{-\gamma c_{t+1}},$$

or

$$-\gamma c_t = \ln\left(\frac{1 + R_{t+1}}{1 + \rho}\right) - \gamma c_{t+1}.$$

Aggregate consumption then satisfies

$$-\gamma C_t = \ln\left(\frac{1 + R_{t+1}}{1 + \rho}\right) - \gamma C_{t+1},$$

so

$$\gamma e^{-\gamma C_t} = \frac{1 + R_{t+1}}{1 + \rho}\gamma e^{-\gamma C_{t+1}} :$$

aggregate consumption satisfies the same Euler equation as each individual's. This is not surprising because this utility function belongs to the HARA class (see the appendix of this chapter).

The Euler condition of each individual can be written in the form

$$\frac{c_{t+1}}{c_t} = 1 + \frac{1}{c_t}\frac{1}{\gamma}\ln\left(\frac{1 + R_{t+1}}{1 + \rho}\right),$$

so consumption growth of the richer individual is faster if $\ln\left((1 + R_{t+1})/(1 + \rho)\right)$ < 0 or $R_{t+1} < \rho$ (which, in light of the Euler equation, implies that individual and aggregate consumption decline between t and $t + 1$). This is not surprising; CARA implies increasing relative risk aversion i.e., a decreasing rate of intertemporal substitution.

b. The Euler condition $\dot{c}(t) = [-u'(c(t))/u''(c(t))]\left(\hat{R} - \hat{\rho}\right)$ reads

$$\dot{c}(t) = \frac{1}{\gamma}\left(\hat{R} - \hat{\rho}\right)$$

and is linear in the change of individual consumption $\dot{c}(t)$, so the change in aggregate consumption is given by $\dot{C}(t) = \frac{1}{\gamma}\left(\hat{R} - \rho\right)$ and does not depend on the distribution. *Proportional* consumption inequality is increasing over time because the proportional growth rate of individual consumption is positively related to consumption levels or, writing

$$\frac{\dot{c}(t)}{c(t)} = \frac{1}{c(t)}\frac{1}{\gamma}\left(\hat{R} - \hat{\rho}\right),$$

if $\hat{R} < \hat{\rho}$. If individuals own stocks $k(0)$ of wealth at time zero, and never earn anything else than the stream of capital income $\hat{R}k(s)$ where $\hat{R}$ is constant, their budget constraints over an infinite planning horizon are

$$\int_0^\infty e^{-\hat{R}s}c(s)ds \leq k(0).$$

Integrating the Euler equation, we have $c(s) = c(0) + \left[(\hat{R} - \hat{\rho})/\gamma \right] s$. When the consumption path satisfies both the Euler equation and the budget constraint (with equality) we have

$$\int_0^\infty e^{-\hat{R}s} \left(c(0) + \frac{\hat{R} - \hat{\rho}}{\gamma} s \right) ds = k(0)$$

or, integrating,

$$c(0) = \hat{R}k(0) - \frac{\hat{R} - \hat{\rho}}{\hat{R}\gamma}.$$

So, the optimal consumption path is

$$c(s) = \hat{R}k(0) - \frac{\hat{R} - \hat{\rho}}{\hat{R}\gamma} + \frac{\hat{R} - \hat{\rho}}{\gamma} s.$$

c. The decentralized equilibria is equivalent to the "social planning" problem of maximizing a weighted sum of individual utility functions, with no constraints on transfers of resources across individuals at a given time t. The first-order conditions of that problem imply that

$$u'(c_t^i)\omega_i = u'(c_t^j)\omega_j$$

for all i, j, and t, where ω_i is the weight of individual i in the social plan's objective. If the rate of return on wealth is constant and there is no other income, the social planner's weights ω^i and ω^j are such that equality of weighted marginal utilities obtains when the optimal market consumption paths of individuals i and j are inserted in their marginal utility functions. So,

$$\gamma e^{-\gamma c^i(t)}\omega_i = \gamma e^{-\gamma c^j(t)}\omega_j$$

$$e^{-\gamma \left(\hat{R}k^i(0) - \frac{\hat{R} - \hat{\rho}}{\hat{R}\gamma} + \frac{\hat{R} - \hat{\rho}}{\gamma} s \right)}\omega_i = e^{-\gamma \left(\hat{R}k^j(0) - \frac{\hat{R} - \hat{\rho}}{\hat{R}\gamma} + \frac{\hat{R} - \hat{\rho}}{\gamma} s \right)}\omega_j$$

$$\omega_i = \omega_j e^{-\gamma \hat{R} \left(k^i(0) - k^j(0) \right)}.$$

As long as $\hat{R} > 0$ (aggregate production is positive), the richer individual receives a larger weight in the social plan. Suppose instead the economy has no productive capital, just an endowment of non-accumulated income flows: individual i earns $W(s)l^i$ at time s, l^i is constant over time, and $W(s) = W(0)e^{\vartheta s}$. The equilibrium interest rate must be such that, in the aggregate, there is no borrowing and no lending: $C(t) = W(t) \int l^i dP = W(t)L$, the economy consumes its endowment. Now, as long as the interest rate and the preference parameters are the same for all individuals, and the utility function is in the HARA class, we know that aggregate consumption satisfies the Euler equation

$$\dot{C}(t) = \frac{1}{\gamma}\left(\hat{R} - \hat{\rho}\right).$$

With $C(t) = W(t)L$, $\dot{C}(t) = \dot{W}(t)L = \vartheta W(t)L$,

$$\hat{R} = \gamma \dot{C}(t) + \hat{\rho} = \gamma\vartheta W(0)e^{\vartheta t}L + \hat{\rho}$$

is the (time-varying) equilibrium interest rate in this economy. It is always higher than the discount rate, so all consumption levels are growing.

As to consumption distribution dynamics, each individual satisfies the Euler condition

$$\dot{c}(t) = \frac{1}{\gamma}\left(\hat{R}(t) - \hat{\rho}\right) = \vartheta W(0)e^{\vartheta t}L,$$

so

$$\frac{\dot{c}(t)}{c(t)} = \frac{1}{c(t)}\vartheta W(0)e^{\vartheta t}L.$$

Since all consumption levels grow at the same rate per unit of time, the proportional growth rate is smaller for individuals who are consuming more, and proportional inequality decreases. The strength of this effect increases over time if $\vartheta > 0$.

As to the relationship of the social planner's weights ω^i and ω^j for individuals i and j to l^i and l^j, note that if each individual consumed his or her own endowment at time t, the social planner's optimality condition

$$\gamma e^{-\gamma w(t)l^i}\omega_i = \gamma e^{-\gamma w(t)l^j}\omega_j$$

with $c_t^i = w(t)l^i$ would read

$$\frac{\omega_i}{\omega_j} = \gamma e^{\gamma w(t)(l^i - l^j)},$$

which *cannot* be satisfied by time-invariant weights if $w(t)$ changes over time and $l^j \neq l^i$. (Note that if the utility function was CRRA, the interest rate would be constant instead, and each individual would indeed consume the endowment at all time. The CARA utility function of this exercise implies constant absolute risk aversion: individuals are disturbed by absolute, rather than percentage, deviations of their consumption from perfect smoothness; since the income path grows at a constant percentage rate, they have incentives to borrow and lend so as to bring their consumption path closer to linear rather than exponential growth.) In fact, individuals would not be satisfying their own Euler conditions if they consumed their wage at all times. The aggregate economy consumes its endowment but the planner, and the market, do transfer resources across individuals at each point in time: only an individual who owns the average endowment of labor ($l^i = L$) has the same Euler equation and budget constraint as the aggregate economy, hence consumes the wage and never has any assets or liabilities vis-á-vis the others. Richer individuals receive a larger welfare weight (or, which is the same, always consume more in market equilibrium); but to obtain $\dot{c}^i(t) = \dot{c}^j(t) = \vartheta W(0)e^{\vartheta t}L$ for all i and j, richer individuals initially borrow from poorer individuals and later repay the (more than exponentially growing) capitalized value of their debt. Thus proportional consumption inequality decreases over time in market equilibrium, and along the planner's optimal path.

d. For the utility function proposed, the optimal consumption levels may be negative at some point in time. For example,

$$c(0) = \hat{R}k(0) - \frac{\hat{R} - \hat{\rho}}{\hat{R}\gamma}$$

would be negative for an individual who is so poor that

$$k(0) < \frac{\hat{R} - \hat{\rho}}{\hat{R}^2\gamma}.$$

Note that as long as $\hat{R} > 0$ each individual (no matter how poor) does own consumable resources, so a negative initial consumption is associated with positive consumption later: as we saw in the previous part, poor individuals tend to be *lenders* in the kind of economy we are studying, because capital income tends to grow at a constant percentage rate if the rate of return is constant. If we impose the $c \geq 0$ constraint and it binds for some individual along the unconstrained path, all answers above are affected, because the solution of this constrained problem does not have the nice properties of unconstrained optimization of HARA utility functions. The consumption function becomes nonlinear, hence distribution matters for aggregate savings.

EXERCISE 10

a. The proposed utility function is in the HARA class only if $\alpha = 1$. In fact, absolute risk aversion

$$\begin{aligned} ARA &= -\frac{u''(c)}{u'(c)} \\ &= \frac{-\sigma\left((c^\alpha - \bar{c})\right)^{-\sigma-1}\alpha c^{\alpha-1}}{(c^\alpha - \bar{c})^{-\sigma}} \\ &= \sigma\frac{\alpha c^{\alpha-1}}{c^\alpha - \bar{c}} \end{aligned}$$

has hyperbolic form $f(x) = \frac{A}{x} + B$ only if $\alpha = 1$.

b. The intertemporal budget constraint reads:

$$k_t = c_t + \frac{c_{t+1}}{1 + R_{t+1}}.$$

The intertemporal utility function is given by $u(c_t) + u(c_{t+1})\frac{1}{1+\rho}$ and, for a utility function such that $u'(c) = (c^\alpha - \bar{c})^{-\sigma}$, the Euler equation reads

$$\frac{(c_t^\alpha - \bar{c})^{-\sigma}}{(c_{t+1}^\alpha - \bar{c})^{-\sigma}} = \left(\frac{1 + R_{t+1}}{1 + \rho}\right)$$

$$c_{t+1} = \left[(c_t^\alpha - \bar{c})\left(\frac{1 + R_{t+1}}{1 + \rho}\right)^{\frac{1}{\sigma}} + \bar{c}\right]^{\frac{1}{\alpha}}$$

inserting this result into the budget constraint we obtain:

$$c_t = k_t - \frac{1}{1 + R_{t+1}}\left[(c_t^\alpha - \bar{c})\left(\frac{1 + R_{t+1}}{1 + \rho}\right)^{\frac{1}{\sigma}} + \bar{c}\right]^{\frac{1}{\alpha}}$$

$$k_t = c_t + \frac{1}{1 + R_{t+1}}\left[(c_t^\alpha - \bar{c})\left(\frac{1 + R_{t+1}}{1 + \rho}\right)^{\frac{1}{\sigma}} + \bar{c}\right]^{\frac{1}{\alpha}}$$

c. Taking the derivative of the expression from b with respect to c_t and k_t we get

$$\frac{\partial k_t}{\partial c_t} = 1 + \frac{1}{1 + R_{t+1}}\frac{1}{\alpha}\left((c_t^\alpha - \bar{c})\left(\frac{1 + R_{t+1}}{1 + \rho}\right)^{\frac{1}{\sigma}} + \bar{c}\right)^{\frac{1-\alpha}{\alpha}}\alpha c_t^{\alpha-1}\left(\frac{1 + R_{t+1}}{1 + \rho}\right)^{\frac{1}{\sigma}}$$

Note that $c_{t+1}^{1-\alpha} = \left((c_t^\alpha - \bar{c})\left(\frac{1+R_{t+1}}{1+\rho}\right)^{\frac{1}{\sigma}} + \bar{c}\right)^{\frac{1-\alpha}{\alpha}}$. This allows us to simplify the above expression and we get

$$\frac{\partial c_t}{\partial k_t} = \frac{1}{1 + \frac{1}{1+R_{t+1}}\left(\frac{c_{t+1}}{c_t}\right)^{1-\alpha}\left(\frac{1+R_{t+1}}{1+\rho}\right)^{\frac{1}{\sigma}}}.$$

Assume $\bar{c} > 0$ and $R_{t+1} > \rho$. Then, the wealthy will follow a steeper consumption path, thus the ratio c_{t+1}/c_t is higher for richer individuals. Hence, if $\alpha > (<)1$ the rich have a higher (lower) MPC $\partial c_t/\partial k_t$. Equivalently, the consumption function is convex (concave) if $\alpha > (<)1$. For $\alpha = 1$ the consumption function is linear, in which case the utility function takes the HARA form.

d. The income expansion path (IEP) is nonlinear because the utility function does not belong to the HARA class (see figure 1).

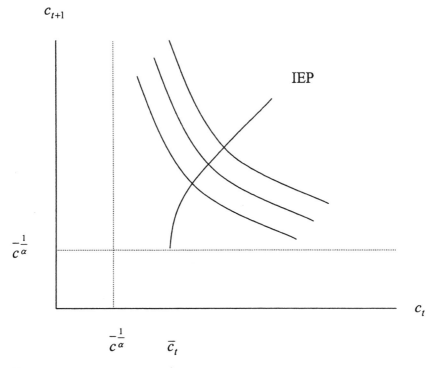

Figure 1. Income expansion path

The slope of the IEP tends to $((1 + R_{t+1}) / (1 + \rho))^{\frac{1}{\alpha\sigma}}$. The distribution of capital affects aggregate accumulation to the extent that the marginal propensity of the rich to consume differs from that of the poor—in a direction that depends on whether α is larger or smaller than unity, as discussed in part c of the answer.

EXERCISE 11

A relationship between the factor composition of income and saving propensity is implicit in the linear specification (2.1), since inserting $y \equiv W\bar{l} + Rk$ in it yields

$$c = \bar{c} + \hat{c}(W\bar{l} + Rk) + \tilde{c}k = \bar{c} + \hat{c}\,W\bar{l} + (\hat{c} + \tilde{c}/R)\,Rk.$$

If we set $\tilde{c} = (1 - \hat{c} - s^p)\,R$ and $\bar{c} = 0$, we get the consumption function assumed in the text. Note that in the model discussed in chapter 1 the propensity to consume out of wealth (or out of accumulated income, Rk) should generally depend on the rate of return R and differs from that relevant to non-accumulated income flows.

The steady-state capital intensity is given by

$$\left(s^p \left(1 - \gamma \right) + s^w \gamma \right) \left(\tilde{f}(\kappa) - \delta \kappa \right)$$
$$= s^p \left(\tilde{f}'(\kappa) - \delta \right) \kappa + s^w \left(\tilde{f}(\kappa) - \kappa \tilde{f}'(\kappa) \right) = 0.$$

If there is exogenous technical progress, the capital intensity is given by (4.7):

$$\bar{\theta} - 1 = \left(s^p \left(1 - \gamma \right) + s^w \gamma \right) \frac{\tilde{f}(\kappa) - \delta \kappa}{\kappa}.$$

EXERCISE 12

With a Leontief production function given, each unit of output is produced by exactly $1/\alpha$ units of capital and $1/\beta$ units of effective labor. If factors are fully employed, $Y_t = K_t \alpha = A_t L \beta$, hence the output/capital ratio is fixed at $Y_t / K_t = \alpha$ and the capital/effective labor ratio is fixed at $K_t / (A_t L) = \beta / \alpha$. Since effective labor grows by a factor θ every period, to provide employment for the $(\theta - 1) A_t L$ new units entering between periods t and $t + 1$ the economy needs to accumulate $\Delta K = (\theta - 1) A_t L \beta / \alpha$ units of capital. Along a full employment growth path capital must simply grow at the same rate as exogenous productivity,

$$\frac{\Delta K}{K} = \frac{(\theta - 1) A_t L \beta / \alpha}{A_t L \beta / \alpha} = \theta - 1.$$

Condition (4.4) reads $\theta = 1 + s^p (1 - \gamma) \alpha$ and requires

$$\gamma = \frac{s^p \alpha - (\theta - 1)}{s^p \alpha}.$$

If growth is positive $(\theta > 1)$ then the income share of non-accumulated factors is lower than unity. This is not surprising: if non-accumulated factors earned all income savings would be zero, but the economy needs positive savings to maintain full employment. Marginal productivity is ill-defined for an economy with Leontief production function and full employment: additional capital has marginal productivity α as long as $K/(AL) < \beta/\alpha$ and it can be combined with unemployed labor, but its marginal productivity is zero if $K/(AL) > \beta/\alpha$. At the full employment configuration, with $K/(AL) = \beta/\alpha$, the partial derivatives of the production function do not exist, hence the value of γ pinned down by the argument above cannot be related to capital's marginal productivity.

EXERCISE 13

The net production function reads: $F(K, L) = K^\alpha L^{1-\alpha} + BK - \delta K$, or

$$F(K/L, 1) = f(k) = (K/L)^\alpha + BK/L - \delta K/L.$$

We derive the net income share of the accumulated factor:

$$
\begin{aligned}
(1 - \gamma) &= \frac{rK}{f(k)} = \frac{\left(\alpha (K/L)^{\alpha-1}/L + B/L - \delta/L\right) K}{(K/L)^\alpha + BK/L - \delta K/L} \\
&= \frac{\alpha (K/L)^{\alpha-1} + B - \delta}{(K/L)^{\alpha-1} + B - \delta} \\
&= 1 - \frac{(1 - \alpha) (K/L)^{\alpha-1}}{(K/L)^{\alpha-1} + B - \delta} \\
&= 1 - \frac{(1 - \alpha)}{1 + (B - \delta) (K/L)^{1-\alpha}}
\end{aligned}
$$

so

$$\frac{\partial(1 - \gamma)}{\partial (K/L)} = \frac{(1 - \alpha)^2}{\left(1 + (B - \delta) (K/L)^{1-\alpha}\right)^2} \frac{1}{L} (B - \delta) > 0, \quad \text{if } B > \delta$$

and

$$\frac{\partial(1 - \gamma)}{\partial (K/L)} < 0, \text{ if } B < \delta.$$

EXERCISE 14

When individuals maximize the discounted (at rate ρ) value of utility flows and marginal utility has constant elasticity as in (4.8), the common growth factor of capital, output, and consumption is

$$\theta = \left(\frac{1 + R}{1 + \rho}\right)^{1/\sigma} = \left(\frac{1 + (1 - \gamma)\frac{Y}{K}}{1 + \rho}\right)^{1/\sigma}.$$

Like (4.4), this is a relationship between the growth rate, the output-capital ratio, and the income shares of accumulated and non-accumulated factors of production. When $\sigma \neq 0$, however, the relationship is nonlinear. Taking θ as given, the discrete-time equations in the text still apply: the saving propensity out of capital income is $s^P = (\theta - 1)/R$, and no wage income is saved. Nonlinearity, however, makes it less straightforward to characterize the impact of γ on the level and the endogenous growth rate of each individual's consumption. In continuous time, the Euler condition for optimal consumption growth reads

$$\frac{\dot{c}(t)}{c(t)} = \frac{u'(c(t))}{-u''(c(t))c(t)}(R(t) - \rho)$$

if $R(t)$ and ρ are the instantaneous (continuously compounded) rate of return on savings and discount rate. If the marginal utility function has constant elasticity σ,

$$\frac{u'(c(t))}{-u''(c(t))c(t)} = \sigma,$$

and along a balanced growth path where $\tilde{R} = \ln(1 + R)$ is constant, the continuous-time growth rate of consumption (and capital and income) is

$$\vartheta = \frac{R - \rho}{\sigma} = \frac{(1 - \gamma)\frac{Y}{K} - \rho}{\sigma},$$

which is linear in γ and Y/K. This is more analytically convenient than the nonlinear form above, and equivalent using the approximation $\rho \approx \ln(1 + \rho)$ and $\vartheta \approx \ln(\theta)$

$$e^{\vartheta} = \left(e^R / e^{\rho}\right)^{1/\sigma} = e^{\frac{R - \rho}{\sigma}}.$$

EXERCISE 15

Consumption per effective unit of labor,

$$\frac{F(K, AL)}{AL} - \vartheta\frac{K}{AL} = f(\kappa) - \vartheta\kappa,$$

is maximized when $f'(\kappa) = \vartheta$. (Here κ denotes capital per effective unit of labor.) In a competitive economy, $f'(\kappa) = \frac{\partial}{\partial K}F(K, AL) = R$ is the income of each capital unit: steady-state investment is equal to capital income $\theta K = RK$, and steady-state consumption is the complementary (wage) share of aggregate income. The balanced growth configuration of an economy where the representative individual maximizes the present value of the logarithm of consumption flows satisfies the Euler condition

$$\vartheta = f'(\kappa) - \rho,$$

or $f'(\kappa) = \rho + \vartheta$. Within such an economy, a portion $\vartheta/R = \left(f'(\kappa) - \rho\right)/R$ of capital income is saved and invested, and all wage income is consumed. As $\rho \to 0$ the result stated obtains: all capital income is invested if saving decisions aim at maximizing average, undiscounted consumption. If $\vartheta = 0$, the only steady state has $f'(\kappa) = 0$, i.e., $\frac{\partial}{\partial K}\tilde{F}(K, AL) = \delta$ if $\tilde{F}(\cdot)$ is the gross production function and δ the depreciation rate. The result is still valid, in that all capital income is invested: there is, however, no capital income.

EXERCISE 16

The median individual must also own the average wealth in order to prefer the same tax rate as the representative individual. Taking the derivative of the indirect utility function (4.22) with respect to τ we get

$$V'(\tau) = \frac{1}{\rho}(1 + (1 - \gamma)(1 - \tau)A)^{-1}(-A(1 - \gamma))$$
$$+ \left(\gamma A \frac{l}{L} + \frac{\rho}{1+\rho}(1 + (1-\gamma)(1-\tau)A)\frac{k_t}{K_t} + \tau(1-\gamma)A\right)^{-1}$$
$$\left(-\frac{\rho}{1+\rho}(1-\gamma)A\frac{k_t}{K_t} + (1-\gamma)A\right).$$

Obviously $V'(\tau)$ decreases in k/K. Therefore, individuals with higher endowment of k given l will prefer a lower tax rate (higher subsidy) τ on capital income. We now evaluate $V'(\tau)$ at $\tau^{RA} = -\gamma/(1-\gamma)$ and $l = L$.

$$V'(\tau^{RA})\big|_{l=L} = \frac{1}{\rho}(1 + A)^{-1}(-A(1 - \gamma))$$
$$+ \left(\frac{\rho}{1+\rho}(1+A)\frac{k_t}{K_t}\right)^{-1}\left(-\frac{\rho}{1+\rho}(1-\gamma)A\frac{k_t}{K_t} + (1-\gamma)A\right).$$
$$= \frac{A(1-\gamma)}{1+A}\left(-\frac{1}{\rho} + \frac{1+\rho}{\rho}\left(\frac{k_t}{K_t}\right)^{-1}\left(-\frac{\rho}{1+\rho}\frac{k_t}{K_t} + 1\right)\right)$$
$$= \frac{A(1-\gamma)}{1+A}\frac{1+\rho}{\rho}\left(\left(\frac{k_t}{K_t}\right)^{-1} - 1\right)$$

We see that $V'(\tau^{RA}) = 0$ if $k = K$.

EXERCISE 17

The factor shares are

$$\gamma = \frac{WL}{Y} = \frac{\partial F(K, L)}{\partial L}\frac{L}{Y} = \frac{1-\alpha}{\alpha(K/L)^\eta + 1 - \alpha}$$

$$1 - \gamma = \frac{RK}{Y} = \frac{\partial F(K, L)}{\partial K}\frac{K}{Y} = \frac{\alpha(K/L)^\eta}{\alpha(K/L)^\eta + 1 - \alpha}.$$

We see that for $\eta = 0$ the factor shares imply a Cobb-Douglas production function, where the shares are constant and given by α and $1 - \alpha$. Thus functional distribution does not change over time. For $\eta = 1$ capital and labor are perfect substitutes and marginal products are constant, so a larger capital stock does not depress the income of each unit of capital: if the young save a lot for old age, they can increase the factor share of capital. If we consider a growing economy where the capital stock is increasing, capital income share will increase. For $\eta < 0$ capital and labor are bad substitutes. For a growing economy the interest rate will fall quickly and thus capital income share will even decrease.

We know that young agents only have labor income and old agents only have capital income. Thus the Gini coefficient is given as follows:

$$G_t = \left| \frac{1+n}{2+n} - \frac{1-\alpha}{\alpha \, (K_t/L_t)^\eta + 1 - \alpha} \right|.$$

For $\eta > 0$ and for a growing economy K/L increases and thus capital share rises. Therefore the Gini coefficient will increase (decrease) if the young agents are poorer (richer) than the old agents.

EXERCISE 18

For discussing overall consumption inequality under the special case when there is no heterogeneity within cohorts we have to consider the consumption ratio of both types of generation, old and young, C_{2t}/C_{1t} in t. The consumption levels of both types in t are given by the following equations:

$$C_{1t} = (1 - s(R_{t+1})) W_t$$

and

$$C_{2t} = (1 + R_t)s(R_t) W_{t-1}$$

where

$$s(R_{t+1}) = \frac{(1 + R_{t+1})^{\frac{1-\sigma}{\sigma}}}{(1 + \rho)^{\frac{1}{\sigma}} + (1 + R_{t+1})^{\frac{1-\sigma}{\sigma}}}.$$

Therefore we can write the consumption ratio as:

$$\begin{aligned}
\frac{C_{2t}}{C_{1t}} &= \frac{(1 + R_t)s(R_t) W_{t-1}}{(1 - s(R_{t+1})) W_t} \\
&= \frac{(1 + aK_t^{\alpha-1})s(aK_t^{\alpha-1})(1 - \alpha)K_{t-1}^\alpha}{(1 - s(aK_{t+1}^{\alpha-1}))(1 - \alpha)K_t^\alpha}.
\end{aligned}$$

Whether there is convergence or divergence in the overall consumption is not clear a priori. Assume a growing economy. On the one hand, the interest rate falls with capital accumulation. This is advantageous for the old generation because it pays higher interest on their savings: $R_{t+1} < R_t$. On the other hand, capital accumulation also implies growing wages $W_{t+1} > W_t$, which is advantageous for the young generation. Additional effects work through the saving rate $s(R)$, which depends on the interest rate and hence also on the accumulated capital stock. Whether the saving rate is increasing or decreasing with capital accumulation depends on the relative sizes of income and substitution effect

$$
\frac{\partial \left(\frac{C_{2t}}{C_{1t}} \right)}{\partial K_{t-1}} = \frac{\left(\frac{\partial R_t}{\partial K_t} \frac{\partial K_t}{\partial K_{t-1}} s(R_t) \frac{W_{t-1}}{W_t} + \frac{\partial \left(\frac{W_{t-1}}{W_t} \right)}{\partial K_{t-1}} (1 + R_t) s(R_t) \right)}{(1 - s(R_{t+1}))}
$$
$$
+ \frac{\frac{\partial s(R_t)}{\partial K_t} \frac{\partial K_t}{\partial K_{t-1}} (1 + R_t) \frac{W_{t-1}}{W_t}}{(1 - s(R_{t+1}))}
$$
$$
- \frac{\frac{\partial (1 - s(R_{t+1}))}{\partial K_{t+1}} \frac{\partial K_{t+1}}{\partial K_t} \frac{\partial K_t}{\partial K_{t-1}} (1 + R_t) s(R_t) \frac{W_{t-1}}{W_t}}{(1 - s(R_{t+1}))^2}.
$$

To see which effects dominate consider the development of C_{2t}/C_{1t} as capital grows. The following three graphs plot C_{2t}/C_{1t} for different values of σ because this parameter determines whether the substitution or the income effect dominates. The other parameters are chosen as follows: $\alpha = 0.3$ and $\rho = 2$.

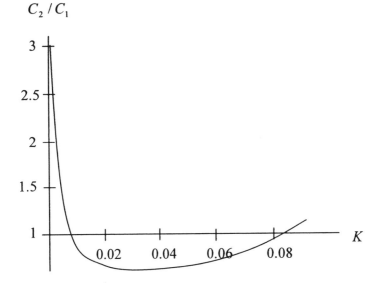

For $\sigma = 0.5$ the substitution effect dominates the income effect. Agents save less if the interest rate falls. Further we know that the fall of the interest rate is high at the beginning of the capital accumulation and hence the saving rate reacts highly. This implies that $\frac{\partial(C_{2t}/C_{1t})}{\partial K_{t-1}} < 0$ for low levels of K. But for high levels of K, the fall of the interest rate will be slower (at least with Cobb Douglas), therefore we get $\frac{\partial(C_{2t}/C_{1t})}{\partial K_{t-1}} > 0$ for high levels of K. Finally note that for $C_{2t}/C_{1t} < (>) 1$ there is convergence (divergence) of overall consumption if $\frac{\partial(C_{2t}/C_{1t})}{\partial K_{t-1}} > 0$. (The steady state is equal to 0.078.)

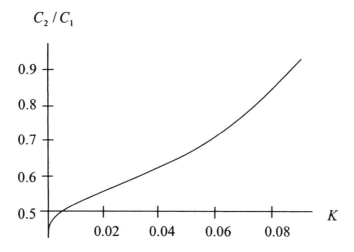

For $\sigma = 2$: the income effect dominates the substitution effect. Agents save more if the interest rate falls. Therefore a large decrease in the interest rate also has a large effect to the saving rate. Hence $\frac{\partial s(R)}{\partial K}$ and $\frac{\partial(W_{t-1}/W_t)}{\partial K_{t-1}}$ will dominate $\frac{\partial R_t}{\partial K_t}$ and therefore $\frac{\partial(C_{2t}/C_{1t})}{\partial K_{t-1}} > 0$. The capital stock has a positive influence on the consumption ratio during the whole capital accumulation. (The steady state is equal to 0.089.)

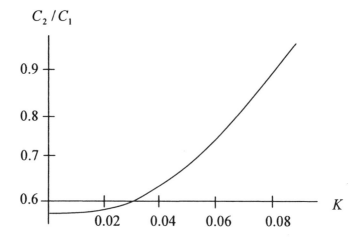

For $\sigma = 1$: the saving rate does not depend on the interest rate. Therefore the decrease of the interest rate at the beginning of the capital accumulation does not affect the saving rate. (The steady state is equal to 0.083.)

EXERCISE 19

Maximizing the objective function

$$U = \frac{1}{1-\sigma}\left(\frac{\beta c_t}{\sigma} - \bar{c}\right)^{1-\sigma} + \frac{1}{1-\sigma}\frac{1}{1+\rho}\left(\frac{\beta(1+R_{t+1})k_{t+1}}{\sigma} - \bar{k}\right)^{1-\sigma}$$

subject to the lifetime budget constraint

$$W_t l + (1+R_t)k_t \le c_t + k_{t+1}$$

yields the first-order conditions

$$\left(\frac{\beta c_t}{\sigma} - \bar{c}\right)^{-\sigma} = \frac{1+R_{t+1}}{1+\rho}\left(\frac{\beta(1+R_{t+1})k_{t+1}}{\sigma} - \bar{k}\right)^{-\sigma}$$

$$k_t = \frac{1}{1+R_{t+1}}\left[\left(\frac{1+R_{t+1}}{1+\rho}\right)^{\frac{1}{\sigma}}c_t + \bar{c}\frac{\sigma}{\beta}\left(\frac{(1+\rho)^{\frac{1}{\sigma}} - (1+R_{t+1})^{\frac{1}{\sigma}}}{(1+\rho)^{\frac{1}{\sigma}}}\right)\right].$$

Inserting k_t into the lifetime budget constraint:

$$W_t l + (1+R_t)k_t = c_t + \frac{1}{1+R_{t+1}}\left[\left(\frac{1+R_{t+1}}{1+\rho}\right)^{\frac{1}{\sigma}}c_t + \bar{c}\frac{\sigma}{\beta}\left(\frac{(1+\rho)^{\frac{1}{\sigma}} - (1+R_{t+1})^{\frac{1}{\sigma}}}{(1+\rho)^{\frac{1}{\sigma}}}\right)\right]$$

$$= c_t \frac{(1+\rho)^{\frac{1}{\sigma}} + (1+R_{t+1})^{\frac{1-\sigma}{\sigma}}}{(1+\rho)^{\frac{1}{\sigma}}} + \frac{1}{1+R_{t+1}}\bar{c}\frac{\sigma}{\beta}\frac{(1+\rho)^{\frac{1}{\sigma}} - (1+R_{t+1})^{\frac{1}{\sigma}}}{(1+\rho)^{\frac{1}{\sigma}}}$$

$$c_t = \frac{(1+\rho)^{\frac{1}{\sigma}}}{(1+\rho)^{\frac{1}{\sigma}} + (1+R_{t+1})^{\frac{1-\sigma}{\sigma}}}\left[W_t l + (1+R_t)k_t\right]$$

$$+\bar{c}\frac{\sigma}{\beta}\frac{(1+R_{t+1})^{\frac{1}{\sigma}} - (1+\rho)^{\frac{1}{\sigma}}}{(1+\rho)^{\frac{1}{\sigma}}(1+R_{t+1}) + (1+R_{t+1})^{\frac{1}{\sigma}}}$$

and

$$s_t = \frac{(1+R_{t+1})^{\frac{1-\sigma}{\sigma}}}{(1+\rho)^{\frac{1}{\sigma}} + (1+R_{t+1})^{\frac{1-\sigma}{\sigma}}}\left[W_t l + (1+R_t)k_t\right]$$

$$-\bar{c}\frac{\sigma}{\beta}\frac{(1+R_{t+1})^{\frac{1}{\sigma}} - (1+\rho)^{\frac{1}{\sigma}}}{(1+R_{t+1})^{\frac{1}{\sigma}} + (1+\rho)^{\frac{1}{\sigma}}(1+R_{t+1})}.$$

Comparing this solution to the OLG model, where individuals inherit no wealth and $k_t = 0$, we see that here lifetime resources include not only the income flow that results from the non-accumulated factor endowment $W_t l_t$ but also inherited wealth, and the resulting income flow $(1 + R_t) k_t$.

EXERCISE 20

a. With $\frac{q}{1+\rho} \equiv \frac{1}{1+\hat{\rho}}$, the solution has the same form as in exercise 19:

$$
\begin{aligned}
c_{1t} = (wl + k_t) \, \frac{(1+\rho)^{\frac{1}{\sigma}}}{(1+\rho)^{\frac{1}{\sigma}} + (1+R)^{\frac{1-\sigma}{\sigma}} q^{\frac{1}{\sigma}}} \\
+ \bar{c} \frac{\sigma}{\beta} \left[\frac{(1+R)^{\frac{1}{\sigma}} q^{\frac{1}{\sigma}} - (1+\rho)^{\frac{1}{\sigma}}}{(1+R)^{\frac{1}{\sigma}} q^{\frac{1}{\sigma}} + (1+\rho)^{\frac{1}{\sigma}} (1+R)} \right],
\end{aligned}
$$

$$
\begin{aligned}
s_t = (Wl + k_t) \left[\frac{(1+R)^{\frac{1-\sigma}{\sigma}} q^{\frac{1}{\sigma}}}{(1+\rho)^{\frac{1}{\sigma}} + (1+R)^{\frac{1-\sigma}{\sigma}} q^{\frac{1}{\sigma}}} \right] \\
- \bar{c} \frac{\sigma}{\beta} \left[\frac{(1+R)^{\frac{1}{\sigma}} q^{\frac{1}{\sigma}} - (1+\rho)^{\frac{1}{\sigma}}}{(1+R)^{\frac{1}{\sigma}} q^{\frac{1}{\sigma}} + (1+\rho)^{\frac{1}{\sigma}} (1+R)} \right].
\end{aligned}
$$

b. With logarithmic preferences ($\sigma = 1$), aggregate savings are given by

$$
S_t = \left[\frac{q}{(1+\rho) + q} \right] (WL + K_t) - \bar{c} \left[\frac{(1+R)q - (1+\rho)}{(1+R)q + (1+\rho)(1+R)} \right]
$$

Recalling that $W_t = (1-\alpha)K_t^\alpha$ and $R_{t+1} = \alpha K_{t+1}^{\alpha-1}$ we can write

$$
\begin{aligned}
K_{t+1} = \left[\frac{q}{(1+\rho) + q} \right] \left[(1-\alpha)K_t^\alpha + K_t \right] \\
- \bar{c} \left[\frac{(1 + \alpha K_{t+1}^{\alpha-1})q - (1+\rho)}{(1 + \alpha K_{t+1}^{\alpha-1})q + (1+\rho)(1 + \alpha K_{t+1}^{\alpha-1})} \right].
\end{aligned}
$$

Recall from the discussion of OLG models with heterogeneous cohorts that it is important to consider whether the steady-state interest rate R^* exceeds or falls short of the discount rate. If $R^* > \frac{1+\rho-q}{q} = 1 + \hat{\rho}$ the term $\frac{(1+\alpha K_{t+1}^{\alpha-1})q - (1+\rho)}{(1+\alpha K_{t+1}^{\alpha-1})q + (1+\rho)(1+\alpha K_{t+1}^{\alpha-1})}$ is positive, hence the steady-state interest rate with $\bar{c} > 0$ is bounded from below: $R^*|_{\bar{c}>0} > R^*|_{\bar{c}=0} > \hat{\rho}$. Instead, if $R^* < \frac{1+\rho-q}{q}$, the interest rate with $\bar{c} > 0$ will be even lower: $R^*|_{\bar{c}>0} < R^*|_{\bar{c}=0} < \hat{\rho}$. It is straightforward to deduce the steady-state interest rate from the aggregate capital stock equation when $\bar{c} = 0$:

$$\left(\frac{R}{\alpha}\right)^{\frac{1}{\alpha-1}} = \left[\frac{q}{1+\rho+q}\right]\left[(1-\alpha)\left(\frac{R}{\alpha}\right)^{\frac{\alpha}{\alpha-1}} + \left(\frac{R}{\alpha}\right)^{\frac{1}{\alpha-1}}\right]$$

$$1 = \left[\frac{q}{1+\rho+q}\right]\left[(1-\alpha)\left(\frac{R}{\alpha}\right) + 1\right]$$

$$R^*|_{\bar{c}=0} = \frac{\alpha}{1-\alpha}\frac{1+\rho+q}{q}.$$

Hence when the steady-state interest rate exceeds $\frac{1+\rho-q}{q}$ it is clear that $R_t > \frac{1+\rho-q}{q}$ also holds for the transition toward the steady state because R is decreasing in a growing economy. Therefore, under our assumptions about the utility function (HARA with $\bar{c} > 0$ and logarithmic preferences), convergence in the distribution of accumulated wealth occurs if $R^* > \frac{1+\rho-q}{q}$ in the transition process. Hence, and similar to the OLG model discussed above, a sufficient condition for convergence in the distribution of accumulated wealth is $\alpha/(1-\alpha) > 1$ or $\alpha < 1/2$.

If the steady-state interest rate falls short of $\frac{1+\rho-q}{q}$ then $R^*|_{\bar{c}>0} < R^*|_{\bar{c}=0} < \hat{\rho}$ holds and therefore divergence in the distribution of accumulated wealth occurs in a neighborhood of the steady state.

c. One characteristic of the steady state is that factor prices do not change, therefore the distribution of wealth will be persistent over time. Let k_v denote the inherited wealth of a dynasty that has lasted for v generations. Then, a share $(1-q)q^v$ of the population inherits capital stock k_v. The (accidental) bequest for generation $v+1$ will be

$$k_{v+1} = (1+R)s_v = (1+R)\frac{q}{(1+\rho)+q}(Wl + k_v).$$

As $k_0 = 0$ by definition, we get an explicit expression for k_v by iterating forward the above expression

$$k_v = \frac{a - a^{v+1}}{1-a}Wl \text{ where } a = (1+R)\frac{q}{(1+\rho)+q}.$$

EXERCISE 21

Computing the marginal productivities in terms of the *net* output measure

$$\tilde{Y} \equiv Y - \delta K = F(K, L) - \delta K,$$

the competitive rental rates $R = 1 - \delta$ and $W = 1$ are fixed (independent of capital accumulation).

If the aggregate saving rate is constant, the proportional growth rate of capital $\Delta K/K = \bar{s}L/K + \bar{s}(1 - \delta)$ approaches the constant $\bar{s}(1 - \delta)$ as capital grows. Thus, the economy can grow forever provided that $\delta < 1$.

If savings are determined as in the standard overlapping generations model, all labor income is earned and all savings are performed by young agents: gross savings amount to a portion $1/(2 + \rho)$ of total wages, not of aggregate income, and are used to purchase the depreciated capital stock from old agents as well as to install new capital (if any). In this simple exercise, wages are constant at L, and

$$K_{t+1} = L/(2 + \rho)$$

for any value of K_t. Far from growing indefinitely, the economy settles immediately in a steady state where the aggregate consumption of young agents is $\frac{1+\rho}{2+\rho}L$, that of old agents is $L\left(1 - \frac{1+\rho}{2+\rho}\right)(1 + R) = K(2 - \delta) = L\frac{2-\delta}{2+\rho}$, their sum

$$\frac{1+\rho}{2+\rho}L + L\frac{2-\delta}{2+\rho} = L + \frac{L}{2+\rho}(1 - \delta) = L + K(1 - \delta)$$

coincides with net output, and capital is constant.

EXERCISE 22

Start with the welfare function

$$V(\tau) = (2 + \rho)\ln\left(W_t l + \frac{S}{1 + (1 - \tau)R}\right) + \ln(1 + (1 - \tau)R)$$

using $W_t L = \gamma A K_t$, $S = \tau R K_{t+1}$, and $R = (1 - \gamma)A$ to get:

$$V(\tau) = \frac{2 + \rho}{1 + \rho}\ln\left(\frac{1+\rho}{2+\rho}\left(\frac{\gamma A K_t}{L}l + \frac{\tau(1 - \gamma)A K_{t+1}}{1 + (1 - \tau)(1 - \gamma)A}\right)\right)$$
$$+ \frac{1}{1+\rho}\ln\frac{1 + (1 - \tau)(1 - \gamma)A}{1 + \rho}.$$

Further use $K_{t+1} = \frac{(1 + (1-\tau)(1-\gamma)A)\gamma A}{(2+\rho)(1+(1-\gamma)A) - \tau(1-\gamma)A}K_t$ which yields:

$$V(\tau) = \frac{2 + \rho}{1 + \rho}\ln\left(\frac{1+\rho}{2+\rho}\left(\frac{\gamma A K_t}{L}l + \frac{\gamma A \tau(1 - \gamma)A K_t}{(2 + \rho)(1 + (1 - \gamma)A) - \tau(1 - \gamma)A}\right)\right)$$
$$+ \frac{1}{1+\rho}\ln\frac{1 + (1 - \tau)(1 - \gamma)A}{1 + \rho}.$$

Differentiate the term with respect to τ:

$$
\frac{\partial V}{\partial \tau} = \frac{2+\rho}{1+\rho} \frac{\frac{\gamma A(1-\gamma)[(2+\rho)(1+(1-\gamma)A)-\tau(1-\gamma)A]+\gamma A\tau(1-\gamma)(1-\gamma)A}{[(2+\rho)(1+(1-\gamma)A)-\tau(1-\gamma)A]^2}}{\gamma \frac{l}{L} + \frac{\gamma A\tau(1-\gamma)}{(2+\rho)(1+(1-\gamma)A)-\tau(1-\gamma)A}}
$$
$$
- \frac{1}{1+\rho} \frac{(1-\gamma)A}{1+(1-\tau)(1-\gamma)A}.
$$

Inserting $\tau = 0$ yields

$$
\frac{\partial V}{\partial \tau} = \frac{L}{l} - 1,
$$

so $\tau = 0$ satisfies the first-order condition for maximization of the welfare of a representative individual with $l = L$. Individuals with lower endowments want a positive tax rate, those with higher endowments a negative one.

EXERCISE 23

The factor rental rates are the marginal productivities of the factors used at the individual level: $r = \alpha k^{\alpha-1} l^{1-\alpha} - 1$, $w = (1-\alpha) k^\alpha l^{-\alpha}$. They are the same across individuals if k/l is, which is ensured by opening at least one of the two factor markets if all production units have the same technology and returns to scale are constant (see exercise 2). In particular, the rate of return would be equalized if families can hire each other's non-accumulated factors ("labor") even when they are prevented from borrowing and lending explicitly.

EXERCISE 24

Writing $\Delta k = y - c = k^\alpha l^{1-\alpha} - k - c$, and recognizing that $k_{t+1} = k_t + \Delta k$,

$$
k_{t+1} = k_t + k_t^\alpha l^{1-\alpha} - k_t - c
$$

shows that $k_{t+1} = k_t^\alpha l^{1-\alpha} - c$ is indeed the individual accumulation constraint. The factor rental rates implied by this situation are marginal productivities at the individual (rather than aggregate) level: $r = \alpha k^{\alpha-1} l^{1-\alpha} - 1$, $w = (1-\alpha) k^\alpha l^{-\alpha}$. Both are heterogeneous across individuals if k/l is. In particular, if $l = L$ (all individuals have the same endowment of non-accumulated factors) then not only the rate of return but also the implicit wage differs across individuals as a function of their accumulated wealth.

EXERCISE 25

a. If the accumulation constraint is $k_{t+1} = (k_t)^\alpha - c_t$, the first-order condition reads

$$\frac{1}{c_t} = \frac{1}{1+\rho} \frac{1}{k_{t+1}}$$

or, recognizing that $k_{t+1} = (k_t)^\alpha - c_t$,

$$\frac{1}{c_t} = \frac{1}{1+\rho} \frac{1}{(k_t)^\alpha - c_t}.$$

Simplifying and solving yields $c_t = \frac{1+\rho}{2+\rho}(k_t)^\alpha$: log linearity of both the objective function and the accumulation constraint implies that the individual consumes a constant fraction of the current capital stock and invests the rest.

Wealth is accumulated according to

$$k_{t+1} = \frac{1}{2+\rho}(k_t)^\alpha$$

and converges to $k = \left(\frac{1}{2+\rho}\right)^{\frac{1}{1-\alpha}}$ from any positive initial condition.

b. More generally, the first-order condition for accumulation is given by

$$u'(c_t) = v'(k_{t+1}) \text{ where } k_{t+1} = f(k_t) - c_t.$$

Total differentiation yields

$$\frac{dk_{t+1}}{dk_t} = f'(k_t) \frac{u''(c_t)}{u''(c_t) + v''(k_{t+1})}.$$

The slope dk_{t+1}/dk_t is positive as long as u and v are concave. The conditions for uniqueness of steady states we have to impose on $u(\cdot)$, $f(\cdot)$, and $v(\cdot)$ are the same as in the standard Diamond model (e.g., $u(x) = (1+\rho)v(x) = \ln(x)$ and $f(k) = k^a$ is sufficient). If the steady state is unique each household must converge to that capital stock irrespective of initial conditions.

EXERCISE 26

Capital and labor are perfectly substitutable: production can use one or the other indifferently.

EXERCISE 27

In the Solow model we should get $K_\infty = s^{1/(1-\alpha)}$. Here we get $K_\infty = [s/(1-s)]^{1/(1-\alpha)}$. The reason is that there are savings from the capital stock—which acts just in the opposite way as the rate of depreciation: δ in the Solow model is equivalent to $1-s$ here. With an increase in $1-s$, more capital is lost to consumption, rather than to technological obsolescence.

EXERCISE 28

a. If individuals can lend and borrow at the same rate, all lifetime consumption paths satisfy the Euler equation

$$\frac{1}{c_{1t}} = (1 + R_{t+1})\frac{1}{c_{2t+1}}.$$

The budget constraint is

$$c_{1t} + \frac{1}{1 + R_{t+1}}c_{2t+1} = PDV(Wl),$$

where, denoting by l_1 and l_2 the labor endowments when young and when old, respectively, the present value of lifetime labor income is given by

$$PDV(Wl) = W_t l_1 + \frac{1}{1 + R_{t+1}}W_{t+1}l_2$$

$$= \begin{cases} W_t\left[1 - x + \frac{W_{t+1}/W_t}{1+R_{t+1}}(1+x)\right] & \text{for the } y/2 \text{ with increasing } l \\ W_t\left[1 + \frac{W_{t+1}/W_t}{1+R_{t+1}}\right] & \text{for the } 1-y \text{ with constant } l \\ W_t\left[1 + x + \frac{W_{t+1}/W_t}{1+R_{t+1}}(1-x)\right] & \text{for the } y/2 \text{ with decreasing } l. \end{cases}$$

Combining the Euler equation and the budget constraint, we get

$$c_t^{y,i} = \frac{1}{2}PDV(Wl) =$$

$$= \begin{cases} \frac{1}{2}W_t\left[1 + \frac{W_{t+1}/W_t}{1+R_{t+1}} + \left(\frac{W_{t+1}/W_t}{1+R_{t+1}} - 1\right)x\right] & \text{for the } y/2 \text{ with increasing } l \\ \frac{1}{2}W_t\left[1 + \frac{W_{t+1}/W_t}{1+R_{t+1}}\right] & \text{for the } 1-y \text{ with constant } l \\ \frac{1}{2}W_t\left[1 + \frac{W_{t+1}/W_t}{1+R_{t+1}} - \left(\frac{W_{t+1}/W_t}{1+R_{t+1}} - 1\right)x\right] & \text{for the } y/2 \text{ with decreasing } l. \end{cases}$$

Aggregating, the terms with x and y cancel out and total consumption by the young is $\frac{1}{2}W_t\left[1 + \frac{W_{t+1}/W_t}{1+R_{t+1}}\right]$, independent of x and y. Savings, the only endogenous choice in this model, are total wages paid to young workers minus consumption. Neither is affected by labor income heterogeneity, so the economy's aggregate equilibrium is the same for all x and all y. Interpretation: the financial market is complete within each generation, and income heterogeneity is completely idiosyncratic within each generation. The different types of individuals do have different lifetime resources and welfare levels if $W_{t+1}/W_t \neq 1 + R_{t+1}$, but with a HARA utility function, this has no implications for macroeconomic aggregate consumption.

b. If $Y_t/K_t = A$ is a given constant, we write $R = (1 - \gamma)A$, $W_t = \gamma A K_t$, $W_{t+1} = \gamma A K_{t+1}$, and aggregate savings by young individuals (who have one unit of labor in the aggregate) are

$$\gamma A K_t - \frac{1}{2}\gamma A K_t \left[1 + \frac{K_{t+1}/K_t}{1 + (1-\gamma)A}\right] = \frac{\gamma A K_t}{2}\left(1 - \frac{K_{t+1}/K_t}{1 + (1-\gamma)A}\right).$$

Since this must be equal to K_{t+1}, the next period's aggregate wealth, we have

$$\frac{K_{t+1}}{K_t} = \frac{\gamma A}{2}\left(1 - \frac{K_{t+1}/K_t}{1 + (1-\gamma)A}\right);$$

solving for the growth factor,

$$\frac{K_{t+1}}{K_t} = \frac{\frac{1}{2}A\gamma}{1 + \frac{1}{2}A\frac{\gamma}{1+A-A\gamma}}$$

$$= A\gamma\frac{1 + A - A\gamma}{2 + 2A - A\gamma}.$$

c. A larger γ implies a smaller rate of return; the income and substitution effects cancel out with a logarithmic utility function, but each generation's representative individual earns labor income when old and saves less when the future is less discounted: this wealth effect implies that savings would be smaller if current and future wages remained unchanged. But a higher γ also implies a larger wage rate when young: this tends to increase the volume of savings, since all savings are performed by the young. In the expression for aggregate savings,

$$\frac{\gamma A K_t}{2}\left(1 - \frac{K_{t+1}/K_t}{1 + (1-\gamma)A}\right),$$

the wealth effect is captured by the γ in the denominator, and the young wage effect is captured by the γ in the numerator of the first term. So, the effect on savings is ambiguous, because both current resources and the saving incentives of the young are affected by γ. The equilibrium effect is further complicated by the fact that the young individuals' future wages are endogenous to their own aggregate savings (K_{t+1} appears in the last expression). Formally, the derivative of the growth rate w.r.t. γ is

$$\frac{d}{d\gamma}\left(A\gamma\,\frac{1+A-A\gamma}{2+2A-A\gamma}\right) = A\frac{1+A-A\gamma}{2+2A-A\gamma} - A\gamma\frac{A(1+A)}{(2+2A-A\gamma)^2}.$$

The first term is positive (γ is less than 1), but the second term can imply that a larger γ decreases growth, as in the Kaldor equation: this is the case if

$$\gamma > \frac{1}{2A^2}\left(4+2\sqrt{2}\right)(A+A^2).$$

d. Individuals who might like to borrow are those with an increasing labor endowment path. Their first-period consumption when borrowing is allowed,

$$c_{1t} = \frac{1}{2}W_t\left[1+\frac{W_{t+1}/W_t}{1+R_{t+1}}+\left(\frac{W_{t+1}/W_t}{1+R_{t+1}}-1\right)x\right],$$

is larger than their first-period income $(1-x)W_t$ if

$$\frac{1}{2}\left[1+\frac{W_{t+1}/W_t}{1+R_{t+1}}+\left(\frac{W_{t+1}/W_t}{1+R_{t+1}}-1\right)x\right] > (1-x)$$

$$2x+\left(\frac{W_{t+1}/W_t}{1+R_{t+1}}-1\right)x > 1-\frac{W_{t+1}/W_t}{1+R_{t+1}}$$

$$x\left(1+\frac{W_{t+1}/W_t}{1+R_{t+1}}\right) > 1-\frac{W_{t+1}/W_t}{1+R_{t+1}}$$

or

$$x > \frac{1+R_{t+1}-W_{t+1}/W_t}{1+R_{t+1}+W_{t+1}/W_t}$$

holds. In this case, the decline in labor endowment is such that wage growth does not allow them to finance desired consumption growth (at rate R) using their labor income only. If we take wages as given for the moment, aggregate consumption by the young is decreased by borrowing constraints: individuals who are constrained consume less, while others consume just as much (because their wages and rate of return are not affected). Higher savings, however, increase future wages in this economy. This makes it less desirable to save: in equilibrium, growth is faster, but savings do not increase as much as in the above argument because lenders save less. Formally, define

$$\frac{W_{t+1}/W_t}{1+R_{t+1}} = \xi$$

and write the expression for savings by the young:

$$\frac{y}{2}\left(W_t(1+x)-\frac{1}{2}W_t[1-\xi x]\right)+(1-y)\left(W_t-\frac{1}{2}W_t[1+\xi]\right).$$

Set this equal to K_{t+1} and recognize that $W_t = \gamma A K_t$, so

$$\xi = \frac{W_{t+1}/W_t}{1 + R_{t+1}} = \frac{\theta}{1 + R_{t+1}},$$

where $W_{t+1}/W_t = K_{t+1}/K_t \equiv \theta$. We obtain

$$\theta = \gamma A \left(\frac{y}{2} \left(\frac{1}{2} + \frac{1}{2}x - \frac{\theta}{1 + R} \frac{1 - x}{2} \right) + (1 - y) \left(\frac{1}{2} - \frac{1}{2} \frac{\theta}{1 + R} \right) \right)$$

with solution

$$\theta = \gamma A \frac{y - yx - 2}{+\gamma A y + \gamma A y x - 2\gamma A - 4(1 + R)} (1 + R),$$

which further calculations could show to be an increasing function of x and y as long as the parameters are such as to make no borrowing a binding constraint.

e. If they take as given the growth rate of wages and the rate of return, the young people who are liquidity constrained would like to be able to borrow and would gladly vote for legislation that would force them to repay; the other young individuals are indifferent. But while the rate of return is indeed fixed at $(1 - \gamma)A$ regardless of whether borrowing is possible in this economy, the voters may realize (like we do when we write down the model) that in the aggregate savings determine the growth rate of wages. Then, individuals who are lenders and do have future labor income actually dislike legislation that eliminates the forced savings (or non-dissaving) of liquidity-constrained individuals, and their positive effect on their own future wages (which are external, rather than incorporated in the lending contract, because this economy has increasing aggregate returns to scale). In fact, even the borrowing-constrained individuals may lose through external effects more than they gain by being able to borrow (a similar phenomenon may occur in Jappelli and Pagano's three-period-life OLG model): the algebra needed to figure out whether this is the case is complex and does not appear worthwhile. Older individuals are indifferent to this kind of legislation, which only has effects after their death. Note, however, that the old-with-increasing-labor-income type of individual would be in favor of repealing this legislation in the *next* period, when they would like to default on their outstanding debt; the other kinds of old individuals (at least those among them who have invested in personal loans rather than in physical capital) would be against it.

EXERCISE 29

Part a

i. The budget constraint for each individual is given by $c_2 = (1 + R)w - c_1$. The first-order condition for utility optimization is

$$\frac{1}{c_1 + 1} = (1 + R) \frac{1}{c_2 + 1}.$$

Using the budget constraint to replace c_2 gives:

$$(1 + R)w - c_1 = (c_1 + 1)(1 + R) - 1$$
$$c_1 = \frac{(1 + R)w - R}{2(1 + R)}$$

and hence

$$c_2 = \frac{(1 + R)w + R}{2}.$$

For $R > 0$ consumption inequality increases between periods 1 and 2, whereas for $R = 0$ consumption inequality does not change between the two periods because $c_1 = c_2 = w/2$. All individuals choose a flat consumption path when the interest rate equals the rate of time preference.

ii. The intertemporal elasticity of substitution is given by $\varepsilon(c) = -\frac{u'(c)}{u''(c)c} = \frac{1+c}{c}$. Hence the intertemporal elasticity of substitution decreases with higher consumption. Therefore, the rich face a lower rate of intertemporal substitution and will choose the flatter consumption path. This is a general result for Stone-Geary preferences with negative subsistence consumption.

Part b

For $x < 1$ $c_1 = c_2 = w/2$; for $x > 1$, $c_1 = w/2 - 1/2$ and $c_2 = w$. Let us compare the implications of these different consumption levels. For $x < 1$ utility is given by $U^{LY} = 2 \log(1 + w/2)$ and for $x > 1$ it is given by $U^{HY} = \log(1/2 + w/2) + \log(w + 1)$. The poor will never choose $x > 1$ because their endowment w_P is equal to unity. It easy to check that for $w_R = 2$, $U^{HY} > U^{LY}$ holds. Therefore the rich choose the high-return investment and $c_{1,R} < c_{2,R}$, hence they follow a steeper consumption path than the poor. Figure 2 displays the endowments of the poor and rich, marking for reference the endowment of an individual who would be just indifferent between the two alternatives (this individual's endowment would be $w = \sqrt{2}$). As the factor return is not equalized for all individuals, the slope of the budget constraint is not the same for the rich and poor individual. For $x < 1$ the slope is one and for $x > 1$ the slope is two. Optimal consumption choices are located where the individual's budget constraint is tangential to the respective indifference curve.

EXERCISE 30

We guess that the optimal solution is of the form: $c_t = (1 + b_t)^{-1} a_t$ where b_t is a constant to be determined. Consumption tomorrow then must equal $c_{t+1} =$

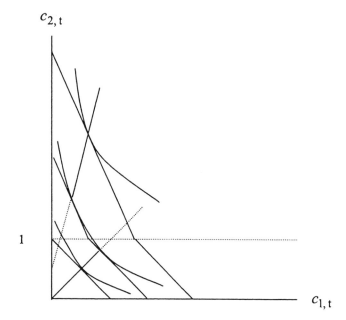

$c_{2,t}$

1

$c_{1,t}$

Figure 2. Savings decision

$(1 + b_{t+1})^{-1} a_{t+1}$. In the optimum the Euler equation (8.5) must hold

$$c_t^{-\sigma} = \beta E_t \left[(1 + r_{t+1}) c_{t+1}^{-\sigma} \right]$$
$$(1 + b_t)^{\sigma} a_t^{-\sigma} = \beta E_t \left[(1 + r_{t+1}) (1 + b_{t+1})^{\sigma} b_t^{-\sigma} (1 + b_t)^{\sigma} (1 + r_{t+1})^{-\sigma} a_t^{-\sigma} \right]$$
$$b_t = \left(\beta E_t \left[(1 + r_{t+1})^{1-\sigma} \right] \right)^{1/\sigma} (1 + b_{t+1}).$$

Iterating the recursive equation forward, we get an explicit expression for b_t

$$b_t = \sum_{j=1}^{\infty} \prod_{m=1}^{j} \left(\beta E_t \left[(1 + r_{t+m})^{1-\sigma} \right] \right)^{1/\sigma},$$

where $\beta E_t \left[(1 + r_{t+m})^{1-\sigma} \right]$ must be smaller than unity such that the geometric sum converges. Recalling the definition of b_t, we get the marginal propensity to consume out of wealth $\hat{c}_t = (1 + b_t)^{-1}$:

$$\hat{c}_t = \left(1 + \sum_{j=1}^{\infty} \prod_{m=1}^{j} \left(\beta E_t \left[(1 + r_{t+m})^{1-\sigma} \right] \right)^{1/\sigma} \right)^{-1}.$$

Note that, apart from the expectation operator and the discount factor $\beta \equiv (1 + \rho)^{-1}$, the marginal propensity to consume has the same form as that valid in equation (3.9) for the certainty case.

EXERCISE 31

With CRRA preferences consumption is linear in assets. Therefore we can insert $u'(c) = c^{-\sigma}$ into the first-order condition of the portfolio decision (8.12). We get

$$E_t \left[(I_{t+1} - r_{t+1}) \left[1 + (I_{t+1} - r_{t+1}) \varphi_{t+1} \right]^{-\sigma} \right] = 0.$$

As in the text let us define $(I_{t+1} - r_{t+1}) \left[1 + (I_{t+1} - r_{t+1}) \varphi_{t+1} \right]^{-\sigma} \equiv g(\varphi_{t+1}, r_{t+1})$. The second derivative of $g(\cdot)$ with respect to r_{t+1} reads

$$\frac{\partial^2 g(\varphi_{t+1}, r_{t+1})}{\partial r_{t+1}^2} = \left[1 + (I_{t+1} - r_{t+1}) \varphi_{t+1} \right]^{-\sigma-2}$$

$$\left[(\sigma - 1)(r_{t+1} - I_{t+1}) \varphi_{t+1} - 2 \right] \sigma \varphi_{t+1}.$$

The sign of the second derivative is determined by the sign of $(\sigma - 1)(r_{t+1} - I_{t+1}) \varphi_{t+1} - 2$. We know that $E_t r_{t+1} > I_{t+1}$. Hence, for $\sigma \gg 1$, the term $(\sigma - 1)(r_{t+1} - I_{t+1}) \varphi_{t+1} - 2$ becomes positive and $g(\cdot)$ is convex in r_{t+1}. If the uncertain asset undergoes an SSD shift, $E_t \left[g(\varphi_{t+1}, r_{t+1}) \right]$ increases for given φ_{t+1}. Therefore the optimal φ_{t+1} is lower as $E_t \left[\partial g(\varphi_{t+1}, r_{t+1}) / \partial \varphi_{t+1} \right] < 0$. On the contrary, if σ is not too high, $g(\cdot)$ remains concave in r_{t+1}. When the high-yield assets become riskier, the optimal share of high-yield assets $1 - \varphi_{t+1}$ increases, as it was in the case of log preferences where $\sigma = 1$.

EXERCISE 32

a. Borrowing and lending is done at the interest rate $R(k) = \partial F / \partial K = \alpha k^{\alpha-1} + A$, where $k = K/L$ is the amount of capital used with each unit of labor; the wage is $w(k) = f(k) - R(k)k = (1 - \alpha)k^{\alpha}$. Given log utility, all individuals' consumption is the same constant fraction of (capital plus present value of wages), but since the present discounted value of wages (same for everybody) is a complex expression there is no closed-form consumption function. **Consumption** grows at the same (slowing-down) rate for all individuals; if $A > \rho$ then initially poor individuals need to save more than rich ones to provide for continuing consumption growth in the far future when wages become a small fraction of optimal consumption, so the relative **wealth** distribution becomes less unequal over time; **income** from labor is always the same for all individuals, capital income may or may not display convergence depending on the parameters: wealth grows faster for poorer individuals, but the rate of return may decline fast enough to reduce their capital income relative to the rich ones. If α is small, then as capital is accumulated the wage grows very little and the declining portion of the rate of return is small (relative to A) so total income must be growing faster for the poor. If neither borrowing nor lending is possible, then each individual uses his own capital, the rate of return is higher for the initially poor ones, the saving rate is the same, so there is convergence of consumption and wealth. Income must also eventually become equalized.

If $\alpha \neq 0$ and $\alpha \neq 1$, then aggregate output is lower when the financial market is closed, because capital is not allocated efficiently across heterogeneous agents. The economy eventually grows at the same asymptotic rate, since financial markets become irrelevant when all inequality disappears. Absent an analytic solution for saving policies, it is difficult to tell which transition has faster growth of aggregate income (which is not so well-defined anyway when there is no aggregate production function, etc.). Under complete markets, the marginal productivity of all units of capital must be the same. The marginal productivity of capital used with each unit of labor is $\alpha k^{\alpha-1}$, if it is equal to $\tilde{A}$ then it means that $\bar{k} = (\alpha/\tilde{A})^{1/(1-\alpha)}$ are in use with each of the L units of labor, the remaining $K - L\bar{k}$ produce $\tilde{A}$ units of output, and the aggregate production function is linear in L and K:

$$F(K,L) = L\bar{k}^{\alpha} + \tilde{A}\left(K - L\bar{k}\right) = \left((\alpha/\tilde{A})^{\alpha/(1-\alpha)} - \tilde{A}(\alpha/\tilde{A})^{1/(1-\alpha)}\right)L + \tilde{A}K.$$

This is valid if the aggregate capital stock is large enough to equip all units of labor, $K \geq L\bar{k}$: otherwise, the linear technology is not used, and

$$F(K,L) = L(K/L)^{\alpha}.$$

This second (Cobb-Douglas) form is valid for a larger range of K levels if $\tilde{A}$ is small, and is, of course, always valid if $\tilde{A}$ is zero. If a constant proportion of output is saved, then the economy grows at a decreasing rate if the capital stock is smaller than $L\bar{k}$; but when capital goes beyond that critical level the production function becomes linear and, as in exercise 8, growth proceeds indefinitely at a constant rate:

$$\Delta Y = \tilde{A}\,\Delta K = \tilde{A}\,sY.$$

b. The problem $\max (c_{1t})^{0.5} + (c_{2t+1})^{0.5}$ subject to $c_{1t} + s = w, c_{2t+1} = (1+R)s$ has solution

$$c_{1t} = \frac{w}{2+R}, \quad s = \frac{(1+R)w}{2+R}.$$

A higher R increases savings, because the intertemporal elasticity of substitution is higher than unity. All savings are performed by young workers, and it must be the case that the savings suffice to at least restore the capital stock which is currently in use but the old want to consume: so, we require

$$\frac{(1+R)w}{2+R} \geq \frac{K}{L}.$$

This is certainly satisfied when K is small: the production function is Cobb-Douglas there, and a small capital-output ratio implies a large w and a small R; hence, the range of output levels consistent with the situation described starts from zero. It does have an upper bound: if $\tilde{A}$ is fairly small, the upper bound where the savings constraint becomes binding is still in the region where the production function is Cobb-Douglas, and the bound on output is complicated to pin down from the condition above (but it is certainly unique, in fact it is the steady state toward which the standard OLG economy with Cobb-Douglas technology converges); if that condition remains satisfied throughout the region where production is Cobb-Douglas, then it means that the Cobb-Douglas steady state is outside of the region: once the economy grows out of it, the wage and rate of return are fixed at

$$w = \left((\alpha/\tilde{A})^{\alpha/(1-\alpha)} - \tilde{A}(\alpha/\tilde{A})^{1/(1-\alpha)}\right), \ R = \tilde{A}$$

the condition above reads

$$K \leq \frac{(1+\tilde{A})\left((\alpha/\tilde{A})^{\alpha/(1-\alpha)} - \tilde{A}(\alpha/\tilde{A})^{1/(1-\alpha)}\right)}{2+\tilde{A}}L \equiv \overline{K},$$

and output can never become larger than

$$\left((\alpha/\tilde{A})^{\alpha/(1-\alpha)} - \tilde{A}(\alpha/\tilde{A})^{1/(1-\alpha)}\right)L + \tilde{A}\overline{K}.$$

c. The substitution effect dominates with this utility function, so idiosyncratic risk reduces the propensity to save if all second-period income accrues from investment in the linear technology. In this economy, however, undiversifiable risk also changes the structure of investment: we need to reconsider how much each individual will invest in the (still safe) technology that uses the labor of a member of the next generation to yield production $\alpha\tilde{k}^\alpha$. If $k - \tilde{k}$ is invested in the risky asset, marginal utility is

$$\left(\sqrt{\alpha\tilde{k}^\alpha + \left(k - \tilde{k}\right)A^i}\right)$$

and depends on the ex post yield A^i of the linear technology. To choose $\tilde{k}$ one should make sure that the marginal return of that investment, $\alpha\tilde{k}^{\alpha-1}$, is equal to the expected return on the risky technology when both are weighted by marginal utility. There is no closed-form solution, but since these individuals are risk-averse they shall surely invest more of their savings in the safe technology. Smaller and less productive savings (because of higher risk and lower average return) imply lower steady-state capital and output. As to distribution, ex post consumption of the old is dispersed by undiversifiable uncertainty; in the absence of intergenerational transfers, there are no other implications.

EXERCISE 33

The Euler equation and the budget constraint imply:

$$c_{1t}^{-\sigma} = c_{2t+1}^{-\sigma}$$
$$c_{1t}^{-\sigma} = \left(W_t l_{1t} + W_{t+1} l_{2t+1} - c_{1t}\right)^{-\sigma}$$
$$c_{1t}^* = \frac{W_t l_{1t} + W_{t+1} l_{2t+1}}{2}.$$

This result holds for an economy without liquidity constraints. Thus an individual wants to consume in both periods the same amount c_{1t}^*. It would be optimal to consume c_{1t}^* in period 1. But the income of the individual in period 1 is only $W_t l_{1t}$. As the individual cannot borrow, she must consume $W_t l_{1t}$ as long as $W_t l_{1t} < W_{t+1} l_{2t+1}$ (see figure 3). In that case the individual will consume all additional income in period 1. If $W_t l_{1t} > W_{t+1} l_{2t+1}$ the individual will be able to do consumption smoothing, and she will consume half of the additional income in period 1 and the other half in period 2: $\partial c_{1t}^* / \partial W_t l_{1t} = 1/2$. Finally note that rich individuals save half of an additional unit of resources, while poor individuals consume all additional income. Therefore income distribution will affect the accumulation.

EXERCISE 34

In the absence of uncertainty and without borrowing constraints, it follows $\mu_t = 0$. The first-order condition (9.2) reads

$$\frac{1}{c_{1t}} = \frac{1+R}{1+\rho} \frac{1}{\left(W_t l_1 - c_{1t}\right)(1+R) + W_{t+1} l_2},$$

to imply

$$c_{1t} = \frac{1+\rho}{2+\rho}\left[W_t l_1 + \frac{W_{t+1} l_2}{1+R}\right].$$

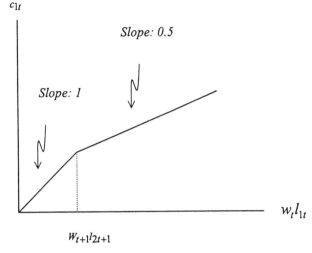

c_{1t}

Slope: 0.5

Slope: 1

$w_t l_{1t}$

$W_{t+1} l_{2t+1}$

Figure 3. Consumption function with liquidity constraints

During a given period t, young agents save

$$W_t l_1 - c_{1t} = W_t l_1 - \frac{1+\rho}{2+\rho}\left[W_t l_1 + \frac{W_{t+1} l_2}{1+R}\right]$$
$$= \frac{W_t l_1}{2+\rho}\left(1 - \frac{1+\rho}{1+R}\theta\frac{l_2}{l_1}\right);$$

their savings are (weakly) positive if

$$\frac{1+\rho}{1+R}\theta\frac{l_2}{l_1} \le 1,$$

and would like to be negative otherwise. Old agents consume all of their income and wealth,

$$c_{2t+1} = (W_{t-1}l_1 - c_{1t})(1+R) + W_t l_2$$
$$= \left(\frac{1}{2+\rho}W_{t-1}l_1 - \frac{1+\rho}{2+\rho}\frac{W_t l_2}{1+R}\right)(1+R) + W_t l_2$$
$$= \frac{1+R}{2+\rho}W_{t-1}l_1 - \frac{1+\rho}{2+\rho}W_t l_2 + W_t l_2$$
$$= \frac{1}{2+\rho}W_t\left(\left(\frac{1+R}{\theta}\right)l_1 + l_2\right),$$

their savings are negative and equal to minus their wealth (inclusive of interest). Aggregate savings are given by:

$$\frac{W_t l_1}{2+\rho}\left(1-\frac{1+\rho}{1+R}\theta\frac{l_2}{l_1}\right)-\frac{W_{t-1}l_1}{2+\rho}\left(1-\frac{1+\rho}{1+R}\theta\frac{l_2}{l_1}\right)$$

$$=\frac{W_t l_1}{2+\rho}\left(1-\frac{1}{\theta}-\frac{1+\rho}{1+R}\theta\frac{l_2}{l_1}+\frac{1+\rho}{1+R}\frac{l_2}{l_1}\right)$$

$$=\frac{W_t l_1}{2+\rho}\frac{\theta-1}{\theta}\left(1-\frac{1+\rho}{1+R}\frac{l_2\theta}{l_1}\right).$$

If the young have positive savings, this expression is positive (since $\theta > 1$) and liquidity constraints are irrelevant. If the young would like to dissave, this is a negative expression, and binding borrowing constraints increase (to zero) both young individuals' savings and old individuals' wealth.

EXERCISE 35

In equation (9.7) in the text, we guessed the value function of the following form $v_t(k_t, Wl_t) = -\frac{B}{\eta}e^{-\eta A[(1+R)k_t+Wl_t]}$. We already confirmed the functional form of the guess and showed that $A = R/(1+R)$. We have still to determine the parameter B. Recall the rewritten value function

$$v_t(k_t, Wl_t) = -\frac{1}{\eta}e^{-\eta z_t}\max_x\left\{e^{-\eta x}+\beta Be^{\eta Rx}E_t e^{-\eta\frac{R}{1+R}Wl_{t+1}}\right\}.$$

To ease notation let $\Xi \equiv E_t e^{-\eta\frac{R}{1+R}Wl_{t+1}}$. The first-order conditions of the maximization problem read

$$e^{-\eta x^*}=\beta BRe^{\eta Rx^*}\Xi.$$

Solving for x yields

$$x^*=-\frac{\ln[\beta BR\Xi]}{\eta(1+R)}\text{ or }e^{-\eta x^*}=(\beta BR\Xi)^{1/(1+R)}.$$

To determine B we reinsert this expression into the value function and use again our guess (9.7)

$$v_t(k_t, Wl_t)=-\frac{1}{\eta}e^{-\eta z_t}\left[(\beta BR\Xi)^{1/(1+R)}+\beta B(\beta BR\Xi)^{-R/(1+R)}\Xi\right]$$

$$B=(\beta BR\Xi)^{1/(1+R)}+\beta B(\beta BR\Xi)^{-R/(1+R)}\Xi$$

$$B=B^{1/(1+R)}(\beta\Xi)^{1/(1+R)}\left(R^{1/(1+R)}+R^{-R/(1+R)}\right)$$

$$B^{R/(1+R)}=(\beta\Xi)^{1/(1+R)}(1+R)R^{-R/(1+R)}.$$

The final step is to find an expression for consumption c_t using our definition $x \equiv c_t - z_t$. We get

$$
\begin{aligned}
c_t &= \frac{R}{1+R}\left[(1+R)k_t + Wl_t\right] + x \\
&= \frac{R}{1+R}\left[(1+R)k_t + Wl_t\right] - \frac{\ln\beta R + \ln\Xi}{\eta(1+R)} - \frac{\ln(\beta\Xi)^{1/R} + \ln(1+R)^{(1+R)/R} - \ln R}{\eta(1+R)} \\
&= \frac{R}{1+R}\left[(1+R)k_t + Wl_t\right] - \frac{1}{\eta R}\ln\left[\beta(1+R)\right] - \frac{1}{\eta R}\ln E_t e^{-\eta\frac{R}{1+R}Wl_{t+1}} \\
&= \frac{R}{1+R}\left[(1+R)k_t + Wl_t\right] - \frac{1}{\eta R}\ln\left[\beta(1+R)\right] + \frac{W}{1+R} - \frac{1}{\eta R}\ln E_t e^{-\eta\frac{R}{1+R}W(l_{t+1}-1)} \\
&= \frac{R}{1+R}\left[(1+R)k_t + Wl_t + \frac{W}{R}\right] - \frac{1}{\eta R}\ln\left[\beta(1+R)\right] - \frac{1}{\eta R}\ln E_t e^{-\eta\frac{R}{1+R}W(l_{t+1}-1)}.
\end{aligned}
$$

EXERCISE 36

We rewrite the maximization problem (9.10) using the guess $v_t(\lambda k_t, \lambda W_t l_t) = v_t(k_t, W_t l_t) + \ln[\lambda]/(1-\beta)\ \forall t$. Define, as in text $x_t \equiv c_t/\lambda$.

$$
\begin{aligned}
v_t(\lambda k_t, \lambda W_t l_t) &= \max_{c_t}\left\{\ln c_t + \beta E_t\left[v_{t+1}((1+R)\lambda k_t + \lambda W_t l_t - c_t, \lambda W_{t+1}l_{t+1})\right]\right\} \\
&= \max_{x_t}\left\{\begin{array}{l}\ln x_t + \ln\lambda + \beta\ln[\lambda]/(1-\beta) \\ +\beta E_t\left[v_{t+1}((1+R)k_t + W_t l_t - x_t, W_{t+1}l_{t+1})\right]\end{array}\right\} \\
\text{s.t. } 0 &\le (1+R)k_t + W_t l_t - x_t.
\end{aligned}
$$

Note that $\ln\lambda + \beta\ln[\lambda]/(1-\beta) = \ln[\lambda]/(1-\beta)$, which is the requested result.

EXERCISE 37

This can be done most easily by writing down the corresponding value equations. The present value of working at a good or a bad site is given by

$$
\begin{aligned}
V_g &= W_g + \frac{1}{1+R}\left((1-p)V_g + pV_b\right) \\
V_b &= W_b + \frac{1}{1+R}\left((1-p)V_b + pV_g\right).
\end{aligned}
$$

We can derive the value difference $\Delta V \equiv V_g - V_b$ of the two states

$$
\begin{aligned}
\Delta V &= W_g - W_b + \frac{1}{1+R}(1-2p)\Delta V \\
\Delta V &= \frac{2p+R}{1+R}(W_g - W_b).
\end{aligned}
$$

The present value of wages of a worker deciding to move is given by

$$V_{move} = W_g - \gamma + \frac{1}{1+R}\left((1-p)V_g + pV_b\right)$$
$$= V_g - \gamma.$$

The worker will move if $V_{move} > V_b$ or $\Delta V > \gamma$. Hence, the critical wage $\hat{W}_g$ where she is indifferent between staying and moving is given by

$$\frac{2p+R}{1+R}(\hat{W}_g - W_b) = \gamma$$
$$W_b + \frac{2p+R}{1+R}\gamma = \hat{W}_g.$$

EXERCISE 38

For given wages W_b and W_g we compare the critical mobility cost allowed such that the worker is still indifferent between staying and moving. Denote by γ_0 the mobility cost with perfect capital markets.

Without capital markets the worker is indifferent if

$$\zeta\left[u(W_g) - u(W_g - \gamma_0/\zeta)\right] = u(W_g) - u(W_g - \gamma),$$

where $\zeta = [1 + \beta(2p-1)]^{-1}$ and, from equation (9.26), $W_b = W_g - \gamma_0/\zeta$. We see directly that the maximum mobility costs are equal, $\gamma_0 = \gamma$, if $\zeta = 1$ or $p = 1/2$ holds. The equation above is derived along the same lines as in the previous exercise: e.g., the utility value of a mover is given by $U_{move} = u\left(W_g - \gamma\right) + \beta\left((1-p)U_g + pU_b\right)$.

We examine the implied change on γ_0 for a given γ when ζ rises (e.g., because p falls). By total differentiation we get

$$0 = d\zeta\left[u(W_g) - u(W_g - \gamma_0/\zeta) - \zeta u'(W_g - \gamma_0/\zeta)\gamma_0/\zeta^2\right]$$
$$+ d\gamma_0\left[\zeta u'(W_g - \gamma_0/\zeta) \cdot 1/\zeta\right]$$
$$\frac{d\gamma_0}{d\zeta} = \frac{u(W_g) - u(W_g - \gamma_0/\zeta) - u'(W_g - \gamma_0/\zeta)\gamma_0/\zeta}{u'(W_g - \gamma_0/\zeta)}.$$

When $u(\cdot)$ is strictly concave (the worker is risk-averse),

$$u(W_g) < u(W_g - \gamma_0/\zeta) + u'(W_g - \gamma_0/\zeta)\gamma_0/\zeta.$$

Inserting this expression into the previous one implies

$$\frac{d\gamma_0}{d\zeta} < 0.$$

Hence, the allowed mobility cost will be higher in the perfect capital market case as long as $\zeta > 1$ or $p < 1/2$.

EXERCISE 39

Expenditures $e(t) = pc(t)N(t)$ grow at rate

$$g_e = g_c + g,$$

where we used the fact that prices remain constant ($p = 1/(1 - \alpha)$). This growth rate depends on growth in the quantity consumed of each good and on growth in variety. We must show that $g_c = 0$ on a balanced growth path.

Rewrite the budget constraint using the fact that wages grow at rate g (since $W(t) = aN(t)$) and the expenditures at rate g_e:

$$\frac{e(0)}{R - g_e} = k(0) + \frac{W(0)l}{R - g}.$$

Aggregate both sides of the latter equation across households and use $K(0) = N(0)aF$ and $W(0) = aN(0)$ to get:

$$\frac{E(0)}{R - g_e} = N(0)aF + \frac{aN(0)L}{R - g}$$

and solve for the ratio of expenditures to variety:

$$\frac{E(0)}{N(0)} = (R - g_e)aF + \frac{R - g_e}{R - g}aL.$$

We focus on the balanced growth path where growth rates are constant. This implies that at each point on the balanced growth path the above ratio is the same. Therefore expenditures grow at the same rate as variety, $g_e = g$, and g_c must equal zero.

EXERCISE 40

a. Writing the labor share as

$$\gamma = \frac{\sigma - (\sigma - 1)\alpha}{\frac{\alpha \rho F}{L} + \sigma + \alpha}.$$

it is evident that it increases in L and decreases in F and ρ. To find the direction of the effect of σ, differentiate the labor share:

$$\frac{\partial \gamma}{\partial \sigma} = \frac{\alpha \left[(1 - \alpha)\frac{\rho F}{L} - \alpha\right]}{\left(\frac{\alpha \rho F}{L} + \sigma + \alpha\right)^2}.$$

For growth to be positive, the numerator $\alpha L/F - (1 - \alpha)\rho$ of the growth rate has to be positive. Hence, this derivative is negative.

To interpret these results, consider the labor shares in each sector. Since profit margins in production are only affected by market power $(1 - \alpha)$, the labor share in that sector only depends on α; in the research sector, the labor share is unity. The labor share of the whole economy therefore depends on the relative distribution of labor on the two sectors: more workers in production decrease the share of labor in total production.

When L increases, the additional workers can be employed either in production or in research. Since their marginal product is decreasing in each sector, they are distributed across both sectors so as to keep marginal productivities equal to each other: the labor share declines or increases depending on whether the research sector absorbs more or less of the labor force increase. Consider then the relationship between population and employment in research. If population is very small, research is unattractive since the marginal value product in production is very high; when population is sufficiently large, the research sector is activated and thereafter grows linearly with population. Therefore, research rises more than proportionally with L, and this explains why a larger L increases the labor share.

Symmetrically, when a larger F makes product innovation more difficult, labor is reallocated out of the research sector and into the production sector, and the labor share shrinks. And when σ increases, people become less willing to substitute consumption between different dates and, in a growing economy, increase current consumption: the production sector must therefore be larger, and the labor share decreases. A larger ρ similarly implies higher current consumption and a smaller research sector.

b. A tax on capital or profits reduces the returns to research investment and the attractiveness of the research sector. The resulting reallocation of workers to the production sector partly offsets the rise in the labor share. Symmetrically, a tax on labor makes research more attractive, and labor reallocation partly offsets the fall in the labor share.

EXERCISE 41

In the denominator of the labor share expression we see the first way of defining the GDP of the economy, as total income:

$$Y = WL + N\Pi.$$

It might appear that the compensation for the researchers is counted twice, as a wage and as a profit. But the profits are the result of past research and researcher wages accrue from current activity. We can see this more clearly if we construct GDP in the two other ways.

Let us proceed with the production side. The economy produces the existing consumption goods and designs for new consumption goods:

$$Y = Npx + \frac{\dot{N}\Pi}{R} = Npx + \frac{gN\Pi}{R}.$$

The first component is obvious. The second is the number of new designs $\dot{N}$ times the value of a design Π/R.

The last method uses the fact that, in a closed economy with no government, GDP is the sum of consumption and savings:

$$Y = C + S.$$

But what is saved in an economy without physical capital? Consumption expenditure is

$$C = E = WL + (R - g)\frac{N\Pi}{R} = WL + N\Pi - \frac{gN\Pi}{R},$$

where we have used the lifetime budget constraint. We see immediately that savings must be

$$S = \frac{gN\Pi}{R},$$

the value of the new designs, which indeed is due to the increase in the assets of the economy corresponding to the investment undertaken.

Since expenditures can also be defined as Npx, the equivalence of the three approaches should be clear.

EXERCISE 42

Final good sector: The first-order conditions are:

$$L_Y (1 - \alpha) x(j)^{-\alpha} = p(j),$$

$$\frac{\alpha Y}{L_Y} = W. \tag{14.1}$$

Intermediate good sector: Maximization of firm j's profit $\Pi = x(j)\left[p(j) - \eta\right]$ yields:

$$p(j) = \frac{\eta}{1 - \alpha}. \tag{14.2}$$

Applying Euler's theorem in the final good sector, the symmetry of the model yields:

$$Npx + WL_Y = Y.$$

Using the wage and price expression from equations (14.1) and (14.2) we can express the number of an intermediate good produced as follows:

$$x = \frac{(1-\alpha)\,Y}{N^{\frac{\eta}{1-\alpha}}}.$$

We then can rewrite profit as:

$$\Pi = \alpha\,(1-\alpha)\,\frac{Y}{N}. \tag{14.3}$$

Consumer: The final good can be used for consumption or for intermediate goods $Y = C + \eta N x$. On a balanced growth path

$$Y_0 e^{gt} = (C_0 + \eta N_0 x)e^{gt} = C_0 e^{gt} + \eta x N_0 e^{gt}$$

must hold. Again, the number of each intermediate good remains constant (this can be reasoned along the lines of the first exercise of this section). The growth rate of consumption, final good, and variety is g. Furthermore, the Euler equation holds:

$$\frac{\dot{C}}{C} = g = \frac{R-\rho}{\sigma}. \tag{14.4}$$

Labor market: Deviating slightly from the derivation in the variety in consumption goods model, we use the labor market to solve the model. The labor employed in research is $L_N(t) = \dot{N}F(t) = gF$. Since full employment requires $L = L_Y + L_N$ we can express employment in the production sector as:

$$L_Y = L - gF. \tag{14.5}$$

Entry and growth: To express growth in terms of the fundamentals we need one last relationship, which is the one of entry:

$$\frac{\Pi}{R} = W(t)F(t),$$

$$\frac{\alpha(1-\alpha)}{\sigma g + \rho}\frac{Y(t)}{N(t)} = \frac{\alpha F}{L_Y}\frac{Y(t)}{N(t)}. \tag{14.6}$$

For the second line I have used equations (14.1), (14.3), and (14.4). We get the growth rate by combining this equation with (14.5):

$$g = \frac{\frac{L}{F} - \frac{1}{1-\alpha}\rho}{\sigma\frac{1}{1-\alpha} + 1}$$

which is familiar from Romer (1990, eq. 13). L is the counterpart to human capital, $1/F$ to δ, and $\frac{1}{1-\alpha}$ to Λ.

Discussion: Let us compare the model of this exercise to the one of the main text. The effects on growth of population L, of research difficulty F, of impatience ρ, and of risk aversion σ is the same in both models. The effect of α is different. In the main text model α is a preference parameter which represents elasticity of substitution between different goods. A higher α, a lower $(1 - \alpha)$, means a lower substitutability between goods and therefore more market power for each firm. In the exercise model, α is a technology parameter which represents substitutability and hence market power in an analogue fashion. However, it represents at the same time the importance of the intermediate goods as a whole in final good production. Remember that $(1 - \alpha)$ is the fraction of output going to the intermediates since technology is Cobb-Douglas. In the main text model, a higher α leads to higher growth as higher market power increases attractiveness of research. In the exercise model, a higher α increases on the one hand market power, but on the other hand decreases the importance of the intermediates. The latter dominates and hence research becomes less attractive. This inconvenient interaction of two important technology parameters can be disentangled by modifying the production function to read

$$Y = (L_Y)^\alpha \left(\int_0^\infty x(j)^{1-\theta} dj \right)^{\frac{1-\alpha}{1-\theta}},$$

where a lower θ indicates increased market power without changing importance of the intermediates.

EXERCISE 43

Let us denote the labor endowment of the poorest client of a firm with $\tilde{\theta}$. The poorest client of a firm is the one that pays his reservation price, whereas the richer clients, who exhibit a higher reservation price, get a positive consumer surplus. Still poorer consumers do not consume the good. The zero-profit condition then might be written as:

$$WF = (1 - G(\tilde{\theta}))L \left(p(\tilde{\theta}) - \frac{W}{a} \right),$$

where $(1 - G(\tilde{\theta}))$ is the fraction of consumers who want to afford the specific good at the reservation price of the critical individual $p(\tilde{\theta})$. As firms are ex ante symmetric, profits must be equal and the equation above must hold for all $\tilde{\theta}$. We solve for the price

$$p(\tilde{\theta}) = \frac{W}{a} + \frac{WF/L}{1 - G(\tilde{\theta})}, \qquad (14.7)$$

which increases in $\tilde{\theta}$. The richer the critical client of a firm, the smaller the firm's market, and the higher the price it sets given the wage level. Note that the price approaches infinity as $\tilde{\theta}$ approaches its upper bound.

To understand the derivation of the market structure, we begin by considering a discrete case where there are n groups of individuals. The budget constraint of an individual i is

$$\theta_i W = \sum_{k=1}^{i} p(\theta_k)[N_k - N_{k-1}],$$

where $N_0 = 0$. N_i is the continuum of products group i consumes. For $N_i - N_{i-1}$ products the group pays its reservation price, for $N_{i-1} - N_{i-2}$ it pays the reservation price of the next poorer group which is a lower price, etc. There are as many group of firms, different in the price to other groups, as there are groups of individuals. We are now ready to switch back to the continuous case:

$$\tilde{\theta} W = \int_{\underline{\theta}}^{\tilde{\theta}} p(\theta)dN(\theta) + p(\underline{\theta})N(\underline{\theta}) = \int_{\underline{\theta}}^{\tilde{\theta}} p(\theta)N'(\theta)d\theta + p(\underline{\theta})N(\underline{\theta}). \quad (14.8)$$

$N(\theta)$ is the continuum of goods consumed by individual θ. Differentiate with respect to $\tilde{\theta}$:

$$W = p(\theta)N'(\theta),$$

solve for $N'(\theta)$, and integrate to obtain

$$N(\tilde{\theta}) = \int_{\underline{\theta}}^{\tilde{\theta}} \frac{W}{p(\theta)} d\theta + N(\underline{\theta}). \quad (14.9)$$

We see whenever the density is nonzero, $p(\tilde{\theta})$ and $N(\tilde{\theta})$ increase strictly in $\tilde{\theta}$. There is "continuous exclusion" and no "clustering exclusion" where similarly endowed individuals consume exactly the same products. An infinitesimally wealthier individual consumes infinitesimally more products.

The mass of products consumed by the poorest in the population can be determined from the budget constraint (14.8) and the price equation (14.7)

$$\underline{\theta} W = p(\underline{\theta})N(\underline{\theta}) = \left(\frac{W}{a} + \frac{WF}{L} \right) N(\underline{\theta})$$

hence

$$N(\underline{\theta}) = \underline{\theta} \frac{aL}{aF + L}.$$

We insert this into (14.9) to solve for the "exclusion profile" $N(\tilde{\theta})$

$$N(\tilde{\theta}) = \underline{\theta} \frac{aL}{aF + L} + \int_{\underline{\theta}}^{\tilde{\theta}} \frac{aL(1 - G(\theta))}{aF + L(1 - G(\theta))} d\theta. \quad (14.10)$$

The product variety in the economy then is given by $N(\bar{\theta})$. We get the general result that more income dispersion implies more variety. To see this from (14.10) we proceed in two steps. (1) Note that $\int_0^z G(\theta)d\theta = \theta G(\theta)|_0^z - \int_0^z \theta g(\theta)d\theta = z - 1$, where z is sufficiently high such that $G(z) = 1$. Hence, if we integrate the distribution function over its whole support the resulting value does not depend on second and higher order moments. (2) The integrand in (14.10) is a concave function of $G(\bullet)$. With more inequality the distribution function becomes flatter, i.e., the values of the distribution function are more concentrated, which implies that the value of the integral must increase.

The overall variety in the economy is not determined from the richest group's income only. This holds true only in the polar case where the setup costs F are zero and $N(\bar{\theta})$ equals $\bar{\theta}a$. When there are positive setup costs F the whole shape of the distribution function matters.

EXERCISE 44

Labor supply L is inelastic. A change in the wage does not affect the quantity of labor desired to supply. When the set of firms N is fixed, there are two possible regimes. The productivity of a worker could be relatively low. This implies that firms, competing for scarce labor, raise the real wage until profits are zero. If there were still positive profits, a firm that could not get any workers would lure in workers by offering higher wages. Hence, prices of mass and exclusive goods are the same. Let us take the price as numéraire. The sets of goods consumed by the rich and the poor, respectively, are given by

$$N_R = \frac{1 - \beta\theta}{1 - \theta}a$$
$$N_P = \theta a,$$

where we used the fact that $w = a$. As profits are zero, the firm sizes are indeterminate.

When productivity is above a certain threshold, the situation switches to another extreme configuration. Each individual does not consume more than one unit of each good. Because the set of goods cannot expand in order to overcome saturation, not all of the labor force is needed anymore if it is sufficiently productive. When do we switch to the latter regime and how is exclusion involved? Consider a rise in productivity. At some point the income of the rich is so high that they could buy more goods than N. This happens when

$$\frac{1 - \beta\theta}{1 - \theta} > \frac{N}{a},$$

i.e., the number of products is relatively small compared to productivity. Not all workers are needed anymore. Therefore, the wage rate falls. But because labor supply is inelastic the wage falls all the way to zero (or more generally the reservation wage), and unemployment arises.

Note that the poor still do not consume all goods. In the former regime prices of all goods were equal, in the latter exclusive goods are more expensive since profits differ from zero. Let us take the mass good price as numéraire ($p = 1$). Profits of both firms have to be equal, with p being the price of the exclusive good:

$$L = L(1 - \beta)p.$$

Wage rate is $w = 0$. Hence, the exclusive good price p is

$$p = \frac{1}{1 - \beta}.$$

The poor agent gets a fraction $\theta < 1$ of average profits. The set of mass consumption goods is

$$N_P = \theta \frac{NL}{L} = \theta N,$$

which is strictly smaller than N and is independent of productivity. Even if $\theta \geq N/a$, a situation where poor people are sufficiently productive to theoretically produce all goods for themselves, they only consume a fraction of the available goods. The imperfect product markets prohibit an outcome where the resources of the economy are employed efficiently. Unemployment u can be derived using product markets equilibrium:

$$(1 - u)aL = \beta L N_P + (1 - \beta)LN,$$
$$u = 1 - [\beta\theta + (1 - \beta)] \frac{N}{a}.$$

Note that higher inequality (either a rise in β, or a fall in θ, or both) raises unemployment.

EXERCISE 45

a. A consumer purchases good j if $j^{-\gamma} \geq \lambda p(j)$ and purchases all goods in the range $[0, N]$ when $p(j) \cdot j^\gamma$ is increasing in j (which will hold in equilibrium). N is determined by the individual's budget constraint $y = \int_0^N p(j)dj$. Firms supplying products in the range $[0, N_P]$ sell to both rich and poor consumers charging a price equal to the willingness of the poor to pay $p(j) = j^{-\gamma}/\lambda_P$, whereas firms supplying products in the range $(N_P, N]$ sell only to rich consumers charging a price equal to the willingness of the rich to pay $p(j) = j^{-\gamma}/\lambda_R$. Note that prices first decrease with j, then jump from $j^{-\gamma}/\lambda_P$ to the higher level $j^{-\gamma}/\lambda_R$ at $j = N_P$ and then decrease thereafter. Decreasing prices reflect the fact that consumers have a higher willingness to pay for lower j (= higher priority) goods and the jump at $j = N_P$ reflects the fact that goods with an index higher than N_P are only purchased by the rich (are exclusive goods), and richer consumers have a higher willingness. Recall also that all firms have the same cost of production, which means that firms producing higher priority goods earn a rent.

b. Calculate first how many firms will enter. The lowest priority good that is actually supplied on the market, good N, will just break even.

$$wF = \left(\frac{N^{-\gamma}}{\lambda_R} - \frac{w}{a}\right)(1 - \beta)L.$$

Furthermore we must have that the firm supplying good N_P, the good with least priority purchased by the poor, is indifferent between selling to the rich at a high price $N_P^{-\gamma}/\lambda_R$ and selling to the whole market at the lower price $N_P^{-\gamma}/\lambda_P$

$$\left(\frac{N_P^{-\gamma}}{\lambda_R} - \frac{w}{a}\right)(1 - \beta)L = \left(\frac{N_P^{-\gamma}}{\lambda_P} - \frac{w}{a}\right)L.$$

In equilibrium both types of consumers exhaust their budget constraints. For the poor we have

$$\theta\frac{wL + \Pi}{L} = \frac{1}{\lambda_P}\frac{N_P^{1-\gamma}}{1 - \gamma},$$

and similarly for the rich we get

$$\frac{1 - \beta\theta}{1 - \beta}\frac{wL + \Pi}{L} = \frac{1}{\lambda_P}\frac{N_P^{1-\gamma}}{1 - \gamma} + \frac{1}{\lambda_R}\frac{N^{1-\gamma} - N_P^{1-\gamma}}{1 - \gamma}.$$

Finally, aggregate profits are just the sum of the profits made by the individual firms

$$
\begin{aligned}
\Pi &= L\int_0^{N_P}\left(\frac{j^{-\gamma}}{\lambda_P} - \frac{w}{a}\right)dj + (1 - \beta)L\int_{N_P}^N\left(\frac{j^{-\gamma}}{\lambda_R} - \frac{w}{a}\right)dj \\
&= L\left[\frac{1}{\lambda_P}\frac{N_P^{1-\gamma}}{1 - \gamma} + \frac{(1 - \beta)}{\lambda_R}\frac{N^{1-\gamma} - N_P^{1-\gamma}}{1 - \gamma} - \frac{w}{a}[(1 - \beta)N - \beta N_P]\right].
\end{aligned}
$$

These are five equations in the six unknowns: $N, N_P, \lambda_R, \lambda_P, w$, and Π. Without loss of generality we can take the marginal cost of product as the numéraire $\frac{w}{a} = 1$. This leaves us with a system of five equations with five unknowns.

EXERCISE 46

a. **Analytical solution**

We express $\underline{p}$ as a function of $\bar{p}$ from the arbitrage condition:

$$\pi_{tot} = \pi_R$$

$$\left[\underline{p} - 1\right]L = \left[\bar{p} - 1\right](1 - \beta)L$$

$$\Longleftrightarrow$$

$$\underline{p} = \bar{p}(1 - \beta) + \beta.$$

The consumption expenditures of a poor consumer relative to those of a rich consumer can be written as:

$$\frac{1 - \beta\theta}{(1 - \beta)\theta} = \frac{pn + \bar{p}(1 - n)}{pn}$$

Using $\underline{p} = \bar{p}(1 - \beta) + \beta$ to replace $\underline{p}$ yields

$$\bar{p} = \frac{\beta}{1 - \beta}\frac{(1 - \theta)n}{\theta - n}.$$

We now insert the expression for $\bar{p}$ in the zero-profit condition and we get a relationship between g and n.

$$WF = \frac{(1 - \beta)(\frac{\beta}{1-\beta}\frac{(1-\theta)n}{\theta-n} - 1)L}{\sigma g + \rho}$$

$$\Longleftrightarrow \frac{WF}{L}(\sigma g + \rho) = \frac{\beta\theta(1 - n)}{\theta - n} - 1.$$

The resource constraint depends on g and n only. We solve it for g and get:

$$L = \frac{1}{a}[\beta Ln + (1 - \beta)L] + Fg$$

$$\Longleftrightarrow g = \frac{L}{F}\left(1 - \frac{1}{a}[\beta n + 1 - \beta]\right).$$

We reinsert into the zero-profit condition to get an explicit solution for n.

$$\frac{WF}{L}\left(\sigma\frac{L}{F}\left(1 - \frac{1}{a}[\beta n + (1 - \beta)\right) + \rho\right) = \frac{\beta\theta(1 - n)}{\theta - n} - 1$$

$$W\sigma - \sigma\beta n - \sigma(1 - \beta) + \frac{\rho WF}{L} + 1 = \frac{\beta\theta(1 - n)}{\theta - n}$$

$$\Longleftrightarrow n = \frac{-\alpha_1 + \sqrt{\alpha_1^2 - 4\sigma\beta\alpha}}{2\sigma\beta}$$

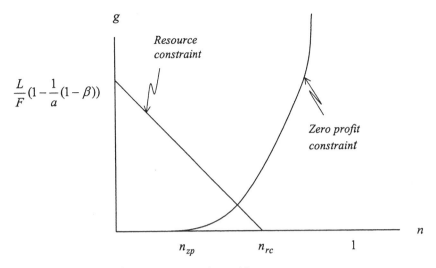

Figure 4. Existence of a positive growth equilibrium

where

$$\alpha_1 = -(W\sigma - \sigma(1-\beta) + \frac{WF}{L}\rho + 1 + \beta\theta(\sigma - 1))$$

$$\alpha = (W\sigma - \sigma(1-\beta) + \frac{WF}{L}\rho + 1 - \beta)\theta$$

To solve for g, insert n in the resource constraint.

For a (unique) equilibrium with positive growth the condition $W\sigma - \sigma(1-\beta) + \frac{\rho WF}{L} + 1 > \beta$ must be fulfilled. To see that this must be the case, note that this implies that $\alpha > 0$ and $\alpha_1 < 0$ and hence $n > 0$.

b. Graphical solution

To get more intuition consider figure 4, where the resource constraint and the zero-profit condition are mapped. Rewrite the zero-profit condition

$$g = \left(\frac{\beta\theta(1-n)}{\theta - n} - 1\right)\frac{L}{WF\sigma} - \frac{\rho}{\sigma}$$

and recall the equation for the resource constraint

$$g = \frac{L}{F}\left(1 - \frac{1}{a}[\beta n + (1-\beta)]\right).$$

It easy to check that—in the relevant range—the zero-profit condition is monotonically increasing in the (n, g) space and approaches infinity at $n = \theta$. We directly see that the resource constraint is monotonically falling.

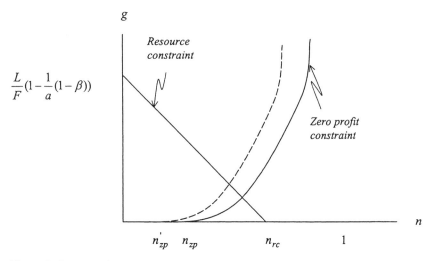

$$\frac{L}{F}\left(1-\frac{1}{a}(1-\beta)\right)$$

Figure 5. Decrease in θ

To determine whether an equilibrium with positive growth exists we have to determine the loci where the two equilibrium curves cross the n-curve. Let us denote them by n_{zp} and n_{rc}. Hence for an equilibrium with positive growth the following condition must hold:

$$n_{zp} < n_{rc}$$

$$\frac{\theta(\frac{\rho WF}{L} + 1 - \beta)}{\frac{\rho WF}{L} + 1 - \beta\theta} < \frac{a - (1 - \beta)}{\beta}.$$

It is easy to check that the latter condition is equivalent to the relation $W\sigma - \sigma(1 - \beta) + \frac{\rho WF}{L} + 1 > \beta$ from above.

If $n_{zp} > n_{rc}$, the growth rate g will be zero and the economy stagnates.

c. Comparative statics

We analyze graphically how the growth rate g and the number of products sold to the poor n depend on distribution parameters β and θ.

Decrease in θ (see figure 5)

As $\frac{\beta\theta(1-n)}{\theta - n}$ decreases in θ, the zero-profit condition curve shifts up when θ decreases. Consequently, $\theta' < \theta$ implies $n'_{zp} < n_{zp}$. On the other side, the resource constraint is unaffected. Therefore an increase in inequality due to a decrease in θ unambiguously increases the growth rate g and reduces n, the number of products sold to the poor.

Increase in β (see figure 6)

Note that an increase in β on the one hand shifts up the resource constraint curve. On the other hand, it also shifts up the zero-profit constraint curve. Hence an increase in inequality due to a higher β implies a higher growth rate, too. However, the impact of a higher β on n is unclear. To see which parameters

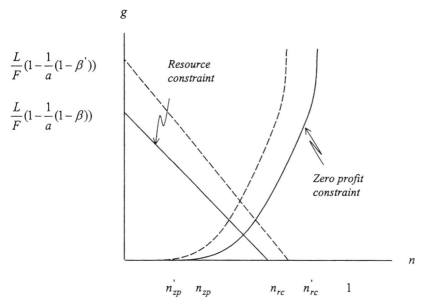

$$\frac{L}{F}(1 - \frac{1}{a}(1 - \beta'))$$

$$\frac{L}{F}(1 - \frac{1}{a}(1 - \beta))$$

Figure 6. Increase in β

determine whether n rises or falls, we differentiate totally the resource and zero-profit constraint:

$$dg = -\frac{L}{F}\frac{1}{a}\beta dn + (1 - n)\frac{L}{Fa}d\beta$$

$$dg = \frac{\theta(1 - n)}{(\theta - n)}\frac{L}{WF\sigma}d\beta + \frac{\beta\theta(1 - \theta)}{(\theta - n)^2}\frac{L}{WF\sigma}dn.$$

Therefore:

$$\frac{dn}{d\beta} = \frac{L}{F}(1 - n)\frac{\frac{\theta}{(\theta - n)}\frac{1}{W\sigma} - 1}{-\frac{L}{F}\frac{1}{a}\beta - \frac{\beta\theta(1 - \theta)}{(\theta - n)^2}\frac{L}{WF\sigma}} <, > 0.$$

Note that an increase in β increases inequality and thus implies a higher price which implies more exclusion (lower n), but on the other hand there are simply fewer rich agents. Therefore a smaller amount is sold at the higher price. Either effect could dominate.

To get a formal intuition why the growth rate rises when inequality increases in the Lorenz sense, we can consider how θ and β affect $\bar{p}$ for a given n. Note that $\frac{\partial \bar{p}}{\partial \theta} < 0$ and $\frac{\partial \bar{p}}{\partial \beta} > 0$ and thus (with n fixed) we get the result that $\frac{\partial \Pi_{tot}(j)}{\partial \theta} < 0$, $\frac{\partial \Pi_R(j)}{\partial \theta} < 0$ and $\frac{\partial \Pi_{tot}(j)}{\partial \beta} > 0$, $\frac{\partial \Pi_{tot}(j)}{\partial \beta} > 0$. The verbal intuition is in the main text.

EXERCISE 47

a. Using the same procedure as in section 11.2.1 we can determine the relative expenditures of poor and rich consumers, which yields an expression in the two endogenous variables m and n

$$\frac{(1-\beta)\theta}{1-\beta\theta} = \frac{pn}{pn+m-n} = \frac{n-\beta\left(1-\frac{b}{a}\right)n}{m-\beta\left(1-\frac{b}{a}\right)n}$$

or

$$m = \left[\frac{1}{\theta} + \frac{b}{a}\frac{\beta}{1-\beta}\frac{1-\theta}{\theta}\right]n.$$

To derive the resource constraint, note that $gF = \frac{(1-\beta)L(1-\frac{b}{a})}{\sigma b} - \frac{\rho}{\sigma}F$ workers are employed in the R&D sector, $\frac{1}{a}[\beta Ln + (1-\beta)L]$ workers are employed to produce consumption goods in monopolistic firms, and $\frac{1}{b}[(1-\beta)L(m-1)]$ workers are employed in the competitive fringe. This allows us to write the resource constraint in terms of the endogenous variables m and n

$$L = \frac{(1-\beta)L(1-\frac{b}{a})}{\sigma b} - \frac{\rho}{\sigma}F + \frac{1}{a}[\beta Ln + (1-\beta)L] + \frac{1}{b}[(1-\beta)L(m-1)]$$

or

$$m = \frac{b}{1-\beta}\left[1+\frac{\rho F}{\sigma L}\right] + \left(1-\frac{b}{a}\right)\left[1-\frac{1}{\sigma}\right] - \frac{\beta}{1-\beta}\frac{b}{a}n.$$

It is most convenient to imagine the solution in a (m,n) diagram, with m as the vertical axis and n as the horizontal axis. The relative budget curve is upward sloping and linear. The resource curve is downward sloping. Its intercept is positive since this is equivalent to $gF \le L$, which means the research sector cannot be greater than population. The intersection of these two curves gives the equilibrium values of m and n.

b. If inequality rises because θ *falls*, a rise in inequality, only the budget curve is affected. It rotates counterclockwise around the origin. The new intersection has a higher m and a lower n. Since the poor are poorer and the rich are richer, the number of mass firms shrinks and the number of exclusive goods rises. Hence, there are more firms producing with the '"inefficient" technology b.

The effect of an increase in β is less clear-cut. The budget curve rotates again counterclockwise. A rise in β (holding θ constant) raises the relative income of the rich. However, the equal profit condition requires that the price of the mass good falls, which implies relative lower expenditures. The two effects do not exactly cancel out; m has to rise given n.

On the one hand, the resource curve shifts upward (higher intercept); on the other, it rotates inward (higher absolute slope). What happens to m given n? Since profit margins shrink, there is less research. Because the rise in demand of the poor for the efficient technology is more than offset by the fall in demand of the rich, less labor is required in the efficient sector. Therefore the inefficient sector must grow, m must rise, for any given n. The total effect of an increase in β on m is clear: m rises. The effect on n is ambiguous: it could either rise or fall.

EXERCISE 48

We insert (12.17) into the instantaneous utility function (12.12) and get

$$
\begin{aligned}
u^*(t) &= -\frac{1}{2} \int_0^n \left(\frac{\eta s}{1+\eta} \frac{j}{e} \right)^{2\eta} j^{-\eta} dj \\
&= -\frac{1}{2} \left(\frac{\eta s}{1+\eta} \frac{1}{e} \right)^{2\eta} \int_0^{\frac{1+\eta}{s\eta} e} j^{\eta} dj \\
&= -\frac{1}{2} \left(\frac{\eta s}{1+\eta} \frac{1}{e} \right)^{2\eta} \int_0^{\frac{1+\eta}{s\eta} e} j^{\eta} dj \\
&= -\frac{1}{2} \left(\frac{\eta s}{1+\eta} \frac{1}{e} \right)^{2\eta} \frac{\left(\frac{1+\eta}{s\eta} e \right)^{1+\eta}}{1+\eta} \\
&= \frac{\eta}{1+\eta} \left(\frac{1+\eta}{\eta s} \right)^{1-\eta} \frac{e^{1-\eta}}{1-\eta}.
\end{aligned}
$$

EXERCISE 49

If the distribution of l is single peaked, $D(Q)$ takes an S shape in figure 13.1. Hence, we obtain, in qualitative terms, the same steady-state equilibria. Of course, and in contrast to the discrete distribution, in the growth process there is a steadily increasing share of consumers buying the luxury good. (For more general distributions, more than three [stable] steady states may arise.)

The share of people buying the luxury good is determined implicitly by the following equation:

$$ Q^* = 1 - F(p_0 + a_1(Q^*)), $$

where $Q^* = D(Q^*)$ holds in steady state.

EXERCISE 50

In this case, the mean income earner is not able to purchase the luxury good: $p_0 + a_1(Q_0) > 1$. The rich are able to purchase the luxury good if their income exceeds the sum of prices of both good 0 and 1 today. Formally,

$$\frac{1 - \beta\theta}{1 - \beta} \geq p_0 + a_1(Q_0).$$

On the other hand the reservation price of the poor $l_P - p_0$ must exceed $a_1((1 - \beta)L)$, so the poor will sooner or later be able to purchase the luxury good. Hence, we must have

$$\theta > p_0 + a_1((1 - \beta)L).$$

Taking these conditions together, trickling down is possible (in the sense that θ can fulfill both conditions above) if the following condition holds:

$$p_0 + a_1(Q_0) \leq \frac{1 - \beta\theta^*}{1 - \beta} < \frac{1 - \beta(p_0 + a_1((1 - \beta)L)}{1 - \beta}$$
$$\Longleftrightarrow p_0 + \beta a_1((1 - \beta)L) + (1 - \beta)a_1(Q_0) < 1.$$

Intuitively, trickling down is more likely if the prices of good 0 and 1 are low today.

EXERCISE 51

The values of marginal revenue products have to equal factor prices and are given by:

$$\frac{\partial Y_0}{\partial H_0} = \alpha A H_0^{\alpha-1} L_0^{1-\alpha} = W_H,$$

$$\frac{\partial Y_0}{\partial L_0} = (1 - \alpha) A H_0^{\alpha} L_0^{-\alpha} = W_L,$$

$$p_1 \frac{\partial Y_1}{\partial H_1} = p_1 \delta A H_1^{\delta-1} L_1^{1-\delta} = W_H,$$

$$p_1 \frac{\partial Y_1}{\partial H_1} = p_1 (1 - \delta) A H_1^{\delta} L_1^{-\delta} = W_L,$$

whereas p_0 is taken as numéraire. When A is relatively low and nobody demands the luxury good, the analysis is equivalent to the one in the main text.

Let us focus on the case where the skilled reach the luxury threshold first ($\alpha + \beta > 1$). Along the lines of the second case in the text, we set demand equal to supply in the basic good sector:

$$\beta [W_L L/\beta] + (1 - \beta)\bar{c}_0 = A H_0^{\alpha} L_0^{1-\alpha}, \tag{14.11}$$

$$\left[1 - (1 - \alpha)\frac{L}{L_0}\right] A H_0^{\alpha} L_0^{1-\alpha} = (1 - \beta)\bar{c}_0,$$

where for the second line we have rewritten the equation using the low skilled wage. Furthermore, we can combine the marginal revenue products to get

$$\frac{1 - \alpha}{\alpha} \frac{H_0}{L_0} = \frac{1 - \delta}{\delta} \frac{H_1}{L_1}.$$

Using the above relationships in combination with the full employment conditions $L_0 + L_1 = L$ and $H_0 + H_1 = H$ we can discuss the effects of a rise in A. We see that a rise in A obviously decreases employment in the basic sector since demand is shifted (in relative terms) toward the luxury sector. Note that skilled workers are used more intensively in the luxury sector, as $H_1/L_1 > H_0/L_0$, and that the factor intensities are proportional to each other. Hence, when employment in the luxury sector rises, factor intensities H_0/L_0 and H_1/L_1 have to fall. If these stayed the same or even increased, the full employment conditions would be violated. This implies that growth raises the skill premium W_H/W_L.

a. Consider the second line of equation (14.11) and take into account that L_0 falls when A rises. Hence, the term in the square brackets falls. Because the right-hand side remains unchanged, the output in the basic sector $AH_0^\alpha L_0^{1-\alpha}$ must rise. Since consumption of the basic good of the skilled remains the same, the unskilled consume more. Therefore their wage must have risen, and at a sufficiently high A, they will be able to consume the luxury good.

Compare this with the case analyzed in the main text. There, the relevant equation is

$$\alpha A H_0^\alpha L^{1-\alpha} = (1 - \beta)\,\bar{c}_0.$$

We see that the production of the basic good $AH_0^\alpha L^{1-\alpha}$ remains the same when A rises. Because the consumption of the basic good of the skilled is constant, consumption of the unskilled must remain the same and they are caught in a "poverty trap."

b. Look at the case where both groups consume the luxury good. The unskilled earn a share $(1 - \alpha)$ of basic production and $(1 - \delta)$ of luxury production. Since growth increases production of the luxury good while leaving production of the basic good unchanged, it enhances welfare for both groups and therefore it is not immiserizing for the unskilled.

When $\alpha + \beta < 1$ and $\delta + \beta < 1$, the unskilled are better off for every A. When the second inequality is reversed, there is leapfrogging: the skilled outrun the initially richer unskilled. To see this consider A is approaching infinity. Then the luxury good sector becomes the absolutely dominant sector. Finally, when both inequalities are reversed, the skilled are always better off. The fourth combination (first inequality reversed but the second not) is impossible because we have assumed $\alpha < \delta$.

EXERCISE 52

When A rises, the economy goes through different "stages of development." At a very low level of A only the unskilled consume a positive amount. The skilled, who are not employed in production of the basic sector, face no demand in the luxury sector and hence earn no wage. The wage of the unskilled is $W_L = A$ (p_0 is the numéraire). The condition for this phase of development is $W_L L/\beta < \bar{c}_0$ which, taking into account that $W_L = A$, we can rewrite as

$$\frac{AL}{\beta} < \bar{c}_0.$$

When A reaches $\bar{c}_0 \beta / L$, the unskilled start to demand the luxury good. Therefore, wages are

$$W_H = p_1 \delta A H^{\delta-1} L_1^{1-\delta},$$
$$W_L = p_1 (1 - \delta) A H^\delta L_1^{-\delta} = A.$$

Using the second equality we can rewrite the price as

$$p_1 = \frac{1}{1-\delta} H^{-\delta} L_1^\delta$$

and hence the skilled wage as

$$W_H = \frac{\delta}{1-\delta} \frac{A L_1}{H}.$$

The next step is to determine employment of unskilled in the luxury sector. Supply equals demand in this sector:

$$A H^\delta L_1^{1-\delta} = \beta \frac{W_L L/\beta - \bar{c}_0}{p_1}.$$

Note that only the unskilled consume the luxury good. Plugging in the appropriate prices and wages, we may rewrite the above equation to get

$$L_1 = \frac{1-\delta}{A} [AL - \beta \bar{c}_0]$$

and rewrite the skilled wage as

$$W_H = \frac{\delta}{H} [AL - \beta \bar{c}_0].$$

This is positive if $AL > \beta \bar{c}_0$, which is exactly the condition that the unskilled have satisfied their basic needs. The skilled wage increases with A and for a sufficiently high level it allows the skilled to consume the luxury good. In the limit as A tends to infinity, which is the long-run equilibrium, we can ignore the basic sector. When $W_H H/(1-\beta) > W_L L/\beta$, which is equivalent to $\beta + \delta > 1$, the skilled become richer than the unskilled for $A \to \infty$. There is leapfrogging. Otherwise, the unskilled stay ahead forever.

References

Abramovitz, Moses, and Paul David (2000) "American Macroeconomic Growth in the Era of Knowledge-Based Progress: The Long-Run Perspective," in Stanley L. Engermann and Robert E. Gallmann (eds.), *The Cambridge Economic History of the United States*, 1–92, Cambridge: Cambridge University Press.

Acemoglu, Daron (1998) "Why Do New Technologies Complement Skills? Directed Technical Change and Wage Inequality," *Quarterly Journal of Economics* 113, 1055–89.

—— (2002) "Directed Technical Change," *Review of Economic Studies* 69, 781–810.

—— (2003) "Labor- and Capital-Augmenting Technical Change," *Journal of European Economic Association* 1, 1–40.

Acemoglu, Daron, and Joshua Linn (2004) "Market Size in Innovation: Theory and Evidence from the Pharmaceutical Industry," *Quarterly Journal of Economics* 119(3), 1049–90.

Acemoglu, Daron, and Robert Shimer (1999) "Efficient Unemployment Insurance," *Journal of Political Economy* 107, 893–928.

Acemoglu, Daron, and Fabrizio Zilibotti (1997) "Was Prometheus Unbound by Chance? Risk, Diversification, and Growth," *Journal of Political Economy* 105(4), 709–51.

—— (2001) "Productivity Differences," *Quarterly Journal of Economics* 116, 563–606.

Adelman, Irma, and Sherman Robinson (1989) "Income Distribution and Development," in H. Chenery and T. N. Srinivasan (eds.), *Handbook of Development Economics*, Vol. 2, Amsterdam: North-Holland.

Aghion, Philippe (2002) "Schumpeterian Growth Theory and the Dynamics of Income Inequality," *Econometrica* 70, 855–82.

Aghion, Philippe, and Patrick Bolton (1992) "Distribution and Growth in Models of Imperfect Capital Markets," *European Economic Review* 36, 603–11.

—— (1997) "A Theory of Trickle-Down Growth and Development," *Review of Economic Studies* 64(2), 151–72.

Aghion, Philippe, Eve Caroli, and Cecilia Garcia-Penalosa (1999) "Inequality and Economic Growth: The Perspective of the New Growth Theories," *Journal of Economic Literature* 37, 1615–60.

Aghion, Philippe, and Peter Howitt (1992) "A Model of Growth through Creative Destruction," *Econometrica* 60(2), 323–51.

—— (1998) *Endogenous Growth Theory*, Cambridge, MA: MIT Press.

Ahluwalia, Montek, Nichola G. Carter, and Hollis Chenery (1976) "Growth and Poverty in Developing Countries," *Journal of Development Economics* 6, 299–341.

Aiyagari, S. Rao (1994) "Uninsured Idiosyncratic Risk and Aggregate Savings," *Quarterly Journal of Economics* 109(3), 659–84.

Aiyagari, S. Rao, and Ellen R. McGrattan (1998) "The Optimum Quantity of Debt," *Journal of Monetary Economics* 42, 447–69.

Alesina, Alberto, and Roberto Perotti (1996) "Income Distribution, Political Instability, and Investment," *European Economic Review* 40(6), 1203–28.

Alesina, Alberto, and Dani Rodrik (1994) "Distributive Policies and Economic Growth," *Quarterly Journal of Economics* 109(2), 465–90.

Alogoskoufis, George, and Frederick van der Ploeg (1990) "On Budgetary Policies and Economic Growth," CEPR Discussion Paper No. 496.

Anand, Sudhir, and Ravi M. Kanbur (1993) "The Kuznets Process and the Inequality Development Relationship," *Journal of Development Economics* 40(1), 25–52.

Andreoni, James (1989) "Giving with Impure Altruism: Applications to Charity and Ricardian Equivalence," *Journal of Political Economy* 97(6), 1447–58.

Angeletos, George-Marios (2004) "Idiosyncratic Investment Risk in the Neoclassical Growth Model," mimeo, MIT.

Angeletos, George-Marios, and Laurent Calvet (2003) " Idiosyncratic Production Risk, Growth and the Business Cycle," mimeo, MIT.

Arrow, Kenneth J. (1962) "The Economic Implications of Learning by Doing," *Review of Economic Studies* 29, 155–73.

—— (1964) "The Role of Securities in the Optimal Allocation of Risk-Bearing," *Review of Economic Studies* 31(2), 91–96 (originally published in French in *Économétrie*, Paris: CNRS, 1953, 41–47).

Asimakopoulos, Athanasios (1988) (ed.) *Theories of Income Distribution*, Boston: Kluwer Academic Publishers.

Atkeson, Andrew, and Robert E. Lucas (1992) "On Efficient Distribution with Private Information," *Review of Economic Studies* 59, 427–53.

—— (1995) "Efficiency and Equality in a Simple Model of Efficient Unemployment Insurance," *Journal of Economic Theory* 66(1), 64–88.

Atkeson, Andrew, and Masao Ogaki (1996) "Wealth-Varying Intertemporal Elasticities of Substitution: Evidence from Panel and Aggregate Data," *Journal of Monetary Economics*, 38(3), 507–34.

Atkinson, Anthony B. (1998) *Poverty in Europe,* London: Blackwell Publishing.

—— (2003) "Top Incomes in the United Kingdom over the Twentieth Century," mimeo, Nuffield College, Oxford University.

Atkinson, Anthony B., and François Bourguignon (2000) "Pauvreté et inclusion dans une perspective mondiale," *Revue d'économie du développement*, 1–2.

—— (2001) "Income Distribution," *International Encyclopedia of the Social and Behavioral Sciences* (Economics/Public and Welfare Economics), 7265–71, Amsterdam: Elsevier.

Atkinson, Anthony B., and Andrea Brandolini (2001) "Promise and Pitfalls in the Use of 'Secondary' Data-Sets: Income Inequality in OECD Countries as a Case Study," *Journal of Economic Literature* 39(3), 771–99.

Attanasio, Orazio, Gabriella Berloffa, Richard Blundell, and Ian Preston (2002) "From Earnings Inequality to Consumption Inequality," *Economic Journal* 112, C52–59.

Auerbach, Alan J., and Lawrence J. Kotlikoff (1987) *Dynamic Fiscal Policy,* Cambridge: Cambridge University Press.

Baland, Jean-Marie, and Debraj Ray (1991) "Why Does Asset Inequality Affect Unemployment? A Study of the Demand Composition Problem," *Journal of Development Economics* 35, 69–92.

Banerjee, Abhijit V., and Esther Duflo (2003) "Inequality and Growth: What Can the Data Say?" *Journal of Economic Growth* 8, 267–99.

Banerjee, Abhijit V., and Andrew F. Newman (1993) "Occupational Choice and the Process of Development," *Journal of Political Economy* 101(2), 274–98.

Banerjee, Abhijit V., Dilip Mookherjee, Kaivan Munshi, and Debraj Ray (2001) "Inequality, Control Rights and Rent-Seeking: Sugar Cooperatives in Maharashtra," *Journal of Political Economy* 109, 138–90.

Banerjee Abhijit V., and Thomas Piketty (2003), "Top Indian Incomes, 1956–2000," mimeo, Harvard University.

Baranzini, Mauro (1991) *A Theory of Wealth Distribution and Accumulation,* New York: Oxford University Press.

Barro, Robert J. (1974) "Are Government Bonds Net Wealth?" *Journal of Political Economy* 82, 1095–1117.

——— (2000) "Inequality and Growth in a Panel of Countries," *Journal of Economic Growth* 5, 5–32.

Barro, Robert J., N. Gregory Mankiw, and Xavier Sala-i-Martin (1995) "Capital Mobility in Neoclassical Models of Growth," *American Economic Review* 85(1), 103–15.

Barro, Robert J., and Xavier Sala-i-Martin (1997) "Technological Diffusion, Convergence and Growth," *Journal of Economic Growth* 2, 1–26.

Barsky, Robert B., Gregory Mankiw, and Stephen P. Zeldes (1986) "Ricardian Consumers with Keynesian Propensities," *American Economic Review* 76, 676–91.

Bekaert, Geert, Campbell R. Harvey, and Christian Lundblad (2004) "Growth Volatility and Financial Liberalization," NBER Working Paper No. 10560.

Bénabou, Roland (1996a) "Equity and Efficiency in Human Capital Investment: The Local Connection," *Review of Economic Studies* 63, 237–64.

——— (1996b) "Heterogeneity, Stratification, and Growth: Macroeconomic Implications of Community Structure and School Finance," *American Economic Review* 86(3), 584–609.

——— (1996c) "Inequality and Growth," in B. S. Bernanke and J. J. Rotemberg (eds.), *NBER Macroeconomics Annual 1996,* 11–73, Cambridge, MA: MIT Press.

——— (1996d) "Unequal Societies: Income Distribution and the Social Contract," *American Economic Review* 90, 96–129.

Bénabou, Roland, and Jean Tirole (2004) "Belief in a Just World and Redistributive Politics," mimeo, Princeton University and University of Toulouse.

Bencivenga, Valerie R., and Bruce D. Smith (1991) "Financial Intermediation and Endogenous Growth," *Review of Economic Studies* 58(2), 195–209.

Benhabib, Jess, and Aldo Rustichini (1996) "Social Conflict and Growth," *Journal of Economic Growth* 1(1), 125–42.

Benhabib, Jess, and Mark M. Spiegel (1994) "The Role of Human Capital in Economic Development: Evidence from Aggregate Cross-Country Data," *Journal of Monetary Economics* 34(2), 143–73.

Bentolila, Samuel, and Gilles Saint-Paul (2003) "Explaining Movements in the Labor Share," *Contributions to Macroeconomics* 3(1), article 9.

Berg, Andrew, and Jeffrey Sachs (1988) "The Debt Crisis: Structural Explanations of Country Performance," NBER Working Paper No. 2607.

Bernhardt, Dan, and Huw Lloyd-Ellis (2000) "Enterprise, Inequality and Economic Development," *Review of Economic Studies* 67, 147–68.

Bernheim, Douglas B. (2000) "Taxation and saving," in Alan J. Auerbach and Martin Feldstein (eds.), *Handbook of Public Economics*, Amsterdam: North-Holland.

Bertola, Giuseppe (1993) "Factor Shares and Savings in Endogenous Growth," *American Economic Review* 83, 1184–98.

——— (1994a) "Theories of Savings and Economic Growth," *Ricerche Economiche* 48, 257–77.

——— (1994b) "Wages, Profits, and Theories of Growth," in Luigi L. Pasinetti and Robert M. Solow (eds.), *Economic Growth and the Structure of Long-Term Development*, 90–108, New York: St. Martin's Press; London: Macmillan Press.

——— (1996) "Factor Shares in OLG Models of Growth," *European Economic Review* 40, 1541–60.

——— (2000) "Macroeconomics of Distribution and Growth," in A. B. Atkinson and F. Bourguignon (eds.), *Handbook of Income Distribution*, chap. 9, Amsterdam: North-Holland.

——— (2004) "A Pure Theory of Job Security and Labor Income Risk," *Review of Economic Studies* 71(1), 43–61.

Bertola, Giuseppe, and Richard Rogerson (1997) "Institutions and Labor Reallocation," *European Economic Review* 41(6), 1147–71.

Binswanger, Johannes (2002) "Government Debt and the Risk Structure of Private Investments with Loss Aversion," mimeo, University of Zurich.

Birdsall, Nancy, David Ross, and Richard Sabot (1995) "Inequality and Growth Reconsidered: Lessons from East Asia," *World Bank Economic Review* 9, 477–508.

Blanchard, Olivier J. (1985) "Debt Deficits and Finite Horizons," *Journal of Political Economy* 92(2), 223–47.

Blinder, Alan S. (1974) "Distribution Effects and the Aggregate Consumption Function," *Journal of Political Economy* 83(3), 447–75.

Bliss, Christopher (2004) "Koopmans Recursive Preferences and Income Convergence," *Journal of Economic Theory* 117, 124–39.

Blundell, Richard, and Ian Preston (1998) "Consumption Inequality and Income Uncertainty," *Quarterly Journal of Economics* 113, 603–40.

Boldrin, Michele (1992) "Dynamic Externalities, Multiple Equilibria, and Growth," *Journal of Economic Theory* 58(2), 198–218.

Bourguignon, François (1981) "Pareto Superiority of Unegalitarian Equilibria in Stiglitz's Model of Wealth Distribution with Convex Saving Function," *Econometrica* 49(6), 1469–75.

—— (1998), "Growth and Inequality in the Dual Model of Development: The Role of Demand Factors," *Review of Economic Studies* 57, 215–228.

—— (2004) "The Poverty-Growth-Inequality Triangle," mimeo, World Bank.

Bourguignon, Francois, Francisco Ferreira, and P. Leite (2003) "Conditional Cash Transfers, Schooling and Child Labor: Micro-Simulating Brazils Bolsa Escola Program," *World Bank Economic Review* 17(2), 229–54.

Bourguignon, François, and Christian Morrisson (1990) "Income Distribution, Development and Foreign Trade: A Cross-Sectional Analysis," *European Economic Review* 34(6), 1113–32.

—— (1998) "Inequality and Development: The Role of Dualism," *Journal of Development Economics* 57, 233–57.

—— (2002) "Inequality among World's Citizens," *American Economic Review* 92(4), 727–44.

Bourguignon, François, and Thierry Verdier (2000) "Oligarchy, Democracy, Inequality and Growth," *Journal of Development Economics* 62, 285–313.

Brunner, Johann K. (1996) "Transition from a Pay-as-You-Go to a Fully-Funded Pension System: The Case of Differing Individuals and Intragenerational Fairness," *Journal of Public Economics* 60, 131–46.

—— (1997) "Optimal Taxation of Income and Bequests," Working paper, Department of Economics, University of Linz, Austria.

Buiter, Willem H. (1993) "Saving and Endogenous Growth: A Survey of Theory and Policy," in A. Heertje (ed.), *World Savings, Theory and Policy*, 64–99, London: Blackwell Publishers.

Caballero, Ricardo (1991) "Earnings Uncertainty and Aggregate Wealth Accumulation," *American Economic Review* 81(4), 859–72.

Carroll, Christopher D. (1992) "The Buffer-Stock Theory of Saving: Some Macroeconomic Evidence," *Brookings Papers on Economic Activity* 1992(2), 61–156.

—— (1997) "Buffer-Stock Saving and the Life Cycle/Permanent Income Hypothesis," *Quarterly Journal of Economics* 112(1), 1–56.

—— (2000) "Why Do the Rich Save So Much?" in Joel B. Slemrod (ed.), *Does Atlas Shrug? The Economic Consequences of Taxing the Rich*, Cambridge, MA: Harvard University Press.

Carroll, Christopher D., and Miles S. Kimball (1996) "On the Concavity of the Consumption Function," *Econometrica* 64(4), 981–92.

—— (2001) "Liquidity Constraints and Precautionary Saving," NBER Working Paper No. 8496.

Casarosa, Carlo (1982) "The New View of the Ricardian Theory of Distribution and Economic Growth," in M. Baranzini (ed.), *Advances in Economic Theory*, Oxford: Basil Blackwell.

Caselli, Francesco, and Jaume Ventura (2000) "A Representative Consumer Theory of Distribution," *American Economic Review* 90(4), 909–26.

Cass, David (1965) "Optimum Growth in an Aggregative Model of Capital Accumulation," *Review of Economic Studies* 32, 233–40.

Castaneda, Ana, Javier Diaz-Gimenez, and Jose-Victor Rios-Rull (2003) "Accounting for the U.S. Earnings and Wealth Inequality," *Journal of Political Economy* 111, 818–57.

Castello, Amparo, and Rafael Domenech (2002) "Human Capital Inequality and Economic Growth: Some New Evidence," *Economic Journal* 112, C187–200.

Chamberlin, Edward H. (1933), *The Theory of Monopolistic Competition*, 4th ed., Cambridge, MA: Harvard University Press.

Chatterjee, Satyajit (1994) "Transitional Dynamics and the Distribution of Wealth in a Neoclassical Growth Model," *Journal of Public Economics* 54, 97–119.

Chen, Shaohua, and Martin Ravallion (2001) "How Did the World's Poorest Fare in the 1990s?" *Review of Income and Wealth* 47, 283–300.

Chou, Chien-fu, and Gabriel Talmain (1996) "Pareto Improving Redistribution in a Growing Economy," *Journal of Economic Growth* 1, 502–23.

Clarke, George R. G. (1995) "More Evidence on Income Distribution and Growth," *Journal of Development Economics* 47, 403–27.

Cochrane, John H. (1991) "A Simple Test of Consumption Insurance," *Journal of Political Economy* 99, 957–76.

Cole, Harold L., George J. Mailath, and Andrew Postlewaite (1992) "Social Norms, Savings Behavior, and Growth," *Journal of Political Economy* 100(6), 1092–1125.

Corneo, Giacomo, and Olivier Jeanne (1999) "Pecuniary Emulation, Inequality and Growth," *European Economic Review* 43, 1665–78.

——— (2001), "Status, the Distribution of Wealth, and Growth," *Scandinavian Journal of Economics* 103, 283–93.

Cowell, Frank A. (2000) "Measurement of Inequality," in A. Atkinson and F. Bourguignon (eds.), *Handbook of Income Distribution*, chap. 9, Amsterdam: North-Holland.

Cremer, Helmuth, and Pierre Pestieau (2003) "Wealth Transfer Taxation: A Survey," CESifo Working Paper No. 1061.

Cutler, David, and Larry Katz (1991) "Macroeconomic Performance and the Disadvantaged," *Brookings Papers on Economic Activity* 2, 1–74.

Dalgin, Muhammed, Devashish Mitra, and Vitor Trindade (2004) "Inequality, Non-homothetic Preferences, and Trade: A Gravity Approach," mimeo, Syracuse University.

Davies, James B., and Anthony F. Shorrocks (2000) The Distribution of Wealth, in A. Atkinson and F. Bourguignon (eds.), *Handbook of Income Distribution*, chap. 11, Amsterdam: North-Holland.

De Janvry, Alain, and Elisabeth Sadoulet (1983) "Social Articulation as a Condition for Equitable Growth," *Journal of Development Economics* 13(3), 275–303.

Deaton, Angus (1991) "Saving and Liquidity Constraints," *Econometrica* 59(5), 1221–48.

——— (2004) "Measuring Poverty in a Growing World (or Measuring Growth in a Poor World)," Working Paper 6/03, Research Program in Development Studies, Woodrow Wilson School, Princeton University.

Deaton, Angus, and John Muellbauer (1980) *Economics and Consumer Behavior*, Cambridge: Cambridge University Press.

Deaton, Angus, and Christina Paxson (1994) "Intertemporal Choice and Inequality," *Journal of Political Economy* 102(3), 437–67.

Debreu, Gérard (1959) "Cardinal Utility for Even-Chance Mixtures of Pairs of Sure Prospects," *Review of Economic Studies* 71.

De Gregorio, José (1996) "Borrowing Constraints, Human Capital Accumulation, and Growth," *Journal of Monetary Economics* 37(1), 49–71.

Deininger, Klaus, and Lyn Squire (1996) "Measuring Income Inequality: A New Database," *World Bank Economic Review* 10(3), 565–92.

——— (1998) "New Ways of Looking at Old Issues: Inequality and Growth," *Journal of Development Economics* 57, 259–87.

Deininger, Klaus, and Pedro Olinto (2001) "Asset Distribution, Inequality and Growth," World Bank Working Paper No. 2375.

Devereux, Michael B., and Makoto Saito (1997) "Growth and Risk-Sharing with Incomplete International Assets Markets," *Journal of International Economics* 42(3–4), 455–73.

Devereux, Michael B., and Gregor W. Smith (1994) "International Risk Sharing and Economic Growth," *International Economic Review* 35(3), 535–90.

De Nardi, Mariacristina (2004) "Wealth Inequality and Intergenerational Links," *Review of Economic Studies* 71(3).

Diamond, Peter A. (1965) "National Debt in a Neoclassical Growth Model," *American Economic Review* 55(5), 1126–50.

Dixit, Avinash K. (1977) "The Accumulation of Capital Theory," *Oxford Economic Papers* 29(1), 1–29.

Dixit, Avinash, and Rafael Rob (1994) "Switching Costs and Sectoral Adjustment in General Equilibrium with Uninsured Risk," *Journal of Economic Theory* 62, 48–69.

Dixit A., and J. Stiglitz (1977) "Monopolistic Competition and Optimum Product Diversity," *American Economic Review* 67, 297–308.

Dollar, David, and Aart Kraay (2002) "Growth Is Good for the Poor," *Journal of Economic Growth* 7, 195–225.

Domar, Evsey D. (1946) "Capital Expansion, Rate of Growth, and Employment," *Econometrica* 14, 137–47.

Drazen, Allan (2000) *Political Economy in Macroeconomics*, Princeton, NJ: Princeton University Press.

Durlauf, Steven N. (1996) "A Theory of Persistent Income Inequality," *Journal of Economic Growth* 11, 75–93.

Dynan, Karen E., Jonathan Skinner, and Stephen E. Zeldes (2004) "Do the Rich Save More?" *Journal of Political Economy* 112, 397–444.

Easterly, William (2002) "Inequality *Does* Cause Underdevelopment," CGD Working Paper 1, Center for Global Development, Institute for International Economics, Washington, DC.

Echevarria, Cristina (1997) "Changes in Sectoral Composition Associated with Economic Growth," *International Economic Review* 38(2), 431–52.

Eicher, Theo, and Cecilia García-Peñalosa (2001) "Inequality and Growth: The Dual Role of Human Capital in Development," *Journal of Development Economics* 66, 173–97.

Engel, Charles, and Kenneth Kletzer (1992) "Distribution of Rents and Growth," Economic Growth Center Discussion Paper No. 656, April.

Engel, Ernst (1857) "Die Productions- und Consumptionsverhältnisse des Königreichs Sachsen," *Zeitschrift des Statistischen Büreaus des Königlich Sächsischen Ministeriums des Inneren*, No. 8 und 9.

Engerman, Stanley L., and Kenneth L. Sokoloff (1994) "Factor Endowments: Institutions, and Differential Paths of Growth among New World Economies: A View from Economic Historians of the United States," NBER Working Paper No. h0066.

——— (2002) "Factor Endowments, Inequality and Paths of Development among New World Economies," NBER Working Paper No. 9259.

Eswaran, Mukesh, and Ashok Kotwal (1993) "A Theory of Real Wage Growth in LDCs," *Journal of Development Economics* 42, 243–69.

Ethier, Wilfred (1982) "National and International Returns to Scale in the Modern Theory of International Trade," *American Economic Review* 73, 389–405.

Falkinger, Josef (1986) *Sättigung—Moralische und psychologische Grenzen des Wachstums*, Tübingen: J.C.B. Mohr (Paul Siebeck).

——— (1990a) "On Growth along a Hierarchy of Wants," *Metroeconomica* 41, 209–23.

——— (1990b) "Innovator-Imitator Trade and the Welfare Effects of Growth," *Journal of the Japanese and International Economies* 4, 157–72.

——— (1994) "An Engelian Model of Growth and Innovation with Hierarchic Consumer Demand and Unequal Incomes," *Ricerche Economiche* 48, 123–39.

Falkinger, Josef, and Josef Zweimüller (1996) "The Cross-Country Engel Curve for Product Diversification," *Structural Change and Economic Dynamics*, 7, 79–97.

Felipe, Jesus, and Franklin M. Fisher (2001) "Aggregation in Production Functions: What Applied Economists Should Know," mimeo, Georgia Institute of Technology, Atlanta and MIT, Cambridge.

Fershtman, Chaim, Kevin M. Murphy, and Yoram Weiss (1996), "Social Status, Education, and Growth," *Journal of Political Economy* 104, 108–32.

Fields, Gary S. (2001) *Distribution and Development: A New Look at the Developing World*, New York and Cambridge, MA: Russell Sage Foundation and MIT Press.

Fields, Gary S., and George H. Jakubson (1993) "New Evidence on the Kuznets Curve," mimeo, Cornell University.

Finkelstein, Amy (2004) "Static and Dynamic Effects of Health Policy: Evidence from the Vaccine Industry," *Quarterly Journal of Economics* 119, 527–64.

Fisher, Franklin M. (1969) "The Existence of Aggregate Production Functions," *Econometrica* 37, 553–77.

Fisher, Irving (1930), *The Theory of Interest, as Determined by Impatience to Spend Income and Opportunity to Invest It*, New York: Macmillan.

Flam, Harry, and Elhanan Helpman (1987) "Vertical Product Differentiation and North-South Trade," *American Economic Review* 77, 810–22.

Flemming, John S. (1978) "Aspects of Optimal Unemployment Insurance," *Journal of Public Economics* 10, 403–25.

Foellmi, Reto (1999) *Monopolistische Preissetzung bei Hierarchischen Präferenzen*, Diploma Thesis, University of Zurich.

—— (2005), *Consumption Structure and Macroeconomics*, Lecture Notes in Economics and Mathematical Systems, vol. 554, Heidelberg/New York: Springer.

Foellmi, Reto, and Manuel Oechslin (2003) "Who Gains from Non-Collusive Corruption?" IEW Working Paper No. 142, University of Zurich.

Foellmi, Reto, and Josef Zweimüller (2002) "Structural Change and the Kaldor Facts of Economic Growth," CEPR Working Paper No. 3300.

—— (2003) "Inequality and Macroeconomics: The Role of Product Market Power" mimeo, University of Zurich.

—— (2004a) "Inequality, Market Power and Product Diversity," *Economics Letters* 82, 139–45.

—— (2004b) "Inequality and Demand-Induced Innovations," mimeo, University of Zurich.

—— (2004c) "Income Distribution, Prices, and Market Size in an Innovative Economy: Demand Composition and the Inequality-Growth Nexus" mimeo, University of Zurich.

Forbes, Kristin (2000) "A Reassessment of the Relationship between Inequality and Growth," *American Economic Review* 90(4), 869–87.

Francois, Joseph F., and Seth Kaplan (1996) "Aggregate Demand Shifts, Income Distribution, and the Linder Hypothesis," *Review of Economics and Statistics* 78, 244–50.

Freeman, Scott (1996) "Equilibrium Income Inequality among Identical Agents," *Journal of Political Economy* 104, 1047–64.

Friedman, Milton (1957) *A Theory of the Consumption Function*, Princeton, NJ: Princeton University Press.

Gabszewicz, Jean Jaskold, and Jacques-François Thisse (1979) "Price Competition, Quality and Income Disparities," *Journal of Economic Theory* 20, 340–59.

—— (1980) "Entry (and Exit) in a Differentiated Industry," *Journal of Economic Theory* 22, 327–38.

—— (1982) "Product Differentiation with Income Disparities: An Illustrative Model," *Journal of Industrial Economics* 31, 115–29.

Gabszewicz, Jean Jaskold, John Sutton, Avner Shaked, and Jacques-François Thisse (1981) "International Trade in Differentiated Products," *International Economic Review* 3, 527–34.

Galor, Oded (2000) "Inequality and the Process of Development," *European Economic Review* 44, 706–12.

Galor, Oded, and Omer Moav (2002) "Das Humankapital: A Theory of the Demise of the Class Structure," mimeo, Hebrew University.

—— (2004) "From Physical to Human Capital Accumulation: Inequality in the Process of Development," *Review of Economic Studies* 71, 1001–26.

Galor Oded, Omer Moav, and Dietrich Vollrath (2003) "Land Inequality and the Origin of Divergence and Overtaking in the Growth Process: Theory and Evidence," mimeo, Brown University.

Galor, Oded, and Harl E. Ryder (1989) "Existence, Uniqueness and Stability of Equilibrium in an Overlapping-Generations Model with Productive Capital," *Journal of Economic Theory* 49, 360–75.

Galor, Oded, and Daniel Tsiddon (1997) "The Distribution of Human Capital and Economic Growth," *Journal of Economic Growth* 2, 93–124.

Galor, Oded, and Joseph Zeira (1988) "Income Distribution and Macroeconomics," Working Paper No. 197, Hebrew University, Jerusalem.

——— (1993) "Income Distribution and Macroeconomics," *Review of Economic Studies* 60, 35–52.

Gancia, Gino, and Fabrizio Zilibotti (2005) "Horizontal Innovation in the Theory of Growth and Development," forthcoming in P. Aghion and S. Durlauf (eds.), *Handbook of Economic Growth*, Amsterdam: North-Holland.

Garcia-Penalosa, Cecilia (1996) "The Paradox of Education or the Good Side of Inequality," *Oxford Economic Papers* 47, 265–85.

Ghatak, Maitreesh, and Neville Nien-Huei Jiang (2002) "A Simple Model of Inequality, Occupational Choice, and Development," *Journal of Development Economics* 69, 205–26.

Ghosh, Sugata, and Sarmistha Pal (2004) "The Effect of Inequality on Growth: Theory and Evidence from the Indian States," *Review of Development Economics* 8(1), 164–77.

Giammarioli, Nicola, Julian Messina, Thomas Steinberger, and Chiara Strozzi, (2003) "European Labor Share Dynamics," EUI Working Paper ECO No. 2002/13, European University Institute, Florence.

Glaeser, Edward L., Jose A. Scheinkman, and Andrei Shleifer (2002) "The Injustice of Inequality," mimeo, Harvard University.

Glass, Amy Joycelin (2001) "Price Discrimination and Quality Improvement," *Canadian Journal of Economics* 34, 549–69.

Glomm, Gerhard, and B. Ravikumar (1992) "Public versus Private Investment in Human Capital: Endogenous Growth and Income Inequality," *Journal of Political Economy* 100(4), 813–34.

Gokhale, Jagadeesh, Laurence J. Kotlikoff, James Sefton, and Martin Weale (2001) "Simulating the Transmission of Wealth Inequality via Bequests," *Journal of Public Economics* 79(1), 93–128.

Gollier, Christian (2001a) *The Economics of Risk and Time*, Cambridge MA: MIT Press.

——— (2001b) "Wealth Inequality and Asset Pricing," *Review of Economic Studies* 68, 181–203.

Gomes, Joao, Jeremy Greenwood, and Sergio Rebelo (2001) "Equilibrium Unemployment," *Journal of Monetary Economics* 48(1) (August), 109–52.

Gordon, Robert J. (2004) "Two Centuries of Economic Growth: Europe Chasing the American Frontier," NBER Working Paper No. 10662.

Greenwood, Jeremy, and Boyan Jovanovic (1990) "Financial Development, Growth, and the Distribution of Income," *Journal of Political Economy* 98, 1076–1107.

Greenwood, Jeremy, and Bruce D. Smith (1997) "Financial Markets in Development, and the Development of Financial Markets," *Journal of Economic Dynamics and Control* 21(1), 145–81.

Grossman, Gene M., and Elhanan Helpman (1989) "Product Development and International Trade," *Journal of Political Economy* 6, 1261–83.

Grossman, Gene M., and Elhanan Helpman (1991) *Innovation and Growth in the Global Economy*, Cambridge, MA: MIT Press.

Grossman, Gene M., and Noriyuki Yanagawa (1993) "Asset Bubbles and Endogenous Growth," *Journal of Monetary Economics* 31(1), 3–19.

Grossman, Herschel I., and Minseong Kim (1996) "Predation and Accumulation," *Journal of Economic Growth* 1(3), 333–50.

Grossmann, Volker (2004) "Risky Human Capital Investment, Income Distribution, and Macroeconomics," mimeo, University of Zurich.

Hahn, Frank H., and R.C.O. Matthews (1964) "The Theory of Economic Growth: A Survey" *Economic Journal* 74, 780–902.

Harrod, Roy F. (1939) "An Essay in Dynamic Theory," *Economic Journal* 49, 14–33.

Heaton, John, and Deborah Lucas (1996) "Evaluating the Effects of Incomplete Markets on Risk Sharing and Asset Pricing," *Journal of Political Economy* 104, 443–87.

Hildenbrand, Werner, and A. Kneip (1999) "Demand Aggregation under Structural Stability," *Journal of Mathematical Economics* 31(1), 81–109.

Houthakker, Hendrick S. (1987) "Engel Curve," in J. Eatwell, M. Milgate, and P. Newman (eds.), *The New Palgrave Dictionary of Economics*, 142–43, London: Macmillan.

Huggett, Mark (1993) "The Risk-Free Rate in Heterogeneous-Agent Incomplete-Insurance Economies," *Journal of Economic Dynamics and Control* 17, 953–69.

——— (1997) "The One-Sector Growth Model with Idiosyncratic Shocks: Steady States and Dynamics," *Journal of Monetary Economics* 39(3), August, 385–403.

Hunter, Linda C. (1991) "The Contribution of Nonhomothetic Preferences to Trade," *Journal of International Economics* 30, 345–58.

Hunter, Linda C., and James R. Markusen (1988) "Per-Capita Income as a Determinant of Trade," in Robert C. Feenstra (ed.), *Empirical Methods for International Trade*, Cambridge, MA: MIT Press.

Irvine, Ian, and Susheng Wang (1994) "Earnings Uncertainty and Aggregate Wealth Accumulation: Comment," *American Economic Review* 84(5), 1463–69.

Jackson, L. Fraser (1984) "Hierarchic Demand and the Engel Curve for Variety," *Review of Economics and Statistics* 66, 8–15.

Jappelli, Tullio, and Marco Pagano (1994) "Saving, Growth and Liquidity Constraints," *Quarterly Journal of Economics* 109, 83–109.

Jones, Larry E., and Rodolfo Manuelli (1990) "A Convex Model of Equilibrium Growth: Theory and Policy Implications," *Journal of Political Economy* 98, 1008–38.

——— (1992) "Finite Lives and Growth," *Journal of Economic Theory* 58(2), 171–97.

Judd, Kenneth (1985) "Short-Run Analysis of Fiscal Policy in a Simple Perfect Foresight Model," *Journal of Political Economy* 93(2), 298–319.

Kaldor, Nicholas (1955) "Alternative Theories of Distribution," *Review of Economic Studies* 23, 83–100.

——— (1956) "Alternative Theories of Distribution," *Review of Economic Studies* 23, 94–100.

——— (1961) "Capital Accumulation and Economic Growth," in F. A. Lutz and D. C. Hague (eds.), *The Theory of Capital*, New York: St. Martin's Press.

Kaldor, Nicholas (1966) "Marginal Productivity and the Macro-Economic Theories of Distribution," *Review of Economic Studies* 33, 309–19.

Kalecki, Michal (1938) "The Determinants of Distribution of the National Income," *Econometrica* 6, 97–112.

——— (1954) *Theory of Economic Dynamics: An Essay on Cyclical and Long-Run Changes in Capitalist Economy,* London: Allen & Unwin Ltd.

Katona, George (1964) *The Mass Consumption Society,* New York: McGraw-Hill.

Keynes, John Maynard (1936) *The General Theory of Employment, Interest, and Money,* reprint, New York: Harcourt Brace Jovanovich, 1964.

Kindleberger, Charles P. (1989) *Economic Laws and Economic History,* Cambridge: Cambridge University Press (Raffaele Mattioli Lectures).

Koeniger, Winfried (2004) "Openness, Innovations and Cross-Country Productivity Differences," mimeo, IZA Bonn.

Kongsamut, Piyabha, Sergio Rebelo, and Danyang Xie (2001) "Beyond Balanced Growth," *Review of Economic Studies* 68, 869–82.

Koo, Hyeng Keun (1999) "Consumption and Portfolio Selection with Labor Income: A Discrete-Time Approach," *Mathematical Methods of Operations Research* 50, 219–43.

Koopmans, Tjalling C. (1965) "On the Concept of Optimal Economic Growth," in *The Economic Approach to Development Planning*, Amsterdam: North-Holland.

Kotlikoff, Lawrence J., and Lawrence H. Summers (1981) "The Role of Intergenerational Transfers in Aggregate Capital Formation," *Journal of Political Economy* 89, 706–32.

Kremer, Michael (2001a) "Creating Markets for New Vaccines: Part I: Rationale," in Adam B. Jaffe, Josh Lerner, and Scott Stern (eds.), *Innovation Policy and the Economy*, Cambridge, MA: MIT Press.

——— (2001b) "Creating Markets for New Vaccines: Part II: Design Issues," in Adam B. Jaffe, Josh Lerner, and Scott Stern (eds.), *Innovation Policy and the Economy*, Cambridge, MA: MIT Press.

Krueger, Dirk, and Fabrizio Perri (2003) "On the Welfare Consequences of the Increase in Inequality in the United States," in M. Gertler and K. Rogoff (eds.), *NBER Macroeconomics Annual 2003*, Cambridge, MA: MIT Press.

Krishna, Kala, and Cemile Yavas (2004) "Immiserizing Growth in a Closed Economy," *Scandinavian Journal of Economics* 106, 143–58.

——— (2005) "When Trade Hurts: Consumption Indivisibilities and Labor Market Distortions," *Journal of International Economics*, forthcoming.

Krusell, Per, Vincenzo Quadrini, and José-Victor Ríos-Rull (1997) "Politico-Economic Equilibrium and Economic Growth" *Journal of Economic Dynamics and Control* 21(1), 23–73.

Krusell, Per, and José-Victor Ríos-Rull (1992) "Vested Interests in a Positive Theory of Stagnation and Growth," *Review of Economic Studies* 63, 301–29.

Krusell, Per, and Anthony A. Smith (1997) "Income and Wealth Heterogeneity, Portfolio Choice, and Equilibrium Asset Returns," *Macroeconomic Dynamics* 1(2), 387–422.

—— (1998) "Income and Wealth Heterogeneity in the Macroeconomy," *Journal of Political Economy* 106, 867–96.

Kurz, Heinz D., and Neri Salvadori (1995) *Theory of Production: A Long-Period Analysis*, Cambridge: Cambridge University Press.

Kuznets, Simon (1955) "Economic Growth and Income Inequality," *American Economic Review* 45(1), 1–28.

Laitner, John (1979a) "Bequests, Golden-age Capital Accumulation and Government Debt," *Economica* 46, 403–14.

—— (1979b) "Household Bequest Behavior and the National Distribution of Wealth," *Review of Economic Studies* 46, 467–83.

—— (1992) "Random Earnings Differences, Lifetime Liquidity Constraints, and Altruistic Intergenerational Transfers," *Journal of Economic Theory* 58, 135–70.

—— (1997) "Intergenerational and Interhousehold Economic Links," in M. R. Rosenzweig and O. Stark (eds.), *Handbook of Population and Family Economics*, vol. 1, 189–238, Amsterdam: North-Holland.

—— (2000) "Structural Change and Economic Growth," *Review of Economic Studies* 67, 545–61.

—— (2002) "Wealth Inequality and Altruistic Bequests," *American Economic Review* 92(2), 270–73.

Lancaster, Kelvin (1979) *Variety, Equity and Efficiency*, Oxford: Basil Blackwell.

Leonardi, Marco (2004) "Product Demand Shifts and Wage Inequality" mimeo, University of Milan.

Lerner, Abba P. (1934) "The Concept of Monopoly and the Measurement of Monopoly Power," *Review of Economic Studies* 3, 157–75.

Levine, David P. (1988) "Marx's Theory of Income Distribution" in A. Asimakopoulos (ed.), *Theories of Income Distribution*, Boston: Kluwer Academic Publishers.

Levy, Moshe, and Sorin Solomon (1997) "New Evidence for the Power-Law Distribution of Wealth," *Physica A: Statistical and Theoretical Physics* 242, 90–94.

Li, Chol-Won (2003) "Income Inequality, Product Market, and Schumpeterian Growth," mimeo, University of Glasgow.

Li, Hongyi, and Heng-fu Zou (1998) "Income Inequality Is Not Harmful for Growth: Theory and Evidence," *Review of Development Economics* 2, 318–34.

Linder, Staffan B. (1961) *An Essay on Trade and Transformation*, Stockholm: Almqvist and Wicksell.

Lindert, Peter H., and Jeffrey G. Williamson (1985) "Growth, Equality, and History," *Explorations in Economic History* 22, 341–77.

Ljungqvist, Lars (1993) "Economic Underdevelopment: The Case of a Missing Market for Human Capital," *Journal of Development Economics* 40, 219–39.

——— (1995) "Wage Structure as Implicit Insurance on Human Capital in Developed versus Undeveloped Countries," *Journal of Development Economics* 46, 35–50.

Ljungqvist, Lars, and Thomas J. Sargent (2004) *Recursive Macroeconomic Theory*, 2nd ed., Cambridge, MA: MIT Press.

Lloyd-Ellis, Huw (1999) "Endogenous Technological Change and Wage-Inequality," *American Economic Review* 89(1), 47–77.

——— (2000) "Public Education, Occupational Choice and the Growth-Inequality Relationship," *International Economic Review* 41, 171–201.

Loury, Glenn C. (1981) "Intergenerational Transfers and the Distribution of Earnings," *Econometrica* 49, 843–67.

Lucas, Robert E. (1988) "On the Mechanics of Economic Development," *Journal of Monetary Economics* 22, 3–42.

Lucas, Robert E., and Edward C. Prescott (1974) "Equilibrium Search and Unemployment," *Journal of Economic Theory* 7, 188–209.

Lucas, Robert, and Nancy Stokey (1984) "Optimal Growth with Many Consumers," *Journal of Economic Theory* 32, 139–71.

Lundberg, Mattias, and Lyn Squire (2003) "The Simultaneous Evolution of Growth and Inequality," *Economic Journal* 113(487), 326.

Maddison, Angus (1987) "Growth and Slowdown in Advanced Capitalist Economies: Techniques of Quantitative Assessment," *Journal of Economic Literature* 25, 649–98.

Mani, Anandi (2001) "Income Distribution and the Demand Constraint," *Journal of Economic Growth* 6(2), 107–33.

Marglin, Stephen A. (1984) *Growth, Distribution, and Prices*, Cambridge, MA: Harvard University Press.

Matsuyama, Kiminori (1992) "Agricultural Productivity, Comparative Advantage, and Economic Growth," *Journal of Economic Theory* 58, 317–34.

——— (2000a) "Endogenous Inequality," *Review of Economic Studies*, 67, 743–59.

——— (2000b) "A Ricardian Model with a Continuum of Goods under Nonhomothetic Preferences: Demand Complementarities, Income Distribution and North-South Trade," *Journal of Political Economy* 108, 1093–1120.

——— (2002) "The Rise of Mass Consumption Societies," *Journal of Political Economy* 110, 1035–70.

——— (2003) "On the Rise and Fall of Class Societies," mimeo, Northwestern University.

McKay, Andrew, and Sarmistha Pal (2004) "Relationships between Household Consumption and Inequality in the Indian States," *Journal of Development Studies* 40, 65–90.

Merton, Robert C. (1971) "Optimum Consumption and Portfolio Rules in a Continuous-Time Model," *Journal of Economic Theory* 3, 373–413.

Moav, Omer (2002) "Income Distribution and Macroeconomics: The Persistence of Inequality in a Convex Technology Framework," *Economics Letters* 75, 187–92.

Modigliani, Franco, and Richard Brumberg (1954) "Utility Analysis and the Consumption Function: An Interpretation of Cross-Section Data," in Kenneth K. Kurihara (ed.), *Post-Keynesian Economics*, 388–436, New Brunswick, NJ: Rutgers University Press.

Mookherjee, Dilip, and Debraj Ray (2002) "Is Equality Stable?" *American Economic Review* 92, 253–59.

——— (2003) "Persistent Inequality," *Review of Economic Studies* 70, 369–93.

Moskowitz, Tobias, and Annette Vissing-Jørgensen (2002) "The Returns to Entrepreneurial Investment: A Private Equity Premium Puzzle?" *American Economic Review* 92, 745–78.

Mueller, Dennis, and Thomas Stratmann (2003) "The Economic Effects of Democratic Participation," *Journal of Public Economics* 87, 2129–55.

Murata, Yasusada (2004) "Non-Homothetic Preferences, Increasing Returns, and the Introduction of New Final Goods," mimeo, Tokio Metropolitan University.

Murphy, Kevin, Andrei Shleifer, and Robert Vishny (1989) "Industrialization and the Big Push," *Journal of Political Economy* 97, 1003–1126.

Nerlove, Marc, and Lakshmi K. Raut (1997) "Growth Models with Endogenous Population: A General Framework," in M. R. Rosenzweig and O. Stark (eds.), *Handbook of Population and Family Economics*, Amsterdam: North-Holland.

O'Donoghue, Ted, and Josef Zweimüller (2004) "Patents in a Model of Endogenous Growth," *Journal of Economic Growth* 9, 81–123.

Obstfeld, Maurice (1994) "Risk-Taking, Global Diversification, and Growth," *American Economic Review* 84(5), 1310–29.

Ogaki, Masao, Jonathan D. Ostry, and Carmen M. Reinhart (1996) "Saving Behavior in Low- and Middle-Income Developing Countries: A Comparison," *International Monetary Fund Staff Papers* 43(1), 38–71.

Ordover, Jansuz A., and Edmund S. Phelps (1979) "The Concept of Optimal Taxation in the Overlapping-Generations Model of Capital and Wealth," *Journal of Public Economics* 12, 1–26.

Pagano, Marco (1993) "Financial Markets and Growth: An Overview," *European Economic Review* 37(3), 613–22.

Panizza, Ugo (2002) "Income Distribution and Economic Growth: Evidence from the U.S. States Data," *Journal of Economic Growth* 7, 25–41.

Partridge, Mark D. (1997) "Is Inequality Harmful for Growth? Comment," *American Economic Review* 87, 1019–32.

Pasinetti, Luigi (1960) "A Mathematical Formulation of the Ricardian System," *Review of Economic Studies* 27, 78–98.

——— (1962) "Rate of Profit and Income Distribution in Relation to the Rate of Economic Growth," *Review of Economic Studies* 29, 267–79.

——— (1981) *Structural Change and Economic Growth*, Cambridge: Cambridge University Press.

———— (1993) *Structural Economic Dynamics,* Cambridge: Cambridge University Press.

Paukert, Felix (1973) "Income Distribution at Different Levels of Development: A Survey of the Evidence," *International Labour Review* 108, 97–125.

Perotti, Roberto (1993) "Political Equilibrium, Income Distribution, and Growth," *Review of Economic Studies* 60, 755–76.

———— (1996a) "Growth, Income Distribution, and Democracy: What the Data Say," *Journal of Economic Growth* 1, 149–87.

———— (1996b) "Inequality and Growth: Comment," in B. S. Bernanke and J. J. Rotemberg (eds.), *NBER Macroeconomics Annual 1996,* 74–82, Cambridge, MA: MIT Press.

Persky, Joseph (1992) "Retrospectives: Pareto's Law," *Journal of Economic Perspectives* 6(2), 181–92.

Persson, Torsten, and Guido Tabellini (1992) "Growth, Distribution, and Politics," *European Economic Review* 36, 593–602.

———— (1994) "Is Inequality Harmful for Growth?" *American Economic Review* 84, 600–621.

———— (1998) "Political Economics and Macroeconomic Policy," in J. Taylor and M. Woodford (eds.), *Handbook of Macroeconomics,* Amsterdam: North-Holland.

———— (2000) *Political Economics: Explaining Economic Policy,* Cambridge, MA: MIT Press.

Piketty, Thomas (1997) "The Dynamics of the Wealth Distribution and the Interest Rate with Credit Rationing," *Review of Economic Studies* 64(2), 173–90.

———— (2000) "Theories of Persistent Inequality and Intergenerational Mobility," in A. Atkinson and F. Bourguignon (eds.), *Handbook of Income Distribution,* chap. 6, Amsterdam: North-Holland.

———— (2003) "Income Inequality in France, 1901–1998," *Journal of Political Economy* 111, 1004–42.

Piketty, Thomas, and Emmanuel Saez (2003) "Income Inequality in the United States, 1913–1998," *Quarterly Journal of Economics* 118(1), 1–39.

Pirttilä, Jukka, and Matti Tuomala (2001) "On Optimal Non-linear Taxation and Public Good Provision in an Overlapping Generations Economy," *Journal of Public Economics* 79(3), 485–501.

Pissarides, Christopher (2001) "Employment Protection," *Labour Economics* 8(2), 131–59.

Plato (360 BC) *Politeia—Der Staat,* translated into German by R. Rufener, Düsseldorf: Artemis und Winkler, 2000.

Pollack, Robert A. (1971) "Additive Utility Functions and Linear Engel Curves," *Review of Economic Studies* 38, 401–13.

Quadrini, Vincenzo (2000) "Entrepreneurship, Saving, and Social Mobility," *Review of Economic Dynamics* 3, 1–40.

Ravallion, Martin (1998) "Does Aggregation Hide the Harmful Effects of Inequality on Growth?" *Economics Letters* 61, 73–77.

———— (2001) "Growth, Inequality and Poverty: Looking Beyond Averages," *World Development* 29(11), 1803–15.

Ray, Debraj (1998) *Development Economics*, Princeton, NJ: Princeton University Press.

Rebelo, Sergio (1991) "Long-Run Policy Analysis and Long-Run Growth," *Journal of Political Economy* 99, 500–521.

—— (1992) "Growth in Open Economies," *Carnegie-Rochester Conference Series on Public Policy* 36, 5–46.

Robinson, Joan (1933) *The Economics of Imperfect Competition*, London: Macmillan.

Robinson, Joan (1956) *The Accumulation of Capital*, London: Macmillan.

Roemer, John E. (1981) *Analytical Foundations of Marxian Economic Theory*, Cambridge: Cambridge University Press.

Romer, Paul M. (1986) "Increasing Returns and Long-Run Growth," *Journal of Political Economy* 94, 1002–37.

—— (1987) "Growth Based on Increasing Returns Due to Specialization," *American Economic Review* 77 (May), 56–62.

—— (1989) "Capital Accumulation in the Theory of Long-Run Growth," in R. J. Barro (ed.), *Modern Business Cycle Theories*, 51–127, Cambridge, MA: Harvard University Press.

—— (1990) "Endogenous Technological Change," *Journal of Political Economy* 98, 71–102.

Rostow, Walt Whitman (1960) *The Process of Economic Growth*, 2nd ed., Oxford: Clarendon.

Saez, Emmanuel (2004) "Income Concentration in Historical and International Perspective," forthcoming in A. J. Auerbach, D. Card, and J. M. Quigley (eds.) *Poverty, the Distribution of Income, and Public Policy: A Conference in Honor of Eugene Smolensky*, New York: Russell Sage Foundation.

Saint-Paul, Gilles (1992a) "Fiscal Policy in an Endogenous Growth Model," *Quarterly Journal of Economics* 107, 1243–59.

—— (1992b) "Technological Choice, Financial Markets and Economic Development," *European Economic Review* 36(4), 763–81.

—— (2004a) "Distribution and Growth in an Economy with Limited Needs," mimeo, University of Toulouse.

—— (2004b) "Are Intellectual Property Rights Unfair?" *Labour Economics* 11, 129–44.

Sala-i-Martin, Xavier (1996a) "Regional Cohesion: Evidence and Theories of Regional Growth and Convergence," *European Economic Review* 40, 1325–52.

—— (1996b) "The Classical Approach to Convergence Analysis," *Economic Journal* 106(437), 1019–36.

—— (2002) "The Disturbing 'Rise' of World Income Inequality," mimeo, Columbia University.

Samuelson, Paul A. (1958) "An Exact Consumption-Loan Model of Interest with or without the Social Contrivance of Money," *Journal of Political Economy* 66, 467–82.

Samuelson, Paul A., and Franco Modigliani (1966) "The Pasinetti Paradox in Neoclassical and More General Models," *Review of Economic Studies* 33, 269–301.

Schmidt-Hebbel, Klaus, and Luis Serven (2000) "Does Income Inequality Raise Aggregate Saving?" *Journal of Development Economics* 61, 417–46.

Schumpeter, Joseph (1939) *Business Cycles: A Theoretical, Historical and Statistical Analysis of the Capitalist Process*, abridged, with an introduction by Rendigs Fels, New York: McGraw-Hill, 1964; reprinted Philadelphia: Porcupine Press, 1989.

Segerstrom, Paul S., Thirumalai C. A. Anant, and Elias Dinopoulos (1990) "A Schumpeterian Model of the Product Life Cycle," *American Economic Review* 80, 1077–91.

Shaked, Avner, and John Sutton (1982) "Relaxing Price Competition through Product Differentiation," *Review of Economic Studies* 49, 3–13.

—— (1983) "Natural Oligopolies," *Econometrica* 51, 1469–83.

Shavell, Steven, and Lawrence Weiss (1979) "The Optimal Payment of Unemployment Insurance Benefits over Time," *Journal of Political Economy* 87, 1347–62.

Sinn, Hans-Werner (1995) "A Theory of the Welfare State," *Scandinavian Journal of Economics* 97, 495–526.

Smith, Adam (1776) *An Inquiry into the Nature and Causes of the Wealth of Nations*, R. H. Campbell, A. S. Skinner, and W. B. Todd (eds.), vol. 2 of *The Glasgow Edition of the Works and Correspondence of Adam Smith*, Oxford: Clarendon Press, 1976.

Solow, Robert M. (1956a) "A Contribution to the Theory of Economic Growth," *Quarterly Journal of Economics* 70(1), 65–94.

—— (1956b) "The Production Function and the Theory of Capital," *Review of Economic Studies* 23, 101–8.

Sraffa, Piero (1960) *Production of Commodities by Means of Commodities: Prelude to a Critique of Economic Theory*, Cambridge: Cambridge University Press.

Steger, Thomas M. (2000) "Economic Growth with Subsistence Consumption," *Journal of Development Economics* 62, 343–61.

Stiglitz, Joseph E. (1969) "Distribution of Income and Wealth among Individuals," *Econometrica* 37(3), 382–97.

Stokey, Nancy (1988) "Learning-by-Doing and the Introduction of New Goods," *Journal of Political Economy* 96, 701–17.

—— (1991a) "Human Capital, Product Quality, and Growth," *Quarterly Journal of Economics* 106, 587–616.

—— (1991b) "The Volume and Composition of Trade between Rich and Poor Countries," *Review of Economic Studies* 58, 63–80.

Stokey, Nancy L., and Sergio Rebelo (1995) "Growth Effects of Flat-Rate-Taxes," *Journal of Political Economy* 103, 519–50.

Storesletten, Kjetil, Chris I. Telmer, and Amir Yaron (2004a) "Consumption and Risk Sharing over the Life Cycle," *Journal of Monetary Economics* 51, 609–33.

—— (2004b) "Cyclical Dynamics in Idiosyncratic Labor Market Risk," *Journal of Political Economy* 112(3), 695–717.

Tamura, Robert (1991) "Income Convergence in an Endogenous Growth Model," *Journal of Political Economy* 99, 522–54.

Topel, Robert H. (1986) "Efficient Labor Contracts with Employment Risk," *Rand Journal of Economics* 17(4), 490–507.

Tornell, Aaròn, and Andrés Velasco (1992) "The Tragedy of the Commons and Economic Growth: Why Does Capital Flow from Poor to Rich Countries?" *Journal of Political Economy* 100(6), 1208–31.

Uhlig, Harald, and Noriyuki Yanagawa (1996) "Increasing the Capital Income Tax May Lead to Faster Growth," *European Economic Review* 40, 1521–40.

Uzawa, Hirofumi (1968) "Time Preference, the Consumption Function, and Optimum Asset Holdings," in J. N. Wolfe (ed.), *Value, Capital, and Growth: Papers in Honor of Sir John Hicks*, Chicago: Aldine Publishing.

Wang, Neng (2003) "Caballero Meets Bewley: The Permanent-Income Hypothesis in General Equilibrium," *American Economic Review* 93, 927–36.

Weil, Philippe (1989) "Overlapping Families with Infinitely Lived Agents," *Journal of Public Economics* 38, 183–98.

Weiss, Matthias (2004) "Skill-Biased Technological Change: Is There Hope for the Unskilled?" mimeo, University of Mannheim.

Williamson, Jeffrey G. (1991) *Inequality, Poverty, and History*, Oxford: Basil Blackwell.

Wolff, Edward N. (1994) "Trends in Household Wealth in the United States, 1962–83 and 1983–89," *Review of Income and Wealth* 40(2), 74–143.

Wright, Randall (1996) "Taxes, Redistribution, and Growth," *Journal of Public Economics* 62(3), 327–38.

Young, Alwyn (1928) "Increasing Returns and Economic Progress," *Economic Journal* 38, 527–42.

Zeldes, Stephen P. (1989) "Optimal Consumption with Stochastic Income: Deviations from Certainty Equivalence," *Quarterly Journal of Economics* 104(2), 275–98.

Zilcha, Itzhak (2003) "Intergenerational Transfers, Production and Income Distribution," *Journal of Public Economics* 87, 489–513.

Zweimüller, Josef (1998) "Aggregate Demand, Non-Linear Engel-Curves, and R&D Investments," mimeo, University of Zurich.

——— (2000) "Schumpeterian Entrepreneurs Meet Engels Law: The Impact of Inequality on Innovation-Driven Growth," *Journal of Economic Growth* 5, 185–206.

Zweimüller, Josef, and Johann K. Brunner (2005) "Innovation and Growth with Rich and Poor Consumers," *Metroeconomica*, 56, 233–62.

Index